Great Britain Public Record Office, Samuel R. Scargill-Bird

A Guide to the Principal classes of Documents

Preserved in the Public Record Office

Great Britain Public Record Office, Samuel R. Scargill-Bird

A Guide to the Principal classes of Documents
Preserved in the Public Record Office

ISBN/EAN: 9783337179762

Printed in Europe, USA, Canada, Australia, Japan

Cover: Foto ©Andreas Hilbeck / pixelio.de

More available books at **www.hansebooks.com**

A

GUIDE

TO THE

PRINCIPAL CLASSES OF DOCUMENTS

PRESERVED IN THE

PUBLIC RECORD OFFICE,

BY

S. R. SCARGILL-BIRD, F.S.A.,

AN ASSISTANT KEEPER OF THE RECORDS.

SECOND EDITION.

LONDON:
PRINTED FOR HER MAJESTY'S STATIONERY OFFICE,
BY EYRE AND SPOTTISWOODE,
PRINTERS TO THE QUEEN'S MOST EXCELLENT MAJESTY.

And to be purchased, either directly or through any Bookseller, from
EYRE AND SPOTTISWOODE, EAST HARDING STREET, FLEET STREET, E.C.; or
JOHN MENZIES & Co., 12, HANOVER STREET, EDINBURGH, and
90, WEST NILE STREET, GLASGOW; or
HODGES, FIGGIS, & Co., LIMITED, 104, GRAFTON STREET, DUBLIN.

1896.

Price Seven Shillings.

INTRODUCTION.

The Public Records of this country have been said to excel all others " in age, beauty, correctness, and authority." For a period of well nigh 800 years they contain, in an almost unbroken chain of evidence, not only the political and constitutional history of the realm and the remotest particulars with regard to its financial and social progress, but also the history of the land and of its successive owners from generation to generation, and of the legal procedure of the country from a time " whereof the memory of man runneth not to the contrary."

Although many of them were buffeted about in civil wars and dissensions, and others hidden away for years in noisome cellars, to be the refuge and food of vermin, they have yet survived to form a magnificent monument of the past, mutilated here and there, it is true, by the ravages of time and neglect, but still speaking with authoritative voice to the centuries to come of the struggles for civil and political liberty and of the social and domestic condition of the English race from its earliest infancy to the present time.

The history of their many vicissitudes, and of the alternate care and neglect with which they have been treated for centuries, has been so exhaustively dwelt upon by previous writers that its repetition here would be both tedious and unnecessary. Suffice it, therefore, to say that within the walls of the stately, albeit unfinished Record Repository, the construction of which on the Rolls Estate was commenced in 1851, are now collected together all the muniments of the Superior Courts of Law anciently preserved in their respective Treasuries (and subsequently in the several Record Offices established in the Tower of London, the Rolls Chapel Office, the Chapter House at Westminster, the King's Mews at Charing Cross, Carlton Ride, and other places of deposit), as well as those of Special or Abolished Jurisdictions from all parts of the country. To these have been added the entire contents of the State Paper Office at Westminster, which was amalgamated with the Public Record Office in 1854, and the Books Papers, and Documents of the various Government Departments to a comparatively recent date.

The charge and superintendence, and, either by the Act itself or by a warrant in pursuance thereof, the custody also of the whole of these was vested in the Master of the Rolls by the Act 1 and 2 Vict., c. 94., known as the " Public Record Act,"

INTRODUCTION.

and by an Order of the Privy Council, dated 5th March 1852, all the Records belonging to Her Majesty, deposited in any office, court, place, or custody other than those named in the Public Record Act were placed thenceforth "under the charge and superintendence" of the Master of the Rolls, subject and according to the provisions of the said Act.

Some idea of the nature and extent of the vast collection now deposited in the Public Record Office may be gathered from the following enumeration of the several Sub-Divisions or groups of Records of which it consists:—*

CONTENTS OF THE PUBLIC RECORD OFFICE.

(1.) Records of the Superior Courts of Law, as follows:—

THE COURT OF CHANCERY.
,,   QUEEN'S BENCH.
,,   COMMON PLEAS.
,,   EXCHEQUER, WITH ITS BRANCHES, ADMINISTRATIVE AND JUDICIAL, AS FOLLOWS:—

THE EXCHEQUER OF PLEAS OR COMMON LAW SIDE.

THE QUEEN'S REMEMBRANCER'S DEPARTMENT OR EQUITY SIDE.

THE LORD TREASURER'S REMEMBRANCER'S DEPARTMENT (INCLUDING THE OFFICE OF THE CLERK OF THE PIPE).

THE AUGMENTATION DEPARTMENT (INCLUDING THE ABOLISHED COURTS OF AUGMENTATIONS AND OF THE GENERAL SURVEYORS OF THE KING'S LANDS).

THE FIRST FRUITS AND TENTHS DEPARTMENT (INCLUDING THE ABOLISHED COURT OF FIRST FRUITS AND TENTHS).

THE RECEIPT DEPARTMENT OR "EXCHEQUER OF RECEIPT" (INCLUDING THE PELLS' AND AUDITORS' OFFICES).

THE TREASURY OF THE EXCHEQUER OR TREASURY OF THE RECEIPT OF THE EXCHEQUER.

THE LAND REVENUE DEPARTMENT.

---

* The enormous bulk of the National Archives will, perhaps, be best exemplified by the statement that one class of documents alone, the Close Rolls of the Court of Chancery, comprises considerably over 19,000 rolls, whilst the Coram Rege and De Banco Rolls, which are also numbered by thousands, are frequently of huge size—a single roll of the Tudor and Stuart periods containing from 500 to 1,000 skins of parchment.

INTRODUCTION.

(2.) Records of Special and Abolished Jurisdictions, as follows:—

HIGH COURT OF ADMIRALTY.

COURT OF CHIVALRY.

HIGH COURT OF DELEGATES.

COURT OF HIGH COMMISSION IN ECCLESIASTICAL CAUSES.

MARSHALSEA AND PALACE COURTS.

PEVERIL COURT.

COURT OF REQUESTS.

COURT OF STAR CHAMBER.

COURT OF WARDS AND LIVERIES.

(3.) Records of the Duchy of Lancaster.

(4.) „ **Palatinate of Durham.**

(5.) „ **Palatinate of Lancaster.**

(6.) „ **Principality of Wales (including the Palatinate of Chester).**

(7.) State Papers and Departmental Records, including:—

RECORDS OF THE ADMIRALTY.

„ AUDIT OFFICE.

„ COLONIAL OFFICE (INCLUDING THE BOARD OF TRADE).

„ FOREIGN OFFICE.

„ HOME OFFICE.

„ LORD CHAMBERLAIN'S DEPARTMENT.

„ TREASURY.

„ WAR OFFICE.

RECORDS OF VARIOUS ABOLISHED OFFICES AND EXPIRED COMMISSIONS.

INTRODUCTION.

In order to afford some guide as to the manner and sequence in which the judicial documents, which constitute the greater part of those described in the present volume, came into existence, a brief sketch of the nature and origin of the Superior Courts of Law and of such of the Special and abolished Jurisdictions as are represented in the Public Records, and also of the duties of the principal Officers attached to such Courts, is appended.* It must be borne in mind that the several Courts are described as they existed prior to the passing of the Supreme Court of Judicature Act of 1873.

A brief account is also given of each of the remaining Sub-Divisions of the Public Records.

DESCRIPTION OF THE COURTS OF LAW.

The term *Court* or *Curia* was originally used to denote simply the Palace or Residence of the King, but came eventually to have a more especial signification, namely, that of the place in which justice was administered. In the process of time the King's Court became subdivided into four branches known as the *Superior Courts*, and generally held at Westminster, consisting of the King's Bench, the Chancery, the Common Pleas, and the Exchequer, all of which were *Courts of Record.*

In addition to these there were numerous Courts having special or limited jurisdiction, some of which were Courts of Record, whilst others were not of Record, and therefore known as *Base Courts.*

A Court of Record was one which had the power to hold pleas according to the course of the Common Law in real, personal, and mixed actions, when the debt or damage in dispute amounted to or exceeded 40s., and, being a King's Court, had authority to fine and imprison; while the *Base Courts* could only hold pleas relating to sums under the amount specified, and could neither impose a fine nor imprisonment, nor were their proceedings enrolled; of this description were the *County Courts, Courts Baron,* &c.

The Rolls of the Superior Courts of Record were of such authority that no proof could be admitted against them, and they were triable only by themselves in pursuance of a *Writ of Error;* whilst in Courts not of Record the proceedings might be denied and tried by a Jury, and a Writ of false judgment be thereupon issued.

All the inferior Courts of Law were regulated by the Court of King's Bench, which took care that they did not exceed their jurisdictions or alter their forms.

* The statements relating to the nature, &c. of the earlier Courts of Law are taken from Sir Thos. Hardy's Introduction to the Close Rolls.

INTRODUCTION.

The Curia Regis or Aula Regis.

This Court took its name from the place in which it was held, the Hall or Court of the King's Palace. It appears to have been of Norman origin, and the name was originally applied to an assembly exercising both legislative and judicial functions, which, under the Norman rule, supplied in all probability the place of the Saxon Wittenagemote or Common Council. In the Curia Regis were discussed and tried all pleas immediately concerning the King and the Realm, and suitors were allowed, upon payment of small fines to remove their plaints from inferior jurisdictions of Saxon origin into this Court, so that, in the reign of Henry I., it had become the regular Court of Appeal from all the Courts of ordinary jurisdiction.

These inferior tribunals, such as the County Courts, Hundred Courts, and Courts Baron, were so numerous as to cause serious inconvenience, and the ignorance or partiality of the judges gave rise to much venality and debasement of the laws. To put a stop to these irregularities " men versed and experienced in the laws and " constitution of the Realm " were appointed in the reign of Henry the First as Itinerant Justices, to go on circuits through every part of the kingdom, and to hear and determine pleas, as well civil and criminal as pleas of the Crown, arising within the several districts assigned to them, and these appointments were finally established and the kingdom divided into six circuits at the Council of Northampton in the 22nd year of Henry the Second.

In the same reign the judicial business of the Curia Regis appears to have been separated from its legislative functions, and the Court definitely established as a legal tribunal.

This step appears to have been taken by the King in consequence of complaints made to him of the partiality of his "Justiciæ" resiant in his Court, whose number he reduced from 18 to 5, and enacted "quod illi quinque " audirent omnes clamores regni et rectum facerent ; et " quod a Curia Regis non recederent, sed ibi ad audi- " endum clamores hominum remanerent, ita ut, si aliqua " quæstio inter eos veniret, quæ per eos ad finem duci " non posset, auditui regi præsentaretur et sicut ei, et " sapientoribus regni placeret, terminaretur."

Here we have the establishment not only of a permanent Court of Justice in the King's Court, but also of a still higher tribunal, that of the KING IN COUNCIL, to whom appeal was to be made in cases of difficulty.

INTRODUCTION.

The jurisdiction of the Curia Regis became eventually
so extensive, and the business transacted therein was of so
miscellaneous a character, that a sub-division of the Court
into distinct Departments became absolutely necessary,
and such a division is believed to have taken place at the
latter end of the reign of Richard the First. "Thence-
" forth pleas touching the Crown, together with common
" pleas of a civil and criminal nature, were continued to
" the Curia Regis; plaints of a fiscal kind were trans-
" ferred to the Exchequer; and for the Court of
" Chancery were reserved all matters unappropriated by
" the other Courts."

A further division took place in the 17th year of King
John, when, by the 11th chapter of Magna Charta, the
Court of Common Pleas was separated from the Curia
Regis and made stationary, being held thenceforward in
Westminster Hall. After this separation the Curia Regis
continued to be the superior Court of Law for all
criminal matters, and became eventually the Court of
King's Bench.

It does not appear at what precise period the change of
title took place, but in the old Calendars the Records are
called rolls of the Curia Regis to the end of the reign of
Henry the Third, after which date they are called rolls of
the King's Bench.

The Concilium Regis, or Select Council.

The Concilium Regis consisted of the Chancellor, the
Treasurer and Barons of the Exchequer, the Judges of
either Bench, the Itinerant Justices and Justices of
Assize, the great officers of State, and such of the
dignified clergy as it pleased the King to summon. There
was another Council with which this has sometimes been
confounded, called the Commune Concilium or National
Assembly, which met at the three great festivals of the
year, and was composed of "all the great men over all
" England, Archbishops and Bishops, Abbots and Earls,
" Thegns and Cniths;" but the Concilium Regis appears
to have been a Select Council chosen from the members
of the more numerous assembly, and exercising peculiar
functions. Thus "it was always about the King, attended
" upon him in all his expeditions, and followed him in all
" his progresses through the kingdom; petitions were
" constantly referred to it, and remedies provided by it
" without delay, and doubtful and intricate points of law
" were there discussed and determined *without waiting for*

INTRODUCTION.

" *the stated meetings* of the Common Council or convoking " an extraordinary assembly." To it, as has been stated, appeal was directed to be made from the Curia Regis by Henry II., and it continued to exercise its judicial functions for upwards of three hundred years until in course of time it came to be superseded by the Court of Chancery, the people finding it more expeditious and satisfactory to address their petitions to the Chancellor direct, knowing that to that high officer they would ultimately be referred.

After the equitable jurisdiction of the Court of Chancery was established, the ancient Council by degrees became extinct in consequence of the greater part of its functions devolving upon the Chancellor. The modern Privy Council appears to have grown out of the Select Council about the reign of Richard the Second.

The Court of Chancery.

The Office of Chancellor was of very great antiquity and of paramount importance.

The Chancellor was originally the King's Principal Secretary, and had the direction and conduct of all foreign affairs, performing most of the business which is now done by the Secretaries of State. He was usually a bishop or prelate, and was the head of the King's Chapel, and in the earlier periods of English history his Confessor. Hence he has been called the Keeper of the King's Conscience. He had the supervision of all charters, letters, and other public instruments, and the custody of the Great Seal. He also supervised and sealed the writs and precepts that issued in proceedings pending in the King's Court and in the Exchequer, and acted together with the Justiciaries and other great officers in matters of revenue at the Exchequer and elsewhere.

His rank in the Council was very high, and to him all petitions addressed to the King in Council were referred in the first instance to decide whether the cases were of sufficient importance for the King's interference, and if not, with the assistance of the other judicial officers, to give the required relief.

The establishment of the Chancery as a Court of Justice seems to have taken place about the end of the reign of Richard I., when the business of the Curia Regis was sub-divided amongst the principal officers of that Court, and its jurisdiction rapidly became very extensive.

INTRODUCTION.

Until the commencement of the reign of Edward III. the Chancellor and other " wise men of the law " were always in attendance on the King to assist him with their advice in cases of difficulty and need. At that time, however, the Chancery ceased to follow the King and became stationary, and consequently the petitions addressed to the King in Council were sent to the Chancellor " in Cancellaria; " and in the 22nd year of Edward III. a writ was addressed to the Chancellor investing him with full power to exercise jurisdiction in matters of *grace* and *favour*, and to this period may be traced the commencement of the Chancellor's independent jurisdiction in matters of equity.

The jurisdiction of the Court of Chancery was of two kinds, *ordinary* and *extraordinary*.

The ordinary jurisdiction was that wherein the Lord Chancellor, &c. in his proceedings and judgments was bound to observe the order and method of the Common Law, and the extraordinary jurisdiction was that which this Court exercised in matters of equity.

The ordinary Court held plea of recognizances acknowledged in the Chancery, on writs of *scire facias* for repeal of letters patent, writs of partition, &c., and also of all personal actions by or against officers of the Court ; and all Original Writs, Commissions of bankruptcy, lunacy, idiotcy, charitable uses, and other Commissions issued out of this Court.

The extraordinary Court, or Court of Equity, proceeded by the rules of equity and conscience, and moderated the rigour of the Common Law, considering the *intention* rather than the words of the law, " equity being the " correction of that wherein the law, by reason of its " universality, is deficient."

A suit to the equity jurisdiction of the Court of Chancery was commenced by preferring a Bill (signed by Counsel) in the nature of a petition to the Lord Chancellor, Lord Keeper, or Lords Commissioners of the Great Seal. If the suit, however, was instituted on behalf of the Crown, or of those whose rights are under its protection, as the objects of a public charity, the matter of complaint was offered by way of an Information presented by the proper officer, usually the Attorney-General.

Except in some few instances, bills and informations subsequent to the reign of Richard III. have been always in the English language ; and a suit thus preferred is therefore commonly termed a suit by *English Bill*, by way of distinction from the proceedings in suits within the ordinary jurisdiction of the Court, which,

INTRODUCTION.

till the statute of 4 Geo. II., were entered and enrolled
in the French or Latin tongue in the same manner as
the pleadings in the other Courts of Common Law.

The proceedings on the Common Law side of Chancery
consist of pleas on matters of record, viz. on Writs of
"Scire Facias" for the repeal of the Letters Patent; on
Writs of partition of land in coparcenary and for dower;
upon recognizances acknowledged pursuant to statute
merchant and statute staple; in traverses of offices found
for the Crown by inquisition; and in matters of lunacy
and idiotcy, &c.

When any fact was disputed on a "Scire Facias,"
&c., and issue was joined thereon, it was transmitted
to the Court of King's Bench for trial, and finally
adjudicated in that Court, and not afterwards returned
into Chancery except when a tenor of the proceedings
was asked for by a Writ of Certiorari. None of the
Records delivered by the Chancellor to the Chief Justice
of the King's Bench were ever remanded back into
Chancery.

It appears from a Petition to Parliament in the second
year of Henry IV. that when an issue of fact was joined
on the Common Law side of Chancery, the Chancellor,
instead of sending the issue to be tried in the Court of
King's Bench, was in the habit of calling the Common
Law Judges into Chancery to assist him in the discussion
of such issues, "to the great delay of the law and the
damage of the people;" but the matter appears to have
been left to the Chancellor's discretion.

But few of these pleas are now extant.

The Principal Officers of the Court of Chancery, in
addition to the Master of the Rolls and the Vice-Chancellors, were as follows:—

The MASTERS IN CHANCERY, to whom references
were made relating to matters of practice, the state of
the proceedings and accounts in Chancery suits, &c.,
whereof they made reports to the Court. They also
executed the orders of the Court, and by their reports
certified in what manner they had executed such orders.
They had the custody of such title deeds and original
instruments as the Court thought fit to place under
their care. Answers and affidavits were also sworn
before them, and they took the acknowledgments of
deeds, recognizances, &c. intended to be enrolled, and
executed all business of that kind. Each Master
executed the orders of reference made to him independently of the other Masters.

INTRODUCTION.

The SIX CLERKS in Chancery, or "Prothonotaries," whose duty it was to receive and file all bills, answers, replications, and other records in causes on the equity side of the Court of Chancery, and to enter memoranda of them in books, from which they were to certify to the Court as occasion should require the state of the proceedings in the various causes.

Each of the Six Clerks was assisted by a certain number of under clerks, or sworn clerks, of whom there were generally ten to each clerk, the whole number being known as the SIXTY CLERKS.

All the Records in the Office of the Six Clerks remained in their respective studies for the space of six terms, in order that the sworn clerks might resort to them when necessary without fee. After that time, they were sorted into bundles and deposited in the Record room.

In addition to these duties the Six Clerks made out certain Warrants and Patents, such as Patents for Ambassadors, Sheriff's Patents, &c.

The Six Clerks were abolished by Stat. 5 & 6 Vict., and their duties transferred to the Clerks of Records and Writs.

The CURSITORS, called also Clerks of Course or *Clerici de Cursu*, made out all original writs and processes returnable in the Court of King's Bench and elsewhere. They were 24 in number, and were abolished by Stat. 5 & 6 Wm. IV., and their duties transferred to the Petty Bag Office.

The CLERKS OF RECORDS AND WRITS were appointed by Stat. 5 & 6 Vict., 1842, to succeed to the duties and Records of the Six Clerks in Chancery.

The REGISTRARS. The duties of the Registrars were to attend the Court and take Minutes of all directions given, and to draw up the decrees, dismissions, and orders, which they entered in Registers.

The "Report Office" was a branch of the Registrars' Office, and in it were received and filed all Reports and Certificates made by the Masters and the Accountant-General. To it on the first day of Michaelmas term in each year were transferred the Decrees and Orders of the previous year, and in the Report Office were kept the Entry Books of Decrees and Orders from the time of Henry VIII., inclusive.

In the Report Office was also kept an account of all moneys, funds, and effects belonging to the suitors of the Court, of which a similar account was kept at the

INTRODUCTION.

Bank of England, and another at the Accountant-General's Office.

The CLERK OF THE HANAPER. The duties of the Clerk of the Hanaper were to get in the several ancient revenues of the Crown made payable to the Clerk of the Hanaper for the time being, and to pay thereout certain salaries and allowances to divers officers of the Court of Chancery by virtue of patents or of warrants under the authority of the Lord Chancellor, &c.

Accounts of these receipts and payments were made up and passed annually before the Commissioners for auditing the public Accounts.

It was also the duty of this Officer to take an account of all patents, commissions, and grants that pass the Great Seal, and to register the same in his office ; to collect the ancient fees thereon, and to account for certain proportions to the King, and to divers officers of the Court of Chancery.

The Hanaper Office was so called from the ancient practice of keeping the writs and returns relating to the business of the subject in a *hamper*, " in hanaperio," while those relating to such matters as immediately concerned the Crown were kept in a little sack or bag, *in parvá bagá*, whence the title of the Petty Bag Office.

The CLERKS OF THE PETTY BAG. These were originally three in number, and a great variety of business passed through their hands. They made out all Writs of Summons to Parliament, and the Writs of Congé d'élire for the electing of Archbishops and Bishops, with the Royal Assents, Patents of Assistance and Restitution of Temporalities thereto belonging, and all patents for the appointment of Collectors of Customs, Searchers, and Tidewaiters.

They also made out all attachments of privilege, and drew up the declarations and pleadings for and against Officers of the Court of Chancery and other privileged persons, and also on traverses of escheats and lunacies. They drew up all proceedings on Writs of Scire facias, and other proceedings on recognizances and bonds enrolled in Chancery, and made out all re-extents and liberates on the Statute Staple. They made out all special Writs of Scire facias to revoke letters patent ; Commissions to inquire of lands purchased by aliens, or given to superstitious uses, or derelict by the sea, and of all estates escheated or forfeited to the Crown for want of an heir, or by attainder, outlawry, or conviction of

INTRODUCTION.

treason or felony ; and Writs of Certiorari for removing Acts of Parliament and other Records into Chancery, which were then filed in the Petty Bag Office for the information of the Court.

They administered the oaths to Solicitors and various officers of the Court of Chancery, and enrolled their admissions. They also enrolled Surrenders of Offices, and until the Stat. 5 & 6 Wm. IV., the Specifications of patent inventions, and transacted a variety of other business. On the abolition of the Cursitors their duties were transferred to this office.

By Stat. 11 & 12 Vict., c. 94., the Clerks of the Petty Bag were reduced to a single Clerk, and the office was finally abolished in 1889.

The CLERK OF THE CUSTODIES. It was the duty of this Officer to make out Commissions of idiotcy and lunacy, and to transact the business connected therewith.

The office was abolished by Stat. 2 & 3 Wm IV., and the duties transferred to the Secretary of Lunatics.

The CLERK OF THE PRESENTATIONS. This officer made out the Letters Patent for grants of all ecclesiastical benefices and dignities (except bishoprics) in the gift of the Crown, of which he kept docket books, the grants being enrolled on the Patent Rolls.

The CLERK OF THE DISPENSATIONS AND FACULTIES. The duties of the Dispensation Office in Chancery were to make out and register confirmations of bishop's commendams, and of dispensations and doctors' degrees granted by the Archbishop of Canterbury, and also to register Masters of Arts' degrees and notarial faculties granted by the Archbishop of Canterbury. These confirmations were then passed under the Great Seal and enrolled on Rolls called Dispensation Rolls.

The CLERK OF THE LETTERS PATENT. This officer was appointed by Letters Patent 16 Jas. I., and his duty was to write and dispatch all grants, confirmations, charters, and letters patent under the Great Seal, the writing whereof did not belong or had not been already granted to any other officer of the Court of Chancery. The office was abolished by Stat. 2 & 3 Wm. IV.

The CLERK OF THE CROWN. The duties of the Clerk of the Crown in Chancery were as follows:—

To continually attend the Lord Chancellor in person or by deputy, to write and prepare for the Great Seal all Commissions for the King's service, viz., Commissions of Lieutenancy, of Justices of Assize, of Oyer

INTRODUCTION.

and Terminer, Gaol Delivery, and Commissions of the Peace, &c.

He also made out all general and special pardons, writs for summoning Peers to Parliament on their creation or succession; and writs for new members of the House of Commons on the occurrence of any vacancy. He received and filed the returns from the Sheriffs of the members of the House of Commons on their election, and certified the said returns to the House. He also received and filed the returns of the 16 Peers elected to represent Scotland, and certified the same to the House; and on the first day of every Parliament he attended the House with the return book of the members of the new Parliament. He also claimed to administer the oaths to the Lord Chancellor, Master of the Rolls, &c., &c.

The EXAMINERS IN CHANCERY. These conducted the examination of all witnesses in Chancery suits who could be examined in London, and took their depositions in writing, which were called Town Depositions.

The CLERK OF INROLMENTS and others.

The Court of King's Bench.

This Court was the remnant of the ancient Curia Regis or King's Court, which changed its title into that of Bancus Regius or King's Bench about the end of the reign of Henry the Third. It was so called because the King used formerly to sit in Court in person, the style of the Court being afterwards continued as *coram ipso rege*. During the reign of a Queen it was called the Queen's Bench, and during the Protectorate of Oliver Cromwell it was styled the Upper Bench.

The Court of King's Bench consisted of a Chief Justice and three puisne Judges, formerly four or five. Although the King occasionally sat himself in this Court, and was always supposed to do so, he did not determine any cause or motion except by the mouth of his Judges, to whom he committed his whole judicial authority. This Court was not, nor could it, from its nature and constitution, be fixed to any certain place, but followed the King's person wherever he went, for which reason all process issuing out of it in the King's name was returnable "ubicunque fuerimus in Anglia," wheresoever we shall then be in England. It was, indeed, for some centuries past usually held at Westminster, being an ancient palace of the Crown, " but might remove with the King to York " or Exeter if he thought proper to command it."

After the division of the Curia Regis, and the establishment of the Court of Common Pleas for the express purpose of determining civil suits, the Court of King's Bench exercised especial jurisdiction in all criminal matters and pleas of the Crown, leaving the judgment of private contracts and civil actions to the Common Pleas and other Courts.

The more modern jurisdiction of the Court was very high and transcendent, and it afterwards took cognizance of both criminal and civil causes; the former in what was called the Crown side or Crown Office, the latter in the Plea side of the Court.

On the Crown side it took cognizance of all criminal causes, from high treason down to the most trivial misdemeanour or breach of the peace. Into this Court also indictments from all inferior Courts might be removed by writ of *certiorari* and tried, either at bar or at *nisi prius*, by a Jury of the County out of which the indictment was brought.

The Plea side or civil branch of this Court originally took cognizance of all actions of trespass or other injury alleged to be committed *vi et armis;* of actions for forgery of deeds, maintenance, conspiracy, deceit, and actions on the case which allege any falsity or fraud; and all actions which savour of a criminal nature although the action is brought for a civil remedy, or which make the defendant liable in strictness to pay a fine to the King as well as damages to the injured party. But the Court might hold plea of any civil action, provided the defendant was an officer of the Court or in the *custody of the Marshal of the Court* for a breach of the peace or any other offence.

And thus in process of time it began by a legal fiction to hold plea of all personal actions whatsoever, it being surmised that the defendant was arrested for a supposed trespass, which he had never in reality committed, and being thus in the custody of the Marshal of the Court, the plaintiff was at liberty to proceed against him for any other personal injury.

The principal Officers of the King's Bench were as follows :—

On the *Crown Side:*

The CLERK OF THE CROWN, or Clerk of the Crown Office, who framed and recorded all Indictments against offenders therein arraigned of any public crime; he also taxed costs, nominated all Special Juries on the Crown

INTRODUCTION.

Side, took recognizances and inquisitions on the death of any prisoner dying in the King's Bench Prison, &c.

The SECONDARY, who drew up the paper books and made an estreat of all fines, &c. forfeited to the Crown.

The CLERK OF THE RULES, the EXAMINER, the CALENDAR KEEPER, and the CLERKS IN COURT.

On the *Plea Side :*

The CHIEF CLERKS.

The SECONDARY, who signed all judgments, &c. and in whose office were filed all writs returned, &c.

The CUSTOS BREVIUM, who filed all original writs and writs in Outlawry, and had several clerks under him for making up Records throughout England.

The CLERK OF THE PAPERS, who made up the Paper Book of "Special Pleas and Demurrers," &c.

The CLERK OF THE DECLARATIONS.

The CLERK OF THE RULES.

The CLERK OF THE BAILS AND POSTEAS.

The CLERK OF THE ERRORS.

The FILACERS, and others.

The Court of Common Pleas.

The Court of Common Pleas was originally a branch of the Curia Regis or King's Court, from which it was separated in the 17th year of King John by one of the clauses of Magna Charta, which directed that the Common Pleas should no longer follow the King, but should be held in a certain place, to wit, in Westminster Hall; and after that period all the writs ran "quod sit coram justiciariis meis apud Westmonasterium," whereas before that the party was required by them to appear "coram me et justiciariis meis," without any addition of place.

The jurisdiction of the Court of Common Pleas was general, and extended itself throughout England. It held plea of all civil causes at Common Law, between subject and subject, in actions real, personal, and mixed; but had no cognizance of pleas of the Crown. The authority of the Court was founded on original writs issuing out of Chancery, which writs were the King's mandates for the Court to proceed in the determination of the causes mentioned therein.

The reason of the original writs issuing out of Chancery was that when the Courts were united, as was formerly the case, the Chancellor held the seal, and when they were divided he, still retaining possession of the seal, continued to seal all original writs.

INTRODUCTION.

There were four Judges of the Court of Common Pleas, who were created by Letters Patent.

The principal officers of the Court were as follows:—

The CUSTOS BREVIUM, whose duty it was to receive and keep all writs returnable therein, and also all records of Nisi Prius, which were delivered to him by the Clerks of the Assize of every circuit, &c. The rolls were filed together by him, and carried into the Treasury of the Records. He also made the copies and exemplifications of all records and writs, &c.

The three PROTHONOTARIES, whose duties were to enter and enrol all declarations, pleadings, judgments, &c., and to make out all judicial writs of execution, writs of privilege, &c.

The SECONDARIES, or assistants to the Prothonotaries, who took the minutes and drew up all orders and rules of Court.

The FILAZERS, who made out all writs and process, such as *capias, alias, pluries,* &c. between the original writ and the declaration, and also all writs of view, &c.

The EXIGENTERS, whose duty it was to make out all writs of exigent and proclamations in actions of outlawry. The writ of exigent or *Exigi facias* was so called because it *exacted* the appearance of the party against whom it was issued within certain days of proclamation, under pain of outlawry.

The CLERK OF THE WARRANTS, who entered all warrants of attorney, enrolled deeds of bargain and sale, and estreated all issues.

The CLERK OF THE ESSOINS, who kept the roll in which were entered all *essoins* or *excuses* for non-appearance in Court by reason of sickness or other just cause of absence.

The CLERK OF THE JURIES, who made out all writs of " habeas corpora juratorum," to compel the appearance of juries, &c.

The CLERK OF THE TREASURY, who kept the Records of the Court and made copies and exemplifications of issues, judgments, &c.

The CLERK OF THE SEALS, who sealed all writs and mesne process, &c.

The CLERK OF THE OUTLAWRIES, who made out all writs of " capias utlagatum," &c.

The CLERK OF THE ERRORS, whose duty it was to allow writs of error returnable in the King's Bench upon proceedings in the Common Pleas, to enter all the proceedings on writs of error, and to make the

transcript of the judgment roll where required, and carry
it to the proper officer of the King's Bench.

The CLERK OF INROLMENTS OF FINES AND RECO-
VERIES, who returned all writs of entry and seisin,
writs of covenant, &c., and enrolled and exemplified
fines and recoveries.

The CLERK OF THE KING'S SILVER, who received
all the *pre* and *post* fines on alienation of lands and
entered an extract of the Fines, with the sums paid
thereon, in books called King's Silver Books.

The CHIROGRAPHER, whose duty it was to engross
all fines and to deliver the several indentures to the
parties, &c.

The Court of Exchequer.

The Court of Exchequer, or " Scaccarium Regis," was
an ancient Court of Record wherein all cases touching the
rights and revenues of the Crown were heard and determined, and where the revenues of the Crown were received.
It was called the Exchequer (*Fr.* " Eschequier," *Lat.*
" Scaccarium ") from the chequered cloth resembling a
chess-board, which covered the table there, and on which,
when certain of the King's accounts were made up, the
sums were marked or scored with counters. It consisted
of two branches: the Administrative portion, which
managed the Royal Revenue, and was subdivided into an
Exchequer of Account and an Exchequer of Receipt, and
the Court or Judicial part of the Exchequer, which was
again subdivided into a Court of Equity and a Court of
Common Law.

The Exchequer of Account consisted of the King's
Remembrancer's Department, the Lord Treasurer's Remembrancer's Department (including the Pipe Office), and
the Land Revenue Department, to which were subsequently added the Augmentation Office and the First
Fruits and Tenths' Department ; the Exchequer of Receipt
comprising the Offices of the Auditors, the Clerk of the
Pells, &c., and the Treasury of the Receipt.

The primary and original business of the Court of
Exchequer was to call the King's Debtors to account, by
bill filed by the Attorney-General ; and to recover any
lands, tenements, or hereditaments, any goods, chattels, or
other profits or benefits belonging to the Crown.

Thus by their original constitution the jurisdiction of the
Courts of Common Pleas, King's Bench, and Exchequer

was entirely separate and distinct; the Common Pleas being intended to decide all controversies between subject and subject; the King's Bench to correct all crimes and misdemeanours that amounted to a breach of the King's peace or an infringement of the Royal Prerogative; and the Exchequer to adjust and recover the King's revenue. The Court of Exchequer was, however, inferior in rank not only to the Court of King's Bench but to the Common Pleas also.

The Court of Equity was held in the Exchequer Chamber, before the Lord Treasurer, the Chancellor of the Exchequer, the Chief Baron, and three puisne Barons. In this Court the clergy for a long time used to exhibit their bills for the non-payment of tithes, they being in point of fact the King's debtors, but in later years a large share of this business was transferred to the Chancery. On the Equity side of the Exchequer the proceedings were by English bill and answer, as in the Court of Chancery, in matters concerning the King the bills being brought by the Attorney-General, and called Informations. The Equity jurisdiction of the Court of Exchequer was abolished in 1841 and transferred to the Court of Chancery.

As by a fiction almost all sorts of civil actions were at a later period allowed to be brought in the King's Bench, in like manner, by another fiction, all kinds of personal actions might be prosecuted in the Court of Exchequer, and this gave origin to the Common Law side of its jurisdiction, which existed originally merely for the benefit of the King's Accountants, and was exercised by the Barons only, and not by the Treasurer or the Chancellor. The writ upon which all proceedings on this side were grounded was called a *quo minus:* in which the plaintiff suggested that he was the King's farmer or debtor, and that the defendant had done him the injury or damage complained of: *quo minus sufficiens existit (by which* he is *the less* able) to pay the King his debt or rent. This surmise of being the King's debtor, however, became eventually a mere matter of form, and the Court was open to all the nation equally; and the same holds good with regard to the Equity side of the Court, for there any person might file a bill against another on the bare suggestion that he was the King's accomptant.

The Court of Exchequer was generally held at Westminster as the usual place of the King's residence, but it has occasionally been held elsewhere at the King's pleasure, as at Winchester, &c.

INTRODUCTION.

The Exchequer, as stated by Coke in his 4th Institute, has been reckoned to consist of seven Courts, viz. :

The Court of Pleas;

The Court of Accounts;

The Court of Receipts;

The Court of Exchequer-Chamber (being the assembly of all the judges of England for difficult matters of law);

The Court of Exchequer-Chamber (for Errors in the Exchequer).

Do. (for Errors in the King's Bench).

The Court of Equity in the Exchequer-Chamber.

The principal officers of the Court of Exchequer were as follows:—

THE LORD TREASURER.

THE CHANCELLOR and UNDER-TREASURER, who had the custody of the Seal of the Court.

THE CHAMBERLAINS, who had the keys of the Treasury in which the Records were kept, including the Domesday Book, &c.

THE KING'S REMEMBRANCER, who had the custody of all manner of informations on penal statutes and entered the rules and orders made thereon. He also called to account all the great Accountants of the Crown, the Collectors of Customs, &c., and made out all writs of privilege and entered judgments on pleas. He also had the custody of all proceedings on English Bills.

THE LORD TREASURER'S REMEMBRANCER, who made out all the Estreats and took an account of all debts of the Sheriffs, and passed their "Foreign Accounts," &c. He also issued out Writs and Process in many cases.

The Lord Treasurer's Remembrancer's office may be properly said to be the office of the Court of Exchequer, wherein the rendering of the *duties* of the Crown to which the subject may be liable was to be enforced at once by proceedings in the nature of final process; whilst on the other hand the office of the King's Remembrancer may be appropriately described as that in which the King's *debts* were recoverable.

Under the words *duties* are comprehended all things due to the King, as *rents*, *fines*, *issues*, *amerciaments*, &c. which were received or levied by the Sheriffs, while the King's *debts*, to the matters concerning which the King's Remembrancer's office was exclusively dedicated, may be taken to mean all such *occasional* debts as were

INTRODUCTION.

not yet reduced to duties and put upon the Roll of the Pipe.

The King's Remembrancer also had the survey and prosecution of all such acts to the injury of the Crown or the public as might be considered in the nature of *torts* or trespasses.

THE COMPTROLLER OF THE PIPE and the CLERK OF THE PIPE, through whose office all accounts and debts due to the King were conveyed, "as water through a pipe."

The CLERK OF THE ESTREATS, who received the estreats from the office of the Lord Treasurer's Remembrancer and copied them out on the Estreat Rolls.

The FOREIGN APPOSER, who apposed, or made a charge on all sheriffs, &c. of their "green wax," (*i.e.*, of the fines, issues, amerciaments, recognizances, &c. certified in estreats annexed to the writ under the seal of green wax), and delivered the same to the Clerk of the Estreats to be put in process.

The three AUDITORS (of RECEIPT, IMPREST, and LAND REVENUE), who received and audited the accounts of the King's Receivers, Collectors, &c. .

The TELLERS, whose business it was to receive and pay all sums of money.

The CLERK OF THE PELLS, so called from his parchment rolls or "Pelles Receptorum."

The CLERK OF THE NIHILS, who made a separate roll of such sums as the sheriff upon process returned "Nihil," &c.

The CLERK OF THE PLEAS, in whose office all officers and privileged persons were to sue and be sued.

The CLERK OF THE SUMMONS, the CLERK OF THE HANAPER, the SECONDARIES of the two Remembrancers, &c., &c.

The "COURT OF THE AUGMENTATIONS OF THE REVENUES OF THE CROWN," established by Henry VIII., with which the "COURT OF THE GENERAL SURVEYORS OF THE KING'S LANDS" was subsequently incorporated, was finally dissolved by Statute 1 Mary, Sess. 2, c. 10., and annexed to the Court of Exchequer by Letters Patent of the same year. The Records of this Court, or rather of the "AUGMENTATION OFFICE" in the Exchequer, form a very considerable and important branch of the Exchequer Records, and are fully described in the present volume, under the several titles of "Crown

INTRODUCTION.

Lands and Rents," " Ministers' and Receivers' Accounts," and "Monastic Foundations, &c." The constitution and functions of the Court are described in the article relating to "Ministers' and Receivers' Accounts."

The "COURT OF FIRST FRUITS AND TENTHS," also erected by Henry VIII., for the regulation of the Ecclesiastical Revenues to which he became entitled on throwing off the Papal Supremacy, was dissolved by Letters Patent of 1 Mary and united to the Court of Exchequer. First Fruits were abolished by Statute 2 & 3 Philip and Mary, c. 4., but revived by Statute 1 Elizabeth, and again put under the survey of the Court of Exchequer. The Records of the FIRST FRUITS' AND TENTHS' OFFICE in the Exchequer are fully described in the present volume, under the title " Ecclesiastical Matters."

SPECIAL AND ABOLISHED JURISDICTIONS.
High Court of Admiralty.

The Court of Admiralty is stated to have been established in the reign of Edward III., although the Lord High Admiral exercised jurisdiction in all maritime affairs from a much earlier period. The office of Admiral is now executed by Commissioners, who, by Statute 2 Will. and Mary, c. 2., are declared to have the same authorities, jurisdictions, and powers as the Lord High Admiral.

The Cinque Ports are, however, exempt from the Admiralty of England, their jurisdiction being vested in the Warden of the said ports.

The High Court of Admiralty, though not a Court of Record, had jurisdiction where the Common Law could give no remedy, and took cognizance of all maritime causes or causes arising wholly upon the sea.

This Court was sub-divided into an Instance Court, a Prize Court, and a Court of Appeal for Prizes.

In the Instance Court proceedings were taken in suits relating to seamen's wages, damage to ships, salvage and droits, and in cases of piracy ; warrants being issued therefrom, on due cause being shown, for the arrest of ships and cargoes, and occasionally of masters and owners.

In the Prize Court, and in the Court of Appeal for Prizes, were decided all cases arising out of prizes taken

from an enemy in time of war, in pursuance of the Prize
Acts usually passed at the commencement of a war, the
provisions of which varied from time to time. In the
Prize Court were also kept Registers of all Letters of
Marque and Reprisal.

There were also Vice-Admiralty Courts in the foreign
dominions of the Crown, from which (except in the case
of prizes) appeals were made to the High Court of
Admiralty, and also to the King in Council.

The appellate jurisdiction from the Instance Court of
Admiralty was vested in the High Court of Delegates.

Court of Arches.

The Court of Arches (*Curia de Arcubus*), so called from
the church in which it was formerly held, St. Mary le
Bow, or *de arcubus*, is a Court of Appeal in ecclesiastical
causes from the courts of the several Bishops or Ordinaries
within the Province of Canterbury, and its jurisdiction
extends to all causes or suits relating to wills, intestacies,
tithes, church rates, marriages, and other matters
cognizable in these Courts.

There are a few proceedings in the Court of Arches of
early dates to be found amongst the Miscellanea of the
Exchequer.

Court of Chivalry.

The Court of Chivalry, Court Military, or Earl Marshal's
Court, which was established by Edward I., was a military
court and court of honour formerly held before the Lord
High Constable and the Earl Marshal of England. When
held before the Earl Marshal only, it was a military court
or court of honour simply, but when before the Lord High
Constable, jointly with the Earl Marshal, it was also a
criminal court. Since the extinction of the office of Lord
High Constable, by the attainder of the Duke of
Buckingham in the reign of Henry VIII., it has been
usually held before the Earl Marshal only in civil
causes.

The jurisdiction of this Court is declared by Statute
13 Rich. II. c. 2., to be " to take cognizance of contracts
" touching deeds of arms or of war out of the realm, and also
" of things which touch war within the realm which cannot
" be discussed by the Common Law ; together with other
" usages and customs to the same matters appertaining."

INTRODUCTION.

It also gave relief to such of the nobility and gentry as felt themselves aggrieved in matters of honour, and corrected encroachments in matters of coat-armour, precedency, and other distinctions of families.

The proceedings in the Court are stated to have been by petition in a summary way, and the trial not by a jury but by witnesses or by combat. A jury, however, appears to have been impannelled in criminal cases, as appears from the " Placita Exercitus Regis " of 24 Edward I.

The last proceedings in this Court were in the year 1631, and are printed in Rushworth's collections. An attempt, however, to revive the Earl Marshal's Court was made in the reign of Queen Anne, in the case of Blunt, which is reported.

The marshalling of coat armour is now in the hands of the Heralds, who were formerly attendants upon this Court.

High Court of Delegates.

The Court of Delegates was established by Henry VIII. in the 25th year of his reign in order to supersede the Papal jurisdiction in appeals from the Ecclesiastical Courts.

It took cognizance of questions of marriage and legitimacy, and of disputes relating to the payment of tithes, fees, obventions, &c., and also of offences against morals and good behaviour, of which the business of the Consistorial Courts chiefly consisted.

In every case of appeal to this Court a Special Commission under the Great Seal was issued out of the Court of Chancery, directed to such persons, called Judices Delegati, as the Lord Chancellor for the time being should see fit to appoint to hear and determine the same.

The Court of Delegates exercised an appellate jurisdiction not only from all the Ecclesiastical Courts but also from the Instance Court of the High Court of Admiralty, This Court was abolished in 1823, and the Processes or Records of the Proceedings were subsequently transferred from the Registrar of the High Court of Admiralty, in whose custody they had previously been, to the Public Record Office.

INTRODUCTION.

Court of High Commission in Ecclesiastical Causes.

This Court was erected and united to the regal power by virtue of the Statute 1 Eliz. c. 1., instead of a large jurisdiction which had previously been exercised under the Pope's authority. It was intended "to vindicate "the dignity and peace of the Church by reforming, "ordering, and correcting the ecclesiastical state and "persons, and all manner of heresies, schisms, abuses, "offences, contempts, and enormities."

Under the shelter of these very general words means were found to vest in the High Commissioners extraordinary and almost despotic powers of fining and imprisoning, which they exercised much beyond the degree of the offence itself, and frequently over offences by no means of spiritual cognizance. In consequence of these abuses this Court was justly abolished by Statute 16 Car. I. c. 2. The Minute Books of the Court of High Commission exist in the Series of Domestic State Papers.

Marshalsea and Palace Courts.

The Marshalsea Court, or Court of the Marshalsea of the King's Household, was originally instituted for the purpose of administering justice between the King's domestic servants.

It was presided over by the Lord Steward and the Earl Marshal, and was at first held in the Aula Regis. Eventually it became a distinct jurisdiction, holding pleas of all trespasses committed within the verge of the Court (12 miles round the royal residence).

The Marshalsea Court was gradually superseded by the erection in the sixth year of Charles I. of a new Court called the "Curia Palatii," or *Palace Court*, with jurisdiction in all manner of personal actions within 12 miles of the Palace of Whitehall, but not extending into the City of London.

The latter Court, together with the ancient Court of Marshalsea, was afterwards held in King Street, in the borough of Southwark, from whence they were removed to Scotland Yard, Westminster.

Both the Courts were finally abolished by Statute 12 & 13 Vict., and the Records directed to be placed under the custody of the Master of the Rolls.

INTRODUCTION.

Peveril Court.

The Court of the Honor of Peveril, which extended into several counties, was of great antiquity, and seems to have comprised both a Tourn and a View of Frankpledge, the former, which was holden twice a year at Nottingham, having jurisdiction to hear and determine all felonies (death of man excepted) and common nuisances.

The latter, which met once in every three weeks, had jurisdiction over those matters which were exempt from the Tourn.

The Bailiwick of the Honor of Peveril was granted in 11 Edward III. to William Eland and his heirs for ever, in whose family it remained until the reign of Henry VIII., when it was alienated by the then heir to Henry Willoughby, together with all profits and charges, and all Records, Evidences, Court Rolls, and Writings concerning and belonging to the said office. In 1607 the office of High Steward of the Honor of Peveril, &c., and the keeping of all courts within the said Honor, was granted by James I. to Sir George and Sir Edward Goring, and, although this lease was disputed by Sir Percival Willoughby, to whom the estate had descended, the Gorings obtained a Decree against him in the Court of Exchequer, by which the lease was confirmed.

In 1672 the office was granted by Charles II. to the Marquis of Worcester and his two sons for the term of their lives, the limits of the Court being then further extended, and a Court of Record appointed to be held every Tuesday, in which should be heard and determined all pleas of debts, trespass, &c., and all personal actions arising within the Honor aforesaid, in which the debts, damages, &c. did not exceed the sum of 50l.

On the death of the last survivor of the three grantees above mentioned, the family of Willoughby once more obtained a grant of the said Stewardship, and in their hands it remained till the Peveril Court was abolished by Statute 12 & 13 Vict. c. 101. The Records of this Court commence about the year 1682.

Court of Requests.

This, sometimes called the "Court of Conscience," was an equity court for poor men's causes, established in the ninth year of Henry the Seventh, the president of the Court being the Lord Privy Seal, who was assisted by the Masters of Requests as the ordinary judges. Originally, this court was intended for the suits of poor men only, which were made to the King by way of supplication, and upon which they were entitled to have right without the

INTRODUCTION.

payment of money ; but before its dissolution it took cognizance of almost all suits that by colour of equity or
supplication to the Prince could be brought before him.
An order was made in Chancery, dated 30 November 1588
referring all poor persons seeking relief in that Court to
the Court of Requests, and further ordinances in 1618–19
refer all plaintiffs suing in *formâ pauperis* to that Court.

Sir Richard Fanshawe, one of the Masters of the Court,
is stated to have asserted it to be the right of his office to
receive all petitions to the King, in opposition to the
Secretary of State, and that such was the practice in the
reign of Charles I., but his claim to do so was disallowed.

The Court was virtually abolished by Statute 16 Car. I.
c. 10 ; but the office of Master of the Requests continued
during the following reign, the last of such appointments
bearing date 12 March, 32 Car. II.

The Records of this Court were removed from the
Palace at Westminster to the Chapter House in 1732, and
finally from thence to the Public Record Office.

Court of Star Chamber.

The Court of Star Chamber, which took its name from
the *Camera Stellata*, the "Starred Chamber," or Council
Chamber of the King's Palace at Westminster, in which it
was held, had its origin in the *Concilium Regis* or Select
Council, for which it was at first but another name.

By the Statutes of 3 Hen. VII. c. 1. and 21 Hen.
VIII. c. 20., the jurisdiction of the Council, or of a part of
the Council, was, however, directed to a particular class of
offences, such as riots and unlawful assemblies, the misdemeanour of sheriffs in the returns and panels of juries,
the giving of liveries signs and tokens, and unlawful main-
tenances ; and this jurisdiction came to be recognised as the
peculiar function of the Court of Star Chamber.

During the reign of Hen. VIII. the action of the Court
appears to have been by no means oppressive, but rather to
have "provided security for the humbler members of the
" community against oppression by their richer or more
" powerful neighbours"; this was, however, afterwards,
as stated by Clarendon, stretched "to the asserting of all
" proclamations and orders of state ; to the vindicating of
" illegal commissions and grants of monopolies ; holding
" for honourable that which pleased, and for just that
" which profited, and becoming both a Court of Law to
" determine civil rights, and a court of revenue to enrich
" the Treasury, the Council table by proclamations en-

INTRODUCTION.

" joining to the people that which was not enjoined by the
" laws, and prohibiting that which was not prohibited,
" and the Star Chamber, which consisted of the same
" persons in different rooms, censuring the breach and
" disobedience to those proclamations by very great fines,
" imprisonments, and corporal severities ; so that any dis-
" respect to any acts of state, or to the persons of states-
" men, was in no time more penal and the foundations of
" right never more in danger to be destroyed."

These abuses led to the final abolition of the Court by Statute 16 Car. 1. c. 10.

The Records of this Court consist of Bills, Answers, Depositions, and other proceedings of great historical and genealogical interest. The Decrees and Orders of the Court are, however, unfortunately no longer extant.

Court of Wards and Liveries.

The Court of Wards was instituted by Statute 32 Hen. VIII. c. 46., to superintend and regulate inquiries upon the death of the King's tenants *in capite* as to the lands of which they died seised, and the name and age of the next heir, &c., in order that the royal claims to the marriage, wardship, relief, primer seisin, and other advantages might be duly enforced, and to take account of the sums received by way of Fines, Compositions, Sales of Wardships, or otherwise. The office of Liveries was united to this Court by Statute 33 Hen. VIII. c. 22.

The judicial Records of the Court consist of original Bills, Answers, and Depositions relating to matters within the jurisdiction of the Court, and of Books of Affidavits, Decrees, Orders, and other Proceedings.

The Accounts, Inquisitions, Surveys, Grants and Sales of Wardship, Leases, and other documents relating to the general business of the Court, are referred to in the present volume, under the head of " Wards and Minors."

The Court of Wards and Liveries was finally abolished by Statute 12 Car. II. c. 24.

RECORDS OF THE DUCHY OF LANCASTER.

The important and valuable private muniments belonging to the Duchy of Lancaster were, by the munificence of Her Majesty, presented to the nation in 1868.

These are entirely distinct from the Records of the County Palatine, which, although *public*, are purely local, whilst the Duchy Records, though *private*, concern the government and

INTRODUCTION.

jurisdiction of the entire dominion of the Duchy, and embrace the County Palatine as a subordinate regality.

The ancient possessions of the Duchy of Lancaster comprise the Honor and County of Lancaster (the Honor extending into the Counties of Lancaster, Norfolk, Suffolk, Lincoln, Nottingham, Leicester, Derby, York, Rutland, and Stafford), the Honors of Leicester and Derby, Bolingbroke, Pickering, Pontefract, Tickhill, Halton, and several others, with various important possessions annexed to it by Acts of the Legislature at various times, as the Honors of Clare and Mandeville, together with the vast possessions of the Earldoms of Hereford and Essex.

Nearly every county in England and Wales is in fact represented as contributing to form part of the territories, and as being to some extent under the jurisdiction of the Duchy of Lancaster,— the Earls, and subsequently the Dukes, of Lancaster, enjoying by grants from the Crown such *Jura regalia* and prerogative rights within their possessions as were communicable to a subject.

The County of Lancaster was elevated by Edward III. in 1351 into a *Palatinate*, with its own Courts of Judicature, as a Court of Chancery, an Exchequer, and Courts of Common Law, but the Records of these Courts relate to the *County* of Lancaster only, and are quite distinct from those of the *Duchy*.

The Chancellor of the Duchy of Lancaster had, however, a special jurisdiction in all matters of equity relating to lands held of the King in right of the Duchy, his Court, which was held in Westminster Hall, being known as the Court of the Duchy Chamber of Lancaster.

An Inventory of the Records of the Duchy of Lancaster, together with a sketch of the history of the Duchy and of the Palatinate, is printed in the Deputy Keeper's 30th Report.

In addition to the Pleadings and other judicial Records of the Court of the Duchy Chamber, the Duchy Records comprise a large collection of Charters and Grants, Ancient Deeds, Leases, Ministers' and Receivers' Accounts, Surveys and Rentals, and other documents analogous to those of the Superior Courts at Westminster, which are described in the following pages, under the titles indicated.

See also the Indexes to the Duchy of Lancaster Records described under the title of "Ayloffe's Calendars."

RECORDS OF THE PALATINATE OF DURHAM.

The Palatinate of Durham has existed from time immemorial by prescriptive right, and, until the year 1836, was vested in the Bishop of Durham for the time being. Within the limits of his diocese the Bishop exercised, conjointly with his ecclesiastical functions, all the temporal rights which belong to a lord palatine. "He had his Courts of Chancery, Common Pleas, and Exchequer,

INTRODUCTION.

" possessing the same powers in the Palatinate as the Sovereign's
" courts had in other parts of the Realm. He had power to levy
" taxes for the defence and service of the Palatinate, to make
" truce with his enemies, to raise troops and impress ships in
" time of war. He sat in judgment of life and death, and could
" inflict capital punishment. He had power to create Palatinate
" barons, to summon them to his councils, and to confiscate their
" lands in case of treason. He possessed all manner of royal
" jurisdictions and rights ; could coin money, grant licences to
" erect castles, build churches, found charities and hospitals,
" create corporations, and grant markets and fairs. Every source
" of profit and every post of honour or service was at his disposal,
" with which the Sovereign could not interfere, nor were royal
" writs allowed to run in the Palatinate without the Bishop's
" sanction."

These extensive liberties and rights were severed from the
Bishopric in 1836 and settled by Act of Parliament on the then
sovereign and his successors.

The Records of the Palatinate of Durham, with the exception
of a few of modern date, which were left behind to facilitate the
transaction of current business, were removed to London and
placed in the Public Record Office, pursuant to a warrant of the
Master of the Rolls, dated 17 November 1868.

They consist of five Divisions :—

(1.) The Prothonotary's Records, comprising the Judicial
Proceedings of the Court of Pleas at Durham.

(2.) The Clerk of the Crown's Records, which consist of
the Indictments, Depositions, and other proceedings at
Assizes.

(3.) The Cursitor's Records, comprising the Chancery Enrolments of the Bishopric, the Inquisitions post mortem,
Registers, &c., and the Halmote Books or Records of the
Halmote Courts, which were formerly held pursuant to the
Bishop's Commission to receive surrenders of copyhold lands,
and to admit such persons as had right thereto, according to
the custom ; to assess and settle all such fines and amercements as arose within the said Courts, and to hear and
determine all suits, complaints, debates, contentions, &c.
between party and party which arose within the said County
or elsewhere within the County Palatinate of Durham. These
Books are further described in the present volume under the
head of " Court Rolls."

(4.) The Registrar's Records, consisting of the Bills,
Answers, and other proceedings in the Court of Chancery at
Durham.

(5.) The Auditor's Records, consisting of the Receiver's
Rolls, Rentals, and counterparts of Leases relating to the
estates of the Bishopric.

INTRODUCTION.

The latter, being claimed by the Ecclesiastical Commissioners
as their private muniments, and necessary for the management
of the estates placed under their control by Act of Parliament,
were, with the exception of a bundle of ancient Sheriffs' Accounts and other documents of a miscellaneous nature, re-trans-
ferred to their custody in 1876.

The earliest of the Records of the Palatinate of Durham, the
Register of Bishop Kellawe, which relates to the affairs of the
Palatinate between the years 1311–1316, has been printed in the
series of "Chronicles and Memorials, &c.," of which it occupies
four volumes.

In the present volume the greater part of the Records have been
classified under the heads "Chancery Enrolments," "Court Rolls,"
"Fines and Recoveries," "Inquisitions post mortem, &c.," and
"Judicial Proceedings."

RECORDS OF THE PALATINATE OF LANCASTER.

The County of Lancaster was erected into a Palatinate by
Edward the Third in the year 1351, when he created Henry
Earl of Lancaster *Duke* of Lancaster, and granted to him, for the
term of his life, Palatinate rights within the said county.

By this charter power was given him to have his Court of
Chancery, and to appoint Justices to hold Pleas of the Crown
and other Pleas touching the Common Law, with all other
liberties and "jura regalia" pertaining to a County Palatine. On
his death, in 1361, the Palatinate was extinguished for about 16
years, but in 1377 it was revived in the person of John of Gaunt,
who had married the sole surviving heiress of the first Duke of
Lancaster, and who had conferred upon him for life "jura regalia"
within the County Palatine, co-extensive with those of the King
elsewhere. By the Acts of 1 Hen. IV. and 2 Hen. V. these "jura
regalia" were extended to all the possessions which had been
annexed to the Duchy.

Under the term "Jura Regalia" the Duke of Lancaster had
the exclusive administration of justice by his courts of equity and
common law in the Duchy and Palatinate of Lancaster.

These courts (closely analogous in their construction and practice
to the King's superior courts) consist of a Court of Chancery, a
Court of Common Pleas for the decision of civil suits, and a Court
of Criminal Jurisdiction.

By the operation of the Judicature Act of 36 & 37 Vict. the
jurisdiction of the Court of Common Pleas at Lancaster has
been transferred to the High Court of Justice. The Court of

INTRODUCTION.

Criminal Jurisdiction in no way differs from that of the ordinary courts.

The Records of these courts were, until their removal to London, in the charge of three several persons in Lancashire, and, except a few of modern date which had been removed to Preston for the convenience of the current business, were preserved in Lancaster Castle.

The Clerk of the Crown had the custody of the criminal proceedings of the Palatinate, the Prothonotary had charge of the Records of the Court of Common Pleas at Lancaster, whilst the Records of the Chancery of the County Palatine were in the custody of the Registrar of that Court.

RECORDS OF THE PRINCIPALITY OF WALES AND OF THE PALATINATE OF CHESTER.

The Records of the Principality of Wales (with the exception of those of the Palatinate of Chester, which are of much earlier origin), may be said to date, with few exceptions, from the establishment of the Courts of Great Sessions of Wales by the Statute of 34 & 35 Henry VIII.

Assizes appear to have been held in Wales in the reign of Edward I., the Statutum Walliæ of 12 Edward I. containing the form of the Patent appointing Justices of Assize for Wales, which, by the same Statute, was divided into seven counties, viz., Snowdon, Anglesey, Caernarvon, Merioneth, Flint, Carmarthen, and Cardigan,—Sheriffs and Coroners being also directed to be appointed for those counties. Of these counties Anglesey, Carnarvon, and Merioneth were generally known as *North Wales*, Carmarthen (to which Pembroke was afterwards joined) as *South Wales*, and Cardigan as *West Wales*.

There are a few Welsh Assize Rolls amongst the Records of the Queen's Bench, and a great number of Accounts of the Chamberlains, Sheriffs, Ministers and Receivers, and other Officers of the Welsh Counties amongst the Records of the Court of Exchequer.

By the Statute of 34 & 35 Hen. VIII. Wales was divided into 12 counties, eight of which, viz., Anglesey, Carnarvon, Carmarthen, Cardigan, Flint, Glamorgan, Merioneth, and Pembroke were of ancient origin ; whilst Brecknock, Radnor, Denbigh, and Montgomery had been recently made by Stat. 27 Hen. VIII.

By the said Statute of 34 & 35 Hen. VIII. sessions were directed to be held twice every year in each of the said counties, to be called the Great Sessions of Wales, which, although similar

INTRODUCTION.

sessions may have been held previously, were finally established by that Statute.

By the same Act the counties of Wales were sub-divided into four circuits, for each of which original and judicial seals were directed to be provided. These were:—

(1.) The CHESTER CIRCUIT, including the counties of Cheshire, Flint, Denbigh, and Montgomery.

(2.) The NORTH WALES CIRCUIT, comprising Anglesey, Carnarvon, and Merioneth.

(3.) The BRECKNOCK CIRCUIT, consisting of Brecknock, Radnor, and Glamorgan.

(4.) The CARMARTHEN CIRCUIT, consisting of Carmarthen, Pembroke, and Cardigan, with the Town of Haverfordwest.

The several proceedings at the Courts of Great Sessions are described in the present volume, under the heads of "Judicial Proceedings" and "Fines and Recoveries" respectively.

The Records of the County Palatine of Chester (which included the County of Flint, that county having from its first conquest been annexed to the Palatinate of Chester for its civil and criminal jurisdiction), although classified amongst the Welsh Records, with which they were in 1854 transferred to the Public Record Office, are of a much more ancient and varied character, the Chamberlain of Chester having had equitable jurisdiction in the Exchequer of Chester from the first existence of the County Palatine, which dates from the reign of Henry III.

The constitution of this Court was somewhat peculiar, and is fully described in Mr. Black's able Report on the Records of Wales and Chester, printed in the Deputy Keeper's First Report. It is therein stated that the Exchequer of Chester was coeval with the existence of the County Palatine, and though principally a *Court of Revenue*, was probably a *Court of Justice* also, before that of the Justiciary was established. Hence, not only were all accounts rendered into it, and process issued thence against the King's debtors within the limits of its jurisdiction, but it was the *Chancery Court* of the Palatinate, and had an exclusive jurisdiction in Equity as fully as the Chancery of England. It possessed also a jurisdiction at Common Law in matters of debt, even for small sums, in the nature of a *Court of Conscience*, and had a peculiar practice of granting writs of protection to poor debtors.

The chief officer of this Court was the Chamberlain of Chester, who had all the powers of a Chancellor, and exercised his judicial functions by a deputy, called the Vice-Chamberlain.

There was also a Baron of the Exchequer, whose business resembled that of a Master in Chancery; but, by the constitution of the Court, the custody of the Records was vested in a third

INTRODUCTION.

officer, called the " Seal Keeper," whose duty it was to have the custody of the Seal of the County Palatine and to seal all writs and processes issuing out of the Baron's office.

The principal Records of the Palatinate of Chester consist of the Chancery Enrolments or " Recognizance Rolls," of Chamberlains' and Ministers' Accounts, Forest Rolls, Court Rolls, and Inquisitions; and of the Rolls of Justices in Eyre, or Assize Rolls, Indictment Rolls, Plea Rolls, Fines and Recoveries, and other Judicial Proceedings, all of which are described in the present volume under the titles of the several classes to which they respectively belong.

RECORDS OF THE STATE PAPER OFFICE.

During the Norman and Plantagenet period the affairs of the State in England were managed by the King's Council, in which the Lord Chancellor exercised the functions of a modern Secretary of State. To him was entrusted the supervision of all Letters, Charters, and other public documents which required the authentication of the Great Seal, and it became the duty of the Prothonotary of the Chancery to draw up, pass under the Great Seal, and enrol all Treaties, Leagues, Ratifications, and other Instruments which passed between the Sovereign of this country and other Sovereigns and States, and also all Commissions, Powers and Orders to Ambassadors, and other documents of a diplomatic nature.

It is therefore to the Patent and Close Rolls, the Treaty Rolls, and other Chancery Enrolments that we must look for the record of State documents prior to the reign of Henry VIII.

Many of the documents from which the enrolments were made, and also much correspondence which does not appear to have been enrolled, were, however, formerly preserved on the Files of the Chancery. These documents have been formed into the class known formerly as " Royal and Historical Letters" and now as " Ancient Correspondence."

In process of time the business of the State began to be exercised in a less formal manner, and to be diverted into other channels, and the King's Secretary (who was at first styled the King's Clerk, then Secretary, afterwards Principal Secretary, and who, probably about the time of Elizabeth, was first called Secretary of State,) was gradually employed to execute much of the business formerly pertaining to the Council.

In the reign of Henry VIII. the King's Principal Secretary had become a person of so great importance that his rank and precedence was determined by Stat. 31 Hen. VIII. c. 10., and the business and correspondence of his office so much increased as to require in the same reign a second Principal Secretary, and

INTRODUCTION.

subsequently a third. Each of these Secretaries, prior to the
establishment of an office for the reception of their papers, as
distinct from those of the Chancery, had the custody of the papers
accumulated in his department.

The State Paper Office, or, as it was originally called, the
"Office of Her Majesty's Papers and Records for business of
" State and Council," was established by Queen Elizabeth in
1578, when Dr. Thomas Wilson was appointed "Clerk of the
Papers." It was erected in order to prevent the "embezzle-
ment" of the papers owing to the frequent changes of Secretaries
of State. and also because it was thought necessary "that a
" certain place should be appointed for them and a fit man chosen
" for registering and keeping them in order, who should be tied
" by oath for the secrecy and safe keeping thereof."

Whenever a Secretary of State or other Minister resigned office
or died it was usual to issue a Warrant for the delivery of his
papers to the Keeper of the Papers, but such papers were frequently "detained" and only recovered by the most indefatigable
exertions on the part of the successive Keepers in hunting them
out. Sir Thomas Wilson, who succeeded to the office in the
beginning of the reign of James I., spared no pains to increase
the importance of his office and to recover any papers which he
judged ought rightly to be in his custody, and the King gave
him every encouragement to do so. In a Memorial issued by
him about the year 1613, it is stated that there were then two
sorts of papers in the State Paper Office, "those that have been
" long kept at Whitehall and those brought from Salisbury House
" by himself since the Lord Treasurer's decease, *which were far
" the greater in number.*"

Notwithstanding this transfer, however, a large mass of papers
appears to have been retained by the Secretaries of the late Lord
Treasurer, one portion of which is now preserved in the Library
of Hatfield House, the other having found its way, after a number
of vicissitudes, into the Lansdowne collection of MSS. in the
British Museum, of which, under the title of "Burghley Papers,"
it forms a most important division. Other extensive collections
of scattered papers which had escaped the vigilance of successive
Keepers of the Papers were made by Sir Robert Cotton in the
reign of James I., by Sir Joseph Williamson in that of Charles
II., and by Robert Harley, afterwards Earl of Oxford, towards
the close of the 17th century. Two of these are well known as the
Cottonian and Harleian collections in the British Museum, whilst
the collection of Sir Joseph Williamson, which was placed by its
originator in the State Paper Office, now forms part of the series
of Domestic State Papers.

The dispersion of State Papers was, however, never entirely
checked, and in addition to the collections above mentioned, they
are to be found in great numbers in the libraries of the Universi-

INTRODUCTION.

ties, in the Lambeth Library, and in almost every private library of note. Those existing in private collections are now, however, being widely made known by means of the invaluable Reports issued from time to time by the Royal Commission on Historical Manuscripts.

No systematic arrangement of the State Papers appears to have been attempted until Sir Thos. Wilson, the nephew of the first " Keeper," succeeded to the office in the beginning of the reign of James I. Previous to that time they were kept in chests, and appear to have been in great confusion. By Sir Thos. Wilson, however, they were " reduced to a set form of library," and placed " in very convenient rooms near the old Banqueting House " at Whitehall.

The plan first adopted by him of dividing the papers under the two heads of " Domestical " and " Foreign," though interfered with many times during the long period which has intervened, by divisions and sub-divisions, is identical with that now in use, and is found, with the additional division of " Colonial," to be the simplest and best for all practical purposes.

The papers relating to Ireland and Scotland, those relating to the former country being especially voluminous, have also been always kept distinct.

But few attempts were made by the early " Keepers " to calendar the State Papers. In 1764 Commissioners were appointed to methodize, regulate, and digest the State Papers, who reported that, although there were catalogues to some, there were no regular calendars, and strongly urged the necessity for the preparation of complete calendars and indexes.

Although they were authorised by a Warrant, dated 16 July 1764, " to make exact calendars and Indexes to all the said Papers " and Records," their proceedings appear to have been confined to sorting and arranging the papers until 1800, when their Commission was revoked, and a small establishment of clerks was allowed to the Keeper of State Papers.

In 1825 a Commission was issued for printing and publishing the documents of the State Paper Office, it having been then considered, as stated (somewhat prematurely) in the Commission, that the documents were in a great measure arranged and indexed.

Under the auspices of this Commission selections of the most important letters of the reign of Henry VIII. were printed in 11 quarto volumes, with Indexes of persons and places.

It was not, however, until the State Papers, by the operation of the Record Act of 1 & 2 Vict. c. 94., and by an Order in Council dated 5th of March 1852, were placed under the charge and superintendence of the Master of the Rolls that any regular system of calendars was adopted. Since that date upwards of 95 volumes of Calendars of the Domestic, Foreign, and Colonial

INTRODUCTION.

Papers, ranging from the reign of Henry VIII. to that of Charles
II., have been published, in which the historical information contained in the original documents is reproduced with a minuteness
of detail sufficient to render access to the original papers almost
unnecessary.

A Calendar of the documents relating to the History of the
State Paper Office down to the year 1800, which are contained
in five volumes known as "State Paper Office Documents," with
an exhaustive introduction by Mr. W. Noel Sainsbury, is printed
in the Appendix to the Deputy Keeper's 30th Report.

In 1871 the Earl of Shaftesbury, through the Royal Commission on Historical Manuscripts, generously presented his collection of Family MSS. to the Public Record Office, and they
have since been arranged by Mr. Noel Sainsbury, whose elaborate
Reports thereon are printed in the Deputy Keeper's 33rd, 34th,
35th, and 39th Reports.

The papers of the Duke of Manchester, which are calendared
in the 8th Report of the Historical MSS. Commission, have also
been deposited in the Public Record Office.

DEPARTMENTAL RECORDS.

The nature and origin of the several Public Departments is
too wide a subject to be here entered upon, and has, moreover,
been most ably and accurately treated in the Materials for the
History of Public Departments, by F. S. Thomas, published in
1846, to which the reader must be referred for information on this
subject.

It will be sufficient for the purpose of this introduction to state
that amongst the " Books, Papers, and Documents " of the several
Government Departments hitherto transferred to the Public
Record Office will be found those of the Home, Foreign, and
Colonial Offices, in continuation of those previously transferred
from the State Paper Office; those of the Admiralty and War
Offices, comprising many thousands of volumes of Muster Rolls
and Pay Lists of the Royal Navy and of the several Regiments,
together with the Log Books, Commission and Warrant Books,
and other official records; the Original Correspondence of Her
Majesty's Treasury from the year 1557, and the Letter, Order,
and Warrant Books from about the year 1667; the Accounts and
other Records of the Audit Office (including those of the Comptroller General of the Exchequer) from the reign of Elizabeth
to that of the present Sovereign, and those of the Lord Chamberlain's Department for a similar period.

A brief description of the more important documents in the
above-mentioned classes, with a statement of the dates up to
which they are open to public inspection, will be found under
the head of "Departmental Records."

INTRODUCTION.

The want of a General Inventory or Descriptive Catalogue of the vast collection of muniments above described has long been felt both by the public and by the officials themselves. The "Hand-book to the Public Records," by F. S. Thomas, a former Secretary of the Public Record Office, published in 1853, although containing much valuable information as to the nature of the several Courts of Law, and the duties of the Officers connected therewith, the greater part of which has been incorporated in the present volume, and treating of some of the principal classes of documents in a thoroughly exhaustive manner, in a great majority of instances merely indicates the existence of certain classes of records without specifying the dates between which they range, or explaining their nature, besides leaving much to be desired in the way of systematic arrangement.

The only other authentic guide to the contents of the Public Record Office is to be found in the Annual Reports of the Deputy Keeper, which, by their bulk alone, extending now to some 50 volumes, and the want of a clearly arranged Subject Index, present a labyrinth of undigested information in which the student may wander to and fro for days without finding the desired clue.

In 1879, at the request of the then Deputy Keeper, Sir William Hardy, I prepared an Alphabetical List of all the Calendars and Indexes in the Public Record Office, which appeared as an Appendix to the Deputy Keeper's 41st Report. On its completion I suggested to the Deputy Keeper that a Descriptive Catalogue of the Records themselves, arranged on a similar plan, would be of great value both to the officials and to the public, and, with his cordial consent, undertook the compilation thereof in such time as could be spared from my official duties as Superintendent of the Legal Search Department. The result, which represents nearly ten years of assiduous though frequently interrupted labour, is now at the service of the public, and will, I trust, do much to smooth the path of both the legal and the literary inquirer.

Owing to the frequent accretion of new matter, and the constant yet never ending progress in the work of classification and arrangement, such an undertaking as the present can hardly ever be either exhaustive or final; it is, however, hoped that a not altogether unsuccessful attempt has been made to put before the reader in a lucid form a general view of the National Archives in their present condition, which will enable him to decide at a glance which and how many of the various classes will be of service to him, at the same time indicating the existing means of reference to each.

Since the first edition of this work was issued, in 1891, considerable progress has been made with the much needed work of classification and arrangement of the Public Records. Upwards of 40 years ago it was stated by Mr. Thomas, in the introduction to his Hand-book to the Public Records, that in dealing with

INTRODUCTION.

these documents "sorting and arranging ought to be the primary
" object. No time ought to be spent in inventorying, calendar-
" ing, or indexing, until the whole arrangement be complete.
" We have *miscellaneous masses* which have been lying in the
" same state for centuries, and they will still so remain unless
" this principle be adopted so as to get the whole into classes in
" chronological order." Notwithstanding this dictum, the wisdom
of which is obvious, very little was done in the way of sortation
and arrangement, although a vast amount of time and labour was
expended on elaborate calendars of certain classes of public
documents, until the appointment, in 1886, of the present Deputy
Keeper, Mr. H. C. Maxwell Lyte, under whose auspices the work
of reducing the Records to a systematic arrangement was begun
in earnest.

In the first place the whole of the Record Rooms (with the
exception of those containing Departmental Records, which have
still to be dealt with) were thoroughly overhauled, their contents,
which were in many cases in the direst confusion, were re-packed,
re-labelled, and catalogued, and the officials were thus for the first
time placed in a position to state definitely whether any Record
or Records of a particular date and class did or did not exist.
This operation, which occupied the best part of two years, was
carried out under my immediate supervision by Messrs. Harley
Rodney and M. S. Giuseppi, of whose energetic and painstaking
performance of a most arduous and disagreeable task I cannot
speak too highly.

In addition to this general arrangement of the Records, huge
masses of so-called Miscellanea have been examined, with the
result that they have been found to contain a great number of
documents belonging to already existing classes. These either
have been, or in process of time will be, incorporated with the
classes to which they belong, so that in the future completely
exhaustive lists of particular classes of documents will be available
for the public use.

Such a series of "Lists and Indexes" has already been begun,
and Inventories of several of the more important classes have been
published. These are described in detail below, and a list
appended of others which are in an advanced state of preparation.

At the same time a New Series of Calendars of the mediæval
Patent Rolls and Close Rolls, which class of enrolments may be
regarded as the very backbone of the National Archives, and also
of the several collections of Ancient Deeds preserved in the
Public Record Office, has been instituted by the Deputy Keeper,
under whose direct supervision they are produced. Twelve
volumes of this series have already been published, of which two
deal with the Patent Rolls of Edward I., one with the Patent
Rolls of Edward II., three with the Patent Rolls of Edward III.,

INTRODUCTION.

one with the Patent Rolls of Richard II., three with the Close Rolls of Edward II., and two with the Ancient Deeds.

The Lists and Indexes already published or in progress are as follows:—

Lists and Indexes.

No. 1. An INDEX to the ANCIENT PETITIONS of the COURTS of CHANCERY AND EXCHEQUER.

This comprises a large collection of Petitions addressed to the King, to the King and Council, to the Parliament, and to the Chancellor and certain other officers of State in the 13th, 14th, and 15th centuries.

They have been brought together from various sources, amongst which may be enumerated the class heretofore known as " Parliamentary Petitions," the " Chancery Files," the Bundles of " Privy Seals, &c.," the " Royal Letters," and the " Miscellanea " of the Courts of Chancery and Exchequer.

No. 2. A LIST of the DECLARED ACCOUNTS of the AUDIT OFFICE and PIPE OFFICE, with a General Index.

This List includes 2,541 Bundles of Public Accounts belonging to the Audit Office Series, and 3,616 Rolls of Duplicate Accounts from the Office of the Clerk of the Pipe They extend in date from about the reign of Henry VIII. to the present time. The Duplicate Accounts from the Pipe Office of a later date than 1714 have been transferred to the Bodleian Library.

No. 3. A LIST of the DOMESTIC STATE PAPERS from the Reign Edward VI. to the Reign of George III.

The object of this List is to furnish clear references to the various volumes of State Papers heretofore existing as distinct series without any uniform system of numeration or description.

No. 4. A LIST of the PLEA ROLLS of the various Courts of Law.

This is an exhaustive List of all the Plea Rolls preserved in the Public Record Office, including the Eyre Rolls, Assize Rolls, Coroners' Rolls, and Gaol Delivery Rolls, with documents subsidiary thereto.

No. 5. A LIST or INVENTORY of ORIGINAL MINISTERS' ACCOUNTS prior to the Reign of Henry VII.

This comprises the very large collection of Bailiffs' and Receivers' Accounts formerly preserved amongst the so-called Miscellanea of the Queen's Remembrancer's Office, with which have been incorporated numerous analogous documents formerly preserved in the Chapter House at Westminster, the Tower of London, and the Office of Land Revenue Records.

It also includes the Ministers' Accounts of the Duchy of Lancaster of an earlier date than Henry VII.

INTRODUCTION.

The contents of the Rolls are fully set out and an Index Locorum is in the press.

No. 6.—A List or Inventory of the Court Rolls preserved in the Public Record Office.

This includes the several series of Court Rolls formerly existing amongst the Records of the Court of Chancery, of the Queen's Remembrancer's Department in the Exchequer, of the Treasury of the Receipt, and of the Augmentation Office, with analogous documents from various collections of Miscellanea.

The contents of the Rolls are shown in detail, and an Index Locorum is annexed.

The following Lists are in preparation :—

A List of Original Accounts of the Exchequer, with documents subsidiary thereto.

This will include all the Accounts relating to expenditure on the Army and Navy, on Ambassadors and Envoys, on the Royal Household and Wardrobe, and on Works and Repairs at the Royal Palaces and other buildings, and to a variety of other subjects connected with the administration of the kingdom, which formerly existed amongst the so-called Miscellanea of the Queen's Remembrancer's Department, the Miscellanea of the Treasury of the Receipt of the Exchequer, and elsewhere.

It has been completed in manuscript.

The original Accounts relating to the Revenue, such as the Customs Accounts and those of the Sheriffs, Escheators, and other Ministers, will form the subject of a separate List.

A List of the Enrolled Accounts of the Exchequer (Lord Treasurer's Remembrancer's Department).

This will include all Accounts, other than those of the Sheriffs, enrolled on the Pipe Rolls, the Chancellor's Rolls, or on the Rolls of Foreign Accounts from the reign of Henry III. to that of Richard III. inclusive.

A List of the Rentals and Surveys preserved in the Public Record Office.

This will include all the Rentals and Surveys hitherto existing amongst the Miscellanea of the Queen's Remembrancer's Department, of the Treasury of the Receipt or Chapter House, and of the Augmentation Office, with references to analogous documents belonging to the well known classes of " Parliamentary Surveys," "Special Commissions," &c., and to the Books of Surveys in the several series of Miscellaneous Books of the Exchequer.

The first portion, dealing with the Rentals and Surveys formerly scattered amongst the Miscellanea, has been completed in manuscript.

INTRODUCTION.

The present volume comprises :—

(1.) A SCHEDULE of the RECORDS of the SUPERIOR COURTS of LAW and of the PALATINATES of DURHAM and LANCASTER, the DUCHY of LANCASTER, and the PRINCIPALITY of WALES, including the Palatinate of Chester.

(2.) A DESCRIPTIVE CATALOGUE of the PRINCIPAL CLASSES of DOCUMENTS in the PUBLIC RECORD OFFICE, arranged under the following heads :—

Accounts.
Acknowledgments of Deeds.
Agarde's Indexes.
Alienation of Lands.
Aliens.
Ambassadors and Envoys.
Annuities.
Apparel.
Army, Navy, and Ordnance.
Attorneys and Solicitors.
Ayloffe's Calendars.
Bankrupts' Estates.
Baronets.
Bonds and Recognizances.
Certificates.
Chancery Enrolments.
Chancery Files.
Channel Islands.
Charities.
Charters and Grants.
Cinque Ports.
Commissions.
Common Prayer Books.
Cornwall, Duchy of.
Coronations.
Coroners' Inquests.
Court or Manor Rolls.
Courts of Justice.
Crown Lands and Rents.
Custos Sigilli.
Deeds (Ancient).
Deeds Enrolled.
Deeds &c., Registries of.
Degrees.
Departmental Records.
Depopulation.
Derelict Lands.
Domesday Book.
Ecclesiastical Matters.
Emigrants.

Escheats, Attainders, and Forfeitures.
Fees of Courts.
Feudal Tenures.
Fines and Recoveries.
Forests, Parks, and Chases.
Fortifications.
France, English possessions in.
Genealogy.
Gentlemen Pensioners.
Grammar Schools.
Guilds and Fraternities.
Hanaper Accounts.
Hospitals.
Hundred Rolls.
Inquisitions.
Ireland.
Jewels.
Jews.
Judicial Proceedings.
Knighthood.
Leases.
Le Neve's Indexes.
Livery of Lands.
Loans and Benevolences.
Manors, Extents of.
Manumissions.
Maps, Plans, and Charts.
Markets and Fairs.
Memoranda Rolls.
Mines.
Ministers' and Receivers' Accounts.
Mint.
Miscellaneous Books.
Miscellaneous Rolls.
Monastic Foundations.
Nomina Villarum.
Oaths of Allegiance, &c

INTRODUCTION.

Palmer's Indexes.
Papal Bulls.
Papists, Recusants, and Nonconformists.
Parliamentary Proceedings.
Partition of Lands.
Petitions.
Piracy.
Post Office.
Prisons.
Privy Council.
Privy Seals, &c.
Rebellions.
Receipts and Issues of the Exchequer.
Registers and Books of Remembrance.
Rentals and Surveys.
Revenue Rolls.
Royal and Historical Letters.
Royalists and Delinquents.

Scotland.
Seals.
Sewers, Laws of, &c.
Sheriffs' Accounts.
Specifications of Patents.
State Papers.
State Prisoners.
Statute Staple.
Surveys.
Taxation.
Tower of London.
Treaties and Diplomatic Documents.
Treatises.
Universities.
Wales.
Wardrobe and Household.
Wards and Minors.
Wills (Royal and Private).
Works and Buildings.

(3.) A GENERAL INDEX:

This work is issued with the sanction of the Deputy Keeper of the Records, to whom and to several of my colleagues I am indebted for much valuable advice and assistance.

For the general scheme and for the accuracy of the details I alone am responsible.

S. R. SCARGILL-BIRD.

Public Record Office,
  25 March 1896.

SCHEDULE OF RECORDS

OF THE

SUPERIOR COURTS OF LAW, &c.*

COURT OF CHANCERY.

Description of Record.	Period embraced.	Number of Bundles, Rolls, or Volumes.
Accountant-General's Certificates -	1726 to 1825 - -	527 Bundles.
Acts of Parliament made in Ireland -	10 Charles I. -	1 Bandle.
Administration Summonses. *See* " Chancery Proceedings."	—	—
Admissions of Officers, Rolls of - (Petty Bag Office.)	39 Elizabeth to 1874	20 Rolls.
Affidavits - - - -	1611 to 1869 - -	2,380 Bundles.
Affidavits, Registers of - -	1615 to 1746 - -	53 Vols.
Awards and Agreements - -	1694 to 1844 - -	15 Bundles.
Bills and Answers. *See* " Chancery Proceedings."	- - -	—
Bishops' Patent Rolls - -	9 George I. to 38 Victoria.	26 Rolls.
Bishops' Patents, Warrants for -	9 George I. to 38 Victoria.	13 Bundles.
Brevia Regia or " Chancery Files " (*Tower Series.*)	Edward I. to Charles II.	Under arrangement.
Brevia Regia or " Chancery Files " (*Petty Bag Series.*)	41 Elizabeth to 31 Victoria.	259 Bundles.
Brevia Regia or " Chancery Files " (*Rolls Chapel Series.*)	- - -	7 Bundles.
Certificates of Guilds -	12 Richard II. -	9 Portfolios.
Certificates (Various) - -	James I. to George III.	8 Bundles.
(Petty Bag Office.)		
Certiorari Bundles - -	James I. to George III.	12 Bundles.
(*Petty Bag Series.*)		
Certiorari Bundles - -	Henry VIII. to George III.	20 Bundles.
(*Rolls Chapel Series.*)		
Chancery Proceedings :—		
(Early) - - -	Richard II. to Philip and Mary.	Under arrangement.
(Series I.) - -	Elizabeth to Charles I.	2,240 Bundles.
(Series II.) Supplementary -	Elizabeth to Charles II.	Under arrangement.
(Six Clerks' Series) :—		
Bridges - -	" Before 1711 " -	640 Bundles.
Collins - - -	Do. - -	610 Bundles.
Hamilton - -	Do. - -	671 Bundles.
Mitford - - -	Do. - -	658 Bundles.
Reynardson - -	Do. - -	487 Bundles.
Whittington - -	Do. - -	546 Bundles.

* N.B.—The number of Bundles, &c. specified in the third column of this Schedule is subject to revision from time to time.

COURT OF CHANCERY—(continued).

Description of Record.	Period embraced.	Number of Bundles, Rolls, or Volumes
Chancery Proceedings (Six Clerks' Series).	1714 to 1758 - -	2,791 Bundles.
Do. do.	1758 to 1800 - -	2,434 Bundles.
Do. do.	1800 to 1842 and Supplementary.	3,193 Bundles.
Chancery Proceedings (Modern Series), "Pleadings," including Bills, Answers, Replications, Administration Summonses, &c. &c.	1842 to 1852 - -	Arranged alphabetically.
Chancery Proceedings, "Administration Summonses."	1852 to 1855 - -	Do.
Chancery Proceedings (Bills only) -	1853 to 1860 -	Do.
Do. do. (Answers only) -	1853 to 1860 -	Do.
Do. do. (Bills, Answers, &c., together).	1861 to 1869 - -	Do.
Charitable Uses, Proceedings relating to :—		
Commissions, Inquisitions, and Decrees.	43 Elizabeth to 8 George II.	60 Bundles.
Commissions, Inquisitions, and Decrees (Supplementary).	- - -	6 Bundles.
Confirmations and Exonerations of Decrees.	8 James I. to 16 George II.	38 Rolls.
Depositions, Interrogatories, &c. -	- - -	19 Bundles.
Exceptions, Answers, and Replications.	- - -	22 Bundles.
Charter Rolls - - - -	1 John to 8 Henry VIII.	207 Rolls.
Clerks in Courts' Books - -	1713 to 1842 - -	138 Vols.
Close Rolls - - - -	6 John to 1883 -	19,207 Rolls.
Commissions, &c. for Fortifications (Crown Office).	Anne to William IV.	1 Bundle.
Common Law Pleadings, or "Placita in Cancellaria." (Tower Series.)	Edward III. to Richard III.	Under arrangement.
Common Law Pleadings - (Rolls Chapel Series.)	Henry VII. to James I.	22 Bundles.
Common Law Pleadings (Proceedings on Scire Facias, &c.). (Petty Bag Office Series.)	Elizabeth to Victoria	93 Bundles.
Common Prayer Books :—		
(Tower Copy) - - -	Charles II. - -	1 Vol.
(Rolls Chapel Copy) - -	Charles II. - -	1 Vol.
County Placita - - - -	John to Edward IV.	42 Portfolios.
Customers' Patents, Warrants for (Petty Bag Office.)	George I. to George III.	6 Bundles.
Darrell and Stonor Papers - -	- - -	1 Bundle.
Deeds (Ancient). Series "C." -	Calendar in progress	—
Decree Rolls - - - -	26 Henry VIII. to 1878.	2,256 Rolls.
Decree Rolls (Supplementary) -	- - -	384 Rolls.
Decrees Enrolled, Docquets of - -	26 Henry VIII. to 1878.	
Decrees and Orders, Entry Books of -	36 Henry VIII. to 1869.	1,158 Vols.
Depositions - - - -	Eliz. to Car. I.	Arranged alphabetically.

COURT OF CHANCERY—(continued).

Description of Record.	Period embraced.	Number of Bundles, Rolls, or Volumes.
Depositions - - - -	(Six Clerks' Series) Bef. 1714.	1,054 Bundles.
Do. - - - -	From 1714 to 1842 (filed with the Chancery Proceedings).	—
Do. - - - -	From 1842 to 1852 (filed with the Chancery Proceedings).	—
Do. - - - -	From 1852 to 1869	65 Bundles.
Do. - - - -	"Sealed" or "Unpublished."	389 Bundles.
Do. - - -	"Town" (taken before the Examiners). Henry VIII. to 1853.	2,504 Bundles.
Docket Books - - - (Patent Office.)	1617 to 1850 - -	19 Vols.
Enrolments (Various) :—		
Almain Rolls - -	22 Edw. I. to 15 Edw. III.	8 Rolls.
Cartæ Antiquæ Rolls -	Ethelbert to Edward I.	45 Rolls.
Confirmation Rolls -	1 Richard III. to 1 Charles I.	113 Rolls.
Coronation Rolls -	Edward II. to Victoria.	13 Rolls.
Dispensation Rolls -	37 Elizabeth to 1745	62 Rolls.
Exchange Rolls -	6 Richard II. to 12 Henry VI.	4 Rolls.
Extract Rolls -	45 Henry III. to 6 Richard II.	31 Rolls.
French Rolls - -	26 Henry III. to 26 Charles II.	208 Rolls.
Irish Rolls - -	1 to 50 Edward III.	3 Rolls.
Liberate Rolls - -	2 John to 14 Henry VI.	147 Rolls.
Norman Rolls - -	2 John to 10 Henry V.	20 Rolls.
Oblata Rolls -	1 to 9 John - -	4 Rolls.
Misæ Roll - -	11 John - -	1 Roll.
Præstita Roll -	12 John - -	1 Roll.
Pardon Rolls - -	22 Edward I. to 2 James I.	46 Rolls.
Protection Rolls -	10 to 35 Edward I. -	4 Rolls.
Redisseissin Rolls -	14 Edward I. to 6 Edward IV.	26 Rolls.
Roman Rolls -	34 Edward I. to 31 Edward III.	22 Rolls.
Scotch Rolls - -	19 Edward I. to 7 Henry VIII.	113 Rolls.
Staple Rolls -	27 Edward III. to 39 Henry VI.	3 Rolls.
Statute Rolls -	Edward I. to Edward IV.	6 Rolls.
Surrender Rolls - -	12 to 20 Charles II.	7 Rolls.
Vascon or Gascon Rolls -	26 Henry III. to 7 Edward IV.	144 Rolls.

COURT OF CHANCERY—(continued).

Description of Record.	Period embraced.	Number of Bundles, Rolls, or Volumes.
Enrolments (Various)—*cont.*		
Welsh Rolls - - - -	5 Edward I. to 23 Edward I.	8 Rolls.
Fine Rolls - - - -	John to 23 Charles I.	553 Rolls.
Forest Proceedings (Ancient) -	John to Henry VIII.	1 Bundle.
Forest Proceedings - -	Henry VIII. to Charles I.	155 Bundles.
Forfeited Estates Papers - -	Pursuant to Statute 1 George I.	Under arrangement.
Gloucester Chartulary - - -	- - - -	1 Vol.
Gloucester Original Charters - -	- - - -	1 Box.
Inquisitions post mortem and ad quod damnum.	Henry III. to Richard III.	68 Vols, and 72 Portfolios.
Inquisitions post mortem and ad quod damnum.	Henry VII. to Charles I., and Miscellaneous.	540 Vols.
Inquisitions " de Rebellibus " -	49 Henry III - -	1 Portfolio.
Lunacy, Commissions and Inquisitions on. (Petty Bag Office.)	Charles I. to 1869 -	37 Bundles.
Memorials of Annuities - -	1813 to 1854 - -	136 Bundles.
Million Bank, Books and Papers of the -	- - - -	1 Bundle.
Miscellaneous Rolls, &c. (Tower Series) :—		
Army and Navy Accounts -	Edward I. to Edward IV.	1 Bundle.
Channel Islands Documents -	Edward I. to Elizabeth.	1 Bundle.
Deeds, &c., Transcripts of -	Henry III. to Edward VI.	1 Bundle.
Ecclesiastical Documents -	Edward I. to 1657 -	1 Bundle.
Ecclesiastical Taxation (of Pope Nicholas).	21 Edward I. - -	1 Bundle.
France, Documents relating to -	Edward I. to Henry VIII.	1 Bundle.
Grants of Markets and Fairs -	John to Henry VI. -	1 Bundle.
Homage Rolls (Scotland) -	19 to 24 Edward I. -	1 Bundle.
Knight's Fees, Inquisitions and Rolls of.	Henry III. to Henry IV.	1 Bundle.
Marshalsey Rolls - - -	Edward I. to Edward II.	1 Bundle.
Proceedings in the Court of Chivalry	9 to 22 Richard II. -	1 Bundle.
Scutage Rolls - - -	John to Edward III.	1 Bundle.
Sewers, Proceedings before Commissioners of.	Edward II. to Henry VI.	1 Bundle.
Special Commissions, Extents, and Inquisitions.	Richard II. to Henry VIII.	1 Bundle.
Treaties and Diplomatic Documents	Henry III. to Henry VII.	1 Bundle.
Wardrobe and Household Accounts	John to Elizabeth -	1 Bundle.
Unclassified Documents - -	Henry III. to Elizabeth.	5 Bundles.
Miscellaneous Rolls, &c. (Rolls Chapel Series.)	- - - -	17 Bundles.
Miscellaneous Rolls, &c. (Petty Bag Office)	- - - -	24 Bundles.
Oath Rolls (Association) - - (Petty Bag Office.)	William III. -	30 Bundles.

COURT OF CHANCERY—(continued).

Description of Record.	Period embraced.	Number of Bundles, Rolls, or Volumes.
Oath Rolls (Various) - (Petty Bag Office.)	Charles II. to Victoria.	36 Rolls.
Oaths, Enrolments of - - (Petty Bag Office.)	Charles II. to William and Mary.	7 Rolls.
Papal Bulls - - - -	John to Henry VIII.	Under arrangement.
Parliament Pawns - - (Petty Bag Office.)	Henry VIII. to Victoria.	4 Bundles.
Parliament Rolls - - -	5 Edward II. to 48 and 49 Victoria.	5,787 Rolls.
Parliamentary and other Proceedings -	Henry III. to Henry VIII.	1 Portfolio.
Parliamentary Writs and Returns - (Petty Bag Office.)	Edward I. to Victoria	272 Bundles.
Patent Rolls - - - -	3 John to 50 Victoria	5,123 Rolls.
Petitions (including Appeal Petitions, 1774 to 1869).	1834 to 1869 - -	1,289 Bundles.
Petitions (Corporation) - -	1834 to 1843 -	3 Bundles.
Petition Books (Lord Chancellors') -	1756 to 1858 - -	43 Vols.
Privy Seals, &c. See " Warrants."	—	—
Registrars' Minute Books - -	1639 to 1869 - -	4,541 Vols.
Remembrance Rolls - - (Petty Bag Office.)	Elizabeth to George III.	85 Rolls.
Remembrance Rolls of Orders - (Petty Bag Office.)	11 Charles I. to 2 George II.	10 Rolls.
Reports and Certificates - -	1544 to 1869 -	2,953 Vols.
Reports and Certificates, Exceptions to -	1756 to 1859 -	47 Bundles.
Reports on Courts of Justice - - (Petty Bag Office.)	1740 to 1864 -	64 Vols.
Sacrament Certificates - - (Petty Bag Office.)	1673 to 1789 - -	33 Bundles.
Scottish Documents - -	Henry III. to Charles II.	2 Portfolios.
Sewers, Laws of, &c. :— (Petty Bag Office.)		
Laws of Sewers - - -	42 Elizabeth to 1831	2 Bundles.
Bedford Level Decrees - -	16–36 Charles II. -	8 Bundles.
Enrolments of Laws of Sewers -	8 Charles I. to 1714	4 Rolls.
Sheriffs' Rolls - - - (Petty Bag Office.)	36 Henry VIII. to 17 Charles I.	3 Bundles.
Sheriffs' Rolls - - (Six Clerks' Office.)	1700 to 1848 -	3 Bundles.
Significavits - - - (Petty Bag Office.)	George II. to 1839 -	12 Bundles (Cursitors' Records, Nos. 752 to 763).
Six Clerks' Cause Books - -	1620 to 1842 - -	102 Vols.
Special Commissions - - (Petty Bag Office.)	James I. to Victoria	21 Bundles.
Specification Rolls - - (Petty Bag Office.)	1712 to 1848 -	287 Rolls.
Specification Rolls - - (Rolls Chapel Office.)	1712 to 1848 -	110 Rolls.
Specifications - - - (Patent Office.)	1852 to 1880 -	1,121 Bundles.
Statutes Staple, Proceedings on - (Rolls Chapel Series.)	Henry VIII. to Anne	46 Bundles.
Statutes Staple, Proceedings on - (Petty Bag Series.)	James I. to George III.	35 Bundles.
Surveys of Church Livings -	Commonwealth -	3 Vols.

d

COURT OF CHANCERY—(continued).

Description of Record.	Period embraced.	Number of Bundles, Rolls, or Volumes.
Swainmote Court Rolls (Windsor Forest.)	2 Edward VI. to 14 Charles I.	21 Bundles.
Vetus Codex, or " Placita Parliamentaria."	Edward I.	1 Vol
Warrants of Attorney to suffer Recoveries. (Petty Bag Office.)	-	751 Bundles (Cursitors' Records, Nos. 1 to 751).
Warrants for the Great Seal:—		
Series I.	Henry III. to Richard III.	1,042 Files.
Series II.	Henry VII. to Henry VIII.	76 Bundles.
Series III.	Edward VI. to Anne	284 Bundles.
Series IV.	George I. to William IV.	294 Bundles.
Series V.	Victoria	85 Bundles.
Writs. See " Brevia Regia."		

COURT OF QUEEN'S BENCH.
(Crown Side.)

Affidavits, General	1716 to 1858	256 Bundles.
Affidavits, Supplementary	1689 to 1737	1 Bundle.
Appearance Books	1725 to 1843	10 Vols.
Assize Rolls, &c.	John to Edward IV.	1,550 Rolls.
Baga de Secretis	Edward IV. to George III.	21 Bags.
Bails (taken in Court)	1687 to 1843	30 Bundles.
Bails (on Certiorari)	1698 to 1843	15 Bundles.
Bails (Amalgamated)	1844 to 1858	15 Bundles.
Bails, Calendar of	6 James I. to 13 William III.	3 Rolls.
Controlment Rolls	1 Edward III. to 1843.	503 Rolls.
Contumace Capiendo, Enrolment of Writs of.	1844 to 1857	1 Roll.
Convicts, Returns of	1785 to 1827	10 Bags.
Coram Rege Rolls	1 Edward I. to 13 William III.	2,149 Rolls.
Coroners' Rolls	Henry III. to Henry VI.	256 Rolls.
Crown Rolls	1 Anne to 22 Victoria.	623 Rolls.
Curia Regis Rolls	5 Richard I. to 56 Henry III.	216 Rolls.
Depositions	1849 to 1857	2 Bundles.
Error, Records in (from Ireland)	George II. and George III.	10 Rolls.
Estreats of Forfeited Recognizances	1603 to 1832	8 Bags.
Gaol Delivery Rolls	Edward I. to Edward IV.	221 Rolls.
Great Doggett Books	6 Charles I. to 1843	17 Vols.
Indictments:—		
(Ancient)	Edward III. to Henry VII.	329 Files.
(London and Middlesex)	1675 to 1845	92 Bundles.
(Out Counties)	1625 to 1845	137 Bundles.
(Amalgamated)	1846 to 1858	52 Bundles.

COURT OF QUEEN'S BENCH—(continued).

(Crown Side)—(continued).

Description of Record.	Period embraced.	Number of Bundles, Rolls, or Volumes.
Inquisitions (Coroners') - - -	1748 to 1767 - -	1 Bundle.
Inquisitions (on Prisoners) -	1747 to 1839 - -	2 Bundles.
Interrogatories - - -	1701 to 1838 - -	6 Bundles.
Judgments, Files of - - -	1734 to 1824 - -	4 Bundles.
Orders and Writs, Records of -	1698 to 1858 - -	70 Bundles.
Outlawry Proceedings -	1739 to 1841 - -	1 Bag.
Papists in Lancaster, Returns of -	George I. - -	1 Bundle.
Posteas - - -	1728 to 1839 - -	43 Bundles.
Process Books - - -	1737 to 1821 - -	8 Vols.
Rule Books - - -	1589 to 1857 - -	70 Vols.
Sacrament Certificates -	1728 to 1828 - -	10 Bags.
Swearing Rolls - - -	1673 to 1858 - -	4 Bags.
Writs Returned. See "Orders and Writs."	—	

(Plea Side.)

Description	Period	Number
Accounts of money paid in and out of Court.	1675 to 1837 - -	30 Vols.
Affidavits of Clerkship - -	1775 to 1848 - -	48 Bundles.
Affidavits of Clerkship (Supplementary)	1804 to 1839 - -	6 Bundles.
Affidavits of Clerkship (of persons not admitted).	1848 - -	1 Bundle.
Affidavits General - -	1733 to 1848 - -	953 Bundles.
Alphabet Books - - -	1751 to 1832 - -	67 Vols.
Appearance Books (in Ejectment) -	1738 to 1836 - -	26 Vols.
Articles of Clerkship (Registered) -	1838 to 1848 - -	38 Bundles.
Attorneys' Certificate Books -	1785 to 1843 - -	61 Vols.
Attorneys' Oath Rolls - -	1750 to 1840 - -	3 Rolls.
Cognovits. See also "Warrants of Attorney."	1825 to 1848 - -	90 Bundles.
Commissions and Depositions -	1832 to 1837 - -	1 Bag.
Common Prayer Book - -	Charles II. - -	1 Vol.
Declarations in Ejectment -	1728 to 1848 - -	138 Bundles.
Doggett Rolls - - -	1390 to 1655 - -	66 Rolls.
Error, Writs and Transcripts of Records in.	- - -	16 Bags.
Essoin Rolls - - -	Edward III. to George III.	76 Rolls.
Extract Rolls - - -	Edward III. to Henry IV.	110 Rolls.
Judgment Rolls - - -	1702 to 1848 - -	1,398 Rolls.
Judgments, Docket Papers of -	1772 to 1839 - -	11 Bundles.
Judgments on Posteas, Entry Books of -	1760 to 1838 - -	16 Vols.
Marshal's Dockets of Commitments -	1730 to 1822 - -	1 Bag.
Marshal's Surrender Books -	1719 to 1838 - -	22 Vols.
Outlawries, Extents and Inquisitions in	George III. to Victoria.	1 Portfolio.
Outlawries, Doggett Books of -	1684 to 1810 - -	3 Vols.
Prisoners' Papers - - -	- - -	1 Bundle.
Rules, Entry Books of - -	1603 to 1848 - -	263 Vols.
Rules (Consent), in Ejectments		
Series I. - - -	1720 to 1842 - -	26 Bundles.
Series II. - - -	1721 to 1836 - -	24 Bundles.

COURT OF QUEEN'S BENCH—(continued).

(Plea Side)—(continued).

Description of Record.	Period embraced.	Number of Bundles, Rolls, or Volumes.
Rules (Prisoners) - - -	1729 to 1838 - -	21 Vols.
Warrants of Attorney - - -	1802 to 1825 - -	335 Bundles.
Do. and Cognovits -	1822 to 1848 - -	1,437 Bundles.
Do. (from various Courts).	1822 to 1825 - -	20 Bundles.
Do. (Supplementary) -	1821 to 1824 - -	5 Bundles.
Writs, Judicial - - - - (Series I.)	1629 to 1848 - -	92 Bundles.
Do. Special Original - - - (Series II.)	1629 to 1844 - -	142 Bundles.
Do. of Habeas Corpus and Recordas -	1649 to 1684 - -	12 Bags.
Do. and Posteas - - -	Elizabeth to William IV.	1 Bundle.
Do. of Replevin - - -	1764 to 1835 - -	4 Portfolios.
Do. of Scire Facias, Enrolments of -	1617 to 1826 - -	8 Bundles.
Do. Precedent Book of, called " Forms of Writs."	George II. - -	1 Vol.

COURT OF COMMON PLEAS.

Acknowledgments of Deeds by Married Women, Certificates of.	1834 to 1855 - -	1,112 Parcels.
Acknowledgments of Deeds by Married Women, Day Books of.	1834 to 1857	16 Vols.
Affidavits, General - - -	1704 to 1829 -	91 Boxes.
Affidavits, General - - -	1830 to 1849 - -	358 Bundles.
Affidavits annexed to Warrants of Attorney for suffering Recoveries.	1774 to 1834 -	62 Bags.
Affidavits to moderate Fines (Alienation Office).	1802 to 1834 - -	—
Appointments of Filazers, &c. - -	1674 to 1831 -	1 Bundle.
Articles of Clerkship (with Affidavits of due execution annexed).	1730 to 1838 -	14 Boxes.
Attorneys :—		
Admission Books - - -	1729 to 1848 - -	4 Vols.
Admission Rolls - - - -	1838 to 1860 -	4 Rolls.
Certificate Books - - -	1786 to 1843 - -	59 Vols.
Oath Rolls - - - -	1789 to 1843 -	16 Rolls.
Do. (Catholics) - -	1791 to 1842 - -	3 Rolls.
Do. (Quakers and Separatists)	1835 to 1842	1 Roll.
Rolls of - - - - -	1730 to 1750 - -	13 Rolls.
Rolls or Books of - - -	1740 to 1853 -	2 Vols.
Do. - - -	1838 to 1843 (pursuant to Stat. 1 & 2 Victoria.)	1 Vol.
Do. - - -	1843 to 1862 (pursuant to Stat. 6 & 7 Victoria.)	1 Vol.
Do. - - -	1830 to 1844 (pursuant to Stat. 1 William IV.).	1 Vol.
Banco, Placita de - - -	1 Edward I. to 24 Henry VII.	987 Rolls.
Commissions - - - -	1834 to 1856 - -	1 Portfolio.
Common Prayer Book - - -	Charles II. - -	1 Vol.

COURT OF COMMON PLEAS—(continued).

Description of Record.	Period embraced.	Number of Bundles, Rolls, or Volumes.
Common Rolls	1 Henry VIII. to Victoria.	3,064 Rolls.
Consents (in Ejectment)	1727 to 1774 (after 1774 filed with the Declarations in Ejectment).	1 Box.
Crown Debts, Register of	1839 to 1848	10 Vols.
Crown Debts, Index to	1839 to 1850	11 Vols.
Declarations in Ejectment	1704 to 1837	27 Boxes.
Docquet Books of Judgments	29 Charles II. to 4 William & Mary.	34 Vols.
	1692 to 1839	198 Vols.
Doggett Rolls	1509 to 1859	1,178 Rolls.
Essoin Rolls	10 Henry III. to 38 George III.	33 Packages.
Extract Rolls	1–17 Edward III.	30 Rolls.
Examinations of Witnesses	1831 to 1849	4 Parcels.
Fines, Concords of	1559 to 1836.	—
Do. Feet of	Richard I. to 1835.	—
Do. Notes of	Edward I. to 1831.	—
Do. Proclamations of	1620 to 1841	3 Vols.
Fines and Recoveries :—		
Enrolment of Writs for	23–24 Elizabeth to 10 Anne.	53 Parcels.
Entries of	1611 to 1835	54 Vols.
Rules to Amend	George III. to William IV.	1 Parcel.
Rules and Orders of Court to pass	1797 to 1834	4 Parcels.
Judgments, Registers of	1838 to 1849	32 Vols.
King's Silver Books	Eliz. to Will. IV.	—
Nisi Prius Records, Entries of	1644 to 1837	22 Vols.
Oath Rolls (Catholics)	1778 to 1829	6 Rolls.
Do. (Clergymen)	1790 to 1836	4 Rolls.
Do. (Qualification)	1780 to 1847	10 Rolls.
Outlawry Books (Exigents)	1821 to 1848	4 Vols.
Outlawry, Reversals of	10 George II. to 1859.	4 Parcels.
Posteas. Series I.	1689 to 1829	261 Bags.
Series II.	1830 to 1852	45 Portfolios.
Recovery Rolls	1583 to 1837	1,004 Rolls.
Remembrance Books :		
Secondaries'	1800 to 1837	} 60 Vols.
Masters'	1838 to 1859	
Remembrance Rolls :—		
(Prothonotaries')	1514 to 1799	Nos. 1 to 1,426.*
(For Recoveries)	1770 to 1834	1,427 to 1,489.
(Of Admissions to prosecute and defend by Guardians.)	1834 to 1859	1,490 to 1491.
Remembrances (Filazers')	1623 to 1691	3 Rolls.
Riders and Final Judgments	Eliz. to Geo. II.	1 Box.
Rules (Consent and Landlords)	1830 to 1852	1 Box.
Tadmarton Inclosure Award	17 George III.	1 Roll.
Warrants of Attorney :—		
To confess judgment	1802 to 1849	238 Bundles.
To sue and defend	1769 to 1837	75 Bags.
Writs :—		
Of Capias, Writs Filed, &c.	1800 to 1859	114 Bags.

* Many of these rolls are wanting. (*See* Deputy Keeper's Report, V., App. II., p. 7.)

COURT OF COMMON PLEAS —(continued).

Description of Record.	Period embraced.	Number of Bundles, Rolls, or Volumes.
Writs—*continued.*		
Of Covenant - - -	Edward III. to William IV.	64 Bags.
Of Entry and Seisin - - -	1801 to 1833 - -	94 Bags.
Of Habeas and Returns - -	1838 to 1842 - -	1 Parcel.
Of Inquiry, &c. - - -	1630 to 1854 - -	222 Packages.

COURT OF EXCHEQUER OF PLEAS.

Accounts of Money paid into and out of Court.	1690 to 1775 - -	3 Vols.
Affidavits General - - -	1830 to 1855 - -	645 Bundles.
Amercements and Issues Forfeited -	1697 to 1740 - -	1 Vol.
Appearance Books - -	28 Elizabeth to 12 Anne.	35 Vols.
Attorneys' Oath Rolls - -	1830 to 1842 - -	1 Bundle.
Bills and Writs - - -	Edward III. to 1855	491 Bundles.
Ejectment, Affidavits and Declarations in.	1778 to 1849 - -	32 Bundles.
Jews' Plea Rolls - - -	3 Henry III. to 14 Edward I.	47 Rolls.
Masters' New Trial Books - -	1848 to 1855 - -	4 Vols.
Minute Books - - -	1657 to 1830 - -	73 Vols.
Order Books - - -	3 Edward VI. to 1830	81 Vols.
Outlawry Books - - -	1832 to 1869 - -	2 Vols.
Placitorum Formulare - -	- - -	1 Vol.
Plea Rolls - - -	Henry III. to 1855 -	1,388 Rolls.
Plea Rolls, Repertories to -	Edward IV. to Henry VII.	1 Package.
Rule Books - - -	1811 to 1854 - -	43 Vols.
Special Paper Book - - -	1847 to 1854 - -	1 Vol.
Term Papers (Orders made Rules of Court, &c.).	1779 to 1785 and 1830 to 1849.	25 Bundles.
Transcripts of Proceedings in Error -	- - -	13 Bundles.
Warrants of Attorney and Cognovits -	1803 to 1855 - -	165 Bundles.
Writ Books - - -	1616 to 1714 - -	15 Vols.
Writs. *See* "Bills and Writs."	—	—
Writs, Inquisitions, Posteas, &c. -	- - -	2 Portfolios.
Writs Returned (London and Middlesex)	1843 to 1855 - -	22 Bundles.
Writs Returned (Out Counties) -	1843 to 1855 - -	22 Bundles.
Writs and Transcripts of Judgments, &c. from the Court of Great Sessions in Wales.	- - -	1 Portfolio.

COURT OF EXCHEQUER.

(Queen's Remembrancer's Department.)

Accounts, &c. (relating to Expenditure and Administration).	Henry III. to James I., and later.	530 Bundles.
Accounts, &c. (relating to Revenue). *See* "Customs Accounts," "Escheators' Accounts," "Ministers' and Receivers' Accounts," "Sheriffs' Accounts," and "Subsidies (Clerical and Lay)."]	—	—
Accounts (Public) Enrolments of -	Elizabeth to 1837 -	530 Rolls.

COURT OF EXCHEQUER.—(continued).
(Queen's Remembrancer's Department)—(continued).

Description of Record.	Period embraced.	Number of Bundles, Rolls, or Volumes.
Accounts of Interest and Dividends due to Suitors.	1820 to 1841 -	86 Vols.
Affidavits (Original) - - -	1572 to 1812 - -	207 Portfolios.
Affidavits of Bailiffs of Liberties claiming Fines.	1830 to 1836 - -	2 Bundles.
Affidavits of Undersheriffs as to sums received for Deodands, &c.	1833 to 1842 - -	2 Bundles.
Alien Priories, &c., Extents of - -	Edward I. to Edward IV.	12 Bundles.
Appearances, Entries of - - -	1588 to 1841 - -	19 Vols.
Army, Assessments for the - -	1645 to 1652 - -	1 Roll.
Army, General and Division Orders -	1811 to 1812 - -	1 Vol.
Army and Navy, Account of Men in the	1719 and 1724-5 -	1 Vol.
Attorneys' Certificate Book - -	- - - -	1 Vol.
Barons and Treasurers of the Exchequer, Names of the.	Edward II. to Elizabeth.	2 Rolls.
Bills and Answers - - -	Elizabeth to 1841 -	2,386 Packages.
Bills against Accountants - - -	Charles I. - -	5 Portfolios.
Bonds - - - - -	Henry VIII. to Elizabeth.	21 Bundles.
Certificates of Residence and Payment of Subsidies.	Elizabeth and James I.	Under arrangement.
Certificates of the Sale and Transfer of Bank Stock.	1820 to 1841 - -	1 Vol.
Certificates as to the Sale of the King's lands.	Commonwealth -	5 Bundles.
Chatham Fortifications, Deeds as to Land for.	1578 to 1718 - -	3 Bundles.
Church Goods, Inventories of - -	Edward VI. - -	10 Bundles.
Claims of Lords of Liberties - -	1837 to 1848 - -	2 Bundles.
Claims as to the River Wey - -	1671 - - -	1 Bundle.
Cleveland, Claims on the estate of the Earl of.	1661 - - -	1 Bundle.
Do. Entry Book of - - -	- - - -	1 Vol.
Concealed Lands, Particulars of -	Hen. VIII. to James I.	1 Bundle.
Conventual Leases - - -	Henry VIII. - -	1 Parcel.
Cornwall, Bailiffs' Accounts of Edmund, Earl of.	24-25 Edward I. -	1 Roll.
Cornwall, Caption of Seisin of the Duchy of.	11 Edward III. -	1 Roll.
Customs, Accounts of Collectors of -	Edward I. to James I.	197 Bundles.
Decrees and Orders, Entry Books of :—		
Series I. (Decrees and Orders) -	1 Elizabeth to 3 James I.	29 Vols.
Series II. (Do.) -	1 Jas. I. to 1 Chas. I.	37 Vols.
Series III. (Do.) -	1 Chas. I. to 13 Chas. II.	30 Vols.
Series IV. (Decrees only) - -	2 James I. to 1841 -	57 Vols.
Series V. (Orders only) - -	13 Chas. II. to 1850	94 Vols.
Decrees and Orders (Original) :—		
Decrees and Orders - -	Elizabeth to 1662 -	129 Portfolios.
Do. (Supplementary) -	- - -	22 Portfolios
Decrees (only) - - - -	1665 to 1841 - -	72 Portfolios and Volumes.

COURT OF EXCHEQUER—(continued).

(Queen's Remembrancer's Department)—(continued).

Description of Record.	Period embraced.	Number of Bundles, Rolls, or Volumes.
Decrees and Orders—*cont.*		
Orders (only) - - -	1664 to 1841 -	139 Portfolios and Volumes.
Deeds (Ancient). Series "D." - -	Calendar in progress.	—
Depositions, taken before the Barons (called " Barons' Depositions ").	Elizabeth to 1841 -	139 Portfolios.
Depositions, taken by Commission -	Elizabeth to 1841 -	306 Portfolios.
Ecclesiastical Documents - -	Henry III. to James I.	14 Bundles.
Escheators' Accounts - - -	Henry III. to James I.	237 Bundles.
Escheators' Inquisitions - -	Henry III. to James I.	42 Portfolios and 1 Box.
Estreats and Affidavits (from Quarter Sessions).	1838 to 1842 - -	19 Bundles.
Estreats, Entries of - - -	- - -	3 Vols.
Do. Miscellaneous - - -	1839 to 1842 -	1 Bundle.
Do. of Deodands, and Affidavits of no Deodands.	1834 to 1842 - -	9 Bundles.
Exchequer Proceedings - - -	Edward I. to James I.	112 Bundles.
Excise Accounts - - -	1829 to 1850 -	19 Bundles.
Excise Extents - - - -	- - -	9 Packages.
Excise Informations - - -	George III. to Victoria.	25 Packages.
Excise Writs and Posteas - - -	- - -	21 Portfolios.
Exhibits - - - -	- - -	55 Packages.
Exmoor Forest Inclosure Award -	58 George III. -	1 Parcel.
Extents and Inquisitions (for Crown Debts).	1685 to 1822 -	98 Portfolios.
Extents and Inquisitions (Miscellaneous)	- - -	10 Portfolios.
Forest Proceedings - - -	Henry III. to James I.	3 Bundles.
Forfeited Lands, Accounts of Commissioners for the Sale of.	Commonwealth -	1 Vol.
Grants, Particulars for - - -	Edw. VI. to James I.	5 Bundles.
Informations of Intrusion (Attorney General *v.* Lord Churchill).	1836 to 1843 -	1 Portfolio.
Informations of Intrusion - -	George II. to Victoria.	1 Portfolio.
Informations, Pleas, and Writs -	Elizabeth to Victoria	10 Packages.
Inventories of Goods and Chattels -	Henry III. to James I.	5 Bundles.
Knights' Fees, Returns of (including the Testa de Nevill.)	Henry II. to Charles I.	6 Bundles.
Leases, Counterparts of Demises (arranged in Counties).	1677 to 1831 -	26 Packages.
Leases (Miscellaneous) - - -	- - -	1 Portfolio.
Licenses to go beyond Seas - -	Elizabeth to Charles I.	1 Bundle.
Lord Mayor and Sheriffs, Mode of presentation of.	1833 to 1842 - -	1 Bundle.
Memoranda Rolls - - - -	1 Henry III. to 13 Victoria.	770 Rolls.
Memoranda Rolls, Repertories to -	- - -	8 Packages.

COURT OF EXCHEQUER—(continued).

(Queen's Remembrancer's Department)—(continued).

Description of Record.	Period embraced.	Number of Bundles, Rolls, or Volumes.
Ministers' and Receivers' Accounts -	Henry III. to Richard III.	562 Bundles,(numbered 740 to 1,301).
Do. do. -	Henry VII. -	1,747 Rolls.
Minute Books (Common) -	1616 to 1821 -	140 Vols.
Minute Books (Exchequer Chamber) -	1695 to 1841	16 Vols.
Miscellanea of the Exchequer (Unclassified.)	John to George III.-	22 Bundles.
Miscellaneous Books - - -	- -	60 Vols.
Miscellaneous Papers in Revenue Causes.	- -	72 Bundles.
Oaths of Allegiance - - -	George I. to William IV.	1 Package.
Ordnance Decrees - - - -	1785 to 1806 -	23 Rolls.
Outlawries - - - -	Charles I. to Victoria	1 Package.
Outlawry Books - - -	1639 to 1841 -	4 Vols.
Parliamentary Proceedings - -	Edward I. to James I.	7 Bundles.
Petitions - - - -	George III. to 1841	15 Portfolios.
Pix, Trials of the - - -	1660 to 1824 -	1 Package.
Rentals and Surveys - - -	- -	322 Rolls and 25 Portfolios.
Replications and Rejoinders - -	- -	10 Bags.
Reports and Certificates - -	1648 to 1841	112 Vols.
Returns of Papists - - -	George I. -	1 Package.
Revenue and other Proceedings (Writs, Indentures of Appraisement, Bonds, &c., &c.).	Various dates -	225 Bundles.
Revenue and other Proceedings, Books relating to.	Various dates -	207 Vols.
Sheriffs' Accounts - - -	Henry III. to James I.	129 Bundles
Sheriffs' Accounts - - -	1832 to 1842 -	11 Bundles.
Solicitors' Roll - - -	1772 to 1841 -	1 Roll.
Special Commissions (Early) -	Edward III. to Philip and Mary.	6 Bundles.
Special Commissions - -	Elizabeth to Victoria	51 Portfolios
Subsidies (Clerical and Lay) -	Henry III. to William and Mary.	266 Boxes.
Summonses of the Pipe -	Edward II. to James I.	7 Bundles.
Suppression Papers -	Henry VIII.	4 Bundles.
Tax Accounts :—		
Land and Assessed Taxes, Parchment Duplicates of.	1688 to 1830 -	1,289 Bags.
Land Tax Duplicates for the year 1798 (selected from the foregoing).	- -	1 Package.
Land and Assessed Taxes, Entries of	1689 to 1835 -	200 Vols.
Do. do. do.	1693 and 1697	2 Vols.
Testa de Nevill. See "Knights' Fees."		
Victuallers' Recognizances -	Elizabeth to James I.	7 Bundles.
Writs, Judicial - -	1666 to 1714 -	13 Bags.
Writs and Posteas - -	William and Mary to 1850.	28 Packages.
Writs of Distringas, &c. -	Edward I. to James I	22 Bundles.

COURT OF EXCHEQUER.

(Lord Treasurer's Remembrancer's Department.)

Description of Record.	Period embraced.	Number of Bundles, Rolls, or Volumes.
Accounts (Declared) - - -	Henry VIII. to 1714	3,616 Rolls. (*See* Lists and Indexes, No. 11).
Board's End Books - - -	1681 to 1833 - -	18 Vols. [*Misc. Books, Vols.* 13 *to* 30.]
Chancellor's Rolls - - -	9 Henry II. to 2 William IV.	612 Rolls.
Drafts of Demises - - -	Elizabeth to George IV.	36 Parcels.
Enrolled Accounts :—		
Customs - - -	Edward I. to Elizabeth.	29 Rolls.
Escheators - - -	Edward II. to James I.	161 Rolls.
Subsidies - - -	Edward I. to Charles I.	74 Rolls.
Wardrobe - - -	Henry III. to Edward VI.	10 Rolls.
Miscellaneous - - -	- - -	21 Rolls.
Estreats - - -	Edward VI. to William IV.	Under arrangement.
Exannual Rolls - - -	Edward I. to George III.	15 Rolls.
Fee-Farm Rents, Certificates of Payments for.	1650 to 1652 - -	1 Vol. [*Misc. Books, Vol.* 12.]
Foreign Accounts - - -	Edward III. to William IV.	23 Rolls and 35 Packages.
Land and Assessed Taxes, Entry Books of:—		
Land Tax - - -	1639 to 1821 - -	10 Vols. [*Misc. Books, Vols.* 31 *to* 10.]
Assessed Taxes - - -	1708 to 1822 - -	11 Vols. [*Misc. Books, Vols.* 42 *to* 52.]
Leases (Crown) Counterparts and Particulars of.	1566 to 1822 - -	28 Portfolios.
Leases, Enrolments of - -	Elizabeth to George III.	4 Rolls.
Leases, Entry Books of - -	1750 to 1812 - -	[*Misc. Books, Vols.* 1–11.]
Leases, Drafts of. *See* "Drafts of Demises."	—	—
Leases, Particulars for - -	1695 to 1803 - -	80 Parcels.
Memoranda Rolls - -	1 Henry III. to 1848	789 Rolls.
Memoranda Rolls, Repertories to	1 Edward I. to 32 Charles II.	4 Cases.
Minute Books of Orders -	3 James II. to 35 George III.	4 Vols. [*Misc. Books, Vols.* 53 *to* 56.]
Miscellaneous Books - - -	- - -	178 Vols.
Miscellaneous Rolls - - -	- - -	8 Parcels.
Nihil Rolls - - -	Charles I. to William IV.	25 Bags.

COURT OF EXCHEQUER—(continued).

(Lord Treasurer's Remembrancer's Department) —(continued).

Description of Record.	Period embraced.	Number of Bundles, Rolls, or Volumes.
Order Books - - -	35 Charles II. to 3 and 4 William IV.	18 Vols. [*Misc. Books. Vols.* 60 *to* 77.]
Originalia Rolls - - -	Henry III. to 1837 -	1,102 Rolls.
Originalia Rolls, Repertories to -	Henry III. to 1824 -	6 Cases.
Pipe Rolls - - -	31 Henry I. to 2 William IV.	676 Rolls.
Pipe Rolls (Norman) - -	30 Henry II. to John	18 Rolls.
Post Fines, Rolls of - -	38 Elizabeth to 1837	34 Bags.
Recusant Rolls (Chancellor's Series) -	34 Elizabeth to 1 and 2 William and Mary.	63 Rolls.
Recusant Rolls (Pipe Series) -	34 Elizabeth to 1 and 2 William and Mary.	82 Rolls.
Repertories (Various) - -	- - -	8 Cases.
Reversion Rolls - - -	Edward III. to Henry VIII.	2 Rolls.
Schedules of the Pipe for Nihil Debts -	William and Mary to George IV.	6 Packages.
Sheriffs' Accounts (of Seizures) -	About Henry VII. to 1660.	170 Rolls.
States and Views of Accounts of Receivers General.	Charles II. to George IV.	52 Vols. [*Misc. Books, Vols.* 79 *to* 130.]
States of Accounts of Sheriffs -	Charles II. to William IV.	16 Vols. [*Misc. Books. Vols.* 131 *to* 146.]
Summons of the Pipe - -	Henry VI. to William IV.	2 Packages.
Tax Accounts - - - -	- - -	30 Packages.
Writs and Inquisitions (for Crown Debts, &c.)	Elizabeth to George IV.	15 Packages.

(Augmentation Department.)

Bills, Answers, &c. of the Court of Augmentations. *See also* "Proceedings."	Henry VIII. - -	2 Vols. [*Misc. Books. Vols.* 20 *and* 23.]
Bills, Answers, &c. of the Court of General Surveyors.	Henry VIII. - -	3 Vols. [*Misc. Books, Vols.* 19, 21, *and* 22.]
Chartularies - - - -	Various dates - -	9 Vols. [*Misc. Books, Vols.* 55 *to* 63.]

COURT OF EXCHEQUER—(continued).

(Augmentation Department)—(continued).

Description of Record.	Period embraced.	Number of Bundles, Rolls, or Volumes.
Church Goods, Inventories of - -	Edward VI. - -	21 Vols. [*Misc. Books, Vols.* 491 to 515.]
Colleges and Chantries, Certificates of -	Henry VIII. and Edward VI.	111 Rolls.
Colleges and Chantries, Particulars for the Sale of.	Henry VIII. and Edward VI.	2 Vols. [*Misc. Books, Vols.* 67 *and* 68.]
Concealments, Particulars of - -	Elizabeth - -	1 Portfolio.
Conventual Leases - - -	Richard II. to Henry VIII.	29 Portfolios.
Court Rolls. *See* Court Rolls General Series. (Lists and Indexes, No. 6).	—	—
Court Rolls, Books of - - -	Various dates - -	8 Vols. [*Misc. Books, Vols.* 79 to 86.]
Decrees and Orders - - -	Henry VIII. to Edward VI.	15 Vols. [*Misc. Books, Vols.* 91 to 105.]
Decrees and Orders of the Court of General Surveyors.	Henry VIII. -	1 Vol. [*Misc. Books, Vol.* 106.]
Deeds (Ancient). Series "B." - -	Calendar in progress.	—
Deeds (Ancient) called "Cartæ Miscellaneæ."	- - - -	24 Vols. [*Misc. Books, Vols.* 31 to 54.]
Deeds of Purchase and Exchange -	Henry VIII. and Edward VI.	21 Boxes.
Deeds of Purchase and Exchange, Enrolments of.	Henry VIII. and Edward VI.	3 Vols. [*Misc. Books, Vols.* 332 to 334.]
Defective Titles, Particulars for the Amendment of.	Elizabeth to Charles I.	6 Vols. [*Misc. Books, Vols.* 87ᴀ to 90.]
Depositions - - - -	Henry VIII. and Edward VI.	26 Vols. [*Misc. Books, Vols.* 108 to 129.]
Duchy of Cornwall :— Accounts, &c. - - - -	Edward III. to Charles II.	7 Portfolios.
Assession Rolls - - -	Edward III. to Henry VII.	1 Box.
Ministers' Accounts. *See* Ministers' Accounts (General Series).	—	—
Miscellaneous Rolls - -	Edward III. to Charles I.	1 Box.
Receipts and Acquittances - -	James I. to Charles I.	7 Vols. [*Misc. Books, Vols.* 69 to 75.]

COURT OF EXCHEQUER—(continued).

(Augmentation Department)—(continued).

Description of Record.	Period embraced.	Number of Bundles, Rolls, or Volumes.
Fee Farm Rents:—		
Certificates and Contracts for the Sale of.	Commonwealth	10 Vols. [*Misc. Books, Vols.* 135 *to* 144.]
Counterparts of Deeds of Sale of	Do.	26 Boxes.
Particulars for the Sale of	Do.	10 Packages.
Grants, Transcripts of	Edward VI. to Charles I.	5 Vols. [*Misc. Books, Vols.* 151 *to* 155.]
Leases, Copies of	Philip & Mary	6 Vols. [*Misc. Books, Vols.* 179 *to* 184.]
Leases and Pensions, Enrolments of	Henry VIII. to James 1.	26 Vols. [*Misc. Books, Vols.* 209 *to* 229, *and* 232 *to* 236.]
Leases, Enrolments of	3 to 43 Elizabeth	8 Boxes.
Do. Particulars for	Henry VIII. to Elizabeth.	42 Portfolios.
Do. Particulars for	Henry VIII. to Elizabeth.	25 Vols. [*Misc. Books, Vols.* 185 *to* 208n.]
Do. Counterparts or Transcripts of	Henry VIII. to James I.	51 Portfolios.
Do. Surrendered to the Crown	Henry VIII. to Edward VI.	9 Portfolios.
Letters Patent and Indentures	Henry VIII.	6 Vols. [*Misc. Books, Vols.* 238 *to* 243.]
Ministers' and Receivers' Accounts	Henry VIII. to Charles 1.	Under arrangement.
Ministers' and Receivers' Accounts, Books of.	Henry VIII. to Edward VI.	41 Vols. [*Misc. Books, Vols.* 268 *to* 308.]
Miscellaneous Books		515 Vols.
Monastic Pensions, Warrants for and Accounts of.	Henry VIII. to Edward VI.	19 Vols. [*Misc. Books, Vols.* 249 *to* 262.]
Offices, Entries of Grants of	Elizabeth to Charles I.	9 Vols. [*Misc. Books, Vols.* 318 *to* 326.]
Do., Particulars for Grants of	Henry VIII. to Charles 1.	5 Vols. [*Misc. Books, Vols.* 157, 158, *and* 309 *to* 311.]

COURT OF EXCHEQUER—(continued).

(Augmentation Department)—(continued).

Description of Record.	Period embraced.	Number of Bundles, Rolls, or Volumes.
Offices, Particulars for Grants of -	Henry VIII. to Charles II.	23 Packages.
Parliamentary Surveys -	Commonwealth -	56 Portfolios.
Particulars for Grants - - -	Henry VIII. to James I.	36 Portfolios.
Particulars for Sale of the Estates of Charles I.	Commonwealth -	22 Boxes.
Proceedings of the Court of Augmentations.	Henry VIII. to Philip & Mary.	15 Parcels.
Rentals and Surveys. *See* General Series.	—	—
Rentals and Surveys, Books of - -	Henry VIII. to James I.	79 Vols. [*Misc. Books, Vols.* 357 *to* 435.]
Surrenders of Monasteries - -	Henry VIII. - -	21 Boxes.
Schools, Particulars of Grants for - -	Edward VI. - -	1 Package.
Treasurers' Accounts - - -	28 Henry VIII. to 1 Mary.	10 Rolls.
Universities of Oxford and Cambridge, Valuations of the.	37 Hen. VIII. -	2 Vols. [*Misc. Books, Vols.* 440 *and* 441.]
Warrants for the delivery of Records -	Henry VII. to Charles I.	1 Box.
Woods, Accounts of Sales of - -	- - -	1 Parcel.
Woods, Accounts of Sales of - -	Henry VIII. to Elizabeth.	6 Vols. [*Misc. Books, Vols.* 457 *to* 461.]

(Treasury of the Receipt.)

Acknowledgments of Supremacy -	Henry VIII. - -	41 Boxes.
Barons' Letter to Pope Boniface and Seals.	29 Edward I. -	2 Cases.
Black Book of the Exchequer -	- -	2 Vols.
Calais, Comptrollers' Accounts - -	Henry VIII. - -	4 Vols.
Calendar of Papal Bulls, &c. - -	- - -	1 Vol.
Deeds (Ancient). Series "A." - -	Calendar in progress.	—
Diplomatic Documents - - -	Henry I. to James I.	Under arrangement.
Domesday Book - - -	A.D. 1086 - -	2 Vols.
Domesday Book, Abbreviation of -	Temp. Edward I. -	1 Vol.
Forest Proceedings - - -	Henry III. to Charles II.	7 Boxes and 2 Bundles.
Indentures of Foundation of Henry VII. Chapel.	- - -	2 Boxes.
Do. do. -	- - -	13 Parcels.
Liber Memorandorum Camerariorum -	- - -	1 Vol.
Miscellaneous Books - - -	- - -	264 Vols.
Parliament Rolls - - -	18 to 35 Edward I. -	10 Rolls.
Placita Aulæ - - - -	Edward I. to Henry VI.	29 Rolls.
Registrum Munimentorum - -	- - -	2 Vols.

COURT OF EXCHEQUER– (continued).

(Treasury of the Receipt)—(continued).

Description of Record.	Period embraced.	Number of Bundles, Rolls, or Volumes.
Scottish Documents - - -	Edward I. to Elizabeth.	102 Packages.
Seals (Loose) - - - -	-	5 Boxes.
Surrenders to Cardinal's College -	Henry VIII. - -	4 Vols.
Survey, Court of. Answers in the -	Henry VIII. to Edward VI.	7 Vols.
Warrants for the Privy Seal or " Privy Signet Bills" :—		
Series I. - - - -	- - -	Under arrangement.
Series II. - - -	Henry VIII. to Charles I.	120 Parcels.
White Book of Cornwall - -	25–39 Edward III. -	1 Vol.
Wills (Royal) - - -	Richard II. - -	1 Box.
	Henry V. - -	1 Box.
	Henry VII. - -	1 Box.
	Henry VIII. - -	1 Box.
Wolsey's Patents - - -	Henry VIII. - -	23 Cases.

(Receipt Department, including the Pells' and Auditors' Offices.)

Account Books (Auditors') - -	1782 to 1834 -	27 Vols.
Account Books (Comptroller Generals')		
Great Britain - -	1835 to 1867 - -	14 Vols.
Ireland (Series I.) - -	1837 to 1867 - -	12 Vols.
Ireland (Series II.) - -	1837 to 1866 - -	5 Vols.
Assignment Books (Auditors') :—		
Series I. - - - -	1622 to 1834 - -	32 Vols.
Series II. - - -	1791 to 1834 -	5 Vols.
Assignment Books (Pells') -	1677 to 1703 -	18 Vols.
Assignment Books (Goldsmiths') :—		
Series I. - - -	1676 to 1713 -	11 Vols.
Series II. - - -	1678 to 1688 -	17 Vols.
Attorney, Warrants of - -	1745 to 1787 and 1801 to 1829.	7 Vols.
Indexes - - -	- - -	4 Vols.
Cash Books (Auditors') -	1800 to 1834 -	35 Vols.
Certificate Books (Auditors') -	1704 to 1834 -	16 Vols.
(Pells') - -	1611 to 1670 -	11 Vols.
(Teller's.)		
Series I. - - -	1610 to 1665 -	14 Vols.
Series II. - -	1831 to 1835 -	5 Vols.
Credits (England) - -	1834 to 1867 -	39 Vols.
Credits (Ireland) - -	1837 to 1867 -	31 Vols.
Debenture Books (Auditors') :—		
Series I. - - -	1619 to 1691 -	24 Vols.
Series II. - - -	1696 to 1834 -	53 Vols.
Debentures (Common) - -	1803 to 1834 -	21 Parcels.
Declaration Books (Auditors') -	1625 to 1691 -	31 Vols.
Declaration Books (Pells') -	1555 to 1792 -	138 Vols.
Declaration Books, *Supplementary* -	10 to 18 Elizabeth -	9 Vols.
Declarations of the State of the Treasury	23 Henry VII. to 38 Henry VIII.	26 Vols.
Entry Books (Auditors') - -	1833 to 1835 -	4 Vols.

COURT OF EXCHEQUER—(continued).

(Receipt Department, including the Pells' and Auditors' Offices)—(continued).

Description of Record.	Period embraced.	Number of Bundles, Rolls, or Volumes.
Exchequer Bills, Certificates of (Public Works).	1834 to 1845 -	6 Vols.
Exchequer Bills, Certificates of (West India Loan).	1833 to 1845 -	2 Vols.
Exchequer Bills Issued, Certificates of -	1666 to 1669 and 1712 to 1862.	56 Vols.
Exchequer Bills authorised to be issued by Parliament, Certificates of.	1714 to 1726 -	8 Vols.
Exchequer Bills, Registers of -	1793 to 1794 -	9 Vols.
Exchequer Bills, Issue Books of :—		
Series I. -	1744 to 1855 and various years.	26. Vols.
Series II. -	1778 to 1833 -	18 Vols.
Exchequer Bills, Warrants for -	1696 to 1698 and 1713 to 1834.	14 Vols.
Exchequer Bills, Paymasters' Certificates of.	1830 to 1834 -	1 Vol.
Exchequer Bills, Accounts and Reports relating to.	1697 to 1731 -	1 Vol.
Gentlemen Pensioners' Rolls -	4 & 5 Philip & Mary to 49 George III.	187 Rolls.
Imprest Books (Pells') -	1684 to 1831 -	15 Vols.
Imprest Certificates (Pells') -	1569 to 1678 -	11 Vols.
Imprest Rolls, General (Auditors') -	1788 to 1834 -	7 Vols.
Irish Military Establishments -	42 Elizabeth to 21 James I.	15 Rolls.
Issue Books (Pells') -	1597 to 1834, and special Issues.	483 Vols.
Issue Rolls (Auditors') -	1 & 2 Edward I. to 19 Edward IV.	357 Rolls.
Issue Rolls (Pells') -	6 Henry VIII. to 37 George III.	1,217 Rolls.
Jewel Rolls -	42 & 43 Elizabeth -	7 Rolls.
Jews Rolls -	John to Edward I. -	38 Rolls.
Jornalia Rolls -	20 Edward I. to 1 Edward II.	33 Rolls.
Liberate Rolls -	10 Henry III. to 31 Edward I.	77 Rolls.
Miscellanea -	-	229 Bundles.
Miscellaneous Books -	-	54 Bundles.
Miscellaneous Rolls -	-	139 Rolls.
Offices and Appointments, Index to	-	2 Vols.
Order Books (Auditors') :—		
Series I. -	1619 to 1697 -	29 Vols.
Series II. -	1760 to 1834 -	150 Vols.
Order Books (Pells') -	1597 to 1697 -	88 Vols.
Orders (Auditors') -	1560 to 1834 -	81 Parcels.
Orders and Treasury Warrants -	1834 to 1865 -	29 Vols.
Orders and Treasury Warrants, Ireland -	1837 to 1867 -	30 Vols.
Patent Books (Auditors') -	1509 to 1834 -	56 Vols.
Patent Books (for Tallies) -	1599 to 1696 -	12 Vols.
Patent Books (Pells') -	1597 to 1834 -	46 Vols.
Patent Rolls (Auditors') -	1609 to 1620 -	9 Rolls.
Patents, Surrenders of -	-	1 Vol.

COURT OF EXCHEQUER—(continued).

(Receipt Department, including the Pells' and Auditors' Offices)—(continued).

Description of Record.	Period embraced.	Number of Bundles, Rolls, or Volumes.
Patent and Privy Seal Rolls (Pells') -	1604 to 1620 -	6 Rolls.
Patents and Privy Seals for Baronets -	1620 to 1701 -	9 Vols.
Payments by Royal Warrant -	1559 to 1586 -	17 Vols.
Posting Books (Pells') - - -		—
Series I. - - - -	See "Privy Seals (Dormant)."	—
Series II. - - -	1718 to 1834 - -	16 Vols.
Privy Seal Books (Auditors') - -	1485 to 1834 -	32 Vols.
Do. (Pells') - -	1597 to 1834 - -	59 Vols.
Do. called "Auditors' Enrolments of Privy Seals."	1620 to 1734 -	7 Vols.
Privy Seal Rolls (Auditors') - -	1611 to 1620 - -	6 Rolls.
Privy Seals Dormant, Books of - -	1597 to 1628 -	20 Vols.
Privy Seals and Warrants for Issues -	Henry III. to William IV.	Under arrangement.
Receipt Books (Auditors') - -	1570 to 1670 and 1709.	128 Vols.
Do. called "Bills of the Day"	1801 to 1866 - -	52 Vols.
Do. do. (Ireland).	1837 to 1867 -	18 Vols.
Receipt Books (Pells') - -	1559 to 1834 (and Special Receipts).	516 Vols.
Receipt Rolls (Auditors') - -	6 Henry VIII. to 10 Elizabeth.	556 Rolls.
Do. (Pells') - -	14 John and 4 Henry III. to 22 George III.	1,112 Rolls.
Receipts, Abbreviates of (Pells') -	1562 to 1643 -	68 Vols.
Revenue, Accounts of the -	1786 to 1834 - -	19 Vols.
Supply Cash Books - - -	1817 to 1833 - -	18 Vols.
Tellers' Bills - - -	Henry VI. to George III.	39 Parcels.
Tellers' Rolls - - -	3 Henry VI. to 16 Charles I.	155 Rolls.
Tellers' Views of Accounts - -	1559 to 1611 -	37 Vols.
Tellers' Views of Receipts and Issues -	1569 to 1608 - -	34 Vols.
Treasurers' Accounts - - -	12 & 13 Edward I. and 14 Edward III. to 20 Henry VII.	19 Rolls.
Treasury Letters :—		
Series I. - - -	1793 to 1834 -	30 Vols.
Series II. - - -	1834 to 1867 -	56 Vols.
Series III. (Ireland) -	1837 to 1867 -	31 Vols.
Treasury Letters. Reference Books (England)	1834 to 1865 -	12 Vols.
Do. do. (Ireland) -	1837 to 1865 -	4 Vols.
Treasury Orders and Warrants -	1547 to 1794 -	22 Portfolios.
Wardrobe Debentures - - -	-	Under arrangement.
Warrant Books (Pells') - -	1617 to 1790 -	45 Vols.
Warrant Books (Auditors') - -	1626 to 1759 -	70 Vols.
Warrants (Original) - - -	1794 to 1831 -	95 Vols.
Warrants for Issues. See "Privy Seals and Warrants for Issues."		

COURT OF EXCHEQUER—(continued).

(First Fruits and Tenths Department.)

Description of Record.	Period embraced.	Number of Bundles, Rolls, or Volumes.
Bishops' Certificates - - -	Elizabeth to 1862 -	40 Portfolios.
Bonds, Entries of - - - -	1658 to 1820 -	153 Vols.
Bonds, Payments of - - -	1692 to 1787 -	9 Vols.
Collectors' Account Book - - -	1666 to 1715 - -	1 Vol.
Commission Books - - -	Henry VIII. to 1684	3 Vols.
Composition Books - - -	1535 to 1795 - -	37 Vols.
Comptrollers' Payment Books - -	1681 to 1799 - -	23 Vols.
Comptrollers' State Books - -	1688 to 1783 - -	15 Vols.
Constat Books - - - -	1717 to 1819 - -	6 Vols.
Constat Books (Remembrancers') -	1793 to 1823 - -	24 Vols.
King's Books or " Liber Valorum " -	- - -	3 Vols.
Ledgers (Canterbury and York) -	1658 to 1838 - -	12 Vols.
Liber Regis. See " Valor Ecclesiasticus."	—	—
Miscellaneous Books - - -	. . -	15 Vols.
Plea Rolls - - - - -	Mary to George II. -	19 Rolls.
Precedent Book - - - -	. . -	1 Vol.
Presentations - - -	1703 to 1786 - -	1 Vol.
Process Books - - - -	29 Henry VIII. to 1817.	13 Vols.
Receivers' Payment Books - -	1795 to 1823 - -	24 Vols.
Remembrancers' Accounts -	33 Hen. VIII. to 1626.	13 Vols.
Remembrancers' Payment Books -	1793 to 1823 - -	21 Vols.
Tenths, Day Books of Receipts of (Canterbury).	1718 to 1838 - -	120 Vols.
Tenths, Day Books of Receipts of (York).	1717 to 1839 - -	121 Vols.
Tenths, Entries of Payment of :—		
Series I. - - - -	1660 to 1705 - -	6 Vols.
Series II. - - -	1717 to 1838 - -	34 Vols.
Series III. - - -	. . -	32 Vols.
(Canterbury and York) - -	. . -	8 Vols.
Valor Ecclesiasticus (Original Returns of the).	Henry VIII. -	18 Vols. and 3 Portfolios.
Valor Ecclesiasticus (Abstracts of the) -	. . -	2 Vols.
Valor Ecclesiasticus (Transcripts of the, called the " Liber Regis.")	. . -	2 Vols.
Writs and Miscellanea - -	Henry VIII. to William IV.	21 Packages.

(Land Revenue Department.)

The Records of the Land Revenue Department transferred to the Public Record Office consist principally of such Public Accounts as were passed before the Auditors of Land Revenue, and are analogous to the Declared Accounts of the Audit Office and Pipe Office. The original Ministers' Accounts and similar documents received from the Land Revenue Office, in continuation of other Ministers' Accounts previously transferred to the

COURT OF EXCHEQUER—(continued).

(Land Revenue Department)—(continued).

Augmentation Office, and thence to the Public Record Office, have been incorporated with the already existing series.

The Public Accounts consist of the following :—

Description of Record.	Period embraced.	Number of Bundles, Rolls, or Volumes.
Alienation Office Accounts :—		
Accounts of Fees for Writs of Entry and Covenant.	44 Elizabeth to 1831	216 Vols.
Receivers' Accounts and Vouchers -	1661 to 1831 -	13 Bundles.
Customs Accounts	-	12 Bundles.
Estreats, Rolls of -	-	126 Bundles.
Fines and Amerciaments, Estreats of	-	23 Bundles.
Greenwich Hospital Accounts -	1702 to 1723 -	13 Vols.
Land Tax, Auditors' Certificates of	1708 to 1800 -	4 Vols.
Land and Assessed Taxes :—		
Auditors' States of	1678 to 1831 -	27 Bundles.
Receiver General's Accounts of	1688 to 1830 -	58 Bundles.
Receivers' Accounts, Drafts of	1704 to 1794 -	19 Vols.
Receivers' Accounts, States of	1701 to 1791	52 Vols.
Recusancy, Accounts of Compositions for.	-	3 Bundles.
Revenues, &c. of Queen Catherine, Accounts of the.	-	14 Bundles.
Revenues, &c. of Queen Henrietta Maria	-	6 Bundles.
Sheriffs' Accounts, Writs, Inquisitions, &c.	-	114 Bundles.
Miscellanea -	-	56 Bundles.

PALATINATE OF DURHAM.

(Chancery Records.)

Account Books (Cursitors') -	1763 to 1841 -	9 Vols.
Account Books (Registrars') -	1720 to 1777 -	3 Vols.
Affidavits (Registrars') -	1657 to 1812 -	26 Bundles.
Bills, Answers, &c. (Registrars') -	1576 to 1840 -	159 Bundles.
Bills of Costs (Registrars') -	1702 to 1775 -	4 Bundles.
Chancery Enrolments -	1333 to 1836 -	106 Rolls (Cursitors' Records, Nos. 29 to 134).
Commissions, Interrogatories, and Depositions (Registrars').	1560 to 1803 -	86 Bundles.
Cursitors' Records -	Various -	211 Vols., Rolls, and Bundles.
Deputy Registrars' Books -	1720 to 1757 -	2 Vols.
Exceptions (Registrars') -	1707 to 1715 -	1 Bundle.
Halmote Court Books -	1349 to 1619 -	17 Vols. (Cursitors' Records, Nos. 12 to 28.)
Inquisitions post mortem -	Henry VI. to Charles I.	27 Bundles (Cursitors' Records, Nos. 164 to 190).
Inquisitions post mortem, Registers of -	Edward II. to James I.	6 Vols. (Cursitors' Records, Nos. 2 to 7).
Interrogatories and Depositions (Cursitors').	1672 to 1768 -	33 Bundles.

PALATINATE OF DURHAM—(continued).

(Chancery Records)—(continued).

Description of Record.	Period embraced.	Number of Bundles, Rolls, or Volumes.
Kellawe's Register -	-	1 Vol.
Members of Parliament, Returns of (Cursitors').	1722 to 1865	4 Bundles.
Miscellanea (Cursitors')	-	58 Bundles.
Orders and Decrees, Entry Books of (Registrars').	1633 to 1850	7 Vols.
Orders, Decrees, and Reports (Original)	1613 to 1778	137 Bundles.
Orders, Decrees, and Reports (Drafts of)	1755 to 1829	8 Bundles.
Papers in various Causes (Registrars') -	-	18 Bundles.
Seals of Writs, Entry Books of (Registrars').	1732 to 1830	16 Vols.
Significavits	1700 to 1765	3 Bundles (Cursitors' Records, Nos. 207 to 209).
Writs of Præcipe quod reddat, &c.	35 Charles II. to 1785.	8 Bundles (Cursitors' Records, Nos. 199 to 206).

(Prothonotary's Records.)

Appearances to Ejectments	Anne to George I. -	1 Bundle.
Attorneys' Clerks, Affidavits of	1750 to 1834 -	3 Bundles.
Cognovits and Warrants of Attorney	1828 to 1853 -	17 Bundles.
Declarations	13–14 Charles II. to 15–16 Victoria.	178 Bundles.
Fines, Concords of	13 Charles II. to 1834.	44 Bundles.
Fines, Feet of	Edward VI. to 1834 -	49 Bundles.
Indexes (Various)	-	1 Bundle.
Judgment Rolls -	20 Henry VII. to 1844.	220 Rolls.
Judgments, Files of	19 Charles I. to 1853	—
Posteas -	1751 to 1865	6 Bundles.
Recoveries, Drafts of	1770 to 1833 -	3 Bundles.
Recoveries, Præcipes for	13 Charles II. to 1833.	35 Bundles.
Writs of the Court of Pleas	-	1 Bundle.

(Clerk of the Crown's Records.)

Assize Calendars. See "Returns of Prisoners."	—	—
Commissions of Gaol Delivery -	1784 to 1876 -	39 Bundles.
Costs of Prosecutions	1828 to 1876	56 Bundles.
Depositions	1843 to 1877	60 Bundles.
Indictments	1713 to 1877	166 Bundles.
Indictment Books	1753 to 1876	7 Vols.
Minute Books	1770 to 1876	10 Vols.
Pardons -	1816 to 1863	2 Bundles.
Recognizances	1843 to 1877	61 Bundles.
Returns of Prisoners	1805 to 1861	6 Bundles

PALATINATE OF LANCASTER.
(Chancery Records.)

Description of Record.	Period embraced.	Number of Bundles, Rolls, or Volumes.
Affidavits	1793 to 1836	9 Bundles.
Affidavits, Entries of	1610 to 1678	4 Vols.
Answers	1474 to 1858	251 Vols. and Bundles.
Appearance Books	1641 to 1703	3 Vols.
Bill Books	Edward IV. to 1734	12 Vols.
Bills	Henry VII. to 1853	136 Vols. and Bundles.
Close Rolls	11 Henry IV. to 9 Edward IV.	3 Rolls.
Consents	1793 to 1836	1 Bundle.
Decrees and Orders, &c.	15 Henry VIII. to 1784.	27 Vols.
Deeds Enrolled	Charles II. to William IV.	1 Bundle.
Exhibits		17 Bundles.
Inquisitions and Decrees as to Charitable Uses, &c.	Commonwealth to George I.	1 Bundle.
Inquisitions post mortem	Henry IV. to Henry VIII.	1 Box.
Interrogatories and Depositions	24 Elizabeth to 1853	273 Bundles.
Lunacy Inquisitions	Charles II. to William IV.	1 Bundle.
Minute Book (Registrar's)	1704 to 1713	1 Vol.
Miscellanea		7 Bundles.
Patent Rolls	4 Richard II. to 21 Henry VII.	10 Rolls.
Replications, &c.	1601 to 1846	21 Bundles.
Warrants	Richard II. to Henry VII.	3 Bundles.
Deed of Amalgamation of the Preston and Wyre and Lancashire and Yorkshire Railway Companies.		1 Box.
Inclosure Award of Walton on the Hill and Fazakerley.	1763	1 Bundle.

(Prothonotary's Records.)

Affidavits of Execution of Articles of Clerkship.	1749 to 1814	2 Bundles.
Affidavits, Pye Books to	1813 to 1838	4 Vols.
Clerks' Articles Books	1749 to 1822	2 Vols.
Declarations, Pye Books to	14 George II. to 11 Victoria.	9 Vols.
Dockets of Issues	41 George III. to 11 Victoria.	6 Vols.
Docket Rolls, &c.	51 Edward III. to 4 William IV.	30 Rolls.
Draft Judgments	20 George II. to 52 George III.	6 Vols.
Draft Posteas	51 George III. to 11 Victoria.	4 Vols.
Fines, &c.	51 Edward III. to 4 William IV.	511 Bundles.

PALATINATE OF LANCASTER—(continued).

(Prothonotary's Records)—(continued).

Description of Record.	Period embraced.	Number of Bundles, Rolls, or Volumes.
Fines, Enrolments of - - -	29 Elizabeth to 4 William IV.	479 Rolls.
Minutes of Rules - - -	7 George II. to 36 George III.	3 Vols.
Minutes of Verdicts - - -	1839 to 1847 - -	1 Bundle.
Panels of Jurors - - -	1811 to 1848 - -	75 Bundles.
Plea Rolls - - - -	2 Henry IV. to 11 Victoria.	767 Rolls.
Precedent Books - - -	- - -	5 Vols.
Remembrance Books - -	8 William III. to 20 George II.	3 Vols.
Rule Books - - -	7 George II. to 8 Victoria.	15 Vols.
Rules, Consent - - -	2 George IV. to 16 Victoria.	1 Bundle.
Rules in Ejectment - -	1811 to 1821 - -	1 Bundle.
Rules of Reference - -	41 George III. to 11 Victoria.	4 Vols.
Sessional Papers - -	Henry VIII. to 1848	219 Bundles.
Sessional Papers, Pye Books to -	Charles II. to George II.	6 Vols.
Writ Books - -	1712 to 1845 - -	22 Vols.

(Clerk of the Crown's Records.)

Assize Rolls - - -	1 Henry VI. to 6 Victoria.	317 Rolls.
Bail Rolls - - -	22-38 Henry VIII. -	16 Rolls.
Coroners' Inquisitions -	14 Charles II. to 3 George IV.	13 Bundles.
Depositions - - -	1808 to 1867 - -	221 Bundles.
Indictments - - -	17 Henry VIII. to 4 William IV.	27 Bundles.
Do. Calendar to -	17 Edward IV. to 35 Henry VIII.	3 Rolls.
Do. and Writs of Assize -	3 Henry VI. to 38 Henry VIII.	22 Bundles.
Minute Books - -	2 James II. to 1823	8 Vols.
Nomina Ministrorum - -	1810 to 1867 - -	215 Bundles.
Order Books - -	10 George II. to 1831	4 Vols.
Outlawry Rolls - - -	Richard II. to 1 Edward VI.	4 Rolls.
Recognizances - -	35 Charles II. to 52 George III.	15 Bundles.
Recognizance Books - -	41 George III. to 8 George IV.	2 Vols.
Rule Books - - -	30 George III. to 2 Victoria.	2 Vols.

DUCHY OF LANCASTER.

Assize Rolls - - -	1-10 Henry Duke of Lancaster.	8 Rolls. [Division xxv., Bundle A.]

DUCHY OF LANCASTER—(continued).

Description of Record.	Period embraced.	Number of Bundles, Rolls, or Volumes.
Chancery Rolls - - -	Henry Duke of Lancaster to Edward IV.	61 Rolls. [Division xxv., Bundles X and Y.]
Charters and Grants (Original) - -	William II. to Henry VII.	Under arrangement.
Court Rolls - - - -	Edward I. to George III.	152 Bundles.
Deeds (Ancient), Series " L." - - -	- - -	Under arrangement.
Extents for Debt - - -	Elizabeth to Charles II.	7 Bundles.
Inquisitions post mortem - -	Henry VIII. to Charles I.	30 Vols.
Judges' Commissions - -	1675 to 1774 - -	9 Bundles.
Judicial Proceedings :—		
Pleadings - - -	Henry VII. to Elizabeth.	213 Vols.
	James I. to 1835 -	208 Bundles.
Depositions, Examinations, &c. .	Henry VIII. to Philip & Mary.	81 Vols.
Depositions, Examinations, &c. -	Elizabeth to George III.	172 Bundles.
Surveys, &c. taken by Commission	Elizabeth to George III.	Under arrangement.
Decrees and Orders (Draft) - -	Henry VIII. to George I.	142 Bundles.
Decrees and Orders, Entry Books of	Edward IV. to 1825	47 Vols.
Affidavits, Reports, &c. - -	Elizabeth to 1800 -	26 Bundles.
Injunctions (Draft) -	12 James I. to 1748	23 Bundles.
Leases :—		
Counterparts of - -	Edward VI. to 1758	61 Bundles.
Draft - - - -	Henry VIII. to 1760	104 Bundles.
Entries and Enrolments of. See " Registers of Grants, &c."	—	
Maps and Plans - - -	- - -	1 Portfolio.
Ministers' Accounts - -	Edward I. to George III.	739 Bundles.
Patents (Draft) - -	Phillip and Mary to George II.	46 Bundles.
Presentations (Draft) - -	Elizabeth to George I.	3 Bundles.
Privy Seals, &c. - -	Henry VII. to George III.	46 Bundles.
Registers of Grants, Leases, &c. -	- - -	105 Vols.
Security Bonds - - -	Henry VIII. to 1716	9 Bundles.
Sewers, Draft Commissions of -	1660 to 1722	3 Bundles.
Sheriffs' Bills - - -	1684 to 1758 -	6 Bundles.
Surveys (Oliver Cromwell's) -	Commonwealth -	3 Bundles.
Do. Books of - -	Elizabeth and James I.	35 Vols.
Do. of Woods - - -	Elizabeth and James	13 Vols.
Do. Drafts of Warrants for	13 Elizabeth to 1785	80 Bundles.
Miscellanea (*Div. xxv.*) - -	- - -	⎫ Under arrangement.
Do. (*Div. xxvi.*) -	- - -	⎬
Do. (*Div. xxvii.*) -	- - -	⎪
Do. (*Div. xxviii*) -	- - -	⎭

COURTS OF WALES AND CHESTER.

Description of Record.	Period embraced.	Number of Bundles, Rolls, or Volumes.
Attorneys' and Solicitors' Admission Rolls.	9 William III. to William IV.	9 Rolls.
Attorneys' and Solicitors' Oath Rolls -	3 George II. to William IV.	17 Rolls.
Bills and Answers (Chester Exchequer)	Henry VIII. to George IV.	102 Portfolios.
Bills and Answers (Chancery) - -	1689 to 1830 - -	55 Portfolios.
Calendar Rolls - - -	Edward III. to Charles II.	22 Rolls.
Coroners' Inquisitions - - -	2 Edward IV. to William IV.	7 Bundles.
Decrees and Orders (Chester Exchequer)	1559 to 1790 - -	78 Bundles.
Decrees and Orders, Entry Books of. See " Miscellaneous Books."	—	—
Docket Rolls - - -	Henry VIII. to William IV.	130 Rolls.
Essoin Rolls - - -	17 Edward III. to 22 Henry VII.	11 Rolls.
Eyre Rolls - -	35 Edward I. to 15 Henry VII.	15 Rolls.
Fines, &c. - - -	Edward I. to William IV.	230 Bundles.
Fines (Supplementary) -	- - -	2 Bundles.
Fines, Concords of (Chester) -	1788 to 1829 - -	9 Bundles.
Fines, Enrolments of:—		
Chester - -	28 Elizabeth to Anne	12 Rolls.
Flint - -	12 Elizabeth to 2 George II.	4 Rolls.
Pembroke - -	29-40 Elizabeth -	1 Roll.
Fines and Amercements (Chester) -	4 Edward II. to 22 Richard II.	3 Rolls.
Fines and Warrants of Attorney (North Wales Circuit).	1789 to 1830 - -	1 Bundle.
Forest Rolls (Chester) -	55 Henry III. to 18 Henry VII.	9 Rolls.
Gaol Files. See " Mainprize Files."		—
General and Special Liveries - -	Elizabeth to Charles I.	1 Bundle.
Inclosure Awards - - -	- - -	1 Bundle.
Indictment Rolls - -	Edward I. to Henry VII.	31 Rolls.
Inquisitions post mortem -	Edward I. to Charles I.	7 Portfolios.
Mainprize Files and Gaol Files -	Elizabeth to William IV.	168 Bundles.
Mainprize Rolls - -	Edward III. to Elizabeth.	33 Rolls.
Plea Rolls :—		
Chester - -	44 Henry III. to William IV.	856 Rolls.
Flint - - -	12 Edward I. to William IV.	592 Rolls.
Denbigh - -	33 Henry VIII. to William IV.	530 Rolls.
Montgomery -	33 Henry VIII. to William IV.	567 Rolls.
Anglesea - -	1 Henry VIII. to William IV.	151 Rolls.
Carnarvon - -	10 Richard II. to William IV.	171 Rolls.

COURTS OF WALES AND CHESTER—(continued).

Description of Record.	Period embraced.	Number of Bundles, Rolls, or Volumes.
Plea Rolls—*cont.*		
Merioneth -	1 Edward VI. to 1 William IV.	191 Rolls.
Brecknock -	34 Henry VIII. to 1 William IV.	450 Rolls.
Radnor -	33 Henry VIII. to 1 William IV.	550 Rolls.
Glamorgan -	33 Henry VIII. to 1 William IV.	560 Rolls.
Carmarthen	33 Henry VIII. to 1 William IV.	463 Rolls.
Pembroke -	34 Henry VIII. to 1 William IV.	521 Rolls.
Cardigan -	33 Henry VIII. to 1 William IV.	450 Rolls.
Quo Warranto Rolls -	27 Edward III. to 15 Henry VII.	6 Rolls.
Privy Seals, Warrants, &c.	Hen. VII. & Hen. VIII.	1 Bundle.
Recognizance Rolls (Chester)	1 Edward II. to 11 George IV.	339 Rolls.
Remembrance Rolls -	James II. to William IV.	69 Rolls.
Ruthin Records (Presentments, Declarations, &c.).	1722 to 1798 -	26 Portfolios.
Sheriffs' Tourn Rolls (Chester) -	31 Edward III. to 18 Edward IV.	7 Rolls.
Sheriffs' Tourn Rolls (Flint) -	16 Edward III. to 1 Edward IV.	1 Roll.
Warrants of Attorney, Rolls of -	17 Edward III. to 31 Henry VIII.	10 Rolls.
Miscellaneous Books (Order Books, Rule Books, Minute Books, &c.).	-	450 Vols.
Miscellaneous Rolls -	-	154 Rolls.

DESCRIPTIVE CATALOGUE.

ACCOUNTS.

Accounts, Original. (Exchequer, Q. R.)

In addition to the extensive and important series of "Ministers' and Receivers' Accounts" of the lands and tenements in the hands of the Crown, and to the "Revenue Rolls" and rolls and books relating to the "Receipts and Issues of the Exchequer," which are fully described under the titles indicated, there are amongst the Miscellanea of the Queen's Remembrancer's Department numerous collections of Original Accounts and "Particulars of Accounts," as rendered to the Exchequer by the Sheriffs, Escheators, Collectors of Customs and Subsidies, and other Revenue officers; of Accounts and subsidiary documents relating to the expenditure on the Army and Navy, on Ambassadors and Envoys, on the royal Household and Wardrobe, and on Works and repairs at the Royal Palaces and other Buildings; and of the issues and profits arising from various Courts and Public Offices, which have been arranged in the present volume under the subjects to which they respectively relate.

Many original Accounts of a similar nature are to be found amongst the Miscellanea of the Treasury of the Receipt of the Exchequer.

An exhaustive Inventory of these Accounts is in progress and will shortly be printed. In the meanwhile a List is appended showing very briefly their nature and extent. It will be seen that they generally terminate with the reign of James I., their places being subsequently supplied in a great measure by the "Declared Accounts," described below.

Alienation Office Accounts. James I.

Army, Navy, and Ordnance Accounts. Henry III. to James I.

Butlerage (Pincerna Regis) Accounts. Edward I. to James I.

Customs, Collectors' Accounts. Edward I. to James I.

Custos Sigilli, Accounts of the. Edward VI. to Elizabeth.

Domus Conversorum, Accounts of the Keeper of the. Edward III. to James I.

ACCOUNTS—(continued).

    Accounts, Original. (Exchequer, Q. R.)—(continued.)

        Equitium Regis (Accounts of the Royal Stables). Edward I. to James I.

        Escheators' Accounts. Henry III. to James I.

        Fines and Amercements, Accounts of. Henry III. to James II.

        Forests (Royal) Issues of the. Henry II. to James I.

        France, Accounts of the English possessions in. Henry III. to Philip and Mary.

        Hanaper, Accounts of the Clerk of the. Edward I. to Elizabeth.

        Irish Exchequer, Accounts of the. Henry III. to Richard III.

        Marshalsea of the King's Household, Accounts of the. Edward I. to Elizabeth.

        Mines (Stannaries), Accounts of. Edward I. to Charles I.

        Mint Accounts. Henry III. to James I.

        Nuncii (Ambassadors, Envoys, and Royal Messengers), Accounts of. Edward I. to Elizabeth.

        Præstita (Accounts of sums advanced to Officers of the Royal Household and others). John to James I.

        Sheriffs' Accounts. Henry III. to James I.

        Subsidies (Clerical and Lay), Accounts of Collectors of. Henry III. to William and Mary.

        Ulnagers' Accounts (of the Subsidy on Cloth). Edward III. to James I.

        Wardrobe and Household Accounts. John to George III.

        Works and Buildings, Accounts of. Henry III. to Elizabeth.

  Accounts, Declared (Audit Office and Pipe Office).

The practice of declaring Accounts before the Lord High Treasurer of England, or before the Chancellor of the Exchequer and two or more of the other Commissioners of the Treasury, appears to have been introduced about the reign of Henry VIII. and to have been fully established in that of Elizabeth. At an earlier date all accounts were rendered at the King's Remembrancer's Office of the Exchequer, amongst the Records of which Department large collections of Original Accounts and "Particulars of Accounts" will be found extending in date from about the reign of John to that of James I. (See above.)

ACCOUNTS— (continued).

ACCOUNTS, DECLARED (AUDIT OFFICE AND PIPE OFFICE)—(continued).

During the period of transition many of these Accounts are analagous to the Declared Accounts.

The system of declaring Accounts when fully established was as follows :—Two copies of each Account were prepared in the Audit Office, the one written on paper and the other on parchment. Both were sent to the Treasury to be declared, where they were registered in volumes known as " Declared Accounts " and " Auditors' States of Accounts." The copy on paper, having been duly signed by the Auditor or Auditors, and by the Lord High Treasurer, Chancellor of the Exchequer, or Commissioners of the Treasury before whom it was declared, was then returned to the Audit Office, and that on parchment, signed in like manner, to the King's Remembrancer's Office, where a " State " or abstract of it was enrolled, and thence to the office of the Lord Treasurer's Remembrancer, where another abstract of it was entered on the Memoranda Rolls under the heading " States and Views of Public Accounts."

Finally, it was forwarded to the Clerk of the Pipe who, until that office was abolished by Statute 3 and 4 William IV., enrolled an abridgment of it amongst the " Foreign Accounts " and retained the original.

An Inventory of the " Declared Accounts " both of the Audit Office and the Pipe Office has been recently printed (Lists and Indexes, No. II., 1893). Those in the Pipe Office series of a later date than 1714, of which duplicates existed in the Audit Office series, were transferred to the Bodleian Library under Rules made in pursuance of the Record Act of 1877. A List of the most important Declared Accounts amongst the Audit Office Records is given on pp. 84–89.

ACCOUNTS, ENROLMENTS OF (EXCHEQUER, Q. R.).

A series of 309 rolls entitled " Enrolments of Public Accounts," and extending from the reign of Elizabeth to 1859. These contain the " States " or Abstracts of the " Declared Accounts "above described, many of the details contained in the Declared Account being omitted. These enrolments formed the official record of the Account in the King's Remembrancer's Office, and warranted the issuing of process from the Exchequer against the Accountants when necessary.

The enrolment of Public Accounts in the Queen's Remembrancer's Office, except in certain cases, was discontinued in accordance with the provisions of the Statute 22 & 23 Vict. c. 21.

ACCOUNTS—(continued).

ACCOUNTS, ENROLMENTS OF (EXCHEQUER, L. T. R.).

The Accounts of the Bailiffs and other Ministers of
lands in the hands of the Crown, and of such Towns and
Boroughs as were not within the receipt of the Sheriffs of
the several Counties, together with those of the Escheators,
Custodes Cambii, Keepers of the Wardrobe, and other
officers were at first enrolled at the end of the Pipe Rolls,
and also of the Chancellor's Rolls in each year under the
heading " Rotulus Compotorum," or " Rotuli Diversorum
Computantium."

As the business of the Exchequer increased, however,
this practice was found inconvenient and cumbrous, and
towards the end of the reign of Edward III. a separate
series of rolls entitled Rolls of " Foreign Accounts " was
formed for the purpose of relieving the Pipe Rolls of such
accounts as were " foreign " to the jurisdiction of the
Sheriffs.

A distinct series of enrolments for the more voluminous
classes of accounts, as those relating to Customs, Escheats,
Subsidies, &c. had, however, already been introduced at a
much earlier period. The enrolments of Accounts in the
Lord Treasurer's Department may therefore be obtained
from the several sources described below :—

(1.) Enrolments on the Pipe Rolls and Chancellor's
Rolls, from Henry III. to Edward III.

(A complete Inventory of all these enrolments is
in progress.)

(2.) Foreign Accounts, Rolls of, 42 Edward III. to
Charles II.

Subsequent to the reign of Charles II. the Foreign
Accounts consist chiefly of enrolments of Tax
Accounts, and, inasmuch as a complete series of the
Declared Accounts has been preserved, are of little
value except as illustrating the process of enrolment in
the Exchequer.

(3.) Enrolled Accounts (Foreign Accounts classified
under Subjects), as follows :—

Customs Accounts. Edward I. to Elizabeth.
Escheators' Accounts. Edward II. to James I.
Subsidies, Aids, &c., Accounts of. Edward I. to
Charles II.
Wardrobe and Household Accounts. Henry III. to
Edward VI.

There are also Miscellaneous Enrolled Accounts,
including—

ACCOUNTS—(continued).

ACCOUNTS, ENROLMENTS OF (EXCHEQUER, L. T. R.)—
(continued).

Accounts of the Agincourt expedition. Henry V.

Purveyance Accounts. Edward III.

Ulnage Accounts. Richard II. to Henry VII.

Contrariants' Lands, Accounts of Edward II.

Queen's Lands, Accounts of. Edward II. to Henry
IV.

Templars' Lands, Accounts of. Edward II.

ACCOUNTS, STATES AND VIEWS OF. (EXCHEQUER, Q. R.)

"States," or brief Abstracts of all the Public Accounts
of the kingdom from Eliz. to 1859 are contained in the
series of rolls entitled "Enrolments of Public Accounts."

The "States and Views of Receivers, &c." from Jas. II.
to Wm. and Mary are contained in two volumes, thus
entitled.

ACCOUNTS, STATES AND VIEWS OF. (EXCHEQUER,
L. T. R.)

The States and Views of Accounts in the Lord
Treasurer's Remembrancer's Department are enrolled on
the "Memoranda Rolls," forming a distinct portion of
each roll.

Repertories to States and Views, 1 Edw. III. to 14
James I.

The "States and Views of Receivers General from
Car. II. to 6 Geo. IV. are contained in 52 Vols. bearing
that title.

ACKNOWLEDGMENTS OF DEEDS.

CERTIFICATES OF THE ACKNOWLEDGMENT OF DEEDS BY
MARRIED WOMEN. (COMMON PLEAS.) 1834 to 1855.

These are the certificates taken in accordance with the
Act of 2 & 3 William IV. "for the abolition of Fines and
Recoveries and the substitution of more effectual means
of assurance." Those of a later date than 1855 are kept
at the Acknowledgment Office.

Alphabetical Index. 1834 to 1855. 22 Vols.

Day Books. 1834 to 1857. 16 Vols.

[The Certificates from 1834 to 1837 inclusive and
Nos. 1 to 700 and 1,020 to 1,087 of the year 1838 were
burnt at the fire which occurred at the Temple in the
year 1838.]

AGARDE'S INDEXES.

A collection so called consisting of Abstracts from and References to the Placita Coronæ, Placita de Juratis et Assisis, Placita de Quo Warranto, &c. (commonly called *Assize and Quo Warranto Rolls*); and from the *Placita Coram Rege, Placita de Banco,* and other records formerly deposited in the Treasury of the Exchequer of Receipt, made at different periods by Arthur Agarde and other officers having charge of the records. 60 vols., as follows:—

Vol. 1 -	Bedford	-	15 Edw. 1. and 4 Edw. 3.	Abstracts of Assize and Quo Warranto Rolls [with Indices Locorum].
	Berks -	-	12 Edw. 1.	
Vol 2 -	Cambridge	-	27 Edw. 1. and 14, 21, & 27 Edw. 1.	Do. [with an Index Locorum for 27 Edw. 1.].
	Cornwall	-	12 Edw. 1. and 30 Edw. 1.	
Vol. 3 -	Cumberland	-	20 Edw. 1. -	Do. [with an Index Locorum].
Vol. 4 -	Dorset -	-	8 Edw. 1. and 16 Edw. 1.	Do. [with Indices Locorum].
	Devon -	-	9 Edw. 1. and 9 & 10 Edw. 1.	
Vol. 5 -	Wilts -	-	Temp. Ric. 1. -	Do. [with an Index Locorum].
Vol. 6 -	Divers Counties		Ric. 1. to Edw. 3.	Abstracts of Placita Coram Rege [with a Table of Contents].
Vol. 7 -	Do.	-	Hen. 4. and Hen. 5.	Do. [with Indices Locorum and Rerum].
Vol. 8 -	Yorkshire	-	15 Hen. 3. and 52 Hen. 3.	Abstracts of Assize and Quo Warranto Rolls [with Indices Locorum and Rerum].
Vol. 9 -	Yorkshire	-	7, 8, & 9 Edw. 1., 7 & 21 Edw. 1., and temp. Edw. 1.	(1.) Abstracts of Assize Rolls, 7, 8, & 9 Edw. 1. [with an Index Locorum]. (2.) Abstracts of Charters by various kings enrolled temp. Edw. 1., and of Assize Rolls, &c., 7 & 21 Edw. 1. [with an Index Locorum]. (3.) Abstracts of Assize Rolls, &c., 7, 8, & 9 Edw. 1. [with an Index Nominum].
Vol. 10 -	Essex -	-	13 Edw. 1. -	Abstracts of Assize Rolls, &c. [with Indices Rerum and Locorum].
Vol. 11 -	Channel Islands		27, 28, & 32 Edw. 1., 2 & 17 Edw. 2., and 5 Edw. 3.	Abstracts of Assize Rolls, &c.

AGARDE'S INDEXES--(continued).

Vol. 12 -	Hertford	6 & 7 Edw. 1. -	Abstracts of Assize Rolls, &c. [with Indices Locorum].
	Hunts -	14 Edw. 1.	
Vol. 13 -	Kent -	7 Edw. 1., 21 Edw. 1., and 6 & 7 Edw. 2.	Abstracts of Assize Rolls, &c. [with Indices Locorum and Rerum]. Printed.
Vol. 14 -	Lancaster	20 Edw. 1. -	Abstracts of Assize Rolls, &c. [with an Index Locorum].
Vol. 15 -	London -	14 Edw. 2. -	Abstracts of Assize Rolls, &c. [with an Index Nominum].
Vol. 16 -	Middlesex	2, 3, & 22 Edw. 1. and 35 Edw. 1.	Abstracts of Assize Rolls, &c. [with Indices Locorum].
	Middlesex, Sussex, Kent, and Surrey.		
Vol. 17 -	Northumberland	21 Edw. 1. -	Abstracts of Assize Rolls, &c. [with an Index Locorum].
Vol. 18 -	Notts -	8 & 9 Edw. 1. and 3 Edw. 3.	Abstracts of Assize Rolls, &c., and of Deeds Enrolled, 3 & 4 Edw. 3. [with an Index Locorum].
Vol. 19 -	Somerset -	8 Edw. 1. -	Abstracts of Assize Rolls, &c. [with an Index Locorum].
Vol. 20 -	Stafford -	21 Edw. 1. -	Do. do.
Vol. 21 -	Surrey, and Divers Counties.	19 & 20 Hen. 3., 39, 43, 47, & 56 Hen. 3.	Do. do.
Vol. 22 -	Surrey and Sussex.	7 Edw. 1. -	Abstracts of Assize Rolls, &c. [with Indices Locorum].
Vol. 23 -	Southampton -	8 Edw. 1. -	Abstracts of Assize Rolls, &c. [with an Index Locorum].
Vol. 24 -	Warwick -	Ric. 1. to Hen. 7.	Extracts from the Feet of Fines for the county of Warwick and from the Feet of Fines of Divers Counties, in which Warwick is included [with an Index Locorum].
		13 Edw. 1. -	Abstracts of Assize Rolls, &c. [with an Index Locorum].
Vol. 25 -	Westmoreland -	20 Edw. 1. -	Abstracts of Assize Rolls, &c. [with an Index Locorum].
Vol. 26 -	Wilts -	9 Edw. 1. -	Do. do.
Vol. 27 -	Notts, Northampton, Guernsey, Bedford, and Derby.	3 & 4 Edw. 3. -	Abstracts of Claims of Liberties, &c., from the Assize and Quo Warranto Rolls.
Vol. 28 -	Hereford and Lancaster.	20 Edw. 1 -	Abstracts of Assize Rolls, &c. [with Indices Locorum].

AGARDE'S INDEXES—(continued).

Vol. 29 -	Various Counties	Ric. 1. -	Abstracts of Placita Coram Rege and of *Feet of Fines*, arranged in counties from Beds to Wilts, &c.
Vol. 30 -	Do. -	1 to 35 Edw. 1. -	Abstracts of Placita Coram Rege, &c., with Indices Locorum et Rerum, arranged under counties. [Printed in the "Abbreviatio Placitorum."]
Vol. 31 -	Do. -	Temp. Edw. 1. -	Abstracts of Placita Coram Rege, &c. [Printed in the "Abbreviatio Placitorum."]
Vol. 32 -	Various Counties	1 to 14 Edw. 1. -	Abstracts of Placita de Banco [with an Index Locorum].
Vol. 33 -	Do. -	15 to 18 Edw. 1.	Do. do.
Vol. 34 -	Do. -	1 to 20 Edw. 2. -	Abstracts of Placita Coram Rege, &c. [Printed in the "Abbreviatio Placitorum."]
Vol. 35 -	Do. -	1 to 22 Edw. 3. -	Abstracts of Placita Coram Rege [with Indices Locorum and Rerum, and a List of Obsolete Words, &c.].
Vol. 36 -	Do. -	23 to 51 Edw. 3.	Do. [with Indices Locorum and Rerum].
Vol. 37 -	Do. -	1 to 22 Ric. 2. -	Do. [with an Index Locorum].
Vol. 38 -	Bucks -	14 Edw. 1. -	} Abstracts of Assize Rolls, &c. [with Indices Locorum].
	Dorset -	8 Edw. 1. -	
	Leicester -	12 Edw. 1. -	
	Divers Counties	9 Edw. 1. -	
	London -	7 to 35 Edw. 1. -	Abstracts of *Deeds and Wills* relating to lands, &c., given in mortmain, enrolled at the *Hustings* in London.
	Somerset -	Edw. 1., 2., and 3.	Abstracts of *Feet of Fines*.
	Surrey -	Hen. 3. -	Do. [with an Index Locorum].
	Kent -	9 Edw. 2. -	A transcript from the "Nomina Villarum" for the county of Kent. A list of the Archbishops of Canterbury and of the Religious Houses in Divers Counties, &c., &c.
Vol. 39 -	Oxford -	Ric. 1. to Hen. 3.	Abstracts of Feet of Fines [with an Index Locorum].
		Hen. 3. and Edw. 3.	Abstracts of Placita Forestæ, &c.
		13 Edw. 1. -	Abstracts of Assize Rolls, &c. [with an Index Locorum].

AGARDE'S INDEXES—(continued).

Vol. 40 -	Westmoreland -	31 Hen. 6. -	A return of the services of free tenants of Thomas Lord Clifford for one whole year.
	Divers Counties	30 Hen. 2. -	Extracts from the "Rotulus de "Dominabus, Pueris et Puel-"lis" for various counties [with an Index Locorum].
	Do. - -	48 Hen. 3. -	Abstracts of Assize Rolls, &c.
	Do. - -	Edw. 1. - -	Do. do.
	Do. - -	28 Edw. 1. -	Extent of the lands, &c., of Edm. Earl of Cornwall.
	Kent - -	6 & 7 Hen. 3. -	Abstracts of Assize Rolls, &c. Copy of an old MS. containing Knights' Fees in Kent. [This vol. contains also "Prece-"dents concerning the cus-"tody of Records, &c., &c.]
Vol. 41 -	Divers Counties	Edw. 1. to Edw. 3.	Abstracts of Placita de Quo Warranto, &c. [with an Index Locorum and Nominum, arranged under counties].
Vol. 42 -	- - -	Edw. 1. to Jas. 2.	Inventory of Coram Rege, King's Bench, and Common Pleas Rolls, &c.
Vol. 43 -	"Adjudicata Placitorum in Banco Regis."	John to Hen. 5.	Abstracts of *Judgments* selected from the Placita Coram Rege, Placita de Banco, &c., with indexes to the subjects, &c., &c.
Vol. 44 -	"Compendium Recordorum."	- - -	A calendar of Treaties and other Diplomatic Documents in the Treasury of the Exchequer of Receipt. [Printed in the 2nd vol. of "Ancient Kalendars," &c.]
Vol. 45 -	Repertory -	- -	An old repertory to certain documents in the Chapter House at Westminster.
Vol. 46 -	Repertory -	- -	A repertory to documents in the Chapter House entitled "Agarde's Repertory."
Vol. 47 -	Court Rolls, &c.	Edw. 3. to Hen. 8.	A calendar of various Court Rolls, Ministers' Accounts, &c., dated 1671, with an Index Locorum.
Vol. 48 -	Index Villaris -	- -	A volume entitled "Nomina "Villarum infra Ducatum "Lancastriæ."

AGARDE'S INDEXES—(continued).

[The following volumes (apparently forming part of Agarde's collection) were, with the exception of Vol. 60, presented to the Public Record Office in 1879 by Sir Charles Isham, Bart.]

Vol. 49 -	Divers Counties	28 to 57 Hen. 3.	Abstracts of Assize Rolls.
Vol. 50 -	Do. -	Temp. Hen. 4. -	Abstracts of Assize Rolls.
Vol. 51 -	Northampton -	3 Edw. 3. -	Abstracts of Assize Rolls, &c. [with an Index Locorum].
Vol. 52 -	Divers Counties	25 to 28 Edw. 1.	Abstracts of Placita de Banco [with an Index Locorum].
Vol. 53 -	Northampton -	Ric. 1. to John -	Abstracts of Feet of Fines [with an Index Locorum].
Vol. 54 -	Do. -	Temp. Hen. 3. -	Do. do.
Vol. 55 -	Divers Counties	Edw. 1. to Ric. 2.	Abstracts of Patent and Charter Rolls, &c. [with an Index Locorum].
Vol. 56 -	Do. -	1 Ric. 2. to 2 Ric. 3.	Abstracts of Inq. post mortem and Inq. ad quod damnum [with Indices Nominum and Locorum].
Vol. 57 -	Kent -	Hen. 3. to Edw. 4.	A calendar of Inq. post mortem and Inq. ad quod damnum.
Vol. 58 -	Dorset -	Various dates -	A book containing Abstracts of Tenures in the county of Dorset, selected from the Inq. post mortem, &c.
Vol. 59 -	- - -	Hen. 8. and Edw. 6.	An Index Nominum referring apparently to particulars of *Deeds of Purchase and Exchange.*
Vol. 60 -	Norfolk -	Ric. 1. - -	Abstracts of Feet of Fines (purchased by the P. R. O. in 1882).

ALIENATION OF LANDS.

Licenses and Pardons for alienation of lands are entered on the Patent Rolls.

Fines for licenses to alienate are entered on the Fine Rolls. (These payments were abolished by Stat. 12 Car. II., Cap. 24.)

Fines "pro licentiâ concordandi" are also entered on the Fine Rolls.

An "**ALIENATION OFFICE**" for the assessment and collection of Fines and other payments for Licenses to agree and Licenses to alienate was established in the reign of Elizabeth when it was called "My Lord of Leicester's Office," because he had the first grant thereof. This

ALIENATION OF LANDS—(continued).

Office was abolished by Stat. 5 & 6 Wm. IV., Cap. 82, the Records being transferred to the Court of Common Pleas and thence to the Public Record Office.

The principal Records of the **ALIENATION OFFICE** are the following :—

ACCOUNTS OF PRE- AND POST- FINES. 1759 to 1794. 4 Vols.

ACCOUNTS OF POST- FINES. 1759 to 1831. 72 Vols.

ACCOUNTS OF POST- FINES. 1788 to 1833.

AFFIDAVITS TO MODERATE FINES. 1802 to 1834. These relate to Fines in the Common Pleas, and state the amount of the Purchase Money, &c.

LICENSES AND PARDONS FOR ALIENATION, ENTRIES OF. 1571 to 1650. 21 Vols.

Index. 1571 to 1650. 9 Vols.

WRITS OF COVENANT, EXTRACTS FROM. 1576 to 1837. 135 Vols.

Index. 1661 to 1835. 102 Vols.

WRITS OF COVENANT, NIL BOOKS. 1668 to 1800. 2 Vols. These contain entries of Writs on which pre-fines were not paid.

WRITS OF ENTRY IN RECOVERIES, EXTRACTS FROM. 1595 to 1835. 33 Vols.

Index. 1660 to 1834. 27 Vols.

See also FINES AND RECOVERIES.

ALIENS.

ACCOUNTS, &C. RELATING TO FOREIGN MERCHANTS. (EXCHEQUER, Q. R.) Edward I. to Henry VIII.

These consist of Accounts of debts owing to various Foreign Merchants residing in London, and of the sums due or paid out of the royal revenues to the Bardi, the Friscobaldi, and similar companies on account of loans advanced by them ; of transactions between the said companies and the Despensers, and other documents of a like nature. Similar accounts exist amongst the Miscellanea of the Treasury of the Receipt.

Descriptive Slips.

See also EXCHANGE ROLLS, p. 40.

Transcripts of Deeds and Grants to the Society of the Bardi of Florence. 12 Edw. II.

[*Misc. Rolls, &c., Chancery, No. $\frac{3}{11}$.*]

ALIENS—(continued).

ACCOUNTS, &c. RELATING TO FOREIGN MERCHANTS, &c.—(continued).

A Writ and Inquisition relating to the goods and debts of the Society of the Scala of Florence. 1 Edw. III.

[*Misc. Rolls, &c., Chancery, No.* $\frac{11}{17}$.]

ALIEN CLERGY, ACCOUNTS OF FINES IMPOSED ON THE. See ALIEN PRIORIES.

ALIEN PRIORIES, EXTENTS, &c. OF. (EXCHEQUER, Q. R.) 22 Edw. I. to 22 Edw. IV.

In addition to Extents of the possessions of the Alien Religious Houses in England, which were seized into the King's hands from time to time whenever a war broke out with the country to which they belonged, these rolls contain Extents of the possessions of laymen who were foreign subjects, and Accounts of Fines imposed on the alien clergy. See also **MINISTERS' AND RECEIVERS' ACCOUNTS.**

ALIEN SUBSIDIES, ROLLS OF. (EXCHEQUER, Q. R.) Edw. III. to Ric. III.

These contain the accounts of the several assessments on Foreigners resident in England between the above dates. Similar accounts of the 14th year of Edw. III. will also be found amongst the " Inquisitiones Nonarum " or Nonæ Rolls.

Descriptive Slips. 1 vol. (Vol. 95 of the Index to Subsidies.)

ALIENS, RETURNS OF. (STATE PAPERS, DOMESTIC.)

There are numerous returns of this kind, the most important of which is one made in Nov. 1571 by the Mayor and Aldermen of London " of all the straungers within London and Southwark and the liberties thereof." [*State Papers, Dom. Eliz. Vol.* 82.] This gives the names of all the foreigners then in London, distinguishing their nations, the wards and parishes in which they dwelt, their trades and occupations, and the churches or congregations frequented by them. The number of persons described amounts to 4,631.

ALIENS, SPECIAL COMMISSIONS RESPECTING THE ESTATES OF. (CHANCERY, PETTY BAG OFFICE.) 15 Charles I. to 8 Victoria. 2 Bundles.

Index.

DENIZATION, LETTERS PATENT OF.

The Letters Patent of Denization are entered on the Patent Rolls. Since August 6, 1844, they are to a great extent superseded by the " Certificates of Naturalization,"

ALIENS—(continued).

DENIZATION, LETTERS PATENT OF—(continued).

which are enrolled on the Close Rolls, although the old practice of taking out Letters Patent was still occasionally followed. The Denizations of an earlier date frequently included a number of persons in a single grant, and are referred to in the Index under the head of " Denizationes " or " Indigenæ " merely. Separate rolls of Denizations for the years 32 Henry VIII., 36 Henry VIII., and 4 Elizabeth, are placed with the Patent Rolls.

The Patent Roll 13 William III., Part 1, No. 8, contains a grant of Denization to one Laugelier and about 200 other persons.

After the revocation of the Edict of Nantes, a number of royal warrants were issued for the denization of the Protestant Refugees to this country. These extend from 1681 to 1688 inclusive, and are contained in an Entry Book amongst the Domestic State Papers which has been printed by the Camden Society. [*Dom. Entry Bk., Car. II., No.* 67.]

NATURALIZATION, CERTIFICATES OF.

These are enrolled on the Close Rolls from Aug. 1844 to Aug. 1870 inclusive, after which date they are registered at the Home Office. Naturalization might also be effected by Letters Patent of Denization and by Private Act of Parliament. The Private Acts of Parliament for this purpose are noticed in the Index to the Parliament Rolls, but the Acts themselves are preserved at the House of Lords.

By an Act of Parliament passed in the 7th year of Queen Anne it was enacted that all Foreign Protestants who subscribed the Oath Rolls in the Courts of Chancery, Queen's Bench, Common Pleas, or Exchequer, should be deemed and taken to be natural-born British subjects. There are in the Queen's Bench Special OATH ROLLS OF NATURALIZATION extending from 1 to 12 Anne.

" NAMES OF PERSONS NATURALIZED IN HIS MAJESTY'S PLANTATIONS IN AMERICA." 1740 to 1761.

Two vols., containing the names, &c. of those who availed themselves of the Act 13 George II. for naturalizing such Foreign Protestants and others as are settled or shall settle in any of His Majesty's Colonies in America.

[*Colonial Office Records* (*Board of Trade*) *Plantations General, Vols.* 59 *and* 60.]

AMBASSADORS AND ENVOYS.

The appointments, powers, and instructions of Ambassadors, together with their correspondence and negotiations,

AMBASSADORS AND ENVOYS—(continued).

are entered on the earlier Patent and Close Rolls, and also on the so-called "Treaty" or Foreign Rolls. See **CHANCERY ENROLMENTS.**

Subsequent to the reign of Henry VII., documents of this nature are to be found amongst the State Papers.

Accounts of monies paid or imprested to Ambassadors appear on the ISSUE ROLLS and ISSUE BOOKS of the Exchequer of Receipt. See **RECEIPTS AND ISSUES OF THE EXCHEQUER.**

There are also original Accounts relating to the expenses of Ambassadors and Royal Messengers as follows :

AMBASSADORS (NUNCII), ACCOUNTS OF. (EXCHEQUER, Q. R.) 23 Edward I. to 13 Elizabeth.

These are Accounts of the expenses of Ambassadors and other persons attached to foreign missions, the nature of which is in some cases indicated. They also include accounts of payments to Royal Messengers for the delivery of Letters, Writs, &c.

Descriptive Slips. 4 Vols. MS.

ACCOUNTS OF AMBASSADORS AND ENVOYS. *" Declared Accounts." Pipe Office and Audit Office.*

ANNUITIES (CHANCERY).

MEMORIALS OF ANNUITIES. 1813 to 1854.

Before 1813 the Annuity Deeds are enrolled in full on the Close Rolls, of which they form a separate branch. After the passing of the Act relative to Annuities in 1813, *Memorials* or Abstracts of the Deeds only are enrolled, forming a distinct class of enrolments. From August 1854 Memorials of Annuities are registered at the Common Pleas Registry of Judgments, &c.

Index. 1777 to 1854. 17 Vols. MS., arranged under the names of the *Grantors.*

Do. 1777 to 1842. 6 Vols. MS., arranged under the names of the *Grantees.* [N.B. The *Registers* of Annuities are retained at the Enrolment Office.]

ANNUITIES (EXCHEQUER).

See **RECEIPTS AND ISSUES OF THE EXCHEQUER.**

APPAREL.

INQUISITIONS CONCERNING APPAREL. (MISCELLANEA, EXCHEQUER, Q. R.). Elizabeth.

These consist of enquiries concerning any violations of the Statute of 4 & 5 Philip and Mary relating to the Keeping of Horses and the Apparel of Men's Wives, &c. *Descriptive Slips.*

Similar documents will be found amongst the " Special Commissions" of the Exchequer, Queen's Remembrancer. See **COMMISSIONS.**

ARMY, NAVY, AND ORDNANCE.

The documents illustrative of the early history of the ARMY and NAVY consist principally of Accounts of payments to the Knights, Esquires, Men-at-Arms, and Archers who served in the Scotch and Welsh wars and in the various expeditions to France, with the Indentures of Covenant entered into by the several Military Leaders and the Lists of their retinues. Amongst these are included several interesting musters of the Army engaged in the expedition of Henry V. which terminated with the Battle of Agincourt.

The personal service enjoined by the Feudal system is also illustrated by the enrolments of the Writs of Summons on the Close Rolls and elsewhere, by the Rolls of the Constables and Earl Marshal of the Army, on which are recorded the names and retinues of those who appeared at the rendezvous and proffered their service, and by the Scutage Rolls, on which are enrolled the Mandates for the relief from the payment of Scutage, &c. of those who either attended personally or by deputy or compounded by a Fine for their absence.

At a later period the Commissions of Array and the Musters taken in pursuance thereof show the available military force in each County, corresponding to a great extent to the modern Militia.

There are also detailed Accounts of the expenses of building and fitting out ships of war, of the Wages of the Mariners and Men-at-Arms, and of the expenses of Garrisons and Fortifications.

The ORDNANCE ACCOUNTS contain many interesting details as to the manufacture and supply of engines and munitions of war, including bows and arrows, corslets, guns, gunpowder, &c.

In addition to the foregoing, special mention may be made of the two interesting volumes containing the Accounts of the Expedition under Martin Frobisher in search of the Meta Incognita, of the Roll of Assessments for the Army throughout England and Wales from 1644

ARMY, NAVY, AND ORDNANCE—(continued).

to 1649 inclusive, and of the volume containing an Account of the number of men in the Army in the year 1719, with the amount of their expenses in pay, &c., and a similar Account relating to the Navy for the year 1724–1725, amongst the Records of the Exchequer, Queen's Remembrancer.

The later Records of the Army and Navy will be found amongst the Records of the War Office and Admiralty respectively, described under the head of **DEPARTMENTAL RECORDS.**

ACCOUNTS, &c. (CHANCERY.)

The following are amongst the Miscellaneous Rolls, &c. (Bundle 1):—

Army and Navy Accounts:

No. 1. Wages, &c. to Knights, Esquires, and foot soldiers in the King's service in Wales. 10 Edw. I.

No. 2. Wages, &c. of soldiers and expenses of the garrison at Hope Castle. 10 Edw. I.

No. 3. An Account of the Wages, &c. of sailors belonging to various ports, entitled "Flota domini Johannis de Boutetort." Edw. I.

No. 4. Names of persons assigned to protect the Sea and various Ports in Norfolk, Suffolk, Essex, and Sussex, &c. 24 Edw. I.

No. 5. Indentures and Memoranda of victuals and stock sent to the King in Flanders and Holland. 25 Edw. I.

No. 6. Payment to the foot soldiers in Wales. 26 Edw. I.

No. 7. Memoranda relating to the receipt of victuals and stock at the Castle of Berwick-on-Tweed. 26-27 Edw. I.

No. 8. Valuation of horses in the possession of various persons. Edw. I.

No. 9. Do. Edw. I.

No. 10. Do. (with names of Arblasters and Esquires). Edw. I.

No. 11. List of horses taken in the Welsh wars. Edw. I.

No. 12. Expenses of the King's horses. Edw. I.

No. 13. Payments to Knights, Esquires, &c. (A fragment.) Edw. I.

No. 14. Indentures between the Admiral of the Fleet and others concerning provisions. 10 Edw. III.

No. 15. Certificates of the number of ships in the ports of Norfolk and Suffolk with the names of their owners. 14 Edw. III.

No. 16. List of Ships taken for the King's service. Edw. III.

No. 17. Do. Edw. III.

No. 18. Do. Edw. III.

No. 19. A List of those who passed the seas with the King. Edw. III.

No. 20. Memoranda of ships and men to be sent to Scotland. Edw. III.

No. 21. An appraisement of a galley of Barcelona, and of the merchandise found in her. 28 Hen. VI.

ARMY, NAVY, AND ORDNANCE—(continued).

ACCOUNTS, &c. (CHANCERY)—(continued).

> No. 22. Examination of witnesses concerning a ship laden with wool, &c., taken by the King's enemies.
>
> 33 Hen. VI.
>
> No. 23. An account of the debts owed by the King to the Captain of Calais and the soldiers and workmen there.
>
> 3 Edw. IV.

ACCOUNTS, &c. (EXCHEQUER, Q. R.)

Army Accounts, &c. (48 Hen. III. to Elizabeth.)

These consist of Accounts of the Constables of military Fortresses for the maintenance of their garrisons and for necessary works and repairs; of the cost of Provisions and Munitions of war, and of the construction and transport of military engines; of the Wages of Bannerets, Knights, Archers, and Men-at-Arms; of the expenses of building and victualling Ships and of the Wages of Mariners.

They also contain Indentures of Military Service, and Muster and Retinue Rolls, giving the names of the Captains or Commanders in the various expeditions, and also of the men-at-arms, hobelars, archers, and others by whom they were accompanied. Amongst these will be found many Retinue Rolls of those who served in the expedition to France in the third year of Henry V., which resulted in the battle of Agincourt; together with a muster of the garrison at Harfleur; Accounts of the Treasurer there from 3 to 7 Henry V.; Accounts relating to the custody of Prisoners of War at the Tower of London, Windsor Castle, and elsewhere; and other documents of the greatest historical interest. The Accounts of a great number of the Commanders in this expedition are enrolled on a large roll amongst the " Enrolled Accounts " of the Pipe Office, but the names of their retinues are only to be found in the foregoing series and amongst the similar accounts belonging to the Treasury of the Receipt of the Exchequer referred to below.

The later documents of this class consist almost entirely of Indentures of Military Service and of Muster Rolls of the troops raised in various counties for service in Ireland and elsewhere.

Descriptive Slips. Hen. III. to Eliz. 10 Vols. MS.

Navy Accounts, &c. Edward III. to Elizabeth.

These consist principally of Accounts of the expenses of fitting out and victualling ships for the King's service and of the wages of mariners, &c.

They also contain Musters and Retinue Rolls of the Men-at-Arms and others embarking on foreign service, corresponding to those amongst the Army Accounts.

ARMY, NAVY, AND ORDNANCE—(continued).

There is a second series of these Accounts from Edw. III. to Hen. VI. described as "Accounts of the Clerk of the Navy," which relate principally to the building and rigging of ships.

(Before Edward III. see "Army Accounts, &c.")
Descriptive Slips. 3 Vols. MS.

Ordnance Accounts, &c. Edward III. to James I.

These relate to the supply and manufacture of military stores and engines of war, as arrows, corslets, guns, saltpetre, gunpowder, &c.

Descriptive Slips.

Provisions, Accounts of. Edward III

These are Accounts of expenses in providing victuals for the Army and Navy in various expeditions and for the garrisons in several castles.

Descriptive Slips.

A General Inventory of all the foregoing Accounts is in progress.

Expenses of the Voyages of Martin Frobisher. Temp. Elizabeth. 2 Vols.

A "Leger Accompt" of the Assessments for the Army received by the Treasurers at War from the several Counties, Cities, and Places in England and Wales from 1644 to 1649. One large roll of paper.

An Account or Estimate of the number of men in the Army in the year 1719, with the amount of their expenses in pay, &c.; and also an Estimate of the charge of the Navy for the year 1724–1725, with the expenses of the Navy Office and a list of pensions and allowances. 1 Vol. MS.

ACCOUNTS, &c. (EXCHEQUER, AUGMENTATION OFFICE.)

Victualling Account. 5 Hen. VIII. [*Misc. Books, Vol.* 4.]

Certificates of the Arrears of Pay and other Allowances due to various Officers and Troops in the service of the Parliament. 1647 to 1652. [*Misc. Books, Vol.* 5.]

Similar Certificates for the Counties of Devon and Cornwall. 1648 to 1650. [*Misc. Books, Vol.* 6.]

Payments to the Officers and others of the Royal Navy. 5 Henry VIII. 1 Vol. [*Misc. Books, Vol.* 315.]

Accounts of the Clerk of the King's Ships. 10 to 17 Henry VII.

ARMY, NAVY, AND ORDNANCE—(continued).

Accounts, &c. (Exchequer, Augmentation Office) —(continued).

Two volumes containing the Accounts of Robert Brigandyn, Clerk of the King's Ships, of all his receipts and expenses for the years 10 to 13 Henry VII. and 16 and 17 Henry VII. respectively. The first volume contains the expenses of fortifying the Dock at Portsmouth, 10-11 Henry VII. [*Misc. Books, Vols.* 316 *and* 317.]

Accounts, &c. (Exchequer, L. T. R.)

Accounts of the Expedition to France which resulted in the Battle of Agincourt. 3 Hen. V.

A large roll, belonging to the series of "Enrolled Accounts," and containing the enrolments of the Accounts of the military leaders who indented to serve the King in his expedition to France, giving the amounts received by them and expended in wages, &c., and also a description of the various royal jewels received by them as pledges for the due payment of the amounts for which they respectively agreed to serve. The *Particulars* of these accounts, giving the names of their retainers, &c., will be found amongst the Miscellanea of the Queen's Remembrancer.

Accounts, &c. (Exchequer, Tr. of the Receipt.)

Army and Navy Accounts, &c. John to Charles I.

These, which include a Muster Roll of the Army of Henry V., taken at Southampton before his second expedition into France in the 5th year of his reign with retinue and other rolls relating thereto, have now been incorporated with the Accounts of the same nature in the Queen's Remembrancer's Department, and included in the General Inventory.

The following are amongst the Miscellaneous Books :—

Vol. 1. Payments and Receipts, Army and Navy.
Hen. VII. and Hen. VIII.
Vol. 2. Charges of the Army and Navy.   3-5 Hen. VIII.
Vol. 3. Army, Navy, and Ordnance Payments, &c.
Hen. VII. and Hen. VIII.
Vol. 4. Payments of the Royal Ordnance, &c.
5 & 6 Hen. VIII.
Vol. 5. Expenses of building the Henry Grace Dieu and other ships.   Hen. VIII.
Vol. 6. Accounts of the Royal Dockyard at Portsmouth.
14-15 Hen. VIII.
Vol. 7. Navy and Ordnance Accounts.   Hen. VII.
Vol. 8. Indentures of the King's Ordnance.   Hen. VII.
Vol. 9. Expenses of the Army to and from France.
Hen. VIII.
Vol. 10. Naval and Ordnance Receipts and Payments.
Hen. VII. and Hen. VIII.
Vol. 11. Expenses, &c. of the Navy.   Hen. VIII.
Vol. 12. Expenses of the Navy.   4 & 6 Hen. VIII.

ARMY, NAVY, AND ORDNANCE—(continued.

ACCOUNTS, &c. (EXCHEQUER, TR. OF THE RECEIPT)—
(continued).

Vol. 13. Inventory of the Stores of the Royal Navy.
6 Hen. VIII.
Vol. 14. Accounts of the sums of money received in aid of
the King's voyage to Scotland. Hen. VII.
Vol. 15. Account of Military Stores. Hen. VII.

ACCOUNTS, &c. (EXCHEQUER OF RECEIPT.)

Accounts of the Military Establishments in Ireland,
and Rolls of the soldiers levied or pressed for service
there, &c. 42 Eliz. to 21 James I. 15 rolls.

ACCOUNTS, &c. (AUDIT OFFICE AND PIPE OFFICE.)

The following Accounts relating to the Army, Navy,
and Ordnance will be found amongst the " Declared
Accounts " of the Audit Office, and similar accounts exist
in the Pipe Office Series. (*See* Lists and Indexes, No. II.)
There are also amongst the Audit Office Records " Establishment Books " of the various forces from 1661 to 1829.

Army Accounts.

Accounts of the Paymaster-General of the Forces.
1652 to 1827.
Accounts of Commanders-in-Chief and Military Governors.
1606 to 1821.
Accounts of Victuals, &c. for Home service. 1565 to 1807.
Do. for garrisons Abroad. 1547 to 1816.
Accounts of Half-Pay, Pensions, and Allowances.
1713 to 1327.
Accounts of Money for Trained Bands and Militia.
1660 to 1674, 1745, and 1813–1827.
Accounts of Vice-Treasurers and Treasurers at War, and
Paymasters of various expeditionary Forces and of
several Garrisons. 1543 to 1826.

Navy Accounts.

Accounts of the Treasurers of " Marine Causes and Affairs,"
and of the Navy. 1558 to 1827.
Accounts of Moneys, &c. arising by the sale of prizes.
1593 to 1813.
Miscellaneous Accounts. 1597 to 1818.

Ordnance Accounts.

Accounts of the Masters and Surveyors of the Ordnance.
1557 to 1632.
Accounts of Lieutenants of the Ordnance. 1561 to 1670.
Accounts of the Treasurers and Paymasters. 1587 to 1827.
Miscellaneous Accounts. 1568 to 1810.

Military Establishment Books.

Establishment Books of the Forces at home and abroad.
1661 to 1829.
Establishment Books of Guards, Garrisons, and Land Forces
in Great Britain. 1729 to 1829.

ARMY, NAVY, AND ORDNANCE—(continued).

ACCOUNTS, &c. (AUDIT OFFICE AND PIPE OFFICE)—
(continued).

> Establishment Books of Guards, Garrisons, and Land Forces
> in Great Britain, Minorca, Gibraltar, and the Planta-
> tions.* 1741 to 1829.

AGINCOURT MUSTER ROLLS. See ACCOUNTS, &c.

COMMISSIONS OF ARRAY. These are enrolled on the
Patent Rolls.

INDENTURES OF WAR. Edw. I. to Henry VII.

These are original Indentures of Covenant between the
King and various nobles and military leaders, by which the
latter agree to furnish a certain number of troops of a
specified character for a fixed period to serve the King in
his expeditions, the Sovereign on his part guaranteeing the
due payment of their wages and expenses. Similar Indentures will be found amongst the Accounts, &c. relating
to the Army and Navy, which contain also the Retinue
Rolls or Lists of the Spearmen, Archers, and others, by
whom the several Lords or Captains fulfilled their part of
the contract.

MILITARY SUMMONS, WRITS OF.

Writs of Summons to Military Service, addressed to the
Barons of the Realm and other Magnates, are enrolled
on the back of the Close Rolls, and also on the Scotch,
Welsh, and Vascon Rolls. Those for the reigns of
Edward I. and Edward II. are printed in Palgrave's
"Parliamentary Writs," &c. For a record of the service
actually performed see SCUTAGE ROLLS, and ROLLS OF
THE MARSHALSEY.

Writs of Summons of the 28th year of Henry III.
and of the 11th and 25th years of Edward I. will be
found amongst the Rolls of the Marshalsey, described
below.

The last of these is a roll of Sheriffs' Returns of
persons having 20 librates of land in the Counties of
Somerset and Dorset, Notts, and Derby, who are summoned to perform military service.

MUSTER AND RETINUE ROLLS.

These will be found amongst the "ACCOUNTS, &c."
above described.

MUSTERS, CERTIFICATES OF.

In the reign of Henry VIII. general Musters of all the
"fencible men" were made at intervals in the several

---

* (Many of these are duplicates of the preceding set.)

ARMY, NAVY, AND ORDNANCE—(continued.)

MUSTERS, CERTIFICATES OF—(continued).

counties, by virtue of Commissions under the Great Seal, and the forces thus called out were assessed to arms according to their substance or property. The " Certificates " or Returns of the Commissioners, therefore, give the names of all the able-bodied men between the ages of 16 and 60 in each township or parish, with a valuation of their possessions in lands or goods, and the amount in money or equipment they were expected to furnish.

Similar Certificates of Musters in this and later reigns will be found in the Domestic Series of State Papers.

The following Books of Musters are amongst the Miscellaneous Books of the Exchequer, Treasury of the Receipt :—

Vol. 16.	Musters in the County of Hereford.		Hen. VIII.
Vol. 17.	Do.	Dorset.	34 Hen. VIII.
Vol. 18.	Do.	Stafford.	Hen. VIII.
Vol. 19.	Do.	South'ton.	14 Hen. VIII.
Vol. 20.	Do.	Denbigh.	Hen. VIII.
Vol. 21.	Do.	Lincoln.	Hen. VIII.
Vol. 22.	Do.	Norfolk.	Hen. VIII.
Vol. 23.	Do.	York, N. R.	
			30 Hen. VIII.
Vol. 24.	Do.	Surrey.	30 Hen. VIII.
Vol. 25.	Do.	Norfolk.	Hen. VIII.
Vol. 26.	Do.	Monmouth.	Hen. VIII.
Vol. 27.	Do.	Worcester.	31 Hen. VIII.
Vol. 28.	Do.	Oxford and Suffolk.	
			Hen. VIII.
Vol. 29.	Do.	Dorset.	30 Hen. VIII.
Vol. 30.	Do.	York, E. R.	
			30 Hen. VIII.
Vol. 31.	Do.	Hereford.	30 Hen. VIII.
Vol. 32.	Do.	York and Ainsty (City of).	
			31 Hen. VIII.
Vol. 33.	Do.	Anglesey and Merioneth.	
			Hen. VIII.
Vol. 34.	Do.	Yorkshire (Craven and Booland).	Hen. VIII.
Vol. 35.	Do.	Worcester.	Hen. VIII.
Vol. 36.	Do.	Do.	Hen. VIII.
Vol. 37.	Do.	York, W. R.	
			26 Hen. VIII.
Vol. 38.	Do.	Do.	Hen. VIII.
Vol. 39.	Do.	Do. E. R.	Hen. VIII.
Vol. 40.	Do.	Northumb'd.	Hen. VIII.
Vol. 41.	Do.	York, N. R.	
			30 Hen. VIII.
Vol. 42	Do.	South Wales.	Hen. VIII
Vol. 43.	Do.	York, W.R.	15 Hen. VIII.
Vol. 44.	Do.	York, N. R.	
			26 Hen. VIII.
Vol. 45.	Do.	Sussex.	Hen. VIII.
Vol. 46.	Do.	Wilts.	Hen. VIII.
Vol. 47	Do.	Beds, North'ton, and Notts.	
			Hen. VIII.

ARMY, NAVY, AND ORDNANCE—(continued).

MUSTERS, CERTIFICATES OF—(continued).

Vol. 48.	Musters in the County of Salop.		Hen. VIII.
Vol. 49.	Do.	North Wales.	Hen. VIII.
Vol. 50.	Do.	Sussex.	30 Hen. VIII.
Vol. 51.	Do.	Dorset.	34 Hen. VIII.
Vol. 52.	Do.	Gloucester.	
			34 Hen. VIII.
Vol. 53.	Do.	Cornwall.	Hen. VIII.
Vol. 54.	Do.	Rutland.	Hen. VIII.
Vol. 55.	Do.	Do.	Hen. VIII.

The following are amongst the Miscellaneous Books of the Augmentation Office :—

Cornwall. A valuation of the lands, goods, and equipment of all the inhabitants in the Hundreds of East, West, Trigge, and Kerrier. Temp. Hen. VIII. [*Vols.* 77 *and* 78.]

Berks. Certificates of Musters in several hundreds. Temp. Hen. VIII. [*Vol.* 464.]

Berks. Account of money " prested " to the King by his subjects in the Co. of Berks, according to the valuation of their substance. [*Vol.* 465.]

Norfolk. Certificates of Musters in the Hundreds of North Grenowe and Holt. [*Vol.* 466.]

ROLLS OF THE MARSHALSEY, or " PROFFERS OF SERVICE."

These are the rolls kept by the Constable or Earl Marshal of the Army, or by their lieutenants, on which were recorded the names of all those who in obedience to the Writs of Military Summons appeared either personally or by deputy at the place appointed, and proffered their service, together with the names of the knights, esquires, sergeants, or others by whom such service was to be performed, the number of their horses, and the nature of their equipment, &c. A roll of this kind was made up on every muster of the King's host, but very few are still extant.

The following is a complete list of these rolls as far as they are known to exist; they are amongst the Miscellaneous Rolls, &c. of the Court of Chancery (Bundle 9). Those stated to be printed will be found in Palgrave's " Parliamentary Writs," &c.

No. 1. 5 Edw. I. Writ of Summons and acknowledgments and Proffers of Service at Worcester. Printed.

No. 2. 10 Edw. I. Acknowledgments and Proffers against Llewellyn, Prince of Wales, and others. Printed.

No. 3. 10 Edw. I. Acknowledgments and Proffers of Service (at Ruthlan). Printed.

No. 4. 10 Edw. I. Another copy of the foregoing.

No. 5. 31 Edw. I. Acknowledgments of service in the army summoned against the Scots.

No. 6. 4 Edw. II. Proffers of Service at Tweedmouth. Printed.

No. 7. 4 Edw. II. Another copy of the foregoing roll.

ARMY, NAVY, AND ORDNANCE—(continued).

ROLLS OF THE MARSHALSEY, &c.—(continued).

No. 8. 16 Edw. II. The Roll of the Summons of the Army at Newcastle-on-Tyne against Robert Bruce and others.

No. 9. 28 Hen. III. A Writ of Summons only.

No. 10. 11 Edw. I. Do.

No. 11. 25 Edw. I. Do. (for the Counties of Somerset, Dorset, Notts., & Derby).

No. 12. A small roll entitled "Nomina Militum destinandorum in Brittaniam. Temp. Hen. III.

No. 13. A roll entitled "Servicium factum domini Regi in Wallia" 29 Henry III., and also "Servicium domini " Regis Edwardi factum apud Wigorniam." 5 Edw. I.

No. 14. Acknowledgments and Proffers of Service at Carlisle. 34 Edw. I.

. SCUTAGE ROLLS.

The Scutage Rolls contain enrolments of the Mandates for the relief from payment of Scutage of such persons as appeared, by inspection of the "Rotuli Marescalcie" or Rolls of the Marshalsey of the Army, to have rendered the service due from them either personally or by sufficient deputies, or who had compounded for the same by payment of a fine. A few accounts relating to the collection of Scutage will be found amongst the Subsidy Rolls and the Miscellanea of the Exchequer.

Scutage Rolls of the following dates will be found amongst the Miscellaneous Rolls, &c. of the Chancery (Bundle 11):—

No. 1. 16 John.

No. 2. 2–15 Hen. III.

(This roll includes Lists of persons summoned to military service at Stamford and Worcester.)

No. 3. 7 Hen. III.

No. 4. 8 Hen. III.

No. 5. 14 Hen. III.

No. 6. 26 Hen. III.

No. 7. 29 Hen. III.

No. 8. 41 Hen. III.

No. 9. 49 Hen. III. to 1 Edw. III. An account of all fines paid for release or respite from military service between the dates specified.

No. 10. 13–18 Edw. I.

No. 11. 31 Edw. I. (Respite of Assizes of Novel Disseisin for those who are in the King's service in Scotland.)

No. 12. 31–35 Edw. I.

No. 13. 31–32 Edw. I.

No. 14. 34 Edw. I. (Letters of General Attorney for those who are in the King's service in Scotland.)

No. 15. 8–11 Edw. II.

No. 16. 8–19 Edw. II.

No. 17. 12–19 Edw. II.

No. 18. 2–11 Edw. III.

No. 19. 20 Edw. III. Letters of Acquittance for sums of money paid by various persons towards the expenses of Archers and Men-at-Arms. A roll of 10 membranes.

ARMY, NAVY, AND ORDNANCE—(continued).

MISCELLANEOUS REFERENCES (CHIEFLY FROM THE DO-
MESTIC STATE PAPERS).

Army.

Minutes of proceedings at Councils of War. 1626 to 1638.
[*S. P. Dom., Car. I., Vol.* 28.]
Entry Book of documents relating to the Council of War.
1638 to 1641. (Calendared.)
[*S. P. Dom., Car. I., Vol.* 396.]
Establishment of the Army, 1640.
[*S. P Dom., Military, Vol.* 1.]
Muster Roll of the Scotch Army in England, 1646.
[*S. P. Dom., Military, Vol.* 2.]
Military Entry Books, 1662 to 1781. 41 Vols.
[*S. P. Dom. Entry Books; and Military Entry Books
of the Home Office.*]
Muster Rolls of German Troops. 1755 to 1766.
[*S. P. Foreign (Various).*]

Navy.

A survey of all the tackle and apparel, cables, anchors, and
other provisions remaining in Her Majesty's ships,
taken at their coming from the seas. 1588.
[*S. P. Dom., Eliz., Vol.* 220.]
A volume containing entries of documents relating to the
Admiralty in the reigns of Elizabeth, James I., and
Charles I., including the names and dates of appointment of all the Lords High Admiral of England from
the reign of Edward II. to the year 1590.
[*S. P. Dom., Eliz., Vol.* 237.]
Report by Sir Robert Cotton on abuses in the Royal Navy.
1608. [*S. P. Dom., Jas. I., Vol.* 41.]
Trinity House Certificates. 1625 to 1638.
Two volumes containing Certificates by the Corporation
of Trinity House, addressed to the Lord High Admiral,
with reference to ships for which warrants were solicited
to enable them to carry pieces of ordnance sufficient for
their defence. They specify the name of the ship, its
tonnage, by whom and where built, the names of the
owner and master, and the number and character of the
Ordnance desired. [*S. P. Dom., Charles I., Vols.* 16 and 17.]
A Register of Warrants for issuing Letters of Marque, from
1628 to 1637. [*S. P. Dom., Car. I., Vol.* 130.]
[Entries of Letters of Marque from 1624 to the end
of the American War will be found amongst the
Records of the High Court of Admiralty.]
Survey of the Navy. 1626-7.
A volume containing minutes of the Special Commissioners appointed to inquire into the state of the Navy
from Dec. 1626 to May 1627. [*S. P. Dom., Car. I., Vol.* 45.]
Survey of all Ships in the Port of London, taken by direction
of the Lords Commissioners of the Admiralty.
[*S. P. Dom., Car. I., Vol.* 137.]
"A brief Abstract, Exposition, and Demonstration of all
parts and things belonging to a Ship and Practique
of Navigation," being a dictionary of Nautical Terms
fully explained. [*S. P. Dom., Car. I., Vol.* 127.]
Entry Book of Instructions to Naval Officers, compiled under
the direction of Sir E. Nicholas. 1625 to 1637.
[*S. P. Dom., Car. I., Vol.* 157.]

ARMY, NAVY, AND ORDNANCE—(continued).

Navy—(continued).

A volume of Collections and Transcripts relating to the Jurisdiction of the Lord High Admiral and of the Court of Admiralty, including the Title of the City of London to the conservancy of the Thames. 1631.
[*S. P. Dom., Car. I., Vol.* 208.]

A volume containing Navy Estimates from 1626 to 1631.
[*S. P. Dom., Car. I., Vol.* 209.]

Minutes of the Lords Commissioners of the Admiralty, from 1632 to 1634. (Calendared.) These include the appointments of Commissioned and Warrant Officers in the Royal Navy. [*S. P. Dom., Car. I., Vol.* 228.]

Do. from 1634 to 1635. (Calendared.)
[*S. P. Dom., Car. I., Vol.* 264.]

Do. from 1637 to 1640. (Calendared.)
[*S. P. Dom., Car. I., Vol.* 353.]

Ordnance.

An account of the stores in the Office of the Ordnance, showing all receipts and issues of the same from 1619 to 1632. [*S. P. Dom., Car. I., Vol.* 227.]

ATTORNEYS AND SOLICITORS.

The Records relating to Attorneys and Solicitors consist of the original Oath Rolls, signed by the Attorneys, &c. on their admission, the Rolls or Books of Attorneys or Alphabetical Registers of the Names and Addresses of the Attorneys admitted in each court with the dates of their admission, &c., the Affidavits of due execution of Articles of Clerkship (to which the Articles themselves are occasionally annexed), Certificate Books, containing the names and addresses of those who took out their annual certificates, with other documents of the like nature. No formal record of the Admissions of Attorneys appears to have been kept prior to the year 1729, when the enrolment thereof was rendered compulsory; but there is amongst the Records of the Common Pleas a rough Catalogue of Attorneys sworn in that Court (apparently drawn up by one of the Secondaries of the Court), entitled "Attornyes jurat" in officio meo, since Hill, 1656," the entries in which have been continued down to 1761. The names are arranged (1.) Alphabetically, and (2.) In Counties.

The Admission Books of the Solicitors of the Court of Chancery and the Rolls or Books of Attorneys of the Courts of Queen's Bench, Common Pleas, and Exchequer of Pleas, of a later date than those deposited in the Public Record Office, were in 1876 placed in the custody of the Clerk of the Petty Bag, and on the abolition of that office in 1889 were transferred to the custody of the Incorporated Law Society.

ATTORNEYS AND SOLICITORS—(continued).

Chancery.

ARTICLES OF CLERKSHIP OF SOLICITORS, REGISTER OF.
At the Office of the Incorporated Law Society.

CERTIFICATES OF ADMISSION OF SOLICITORS AND AT-
TORNEYS. Geo. I. to Geo. III. See **CERTIFI-
CATES.**

ROLLS OR BOOKS OF SOLICITORS, from 1736. At the
Office of the Incorporated Law Society.

Queen's Bench.

ARTICLES OF CLERKSHIP, AFFIDAVITS OF DUE EXECU-
TION OF.

Series I. 1775 to 1817. (Registered Nos. 3,001* to
20,000.) In bags 1 to 20, inclusive.

Series II. 1817 to 1834. (Registered Nos. 1 to
15,000.) In bags 21 to 32 inclusive.

Series III. 1834 to 1839. (Registered Nos. 1 to 2,993.)
In bag 33.

1840 to 1848. In bags 34 to 48 inclusive.

Series IV. 1804 to 1839. Supplementary Bundles,
in 6 bags.

Series V. 1838 to 1848. Articles registered pursuant
to Statute 34 George III. 32 bags.

Note.—There are no affidavits of execution of an earlier
date than 1775. The numbers missing in the above series
will be found in Supplementary Bundles, as follows :—

From 1810 to 1832. In bag 20.

From 1804 to 1839. In Series IV. Bags 1 to 6.

ARTICLES OF CLERKSHIP, REGISTER OF. 1749 to 1837.
6 Vols.

Alphabetical Index 1749 to 1845. 6 Vols. (This refers
by number either to the Register or to the Affidavits
themselves.)

CERTIFICATE BOOKS. 1785 to 1843. These contain the
names and addresses of Attorneys who took out their
annual certificates.

OATH ROLLS OF ATTORNEYS. 1750 to 1840. 3 rolls. The
original rolls signed by the Attorneys on their admission.

RESIDENCE BOOKS. 1790 to 1828. 2 Vols.

ROLLS OR BOOKS OF ATTORNEYS. 1729 to 1842. 5 Vols.
Do. 1790 to 1838. 2 Vols., called " Public," and giving
the names of the Attorneys only, without the addresses.

Abstract Roll of Attorneys. 1729 to 1814. 1 Vol.

Roll of Welsh Attorneys. 1830 to 1834, containing the
names of those who signed the roll, pursuant to Statute 1
William IV. 1 Vol.

---

* There are no Affidavits corresponding to the first 3,000 Nos. in the Register.

ATTORNEYS AND SOLICITORS—(continued).

Common Pleas.

ARTICLES OF CLERKSHIP. 1730 to 1838.
—— REGISTER OF. 1756 to 1867. 2 Vols.
—— REGISTER OF. 1843 to 1863. 1 Vol. (This volume relates to the Articles registered pursuant to Stat. 6 and 7 Vict.).

ADMISSION BOOKS. 1729 to 1848. 4 Vols.

ADMISSION ROLLS. 1838 to 1860. 4 Rolls.

CERTIFICATE BOOKS. 1786 to 1843. 59 Vols.

OATH ROLLS. 1790 to 1843. 16 Rolls.

Do. (CATHOLICS.) 1791 to 1842. 3 Rolls.

Do. (QUAKERS.) 1835 to 1842. 1 Roll.

ROLLS OF ATTORNEYS. 1730 to 1750. 13 Rolls.

ROLLS OR BOOKS OF ATTORNEYS. 1740 to 1853. 2 Vols.

Do. 1838 to 1843. (Signed pursuant to Statute 1 & 2 Vict. 1838.) 1 Vol.

Do. 1843 to 1862. (Signed pursuant to Statute 6 & 7 Vict. 1843.) 1 Vol.

Do. 1830 to 1844. (The Roll of Welsh Attorneys, signed pursuant to Statute 1 William IV.) 1 Vol.

Exchequer of Pleas.

OATH ROLLS. 1830 to 1842. 3 Rolls.

Do. (CATHOLICS.) 1831 to 1837. 1 Roll.

Do. (QUAKERS.) 1831 to 1845. 1 Roll.

ROLL OR BOOK OF ATTORNEYS. 1830 to 1836. 1 Vol.

Do. (WALES AND CHESTER), pursuant to Statute 1 Wm. IV. 1830., 1 Vol.

Exchequer, Queen's Remembrancer.

ROLLS OR BOOKS OF ATTORNEYS. 1729-1730, and 1794 to 1841. 2 Vols.

Wales and Chester.

ADMISSIONS OF ATTORNEYS.
Chester. 9 Will. III. to 2 Geo. II.
North Wales Circuit. 7 Geo. I. to 8 Geo. IV.

ADMISSIONS OF SOLICITORS.
Chester. 44 Geo. III. to 11 Geo. IV.

ARTICLES OF CLERKSHIP, AFFIDAVITS OF EXECUTION OF.
Chester. 25 Geo. III. to 1 Will IV.
Chester Circuit. 17 to 55 Geo. III.
Brecon Circuit. 46 Geo. III. to 1 Will. IV.
Carmarthen Circuit. 23 Geo. II. to 44 Geo. III.

ATTORNEYS AND SOLICITORS—(continued).

Wales and Chester—(continued).

ARTICLES OF CLERKSHIP, FILES OF. (Chester.) 1 to 8 Geo. II.
> Do. (Chester Circuit.) 5 to 9 Geo. II.

ARTICLES OF CLERKSHIP, REGISTERS OF.
> Brecon Circuit. 36 Geo. III. to 1 Will. IV.
> Carmarthen Circuit. 34 Geo. III. to 1 Will. IV.
> North Wales Circuit. 21 Geo. II. to 1 Will. IV.
> Montgomery. 37 Geo. III. to 1 Will. IV.

OATH ROLLS.
> Attorneys and Solicitors.
>> Chester Circuit. 3 Geo. II. to 1 Will. IV.
>
> Attorneys.
>> North Wales Circuit. 24 Geo. II. to 11 Geo. IV.
>> Brecon Circuit. 31 Geo. III. to 1 Will. IV.
>> Carmarthen Circuit. 13 Geo. III. to 10 Geo. IV.
>> Denbigh and Montgomery. 3 Geo. II. to 1 Will. IV.

Palatinate of Durham.

ATTORNEYS' OATH ROLL. 1730 to 1837.
> [*Cursitor's Miscellanea, No.* 12.]

AFFIDAVITS MADE ON THE TAKING AND BINDING OF ATTORNEYS' CLERKS. 1750 to 1834. 3 Files.

ATTORNEYS' CERTIFICATES, INDEX TO. 1785 to 1842.
> A volume containing the names and addresses of persons enrolled Attorneys in the Court of Pleas at Durham, registered pursuant to Stat. 25 Geo. III.
> [*Prothonotary's Indexes, No.* 4.]

Palatinate of Lancaster.

AFFIDAVITS OF EXECUTION OF ARTICLES OF CLERKSHIP 1749 to 1814. 2 Bundles.

CLERKS' ARTICLE BOOKS. 1749 to 1852. 2 Vols.

AYLOFFE'S CALENDARS.

A collection of miscellaneous references to the Duchy of Lancaster Records, compiled by Benjamin Ayloffe, the Keeper of the Records, and known by his name. 10 vols., as follows :—

Vol. 1. "Great Ayloffe. 1692." This volume contains, in addition to a general view of the records in the Duchy Office, a great variety of references to Grants, Inquisitions, Surveys, Privy Seals for Grants of Offices and other matters, with memoranda as to the business and jurisdiction of the Duchy. The references have, however, in most cases been superseded by later calendars. Folios 195 to 265 inclusive comprise a valuable *Index to Decrees and Orders* relating to Commons, Mills, Tolls, Fisheries, Tithes, Enclosures, &c., arranged under *Counties* and Names of *Places*, from Edw. 4. to 17 Chas. 1.

AYLOFFE'S CALENDARS—(continued).

Vol. 2. "Ayloffe. 1695." Contains an account of *Depositions and Surveys* relating to Commons, Boundaries, Mills, &c., from Hen. 7. to 1668, *selected* from the respective calendars for their special interest. Also a selection of *Special Warrants* and *Special Commissions* for Surveys, &c., from Eliz. to Chas. 2.

Vol. 3. "Ayloffe. 1704." Contains a calendar of *Decrees and Orders* from 1660 to 1687, arranged under *Counties* and *Places*, with a list of *Decrees* as to the *Title of Lands*, &c., in the Duchy jurisdiction, from Edw. 4. to Eliz., and an account of the names of the *Grantees* in *Feefarm*, from Eliz. to Chas. 1., &c., &c.

Vol. 4. "Ayloffe. 1712." Contains a *Calendar* of *Pleadings*, Edw. 6. and Mary. *Superseded* by the printed calendar.

Vol. 5. "Ayloffe. 1715." Contains a *Collection* of all the *Grants of Lands* in the counties of *Northumberland, Cumberland, Westmoreland,* and *Lancaster,* from the creation of the Duchy to 1715. [The grants mentioned are all indexed in the vol. entitled "Index to Grants in Fee."]

Vol. 6. "Ayloffe. 1718." Contains a *Calendar* to the *Counterparts of Leases* granted by the late Queen Mother and the late Queen Dowager, from 1641 to 1705.

Vol. 7. "Ayloffe. 1718." A rough note book entitled "Directions for Searches."

Vol. 8. "Ayloffe." A collection of divers searches, &c. This vol. contains notes respecting *various searches* made in the Duchy Records, with *references* to the documents, and an *Index* to the *Matters* and *Places* mentioned.

Vol. 9. "Ayloffe." A vol. entitled "Particulars of Duchy Leases," 1661 to 1716, giving full particulars of the leases during the above period, with observations thereon.

Vol. 10. "Ayloffe." A calendar to the *Grants in Boxes. Superseded* by the calendar printed in the Deputy Keeper's Reports.

BANKRUPTS' ESTATES.

The Conveyances of Bankrupts' Estates are enrolled on the Close Rolls, and appear in the Index to "INDENTURES" under the name of the First Commissioner in Bankruptcy for the time being. They are, however, referred to in the "CLOSE ROLL" Index under the name of the Bankrupt. The Commissions, Orders, and all other proceedings in Bankruptcy are kept at the Bankruptcy Court.

BARONETS.

The Creations of Baronets are enrolled on the Patent Rolls.

On the 11th Aug. 1623 Sir Thomas Playters was created a Baronet by warrant under the Royal Sign Manual, and a Memorandum in the Docquet Book of that date states that "it was the last of that nature His " Majesty resolveth to grant, as by his express pleasure " is signified and entered in the Book of Caveats at the " Signet Office."

The following documents also bear on this subject :—

PATENTS AND PRIVY SEALS FOR BARONETS, ENTRIES OF. (EXCHEQUER OF RECEIPT.) James I. to James II.

BARONETS—(continued).

9 Vols., containing accounts of the sums paid by various persons for Patents of Baronetcy.

PATENTS FOR BARONETCIES, LIST OF. 15 to 37 Charles II. [*Misc. Rolls, Chancery, No. $\frac{12}{13}$.*]

A List of the Creations of Baronets in the reigns of James I. and Charles I., compiled from the Indexes to the Patent Rolls, &c., is printed in the 47th Report, App., pp. 125-138.

BONDS AND RECOGNIZANCES.

Chancery.

The Recognizances and Bonds enrolled in the Court of Chancery from the reign of Henry VIII. to the present time are entered on the Close Rolls, of which in later years they form a distinct branch. See **DEEDS ENROLLED.**

For Recognizances and obligations of debt under the Statute Staple of 27 Edw. III., see **STATUTE STAPLE.**

Exchequer, Queen's Remembrancer.

BONDS AND OBLIGATIONS. Henry VIII. to Elizabeth These relate principally to the payments of sums due to the Collectors of Customs and Subsidies and other officers of the Exchequer and of the Royal Household, and to the delivery of Cargoes at various ports, &c., &c.
Descriptive Slips.

BONDS, SPECIAL. 1608 to 1835. 17 Packages. These are bonds entered into by persons on their admission to employment under the Crown.
Index. Car. II. to Jas. II.

Exchequer, Augmentation Office.

MEMORANDA, OBLIGATIONS, &c. Temp. Henry VIII. 1 Vol. [*Misc. Books, Vol. 263.*]
RECOGNIZANCES, ENTRIES OF. 34-35 Hen. VIII. 1 Vol. [*Misc. Books, Vol. 352.*]
MEMORANDA OF THE DELIVERY OF OBLIGATIONS TO THE TREASURER OF THE COURT OF AUGMENTATIONS. Edward VI. 1 Vol. [*Misc. Books, Vol. 327.*]

Duchy of Lancaster.

SECURITY BONDS. Hen. VIII. to 1716. 9 Bundles.

Palatinate of Chester.

BONDS, &c. See **CHANCERY ENROLMENTS.**

CERTIFICATES.

Chancery.

CERTIFICATES OF STATUTES STAPLE AND EXTENTS THERE-
ON. See **STATUTE STAPLE.**

CERTIFICATES OF THE ACCOUNTANT-GENERAL AND OF
THE MASTERS AND CHIEF CLERKS IN CHANCERY. See
JUDICIAL PROCEEDINGS.

CERTIFICATES, VARIOUS. (PETTY BAG OFFICE.) Eight
bundles, as follows:—

No. 1. Certificates, Licences, and Presentments of Taverns
and Cookshops in the City of London, temp. Jac. I. and
Car. I.

No. 2. Certificates of Delinquents' Estates sequestrated
during the Commonwealth.

No. 3.   Do.   Do.

No. 4. Certificates of Recusants' Estates sequestrated, 1650.

No. 5. Certificates of Surrenders of Offices. Car. II. and
Jas. II.

No. 6. Certificates of Popish Recusants and of Persons concealed. Anne and George I.

No. 7. Certificates of the Admission of Solicitors and
Attorneys. Geo. I. to Geo. III.

No. 8. Certificates of Qualification of Members of Parliament. Geo. I. to Geo. III.

CERTIFICATES OF PERSONS RECEIVING THE SACRAMENT
PURSUANT TO THE TEST ACT. See **OATHS OF
ALLEGIANCE, &c.**

Common Pleas.

CERTIFICATES OF ACKNOWLEDGMENT OF DEEDS BY
MARRIED WOMEN.

See **ACKNOWLEDGMENTS OF DEEDS.**

Exchequer, Queen's Remembrancer.

CERTIFICATES OF SALE OF THE LANDS OF CHARLES I.,
&c. See **CROWN LANDS.**

CERTIFICATES OF THE SALE AND TRANSFER OF BANK
STOCK, &c. See **JUDICIAL PROCEEDINGS.**

Exchequer, Augmentation Office.

CERTIFICATES OF COLLEGES, CHANTRIES, FREE
CHAPELS, &c. See **MONASTIC FOUNDATIONS,
&c.**

Exchequer, First Fruits Department.

CERTIFICATES OF INSTITUTION TO BENEFICES, CALLED
" BISHOPS' CERTIFICATES." See **ECCLESIASTI-
CAL MATTERS.**

CHANCERY ENROLMENTS.

In addition to the Charter, Patent, Close, and Fine Rolls, which may be considered to be the four great classes of Chancery Enrolments, separate rolls were formed of various classes of documents relating both to the domestic and foreign relations of the country, of which the Lord Chancellor had cognizance in his capacity as Secretary of State or otherwise. Such were the Foreign or Treaty Rolls relating to the affairs of the French Provinces, and to diplomatic and military relations with Ireland, Scotland, Wales, and with various foreign countries; the Cartæ Antiquæ Rolls, containing transcripts of various early charters ; the Coronation Rolls, Confirmation Rolls, Extract Rolls, Liberate and Præstita Rolls, Pardon Rolls, Protection Rolls, and Redisseisin Rolls ; the Statute Rolls, on which the legal enactments of the several Parliaments were formally drawn up and enrolled, the Staple Rolls, and many others brought together in the present volume, under the general title of **" CHANCERY ENROLMENTS (VARIOUS)."** [The " Decree Rolls " and " Parliament Rolls " of the Court of Chancery are described under the heads of **JUDICIAL PROCEEDINGS** and **PARLIAMENTARY PROCEEDINGS** respectively.]

CHARTER ROLLS. 1 John to 8 Henry VIII.

The instruments by which the Sovereigns of England made grants and expressed their intentions to their people were of three kinds, called respectively Charters, Letters Patent, and Letters Close. " By the first their more " solemn acts were declared, by the second their more " public directions promulgated, and by the third they " intimated their private instructions to individuals."

The Royal Charter was the form of instrument employed by the Sovereign in granting liberties, privileges, immunities, and exemptions, and also lands, tenements, and other possessions, both to corporations and to private individuals. Charters were distinguished from the Letters Patent by their being always executed in the presence of witnesses whose attestation was necessary to the validity of the document, and by their being addressed " To the archbishops, bishops, abbots, priors, earls, barons, &c.," instead of simply, " To all to whom these presents shall come." They are of two kinds : — (1) Original grants of lands, tenements, liberties, &c. (2.) Charters of confirmation or inspeximus of previous grants. The latter may again be subdivided into two classes : Charters confirming previous grants without reciting them ; and charters reciting in full others previously granted, and ratifying and confirming the same, sometimes .with the

CHANCERY ENROLMENTS--(continued).

CHARTER ROLLS—(continued).

addition of further privileges. Confirmations of charters prior to 1 Ric. III. are entered both on the Patent and Charter Rolls, and also on the Cartæ Antiquæ. From 1 Ric. III. to 1 Car. I. they are entered on the Confirmation Rolls, and subsequent to the latter date again on the Patent Rolls. The Charter Rolls terminate in the 8th year of Henry VIII., when that class of instrument was discontinued, all further grants from the Crown being made in the form of Letters Patent. The documents entered on the Charter Rolls consist chiefly of Charters of Foundation and Incorporation; Grants of Lands, Liberties, and Privileges to Cities, Towns, Civil and Religious Corporations, and to individuals; Grants of Markets, Fairs, and Free-Warren, &c., &c. [See Introduction to the printed volume of Charter Rolls.]

Inventory. John to Henry VIII. Report II., App. II., pp. 2–7; and Report III., App. II., p. 142.

Transcript in full. 1–18 John. Printed by the Record Commission (with an Introduction and General Index).

Calendar. John to Edw. IV. Printed (with Indices Locorum and Nominum).

Do. Ric. III. to Henry VIII. MS. (Incorporated with the MS. Calendar to the Patent Rolls. Vol. 4.)

See also **PALMER'S INDEXES.**

PATENT ROLLS. 3 John to 50 Victoria. The Patent Rolls derive their name from the "Litteræ Patentes," or Letters Patent, of which they are the formal enrolments.

The Letters Patent were, as their name implies, written upon open sheets of parchment, with the Great Seal pendent at the bottom, being thus distinguished from the "Litteræ Clausæ," or Letters Close, which, being of a less public nature, and addressed to individuals, were *closed* or folded up.

During the reigns of the Plantagenets the Patent Rolls contain documents of a most diversified and interesting nature, relating principally to the Prerogatives of the Crown, to the Revenue, and to the different branches of Judicature; to Treaties, Truces, Correspondence, and Negociations with Foreign Princes and States; Letters of Protection, of Credence and of Safe Conduct; Appointments, and Powers of Ambassadors, &c.

In addition to these documents of an essentially public nature they also contain Grants and Confirmations of Liberties, Offices, Privileges, Lands, and Wardships, both

CHANCERY ENROLMENTS—(continued).

PATENT ROLLS—(continued).

to public bodies and private individuals ; Charters of Incorporation ; Licenses for the election of Bishops and other Ecclesiastical Dignitaries ; Restitutions of Temporalities : Presentations to Churches and Chapels ; Creations of Nobility ; Special and General Pardons, Special Liveries ; Licenses and Pardons for Alienation : Crown Leases : Proclamations, and all manner of Commissions, documents of the last two classes being entered on the back of the rolls.

By the Statute of 1 Anne, cap. 7, which provides for the establishment of the Civil List, the power of the Crown to dispose of its Land Revenue was restrained, and it was enacted " That no grant shall be made by the Crown of any " manors, messuages, lands, tenements, rents, tithes, woods, " or other hereditaments (advowsons of churches and " vicarages only excepted), for any longer term than one " and thirty years or three lives." From and after this date, therefore, the contents of the Patent Rolls consist principally of Grants of Offices and Pensions : Creations of Nobility : and Letters Patent of Invention and Denization. Subsequent to the year 1725 the Appointments of Bishops, Congés d'Elire, and Writs of Restitution of Temporalities are enrolled on a distinct set of rolls called " Bishops' Patent Rolls."

Inventory. 3 John to 45 Eliz. Printed. Reports II., App. II., p. 7 ; III., Ap. II., p. 142 : and VI., App. II., p. 203.

Transcript in full. 3 to 18 John. Printed, in 1 Vol. folio, with an Introduction, and Indices Nominum and Locorum. (The Introduction contains also an *Itinerary of King John.*)

Calendar. John to Edw. IV. Printed, in 1 Vol. folio, with Indices, Rerum, Nominum, and Locorum. (This Calendar consists of *selections only.*)

Do. 1 Hen III. Printed. Reports XXVI., App., pp. 66–86.

Do. 1 to 57 Hen III. 3 Vols. MS.

Do. 1 to 9 Edw. I. Printed. Reports XLII. to L., inclusive.

Do. 10 to 29 Edw. I. Printed, in 2 Vols. (1893–94.)

Do. 1 to 6 Edw. II. Printed (1894).

Do. 1 to 8 Edw. III. Printed, in 2 Vols. (1891–93.)

Do. 1 to 4 Ric. II. Printed (1894).

Do. Edw. V. and Ric. III. Printed, Report IX. App. II., pp. 1–147.

CHANCERY ENROLMENTS—(continued).

PATENT ROLLS—(continued).

Calendar 1–6 Henry VII. Printed in Campbell's "Materials for the History of the reign of Henry VII."

Do. 1–30 Hen. VIII. Printed in "Letters and Papers."

Calendars and Indexes. Edw. V. to 50 Vict. 56 Vols. MS.

See also **PALMER'S INDEXES.**

A List of the *Creations of Peers and Baronets,* from Richard III. to Charles I., compiled from the Indexes to the Patent Rolls, &c., is printed in the 47th Report, App. pp. 78–138.

CLOSE ROLLS. 6 John to 1883. The Rotuli Litterarum Clausarum or Close Rolls, which are so called in contradistinction to the Rotuli Litterarum Patentium or Patent Rolls, contain the enrolments of all mandates, letters, and writs of a private nature; that is to say, such as were addressed in the King's name to individuals, and were folded or *closed up;* the Litteræ Patentes being, on the other hand, addressed to all persons, and delivered *open,* with the Great Seal attached to the bottom.

On the Close Rolls are enrolled documents of the most varied description, touching the royal prerogatives, the revenue, and the several branches of the judicature; "such " as orders for the observance of treaties and truces, con- " cerning aids, subsidies, tallages, restitutions of posses- " sions, assignments of dower, and acceptances of homage; " for the repairing, fortifying, and provisioning of castles; " writs and mandates respecting the coin of the realm " the affairs of the royal household, and the payment of " salaries and stipends; commitments, pardons, and deli- " veries of State prisoners, &c. On the back of the rolls " are summonses to and prorogations of parliaments, great " councils, and convocations, writs of summons for the " performance of military and naval services; copies of " letters to foreign princes and states; proclamations; " prohibitions; orders for regulating the coinage of the " kingdom, and the sale of wine and other necessaries; " for receiving knighthood, providing ships, raising and " arraying forces, and furnishing provisions; for paying " knights, citizens, and burgesses for attendance in par- " liament; liveries and seizins of lands; enrolments of " private deeds, of awards of abitrators, and of various " other documents." [See Sir Thomas Hardy's admirable and exhaustive introduction to the printed volume of Close Rolls.]

CHANCERY ENROLMENTS—continued.

CLOSE ROLLS—(continued).

The more modern Close Rolls, that is to say, those from the reign of Henry VIII. to the present time, consist of the ordinary enrolments in Chancery, such as Deeds of Bargain and Sale, Conveyances, Disentailing Deeds, Deeds enrolled for Safe Custody, Conveyances in Trust for Charitable Purposes, Recognizances, Specifications of Inventions, Memorials of Annuities, Memorials of Assurance Companies, Certificates of Naturalization, Deeds relating to Change of Name, &c., &c. Of these enrolments the Recognizances Memorials of Annuities, and Specifications of Inventions form distinct branches of the series of Close Rolls. See **DEEDS ENROLLED.**

Inventory. John to Eliz. Printed. Reports II.,App. II., pp. 17–24; III.,App. II.,pp. 148–151; and IV., App.II., pp. 99–103.

Transcript in full. 6 John to 11 Hen. III. Printed (with an Introduction and Indices Nominum and Locorum). 2 Vols. folio.

Calendar. 12 Hen. III. Printed. Report XXVII., App., pp. 48–93.

Do. 13 Hen. III. to 3 Edw. I. 11 Vols. MS.

Calendar. 1 to 16 Edw. II. Printed in 3 Vols. (1892–94.)

Indexes. John to 1848. 84 Vols. MS. (From 1 Hen. III. to the end of Edw. IV. these Vols. contain *selections* only.)

See also **PALMER'S INDEXES.**

FINE ROLLS. John to 23 Charles I. The Rolls upon which were entered the sums of money (or other property, such as palfreys, harriers, falcons, &c.) offered to the King by way of oblation or fine for the passing or renewal of charters or grants, and for the enjoyment of lands, offices, wardships, exemptions, liberties, privileges, and other marks of the royal favour, were called the Oblata or Fine Rolls. The first of these appellations fell into disuse after the reign of John, the latter only being thenceforward retained. There are "Oblata Rolls" for the first, second, third, and ninth years of King John; and "Fine Rolls" for the sixth, seventh, fifteenth, seventeenth, and eighteenth years of that reign. From that date to the year 1641, when it terminates, the series is, with one or two exceptions, complete. The Fine Rolls as documents of historical and genealogical importance rank next to the three great classes of Charter, Patent, and Close Rolls, to the latter of which, indeed, they bear some resemblance, many of the

CHANCERY ENROLMENTS—(continued).

FINE ROLLS—(continued).

entries on the early Close Rolls belonging more properly to this series.

By the entries on these rolls the receipt of fines or oblations appears to have constituted a great source of wealth to the Crown, no pretext being too trivial for the extortion of an apparently voluntary payment, and the royal favour and interference being solicited and obtained in matters of the most private nature, as, for instance, in cases of " conjugal infidelity " and in cases respecting the exercise of " matrimonial rights." The more general occasions on which fines were paid were, however, to procure grants and confirmations of liberties and franchises of various kinds, and of markets and fairs, free warren, &c. ; for exemptions from tolls, &c.; for livery of lands ; for grants of wardships and marriages ; for licenses " alienandi et concordandi " ; for exoneration from knighthood ; for letters of safe conduct ; for pardons of trespasses and misdemeanours ; and for the expedition of justice, the stopping or delaying of trials or judgments, and their removal from inferior tribunals to the King's Court. On the Fine Rolls were also entered the patents for the appointment of sheriffs, escheators, customers, comptrollers, searchers, and other officers in the gift of the Lord Treasurer ; writs for livery of lands on the heir attaining his majority, entitled " de homagio capto "; writs " de custodia commissa "; " de terris captis in manum regis"; with writs " de diem clausit extremum," " ad quod damnum," and its of inquiry on amortising lands, &c., &c.

Inventory. 6 John to 23 Charles I. Printed. Report II., App. II., p. 24 ; and Report III., App. II., p. 135.

Transcript in full. John. Printed. 1 Vol. 8vo, entitled " Rotuli de Oblatis et Finibus."

Selections. Hen. III. Printed. 2 Vols. 8vo, entitled " Excerpta e Rotulis Finium."

Do. 1 Edw. I. to 7 Edw. II. 5 Vols. MS.

Calendar. Edw. V. to Car. I. (with Indices Locorum et Nominum). See " Palmers Indexes," Vols. 75, 76, and 77.

CHANCERY ENROLMENTS (VARIOUS).

ALMAIN ROLLS. 22 Edw I. to 15 Edw. III. A branch of the " Treaty Rolls " consisting of eight rolls relating to negotiations, alliances, treaties, &c. in Germany and Flanders. The rolls of Edward I. relate to negotiations between himself and Adolph King of the Romans, John Duke of Brabant, Guy Earl of Flanders, John Earl of

CHANCERY ENROLMENTS (VARIOUS) —
(continued).

ALMAIN ROLLS—(continued).

Holland, &c. Those of Edward III. relate to the great confederacy formed by him against Philip of Valois in the prosecution of his claim to the crown of France.

Inventory. Report II., App. II., p. 45.

CARTÆ ANTIQUÆ ROLLS. Ethelbert to Edward I. These are the most ancient records of the Court of Chancery, and consist of Transcripts, made apparently in the 12th and 13th centuries, of grants and charters of various dates, from the reign of Ethelbert to that of Edward the First inclusive.

Inventory. Report II., App. II, p. 1.

Calendar and Index Locorum. Printed in " Ayloffe's Calendar of Ancient Charters," &c.

See also the " Calendar of Royal Charters," printed in Report XXIX., App., pp. 7–48 ; and Report XXX., App., pp. 197–211.

CONFIRMATION ROLLS. 1 Ric. III. to 1 Car. I. These rolls contain confirmations of Charters to cities, boroughs, or other corporate or politic bodies, and also to private individuals. Before 1 Ric. III. confirmations are entered on the Charter and Patent Rolls, and subsequent to 1 Charles I. again on the Patent Rolls.

Inventory. 1 Ric. III. to 1 Car. I. Printed. Report IV., App. II., p. 104.

Calendar. 1 Ric. III. to 1 Car. I. 1 Vol. MS.

CONTRABREVIA ROLLS. See NORMAN ROLLS.

CORONATION ROLLS. Edw. II. to Vict. These contain the Commissions and proceedings of the Commissioners appointed to hear and determine claims of service to be performed at Coronations, and also the oath taken and the declaration made and signed by the King or Queen when crowned. The series is imperfect, Coronation Rolls existing for the following sovereigns only :—Edw. II., Hen. IV., Hen. V., James I., Charles II., James II., Wm. and Mary, Anne, George I., George II., George IV., William IV., and Victoria.

DISPENSATION ROLLS. 37 Elizabeth to 1747. These are the records of the Clerk of the Dispensations and Faculties in Chancery, and consist of enrolments of the confirmations of Bishops' Commendams, of Dispensations, and Notarial Faculties, and of Doctors' and Masters of Arts' degrees granted by the Archbishop of Canterbury. The office of

CHANCERY ENROLMENTS (VARIOUS) —
(continued).

DISPENSATION ROLLS—(continued).

Clerk of the Dispensations was abolished by Stat. 2 & 3 Wm. IV., c. 111, and the duties transferred to the Secretary of Presentations.

EXCHANGE ROLLS. 6 Richard II. to 12 Henry VI. The Exchange Rolls contain the licenses from the King to foreign merchants residing in England to give letters of exchange on their houses abroad, so that no gold or silver should pass out of the kingdom. They contain also a few licenses to go beyond the seas. There are four rolls only, the dates of which are respectively 6 to 17 Ric. II., 2 to 14 Hen. IV., 1 & 2 Hen. VI., and 3 to 12 Hen. VI.

EXTRACT ROLLS. 45 Henry III. to 6 Richard II. The Extract Rolls, or " Extracta Donationum," contain abstracts from the Charter, Patent, and other Rolls of gifts and grants from the Crown. (Two rolls apparently belonging to this series, found amongst the Miscellaneous Rolls, Chancery, and containing " Extracta Donationum," from 3–8 Edw. II. ; and " Extracta Patentium," 8–9 Edw. II., have been added to it).

Inventory. Report II., App. II., p. 37.

FRENCH ROLLS. 26 Henry III. to 26 Charles II. The French Rolls form a branch of an important series of enrolments relating to Foreign Countries, which at the time of their deposit in the Tower of London were generally described as " Treaty Rolls." In earlier periods they were, however, divided into the several classes of Almain, French, Norman, Vascon, Roman, Welsh, Irish, and Scotch Rolls, according to the countries to which they respectively related.

From the reign of Edward V. to that of Henry VII. these classes were reduced to two, namely the French and the Scotch Rolls, and the latter being discontinued about the seventh year of Henry the Eighth, the French Rolls only continued to be made up after that date. On them, however, were enrolled diplomatic and other documents relating to European countries generally.

The earliest French Roll is dated 16 Henry III., but the regular series does not begin till 1 Edward II., and during several years of that reign the French and Roman affairs are mixed, part of the French Roll being devoted to documents relating to Rome and *vice versa.* The earlier French Rolls contain all charters, grants, writs, mandates, and other documents relating to those provinces of France which were under the English rule ; those of a

CHANCERY ENROLMENTS (VARIOUS) — (continued).

FRENCH ROLLS—(continued).

later date consisting chiefly of enrolments of treaties and negociations, commissions, powers and orders to ambassadors, and licenses for the mustering of ships' crews, and the transport of wines, &c. There are distinct rolls for the Provinces of Normandy and Gascony, described respectively as Norman, and Gascon or Vascon Rolls. The regular series of French Rolls terminates with the 22nd year of James the First, the last document of this class consisting of an enrolment of the Treaties of Breda, and of the ratification thereof, dated 19 Charles II. and 26 Charles II. respectively.

Inventory. 26 Hen. III. to 26 Car. II. Printed Report II., App. II., p. 42 ; and Report III., App. II. p. 40.

Calendar. John to Hen. VI. See Carte's " Catalogue of the Gascon, French, and Norman Rolls." *Selections only.* 2 Vols.

Do. 1 to 10 Hen. V. Printed. Report XLIV., App., pp. 545–638.

Do. 1 to 49 Hen.VI. Printed. Report XLVIII., App., pp. 217–450.

See also **FRANCE, ENGLISH POSSESSIONS IN.**

GASCON ROLLS. See VASCON ROLLS.

IRISH ROLLS. 1 to 50 Edward III. The " Rotuli Hiberniæ " or Irish Rolls, which were formerly deposited in the Tower, consist of three rolls, the first of which extends from the 1st to the 12th year of Edward the Third, and contains such Charters, Grants, and other documents which passed the Great Seal as relate to Ireland. The other two rolls contain " Memoranda de Hibernia " from the 47th to the 50th of Edward III. relating to the aid solicited by that King from his Parliament in Ireland, " to enable him to support the wars undertaken for the " preservation and defence of that kingdom," and consisting of the Writs thereupon issued to the Archbishops, Bishops, and other magnates of the Realm, directing the election of representatives from every diocese, county, city, and borough to appear before the King and his Council, with the returns thereto ; and of Articles of complaint against the King's ministers in that country, with the Inquisitions taken thereon, &c., &c. These two rolls are fully described and partially printed in Ayloffe's " Calendars of Ancient Charters, &c."

CHANCERY ENROLMENTS (VARIOUS). —
(continued).

LIBERATE ROLLS. 2 John to 14 Henry VI. The Liberate Rolls derive their name from the Writs of " Liberate," which are recorded on them. They consist of precepts to the Treasurer and other officers of the Exchequer to " Deliver" out of the Treasury such sums of money as were required for the payment of pensions, salaries, and stipends, and for the various expenses of the State and of the Royal Household. They also contain Writs of " Allocate " and " Computate," directing sums of money to be " allowed" or " reckoned " in accounting with the several officers and ministers of the Crown and others; and Writs to Sheriffs for the delivery of lands or goods which had been extended, &c. From 6 John to 9 Henry III. inclusive there are no Liberate Rolls, the Writs of that description being enrolled amongst the other writs on the Close Rolls. They recommence in the 10th year of Henry III., and are continued from that date to the 14th year of Henry VI., after which time no roll of that description appears to have been made up. There are also Liberate Rolls from 10 Henry III. to 33 Edward I. amongst the Records of the Exchequer of Receipt (Pells). See also NORMAN ROLLS and VASCON ROLLS.

The Liberate Rolls of King John, namely of the 2nd, 3rd, and 5th years of his reign, have been printed in full, together with the Misæ Roll of the 11th and the Præstita Roll of the 12th years of the same reign.

Inventory. Report II., App. II., p. 29.

Transcript in full. 2 to 5 John. Printed in 1 Vol. 8vo, entitled " Rotuli de Liberate ac de Misis et Præstitis."

MISÆ ROLL. 11 John. This Roll contains an account of the daily *expenses* of the Court of King John during the 11th year of his reign. " The value of gold, silver, jewellery, " and arms ; the prices of robes, dresses, wines, provisions, " and the various other articles used in domestic economy ; " the presents made to distinguished individuals ; the salaries " and pensions to the Officers of State and others in the " Royal household ; the expenses of Ambassadors and " Messengers ; and the money bestowed in alms and obla- " tions are all registered on the Misæ Roll with scrupulous " exactness." This is the only Roll of its class now extant with the exception of one for the 14th year of King John, preserved amongst the WARDROBE ACCOUNTS of the Exchequer, Q. R., which is printed in Cole's " Selec-

CHANCERY ENROLMENTS (VARIOUS) —
(continued).

MISÆ ROLL.—(continued).

" tions from the Records of the Exchequer, Queen's
" Remembrancer."

Transcript in full. Printed in the volume entitled,
" Rotuli de Liberate, ac de Misis et Præstitis."

NORMAN ROLLS. 2 John to 10 Henry V. The Norman
Rolls contain the enrolments of such Letters Patent, and
Close, Writs, Mandates, and other instruments passing
under the Great Seal, as related to the Duchy of Normandy, whilst it was under the dominion of the English
Crown; and also of Chirographs, Concords, and other
documents executed in the King's Court of Exchequer at
Caen. They also contain Treaties and other documents
of a diplomatic character between the Kings of England and
the Dukes of Brittany, Burgundy, and others. The series
of Norman Rolls is very irregular, seven rolls only of the
reign of King John being now in existence. These consist
of a Charter Roll, a Liberate Rolls and an Oblata Roll for
the second year of his reign; two rolls called "Contrabrevia," containing entries similar to those in the Close
Rolls, for the second and fourth years respectively; a
Close Roll for the fifth year; and for the sixth a roll entitled " Rotulus de Valore Terrarum Normannorum," which
specifies the value of the lands in England, which were held
by the Normans then in rebellion, and which thereby
became escheated to the English Crown. In the fifth
year of King John, Normandy becoming re-united to the
Crown of France, the records relating to that province
were discontinued until its invasion and re-conquest by
Henry the Fifth, when the series recommences as
" Norman Patent Rolls," and as such is continued to the
end of that King's reign. Between the reigns of John and
Henry the Fifth there are, however, with the Norman
Rolls two rolls dated respectively 46 & 47 Henry III.
and 20 Edward III., the former of which consists of a
few writs of Liberate issued during the King's absence in
France and relating chiefly to his expenses there, the latter
containing the Patents and Charters granted by Edward
the Third whilst occupied in the siege of Calais, which
consist chiefly of General Pardons and other rewards for
services during the war with France. The Norman Rolls
of the reign of Henry the Fifth consist principally of
letters of safe-conduct and protection, grants and confirmations of their estate to such as voluntarily surrendered
to him or to his commanders, restitutions of their temporalities to such convents as recognized his authority, and of

CHANCERY ENROLMENTS (VARIOUS) —
(continued).

NORMAN ROLLS—(continued).

grants to his followers of the castles and estates of such Normans as were slain or remained in open rebellion, and of Grants of Officers, Commissions of Array, Presentations to ecclesiastical benefices, &c. In addition to the Norman Rolls the Patent and Charter Rolls of the first five years of King John contain numerous entries relating to the Anglo-French provinces ; and there are amongst the Miscellaneous Rolls of Chancery three rolls dated 21 Edw. I. relating to injuries done by the Normans to the King's subjects in Saintonge, Bayonne, the Cinque-Ports, and elsewhere. There are also amongst the Exchequer Records a collection of Norman Pipe Rolls of various dates from 30 Henry II. to King John. These are placed with the Pipe Rolls, and have been printed in full by the Society of Antiquaries.

The Norman Rolls from 2 John to 5 Hen. V. have been printed in full by Sir Thos. Hardy under the direction of the Record Commissioners ; and to those from 6 to 10 Hen. V. a calendar has been made and printed in Report XLI., App. I., pp. 671–810 ; and Report XLII., App., pp. 313–472. Reference to these Rolls will also be found in Carte's " Catalogue des Rolles Gascons, Normands, et Francais," in 2 Vols. folio.

OBLATA ROLLS. See FINE ROLLS (p.   ).

PARDON ROLLS. 22 Edward I. to 2 James I. These contain the enrolments of General Pardons granted between the foregoing dates. The series is, however, imperfect. General and Special Pardons and Pardons for Alienation are also entered on the Patent Rolls. (A roll of pardons from 7 to 11 Hen. VIII., found amongst the Miscellaneous Rolls, Chancery, has been added to this series.)

Inventory. Report II., App. II., p. 36 ; and Report III., App. II., p. 139.

PASSAGE ROLLS. A roll entitled " Rotulus Passagii," containing mandates to the " Custodes Passagii " in the various ports to permit the persons therein specified to go beyond the seas. 14–15 Edw. III.

[*Misc. Rolls, Chancery, No. $\frac{11}{13}$.*]

A similar roll for the years 1–2 Ric. II.

[*Do.*   *No.* $\frac{18}{5}$.]

PRÆSTITA ROLL. On the Præstita Roll, so called from the word *præstitum*, were entered the sums of money which issued out of any of the Royal Treasuries by way of imprest, advance, or accommodation, and which had to be repaid or otherwise accounted for. This is the only roll

CHANCERY ENROLMENTS (VARIOUS) —
(continued).

PRÆSTITA ROLL.— (continued).

of the kind amongst the Chancery enrolments, but other rolls of a similar character exist amongst the Miscellanea of the Exchequer, Queen's Remembrancer.

Transcript in full. Printed in the vol. entitled " Rotuli de Liberate, ac de Misis et Præstitis."

PROTECTION ROLLS. 10 to 34 Edw. I. These consist of four rolls containing the enrolments of Letters of Protection granted to such persons as were about to proceed to the wars in Scotland and elsewhere on the King's service. There is also amongst the Vascon Rolls a roll of Protections dated 22 Edward I.

REDISSEISIN ROLLS. 14 Edward I. to 39 Henry VI. These contain the Writs to Sheriffs for the restoration of persons to lands, &c. of which they had been unlawfully dispossessed, and in respects of which judgments had been obtained in actions of novel disseisin. There was also amongst the " Miscellaneous Rolls " a Redisseisin Roll dated 1-6 Edw. IV. (now added to this series). Transcripts of these writs were sent into the Exchequer and enrolled on the " ORIGINALIA ROLLS." The contents of the Redisseisin Rolls are almost entirely reproduced in the " Rotulorum Originalium Abbreviatio," printed by the Record Commissioners.

ROMAN ROLLS. 34 Edward I. to 31 Edward III. The Roman Rolls form a branch of the so-called " Treaty Rolls," and consist chiefly of letters to various Popes and Cardinals touching the ecclesiastical affairs of the kingdom. Matters relating to Roman affairs will also be found on the French Rolls during the reign of Edward the Second and *vice versâ*.

Inventory. 34 Edw. I. to 31 Edw. III. Printed. Report II., App. II., p. 45.
See also Carte's " Catalogue of Gascon Rolls, &c.," Vol. II.

SCOTCH ROLLS. 19 Edward I. to 7 Henry VIII. The " Rotuli Scotiæ " or Scotch Rolls form a branch of the series formerly known as " Treaty Rolls," and contain the enrolments of negotiations, treaties, and truces between the kingdoms of England and Scotland ; of documents relating to the disputed succession to the Crown of Scotland on the death of Margaret of Norway ; to the claims of Edward I. as superior Lord of Scotland, and the contest between Balliol and Bruce and the other competitors to the Scottish throne ; of precepts to the Lords Marchers

CHANCERY ENROLMENTS (VARIOUS)·—
(continued).

SCOTCH ROLLS—(continued).

and others for levying troops, orders for garrisoning, fortifying, and victualling castles, and other preparations for the wars with Scotland ; of negotiations relating to prisoners of war and their ransom ; letters of protection and safe-conduct ; grants of estates, &c. to Scottish partisans ; attainders and pardons ; orders for raising money by levying customs and other duties ; licenses to English and Scottish merchants ; grants of benefices ; and other documents of a miscellaneous nature relating to Scottish affairs. See also the " HOMAGE ROLLS " and " SCOTTISH DOCUMENTS " described under the heading **SCOTLAND.**

Transcript in full. Printed by the Record Commissioners in 2 Vols. folio, with Indexes of names and places.

Calendar. Printed in Ayloffe's " Calendar of Ancient Charters, &c."

SPECIFICATION ROLLS. See **SPECIFICATIONS OF PATENT INVENTIONS.**

STAPLE ROLLS. 27 Edw. III. to 39 Hen. VI. Three rolls, formerly deposited amongst the Records in the Tower of London, contain the appointments of Mayors and Constables of the Staple in various towns, Licenses to transport wools, &c. from one town to another, and other orders and proclamations relating to the business of the Staple. The first of these rolls contains also the " Ordinatio Stapulorum " or " Statute of the Staples " of 27 Edw. III., which is printed in " Statutes of the Realm," Vol. 1, p. 332.

See also **STATUTE STAPLE.**

STATUTE ROLLS. 6 Edw. I. to 8 Edw. IV. These are Records of Chancery on which were entered the several Statutes when drawn up in form, for the purpose of being proclaimed and published ; the Statutes being framed upon such original Petitions and Answers, or entries thereof on the Parliament Rolls, as related to Public Concerns. The regular series of Statute Rolls consists of six rolls extending from 6 Edw. I. to 8 Edw. IV., with an interruption from 8 to 23 Henry VI.

There is evidence of the existence of Statute Rolls of a later date than 8 Edward IV., for the Statutes from that date to 4 Henry VII. inclusive are inserted in the early Printed editions in a form manifestly copied from complete Statute Rolls, and similar copies are found in several Manuscript collections ; but there is reason to conclude that the making up of the Statute Roll entirely ceased with the Session 4 Henry VII., as no such roll of a later

CHANCERY ENROLMENTS (VARIOUS) —
(continued).

STATUTE ROLLS—(continued.)

date, nor any evidence of the existence thereof, has been discovered. It may be observed that in the following Session, that of 7 Henry VII., Public Acts were for the first time printed from the several Bills passed in Parliament, and not as part of one general Statute drawn up in the ancient form.

In addition to the six rolls above mentioned there are amongst the Tower Records Transcripts of Statutes, apparently sent into the Chancery for the purpose of being exemplified under the Great Seal, which supply the deficiency of the Statute Roll for certain periods.

See PARLIAMENTARY PROCEEDINGS.

SURRENDER ROLLS. 12 to 20 Charles II. These are seven rolls containing Surrenders of Offices and Fee-Farm Rents, with a few conveyances of lands, &c. from private individuals to the Crown. They are calendared in the volume entitle "Rotuli Regis Caroli, &c."

See also "SPECIFICATION AND SURRENDER ROLLS," described under the title of SPECIFICATIONS OF PATENT INVENTIONS.

TREATY ROLLS. See ALMAIN, FRENCH, ROMAN, AND VASCON ROLLS.

VASCON ROLLS. 26 Henry III. to 7 Edward IV. The Vascon or Gascon Rolls form a branch of the series of Rolls preserved in the Tower of London, relating to the affairs of the French provinces and other foreign countries, and generally known as Treaty Rolls. They contain Treaties, Truces, Orders, Summonses, letters of safe-conduct and protection, and Grants of offices, lands, &c. relating to Gascony, whilst that province was under the dominion of the Kings of England. The earliest Vascon Rolls are of the 26th, 27th, and 39th years of Henry the Third, but the regular series does not begin till 3 Edward I., from which period it extends to the seventh year of Edward IV. There are also amongst the regular series of Charter and Patent Rolls, rolls relating to the affairs of Gascony, and also containing such Charters and Grants as were made by the King when in France, dated 37 & 38 and 39 Henry III. respectively. See also the "GASCON PETITIONS," &c., described under the title FRANCE, ENGLISH POSSESSIONS IN. Selections from the Vascon Rolls are printed by Carte in his "Catalogue des Rolles Gascons, Normans, et Francais."

Transcript in full. 26 to 38 Hen. III., entitled "Rôles " Gascons, transcrits et publiés par Francisque Michel. " Tom. 1. A.D. 1242–1254."

CHANCERY ENROLMENTS (VARIOUS) — (continued).

" WATSON'S ROLL." A Patent Roll of divers years of Elizabeth, containing certain grants and other instruments which had been kept in his possession by one Watson, a clerk of the Great Seal between the 30th and 40th years of Elizabeth, on whose death they were found and enrolled. It is now placed with the regular series of the Patent Rolls. (Indexed in the volume entitled " De diversis annis.")

WELSH ROLLS. 5 Edward I. to 23 Edward I. The Welsh Rolls commence with the proceedings relating to the Treaty between Edward I. and Llewellyn, Prince of Wales, concluded at Aberconway in the year 1277. From that date they contain all the instruments which passed the Great Seal touching the Principality and its Marches, until that country was thoroughly subdued and incorporated with England.

Calendar. 5 to 23 Edw. I. See Ayloffe's " Calendar of Ancient Charters, &c."

CHANCERY ENROLMENTS (PALATINATE OF CHESTER).

PATENT OR REMEMBRANCE ROLLS OF THE PALATINATE OF CHESTER, CALLED " RECOGNIZANCE ROLLS." 1 Edw. II. to 1 Will. IV. These rolls contain the enrolments of Charters, Letters Patent, Fines, Deeds, Wills, and other important matters relating to the Palatinate. They appear to have been denominated " Recognizance Rolls " because the recognizances for debt are generally entered on the first membrane.

Inventory. Report XXI., App. pp. 27–32.

Alphabetical Calendar. Printed in Reports XXXVI., XXXVII., and XXXIX.

CHANCERY ENROLMENTS (PALATINATE OF DURHAM).

CHANCERY ROLLS OF THE PALATINATE OF DURHAM. From the Pontificate of Bishop Bury to that of Bishop Maltby. 1333 to 1836. [*Cursitors' Records, Nos. 29 to 134.*] These rolls contain enrolments of the recognizances of debts in the Chancery of Durham, of Letters Patent, Charters. Pleas and Processes, Commissions, Pardons, Grants of Wardship and other Grants, Licenses to Alienate, Inquisitions, Private Deeds, Leases, Releases, and other documents of a similar nature.

CHANCERY ENROLMENTS (PALATINATE OF DURHAM)—(continued).

CHANCERY ROLLS OF THE PALATINATE OF DURHAM—(continued).

Calendars of these Rolls from the commencement to the end of James I. have been printed as follows:—

Report XXXI., App. I., pp. 42-168. Bps. Bury and Hatfield (1333-1366).

Report XXXII., App. I., pp. 265-330. Bps. Hatfield and Fordham (1366-1388).

Report XXXIII., App. I., pp. 43-210. Bps. Skirlaw and Langley (1388-1437).

Report XXXIV., App. I., pp. 163-264. Bp. Neville (1438-1457).

Report XXXV., App. I., pp. 76-156. Bps. Booth and Dudley (1457-1483).

Report XXXVI., App. I., pp. 1-160. Bps. Sherwood, Fox, Severs, Bainbridge, Ruthall, and Wolsey (1485-1529).

Report XXXVII., App. I., pp. 1-171. Bps. Tunstall, Barnes, Hutton, and Matthew (1530-1606).

Report XL., App., pp. 480-520 Bp. James (1606-1617).

INROLMENTS OF DEEDS. Phil. & Mary and Elizabeth. A bundle of 33 Instruments.

[*Cursitors' Records, No.* 156.]

Do. 5 to 36 Elizabeth. A bundle of 126 Instruments.

[*Cursitors' Records, No.* 155.]

CHANCERY ENROLMENTS (PALATINATE AND DUCHY OF LANCASTER).

Palatinate of Lancaster.

PATENT ROLLS.

No. 1. 5-11 John D. of Lanc. (4-10 Ric. II.)
No. 2. John D. of Lanc. and Hen. IV. (fragments).
No. 3. 1-7 Hen IV.
No. 4. 11-13 Hen. VI.
No. 5. 14-18 „
No. 6. 20-22 „
No. 7. 23-28 „
No. 8. 1-5 Hen. VII.
No. 9. 17-20 „
No. 10. 21 „

Calendar. Report XL., App., pp. 521-545.

CHANCERY ENROLMENTS (PALATINATE AND DUCHY OF LANCASTER)—(continued).

Palatinate of Lancaster—(continued).

CLOSE ROLLS.

No. 1. 11–14 Hen. IV.
No. 2. 31–36 Hen. VI.
No. 3. 1–9 Edw. IV.

Calendar. Report XXXVII., App., pp. 172–179.

The following Chancery Rolls of the Palatinate of Lancaster, are deposited with the Miscellaneous Records of the Duchy of Lancaster (Div. XXV.) :—

LETTERS PATENT, LETTERS CLOSE, CHARTERS, AND FINES, ROLLS OF.

4 Henry, D. of Lancaster. 1 roll.
[*Chancery Rolls, D. of Lanc., No.* 1.]
4–11 Henry, D. of Lancaster. 1 roll.
[*Do.* *No.* 2.]
1–12 John, D. of Lancaster. 1 roll.
[*Do.* *No.* 3.]
1–2 Henry IV. (fragment). 1 roll.
[*Do.* *No.* 4.]
3–12 Henry IV. 1 roll.
[*Do.* *No.* 5.]
1–10 Henry V. 1 roll.
[*Do.* *No.* 6.]
1–18 Henry VI. 1 roll.
[*Do.* *No.* 7.]

Calendar. Report XXXII., App. I., pp. 331–365 ; and Report XXXIII., App. I., pp. 1–42.

Duchy of Lancaster.

LETTERS PATENT, WARRANTS, GRANTS, LEASES AND COMMISSIONS, ROLLS OF.

19–39 Henry VI. 22 rolls.
[*Chancery Rolls, D. of Lanc., Nos.* 8 to 29.]
1–11 Edward IV. 11 rolls.
[*Do.* *Nos.* 30 to 40.]
12–17 Edward IV. 6 rolls.
[*Do.* *Nos.* 41 to 46.]

WARRANTS, ROLLS OF (RELATING TO OFFICES AND MATTERS OF REVENUE).

12–18 Edward IV 6 rolls.
[*Do.* *Nos.* 47 to 52.]

INDENTURES, LEASES, HOMAGES, &c., ROLLS OF

19–39 Henry VI. 1 roll.
[*Do.* *No.* 53.]
1–18 Edward IV. 5 rolls.
[*Do.* *Nos.* 54 to 58.]

CHANCERY ENROLMENTS (PALATINATE AND DUCHY OF LANCASTER)—(continued).

Duchy of Lancaster—(continued).

PRESENTATIONS, ROLLS OF.

19–38 Hen. VI. 1 roll.

[*Do.* *No.* 59.]

1–17 Edward IV. 2 rolls.

[*Do.* *Nos.* 60 *and* 61.]

CHANCERY FILES.

The documents originally preserved " *in Filaciis* " or on the Files of Chancery, consisted of warrants or drafts for the original Writs, &c. issued by the authority of the Lord Chancellor under the Great Seal, most of which were subsequently enrolled on the Patent, Close, and Fine Rolls, or on the Treaty Rolls, Pardon Rolls, Protection Rolls, and other Miscellaneous Rolls of the Court of Chancery.

The more important of these documents appear to have been removed at various times, and formed into distinct classes, such as the Royal Letters, Privy Seals, &c., the residue consisting principally of Writs of Certiorari and other Writs returnable into Chancery, Judicial Writs of various kinds, Writs and other documents relating to proceedings under the Statute Staple, and of Warrants for Pardons, Protections, and Safe-Conducts, with other documents of minor importance.

CHANCERY FILES. (TOWER SERIES.)

The Tower Series of CHANCERY FILES extends in date from the reign of Edward I. to that of Charles II., and their present contents may be briefly summarized as follows :—

WRITS of three kinds, *i.e.,*

(1.) WRITS JUDICIAL, including :—

Writs of Attachment ;

    „   Scire Facias ;

    „   Subpœna ;

    „   Corpus cum Causa ;

    „   Assumpsit ;

    „   Levari facias ;

    „   de Custodia Pacis ;

    „   de Odio et Atia ;

    „   Distringas.

(2.) WRITS OF CERTIORARI WITH THE RETURNS THERETO.

(3.) WRITS ENROLLED, consisting of :—

Writs of Allocate and Liberate ;

    „   Dedimus Potestatem ;

    „   Mort d'Ancestor ;

    „   Novel Disseisin ;

    „   Præcipe quod reddat ;

    „   Appointment of Coroners, Verderers, &c.

    „   Appointment of Justices of Assize.

CHANCERY FILES—(continued).

LETTERS AND WARRANTS OF ATTORNEY.

WRITS, RECOGNIZANCES AND OTHER PROCEEDINGS ON THE STATUTE STAPLE.

CHANCERY FILES. (PETTY BAG OFFICE SERIES), OR " BREVIA REGIA."

The Bundles of " BREVIA REGIA," formerly in the Petty Bag Office, which extend in date from 41 Elizabeth to 31 Victoria, are very similar in nature to the "Chancery Files," of which they may in fact be said to form a continuation.

These contain Writs of Certiorari with the Returns thereto ; Writs of Scire Facias ; of ad quod Damnum; of Dedimus Potestatem (to swear Masters Extraordinary in Chancery, Justices of the Peace, Sheriffs, &c.); Writs for electing Coroners, Verderers, and Regarders of Forests; Writs of Summons to Serjeants-at-Law ; &c., &c.

Indexes. Eliz. to 16 Vict. 11 Vols. MS.

CHANCERY FILES. (ROLLS CHAPEL OFFICE SERIES).

Documents of a nature very similar to the foregoing will also be found amongst the Miscellaneous Bundles from the Rolls Chapel Office, formerly known as the " Arrow Bundle," the " Horn Bundle," and so on, which no doubt originally constituted a branch of the Chancery Files.

CHANNEL ISLANDS.

CHANNEL ISLANDS DOCUMENTS (CHANCERY).

The following are amongst the Miscellaneous Rolls, &c. (Bundle 2.)

No 1. A roll of Inquisitions relating to Tenures, in the Island of Jersey. 2 Edw. I.

No. 2. A similar roll for the Island of Guernsey. 2 Edw. I.

No. 3. Presentments of Jurors in various parishes in Jersey and Guernsey, with Transcripts of Charters relating to the Liberties of the Island of Guernsey. Temp. Edw. 1.

No. 4. The Petition of the inhabitants of Jersey against the Ministers of the King and of Otto Grandison. 2 Edw. II.

No. 5. A roll of similar petitions addressed to the King and Council. 2 Edw. II.

No. 6. A Transcript of the King's Writs, &c., relating to the Pleas and complaints against his ministers and those of Otto Grandison. [The Pleas, together with these Writs are enrolled in full on the Assize Rolls.] 2 Edw. II.

No. 7. A Transcript of Proceedings before the Bailiff, &c. of Jersey, relating to the Manor of Wyncelays. 9 Edw. [III.]

No. 8. Inquisitions concerning Manors, Lands, Advowsons, &c. in Jersey, which ought to be escheated to the king. 7 Hen. VIII.

No. 9. Commission and Inquisition concerning the Ancient Customs of the Island of Guernsey. 21 Eliz.

CHANNEL ISLANDS—(continued).

CHANNEL ISLANDS DOCUMENTS (EXCHEQUER, Q. R.).

Edward III. to Elizabeth. These consist of Accounts, Extents, and Inquisitions relating to the Issues of the aforesaid Islands, and to their rights, privileges, and customs, respecting which very minute information is given. Nearly the whole of these belong to the reign of Edward III. Many similar documents will be found amongst the Miscellanea of the Treasury of the Receipt.

Descriptive Slips.

Assize Rolls relating to the Channel Islands, from Edw I. to Edw. III., will be found in the General Series of Eyre and Assize Rolls. (See Lists and Indexes, No. IV., 1894.)

For State Papers relating to the Channel Islands see printed Calendars of Domestic State Papers, and also List of Volumes of State Papers. (Lists and Indexes, No. III., 1894.)

CHARITIES.

CHARITABLE USES, PROCEEDINGS RELATING TO (CHANCERY, PETTY BAG OFFICE).

These consist of—

1. Commissions, Inquisitions, and Decrees of Commissioners appointed under the Statute 43 Eliz. to inquire respecting lands given to Charitable Uses. 43 Eliz. to 8 Geo. II. 60 Bundles.

2. Inrolments of the Confirmations and Exonerations of Decrees by the said Commissioners. 8 Jas. I. to 1743. 37 Parts or Rolls.

3. Depositions, Interrogatories, &c. 23 Bundles.

4. Exceptions, Answers, and Replications to Decrees. 21 Bundles.

Calendar. I Vol. MS.

CHARITABLE TRUSTS, PETITIONS AND REPORTS ON, &c.

A volume entitled "Corporation Reports," 1836 to 1848, amongst the Reports and Certificates of the Court of Chancery, contains Reports by the Masters in Chancery relating to Charitable Trusts in various Boroughs throughout England, arranged alphabetically under the names of the Boroughs or "Corporations." *Index.* 1 Vol. MS.

There is also a set of Petitions for the appointment of Charity Trustees, with an *Index* in 1 Vol. MS.

Schemes for the Administration of Charities will also be found amongst the Masters' Reports in Chancery.

CHARITIES, TRUST DEEDS RELATING TO. Enrolled on the Close Rolls of Chancery subsequent to Statute 9 Geo. II. cap. 36.

Calendar. 9 Geo. II. to 1865. Printed as an Appendix to the Deputy Keeper's Thirty-second Report.

CHARITIES—(continued).

CHARITABLE USES, &c., INQUISITIONS AND DECREES RESPECTING. (PALATINATE OF LANCASTER.)

Commonwealth to George I. 1 Bundle.

MINUTE BOOK OF COMMISSIONERS APPOINTED TO INQUIRE INTO THE EXECUTION OF THE LAWS FOR THE RELIEF OF THE POOR AND THE ADMINISTRATION OF GIFTS FOR PIOUS USES. 1631.

[*S.P. Dom. Car. I. Vol.* 213.]

ORPHAN'S FUND. ACCOUNTS OF THE CHAMBERLAINS OF THE CITY OF LONDON. 1694 to 1826.

[*Audit Office, " Declared Accounts." Bundles* 1907 *to* 1921.]

CHARTERS AND GRANTS (ROYAL).

The term Charters, or Cartæ, was originally applied to deeds of gift and covenants between private persons, and signified any deed or writing by which lands, tenements, or privileges were conveyed from one person to another. The *Royal Charter* on the other hand was the instrument employed by the sovereign in granting liberties, privileges, immunities and exemptions, and also lands, tenements, and other possessions, both to private individuals, and to towns and other corporate bodies. Like the Letters Patent —from which they were distinguished by being always executed in the presence of witnesses, and also by a slight variation in the form of the address, that of the Charter being "To the Archbishops, Bishops, Abbots, Priors, Earls, Barons, &c. greeting," whilst that of the Patent was, "To all to whom these Presents shall come."—the Royal Charters were passed under the Great Seal, and from 1 John to 8 Henry VIII. were enrolled on a distinct set of rolls, denominated Charter Rolls. From the latter date, the Charter Rolls were discontinued, all grants from the Crown being thenceforward made in the form of Letters Patent, and enrolled with other instruments passing the Great Seal on the Patent Rolls.

The Royal Charters were of two kinds :

1. *Original Charters,* referring to lands, tenements, and liberties not before granted.

2. *Charters of Confirmation,* or of *Inspeximus and Confirmation,* the first of which simply confirmed previous grants without reciting them ; whilst the second recited the previous charters verbatim,—each recital being preceded by the words " Inspeximus quandam cartam in hec verba "—and then ratified and confirmed them, sometimes with additional liberties and privileges.

CHARTERS AND GRANTS (ROYAL)—(continued.)

Grants from the Crown of Lands, Tenements, Honours Dignities, Annuities, Pensions, Wardships, Liberties, and Privileges, together with Crown Leases, Licenses of various kinds, and at a later period, Charters of Incorporation, &c., were made in the form of Letters Patent, and enrolled on the Patent Rolls of the Court of Chancery or on the several Records of the Court of Exchequer, relating to the Revenues of the Crown.

Until the fifth year of Richard II. no enrolment or exemplification could be received in evidence in either of the King's Courts, the production of the original instrument under the Great Seal being always required. Owing, however, to the tumults and insurrections in the Kingdom, many persons having been deprived by fire or otherwise of their deeds and evidences, it was in that year enacted that persons so situated should have copies or "exemplifications" under the Great Seal of such Charters, Deeds, and Muniments as were enrolled in the several courts, such exemplifications to have the full force and effect of the original documents. It was not, however, till the reign of Edward the Sixth that an Act of Parliament was passed rendering an exemplification, constat, or enrolment of all Letters Patent granted since the 27th year of Henry VIII. of the same force and effect, and as valid as the original Patent, which Act was confirmed and amplified by Elizabeth in the 13th year of her reign. From that time to the present, the Courts have not only received copies of enrolments made since 27 Henry VIII. as evidence, but also attested copies of all records made at any time before that period.

The power of the Crown to dispose of its Land Revenue by Grant was limited by the Statute 1 Anne, cap. 7, which, whilst providing for the Civil List of that reign, enacted that no grant shall be made of any manors, lands, tenements, rents, tithes, woods, or other hereditaments (advowsons of churches and vicarages only excepted) whether belonging to the Crown in right of the Crown of England, or as part of the Principality of Wales, or of the Duchy or County Palatine of Lancaster, for any longer term than thirty-one years, or three lives.

This, however, did not disable the Crown from granting away or restoring estates forfeited for treason or felony, or acquired by purchase from the Privy Purse, or otherwise privately obtained.

The following are the principal classes of records on which the enrolments of Grants and Charters are to be found.

CHARTERS AND GRANTS (ROYAL)—(continued).

Chancery.

1. The CARTÆ ANTIQUÆ ROLLS which contain transcripts of Charters and Grants from the time of Ethelbert to the reign of Edward I.

2. The CHARTER ROLLS from 1 John to 8 Hen. VIII. (Subsequent to 8 Hen. VIII. the Charters are enrolled on the Patent Rolls.)

3. The CONFIRMATION ROLLS from 1 Ric. III. to 1 Car. I.

(Before 1 Ric. III. the Confirmations of Charters are enrolled on the Charter and Patent Rolls, and subsequent to the latter date, again on the Patent Rolls.)

4. The EXTRACTA DONATIONUM or EXTRACT ROLLS from 45 Hen. III. to 6 Ric. II.

5. The PATENT ROLLS from 3 John to 50 Victoria.

See **CHANCERY ENROLMENTS.**

For Leases of Crown Lands, and Sales of *Fee-Farm Rents*, see also **LEASES** and **CROWN LANDS AND RENTS** respectively.

Exchequer.

1. THE ORIGINALIA AND MEMORANDA ROLLS.

Transcripts of all Grants, Leases, &c., in which any rent was reserved, or for which any service was to be rendered to the Crown, were transmitted to the Exchequer for enrolment on the " ORIGINALIA ROLLS," in order that such rents or payments might be duly put in charge by the officers of that Court, and enrolments of Charters and Grants are frequently to be found on the " MEMORANDA ROLLS," both of the Queen's Remembrancer and of the Lord Treasurer's Remembrancer, and also on the Great Rolls of the Exchequer or " PIPE ROLLS."

2. THE PATENT AND PRIVY SEAL BOOKS AND ROLLS.

Grants of Offices, Annuities, Pensions, and all Letters Patent authorising any payment to be made at the Receipt of the Exchequer since the beginning of the reign of Henry VIII., are entered or enrolled in the Patent and Privy Seal Books and Rolls of the Pells' and Auditors' Departments. See **RECEIPTS AND ISSUES OF THE EXCHEQUER.**

Grants and Charters under the Seals of the Duchies of Lancaster and Cornwall and of the Palatinates of Chester, Durham, and Lancaster form distinct series of enrolments.

There are also amongst the Miscellanea various collections of Royal Charters and Letters Patent, both originals

CHARTERS AND GRANTS (ROYAL)—(continued).

Exchequer—(continued).

PATENT AND PRIVY SEAL BOOKS AND ROLLS—(continued).

and transcripts, a list of which is given below ; as also of the " PARTICULARS FOR GRANTS " and " TRANSCRIPTS OF GRANTS " amongst the Records of the late Augmentation Office and elsewhere.

Various Collections.

CHARTERS AND LETTERS PATENT, ORIGINAL AND TRAN-SCRIPTS. (CHANCERY.)

The following are amongst the " Miscellaneous Rolls, &c." (Chancery) : —

Grants and Letters Patent of Queen Philippa, from 4 to 10 Edw. III. No. $\frac{11}{12}$.

A file of Grants and Claims of Markets and Fairs, Free Warren, &c. John to Hen. VI. Bundle 6.

> [*The latter is calendared in Palmer's Indexes,*
> *Vol.* 106.]

Do. (EXCHEQUER, Q. R.)

Henry I. to James I. Two bundles entitled " DEEDS (VARIOUS)," containing, *inter alia*, very early Transcripts of Royal Charters to Religious Houses, &c. with a few original Charters of a similar description. The original Deeds formerly in this collection are now included in ANCIENT DEEDS, SERIES D.

Descriptive Slips.

Do. (EXCHEQUER, Q. R.)

Edward VI. to George I. A few documents only, relating principally to the Jointures of Henrietta Maria, Queen of Charles I., and of Catherine of Portugal, the Queen of Charles II. Several of these are splendidly illuminated.

Descriptive List. Report XX., App., p. 146.

Do. (EXCHEQUER, AUGMENTATION OFFICE.)

Two large volumes entitled " CHARTÆ ANTIQUÆ DIVERSORUM REGUM," Ric. II. to Car. II., containing original Royal Charters of various dates, Transcripts of Papal Bulls, and other documents relating to the several Religious Houses.

> [*Misc. Books, Vols.* 29 and 30.]

Do. (EXCHEQUER, TREASURY OF THE RECEIPT.)

Transcripts of Charters are contained in the two volumes known as the " Registrum Munimentorum."

See **REGISTERS AND BOOKS OF REMEM-BRANCE.**

CHARTERS AND GRANTS (ROYAL)—(continued).
Various Collections—(continued.)
CHARTERS AND LETTERS PATENT, &c.—(continued).

There is also amongst the Chapter House Records an original CHARTER OF ALFONSO, KING OF CASTILE, dated 1 Nov. 1254, conferring knighthood on Prince Edward, the eldest son of Henry III. This is finely illuminated and has a golden seal attached.

Many Transcripts of Charters and Grants relating to Religious Foundations are also to be found amongst the MISCELLANEOUS BOOKS of the Chapter House. These are described under the head of **MONASTIC FOUNDATIONS, &c.**

Grants, Particulars for, &c.
GRANTS, PARTICULARS FOR. (EXCHEQUER, AUGMENTA-TION OFFICE.)

Henry VIII. to James I., and Miscellaneous.

These consist of the "Requests to Purchase" which were addressed in writing to the Commissioners appointed for the Sale of the possessions of the late dissolved Monasteries, and of other lands in the hands of the Crown, by all persons wishing to acquire any portion of such lands, accompanied by "Particulars" of the property required, giving a full description of the premises and their value, stating to what monastery or individual they had belonged before being seized into the King's hands, what leases, if any, had been made thereof, and what fines were payable thereon. These particulars were examined by the Officers of the Crown, who certified to their correctness, whereupon the "fiat dimissio" was issued. They are contained in 36 portfolios.

Inventory. Henry VIII. Printed. Report IX., App. II., pp. 148–232, and Report X., App. II., pp. 223–309. Arranged alphabetically under the names of the Grantees.

Index Locorum. Henry VIII. 4 Vols. MS.
Calendar and Index Locorum. Edw. VI. 3 Vols. MS.
Do.   do.   Ph. & Mary to James I. 2 Vols. MS.

Particulars for Grants of the Manor of Boxley and others, in Kent, to Thos. Wyatt. Henry VIII.
[*Misc. Books, Vol.* 156]

Do.   (MISCELLANEA, EXCHEQUER Q. R.)

Edward VI. to James I. These are of a similar nature to the Particulars for Grants amongst the Records of the Court of Augmentations, many of them being Books or Portions of Books of Enrolment of such Particulars.
Descriptive Slips.

CHARTERS AND GRANTS (ROYAL)—(continued).

Grants, Particulars for, &c.—(continued).

GRANTS, PARTICULARS FOR. (EXCHEQUER, TR. OF THE RECEIPT.)

Edward VI. 2 Vols., with an Index in 1 Vol. These relate chiefly to the Possessions of Colleges and Chantries.

[*Misc. Books, Vols.* 258, 259, *and* 260.]

Do. (STATE PAPER OFFICE). Charles I. 13 cases. See printed "Calendars of State Papers."

GRANTS OF OFFICES, PARTICULARS FOR. (AUGMENTATION OFFICE.)

See **OFFICES AND APPOINTMENTS.**

GRANTS, TRANSCRIPTS OF. (EXCHEQUER, AUGMENTATION OFFICE.)

Edward VI. to Chas. I. Five volumes, containing copies, on paper, of various Grants and Indentures.

[*Misc. Books, Vols.* 151 to 155.]

GRANTS OF ARMS. 1509 to 1583 and 1647.

A case containing a few original Grants of Arms, some of which are finely illuminated. [*S. P. Dom. Miscellaneous. Vol.* 1.]

Grants of Land in the Colonies.

These are registered in the Offices of the Secretaries of the several Colonies. The following volumes, containing entries of such grants will be found amongst the Colonial Office Records:—

GRANTS OF LAND.— Carolina. 1674 to 1765. [*Col. Entry Books, Vol.* 23.]

„ „ New York. 1665 to 1765. [*Col. Entry Books, Vol.* 71.]

„ „ To Discoverers in America. From Henry VII. [*Col. Papers, America and West Indies, Vol.* 627.]

„ „ North Carolina. 1725 to 1760. [*Board of Trade Papers, Carolina, North, Vol.* 42.]

„ „ Georgia. 1760 to 1768. [*Board of Trade Papers, Georgia, Vol.* 52.]

„ „ Jamaica. 1754. "List of Land-holders." [*Board of Trade Papers, Jamaica, Vol.* 148.]

„ „ Plantations General. 1752 to 1771. [*Board of Trade Papers, Plantations General, Vol.* 57.]

CHARTERS AND GRANTS OF THE DUCHY OF LANCASTER.

ROYAL CHARTERS. William II. to Henry VII. 9 boxes.
    Calendar. William II. to Richard II. Printed.
Report XXXI., App., pp. 1–41. This Calendar refers
to those Charters only which passed the Great Seal of
England. When not otherwise referred to in the Calendar
as "Ancient Transcripts," the Original Charters, with, in
most cases, the Great Seal attached, are indicated.

    Do. William II. to Edward III. 3 Vols. MS.
called " The Register of Royal Charters."

THE GREAT COWCHERS, OR "CARTÆ REGUM." Henry
III. to Richard II.

Two large and handsomely illuminated volumes, containing enrolments of Charters and Grants relating to the
possessions of the Duchy between the foregoing dates,
together with Perambulations and Pleas of the Forests in
Lancashire and Yorkshire. A duplicate of the first of
these volumes exists amongst the Miscellaneous Books of the
Exchequer, Q. R. (Vol. 8); the handwriting is, however,
apparently of a much earlier period than that of the Great
Cowchers, and the whole volume is splendidly rubricated.
It is described on the fly-leaf as " Liber Johannis
Maynard," by whom it is stated to have been delivered
into Court on the 2nd June, 26 Charles II.
    Calendar and Index. 2 Vols., MS.

GRANTS, REGISTERS OF, as follows :—

    John to Edward IV. 9 Vols. (*Div. xi., Nos.* 11 *to* 19.)
        Calendars and Indices Locorum in two Vols., entitled
        " *Abstracts and Indexes of Registers.*"

    Richard III. 1 Vol. (*Div., xi., No.* 20.)
        Calendar at the commencement of the Vol.

    Henry VII. 1 Vol. (*Div., xi., No.* 21.)
        Calendar at the commencement of the Vol.

    Henry VIII. 1 Vol. (Div. xi., *No.* 22.)
        Index in the Vol. entitled, " *Index to Patents, Hen*
        VIII. to 1760."

    Edw. VI., Phil. and Mary and 1–10 Eliz. 1 Vol. (*Div.
    xi., No.* 23.)
        Index in the Vol., entitled " *Index to Patents,*"
        Hen. VIII. to 1760.

    Jas. I to Will. III. 1 Vol. (*Div. xi., No.* 24.) Con-
    taining Grants, Patents, Exemplifications of Decrees
    &c.
        Index at the commencement of the Vol.

CHARTERS AND GRANTS OF THE DUCHY OF LANCASTER—(continued).

GRANTS, REGISTERS OF—(continued).

Eliz. to Geo. I. (Surrenders, &c.) 1 Vol. (Div., xi., No. 25.) Containing Surrenders, Grants, Leases, &c., chiefly between the reigns of Eliz. and Geo. I., with a few transcripts of documents of a much earlier date. (*Index in the Vol.*)

1711 to 1730 1 Vol. (*Div., xi., No.* 26.)

4 to 14 Geo. II. 1 Vol. (*Div. xi., No.* 27.)

Register of Grants, &c., relating to the Manor of Daventry. 59 Edw. III. (*Div. xi., No.* 9.)

Extracts of Charters, &c. relating to the Manor of Langeney, in the Rape of Pevensey, co. Sussex, Temp. Edw. IV. (*Div. xi., No.* 10.)

Leases, Patents, Commissions, and Presentations. 13 to 44 Eliz. (*Div. xi., No.* 99.)

Leases granted by the Earls of Hereford and Rutland. Temp. Henry VIII. (*Div. xi., No.* 100.)

Grants, 20 James I. to 14 Charles I. (*Div. xi., No.* 102.)

Grants to the City of London; temp. Car. I. (An abstract of the Grant to Edward Ditchfield and others, as Trustees for the City of London, 4 Car. I., so far as it relates to the Duchy of Lancaster). (*Div. xi., No.* 104.)

GRANTS AND LEASES, AUDITORS' ENTRY BOOKS OF.

North Auditor's Books. Henry VII. to 1765. 35 Vols.

South Auditor's Books. Henry VIII. to 1767. 22 Vols.

List. Report XXX., App., p. 5.

ORIGINAL PRIVY SEALS AND SIGNED BILLS FOR GRANTS. 1 Hen. VII. to 1767. 43 Bundles.

Index, 1 *Vol., entitled, " Index to Grants in Fee."*

DRAFT PATENTS (WITH THE PARTICULARS ANNEXED). Phil. & Mary to Geo. II. 46 Bundles. These appear to relate to Grants of Offices only.

CINQUE PORTS.

A volume relating to the Jurisdiction and Customs of the Cinque Ports, including a long and curious collection of bye-laws entitled " The Custumal of Rye." 1578.

[*S.P., Dom. Eliz., Vol.* 128.]

62

COMMISSIONS.

Commissions of Array, Commissions of Lords Lieutenant of Counties, of Justices of the Peace, of Oyer and Terminer, of Gaol Delivery, and Special Commissions of all kinds are enrolled on the back of the Patent Rolls.

Commissions for opening and proroguing Parliament, for giving the Royal Assent to Bills, with Commissions of the Peace, Commissions of Sewers, and other Miscellaneous Commissions of more modern dates, are preserved at the Crown Office in Chancery.

Chancery.

COMMISSIONS FOR BETTER FORTIFYING AND SECURING HARBOURS AND DOCKS, &c. (from the Crown Office). See **FORTIFICATIONS.**

COMMISSIONS OF BANKRUPTCY. These are kept at the Bankruptcy Offices in Lincoln's Inn.

Do. OF FORFEITED ESTATES, &c. See **ESCHEATS, ATTAINDERS, AND FORFEITURES.**

Do. OF LUNACY AND IDIOTCY. See **LUNACY.**

Do. OF SEWERS. See **SEWERS.**

SPECIAL COMMISSIONS (CHANCERY, PETTY BAG OFFICE). James I. to Victoria. 18 Bundles, containing Commissions of Enquiry respecting estates forfeited to the Crown, and various other matters, with the Inquisitions and traverses thereon. They are arranged under the following heads :—

ALIENS. 15 Geo. 2 to 9 Vict.

CONCEALED LANDS. Car. II. to Wm. & Mary.

DEPOPULATIONS. 5 James I.

DERELICT LANDS. James II. to Vict.

ESCHEATS (FOR WANT OF AN HEIR). 6 Car. I. to 52 Vict.

FORFEITURES OF OFFICES. 5 Car. I. to 4 Will. IV.

MISCELLANEOUS INQUIRIES.

MURDERS AND FELONIES. 12 Car. I. to Victoria.

PERAMBULATIONS OF FORESTS. Car. I.

PORTSMOUTH HARBOUR, &c. Anne.

SUPERSTITIOUS USES, LANDS GIVEN TO. 33 Car. II. to 11 Wm. III.

SURVEY OF THE MANOR OF EAST GREENWICH. 1696.

TREASON. 5 Car. I. to Anne.

Index. 1 Vol. MS.

Exchequer, Queen's Remembrancer.

SPECIAL COMMISSIONS. Elizabeth to Victoria, and Miscellaneous.

These are Commissions of Inquiry with the Returns thereto relating to CONCEALED LANDS, the POSSESSIONS OF

COMMISSIONS—(continued).

Excheqeur, Queen's Remembrancer—(continued).

SPECIAL COMMISSIONS—(continued).

PERSONS ATTAINTED and of DEBTORS TO THE CROWN; ENCROACHMENTS and INTRUSIONS; TITHES, WOODS, MARSH LANDS, SEA BANKS, MILLS; the BOUNDARIES OF PORTS, &c., &c., and abound with Legal and Topographical information of the highest value and interest.

Descriptive Catalogue. Elizabeth to Victoria. Report XXXVIII. App., pp. 1–149. (Those of a date prior to Elizabeth, of which there are very few, are described in a Manuscript List referred to below.)

SPECIAL COMMISSIONS. Edward II. to Edward VI.

Four parcels amongst the Miscellanea (Nos. 818 to 821) containing documents of a similar nature to those above described.

Descriptive List.

Many Special Commissions of Inquiry with the Returns are enrolled on the Memoranda Rolls of the Exchequer, both of the Queen's Remembrancer's and Lord Treasurer's Remembrancer's Departments.

Duchy of Lancaster.

COMMISSIONS, ORDERS, &c., ENTRY BOOKS OF. 1 Henry VIII. to 44 Elizabeth. 4 Vols. (*Div. xi., Nos.* 95 *to* 98.) *Index.* 1 Vol. MS.

COMMISSIONS FOR SPECIAL PURPOSES. 30 to 32 Eliz. 1 Bundle.

JUDGES' COMMISSIONS. 1675 to 1774. 9 bundles, containing Bills under the Royal Sign Manual, for Commissions appointing the Judges in the County Palatine of Lancaster.

COMMON PRAYER BOOKS.

Five Sealed Copies of the Book of Common Prayer, deposited pursuant to the Act of Uniformity, 14 Car. II. are amongst the Records of the following Courts.

Chancery. (Tower Series.)   1 copy.
Do.   (Rolls Chapel Series.)   „
Queen's Bench.   „
Common Pleas.   „
Exchequer, Queen's Remembrancer   „

CORNWALL, DUCHY OF.

The following documents relating to the Revenues, &c. of the Earldom and Duchy of Cornwall are amongst the Records of the Exchequer.

CORNWALL, DUCHY OF—(continued).
Exchequer, Augmentation Office.

ACQUITTANCES. James I. to Charles I.

Seven volumes containing the Receipts or Acquittances given by the Receivers of the Duchy to the Bailiffs, Reeves, and Farmers of the various Manors for the rent due from them, and also the Receipts of various Officers of the Duchy for their salaries and allowances.

[*Misc. Books, Vols.* 69 *to* 75.]

ASSESSION BOOK. 9 Elizabeth.

An Arrentation or " Assessment" of all lands, &c. in the Counties of Devon and Cornwall belonging to the Duchy of Cornwall and let on lease by the Commissioners or " Assessors" appointed for that purpose by Letters Patent dated 30 May, 9 Elizabeth.

[*Misc. Books, Vol.* 15.]

ASSESSION ROLLS. Edward III. to HENRY VII. 15 Rolls.

These contain the Arrentation or Assessment of all the " Assessionary" lands belonging to the Duchy, the leases of which were renewed or new leases granted every seven years. They give the names of all the Tenants, distinguishing them as " liberi" or " nativi," the amount of land, &c. taken by each, the rent payable therefor, and the name of the previous tenant.

LETTERS FROM SIR JULIUS CÆSAR AND OTHERS RELATING TO ESTATES IN THE DUCHY OF CORNWALL. 1612 to 1621. One volume.

[*Misc. Books, Vol.* 76.]

MISCELLANEOUS ACCOUNTS AND PAPERS. Edward III. to Charles II. 7 Portfolios.

These contain Miscellaneous Letters and Papers relating to the Woods and Revenues of the Duchy, Drafts (on paper) of Receiver's and Receiver Generals' Accounts, of Accounts relating to the Stannaries, and of Assession Rolls, with a few Articles of Inquiry at Assessions and the returns thereto.

MINISTERS' ACCOUNTS. 12 Edward III. to 1650.

See **MINISTERS' AND RECEIVERS' ACCOUNTS.**

STANNARY ROLLS. Edward I. to Philip and Mary.

Accounts of the Cunagium Stanni in Cornwall and Devon. 1 Box, containing 24 Rolls.

CORNWALL, DUCHY OF—(continued).

Exchequer, Augmentation Office—(continued).

MISCELLANEOUS ROLLS. Edw. III. to Charles I.

A box containing a few accounts relating to the Duchy of Cornwall, with Articles of Inquiry as to the Customs of Manors, &c., administered at the " Assessions" and the Returns thereto, belonging chiefly to the reigns of James I. and Charles I. See also MISCELLANEOUS ACCOUNTS AND PAPERS.

VALUATIONS OF SPIRITUALITIES AND TEMPORALITIES. [Henry VIII.] Two volumes containing a valuation taken by the Royal Commission of all the lands and goods, &c. in the Hundreds of East, West, Trigge, Kerrier, and others, in the County of Cornwall, apparently for the purpose of assessing a military levy.

The names of the inhabitants in each parish are given with the value of their goods, &c. and the amount to be levied from each in money or equipment.

[*Misc. Books, Vols.* 77 *and* 78.]

Exchequer, Queen's Remembrancer.

ACCOUNTS OF THE BAILIFFS OF EDMUND EARL OF CORNWALL. 24–25 Edward I. 1 Roll. Apparently an Exchequer Roll of the Earldom.

"CAPTIO SEISINÆ DUCATUS CORNUBIÆ." 11 Edward III. A survey or return of the whole of the possessions of the Duchy made by the Commissioners assigned in the 11th year of Edward III., to take seisin thereof to the use of the King's eldest son. 1 Roll.

Exchequer, Treasury of the Receipt.

COUNCIL BOOK OF THE DUCHY OF CORNWALL. 25–39 Edward III. This volume which is also known as the " White Book of Tenures in Cornwall," contains entries of all Writs, Warrants, &c. directed to the Seneschal and others of the Duchy of Cornwall, by Edward the Black Prince, from the 25th to the 39th year of Edward III.; and of the Petitions and other Proceedings before the Council of the Duchy during the same period.

RECEIVER GENERAL'S ACCOUNTS relating to the Duchy of Cornwall. Henry VII. and Henry VIII.

[*Misc. Books, Vol.* 56.]

CHARTERS, &c., TRANSCRIPTS OF.

A volume containing Transcripts of all Charters, Deeds, &c. belonging to Edmund late Earl of Cornwall. Temp. Edw. I. [*Misc. Books, Vol.* 57.]

CORONATIONS.

CORONATION ROLLS. (CHANCERY.) Edward II. to Victoria.
These contain the Commissions and Proceedings of the Commissioners appointed to hear and determine claims of service to be performed at Coronations, and also the oath taken and the declaration made and signed by the Sovereign when crowned.

The series is imperfect, Coronation Rolls existing for the following sovereigns only : Edward II., Henry IV., Henry V., James I., Charles II., James II., William and Mary, Anne, George I., George II., George IV., William IV., and Victoria.

The Coronation Oath of George III , and the Certificate of the Archbishop of Canterbury attached, and the Commissions for holding the Court of Claims at the Coronations of George IV., William IV., and Victoria, with the original Petitions and Claims are at the Chancery Crown Office.

Matters relating to Coronations are also enrolled on the early Close Rolls.

An account of the Coronation of Queen Eleanor (of Provence) in the 20th year of Henry III., with the claims of service thereat, is contained in the Red Book of the Exchequer. [Fol. 232.]

An account of the ceremony to be observed at the Coronation of Edward III., &c., will be found amongst the Miscellaneous Rolls, &c., Chancery. [No. ⅓⁸.]

The proceedings at the Coronation of Richard II. are enrolled on the Close Roll of 1 Rich. II., m. 45.

Those at the Coronation of Charles II. are amongst the Domestic State Papers. [Vol. xxxv., No. 38.]

Much information relating to the Ceremonies to be observed at Coronations, &c. will be found in the Records of the Lord Chamberlain's Department.
See **DEPARTMENTAL RECORDS.**
See also **WARDROBE AND HOUSEHOLD.**

CORONERS' INQUESTS.

By the Statute " de Officio Coronatoris," 4 Edward I., when any person was slain or died suddenly, the King's coroner was to summon a jury who were to inquire into the circumstances occasioning the death, and if any person were found guilty of the murder by this Inquisition the Coroner was to commit him to prison, and the witnesses were to be bound over to appear at the next assizes.

The Inquisition, whether the return was murder, manslaughter, or otherwise, was to be enrolled and returned to the Justices Itinerant at the next Gaol Delivery, or to be certified into the Court of King's Bench.

CORONERS' INQUESTS—(continued).

There are Coroners' Rolls from Edward I. to Henry VI., inclusive, amongst the Records of the Queen's Bench, and Coroners' Inquisitions of a later date will be found in the Bundles of Indictments of that Court. See **JUDICIAL PROCEEDINGS.**

From about 1760 the Coroners' Inquests are filed with the Clerks of the Peace of the several counties.

There are also distinct collections of Coroners' Inquests amongst the Records of the Queen's Bench, Crown Side, as follows :—

CORONERS' INQUISITIONS POST MORTEM.

1748 to 1767. 1 Bag, containing Inquisitions post mortem taken before the Coroners in various counties. (Those of an earlier date will be found on the bundles of Indictments.)

CORONERS' INQUISITIONS POST MORTEM (ON PRISONERS).

1747 to 1839. 2 Bags, containing Inquisitions post mortem on the prisoners who died in the King's Bench Prison.

COURT OR MANOR ROLLS.

The principal collections of Court Rolls or Manor Rolls existing in the Public Record Office are those of the Augmentation Office, those of the Duchy of Lancaster (calendared in the Deputy Keeper's 43rd Report), the Halmote Court Books of the Palatinate of Durham, and the Court Rolls belonging to the several Welsh Jurisdictions, Inventories of which have been printed in the 21st and 22nd Reports.

These (with the exception of the Halmote Court Books of Durham, referred to below), together with the numerous Court Rolls formerly existing amongst the various classes of Miscellanea or mixed with the Ministers' and Receivers' Accounts, have now been formed into one large series, an Inventory of which is in the press.

There are also various Books containing Court Rolls, as follows, all of which are referred to in the printed inventory :—

COURT ROLLS, RENTALS, &c., IN VARIOUS COUNTIES, TRANSCRIPTS OF. (EXCHEQUER, AUGMENTATION OFFICE.)

Edward III. to Elizabeth. 8 volumes.

[*Misc. Books, Vols. 79 to 86.*]

COURT ROLLS OF NEWTON, Co. LANC, &c.

Henry VIII. to Charles I. 1 Vol.

[*Misc Books, Vol. 134.*]

COURT OR MANOR ROLLS—(continued).

COURT ROLLS OF LANGENEY, &c. IN THE RAPE OF PEVEN-
SEY, Co. SUSSEX.   Edw. IV. to Hen. VI.
[*Registers of Grants, &c. D. of Lanc., Div. xi., No.* 10.]

HALMOTE COURT BOOKS (PALATINATE OF DURHAM.]
From the Pontificate of Bishop Hatfield to that of
Bishop Neil.   1349 to 1619.   17 Vols.   (Cursitor's
Records, Nos 12 to 28.)

The Halmote Courts were holden pursuant to the
Bishop's Commission under the Great Seal of the Palatinate before the Escheator of the Palatinate and other
persons thereto appointed, to receive surrenders of copyhold lands, and to admit such persons as had a right
thereto according to the custom ; to assess and settle all
such fines and amercements as arose within the said Courts
and to hear and determine all suits, complaints, &c. between
party and party which arose within the said county or elsewhere within the Palatinate of Durham.

Indexes.   1523 to 1587.   (Prothonotary's Indexes,
No. I.)   This is an ancient index containing (*inter alia*)
complete indexes to the Halmote Court Books of :—

(1.) Bp. Wolsey.   1523–1529.   (No. 22.)
(2.) Bp. Tunstall.   1530–1559.   (No. 23.)
(3.) *Sede vacante.*   1559–1576 and Bp. Barnes.   1577–
1587.   (No. 24.)

COURTS OF JUSTICE, REPORTS ON.

REPORTS OF COMMISSIONERS UPON INQUIRIES RESPECT-
ING COURTS OF JUSTICE. (CHANCERY, PETTY BAG
OFFICE).   1740 to 1864.   64 Reports.

CROWN LANDS AND RENTS.

During the earlier portion of the Feudal Period the
revenue of the Crown was derived to a very great extent
from its landed estates, and from the proceeds of the
forests, parks, and chases, the ownership of which formed
a part of the Royal Prerogative.   The Ancient Demesne
of the Crown, as recorded in Domesday Book, consisted of
1,422 Manors, besides lands in Middlesex and Shropshire,
the greater part of which descended to the Conqueror from
Edward the Confessor and his immediate relatives and
adherents.   A considerable distinction was made between
Ancient Demesnes of the Crown and those lands which it
acquired by its lucrative properties, viz., by Escheat, Forfeiture, or otherwise.   It appears to have been understood
that the Sovereign might dispose of the latter at pleasure,
but to alienate the Ancient Demesnes of the Crown was
considered not only inexpedient but even "impious."

CROWN LANDS AND RENTS—(continued)

No absolute restriction was, however, imposed on the Sovereign in this respect, exorbitant alienation on his part being generally counterbalanced by the action of his Parliament, which when further supplies were demanded seldom failed to *resume* what had been too lavishly disposed of.

The greater part of the Conqueror's possessions were dissipated by his immediate successor, who was, however, compelled to resume the grants he had made, and in consequence of similar profusion *Acts of Resumption* were passed in almost every reign during the 12th, 13th, and 14th centuries.

The lands accruing to the Crown in earlier times by *Escheat or Forfeiture* were very extensive. Amongst the more important of these Forfeitures may be mentioned the " *Terræ Normannorum,*" or lands held by the Normans in England which, on the separation of Normandy from the Crown of England, in the reign of Henry II., became vested in the King of England as having being forfeited by his rebellious subjects.

On the expulsion of the *Knights' Templars* from England in the reign of Edward II., their possessions were confiscated to the Crown, and formed a very important addition to the Royal revenues, the accounts of which occupy three large rolls.

The possessions of the *Alien Priories,* which were generally seized into the King's hands, on the breaking out of a war between England and France (being however restored to their owners on the conclusion of peace), were finally confiscated and placed at the King's disposal on the suppression of those houses in the second year of Henry V.

A very large increase of revenue accrued to the Crown by the dissolution of the Religious Houses in the reign of Henry VIII., for the collection and administration of which two new courts were erected, called respectively the *Court of General Surveyors* and the *Court of the Augmentations of the Revenues of the Crown.* The Records of these two courts, especially of the latter, are exceedingly voluminous and important, comprising *Accounts and Surveys of the Possessions of the Religious Houses* throughout England and Wales, with Deeds and other documents relating to the acquisition of land by *Purchase* or *Exchange* during the reigns of Henry VIII. and Edward VI.

The greater part of the Estates thus acquired were however alienated during the same reign, and soon after the accession of Edward the Sixth it became necessary to provide by further confiscation for the expenses of the kingdom, and accordingly the Estates of the Colleges, Chantries, Free Chapels, &c., to the number of over 2,374,

CROWN LANDS AND RENTS—(continued).

were seized into the King's hands. See **MONASTIC FOUNDATIONS, &c.**

The grants of Crown Lands made during the reign of Elizabeth were very numerous, as, in order to avoid un-popularity with her subjects by asking for supplies, she disposed of a considerable part of her domains, and an even greater profusion was exercised during the reign of James I. The extensive Surveys taken during the latter reign, which are now in the Land Revenue Office, tend, however, to show that great attention was paid to the management and improvement of estates as long as they remained in the hands of the Crown.

Charles the First, in his endeavour to support the expenses of his Government, without the aid of Parliament, sold many of the Estates of the Crown. At one time he borrowed 320,000*l.* from the City of London on the security of the Crown Lands, grants thereof being afterwards made for the repayment of the money. These grants, which were made to *Edw. Ditchfield and others* as *Trustees for the City*, in the 4th year of Charles I., occupy three entire Patent Rolls, each consisting of three parts.

Another method of raising money, which was frequently made use of during the reigns of Elizabeth, James I., and Charles I., was, by the discovery or pretended discovery of "*Concealed Lands*," that is to say, of lands which should be in the possession of the Sovereign, but which either by purchase, descent, or otherwise had come into the hands of private persons, whose titles thereto were altogether defective, to whom re-grants were offered on their compounding for the same with the Commissioners who were from time to time appointed for that purpose.

Almost all the Landed Estates of the Crown, together with the *Fee-Farm Rents* reserved on Grants from the Crown, were sold during the Commonwealth, being vested in Trustees for that purpose, by whose direction elaborate and careful Surveys of the Crown lands were taken, which form the collection known as *Parliamentary Surveys.* There are also amongst the Records of the Augmentation Office *Particulars and Contracts for the sale of Crown Lands and Fee-Farm Rents*, together with the *Minute Books of the Trustees* and other important documents of a similar nature.

Immediately after the Restoration all the sales made during the Commonwealth were declared void, and the King restored to the possession of his honours, lands, and hereditaments.

The Revenue is, however, supposed to have suffered largely by *concealments*, and by forbearance or favour to

CROWN LANDS AND RENTS—(continued).

bonâ fide purchasers, and to those who had promoted the Restoration.

Some different provision for the support of the Government being found necessary, the Feudal Tenures were abolished soon after the Restoration, and a permanent income of 1,200,000*l.* per annum settled on the King, of which the Royal demesnes, though much reduced in value, formed a part.

This income, however, being found altogether inadequate to his expenses, Acts were obtained in the 22nd and 23rd years of his reign, enabling him to dispose of the *Fee-Farm Rents* which, to a considerable extent, remained the Royal property. These rents were accordingly vested in Trustees for that purpose, by whom extensive sales were made, the *Deeds of Bargain and Sale* being enrolled on the Close Rolls.

The Land Revenue of the Crown underwent little change during the reign of James II., but the rewards bestowed by William III. on those who had aided in the Revolution, diminished it as effectually as the prodigality of Charles II. These frequent alienations of the Royal domains did not fail to draw the public attention, and in the first year of Queen Anne what is known as the *Civil List Act* was passed, by which it was enacted that no grant should be made of any manors, lands, tenements, &c. belonging to the Crown (advowsons of churches and vicarages only excepted) for a longer period than 31 years, or three lives.

This, however, did not apply to estates forfeited by treason or felony, or acquired by purchase out of the Privy Purse.

The several classes of documents illustrating the subject of Crown Lands and Fee-Farm Rents may be arranged under the following heads : (The Leases of Crown Lands, &c., are described under the head of **LEASES.**)

(1.)—Accounts, &c., relating to Crown Lands.

The various series of Accounts of the lands in the hands of the Crown, including the possessions of the dissolved monasteries, &c., are fully described under the head of **MINISTERS' AND RECEIVERS' ACCOUNTS.**

The following Account Books, Ledgers, and other documents belonging to the Augmentation Office are, however, of a distinct nature, and contain much general information respecting the transactions of that Department.

CROWN LANDS AND RENTS—(continued).
(1.)—Accounts, &c.—(continued).

ACQUITTANCES, ENROLMENTS OF.

34 Henry VIII. to 7 Edward VI.

A large volume containing enrolments of the "Bills of Acquittance" or Receipts given by the Treasurer of the Court of Augmentations, for the sums of money received by him as payments for grants from the Crown of the sites and possessions of the dissolved monasteries, &c. The names of the grantees, dates of the grants, and descriptions of the premises are fully set out.

[*Misc. Books, Vol.* 1.]

ESTABLISHMENT OF THE NEW COURT OF AUGMENTATIONS.

A copy of the Letters Patent, dated 38 Henry VIII., dissolving the old Courts of Augmentations and of General Surveyors, and establishing a new "Court of Augmentations."

[*Misc. Books, Vol.* 17.]

MEMORANDA RESPECTING THE COLLECTING OF RENTS IN VARIOUS COUNTIES.

Edward VI. and Philip and Mary. 4 Vols.

[*Misc. Books, Vols.* 264 *to* 267.]

WRITS OF PRIVY SEAL directing the payment to the Receiver of the Court of Augmentations of the ARREARS DUE FROM VARIOUS ACCOUNTANTS. 33 Henry VIII. 1 Vol.

[*Misc. Books, Vol.* 331.]

RECEIPT BOOKS OR LEDGERS OF THE TREASURER OF THE COURT OF AUGMENTATIONS. 33 Henry VIII. to 1 Mary. 14 Vols.

[*Misc. Books, Vols.* 336 *to* 349.]

MISCELLANEOUS LETTERS AND PAPERS. Hen. VIII., &c. 10 Vols.

[*Misc. Books, Vols.* 472 *to* 481.]

The following Accounts are amongst the "Declared Accounts," of the Audit Office :—

ACCOUNTS OF THE RECEIVER OF THE MONEY ARISING FROM THE SALE OF DUNKIRK. 1662.

[*Bundles* 848 *and* 849.]

ASSART LANDS, ACCOUNTS OF MONEYS ARISING FROM. 1605 to 1616.

[*Bundle* 354.]

ACCOUNTS OF THE RECEIVER OF MONIES ARISING FROM THE SALE OF CROWN LANDS. 1561 to 1592.

[*Bundle* 493.]

CROWN LANDS AND RENTS—(continued).

(1.) Accounts, &c.—(continued).

Auditors' Certificates of the Revenues of Queen Henrietta Maria from Lands in various parts of England. 1633.

[*S. P. Dom. Car. I., Vol.* 235.]

(2.)—Bargains and Sales of Crown Lands and of Fee-Farm Rents.

The Bargains and Sales of Crown Lands and of the Estates of the so-called " Delinquents " made by Commissioners during the Commonwealth are enrolled on the Close Rolls, as are also the sales of Fee-Farm Rents by Lord Hawley and other Trustees in the reign of Charles II. [See "Palmer's Indexes," Vol. 78 and 79, and Vol. 72 respectively.]

The Particulars for Sale of the Estates of Charles I., and also of the Fee-Farm Rents belonging to the Crown, with the Certificates, Contracts, and other documents relating thereto are as follows :—

Particulars for the Sale of the Estates of Charles I., the Queen, and Prince (Augmentation Office). Commonwealth. 22 Boxes.

Index. 1 Vol. MS.

Contracts for the Purchase of the Lands, &c. of the late King and Queen. (Augmentation Office.) 1649 to 1653. 2 Vols.

[*Misc. Books*, Vols. 173 and 174.]

Certificates relating to the sale of Crown Lands (Exchequer, Q. R.) Commonwealth. 5 Bundles.

Minute Book of the Trustees for the Sale of Crown Lands. (Augmentation Office.) 1649 to 1659.

[*Misc. Books.* Vol. 314.]

Minute Book of Commissioners for the Sale of His Majesty's Lands in Fee-Farm. Dec. 2, 1626, to June 26, 1627.

[*S. P. Dom. Car. II.* Vol. 79.]

(3.)—Concealed Lands.

Particulars for the Amendment of Defective Titles. (Augmentation Office.) James I. and Charles I.

These are particulars for new grants or leases taken by virtue of warrants issued by the Commissioners appointed from time to time for the compounding of defective titles. Commissions of this nature were of frequent occurrence during the reigns of Elizabeth, James I., and Charles I.]

CROWN LANDS AND RENTS—(continued).
(3.)—Concealed Lands—(continued).

and generally set forth that, it having come to the knowledge of the Sovereign that many of his liege subjects were
in possession by purchase, descent, or otherwise, of lands
and hereditaments formerly belonging to the Crown of
which they held either imperfect grants or no grants at all,
he, out of consideration for their welfare and in order to
prevent costly law suits, and probable total loss of such
lands and hereditaments, empowered certain Commissioners
to compound with such persons for a certain sum of ready
money to be by them paid into the Exchequer, and thereupon to issue to them in the King's name new grants or
leases of the premises thus putting them in secure possession of their estates at a comparatively small cost. This
apparent generosity on the part of the Sovereign was
extensively applied for the purpose of raising money
both by himself and by unscrupulous informers who
obtained from the Commissioners what have been termed
"Fishing" grants, that is to say, grants of lands already
held by other persons whose titles they alleged to be
defective, and from whom they extorted large sums for a
re-transfer of their estates.* Several grants of this description were made in the 33rd and 34th years of Elizabeth
to two persons named Wm. Tipper and Edw. Dawe, who
were particularly active in the discovery of so-called
"Concealed Lands." The "Particulars" above mentioned
are contained in seven volumes.

[*Misc. Books, Nos.* 87*a to* 90, *and No.* 159.]

PARTICULARS OF CONCEALMENTS. (AUGMENTATION OF
FICE.) Elizabeth.

One Portfolio, containing particulars for the letting or
sale of lands in various counties, which had been found to
have been concealed from the Queen's Majesty, or from
her progenitors, by Certificates or Inquisitions thereof
taken and remaining in the custody of the Queen's
Remembrancer or Lord Treasurer's Remembrancer
respectively.

ACCOUNTS, &C. RELATING TO CONCEALED LANDS.
(MISCELLANEA EXCHEQUER, Q. R.) Henry VIII. to
James I.

These consist of Accounts of lands, &c., "recovered to
the use of the Lord the King," whose title thereto had
hitherto been concealed, and of Certificates, Inquisitions,
and Informations respecting "Concealed Lands" in divers
counties.

Descriptive Slips.

---

* *Vide* "History and Law of the Foreshore," by Stuart A. Moore, p. 171.

CROWN LANDS AND RENTS—(continued).

(3.) Concealed Lands—(continued).

SPECIAL COMMISSIONS RESPECTING CONCEALED LANDS, &c. (EXCHEQUER, Q. R.). Eliz. to Victoria. See **COMMISSIONS.**

SPECIAL COMMISSIONS CONCERNING CONCEALED LANDS. (CHANCERY PETTY BAG OFFICE.) Car. II. to Wm. & Mary. 1 Bundle.
Index.

(4.)—Fee-Farm Rents.

PARTICULARS FOR THE SALE OF FEE-FARM RENTS. (AUGMENTATION OFFICE.) Commonwealth. 10 Packages.
Calendar with Index Locorum. 2 Vols. MS. (The second of these volumes relates chiefly to the Fee-Farm Rents belonging to the Duchy of Lancaster.)

COUNTERPARTS OF DEEDS OF SALE OF FEE-FARM RENTS. (AUGMENTATION OFFICE.) Commonwealth. 26 Boxes.
Calendar 2 Vols. MS. with an *Index Locorum* at the end of each Vol.

CERTIFICATES AND CONTRACTS FOR THE SALE OF FEE-FARM RENTS IN VARIOUS COUNTIES, WITH OTHER PAPERS RELATING THERETO. (AUGMENTATION OFFICE.) Commonwealth. 10 volumes, including a Minute Book of the Trustees (Vol. 139).
[*Misc. Books, Vols.* 135 to 144.]

PARTICULARS OF FEE-FARM RENTS. (DUCHY OF LANCASTER.) Temp. Commonwealth. 2 Bundles.
[*Div. xii. Bundles* 44 *and* 45.]
Calendar, 1 Vol. MS. This Calendar refers also to those Particulars in the Augmentation Office which relate to the Duchy of Lancaster.

CERTIFICATES OF PAYMENTS FOR FEE-FARM RENTS. (EXCHEQUER, L. T. R.) 1650 to 1652.
A volume of 423 pages containing entries of Certificates to the Treasurers of Fee-Farm Rents by the " Registrar Accomptant " of the receipts due to various persons for sums paid on account of purchases of Fee-Farm Rents. Index of persons at the commencement.

See also **Bargains and Sales of Crown Lands, &c.**

(5.)—Purchases and Exchanges.

ACTS FOR THE ASSURANCE OF PURCHASES AND EXCHANGES (AUGMENTATION OFFICE.) 1–28 Henry VIII.
A volume containing Transcripts of all Acts of Parliament for the assurance to the King of all such manors,

CROWN LANDS AND RENTS—(continued).

(5.) Purchases and Exchange—(continued).

lands, and tenements under the survey of the Court or Augmentations as were acquired by him by purchase or exchange or otherwise since the first year of his reign. A copy of the Act establishing the Court of Augmentations is prefixed.

[*Misc. Books, Vol.* 2.]

PURCHASE AND EXCHANGE, DEEDS OF. (AUGMENTATION OFFICE.) Henry VIII. to Edward VI. 21 Boxes.
Index, 2 Vols. MS.

PURCHASE AND EXCHANGE, ENROLMENTS OF DEEDS OF. (AUGMENTATION OFFICE.) 31 to 38 Henry VIII. and 1 to 7 Edw. VI. 3 Vols.

[*Misc. Books, Vols.* 332 *to* 334.]

INDENTURES, TRANSCRIPTS OF. (AUGMENTATION OFFICE.) 2 to 28 Henry VIII. Transcripts of Conveyances to Henry VIII. 1 Vol.

[*Misc. Books, Vol.* 162.]

21 to 25 Henry VIII. Transcripts of Indentures of Bargain and Sale by Sir Edward Seymour and others. 1 Vol.

[*Misc. Books, Vol.* 163.]

DEEDS OF BARGAIN AND SALE, ENROLMENTS OF. (EXCHEQUER, Q. R.) 35–37 Henry VIII. 2 Vols.

[*Misc. Books, Vols.* 33 *and* 34.]

(6.)—Resumed Lands

ACCOUNTS OF RESUMED LANDS (CHANCERY).

A roll, entitled, "De donationibus et concessionibus per " Regem factis in manibus ejus resumendis. 3–5 Edw. " II.," consisting of Writs to the Escheators Citra and ultra Trentam, directing them to resume into the King's hands all lands, rents, custodies, marriages, &c. granted by him since the 16th day of March in the third year of his reign, a schedule of which is annexed to each writ.

[*Misc. Rolls, &c., No.* $\frac{16}{22}$.]

Do. (EXCHEQUER, Q. R.) Henry VI.

These are Accounts of the Escheators and others in various counties of the revenues and emoluments arising from the lands and possessions seized into the King's hands by virtue of an Act of Resumption passed in the 29th year of Henry VI.

Descriptive Slips.

Note. Grants of lands, demesnes, &c. made by Henry III. to his son Edward I., as well in England and Wales, as beyond the seas, and also Grants and Conveyances to the Crown temp. Edw. I., are entered in the "REGISTRUM MUNIMENTORUM" of the Exchequer, Treasury of the Receipt. See **REGISTERS AND BOOKS OF REMEMBRANCE.**

CUSTOS SIGILLI.

ACCOUNTS OF THE CUSTOS SIGILLI. (MISCELLANEA, EXCHEQUER, Q. R.) Edward VI. to Elizabeth.

These are the Accounts of the Keeper of the Seal in the Court of *Chancery*, who was appointed by the Clerks of the Hanaper as their Deputy to receive the Fees arising from that seal; and also of the Keeper of the Seal in the Court of *Common Pleas*. They show little more than the gross receipts and incidental expenses.

Descriptive Slips.

DEEDS (ANCIENT).

There are amongst the Public Records very large collections of Conveyances, Bonds, Agreements, and other Deeds, mostly between private persons, many of which are of very early date, and which have hitherto been altogether undescribed. These have now been formed into several Series, as follows, and a Descriptive Catalogue of the whole collection is in progress, two volumes of which have already been issued (1890–1894).

Series A. Ancient Deeds of the Treasury of the Receipt of the Exchequer, formerly preserved in the Chapter House.

Series B. Ancient Deeds, formerly in the Augmentation Office of the Exchequer.

Series C. Ancient Deeds belonging to the Court of Chancery, formerly preserved in the Tower of London and the Rolls Chapel.

Series D. Ancient Deeds belonging to the Queen's Remembrancer's Office of the Exchequer.

Series E. Ancient Deeds belonging to the Office of Land Revenue Records.

In addition to the foregoing Series there are several collections of Ancient Deeds to which Calendars or partial Calendars, already exist. A List of these is appended.

Exchequer, Augmentation Office.

" CHARTÆ MISCELLANEÆ." 24 Vols.

[Miscellaneous Books, Vols. 31 to 54.] The first 20 of these volumes are calendared in 1 Vol. MS. with an *Index Locorum*; the remainder are not yet calendared.

DEEDS AND CHARTERS, PRECEDENT BOOK OF.

A volume entitled " Liber de diversis modis faciendi Cartas," containing Transcripts of Indentures, Deeds, and Writings of various kinds.

[*Misc. Books, Vol. 330.*]

Court of Wards and Liveries.

DEEDS, CHARTERS, AND EVIDENCES. Edw. I. to Car. I.

A collection of 4,698 Charters, Deeds, Evidences, and other Writings belonging to the Court of Wards and Liveries.

Inventory and Index. Report VI., App. II., pp. 1–87.

DEEDS (ANCIENT)—(continued)
Duchy of Lancaster.

"GRANTS (IN BOXES)."

A collection of Ancient Deeds and Charters consisting of 22 Boxes lettered A. to M. A Calendar of the contents of "Box A." (4 boxes), the dates of which extend from Hen. I. to Hen. VI., is printed in Report XXXV., App., pp. 1–41. A similar Calendar of the contents of "Box B." (4 boxes), which consist of Deeds and Charters relating to Furness Abbey and to the Priories of Conished, Cartmel, and Burscough, is printed in Report XXXVI., App., pp. 161–205. A Calendar of "Box C." (2 boxes) is placed in the Search Room.

N.B.—The printed Calendars also contain references to such Deeds and Charters as, being without seals, are not placed in the Boxes, but bound up in the three volumes called "Cartæ Miscellanæ."

CARTÆ MISCELLANEÆ.

Three volumes containing such Ancient Deeds and Charters belonging to the class known as "Grants in Boxes" as had lost their seals, and were in consequence collected together and bound in volumes.

These are included in the Calendar to the "Grants (in Boxes)."

The following TRANSCRIPTS OF ANCIENT DEEDS AND CHARTERS are amongst the "Miscellaneous Rolls, &c. Chancery."

(Bundle 3.)

No. 1. Transcripts of the Deeds and Charters of Robert Walerand. 52 Hen. III.
No. 2. Ditto. of Peter de Sabaudia. Temp. Hen. III.
No. 4. Ditto of John de Poudreham de Wyteston. 5 Edw. II.
No. 5. Transcripts of the Charters and Muniments of the Archbishop of Dublin. 6 Edw. II.
No. 6. Extracts from the Charters, &c. deposited in the Priory of Malton relating to the De Vescys of Kildare. 9 Edw. II.
No. 11. Transcripts of Deeds and Grants made to the Society of the Bardi of Florence in Lombard Street. 12 Edw. II.
No. 12. Transcripts of Deeds, &c. relating to the Church of St. Giles, Cripplegate. 14–32 Edw. III.
No. 15. Ditto relating to the Chantry of St. Mary in the Church of St. Dunstan's in the West. 49 Edw. III.
No. 16. Transcripts of Deeds and Charters to the Butillers and others. (A fragment.) Temp. Edw. III.

(Bundle 4.)

No. 22. Charters, &c. relating to the foundation of a Carthusian Priory at Eppworth in the Isle of Axholme. 3 Hen. IV.

DEEDS ENROLLED.
Chancery.

Deeds and conveyances between private persons are enrolled on the Close Rolls from a very early date. See **CHANCERY ENROLMENTS.**

Under the general title of "INDENTURES," a great variety of documents are enrolled on the Close Rolls from the reign of Elizabeth to the present time. These include Deeds of Bargain and Sale ; Deeds of Lease and Release ; Disentailing Deeds ; Conveyances in Trust for Chapels, Schools, and Charitable Purposes ; Conveyances under the Queen Anne's Bounty Act for the Augmentation of Curacies, &c. ; Deeds of Settlement of Ecclesiastical Districts and Parish Boundaries ; Awards respecting Inclosures, &c. ; Conveyances of Bankrupts' Estates ; Deeds Poll relating to Change of Name ; Certificates of Naturalization ; Consents : Memorials of Annuities ; Memorials of the Names of Trustees, &c. of Assurance Companies ; Specifications and Disclaimers of Patents ; Recognizances and Bonds of Receivers and Official Liquidators, and other documents of a similar nature.

Of these enrolments, the Memorials of Annuities, Specifications and Disclaimers of Patents (from 1849 to 1853 only), and the Recognizances and Bonds form distinct branches.

INDEX TO INDENTURES, &c. 1573 to 1887. 71 Vols. MS. These Indexes are arranged alphabetically under the names of the *Grantors* (Cross-references under the names of the *Grantees*, and in some cases under the names of *Places*, will be found in the " Index to Close Rolls ").

The RECOGNIZANCES and BONDS are indexed in the same books as the INDENTURES till the year 1871, but under a distinct heading. After that date the Indexes are separate. There is also a separate Index to the SPECIFICATIONS from 1849 to 1853 ; and to the " MEMORIALS OF ANNUITIES," from 1777 to 1854 inclusive. [These ceased to be enrolled on the Close Rolls in 1813.] A Calendar of the " TRUST DEEDS," from 11 George II. to 1865, arranged alphabetically under names of *Places*, is printed as an Appendix to Report XXXII.

There is also an Index in 2 Vols MS. to the " DEEDS, WILLS, &c., ENROLLED FOR SAFE CUSTODY," from William and Mary to George II. inclusive, many of which are of a much earlier date than that of their enrolment.

Queen's Bench, Crown Side.

Deeds between private persons are frequently enrolled on the earlier Coram Rege Rolls. See **JUDICIAL PROCEEDINGS.**

DEEDS ENROLLED—(continued).

Queen's Bench, Crown Side—(continued).

There is amongst the Assize Rolls, &c. a roll (No. 556) containing Abstracts of Deeds and Wills relating to lands given in Mortmain from 7 Edward I. to 38 Edward III. inclusive, which are enrolled at the Hustings of the City of London.

Queen's Bench, Plea Side.

Deeds are enrolled on the Placita Coram Rege or Crown Rolls till 1702, after which date they appear in the Plea Rolls, which thenceforward formed a distinct class.

From 1390 to 1595 the Deeds enrolled are indexed in the "DOGGETT ROLLS;" from 1595 to 1648 in the "SPECIAL REMEMBRANCE ROLLS;" from 1648 to 1655 they are again entered in the "DOGGETT ROLLS," and afterwards in the DOGGETT BOOKS under the head of "SPECIAL REMEMBRANCES."

Common Pleas.

Deeds enrolled in the Court of Common Pleas are on the PLACITA DE BANCO or PLEA ROLLS till Easter 25 Elizabeth, when those rolls were subdivided into "COMMON ROLLS" and "RECOVERY ROLLS," the Deeds being thenceforward enrolled on the latter, of which they form a distinct portion in each Term. On the abolition of Fines and Recoveries in 1834 the Deeds were again enrolled on the Plea or Common Rolls.

Indexes.

Before 20 Hen. VII. See "AGARDE'S INDEXES."

From 20 Hen. VII. to 31 Hen. VIII. See "RECOVERY INDEX," Vol. I.

From 1555 to 1836, there is a *Calendar* in 5 Vols. MS.

Exchequer of Pleas.

Deeds enrolled are on the PLEA ROLLS, and are indexed in the same Calendars and Docket Books as the Pleadings. See **JUDICIAL PROCEEDINGS**

Exchequer, Queen's Remembrancer's and Lord Treasurer's Remembrancer's Departments.

For Deeds enrolled, see **MEMORANDA ROLLS OF THE EXCHEQUER.**

Exchequer, Augmentation Department.

Enrolments of Deeds of Bargain and Sale, or of the Purchase and Exchange of Lands by the Crown, in. volumes. See **CROWN LANDS.**

DEEDS ENROLLED—(continued)

Palatinate of Lancaster.

DEEDS, DECREES, &c., ENROLMENTS OF (CHANCERY) Car. II. to Will. IV. 1 Bundle.

Deeds enrolled in the Court of Common Pleas at Lancaster are on the Plea Rolls. See **JUDICIAL PROCEEDINGS.**

Palatinate of Chester.

Deeds are enrolled on the PLEA ROLLS and also on the " RECOGNIZANCE ROLLS."

Calendar to Deeds, &c. enrolled on the Plea Rolls. Hen. III. to Hen. VIII. Printed. *Vide* Reports XXVI. to XXX. inclusive.

Calendar to the Recognizance Rolls of the Palatinate of Chester. I Edw II. to 11 Geo. IV. Printed. *Vide* Reports XXXVI. to XXXIX. inclusive.

Palatinate of Durham.

Deeds enrolled in the Court of Pleas at Durham will be found on the PLEA ROLLS. For Deeds enrolled in the Chancery of the Palatinate, see **CHANCERY EN- ROLMENTS.**

Principality of Wales.

Deeds enrolled are entered on the PLEA ROLLS of the several Counties. See **JUDICIAL PROCEEDINGS.**

Various Courts (Inclosure Awards).

The Awards of Commissioners appointed to inclose, set out and allot the open Commons and other Lands in England and Wales were, by the several Inclosure Acts under which they were made, generally directed to be enrolled *either* with the Clerk of the Peace for the County, *or* in one of the Courts of Chancery, Common Pleas, Queen's Bench, Exchequer, &c.

A List of those enrolled in the several Courts of Law (including those enrolled in the Duchy of Lancaster Office) is printed in the Appendix to the 27th Report. In a great majority of instances, however, they will be found to be enrolled with the Clerks of the Peace.

Many Inclosure awards for the County of Durham are recited in the Registrars' Entry Books of Orders and Decrees.

DEEDS, &c., REGISTRIES OF.

The earliest Act for the Registration of Deeds was passed in the 27th year of Henry VIII. This was supple- mented, and an omission therein supplied, by an Act of the

DEEDS, &c., REGISTRIES OF—(continued).

5th year of Elizabeth, entitled "An Act for the enrolment of Indentures of Bargain and Sale in the Queen's Majesty's Courts," including the Counties Palatine or Lancaster and Chester and the Bishopric of Durham. Separate Registries of Deeds were subsequently established as follows:—

For Conveyances relating to the fens called Bedford Level. 15 Car. II.

For the West Riding of Yorkshire (Registry at Wakefield). 2 & 3 Anne.

For the East Riding of Yorkshire (Registry at Beverley). 6 Anne.

For the North Riding of Yorkshire (Registry at North-. allerton). 8 Geo. II.

For the County of Middlesex. 7 Anne.

There are also distinct Registries of Deeds for Scotland and Ireland.

Deeds were also frequently enrolled with the Clerks of the Peace for the several counties.

In the Second Report of the Commissioners on Public Records (1800), p. 629, is given a list of the Records generally to be found in the custody of the Clerks of the Peace of the several counties of England and Wales, amongst which appear the following:—

PROCEEDINGS AT THE COURTS OF QUARTER SESSIONS, in some counties from about the reign of Elizabeth, in others from a much later period.

INROLMENTS AND REGISTERS OF DEEDS AND INCLOSURE AWARDS, from about the reign of Queen Anne (those for the county of Northampton begin in the reign of Elizabeth).

LISTS OF FREEHOLDERS LIABLE TO SERVE ON JURIES, AND POLL BOOKS OR REGISTERS OF VOTERS, from about 1760 (for Northampton from 1669).

LAND TAX ASSESSMENTS, from about 1780.

COUNTY RATE BOOKS.

REGISTERS OF LICENSES FOR ALE HOUSES, DROVERS, HIGLERS, &c.

CORONERS' INQUESTS.

CERTIFICATES FOR REGULATING BUILDINGS AND PARTY WALLS, pursuant to Stat. 14 Geo. III.

QUALIFICATION ROLLS OF JUSTICES, MILITIA OFFICERS, AND DEPUTY LIEUTENANTS, WITH THEIR SACRAMENT CERTIFICATES.

DEEDS, &c., REGISTRIES OF—(continued).

QUALIFICATIONS OF DISSENTING MINISTERS AND OF ROMAN CATHOLICS UNDER CERTAIN STATUTES; AND REGISTERS OF THE ESTATES OF ROMAN CATHOLICS AND OF BARGAINS AND SALES BY THEM, AND OF THE HOUSES OF WORSHIP OF DISSENTERS AND ROMAN CATHOLICS.

In many counties these records are however very defective.

DEGREES GRANTED BY THE ARCHBISHOP OF CANTERBURY.

The "DISPENSATION ROLLS" contain enrolments by the Clerk of the Dispensations and Faculties of all Doctors' Degrees granted by the Archbishop of Canterbury.
See **CHANCERY ENROLMENTS (VARIOUS).**

DEPARTMENTAL RECORDS.

Admiralty.

The principal records of the Admiralty deposited in the Public Record Office, which are open to public inspection up to 31 Dec. 1799, consist of the following classes :—

SECRETARY'S DEPARTMENT.

Admirals' Despatches, from about 1705 to 1839 (arranged according to the several Stations).
Admirals' Journals, from about 1744 to 1839.
Captains' Journals, from about 1806 to 1842.
Commission and Warrant Books, from 1694 to 1815. These contain the appointments of all Officers of the Navy, both Commissioned Officers and Warrant Officers.

Letter Books (Lords of the Admiralty), from about 1688 to 1815.
Do. (Secretary of the Admiralty), from about 1688 to 1815.
Orders and Instructions, Entry Books of, from about 1665 to 1815.
Orders in Council, from about 1688 to 1815.

ACCOUNTANT-GENERAL'S DEPARTMENT.

Half-Pay Books, from about 1700 to 1832.
Log Books, from the reign of Charles II. to 1885.
Pay Books, from about 1680 to 1855.
Muster and Victualling Books, from about 1680 to 1875.

F 2

DEPARTMENTAL RECORDS—(continued).

Audit Office.

The Audit Office Records consist principally of the
"Declared," or Audited Accounts, relating to a great
variety of subjects, a list of the most important of which
is given below. They also include Military Establishment
Books of the various Forces at home and abroad, and a
great number of books of accounts and other volumes of
too miscellaneous a description to be here detailed. They
are open to public inspection to the end of the year 1821
only.

An Inventory of the "Declared Accounts" of the
Audit Office, including the Duplicate Series of the Pipe
Office, has been recently printed. (Lists and Indexes,
No. II., 1893.)

DECLARED ACCOUNTS.

African Company (Royal). Accounts of Moneys
imprested to the Company at the Exchequer for the
support of trade, &c. 1729 to 1749.

Do. Account of his Majesty's Adventure in. 1661.

Agents for Special Services, Accounts of. 1563–1574,
1620 to 1638, 1683, and 1796 to 1819.

Ambassadors and Envoys, &c. Accounts of. 1566 to
1827.

Army, Accounts of the Paymasters-General of the
Forces. 1652 to 1827.

Do. of Commanders-in-Chief and Military
Governors. 1606 to 1821.

Army, Accounts of Victuals, &c. for home service.
1565 to 1814.

Do. for garrisons abroad. 1547 to 1820.

Do. of Half-pay, Pensions, and Allowances. 1713
to 1827.

Do. of money for Trained Bands and Militia.
1660 to 1674, 1745, and 1808 to 1827.

Do. of Vice-Treasurers and Treasurers at War,
and Paymasters of various expeditionary Forces and of
several garrisons. 1543 to 1826.

Assart Lands, Accounts of moneys arising from. 1605
to 1616.

Attainders, Forfeitures, &c. Accounts of the Receivers
and Collectors of the Revenues arising from the estates of
Popish Recusants and of persons convicted of High
Treason, &c. 1557, 1602 to 1605, and 1627 to 1734.

DEPARTMENTAL RECORDS—(continued)
Audit Office—(continued).
DECLARED ACCOUNTS—(continued).

Bishops' Lands, &c., Proceeds of the sale of. Treasurer's Accounts. 1646 to 1660.

Butlerage. Accounts of the Chief Butler of England. 1554 to 1673.

Captives, Redemption of. Accounts of money collected for the redemption of captives at Algiers, Morocco, &c. 1653 to 1725.

Chamber, Treasurer of the, and Master of the Posts. Accounts of. 1558 to 1782.

Churches. Accounts of the Treasurers of the Fund for building new churches in London and Westminster. 1712 to 1741.

Civil List Deductions. Accounts of the Receivers-General. 1721 to 1811.

Commissariat Accounts. 1596 to 1828.

Commonwealth Accounts:

>Accounts of the Commissioners for Advance. 1653 to 1654.
>Accounts of Moneys for the use of the State. 1653 to 1657.

Crown Lands. Accounts of the Receiver of moneys arising from the sale of certain Crown Lands. 1561 to 1592.

Customs:

>Accounts of the Farmers, Commissioners, Collectors, and Comptrollers-General of the Customs. 1602 to 1827.
>Accounts of Receivers-General and Cashiers. 1672 to 1827.
>Account of the Comptroller-General in Barbadoes, and the Leeward Islands. 1684–1685.

Dunkirk, Sale of. Accounts of the Receiver of the money arising from the sale of Dunkirk. 1662.

Exchequer Bills:

>Accounts of the Trustees for advancing money 1697 to 1724.
>Accounts of the Receivers of the money for purchasing Exchequer Bills. 1698 to 1703.
>Accounts of the Receivers of the money for discharging the Interest on Exchequer Bills. 1709 to 1720.
>Accounts of the Paymasters of Exchequer Bills. 1723 to 1828.

DEPARTMENTAL RECORDS—(continued).

Audit Office—(continued).

DECLARED ACCOUNTS—(continued).

Excise :

Accounts of the Commissioners and Governors of Excise (Cash Accounts). 1647 to 1841.*

Do (General Accounts). 1683 to 1849.*

Faculties, Accounts of the Clerk of the. 1573 to 1641.

First-Fruits and Tenths. Accounts of the Remembrancers and Receivers. 1558 to 1827.

Forests, &c. Accounts of the deer in the Royal Parks and Forests. 1616 to 1674.

Governors, Agents, &c., Accounts of:
Alderney. 1793–1806.
Bahamas. 1798–1827.
Barbadoes 1789–1814.
Bermuda. 1782–1811
Canada (Upper). 1791–1820.
Cape Breton. 1746–1820.
Carolina. 1776–1779.
Florida (East). 1772–1786.
Florida (West). 1764–1781.
Georgia. 1752–1783.
Gibraltar. 1714–1810.
Guernsey and Alderney. 1793–1827.
Jamaica. 1660–1675.
Jersey. 1793–1827.
New Brunswick. 1784–1827.
Newfoundland. 1794–1827.
New South Wales. 1786–1827
Nova Scotia. 1752–1827.
Prince Edward's Island. 1780–1827.
Sierra Leone. 1808–1825.
Virginia. 1754–1757.
West Indies. 1760–1827.
&c. &c.

Hackney Coaches, Receiver-General's Accounts of the Duty on. 1694 to 1828.

Hanaper, Accounts of the Clerks of the. 1562 to 1827.

Hawkers' Licenses. Receivers and Commissioners' Accounts of. 1697 to 1828.

Hearth Tax. Accounts of the Receivers and Managers, &c. 1673 to 1684.

Horse, Masters of the. General Accounts. 1603 to 1813.

* These are open to inspection down to 1841.

DEPARTMENTAL RECORDS—(continued).
Audit Office—(continued).
DECLARED ACCOUNTS—(continued).

Hospitals:

 Accounts of the Receivers-General and Paymasters of Chelsea Hospital. 1680 to 1827.

 Accounts of the Agents for the Out-Pensioners of Chelsea Hospital. 1754 to 1826.

Hospitals and Infirmaries (Various), Accounts of. 1653 to 1809.

Household. Accounts of the Comptroller of the Queen Mother's Household. 1668–1669.

Indians (North American). Agents' Accounts for purchasing presents, &c. for the Indians in the neighbourhood of his Majesty's Colonies. 1755 to 1785.

Jewels and Plate. Accounts of the Master and Treasurer of the Crown Jewels, &c. 1546 to 1639.

Lancaster, Palatinate of. Accounts of the Receiver of the moneys arising as Pre-Fines on Writs of Covenant, &c. 1649 to 1658.

Lotteries, Annuities, &c. Accounts of Paymasters and Receivers. 1694 to 1828.

Marriages, Births, and Burials. Accounts of the Receivers-General of Duties on Marriages, Births, and Burials (and also on Bachelors and Widowers) in certain counties and precincts. 1695 to 1706.

Mint:

 Accounts of the Wardens. 1536 to 1815.

 Accounts of the Masters and Workers. 1626 to 1827.

 Accounts of Purchases and Sales of Tin. 1603 to 1725.

 Miscellaneous Accounts and Expenses. 1547 to 1822.

Navy:

 Accounts of the Treasurers of the "Marine Causes and Affairs," and of the Navy. 1558 to 1827.

 Accounts of moneys, &c. arising by the sale of Prizes. 1593 to 1813.

  [There are also Warrants to the Cashier-General and Deputy Treasurers for Prizes, from 1664 to 1670.]

 Miscellaneous Accounts. 1597 to 1818.

DEPARTMENTAL RECORDS—(continued)

Audit Office—(continued).

DECLARED ACCOUNTS—(continued).

Ordnance :

Accounts of the Masters and Surveyors. 1557 to 1632.

Accounts of Lieutenants of the Ordnance. 1561 to 1670.

Accounts of the Treasurers and Paymasters. 1587 to 1827.

Miscellaneous Accounts. 1568 to 1640.

Orphans' Fund. Accounts of the Chamberlains of the City of London. 1694 to 1826.

Pensions. Accounts of the Paymaster of several of Her Majesty's Pensions. 1684 to 1782.

Post Office. Accounts of the Masters and Comptrollers of the Posts. 1566 to 1639.

Accounts of the Receivers-General. 1695 to 1827.

Do. of the Accountants General. 1746–1827.

Privy Purse. Accounts of the Keeper of the Privy Purse, and of the Receiver-General of the Revenues of Henry Prince of Wales. 1603 to 1688.

Progresses (Royal), Accounts of the Expenses of. 1603 to 1687.

Protestants in Piedmont and Poland. Accounts of the Treasurers. 1655 to 1660.

Recusants. See "Attainders, Forfeitures, &c."

Do. Accounts of moneys received from the principal recusant Clergy for providing horses and lances for Her Majesty's service in the Low Countries. 1585 to 1589.

Revenues (Various) in Minorca, Quebec, Upper and Lower Canada, the Isle of Man, &c. Receiver-General's Accounts. 1727–1825.

Revels, Accounts of Masters of the. 1572 to 1670.

Robes, Accounts of the Masters and Gentlemen of the. 1605 to 1812.

Mistress of the Queen's Robes, Accounts of. 1606 to 1714.

Salt, Duties on—

Cash Accounts. 1694 to 1798.

General Accounts. 1694 to 1798.

Scots. Mary Queen of. Accounts of the expenses of her diet, &c. and also of her funeral expenses. 1684–1687.

Seals. Account of the Graver of the Mint for making seals for the late Queen Elizabeth and for James I. on his accession. 1600–1609.

Secret Service Accounts. 1779–1828.

DEPARTMENTAL RECORDS—(continued).

Audit Office—(continued).

DECLARED ACCOUNTS—(continued).

Settlers in America. Account of the contractor for victualling the settlers in Nova Scotia. 1749-1751.

Do. Expenses of transporting foreign Protestants from Holland to Nova Scotia. 1751-1753.

Spaniards cast on the coast of Dorset. Expenses of Diet, Lodging, &c. 1628-1629.

Stamp Duties—

Cash Accounts. 1694 to 1827.

General Accounts. 1709 to 1827.

Tenths of the Clergy. (Queen Anne's Bounty.) Accounts of the Collectors or Receivers. 1713 to 1826.

Tents, Hales, and Pavilions, Accounts of the Masters of the. 1560 to 1676.

Tower of London. Expenses of State Prisoners and pay of the Garrison. 1551 to 1553.

Tower of London. Accounts of the Masters and Keepers of the Armoury. 1556 to 1686.

Toyles, Accounts of the Masters of the. 1560 to 1630.

Trade. Expenses of the Council for Trade and Plantations. 1696 to 1728.

Transport Service, Accounts of the. 1589 to 1744.

Treasury Solicitor, Accounts of the. 1657 to 1827.

Wardrobe. Accounts of the Masters or Keepers of the Great Wardrobe. 1558 to 1782. There are also six volumes containing Accounts of the expenses of Funerals and Coronations from 1619 to 1714.

Wine Licenses. Accounts of Commissioners and Agents. 1616 to 1757.

Works and Buildings (Public). Accounts of Surveyors and Paymasters. 1563 to 1827.

Works and Buildings (Miscellaneous). Royal Parks, Palaces, &c. 1573 to 1724.

Works (Military) and Fortifications. Accounts of the Paymasters of Works and Repairs and also of the Garrisons and Pensioners. 1541 to 1810.

Colonial Office.

The Records of the Colonial Office are with some exceptions open to public inspection up to 31 December 1802.

The papers for the following periods have been calendared in the printed "Calendars of State Papers, &c."

1574 to 1676—"America and West Indies,"

1513 to 1634—"East Indies, China, and Japan," and the papers are arranged for calendaring to the year 1688 inclusive.

DEPARTMENTAL RECORDS—(continued).

Colonial Office—(continued).

The remaining documents are arranged as follows :

(1.) Colonial Entry Books, from about James I. to William III. (Those of an earlier date than 1674 are referred to in the printed calendars.)

(2.) Correspondence, &c. relating to America and the West Indies from 1689.

(3.) "Board of Trade Papers," from about 1689. A collection of papers relating solely to Colonial matters, originally transmitted from the Board of Trade, but considered as belonging to the Colonial Series. These include *Acts* and *Minutes of Council and Assembly* of the various Colonies.

(4.) "Colonial Office Transmissions." From 1686. These include Colonial Military Returns, &c., from about 1810.

(5.) Colonial Correspondence relating to—
The East Indies, from 1570 to 1849 (calendared prior to 1634) ; and to other Colonies, from about 1700 to 1849.

[A printed List of the Colonial Office Records open to public inspection is issued for use in the Search Rooms.]

Foreign Office.

The Foreign Correspondence from the years 1547 to 1577 inclusive, has been arranged chronologically and calendared in the printed "Calendars of State Papers, &c." Subsequent to the latter date, the papers are arranged according to the several countries to which they relate. They extend in date to the year 1847, and are, with some exceptions, open to public inspection to 31 December 1802. The "Royal Letters" of each State are placed at the commencement of the particular series, and there are also, in some instances, a few transcripts of treaties and other documents of an earlier date than 1547.

There is also a collection of "Foreign Entry Books" from 1603 to 1688 ; of Books and Papers relating to the "Levant Company" from James I.; of papers relating to "Military Auxiliary Expeditions" in Flanders and Germany from 1695 to 1763 ; of "Treaties" and "Treaty Papers," from about 1544, with a few transcripts of earlier dates ; and of miscellaneous Correspondence and Despatches known as "Foreign Various."

[A printed List of the Foreign Office Records open to public inspection is issued for use in the Search Rooms.]

DEPARTMENTAL RECORDS—(continued).

Home Office.

The greater part of the Home Office Records prior to the year 1688 have been classified under the head of "State Papers (Domestic Series)." See **STATE PAPERS, CALENDARS OF.** Those subsequent to the reign of James II. are arranged under the following (principal) heads, and are open to public inspection down to 31 December 1772.*

Admiralty Correspondence, &c. 1689 to 1830.
Admiralty Entry Books. 1693 to 1836.
Caveats (against making Grants and Presentations). Entries of. 1668 to 1710.
Channel Islands:
    Correspondence, &c. 1694 to 1830.
    Entry Books. 1748 to 1817.
Church Books. 1688 to 1828. These contain entries of Royal Warrants for Conge's d'Elire, Restitution of Temporalities, Presentations, and other Ecclesiastical Preferments, and of Proclamations and Addresses relating to Ecclesiastical matters.
Church Books (Scotland). 1724 to 1808.
Council Office. Minutes and Correspondence. 1696 to 1830.
Criminal Papers. 1707 to 1849.
    Do. Registers. 1791 to 1866.
Docquets. 1549 to 1806.
Domestic Correspondence. 1689 to 1840.
    Do. Entry Books (with Index). 1706 to 1772.
Foreign Office. Commissions and Instructions to Ambassadors. 1664 to 1670.
Ireland, Correspondence, &c. 1685 to 1831. See also "Letter Books."
Ireland, Entry Books. 1716 to 1827.
Isle of Man, Correspondence, &c. 1761 to 1835.
    Do. Entry Books, 1765 to 1817.
Law Papers (Attorney and Solicitor-General's Reports, Opinions, &c.). 1684 to 1768 (with Calendar).
Law Reports. 1757 to 1834.
Letter Books (King's). 1688 to 1806.
    Do. do. (Ireland). 1681 to 1828.
    Do. (Secretary's). 1688 to 1782.
    Do. (Scotland). 1713 to 1725.
    Do. (Signet Office). 1627 to 1747.
    Do. do. (Irish). 1747 to 1827.

* A Calendar of the Home Office Records from 1760 to 1772 inclusive, has been published in the series of "Calendars of State Papers, &c."

DEPARTMENTAL RECORDS—(continued).

Home Office—(continued).

Military Commissions. 1706 to 1772. A small collection of original Military Commissions of various dates.

Military Entry Books. 1679 to 1831.

Militia Correspondence, &c. 1694 to 1820.

Ordnance :

Correspondence, &c.	1732 to 1830.
Entry Books.	1760 to 1855.
Passes (for ships).	1625 to 1784.
Petitions, Reports, &c.	1636 to 1830.
Post Office Correspondence.	1704 to 1830.

Precedent Books. Car. II. to 1782.

Regencies, Correspondence, &c. 1689 to 1779.

Do. Lords Justices' Warrants, Minutes, &c. 1695 to 1752.

Scotland, Correspondence, &c. 1688 to 1830.

Index, 2 Vols. MS.

Do. Warrants for, see " Warrant Books."

Signet Bills.	1661 to 1851.
Docquets.	1584 to 1835.
Indexes.	1584 to 1829.

Signet Office Letter Books, see " Letter Books."

Treasury and Customs, Correspondence, &c. 1729 to 1830.

Treasury Entry Book. 1763 to 1815.

Volunteer Corps, Correspondence, &c. 1745 to 1822.

War Office Correspondence, &c. 1716 to 1823.

Warrant Books. Elizabeth to 1829.

Do. (for Scotland). 1670 to 1829.

Warrants (Lord Justices'), &c. See " Regencies."

[A printed List of the Home Office Records open to public inspection, is issued for use in the Search Rooms.]

Lord Chamberlain's Department.

The principal Records of the Lord Chamberlain's Department, which are not open to inspection without permission from that Department, consist of volumes of Accounts, &c., as follows :—

Accounts of the Keeper of the Great Wardrobe. 1557 to 1782.

Appointment Books. 1660 to 1820.

Ceremonies, Records of Masters of the. 1612 to 1846.

Coronations, Accounts, &c. relating to. Edward IV. to William IV.

Establishment Books of the Household. 1641 to 1759.

Funerals and Mourning, Accounts of. 1499 to 1837.

Jewels and Plate, Accounts of. 1660 to 1839.

Palaces, Accounts and Estimates for. 1802 to 1846.

DEPARTMENTAL RECORDS—(continued.)

Lord Chamberlain's Department – (continued).

Precedent Books. 1625 to 1733.
Recognizances, Entry Books of (with Indexes). 1533 to 1775.
Salaries, &c., Accounts of. 1667 to 1782.
Theatres, Patents and Licenses for, &c. 1660 to 1820.
Warrants, of various kinds. 1628 to 1828.

Treasury.

The Records of the Treasury are open to public inspection to 31 Dec. 1759, and include the following principal classes :

Appointment Books. 1705 to 1723.
Correspondence (Original). 1557 to 1862.*
Crown Lease Books. 1726 to 1758 (Prior to 1726, see " Warrants not relating to money ").
Declared Account Books, 1685 to 1767.
Disposition Books (Public and Civil List). 1679 to 1834. Entries of Letters authorizing the disposition of money at the Exchequer.

Fee Books. 1711 to 1851.
Irish Books. 1670 to 1749.
Letter Books. 1667 to 1862.
        Do.   (Customs and Excise). 1667 to 1856.
Minute Books. 1667 to 1862.
Money Books from 1667 to 1839.
North Britain Books. 1690 to 1856.
Order Books. 1667 to 1831.
Reference Books. 1679 to 1819.
Warrant Books, as follows :
        Warrant Books (Early), 1634 to 1666.
        Money Warrants. 1667 to 1849.

King's Warrants and Privy Seals from 1667 to 1842. (These correspond with the Pells' Privy Seal Books.)

Warrants not relating to money. 1667 to 1849. These contain Treasury constitutions and appointments; commissions and instructions; constats, particulars, and other documents relating to Crown Leases (prior to 1726); with reports of various kinds.

Warrant Books (Lord Chamberlain's). 1715 to 1733.

---

* A Calendar of the Treasury Papers from 1557 to 1728, inclusive, has been printed in the series of " Calendars of State Papers, &c."

DEPARTMENTAL RECORDS—(continued).

War Office.

The War Office Records deposited in the Public Record Office are open to public inspection, with a few exceptions down to June 19, 1837. The classes which are of the most general interest to the public are as follows :—

1. The Muster Rolls and Pay-Lists of the various regiments of Horse and Foot from about 1760 to 1837.

   Do. of Foreign Corps from about 1795 to 1817.

   Do. of the Militia from about 1780 to 1837.

   Do. of the Fencible Cavalry and Infantry from 1794 to 1802.

   Do. of the Volunteers from 1798 to 1814.

2. General Monthly Returns for various Foreign Stations from 1812 to 1837.

   Do. of Militia from 1760 to 1837.

   Do. of Fencibles, Yeomanry, and Volunteers, from about 1795 to 1804.

   Do. of Foreign Corps from about 1800 to 1807.

3. Commission Ledgers, containing the Appointments and Promotions of Officers, from about 1680 to 1805. (There is a gap between the years 1748 and 1760.)

4. Inspection Returns from 1750 to 1837.

5. Marching Orders (volumes containing Orders for the marching and removal of the forces) from 1683 to 1837.

6. Establishment Books from 1702 to 1837.

7. Miscellany Books from 1683 to 1820.

8. Original Correspondence from 1758 to 1837.

9. Ordnance : King's Warrant Books from 1642 to 1837.

Abolished Offices, &c.

The Records of the following Abolished Offices and Expired Commissions of Inquiry, &c., all of which are under the special control of H.M. Treasury, and can only be inspected by the express permission of that Department, have also been deposited in the Public Record Office :—

ABOLISHED OFFICES.

Masters in Chancery (deposited pursuant to Stat. 40 & 41 Vict. cap. 55).

Metropolitan Buildings, Registrar of.

Royal African Company (transferred with the Records of the Treasury).

Slave Registration Department.

DEPARTMENTAL RECORDS—(continued).

Abolished Offices, &c.—(continued).

EXPIRED COMMISSIONS OF INQUIRY, &c.

American Loyalist Claims.
Boundaries (Municipal).
    Do.   (Parliamentary).
Caledonian Canal.
Cattle Plague.
Census.
Civil List Inquiry.
Courts of Justice.
Customs, Excise, and Public Revenue.
Education.
Fees of Public Offices.
French Refugees.
Foreign Claims (Danish, French, German, and Spanish).
Highland Roads and Bridges.
Holyhead Road and Harbour.
Irish Reproductive Loan Fund.
Oxford University.
Polish Refugees.
Port of London Compensation.
Potato Crop Returns.
Public Accounts.
Public Schools.
Public Records.
Royal Gardens.
Royal Military Canal and Roads.
Scottish Harbours.
Slave Compensation.
State Papers, Publication of.
Surinam Absentee Estates.
Tyne River.

DEPOPULATION.

Commissions to inquire into Depopulations, with the Returns thereto. 5 James I. 1 Bundle. Amongst the "SPECIAL COMMISSIONS" of the Chancery (Petty Bag Office). See **COMMISSIONS**.

DERELICT LANDS.

Commissions of Inquiry concerning Derelict Lands, with the Returns thereto. Car. I. to Vict. 1 Bundle. Amongst the "SPECIAL COMMISSIONS" of the Chancery (Petty Bag Office). See **COMMISSIONS**.

DOMESDAY BOOK.

DOMESDAY BOOK. (EXCHEQUER, TREASURY OF THE RE-CEIPT.)

This important and unique survey of the greater portion of England is the oldest and most valuable record in the national archives, having been completed in the year 1086. Its compilation was determined upon at Gloucester by William the Conqueror, in council, in order that he might know what was due to him, in the way of tax, from his subjects, and that each at the same time might know what he had to pay. It was in fact compiled as much for their protection as for the benefit of the Sovereign. The commissioners appointed to make the survey were to inquire the name of each place; who held it in the time of King Edward the Confessor; the present possessor; how many hides were in the manor; how many ploughs were in demesne; how many homagers; how many villeins; how many cottars; how many serving men; how many free tenants; how many tenants in soccage; how much wood, meadow, and pasture; the number of mills and fish-ponds; what had been added or taken away from the place; what was the gross value in the time of Edward the Confessor; the present value; and how much each free-man or soc-man had, and whether any advance could be made in the value. Thus could be ascertained who held the estate in the time of King Edward; who then held it; its value in the time of the late king; and its value as it stood at the formation of the survey. So minute was the survey, that the writer of the contemporary portion of the Saxon Chronicle records, with some asperity, " So very narrowly " he caused it to be traced out, that there was not a single " hide, nor one virgate of land, nor even, it is shame to " tell, though it seemed to him no shame to do, an ox, nor " a cow, nor a swine was left, that was not set down."

The Domesday Survey is in two parts or volumes. The first, in folio, contains the counties of Bedford, Berks, Bucks, Cambridge, Chester and Lancaster, Cornwall, Derby, Devon, Dorset, Gloucester, Hants, Hereford, Herts, Huntingdon, Kent, Leicester and Rutland, Lincoln, Middlesex, Northampton, Nottingham, Oxford, Salop, Somerset, Stafford, Surrey, Sussex, Warwick, Wilts, Worcester, and York. The second volume, in quarto, contains the counties of Essex, Norfolk and Suffolk, and appears to consist of the Transcripts in full of the Original Returns for those counties, giving details as to the live-stock on each manor which are generally omitted from the Survey in its final form as transcribed in the Exchequer. Similar Transcripts of the Original Returns for several counties, known as the Exeter Domesday, are preserved in the Library of the Dean and Chapter of Exeter, and the

DOMESDAY BOOK—(continued).

"Inquisitio Eliensis," a copy of which is preserved in the British Museum, appears to be of the same nature. For some reason left unexplained, many parts were left unsurveyed; Northumberland, Cumberland, Westmoreland, and Durham, are not described in the survey; nor does Lancashire appear under its proper name; but Furness and the northern part of Lancashire, as well as the south of Westmoreland, with a part of Cumberland, are included within the West Riding of Yorkshire. That part of Lancashire which lies between the Ribble and Mersey, and which at the time of the survey comprehended 688 manors, is joined to Cheshire. Part of Rutland is described in the counties of Northampton and Lincoln.

Domesday Book was printed *verbatim et literatim* during the last century, in consequence of an address of the House of Lords to King George III. in 1767. It was not, however, commenced until 1773, and was completed early in 1783.

In 1816, an additional volume was published under the direction of the Record Commissioners, containing Records supplementary to the Domesday Survey, consisting of :—

(1.) The "EXON DOMESDAY," the original of which is preserved amongst the muniments of the Dean and Chapter of Exeter Cathedral. This volume comprises the counties of Wilts, Dorset, Somerset, Devon, and Cornwall, and is supposed to contain so far as it extends, an exact Transcript of the original Returns made by the Commissioners at the time of the General Survey from which the Great Domesday itself was compiled.

(2.) The "INQUISITIO ELIENSIS," a document similar in nature to the foregoing, relating to the property of the Monastery of Ely. It is preserved in a Register of the Monastery remaining among the Cottonian MSS. in the British Museum [Tiberius A. VI.], and belongs apparently to the twelfth century. Another copy of this Inquisition is contained in the Chartulary of Ely preserved at Trinity College, Cambridge.

(3.) The "WINTON DOMESDAY," now in the Library of the Society of Antiquaries, consisting of a Survey taken before William, Bishop of Winchester, between the years 1107 and 1128, for the purpose of ascertaining what lands were held in Winchester by Edward the Confessor as of his own demesne.

(4.) The "BOLDON BOOK," or Survey of the Palatinate of Durham, taken by command of Hugh Pudsey, Bishop of Durham, in the year 1183. This

DOMESDAY BOOK—(continued).

volume apparently took its name from the village of Boldon, near Sunderland, reference to which is frequently made in the Survey. The original Manuscript is lost, but there are four copies now extant: one, formerly in the Auditor's Office, Durham, now in the Public Record Office; one in the Library of the Dean and Chapter of Durham; one in the Bodleian Library; and one amongst the Stowe MSS. at the British Museum.

An *Introduction* to Domesday Book, by Sir H. Ellis, with Indexes of Tenants-in-Chief and Under-Tenants, &c., was published in 1833 in 2 Vols. 8vo.

A *Fac-simile* of Domesday Book, taken by Photozincography, was completed in 1863. It is in 33 Parts, one for each County.

DOMESDAY BOOK, ABBREVIATION OF. (EXCHEQUER, TREASURY OF THE RECEIPT.) An abridgment of Domesday Book in one very beautiful volume, apparently compiled early in the reign of Edward I.

DOMESDAY BOOK, ABSTRACT OF. (EXCHEQUER, Q. R.) A volume described as a " Breviate of Domesday with other matters," being a transcript of Domesday Book, omitting the enumeration of villeins, bordarii, and stock, and containing various Notes and Memoranda of historical and other matters.

[*Misc. Books, Exchequer, Q.R., Vol.* 1.]

ECCLESIASTICAL MATTERS.

The documents relating to the History and Revenues of the Church (exclusive of those directly concerning the dissolved monasteries, &c., and their possessions, which are described under the head of **MONASTIC FOUNDATIONS, &c.**) consist of the Appointments to Bishoprics, with the Congés d'élire, Writs of Restitution of Temporalities, and other documents subsidiary thereto; of Accounts of the Temporalities of the several Bishoprics whilst in the hands of the Crown during the vacancies of their respective Sees, from Hen. III. to Car. I inclusive; of Inventories of the Goods, Plate, Jewels, Vestments, Bells, &c., of all Churches, Chapels, Guilds, Fraternities, or Brotherhoods, throughout England, taken by the Commissioners appointed for that purpose in the reign of Edward VI.; of Documents relating to the Bargains and Sales of Church Lands by the Commonwealth; Accounts and other documents relating

ECCLESIASTICAL MATTERS—(continued).

to the payments and compositions for First-Fruits and Tenths; Certificates by the Bishops of the several Dioceses of the Institutions made by them to the livings within their respective Sees, from the reign of Elizabeth to the present time; the Accounts and Deeds relating to the Augmentation of poor livings under the Statute of Queen Anne, known as Queen Anne's Bounty; Enrolments of Presentations to Livings in the gift of the Crown and of the Duchy of Lancaster; the Original Renunciations of the Papal Supremacy by the Clergy throughout England in the reign of Henry VIII.; Accounts of Clerical Subsidies and Imposts from Hen. III. to Will. & Mary; with Surveys and Valuations of Ecclesiastical Benefices of various dates, including the celebrated Taxation of Pope Nicholas in the reign of Edward I., the Nonæ Rolls or Inquisitiones Nonarum of 14 and 15 Edw. III., which specify the value of every benefice, stating whether and by how much it exceeded or fell short of the valuation of Pope Nicholas, with the reasons for such variation, the Valor Ecclesiasticus of 26 Henry VIII., a few of the Original Surveys taken during the Commonwealth, and many other Records of a miscellaneous character illustrating the condition of the Church from a very early period.

They may be classified as follows:

<small>BENEFICES, INSTITUTIONS AND PRESENTATIONS TO.</small>

Bishops' Certificates of Institutions to Church Livings (Exchequer, First-Fruits and Tenths Department.) Eliz. to 1862. 40 Portfolios. These are the Certificates of the induction of Clerks to Livings made by the Bishops of the several Dioceses to the Barons of the Exchequer. The Returns were made half-yearly and are arranged according to Dioceses. They generally give the name of the last incumbent and also the name of the patron. See also the "Composition Books" described under the head of FIRST FRUITS AND TENTHS.

Abstracts called "Institution Books," in three series:—

Series A. 1556 to 1660. 5 Vols.
  „ B. 1660 to 1720. 7 Vols.
  „ C. 1720 to 1838. 3 Vols.

Institutions to Livings. (Court of Wards and Liveries.) 19 Jas. I. to 27 Car. I. A volume containing the Institutions to Livings the presentation of which was in the hands of the Crown owing to the minority of the Wards.

[*Misc. Books, Court of Wards, Vol.* 355.]

Presentations to Livings in the gift of the Crown. (Chancery) Enrolled on the Patent Rolls.

Index. 1 Edw. I. to 24 Edw. III. 1 Vol. MS.

ECCLESIASTICAL MATTERS—(continued).

BENEFICES, INSTITUTIONS AND PRESENTATIONS TO—(continued).

Presentations. (Exchequer, First Fruits and Tenths.) 1703 to 1786. 1 Vol.

Presentations to Benefices. (Duchy of Lancaster.) Inrolments of Presentations will be found in the Registers of Grants, Patents, &c.

There are also Rolls of Presentations as follows :—
19–38 Henry VI. 1 Roll.
[*Chancery Rolls, D. of Lanc., No.* 59.]
1–17 Edward IV. 2 Rolls.
[*Do., Nos.* 60 & 61.]
Draft Presentations. Eliz. to Geo. I. 3 Bundles.

BENEFICES, &C., RETURNS OF :

The following are amongst the Chancery Miscellaneous Rolls, &c. (Bundle 4):—

No. 7. Certificate of the Sheriff of Cornwall of the number of Churches, Chapels, and Prebends in that County. 45 Edw. III.
No. 9. A similar Certificate from the Sheriff of Wilts. 45 Edw. III.
No. 9. A similar Certificate from the Bishop of Coventry and Lichfield. 45 Edw. III.
No. 10. Names of Churches in the Deaneries of Wylforde, Lose, Saunford, Ipswich, and Waynford. Edw. III.
No. 11. Account of Ecclesiastical Benefices in England held by *Roman Cardinals.* Edw. III.
No. 12. Return of the value of Churches, Chapels, Rectories, Parsonages, &c. in the County of Wilts. 3 Edw. VI.
No. 13. Presentments of Jurors appointed to inquire concerning Ecclesiastical Benefices in the Counties of Cambridge, Derby, and Wilts. 1650.
No. 14. A Commission to ascertain the number and value of Churches, Chapels, &c. in the County of Wilts. 1650.
No. 15. A Commission to inquire concerning Ecclesiastical Benefices in various Parishes in the County of Southampton. 1657.
No. 16. A Commission and Presentment of Jurors concerning Ecclesiastical Benefices in the Parishes of St. Helen and St. Nicholas, in Abingdon, Berks. 1657.
No. 17. A List of Parishes in different Counties. 1657.

BISHOPRICS, HENRY THE EIGHTH'S SCHEME OF.

A book containing a scheme for certain new Bishoprics and Colleges to be erected by Henry the Eighth from the revenues of the dissolved monasteries, &c., showing the amounts to be expended in stipends, &c.
[*Misc. Books (Augmentation Office), Vol.* 24.]

BISHOPS' PATENT ROLLS. CHANCERY (PETTY BAG OFFICE).

9–10 Geo. I. to 38 Victoria. These Rolls include the Congés d'élire and Royal Assents to the appointments of Bishops, and also the Patents of Assistance and Writs of Restitution of Temporalities.

ECCLESIASTICAL MATTERS—(continued).

BISHOPS' PATENT ROLLS. CHANCERY (PETTY BAG OFFICE)
—(continued).

The patents of "Searchers" and "Customers," though
of a very different nature, were also formerly entered on
these Rolls.

At an earlier period, the Patents relating to Bishops'
appointments were entered on the general Patent Rolls,
and these of Officers of Customs on the Fine Rolls.

BISHOPS' PATENTS. CHANCERY (PETTY BAG OFFICE).
George I. to 38 Victoria. These are the original Warrants
or Privy Seal Bills for the Congés d'élire and Royal
Assents to the appointment of Bishops and consist of 13
Bundles or Parts. They are enrolled, together with the
"Customers' Patents," on the "BISHOPS' PATENT ROLLS."

BISHOPS' TEMPORALITIES, ACCOUNTS OF. Henry III.
to Charles I.
See **MINISTERS' ACCOUNTS, &c.**

BISHOPS' LANDS, PROCEEDS OF THE SALE OF. (Treasurers'
Accounts), 1646 to 1660.
[*Audit Office Declared Accounts, Bundle* 367.]

CHURCH GOODS, INVENTORIES OF. (MISCELLANEA, EX-
CHEQUER, Q. R.) Edward VI.
These are Inventories, taken by the Commissioners
appointed for that purpose in the 6th year of Edward the
Sixth, of all manner of "goodes, plate, juells, vestyments,
" bells, and other ornyments within every paryshe belonging
" or in any wyse apperteyning to any Churche, Chapell,
" Brotherhed, Gylde, or Fraternytye within this our Realme
" of Englond;" together with Indentures of the delivery of
such goods and ornaments as were allowed to remain in
the hands of the Churchwardens for the use of the several
churches.

There are also a few Returns to similar Commissions
issued in the second year of the same reign.
Catalogue. Report VII, App. II., pp. 315–336; and
Report IX., App. II., pp. 237–242.
Descriptive Slips. 4 Vols. MS.

Do. (EXCHEQUER AUGMENTATION OFFICE.)
Edward VI. 21 Vols. [*Misc. Books, Vols.* 495 *to* 515.
Descriptive Slips (as above).

Do. (LAND REVENUE OFFICE.)
Henry VIII. to Philip and Mary.
Descriptive List.

CHURCH LANDS, DEEDS OF BARGAIN AND SALE OF.
Temp. Commonwealth. Enrolled on the Close Rolls
See " Palmer's Indexes." Vols. 78 to 81.

ECCLESIASTICAL MATTERS—(continued)

CHURCH LANDS, ABSTRACTS OF LEASES OF. (Lands belonging to the Archbishopric of Canterbury.) 1583 to 1600. [*S. P., Dom., Elizabeth. Vol.* 277. (*Calendared.*)]

CHURCH LIVINGS, SURVEYS OF. See SURVEYS AND VALUATIONS.

CLERICAL SUBSIDIES, ACCOUNTS OF. (MISCELLANEA, EXCHEQUER, Q. R.) Hen. III. to Will. and Mary.

These consist principally of the Accounts of the Collectors of the Subsidies granted by the Clergy in the several Dioceses, and give the amount assessed on each Benefice and sometimes the name of the person by whom it was paid. They include some of the original Rolls of the Taxation of Pope Nicholas.

Descriptive Slips. 26 Vols.

CLERICAL CONTRIBUTIONS AND SUBSIDIES, ACCOUNTS OF, CALLED "CLERGY DIOCESAN RETURNS" (AUDIT OFFICE).

Accounts of the benevolent contribution of three shillings in the pound on the annual value of each Archbishopric, Bishopric, Deanery, &c., from 1587 to 1589.

Accounts of the Archbishops and Bishops of the annual payments of Tenths on Benefices and Promotions. 29 Henry VIII. to 10 Charles I.

Accounts of Receivers-General of the Tenths of the Clergy. 1647 to 1659.

Accounts of the Archbishops and Bishops of the subsidies paid in their several Dioceses. 33 Henry VIII. to 2 & 3 Ph. and Mary.

ECCLESIASTICAL DISTRICTS.

Deeds for the settlement of Ecclesiastical Districts and of Parish Boundaries are enrolled on the Close Rolls.

See **DEEDS ENROLLED.**

ECCLESIASTICAL DOCUMENTS (CHANCERY). Henry III. to James I.

Petitions for secular aid against excommunicated persons, &c. 26 parcels.

Petitions for the arrest of vagabond monks. 2 parcels.

ECCLESIASTICAL DOCUMENTS (EXCHEQUER). Henry III. to James I.

These consist principally of Transcripts of Proceedings in various courts relating to Ecclesiastical Matters and of documents touching the possession of Church Lands and Tithes.

They also include accounts of the Fines and Penalties imposed by the Commissioners for Ecclesiastical causes in the reigns of Elizabeth and James I., and of Bonds given by various persons for personal appearance, or that they would not confer with Jesuits, seminary priests, or known recusant .

ECCLESIASTICAL MATTERS—(continued).

ECCLESIASTICAL PETITIONS (CHANCERY). Henry III. to
Eliz. 51 Files.

These consist of Petitions for Congés d'élire, Royal
Assents, and Restitution of Temporalities.

ECCLESIASTICAL PREFERMENTS, ENTRY BOOKS OF LETTERS,
WARRANTS, &c. RELATING TO. Chas. II. to 1828.

These include Presentations, Congés d'élire, Dispensations, and other Documents of a similar nature.

[State Papers (Domestic), Entry Books. Charles II. to
James II., and Home Office, Church Books, 1688 to 1828.]

ECCLESIASTICAL TAXATIONS.

Taxation of Pope Nicholas. (Exchequer, Q. R.) 21
Edward I.

The two volumes bearing this title contain a valuation
of all the Ecclesiastical Benefices in the Provinces of York
and Canterbury respectively, made by command of Edward I. and completed about the year 1291. In 1288
Pope Nicholas the Fourth, from whom the valuation takes
its name, granted all the tenths due from the Clergy to the
King for six years in order to defray the expenses of an
expedition to the Holy Land, and this valuation was then
begun by the Royal precept, in order that the said tenths
might be collected to their full value. Until the Survey
taken in the 26th year of Henry the Eighth called the
" Valor Ecclesiasticus " the " Taxation of Pope Nicholas,"
or " Taxatio Ecclesiastica," regulated the amount of the
taxes due both to King and Pope.

A certified copy of this valuation exists amongst the
Miscellaneous Rolls of the Court of Chancery and
the Original Returns for several Dioceses will be found
amongst the Clerical Subsidies.

The two volumes above described have been printed in
full by the Record Commissioners in 1 Vol. folio.

See also NONÆ ROLLS.

Ecclesiastical Taxations of Ireland.

Two Ecclesiastical Taxations of Ireland, dated respectively A.D. 1302 and A.D. 1306, are deposited with the
" Irish Exchequer " Documents amongst the Miscellanea
of the Exchequer Queen's Remembrancer.

These have been printed, in extenso, in the Calendar of
" Documents relating to Ireland."

The following Ecclesiastical Taxations, &c. are amongst
the Miscellaneous Books of the Exchequer, Treasury of
the Receipt:—

Vol. 58. A Taxation of the Ecclesiastical Benefices in
the Diocese of Coventry and Lichfield.

ECCLESIASTICAL MATTERS— (continued).

ECCLESIASTICAL TAXATIONS—(continued).

Vol. 60. A Taxation of the Ecclesiastical Benefices in the Diocese of Rochester. 15th Cent.
Vol. 61. Do. in the Archdeaconry of Richmond. Hen. VIII.
Vol. 62. Do. in the Diocese of Lincoln. Hen. VI.

FIRST FRUITS AND TENTHS.

The *primitiæ* or first fruits were the profits of every spiritual living for the first year after avoidance, which were in ancient times given to the Pope throughout all Christendom. On the rejection of the Papal Supremacy in the reign of Henry VIII. they were vested in the King by Statute 26 Hen. VIII. c. 3, and a new Valuation was then made called the VALOR ECCLESIASTICUS, by which the Clergy are at present rated.

A Court was erected in the 32nd year of Henry VIII. for the administration of this revenue, but it was soon afterwards dissolved, and in the first year of Queen Mary the Office of First Fruits and Tenths was made a branch of the Exchequer.

In the second year of Queen Anne that sovereign restored to the church what had at first been indirectly taken from it, not by remitting the payment of First Fruits and Tenths entirely, but by applying the sums received from the larger benefices to make up the deficiencies of the smaller; for this purpose she granted a Charter, afterwards confirmed by Statute, whereby all the revenue of the first fruits and tenths is vested in Trustees to form a perpetual fund for the Augmentation of poor livings under 50*l.* a year. This is usually called "Queen Anne's Bounty," and has been further regulated by subsequent Statutes. By Statute 1 Vict. c. 20 the Office of First Fruits and Tenths was abolished, the collection of the revenue being placed entirely under the management of the Governors and Treasurer of Queen Anne's Bounty.

The following are the principal Records belonging to the Office of the First Fruits and Tenths:—

Bishops' Certificates of Institutions to Benefices. Elizabeth to 1862.
Bonds, Entries of. 1658 to 1820. 153 Vols. Entries of the date of the quarterly payments of composition.
Bonds, Payments of. 1692 to 1787. 12 Vols.
Certificates of all Church Livings not exceeding the yearly value of 50*l.* 5 Anne. 1 Portfolio. These Certificates were returned into the

ECCLESIASTICAL MATTERS—(continued).

FIRST FRUITS AND TENTHS—(continued).

Exchequer pursuant to the Statute of 5 Anne, by which all such livings were discharged from the payment of the First Fruits and Tenths. A complete Abstract of these is given in Ecton's "Liber Decimarum." 2 Vols.

Collectors' Account Book. 1666 to 1715. 1 Vol.

Commission Books. Henry VIII. to 1684. 3 Vols., containing entries of various Commissions relating to First Fruits and Tenths.

Composition Books. 1535 to 1795. 31 Vols.

These contain entries of the Compositions for First Fruits paid by incumbents on their induction, giving the date of such payment and the names of the sureties.

Indexes. (County Arrangement):
  Series I. 1536 to 1660. 2 Vols.
  Series II. 1684 to 1838. 8 Vols.
  Series III. 1684 to 1838. 6 Vols.
  Do. (Arranged under Incumbents' names):
  Series I. 1656 to 1684. 2 Vols.
  Series II. 1658 to 1798. 8 Vols.

Comptrollers' Payment Books. 1681 to 1799. 23 Vols.

Comptrollers' State Books. 1688 to 1783. 15 Vols.

Constat Books. 1717–1819. 6 Vols.
  Do. (Remembrancers'). 1793–1823. 24 Vols.

Day-Books of Receipts of Tenths.
  Canterbury. 1718 to 1838. 120 Vols.
  York. 1717 to 1839. 121 Vols.

King's Books or Liber Valorum. 3 Volumes containing extracts from the Valor Ecclesiasticus made from the original returns when they were complete, and supplying their places where now defective.

Ledgers. *Canterbury and York.* 1658 to 1838. 12 Vols.

"Liber Decimarum." Two volumes compiled from the original Books and Rolls in the First Fruits and Tenths Office, by John Ecton, Receiver-General of Tenths in the year 1709, and containing an account of the yearly Tenths charged on all benefices, and also of such livings as were discharged from the payment of First Fruits and Tenths by Statute 5 Anne.*

---

* See also the "Thesaurus Rerum Ecclesiasticarum by John Ecton, Esq.," with additions, &c. by Browne Willis, LL.D , printed in 1754.

ECCLESIASTICAL MATTERS—(continued).

FIRST FRUITS AND TENTHS—(continued).

>Receivers' Payment Books. 1759 to 1823. 24 Vols.
>
>Remembrancers' Payment Books. 1793 to 1823. 21 Vols.
>
>Remembrancers' Accounts of First Fruits. 32 Hen. VIII. to 1626. 13 Vols.
>
>Tenths, Entries of Payments of. 1660 to 1705. 6 Vols.
>
>Do. 1717 to 1838. 66 Vols.
>
>Valor Ecclesiasticus, Original Returns of the. 26 Hen. VIII. 3 Portfolios and 18 Vols.
>
>Do. Abstracts of the. 2 Vols.
>
>Do. Transcripts of the, known as the " Liber Regis." 2 Vols.

See also QUEEN ANNE'S BOUNTY RECORDS.

FIRST FRUITS AND TENTHS. Treasurer's Account, 1552.

An account of arrears due on 1st Feb. 1552, giving the names of the various benefices, and of the incumbents, with the amounts due from each.

>[*State Papers, Dom., Edw. VI. Vol.* 16.]

Accounts of the Remembrancers and Receivers of First Fruits and Tenths from 1558 will be found amongst the " Declared Accounts " of the Audit Office and Pipe Office. See **DEPARTMENTAL RECORDS.**

NEW CHURCHES.

Accounts of the Treasurers of the Fund for building New Churches in London and Westminster. 1712 to 1741. [*Audit Office, " Declared Accounts," Bundles* 437 *to* 439.]

NONÆ ROLLS. (EXCHEQUER, Q. R.) 14 and 15 Edw. III.

The " Nonæ Rolls" or " Inquisitiones Nonarum," which are placed with the Lay Subsidies, are Inquisitions taken on the oath of the Parishioners in every parish for the purpose of assessing a subsidy of a ninth and a fifteenth, granted to the King in the fourteenth year of Edw. III. in aid of the expenses of his wars. The subsidy consisted of a *ninth* of the corn, wool, and lambs in each parish, and in Cities and Boroughs a *ninth* of all moveables, whilst from Foreign Merchants, those who dwelt in Forests and Wastes, and " those who lived not of their grain or store," a *fifteenth* only was demanded.

These Inquisitions specify the value of every ecclesiastical benefice throughout England, comparing it with the Valuation of Pope Nicholas in 1291, and stating whether

ECCLESIASTICAL MATTERS—(continued).

NONÆ ROLLS—(continued).

it exceeded or fell short thereof with the causes of such variation. Many of these Rolls have been printed by the Record Commissioners in the volume entitled " Nonarum Inquisitiones," the introduction to which contains a full description of the manner in which the assessment was made. A detailed account of the Nonæ Rolls, distinguishing such as are not printed, is contained in the " Inventory of Accounts, Assessments, &c.," printed in the Second Report, App. II., pp. 132–189.

QUEEN ANNE'S BOUNTY RECORDS.

The Records transferred from the Queen Anne's Bounty Office to the Public Record Office consist of 40 Bundles of Writs and Returns, Bonds, Obligations, and other documents, relating to the payment of First Fruits and Tenths, including a List of Presentations to Benefices under the jurisdiction of the Dean of Salisbury, dated 1712, a grant of an annuity of 1,000l. to the Duchess of Portsmouth in 1681, and other documents of a miscellaneous nature.

Conveyances under the Queen Anne's Bounty Act for the Augmentation of small Livings are enrolled on the Close Rolls. They will be found in the Close Roll Index under the heading, " Bounty of Queen Anne," and are also referred to under the name of the Living, &c. augmented.

RENUNCIATIONS OF PAPAL SUPREMACY.

The original Renunciations of the Papal Supremacy by the Clergy in divers dioceses throughout England. Temp. Henry VIII. 2 Vols.
[*Misc. Books, Exch. Tr. of the Receipt, Vols. 63 and 64.*]

SIGNIFICAVITS. (PETTY BAG OFFICE, CURSITORS' RECORDS.) George II. to Victoria. 12 Bundles.

These are Certificates from the Ecclesiastical Courts whereon Writs "de excommunicato capiendo" and "de contumace capiendo" were issued. For similar documents of an earlier date see ECCLESIASTICAL DOCUMENTS (CHANCERY), p. 102.

SURVEYS AND VALUATIONS.

Bangor and St. Asaph, Valuations of the Bishoprics of. 27 Henry VIII. A collection of original valuations of the Rectories, &c., within the Dioceses of Bangor and St. Asaph. Printed in the Valor Ecclesiasticus. (Vol. 6.)
[*Misc. Books, Augmentation Office, Vol. 362.*]

ECCLESIASTICAL MATTERS—(continued).

SURVEYS AND VALUATIONS—(continued).

Canterbury, Valuation of the Province of. 28 Elizabeth. A valuation of all ecclesiastical benefices, &c. within the Province of Canterbury, taken in the year 1576 for the purpose of assessing a "benevolence."

[*Misc. Books. Exchequer, First Fruits, &c., Vol.* 1.]

Durham, Survey of the Bishopric of. "Temp. Thomæ Hatfield Episcopi." This survey contains also a copy of the Boldon Book.

[*Rentals and Surveys, Portf.* 21, *No.* 28.]

Durham, Rental of the lands, &c. of Thomas Langley, Bishop of. Anno 1418.

[*Rentals and Surveys, Portf.* 21, No. 29.]

Exeter, &c., Valuation of the Bishopric of. Henry VII. A volume containing valuations of the Bishopric of Exeter, "anno 2do Episcopi Redmayn" (A.D. 1496); and of the manors, lands, &c. assigned by Henry the Eighth for the endowment of the Bishopric of Bristol, the Cathedral Church of Bristol, the College of Rochester, and the Cathedral Churches of Worcester and Winchester.

[*Misc. Books, Augmentation Office, Vol.* 389.]

Hereford, Ecclesiastical Taxation of the Bishopric of. A Register or Valuation of the Tithes of Ecclesiastical Benefices in the Diocese of Hereford, with other documents. 1 Vol.

[*Misc. Books, Augmentation Office, Vol.* 489.]

Norwich, Visitation of the Archdeaconry of. 42 Edward III. A Visitation and Register of Ornaments of all the Churches within the Archdeaconry of Norwich made by William de Swynflete, Archdeacon, Anno Domini 1368, This register includes a valuation of each benefice with an account of the Sinodals, Peter's Pence, &c. due therefrom, and a detailed statement of all the vestments, ornaments, missals, &c., thereto belonging.

The volume is slightly rubricated and contains 150 leaves of parchment.

[*Misc. Books, Exchequer Q. R., Vol.* 30.]

York, Visitation of the Archbishopric of. 1559.

[*State Papers, Domestic, Eliz., Vol.* 10.]

Valuations of Rectories, &c. A volume containing—

(1.) A valuation of the Leases of Rectories granted by Henry VIII. in various counties with the names of the Grantees, &c.

(2.) An account (imperfect) of the Fee-Farm Rents, Stipends, &c., sold by Order of the Trustees of the Commonwealth in 1650.

[*Misc. Books, Augmentation Office, Vol.* 175.]

ECCLESIASTICAL MATTERS—(continued).

Valuations of Spiritual Promotions. A volume, formerly in the State Paper Office, entitled, "The number and value of all Spiritual Promotions as certified in King Henry the Eighth's time," being an epitome of the Valor Ecclesiasticus arranged under Counties.

[*Misc. Books, Exch. Tr. of the Receipt, Vol. 65.*]

SURVEYS OF CHURCH LIVINGS (CHANCERY), Commonwealth. 3 Vols.

These contain the presentments of the Inhabitants of various Parishes throughout England of the number and value of the Ecclesiastical Benefices therein, with the names of the Incumbents, &c., made pursuant to an Ordinance of Parliament dated 20th December 1649.

Vol. 1 contains the Returns for the Counties of Berks, Bucks, Essex, Gloucester, Hertford, Lancaster, and Lincoln;

Vol. 2, the returns for the County of Dorset only;

Vol. 3 contains the Returns for the Counties of Middlesex, Norfolk, Northumberland, Oxford, Sussex, Westmoreland, Wilts, and Yorkshire.

The above are the only original returns known to exist, but there are in the Lambeth Library 24 large volumes, consisting chiefly of official copies of these returns, which were made shortly after the originals, and which in many cases supply their places where wanting. See also BENEFICES, RETURNS OF.

VALOR ECCLESIASTICUS (EXCHEQUER, FIRST FRUITS AND TENTHS). Henry VIII.

The important Record, known as the Valor Ecclesiasticus, consists of a survey or valuation of all Ecclesiastical Benefices throughout England and Wales taken by virtue of a Commission issued in the 26th year of Henry VIII. in order to carry into effect the Statute giving the First Fruits and Tenths to the King. The Returns were made either in the form of books or on rolls of paper or parchment, and are contained in 3 Portfolios and 18 Volumes. Those for the Diocese of Ely, a great part of the Diocese of London, the Counties of Berks, Rutland, and Northumberland, and a great part of the Diocese of York, including the Deaneries of Rydal and Craven, are wanting. This deficiency is, however, to some extent supplied by the Abstracts contained in 3 volumes known as " King's Books " or the "Liber Valorum " which were compiled from the original Record when it was entire for the

ECCLESIASTICAL MATTERS—(continued).

Valor Ecclesiasticus, &c.—(continued).

use of the First Fruits Office, and by the beautiful Transcript on vellum of Portions of the Valor known as the "Liber Regis" and consisting of two large volumes. The Valor Ecclesiasticus has been printed by the Record Commission in six volumes, folio.

See also Surveys and Valuations.

Miscellaneous.

The following documents relating to Ecclesiastical Matters are amongst the Chancery Miscellaneous Rolls (Bundle 4) :—

No. 1. A File of Writs and Memoranda relating to Fines paid by the Clergy for protections. 25 Edw. I.
No. 2. A Roll of Writs to the Sheriffs of various Counties directing the restitution to numerous prelates and other ecclesiastics of lay fees which had been seized into the King's hands. 25 Edw. I.
No. 3. A Roll containing Transcripts of Proceedings relating to the Liberties of Battle Abbey, returned pursuant to a Writ of Certiorari. 29 Edw. III.
No. 4. A Roll containing the names of the Alien Clergy who had paid fines at the Exchequer. Temp. Edw. III.
No. 5. A Notarial Instrument relating to the disputes between the Dean and Chapter of Lincoln. 9 Hen. V.
No. 6. A Petition and Warrant for the grant of certain liberties, &c. to the Archbishop of York. 22 Hen. VI.

See also Benefices, Returns of.

EMIGRANTS.

Licenses to pass beyond the Sea. (Miscellanea, Exchequer Q. R.) Elizabeth to Charles I.

These consist of Returns of the names, ages, &c. of soldiers who took the oath of allegiance preparatory to going on foreign service, principally to the Netherlands, and also of Registers of all the passengers embarking from London and other ports for New England and other American Colonies about the year 1635. Those relating to the American settlers have been published by J. Camden Hotten, under the title "Original Lists of Persons of Quality, &c."

Descriptive Slips.

List of Emigrants to Nova Scotia. 1748 to 1749.

[*Colonial Office Records (Board of Trade) Nova Scotia, Vol.* 46.]

ESCHEATS, ATTAINDERS, AND FORFEITURES.

Prior to the reign of Henry III. the revenue arising from Escheated or Forfeited Lands was answered for by

ESCHEATS, ATTAINDERS, &c.—(continued).

the Sheriffs of the several counties, and accounted for by them on the Great Rolls of the Exchequer or Pipe Rolls under the title "De purpresturis et Escaetis." Towards the end of the reign of Henry II., however, a separate account appears to have begun to be kept of the Escheats in various counties, and subsequently distinct officers were appointed for the management of these revenues, who were called "Custodes Escaetarum" or "Custodes Escaetriæ," and afterwards "Escheators."

About the end of the reign of Henry III. the whole kingdom was divided into two Escheatries, "Citra Trentam" and "Ultra Trentam," and this arrangement appears to have continued, with a short interval, till 8 Edward III., when the Escheatry south of Trent was formed into seven Escheatries, and the district north of Trent (exclusive of Lancashire) formed an eighth Escheatry, as follows :—

1. Surrey, Sussex, Kent, and Middlesex.
2. Hants, Wilts, Oxford, Berks, Bedford, Buckingham.
3. Norfolk, Suffolk, Cambridge, Huntingdon, Essex, Hertford.
4. Warwick, Leicester, Nottingham, Derby, Lancaster.
5. Lincoln, Northampton, Rutland.
6. Gloucester, Worcester, Hereford, Salop, Stafford, and Marches of Wales.
7. Cornwall, Devon, Somerset, and Dorset.
8. Northumberland, Cumberland, Westmoreland, York (and for a time Lancaster).

As the business of the Exchequer increased several new divisions arose from time to time (each with an independent Escheator), until about the reign of Henry V., when the division of the country into Escaetorial districts became complete, no alteration having been made since that reign, except that particular cities or towns obtained the privilege of having each its own Escheator.

The office of Escheator appears to have disappeared with the abolition of Feudal Tenures at the Restoration, inquiries respecting estates forfeited to the Crown from about the 5th year of Charles I. to the present time being made by virtue of Special Commissions for that purpose issued out of the Court of Chancery and returnable into the Petty Bag Office.

The following classes of Records relate more especially to lands, &c. forfeited by Escheat, Attainder, or otherwise.

See also the titles "INQUISITIONS POST MORTEM," "MINISTERS' AND RECEIVERS' ACCOUNTS," "PAPISTS, RECUSANTS, &c.," "ROYALISTS AND DELINQUENTS," and "SURVEYS AND RENTALS."

ESCHEATS, ATTAINDERS, &c.—(continued).

ESCHEATORS' ACCOUNTS AND INQUISITIONS. (EXCHEQUER Q. R.) Henry III. to James I.

The earlier Escheators' Accounts contain full particulars as to the property accounted for, stating where it was situated, its extent and value, and the reasons why it was seized into the King's hands, the matter therein containe l being uniformly distributed under the heads "Old Escheats," "New Eschents," and "Goods of Outlaws, Felons, and Fugitives." An alteration in the mode of making up these accounts took place about the 20th year of Elizabeth, subsequent to which date all particulars are omitted.

The "Escheators' Inquisitions" are contemporary Transcripts of the Inquisitions post mortem taken before the Escheators *virtute officii* or otherwise, and returned into the Court of Chancery, of which series they frequently supply the deficiencies. They were not unfrequently returned in the same pouch with the Escheators' Accounts, but have now been arranged in two Series, extending from Henry III. to Richard III., and from Henry VII. to James I. respectively.

Calendar to the "Escheators' Accounts and Inquisitions." Henry III. to James I. 10 Vols. MS.

Do. Henry VII. to James I. Printed. Report X., App. II., pp. 1–222.

Index Nominum. Hen. VII. to James I. 1 Vol. MS.

ESCHEATORS' ACCOUNTS, ENROLMENTS OF. (EXCHEQUER L. T. R.) 17 Edward II. to 21 James I. 161 Rolls.

Repertories. 1 Edward II. to 21 Henry VI. Prior to 17 Edward II. the Enrolments of Escheators' Accounts appear on the PipeRolls and Chancellors' Rolls respectively.

An Inventory of these and other Foreign Accounts is in progress.

Repertory. Edw. III. to Eliz. 1 Vol. MS. entitled "Repertory of Escheators' Accounts, including vacant Abbies and Priories." From Edw. III. to Edw. IV., this volume gives the names of the escheators only, but from Ric. III. to Eliz., it gives not only the escheators' names, but also those of the persons whose lands were taken, and of the vacant abbeys, &c. whose possessions were seized into the King's hands during such vacancy.

FELONS' GOODS, INQUISITIONS CONCERNING. (MISCELLANEA, EXCHEQUER Q. R.) Henry IV. to Henry VI.

These consist of Writs and Inquisitions relating to the goods and chattels of felons and outlaws in various counties.

Descriptive Slips.

ESCHEATS, ATTAINDERS, &c.—(continued).

FORFEITED ESTATES, MISCELLANEOUS ACCOUNTS RELATING TO. (MISCELLANEA, EXCHEQUER Q. R.) Richard II. to Edward IV.

Two bundles entitled " Miscellaneous Files and Parcels of Accounts," and containing accounts of the *Farmers of Forfeited Estates* or of forfeited goods and chattels in various counties of the *surplus receipts* over and above a certain value ; together with a few accounts of Sheriffs and of collectors of Customs and searchers in various ports.
Descriptive Slips.

FORFEITED GOODS, &c., ACCOUNTS OF. (MISCELLANEA, EXCHEQUER Q. R.) Edward I. to Edward III.

These are principally Accounts of the goods and chattels of " Felons, Fugitives, and Outlaws," and appear to be subsidiary to the Escheators' Accounts.
Descriptive Slips.

FORFEITURES (VARIOUS).

(1.) Lands of the Earl of Leicester and his followers (confiscated by the Dictum de Kenilworth. Temp. Henry III.).

a. A Roll entitled " Terræ rebellium datæ fidelibus," containing brief notices of the lands forfeited, with the names of the persons to whom they had been given. [*Miscellanea, Exchequer, Treasury of the Receipt.*]

b. A Roll entitled " De terris duellionum a rege diversis personis concessis," 50 Hen. III.
[*Misc. Rolls, &c., Chancery, No. ⁹⁄₉.*]

c. " Inquisitiones de Rebellibus." 49 Hen. III. One Portfolio, placed with the Inquisitions post mortem.

(2.) Lands of the Normans. (Confiscated temp. Henry III.)

A Roll entitled " Terræ Normannorum seisitæ in manum Domini Regis," containing an account of the grants of custody of certain lands formerly belonging to the Normans, which had been seized into the king's hands on the separation of Normandy from the English Crown. [*Miscellanea, Exchequer, Treasury of the Receipt.*]

The foregoing is printed in full in Hunter's " Rotuli Selecti."

(3.) Lands of the " Contrariants." (Temp. Edward II.)

The Accounts relating to the possessions of Thomas, Earl of Lancaster, and his adherents, who in respect of their great power and influence instead of being described as " Rebels " or " Traitors " were called " Contrariants," have now been incorporated in the General Series of

ESCHEATS, ATTAINDERS, &c.—(continued).

FORFEITURES (VARIOUS)—(continued).

"Ministers' and Receivers' Accounts," a detailed List of which has recently been issued.

There are also amongst the records of the Exchequer, L. T. R., Enrolled Accounts of the "Contrariants' Lands" from 14 to 20 Edward II., consisting of three large rolls.

Grants by the King of the Lands, &c. forfeited by the Contrariants are enrolled on a Patent Roll of 15 & 16 Edward II., entitled, "Cartæ de Terris Forisfactis."

(4.) Lands of the Duke of Ireland and others. (Attainted 11 Richard II.)

A File of Inquisitions and extents of the lands and possessions of Alexander Nevill, Archbishop of York; Robert de Vere, Duke of Ireland; Michael de la Pole, Earl of Suffolk; Sir Robert Tresilian, Sir Nicholas Brembre, and others attainted by Act of Parliament, 11 Richard II.

[*Misc. Rolls, &c., Chancery, Bundle* 13, *File* 2.]

. Inventories of the goods and chattels of De Vere, Duke of Ireland, and other attainted persons. 11–12 Richard II.

[*Misc. Books, Exchequer, Tr. of the Receipt, Vol. 66.*]

Inquisitions "De Forisfacturis," a Portfolio placed with the Inquisitions post mortem and referring to the possessions of the under-mentioned persons :—

11 Ric. II.	Michael de la Pole, Earl of Suffolk.
	Alexander Nevill, Archbp. of York.
	Sir Robert Tresilian.
12 Ric. II.	John de Nevill of Raby.
13 Ric. II.	Roger de Clifford.
	John de Hastings, Earl of Pembroke.
14 Ric. II.	Ralph Basset de Drayton.
15 Ric. II.	Hugh de Courtenay, Earl of Devon.
16 Ric. II.	Thomas, Earl of Stafford.
19 Ric. II.	Henry Grey de Wilton.
	William la Zouche de Haringworth.
	John de Carey (attainted 11 Ric. II.)
20 Ric. II.	Thomas de Holand, Earl of Kent.
	W. de Montacute, Earl of Salisbury.
	John de Wellington.
21 Ric. II.	Richard, Earl of Arundel.
	Thomas, Duke of Gloucester.
	Thomas, Earl of Warwick.
	Thomas Mortymer.
	Thomas, Archbp. of Canterbury.
	John de Cobham.
	Ralph de Drayton.
22 Ric. II.	Roger Mortimer, Earl of March.
	Henry Percy, Earl of Northumberland.
	Thomas, Earl of Stafford.

ESCHEATS, ATTAINDERS, &c.—(continued).

FORFEITURES (VARIOUS)—(continued).

The foregoing are included in the printed Calendar of Inquisitions post mortem.

The Accounts relating to the possessions of the Knights Templars (confiscated by Edward II.) and of the Alien Priories (confiscated by Henry V.) are described under the head of **MINISTERS' AND RECEIVERS' ACCOUNTS.**

The following documents relating to Attainders are amongst the Miscellaneous Rolls (Chancery) :—

No. ⅐. The Pronunciation of Judgment on Roger Mortimer the elder and Roger Mortimer the younger.   16 Edw. II.
No. ⅑. The Pardon of Humphrey, Duke of Gloucester, and Alianora his wife.   Temp. Hen. VI.

The following are amongst the Records of the Augmentation Office :—

Letters and Papers relating to Anthony Wydvill, Earl Rivers, and others. Temp. Edward IV. 1 Vol.
    [*Misc. Books. Vol.* 486.]
Inventories of the goods of William Leighe of Middleton, co. York, and others, attainted. 33 Henry VIII.
    [*Misc. Books. Vol.* 171.]

See also **REBELLIONS.**

FORFEITED ESTATES, &c., COMMISSIONS OF INQUIRY RESPECTING. (CHANCERY, PETTY BAG OFFICE.) James I. to Victoria.

These consist of Special Commissions to inquire respecting estates forfeited to the Crown for various causes, with the Inquisitions and Traverses thereon. They are arranged in bundles under the following heads :—

Aliens, Estates acquired by. 15 Car. I. to 8 Victoria.
Concealed Lands. Car. II. to Will. and Mary.
Depopulations, or lands, &c. laid waste in various counties. 5 James I.
Derelict Lands, or lands reclaimed from the sea. Car. I. to Victoria.
Escheats (for want of heirs). 6 Car. I. to 1889.
Forfeitures of Offices. 5 Car. I. to 4 William IV.
Murders and Felonies, Lands, &c. forfeited for. 12 Car. I. to Victoria.
Superstitious Uses, Lands given for. 33 Car. II. to 11 Wm. III.
Treason, Lands, &c. forfeited for. 5 Car. I. to Anne.
    Index. 1 Vol. MS.

FORFEITED ESTATES PAPERS. Pursuant to Statute 1 George I.

These are the Books, Papers, and Proceedings of the Commissioners appointed pursuant to an Act of Parlia-

ESCHEATS, ATTAINDERS, &c.—(continued).

ment in the first year of the reign of George I., entitled,
" An Act for appointing Commissioners to inquire of the
" Estates of certain Traitors, and of Popish Recusants, and
" of Estates given to Superstitious Uses, in order to raise
" money out of them severally for the use of the Publick."
They consist, in addition to the Reports, Minutes, and
other proceedings of the Commissioners, of Rentals of and
deeds relating to the Estates of all the persons attainted
during the rebellion of 1715, complete lists of whom are
given, with the claims of creditors thereon, &c., &c.; of
Lists of the Popish Recusants who had registered their
estates in the several counties in England and Wales,
arranged in counties and also alphabetically; and of Informations, &c. respecting Lands given to Superstitious Uses.
Inventory. Report V., App. II., pp. 97–130.

FEES OF COURTS, &c.

Minutes of the Commissioners appointed to inquire
into the Fees taken in every Court, Parish Church, and
in every Office in England and Wales. (Exchequer
Queen's Remembrancer.) 1627 to 1636. 4 Vols.

FEUDAL TENURES.

When the levying of Scutage in lieu of military service
became a recognized institution, which appears to have
taken place in the reign of Henry II., the amount of
service due from each Tenant in Capite was at first ascertained by *Certificates,* rendered to the Exchequer by the
Tenants themselves, of the number of Knights' Fees for
which they were liable, by which the Officers of the
Exchequer were guided in making their assessment.
Transcripts of the Certificates sent in by the Tenants in
Capite in the 14th year of Henry II., when a levy was
made on all the Knights' Fees throughout the kingdom in
aid of the marriage of the King's daughter, are contained
in the " Red Book" of the Exchequer (fol. 83–122), but two
only of the original Certificates are now known to exist.

Another copy of these Certificates (printed by Hearne)
is contained in the Black Book of the Exchequer, known
as the " Liber Niger Parvus."

The Red Book contains also (fol. 47–81) a return of all
the Scutages levied between the 2nd year of Henry II.
and the 13th year of King John which was compiled from
the Great Rolls of the Exchequer by Alexander de
Swereford in the reign of Henry III. as a guide for future
assessments. See **REGISTERS AND BOOKS OF
REMEMBRANCE.**

FEUDAL TENURES—(continued).

At a later period Inquisitions were taken from time to time concerning the Knights' Fees and Serjeanties in the various counties from which Returns or "Books of Knights' Fees" were subsequently compiled, the chief of which are well known as the "Testa de Nevill" or "Liber Feodorum," in the reigns of Henry III. and Edward I. "Kirkby's Quest" or Inquest of the 24th year of Edward I., and the "Book of Aids," which contains a Record of the Knights' Fees throughout the greater part of the kingdom in the reigns of Edward III. and Henry IV. Many of these Inquisitions exist amongst the Miscellanea of the Queen's Remembrancer, including a Survey or Return made in the 31st year of Henry II. of all wardships, reliefs, and other profits due to the King from the *Widows and Orphans* of his Tenants in Capite which is generally known as the "Rotulus de Dominabus" or "Ladies' Roll."

Inquisitions were also frequently taken for the purpose of ascertaining the names of persons in the several counties holding 20 librates of land or upwards, who were thereby rendered liable to knight-service and became subject to Fine or Composition for neglecting to take upon themselves the order of Knighthood, many of which will be found amongst the Chancery Miscellaneous Rolls and elsewhere as referred to below.

The various documents bearing on this subject, which furnish invaluable evidence as to the Feudal Tenures throughout England, are indicated in the following List:—

AIDS, BOOK OF. Edward III. and Henry IV.

A large volume containing Particulars of the Accounts of the Collectors of the Aid granted for making the King's eldest son a knight in the 20th year of Edward III., and also of an aid towards marrying the King's eldest daughter granted in the 3rd year of Henry the Fourth. The tenures of the persons contributing to the several Aids are described with great minuteness, the volume forming a most valuable Record of the Knights' Fees throughout the greater part of the kingdom.

[*Misc. Books, Exchequer, Q. R., Vol. 3.*]

KIRKBY'S QUEST. 24 Edward I.

An account of all the Knights' Fees, held from the King in Capite or from others in various Counties, according to Inquisitions thereof taken by John de Kirkeby the King's Treasurer and others thereto assigned in the 24th year of Edward I.

[*Misc. Books, Exchequer, Q. R., Vol. 17.*]

Transcripts of Kirkby's Quest for the County of York will also be found in the Miscellaneous Books of the

FEUDAL TENURES—(continued).

KIRKBY's QUEST—(continued).

Exchequer, Treasury of the Receipt. [*Vols.* 67 *and* 68.]

Fragments of the original Inquisitions for several Counties exist amongst the Subsidy Rolls, Exchequer, Queen's Remembrancer. [*Subs. Roll, No.* $\frac{240}{251}$.]

KNIGHTS' FEES, BOOK OF. 6 Henry VI.

A volume containing transcripts of Inquisitions as to the Knights' Fees, &c. in various Counties, taken in the 6th year of Henry the Sixth for the purpose of levying the Subsidy granted in that year.

[*Misc. Books, Exchequer, Q. R., Vol.* 4.]

SERJEANTIES, ROLLS OF. (EXCHEQUER, L. T. R.) Henry III. and Edward I.

There are amongst the Miscellaneous Rolls of the Lord Treasurer's Department two large Rolls containing Returns of all the Serjeanties throughout England in the reigns of Henry III. and Edward I., stating whether they were rented or alienated, wholly or in part, with the names of the Tenants and the rent paid by them, &c. The substance of these Rolls appears to be printed in the " Testa de Nevill."

TESTA DE NEVILL, OR LIBER FEODORUM. Henry III. and Edward I.

The two volumes, known as "Testa de Nevill," contain Transcripts, compiled apparently about the end of the reign of Edward II., of Inquisitions taken temp. Henry III. and Edward I. concerning the Nomina Villarum, Serjeanties, and Knights' Fees in the several Counties throughout England. They appear to have derived their title from Ralph de Nevill, who was an Accountant in the Exchequer and Collector of Aids in the reign of Henry the Third, or from Jollan de Nevill a Justice Itinerant of the same reign. They contain an account of all Fees holden either immediately of the King, or of others who held of him in Capite, and also of Fees holden in Frankalmoigne with the values thereof respectively; of all Serjeanties holden of the King, distinguishing such as were rented or alienated, with the values of the same; of all Widows and Heiresses in Capite whose Marriages were in the gift of the King with the values of their lands; of all Churches in the gift of the King, stating in whose hands they were; of all Escheats, as well of the lands of Normans as others, stating in whose hands they were and by what

FEUDAL TENURES—(continued).

TESTA DE NEVILL OR LIBER FEODORUM, &c.—(continued).

services holden ; and of the Amounts paid for Scutage and Aid, &c. by each Tenant.

[*Misc. Books, Exchequer, Q. R., Vols. 5 and 6.*]

Some of the original Rolls from which these two volumes were compiled will be found amongst the Miscellanea of the Exchequer Queen's Remembrancer ; and a portion of a Roll amongst the Miscellanea of the Treasury of the Receipt bearing the same name, appears to be the original document from which many of the entries have been copied. See also SERJEANTIES, ROLLS OF.

These volumes have been printed in full by the Record Commissioners in 1 Vol., folio, with Indices Locorum and Nominum.

TENURES AND KNIGHTS' FEES APPERTAINING TO THE DUCHY OF LANCASTER IN VARIOUS COUNTIES, BOOKS OF. 3 Vols.

[*Duchy of Lancaster Records. Div. XVIII., Vols. 31 to 33.*] See also "Miscellaneous Records, Duchy of Lancaster." [Div. XXV. and Div. XXVI.].

KNIGHTS' FEES, INQUISITIONS, &c. CONCERNING. (MISCELLANEA, EXCHEQUER, Q. R.) Henry II. to Edw. I.

These consist of Returns of the names of persons holding Knights' Fees in various Counties, including the "*Rotulus de dominabus, pueris et puellis*" of 31 Henry II., which was a survey taken to ascertain "the wardships, reliefs, and other profits due to the King from the widows and orphans of his tenants in Capite, minutely describing their ages and heirship, the quantity and value of their lands and of the cattle and stock upon them," &c. This Roll has been printed by Stacey Grimaldi for the Society of Antiquaries.

Descriptive Slips.

Many Inquisitions concerning Knights' Fees will also be found amongst the Subsidy Rolls. [See Descriptive Inventory in Report II., App. II , pp. 132–189 *et seq.*]

KNIGHTS' FEES, INQUISITIONS, &c. CONCERNING. (MISCELLANEA, EXCHEQUER,Q.R.) Henry III. to Henry VIII.

These consist of Returns of the names of persons holding Knights' Fees in various Counties, and also of those who held 20 or 40 librates of land, and had not taken upon themselves the order of Knighthood. They are at present placed in two Bundles, entitled " Feudal Service."

Descriptive Slips.

FEUDAL TENURES—(continued).

KNIGHTS' FEES, INQUISITIONS, &c.—(continued).

Inquisitions concerning Knights' Fees in various Counties will also be found amongst the Miscellaneous Rolls of the Exchequer, Lord Treasurer's Remembrancer.

KNIGHTHOOD, COMPOSITIONS FOR. (EXCHEQUER OF RECEIPT.) 1630 to 1632.

A volume containing the names of persons throughout England who compounded for not taking the Order of Knighthood, with the sum paid by each, arranged under Counties.

There is also amongst the Miscellanea of the Exchequer of Receipt an original Roll containing similar Accounts for the Counties of *York* and *Cumberland*.

The following documents relating to Knights' Fees are amongst the Miscellaneous Rolls, Chancery (Bundle 8):—

No. 1. Returns of the names of persons holding 15 librates of land and upwards who ought to be knights.
40 Hen. III.

No. 2. A Roll containing Writs of respite from taking up knighthood, and also Writs relating to the payment of the "Saladin Tithe," and memoranda relating to a Treaty with Sicily. 41 & 42 Hen. III.

No. 3. A Roll containing Extracts from the "Liber Feodorum." Temp. Edw. 1.

No. 4. A File of Writs and Returns of Sheriffs of the names of persons in various counties holding 40 librates of land, &c. 6 Edward II.

No. 5. Do. 18 Edward II.
No. 6. Do. 19 Edward II.
No. 7. Do. 8 & 9 Edward III.

No. 8. Extracts from the Red Book of the Exchequer and the Liber Feodorum of all the Knights' Fees belonging to Edmund Earl of Chester. 11 Edw. III.

No. 9. A File of Writs and Returns of persons holding "centum solidatas terræ vel redditus," &c.
18 Edw. III.

No. 10. Extracts from the Red Book of the Exchequer of the names of all the Tenants in Capite in Norfolk, Suffolk, Essex, Herts, Cambridge, and Hunts. 45 Edw. III.

No. 11. A List of all the Knights' Fees, &c. of Hugh Courtenay, late Earl of Devon. Edw. III.

No. 12. Lists of all the Knights' Fees, &c. of Thomas Mowbray, late Duke of Norfolk (2 rolls). 1 Hen. IV.

Lists of Knights' Fees will also be found amongst the DEEDS OF PARTITION. See **PARTITION OF LANDS.**

The following are amongst the Miscellaneous Books of the Exchequer, Treasury of the Receipt :—

Vol. 69. Extents of Knights' Fees, &c. belonging to the Honor of Richmond. 9–10 Edw. I.

70. List of Knights' Fees in the County of Kent.
Temp. Edw. II.

71. Transcript of part of the "Testa de Nevill" (Edw. 1.) relating to Lincolnshire ; and a "Ledger Book" of the Abbey of Barlinges. (Edw. II to Hen. V.)

FEUDAL TENURES—(continued).

72. A volume entitled "Feoda in Capite," containing an account of all Knights' Fees in the Counties of Devon. Lincoln, Cumberland, Kent, and Bucks, compiled by the Master of the Court of Wards and Liveries.
34 Hen. VIII.

73. An account of all the Knights' Fees in the County of Kent, temp. Edw. III., including those of the Castle of Dover.
35 Hen. VIII.

74. An account of the Tenures of Manors in the County of Gloucester.
18 Eliz.

FINES AND RECOVERIES.

FINES.

A Fine (*Finis, or Finalis Concordia*), so called from the words with which it begins, and also from its effect in putting a *final end* to all suits and contentions, was an amicable agreement or composition of a suit (whether real or fictitious) made between the parties with the consent of the judges, and enrolled amongst the Records of the Court in which the suit was commenced, and by which freehold property might be transferred, settled, or limited. These Fines, or Final Agreements, are said to be of equal antiquity with the first rudiments of the law, instances having been produced of them even prior to the Norman invasion, and they no doubt originated in actual suits for recovering the possession of lands or other hereditaments, the possession thus gained being found so sure and effectual that fictitious actions were soon introduced for the sake of obtaining the same security. The Records of these actions exist in an almost unbroken series from the reign of Richard I. to the year 1834, when a Statute was passed " For the abolition of Fines and Recoveries and the " substitution of more simple modes of assurance."

The Records of Fines consist of the following branches, each of which represents one step in the proceedings :—

1. The *Writ of Covenant.*—This is a writ of Precipe sued out of the Court of Common Pleas the foundation of which is a supposed agreement or covenant between the parties, the fulfilment of which has been neglected, and forms the commencement of the suit. From this writ a fine was due to the King of one-tenth of the annual value of the lands, which was called the *primer fine.* Then followed the *licentia concordandi*, or leave to agree between the parties, for which, the suit having already been commenced and pledges to prosecute given, another fine was due to the King, which was called the *post fine* or " King's Silver." This was half as much again as the *primer fine*, that is three-twentieths of the supposed annual value.

2. *The Concord.*—This is the actual agreement signed by the parties after the leave to agree had been duly obtained and was either acknowledged in open Court or before two or more Commissioners specially appointed for

FINES AND RECOVERIES—(continued).

the purpose. In the latter case there are annexed to it the Writ of *Dedimus Potestatem,* containing the appointment of the Commissioners, and an affidavit verifying the taking of the acknowledgment.

The Concord being the complete Fine has been held to be the *principale recordum,* and the Fine was held to be of that term in which the Concord was made.

3. The *Note of the Fine.*—This was made out by the Chirographer from the Concord, and from this and the other proceedings he drew up the *Chirograph* or *Foot of the Fine,* which, with the previous proceedings annexed, was then deposited with the Custos Brevium, the Notes being retained by the Chirographer, by whom they were filed in Terms

4. The *Foot* and *Indentures of Fine.*—The Foot or conclusion of the Fine, sometimes called the Chirograph, begins with the words "Hæc est finalis concordia," "This is the final agreement," and recites the whole proceedings, the Fine being then completely levied.

In order to render the Fine more universally public and less liable to be levied by fraud, it was enacted that the Fine after engrossment should be openly read and proclaimed in Court sixteen times, viz., four times in the Term in which it was levied, and four times in each of the three succeeding Terms. This was reduced by Stat. 31 Eliz. to once in each of the four Terms, and these proclamations were endorsed on the Chirograph or Foot of the Fine.

In addition to the Foot, two Indentures, or Transcripts thereof, were engrossed by the Chirographer on the same piece of parchment, which was then divided into three indented portions, the Foot, between which and the two Indentures the word "Cyrographum" was written, being retained by the Custos Brevium, and the Indentures being given out to the respective parties to the Fine. The annexed diagram will show the manner in which this was done, and also how the Chirograph and the two Indentures can be made to verify each other :—

Foot and Indentures of Fine.

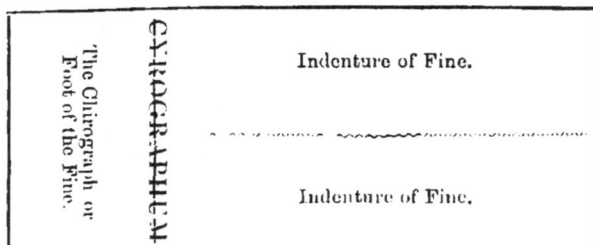

FINES AND RECOVERIES—(continued).

A *Recovery* in its most extensive sense is a restitution to a former right by the solemn judgment of a Court of Justice. What is generally termed a *Common Recovery* was, however, a judgment in a fictitious suit brought against the tenant of the freehold, which was obtained in consequence of a default made by the person last vouched to warranty in such fictitious suit. It is stated to have owed its origin to a practice introduced by the Religious houses in the reign of Edward I. of bringing actions for the recovery of lands, to which they set up a fictitious title, in order by so doing to elude the Statute of Mortmain and obtain, by a sentence of the law, those lands which they were otherwise precluded from acquiring.

It was not, however, till the reign of Edward IV. that Common Recoveries were generally introduced and recognised as an ingenious and effectual means of putting an end to all fettered inheritances and of barring estates tail and all remainders and reversions expectant thereon.

Though a Recovery, generally speaking, was a more extensive species of conveyance than a Fine to guard an estate against all claims and incumbrances, the operation of each was frequently necessary in aid of the other. A Fine was thus often levied for the purpose of creating a good Tenant to the Præcipe on which the Recovery was suffered, while a Recovery was suffered in order to operate as a discontinuance of an estate-tail, or for the purpose of barring remainders or reversions consequent thereon, and such a conveyance by Fine and Recovery *barred all the world.*

A Fine is technically said to be *levied*, a Recovery to be *suffered.* These terms have, however, not unfrequently been confounded.

Recoveries were of two kinds, either by *single* or by *double voucher*, and were effected in the following manner:—

Suppose A.B. to be the Tenant-in-tail in possession of a freehold, and to be desirous of barring all entails, &c. thereon, and of conveying the same in fee-simple to C.D.

The first step in the proceedings is for C.D., who is then called the *Demandant*, to bring an action against A.B. for the recovery of the lands in question, alleging that the Tenant has no legal title thereto, but that he only came into possession after one *Hugh Hunt* had turned him, the Demandant, out therefrom. This he does by suing out a writ called, from its initial words, " Præcipe quod reddat." The Tenant appears thereto and defends his right, " vouching," or calling to warranty a third person, who was hence called the *Vouchee.* The *Demandant* then craves leave of the Court to *imparl*, or confer with the Vouchee in private, after which he returns again to the

FINES AND RECOVERIES—(continued).

Court, but the Vouchee, although solemnly called, "cometh "not again, but departeth in contempt of Court," and makes default, whereupon judgment is given for the *Demandant* to recover the lands in question against the Tenant, who on his part may recover lands of equal value from the *Vouchee ;* but the latter having no lands of his own, being usually the Crier of the Court (who from being frequently thus vouched is called the *Common Vouchee*), the Tenant has only a nominal recompense, and the lands become absolutely vested in the *Demandant* by Judgment of the common law, a writ being directed to the Sheriff of the County to deliver seisin thereof.

The Recovery above described is by a *single* voucher only ; the Recovery by *double* voucher differed from this by the estate being first conveyed, either by Fine or by Indenture, to some indifferent person against whom the Præcipe or Writ was issued, and who was thence called the *Tenant to the Præcipe.* He vouched or called to Warranty the actual *Tenant-in-tail,* who in his turn vouched the *Common Vouchee,* who made default as before. This was much the more effective and common form of Recovery, for if the Recovery were had against the Tenant-intail directly, it barred only such estate in the premises as he was then actually seised of ; whilst if the Recovery were brought against another person, and the Tenant-intail were called to Warranty, he thereby barred every *latent* right and interest he might have therein.

As the most usual form of Fine, that "sur cognizance de droit come ceo, &c.," conveys an absolute estate without any limitations to the cognizee, and as Common Recoveries do the same to the Recoveror, these assurances could not be made to answer the purpose of family settlements unless their force and effect were subjected to the declaration of other more complicated deeds wherein particular uses can be more particularly expressed. If these deeds are made previous to the Fine or Recovery, they are called deeds to *lead* the uses ; if subsequent, Deeds to *declare* them ; and the Fine, when levied or the Recovery when suffered, shall enure to the uses so specified, and to no other. For although the Cognizee or Recoveror has a Fee-Simple vested in him by the Fine or Recovery, yet by the operation of this Deed he becomes a mere instrument or conduitpipe, seized only to the use of the persons specified in the settlement in successive order, such uses coming immediately into execution.

The enrolment of Deeds to lead or declare uses was not compulsory, and, such Deeds being generally of a more or less confidential nature, was not often resorted to. They

FINES AND RECOVERIES—(continued).

RECOVERIES—(continued).

might, however, be enrolled in any Court of Law within six months of the date of their execution.

The following List embraces the principal documents relating to Fines and Recoveries amongst the Records of the Courts of Common Pleas, and in the several Courts of the Principality of Wales and of the Counties Palatine of Chester, Durham, and Lancaster :—

Common Pleas.

AFFIDAVITS TO MODERATE FINES (ALIENATION OFFICE). 1802 to 1834. These state the amount of the Purchase Money, &c.

AFFIDAVITS ON WARRANTS OF ATTORNEY FOR SUFFERING RECOVERIES. 1774 to 1834.

FINES, FEET OF. Richard I. to 6 William IV. From Richard I. to Henry VIII., the Feet of Fines are arranged alphabetically in Counties. Subsequently to the latter reign, they are arranged chronologically Term by Term.

FINES, CONCORDS OF. 1 Eliz. to 6 Will. IV.

FINES, NOTES OF. Edward I. to 4 Will. IV.

FINES, PROCLAMATIONS OF. 1620 to 1841. 3 Vols.

FINES AND RECOVERIES, INROLMENTS OF WRITS FOR. 23–24 Eliz. to 10 Anne.

KING'S SILVER BOOKS. Eliz. to Will. IV. These books contain Abstracts of the Fines, giving the names of the parties and full particulars of the premises. Before George I. the series is very imperfect.

KING'S SILVER ENROLMENTS. These are entries of the payment of King's Silver enrolled on the Recovery Rolls, of which they form a distinct section.

RECOVERY ROLLS OR " PLACITA TERRÆ." Easter, 25 Elizabeth to 1837. 1004 rolls. Before Easter, 25 Elizabeth, see "Placita de Banco," or "Common Rolls." The Recovery Rolls consist of three portions :

1. Enrolments of "Common Recoveries" and also of Real Recoveries, or "Writs of Right."
2. Enrolments of the payment of King's Silver for license to levy Fines.
3. Enrolments of Deeds and other Instruments.

The last two rolls, extending from 1834 to 1837, consist of Pleas of Land and Deeds Enrolled only.

FINES AND RECOVERIES—(continued).

Common Pleas—(continued).

REMEMBRANCE ROLLS FOR RECOVERIES. 1770 to 1850.

These contain entries of præcipes for suffering common Recoveries with the record of the Tenants' appearances in Court, the names of the Demandants, Tenants, and Vouchees, and the particulars of the lands to be passed.·

The last of these Rolls, extending from 1834 to 1850, contains enrolments of admissions to prosecute and defend by guardians.

RULES TO AMEND FINES AND RECOVERIES. Geo. III. to Will. IV.

RULES AND ORDERS TO PASS FINES AND RECOVERIES. 1797 to 1834.

WARRANTS OF ATTORNEY FOR SUFFERING RECOVERIES. See AFFIDAVITS ON WARRANTS OF ATTORNEY.

WRITS OF COVENANT. 1 Edw. III. to 1834.

WRITS OF COVENANT, EXTRACTS FROM. (ALIENATION OFFICE.) 1576 to 1837. 135 Vols.
Indexes. 102 Vols.

WRITS OF ENTRY IN RECOVERIES, EXTRACTS FROM (ALIENATION OFFICE.) 1595 to 1835. 33 Vols.
Indexes, 1660 to 1834. 27 Vols.

The means of reference to Fines and Recoveries are as follows :—

Feet of Fines, Transcripts of. Ric. I. and John. *Bedford to Dorset.* Printed in 2 Vols. 8vo.

Do. *Ebor to Warwick.* 7 Vols. MS.

Feet of Fines, &c., Indexes to (for certain Counties). Ric. I. to Hen. VIII. 37 Vols. See **LE NEVE'S INDEXES.**

Feet of Fines, Index to. 1 Hen. VIII. to 58 Geo. III.
56 Vols. MS.

Do. 58 Geo. III. to 1839. 5 Vols. MS., called " Index to Notes of Fines."

Do. 1611 to 1835, 54 Vols. MS., called " Entry Books of Fines, and of Writs of Entry in Recoveries."

Recoveries, Indexes to. 7 Hen. VIII. to 5 Will. IV. 37 Vols.
M.S.

Welsh Courts.

The original WRITS, CONCORDS, and frequently the CHIROGRAPHS OF FINES and the PRÆCIPES and WARRANTS OF ATTORNEY, &C. FOR RECOVERIES are arranged in Files or Bundles for the following Counties ; the Recoveries being also enrolled in full on the PLEA ROLLS :

Anglesey. 1 Jas. II. to 11 Geo. IV.

Brecon. 1 Eliz. to 1 Will. IV.

FINES AND RECOVERIES—(continued).

Welsh Courts—(continued).

Cardigan. 2 Edw. VI. to 1 Will. IV.
Carmarthen. 2 Eliz. to 1 Will. IV.
Carnarvon. 1 Jas. I. to 11 Geo. IV.
Denbigh. 3 & 4 Phil. and Mary to 1 Will. IV.
Flint. Hen. VI. to 1 Will. IV.
Glamorgan. 34 Hen. VIII. to 1 Will. IV.
Merioneth. 7 Jas. I. to 1 Will. IV.
Montgomery. 1 Eliz. to 1 Will. IV.
Pembroke. 2 & 3 Phil. and Mary to 11 Geo. IV.
Radnor. 1 Mary to 1 Will. IV.

The means of reference are as follows :—

Docket Books of Fines and Recoveries.

(Anglesea, Carnarvon, and Merioneth.) 1803 to 1830. 1 Vol.
(Brecon, Radnor, and Glamorgan.) 1686 to 1830. 5 Vols.
(Cardigan.) 1739 to 1830. 3 Vols.
(Carmarthen.) 1792 to 1815. 2 Vols.
(Denbigh.) 1792 to 1806. 1 Vol.
(Flint.) 1 Eliz. to 1 Will. IV. See " Docket Books, Chester and Flint."
(Montgomery.) 1790 to 1830. " Entry Book." 1 Vol.
(Pembroke.) 1739 to 1798. 1 Vol.

Remembrance Rolls of Recoveries.

(Cardigan.) 1 Jas. II. to 1 Will. IV.
(Carmarthen.) 1657 to 1 Will. IV.
(Pembroke.) 1 Anne to 1 Will. IV.

N.B.—The Docket Rolls and Docket Books of *Pleas* also contain entries of Fines and Recoveries. See **JUDICIAL PROCEEDINGS.**

Palatinate of Chester.

FINES AND WARRANTS OF ATTORNEY, &c., FOR RECOVERIES. 1 Edw. I. to 1 Will. IV.

These are Files or Bundles containing the original Writs, Concords, and frequently the Chirographs of the Fines and the Præcipes and Warrants of Attorney for Recoveries.

Calendar. Edw. I. *Printed.* Report XXVIII. App., pp. 6–19.

Docket Books of Fines and Recoveries. 1 Henry VIII. to 1 Will. IV. 12 Vols. MS.

FINES, ENROLMENTS OF (CHESTER). 28 Elizabeth to Anne.

FINES AND RECOVERIES—(continued).
Palatinate of Chester—(continued).

FINES, ENROLMENTS OF (FLINT). 12 Elizabeth to 2 George II.

Do. (PEMBROKE). 29–40 Elizabeth.

RECOVERIES, ENROLMENTS OF. 1 Hen. VIII. to Will. IV.

The Recoveries are enrolled in full on the Plea Rolls, reference to them being made by means of the "Docket Books of Fines and Recoveries."

Palatinate of Durham.

FINES, FEET OF. Edw. VI. to 1834. 44 Bundles.

FINES, CONCORDS OF. 13 Chas. II. to 1834. 44 Bundles.

RECOVERIES, PRÆCIPES FOR. 13 Chas. II. to 1833. 35 Bundles.

RECOVERIES, DRAFTS OF. 1770 to 1833. 3 Bundles.

The Recoveries are enrolled at length on the Judgment Rolls.

Index to Fines. Hen. VI. to 31 Eliz. 1 Vol.
[*Prothonotary's Indexes, No.* 1.]

WRITS OF PRÆCIPE QUOD REDDAT, WARRANTS OF ATTORNEY, WRITS OF DEDIMUS POTESTATEM, AND OTHER PROCEEDINGS IN RECOVERIES (CURSITORS'). 35 Car. II. to 1785. 8 Bundles.

Palatinate of Lancaster.

FEET OF FINES, CONCORDS, &c. In bundles. From John of Gaunt (1362) to 4 Will. IV.

FINES, ENROLMENTS OF. 29 Eliz. to 4 Will. IV. Before 29 Elizabeth the Fines are enrolled on the Plea Rolls.

RECOVERIES. The Recoveries are enrolled in full on the Plea Rolls.

Indexes as follows:—

Docquet Rolls. 1362 to 34 George II. These refer to the Pleadings as well as to the Fines and Recoveries.

Docquet Rolls of Fines and Recoveries. 1 to 52 George III. Referring to Fines and Recoveries only.

Docquet Rolls of Fines. 1 to 27 George II. Referring to Fines only.

Docquet Books. 49 George III. to 4 William IV. 2 Vols. MS. called "Draft Docquets of Fines and Recoveries."

FORESTS, PARKS, AND CHASES.

A *Forest* was a portion of territory consisting both of woodlands and pastures circumscribed by certain metes and bounds within which the right of hunting was reserved exclusively to the King, and subject to a code of special laws frequently of exceptional severity. It had its own Courts for the administration of the Forest Laws, consisting of a Court of Justice Seat, a Court of Swainmote, and a Court of Attachments. The first of these was presided over by a Justice in Eyre of the Forests, who went his circuit once in every three years for the purpose of trying the offences presented at the two inferior courts, of which, the Court of Swainmote was held three times a year, and the Court of Attachments, or Woodmote Court, every forty days. The Justices in Eyre were appointed early in the reign of Henry II., and were two in number, one for the North and one for the South side of Trent. The principal Officers of the Forest were the *Verderers*, who acted as judges of the Swainmote Court and directors of all the other officers; the *Regarders*, who made a regard or Survey of the Forest every third year to inquire concerning all offences against the Forest Laws, and concerning *Assart Lands*, or lands cleared of forest growth and put under cultivation, for which Fines or Rents were due to the King, and *Purprestures* or encroachments of any kind for which similar payments were exacted; the *Agistors*, who regulated the sums paid for the Agistment or pasturage of cattle; Foresters, Woodwards, and others.

A *Chase* was, like a Forest, unenclosed and defined by metes and bounds only, but it had no particular laws or courts, offenders therein being punished according to the Common Law of England, nor had it the same officers as a Forest, but only Keepers and Woodwards.

A *Park* was of the same nature as a Chase, with the exception that it was always enclosed by a wall or pale. Finally, Parks and Chases might be held by any subject, whilst a Forest could, strictly speaking, only be held by the King, who alone could create a Justice of the Forest. The Royal Forests were 69 in number, besides thirteen Chases and more than seven hundred Parks. With the exception of the New Forest, which was formed by William the Conqueror, the origin of the Royal Forests cannot be exactly traced.

The bounds of the Forests were largely increased during the reigns of Henry II., Richard I., and King John, but by the Chartæ de Foresta of the second and ninth years of Henry III. it was enacted that the Royal Forests should be reduced to their ancient limits, and that those portions

FORESTS, PARKS, AND CHASES—(continued).

which were not the ancient demesne of the King should be
disafforested. In order to carry this into effect several
Perambulations of the Forests were made during the reigns
of Henry III. and Edward I., which were subsequently
confirmed by Statute 1 Edw. III., c. 1.

Perambulations of the Royal Forests were also made in
the 17th year of Charles I.

The Accounts relating to the Royal Forests and of the
Issues of Assarts and Purprestures were enrolled at first
on the Pipe Rolls, and subsequently on the Rolls of
Foreign Accounts. A very large collection of original
Accounts of the Foresters, or "Custodes Forestarum,"
also exists amongst the Miscellanea of the Exchequer.

Subsequent to the establishment of the Court of General
Surveyors of the King's Lands and of the Court of
Augmentations the management of the Royal Forests was
vested in the hands of Special Officers belonging to those
Courts, and the Accounts relating thereto will be found in
the General Series of **MINISTERS' AND RE-
CEIVERS' ACCOUNTS.**

The following classes of Records relate to this subject:—

ACCOUNTS, &c. RELATING TO THE ROYAL FORESTS. (MIS-
CELLANEA, EXCHEQUER, Q. R.) Henry II. to James I.

These consist of Accounts of the Issues of the Royal
Forests, Presentments, and Certificates of Wastes and
Spoils, Proceedings in the Forest Courts, &c., &c.

Calendar. 1 Vol. MS.

Accounts of the deer in the Royal Parks and Forests,
1616 to 1674. [*Audit Office, "Declared Accounts,"
Bundles 846 and 847."*]

PLACITA FORESTÆ OR FOREST PROCEEDINGS. (CHANCERY.)
John to Charles I.

These consist of Perambulations, Claims, Presentments,
and other proceedings before the Justices in Eyre of the
Forests, Enrolments of Grants and Deeds relating to lands
in the Royal Forests, and other documents of a similar
nature. Those of an early date, *i.e.*, from John to Edward
III., are in one Bundle entitled " De Antiquis Forestis;"
those from Henry VIII. to Charles I. consist of 155
Bundles, of which, as well as of the earlier proceedings, an
Inventory is printed in Report V., App. II., pp. 46–56.

Two Perambulations of the Forests dated 7 Edward I.
and 29 Edward I. formerly amongst the Miscellaneous
Rolls have been added to the Bundle "De Antiquis
Forestis"; and a Bundle of Perambulations dated 17
Charles I. will be found amongst the "Special Com-
missions," &c. formerly in the Petty Bag Office.

FORESTS, PARKS, AND CHASES—(continued).

PLACITA FORESTÆ, &c.—(continued).

There are also "Swainmote Court Rolls" of Windsor Forest, from 2 Edw. VI. to 14 Charles I, an *Inventory* of which is printed in Report V., App. II., pp. 57–59 *Index.* 1 Vol. MS.

Do. (EXCHEQUER, TREASURY OF THE RECEIPT.) Henry III. to Charles II.

These consist of Pleas, Inquisitions, Claims, Perambulations, and other proceedings relating to the Royal Forests of various dates. They were formerly deposited with the so-called "County Bags" of Miscellanea. There is also a box containing Perambulations and Inquisitions "de statu Forestarum" in Divers Counties.

Calendars. 3 Vols. MS.

The following are amongst the Miscellaneous Books of the Exchequer, Treasury of the Receipt :—

Vol. 75. Transcripts of "arrentations." or demises of assarts and wastes, &c., in divers Forests. 9–35 Edw. I.
76. Perambulations, Pleas, &c. relating to Sherwood Forest. Hen. III. to Edw. III.
77. The "Black Book of the Forests"; a "perfect view and declaration" of every head of game, &c. in all the King's Forests north of Trent. 30 Hen. VIII.

Do. (DOMESTIC STATE PAPERS.)

A Book of Orders concerning the Royal Forests. 1637 to 1648. (Calendared.)

[*S. P. Dom, Car I., Vol. 384.*]

Do. (DUCHY OF LANCASTER.)

Pleas and Claims relating to divers forests in Lancashire and Yorkshire; Chute Forest in Wiltshire; the High Peak in Derbyshire; Pickering in Yorkshire; Waltham Forest in Essex, and others. Edw. I. to Hen. VII.

[*Misc. Records, Duchy of Lanc., Div. XXV., Bundle F.*]

Surveys, &c., relating to the Castle and Forest of Knaresborough, &c., co. York. Edw. IV. to Geo. III.

[*Misc. Records, Duchy of Lanc., Div. XXVI., Bundle 29.*]

See also the "GREAT COWCHERS" or CARTÆ REGUM.

PLACITA FORESTÆ OR FOREST PROCEEDINGS. (WELSH RECORDS.)

Forest Rolls. Chester. 55 Hen. III. to 18 Hen. VII. These contain Pleas of the Forest, Charters, and other proceedings relating to the Forests of Macclesfield, Delamere, Wirrall, Rudheath, and Overmarsh.

FORTIFICATIONS.

COMMISSIONS, &c. FOR PUTTING INTO EXECUTION ACTS FOR THE BETTER SECURING AND FORTIFYING THE DOCKS AND HARBOURS AT PORTSMOUTH, CHATHAM, AND PLYMOUTH, &c. (CHANCERY, CROWN OFFICE), Anne to Will. IV.

No. 1. Commission and Return, dated Sept. 1, 1714, for the docks, &c. at Portsmouth, Chatham, and Harwich.

No. 2. Ditto dated July 27, 1758, for the docks, &c. at Portsmouth, Chatham, and Plymouth.

No. 3. Ditto dated Dec. 14, 1759, for the docks, &c. at Milford Haven.

No. 4. Commission and Return, dated Sept. 17, 1760, for removing the gunpowder magazine from Greenwich to Purfleet.

No. 5. Decree, dated Nov. 8, 1762, for the docks, &c. at Milford Haven.

No. 6. Commission and Return, dated July 19, 1762, for securing lands in Kent, Sussex, and Southampton.

No. 7. Ditto dated Aug. 26, 1780, for the docks, &c. at Plymouth and Sheerness.

No. 8. Ditto dated Aug. 26, 1780, for the docks, &c. at Chatham.

No. 9. Ditto dated Aug. 26, 1784, for the docks, &c. at Portsmouth, and the gunpowder magazine at Faversham.

No. 10. Ditto dated June 24, 1786, for the magazine, &c. at Faversham.

No. 11. Ditto dated Sept. 30, 1784, for the docks, &c. at Portsmouth and Plymouth.

No. 12. Ditto dated Feb. 24, 1831, for the docks, &c. at Gosport.

COMMISSIONS OF INQUIRY RESPECTING PORTSMOUTH HARBOUR, &c. (CHANCERY, PETTY BAG OFFICE.) Anne. 1 Bundle.

DEEDS, &C., RELATING TO THE PURCHASE OF LAND FOR THE FORTIFICATIONS AT CHATHAM. (EXCHEQUER, Q. R.) 1578 to 1715. (3 Parcels containing 110 documents.)

ORDNANCE DECREES. (EXCHEQUER, Q. R.) 1785 to 1806. 23 Rolls containing enrolments of the Decrees made under several Statutes for transferring lands for the service of the Board of Ordnance, in erecting Fortifications, &c. (A List of these Rolls is contained in the volume entitled " Index to Papers.")

FRANCE, ENGLISH POSSESSIONS IN.

For a description of the FRENCH, GASCON, and NORMAN ROLLS respectively, see **CHANCERY ENROL- MENTS (VARIOUS).**

ACCOUNTS AND OTHER DOCUMENTS RELATING TO THE ENGLISH POSSESSIONS IN FRANCE. (MISCELLANEA, EXCHEQUER, Q. R.) Henry III. to Henry VIII.

These consist of 51 Parcels, entitled "Realm of France"; containing, in addition to the Accounts of the Constables and Controllers of Bordeaux, Calais, and other towns, and of the Collectors of Customs and other dues in various ports, Accounts of the Seneschals and Governors of the French provinces under the English rule, that is to say, Aquitaine or Gascony, Ponthieu, the district of Calais and the Marches, and for certain short periods parts of Brittany and Normandy.

Calendar. 1 Vol. MS.

Many documents of a similar nature to the foregoing formerly amongst the Miscellanea of the Treasury of the Receipt will be added to this series.

The following are amongst the Miscellaneous Books of the Treasury of the Receipt :—

Vol. 78. Accounts of payments made by the Constable of Gascony. 4 Edw. II.
Vol. 79. Accounts relating to Harfleur and Ponthieu. Hen. V. and Edw. III.
Vol. 80. Accounts of Ponthieu and Gascony. [Edw. III.]
Vol. 81. Accounts, &c. relating to Gascony. [Edw. III.]
Vol. 82. Accounts of the Bishopric of Tournay. 23 Hen. VII.
Vol. 83. Original Examinations in the Chancery of Brittany. Hen. VIII.

CALAIS, ACCOUNTS RELATING TO. Henry IV.
[*Misc. Books, Augmentation Office, Vol. 335.*]

CALAIS, ACCOUNTS OF LANDS PURCHASED AND EXCHANGED. (EXCHEQUER, AUGMENTATION OFFICE.) 32 Henry VIII. to 5 Edward VI.

These are incorporated in the General Series of "Ministers' and Receivers' Accounts."

CALAIS AND THE MARCHES, ACCOUNTS RELATING TO. (MISC. BOOKS, EXCHEQUER, L. T. R.)

36 Hen. VI. Account of Sir John Cheyne, Receiver and Victualler of Calais.

22 Edw. IV. Comptroller's Account of the Office of Treasurer.

36–37. Hen. VIII. Comptroller's Account of the Office of Victualler.

FRANCE, ENGLISH POSSESSIONS IN—(continued).

CALAIS, COMPTROLLERS' ACCOUNTS. (EXCHEQUER, TREASURY OF THE RECEIPT.) Henry VII. and Henry VIII.

These are bound in four very large volumes. There are also several bundles of Indentures witnessing the receipt by the Treasurer of Calais from the Collectors of Customs in various ports of the sums of money assigned for the expenses of Calais, with bonds of merchants and other documents relating thereto.

Treasurers' and Comptrollers' Accounts of the Town and Marches of Calais from 8 to 18 Henry VII. will be found amongst the Receiver-Generals' Accounts of the Duchy of Lancaster. See Report XXX., App., pp. 35-38.

CALAIS AND THE MARCHES, SURVEY OF.

A new Survey of Calais and the Marches taken in the year 1556, and entitled "The description of the limytes, " wayes, rivers, watergangs, and perambulacons and par- " ticous of parisshes of the same, by measure from pointe " to pointe directed by compas maryne by the Low " Countrie measure." Two very large volumes.

[*Misc. Books, Augmentation Office, Vols.* 371-372.]

CALAIS, LAWS, LIBERTIES, AND PRIVILEGES OF. 1 Henry VIII. 1 Vol.

[*D. of Lanc. Div. xxr. M. 23.*]

PONTIVY AND MONSTROILL, ACCOUNTS OF NICHOLAS DE LOUTH, THE KING'S TREASURER OF THE LORDSHIPS OF. Edward III. 2 Vols.

[*Misc. Books, Augmentation Office, Vols.* 437-438.]

GASCON PETITIONS (CHANCERY). Edw. I. to Edw. III.

These have been incorporated with the Parliamentary Petitions or Petitions to King and Council, and consist of Petitions on various subjects addressed to the King in Council, from his subjects in Gascony and other French Provinces.

Calendar. Edw. II. 1 Vol. MS.

The following documents relating to the French Provinces are amongst the Miscellaneous Rolls, Chancery:

FRANCE, DOCUMENTS RELATING TO. (CHANCERY.) Bundle 5.

No. 1. Petition of the Steward of Saintonge, complaining of the injuries inflicted by the Normans on English subjects in Saintonge, Bayonne, the Cinque Ports, Ireland, and elsewhere. 21 Edw. I.

FRANCE, ENGLISH POSSESSIONS IN—(continued).

FRANCE, ENGLISH POSSESSIONS IN—(continued).

FRANCE, DOCUMENTS RELATING TO, &c.—continued.

No. 26. Transcripts of Letters by the King of France renouncing a maletolt granted to him by the town of Bordeaux. 3 Edw. II.

No. 27. Proceedings between the King of England, as Duke of Aquitaine, and the Lord de Caumont, concerning the "locus de Gontant." 6 Edw. II.

No. 28. A Notarial Instrument relating to proceedings in the Court of the King of France by the Proctor of the King of England relating to the Castle of Agen.
16 Edw. II.

No. 29. Proceedings before the Bishop of Winchester and others, Commissioners of the King of England, appointed to receive the oaths of the Steward, Nobles, and others of Gascony. 16 Edw. II.

No. 30. Enrolment of Writs of Dedimus Potestatem to Ralph Basset de Drayton and others to receive into the King's peace all persons of the Duchy of Aquitaine who are willing to return to their allegiance.
18 Edw. II.

No. 31. A Notarial copy of the Will of the Count of Poitou and Toulouse. 55 Hen. III.

No. 32. Transcripts of the donations made to Stephen de Montferrand by the Lady Margaret his wife, in Gascony. Aquitaine, &c. 3 Edw. I.

No. 33. The Petition of Hugh, Earl of March, for the restoration of his lands in Saintonge, &c. Edw. I.

No. 34. Transcripts of instruments relating to the possessions of the said Earl of March. Edw. I.

No. 35. A Petition from the Mayor, &c. of the Town of Libourne concerning the losses sustained by them, with the reply thereto. Hen. VI.

No. 36. Extents of the lands, &c. belonging to the Castles and Lordships of Merke, Calais, Sandgate, Guisnes, &c. 10 Hen. V.

No. 37. An Inquisition concerning the state of houses and buildings at Calais. 20 Hen. VIII.

See also the "REGISTRUM MUNIMENTORUM," described under the head of **REGISTERS AND BOOKS OF REMEMBRANCE, and TREATIES AND DIPLOMATIC DOCUMENTS.**

GENEALOGY.

Records of almost every kind may be said to bear indirectly on the subject of genealogical inquiry, but there are certain classes of documents especially rich in information respecting the descent of families, and the ownership of land, the chief of which may be briefly indicated as follows:

(1.) The INQUISITIONS POST MORTEM, extending from the reign of Henry III. to that of Charles II.

These were held on the death of any person holding or supposed to hold lands or tenements as a tenant in capite from the Crown, and state the extent and value of the

GENEALOGY—(continued).

lands so held, the date of the death of the proprietor, and and the name, age, and relationship of the next heir.

(2.) The FINE ROLLS, extending from the reign of John to that of Charles I., and containing entries of all writs for the livery of lands, grants of wardships and marriages, and other documents incidental to the Feudal Tenures.

(3.) The INQUISITIONS and BOOKS OF KNIGHT'S FEES from Henry II. to Elizabeth, which state the number of Fees held by the tenants in capite throughout England, according to the returns made thereof from time to time, for the purpose of levying Scutages and other feudal imposts; together with lists of persons in the various counties holding such a quantity of land as qualified them for the order and duties of knighthood.

These are fully described under the head of **FEUDAL TENURES.**

(4.) The PARLIAMENTARY WRITS and WRITS OF SUMMONS TO MILITARY SERVICE.

The Writs of Summons of Peers, Writs and Returns of Members of the House of Commons, Writs of Summons, Commissions of Array, and other documents relating to Military service (including the Scutage and Marshals' Rolls), for the Reigns of Edward I. and Edward II. have been transcribed from the various classes of Records on which they are enrolled and published, together with a Chronological Abstract and Calendar thereof, in 4 Vols. or parts, edited by Sir F. Palgrave.

There are also 55 Vols. of similar Transcripts in MS. extending from Edw. III. to Edw. IV., and a Chronological Abstract from 1 to 51 Edw. III. in 8 Vols.

(5.) The ACCOUNTS, MUSTER ROLLS, RETINUE ROLLS, and other documents relating to the ARMY AND NAVY from John to Elizabeth, which include Lists of the Knights, and Men-at-arms who served in the Scotch and Welsh wars, the Musters of the Army of Agincourt, and many similar documents.

These are fully described under the title **ARMY AND NAVY.**

(6.) The CHIROGRAPHS or FEET OF FINES, which extend in an almost unbroken series from Richard I. to William IV., and contain the evidence of almost every transfer of land or other hereditaments which took place between those dates. See **FINES AND RECOVERIES.**

(7.) The large collections of ANCIENT DEEDS, a Descriptive Catalogue of which is in progress, two volumes having been already issued (1890–1894).

GENEALOGY—(continued).

(8.) The SUBSIDY ROLLS or Accounts of the Collectors of Lay and Clerical Subsidies and other imposts, from Henry III. to Wm. and Mary.

In many of these Rolls the assessments are set out in full, the names being given of all the persons in each Parish contributing to the Subsidy, Poll Tax, or other levy, with the amounts at which they were assessed, in lands or in goods. They also include voluminous accounts of the *Hearth Tax* levied in the reign of Charles II., specifying the number of Hearths paid for by each contributor. These are further described under the head of **TAXATION.**

(9.) The ROYALIST COMPOSITION PAPERS, or Proceedings of the Committee for compounding with the Royalist nobility and gentry for the estates forfeited by them during the Commonwealth, which are full of interesting particulars respecting those who favoured the Royal cause. See **ROYALISTS AND DELINQUENTS.**

(10.) The FORFEITED ESTATES PAPERS. Temp. George I.

These papers contain complete lists of all the persons attainted during the rebellion of 1715, with Rentals and Deeds relating to their estates ; lists of all Popish Recusants who had registered their estates, pursuant to the Statute of 1 Geo. I., arranged under counties, and also alphabetically ; and a large collection of informations respecting lands given to Superstitious Uses, all of which are genealogically valuable and interesting.

An *Inventory* of these Papers is printed in Report V., App. II., pp. 97–130.

(11.) The CHANCERY PROCEEDINGS, or Pleadings and Depositions in Chancery Suits, from the reign of Elizabeth to the present time.

These are indexed, and frequently contain statements of family relationship extending over several generations. See **JUDICIAL PROCEEDINGS.**

In addition to the foregoing, attention may be directed to the ROTULUS DE DOMINABUS or "Ladies' Roll" of 31 Henry II., printed by Stacy Grimaldi for the Society of Antiquaries ; to the CALENDARIUM GENEALOGICUM or Calendar of Heirs, Henry III. and Edw. I., extracted from the Inquisitions post mortem and the Fine Rolls, printed in the Series of "Calendars of State Papers, &c." ; the Calendar of PROOFS OF AGE, temp. Edward III., printed in Report III., App. II., p. 202, and Report IV., App. II., p. 131 : and to the HUNDRED ROLLS, the ASSIZE AND QUO WARRANTO ROLLS, the ABBREVIATIO PLACITORUM, and other publications of the Record Commissioners.

GENEALOGY—(continued).

The Rolls of Common Law Proceedings, although full of invaluable information, are too bulky to invite the attention of the genealogical inquirer, and the absence of complete indexes renders an exhaustive search almost impracticable ; but the REDISSEISIN ROLLS of the Court of Chancery, which contain enrolments of all writs to the Sheriffs of Counties to re-deliver to successful plaintiffs the lands and tenements of which they had been unjustly deprived, are well worth attention, as containing abstracts of pleadings relating to land. The greater portion of these Rolls are printed in the volumes entitled, "Rotulorum Originalium Abbreviatio." See **CHANCERY ENROLMENTS (VARIOUS).**

The various series of COURT ROLLS described in the present work, are full of information respecting copyhold tenures.

There are amongst the collection known as "Palmer's Indexes" two folio volumes, entitled respectively "Primus Liber Cedularum" and "Secundus Liber Cedularum" (Vols. 102 and 103), which contain a collection of materials touching the descent of families from 1 Hen. VIII. to 28 Elizabeth, referring apparently to books at the "Herald's College."

A collection of "Genealogical Notes" extracted principally from the Coram Rege and De Banco Rolls, comprising 17 folio volumes, each volume being carefully indexed, was acquired by the Public Record Office from the representatives of the late General Harrison in 1891, and five more volumes by the same compiler were subsequently presented to the office by J. C. C. Routh, Esq. These volumes have been placed in the Search Rooms for the public use.

The "Golden Grove Book," a Genealogical and Heraldic collection relating to Wales, in 4 Vols., belonging to the Earl of Cawdor, was in 1870 conditionally deposited by him in the Public Record Office for public use.

The following documents relating to the history of private families will be found amongst the "Miscellaneous Rolls," Chancery.

The Pedigree of Lord Fitzhugh. Hen. VI. (No. ¹⁹.)
Letters, &c. relating to the families of Darell, Stonor, &c.
Edw. IV.—Eliz.
Papers relating to the title of Lord Rutland and Wm. Darrell, Esq., to the Manor of Chilton Foliot, co. Wilts.
Hen. VI.—Eliz.

The following, relating chiefly to former Officers of the Court of Exchequer, are amongst the "Miscellanea" of the Exchequer, Queen's Remembrancer.

Fanshaw Papers. Hen. VIII. to Jas. I.

GENEALOGY — (continued).

Hencage Papers. Hen. VIII. and Edw. VI.
Holland Papers. James I.
Stonley Papers. Elizabeth.

There are also amongst the Records of the Augmentation Office the following Chartularies of private families (Calendared in Report VIII., App. II., pp. 147–166):—

A Register of the Muniments of the family of Beauchamp of Hacche, Co. Somerset. Hen. III. to Edw. III.
Do.   of the family of Hull or Hyll, of Spaxton,
Co. Somerset.   Hen. III. to Edw. IV.

GENTLEMEN PENSIONERS.

GENTLEMEN PENSIONERS ROLLS.   (EXCHEQUER OF RECEIPT.) 4 & 5 Philip and Mary to 49 George III.

These contain yearly or quarterly accounts of the Wages due at the Receipt of the Exchequer to the Captain and other Officers and to the Band of " Gentlemen Pensioners " whose names are specified, with the amounts due to each.

GRAMMAR SCHOOLS.

SCHOOLS, DOCUMENTS RELATING TO.   (EXCHEQUER, AUGMENTATION OFFICE.) Edward VI.

A Package, containing :—

(1.) A File of Warrants by the Commissioners appointed in the 2nd year of Edward VI. to take order for the maintenance and continuance of schools and of " preachers, priests, and curates of necessitie " and for the payment of the stipends, &c. allowed by the said Commissioners.

(2.) 14 Rolls of Particulars for Grants of lands and tenements in various counties towards the erection and maintenance of Free Grammar Schools, dated 5 Edward VI.

Licenses for the foundation of Grammar Schools, &c. are enrolled on the Patent Rolls.

GUILDS AND FRATERNITIES.

GUILDS, CERTIFICATES OF. (CHANCERY.) 12 Richard II.

These are the Returns made to the King in Council, pursuant to Statute, 12 Ric. II., as to the *Ordinances, Usages*, and *Property*, &c. of the various *Guilds and Brotherhoods* throughout England. They are contained in 9 Portfolios, placed with the Miscellaneous Rolls of the Court of Chancery. A List of these Certificates arranged under Counties has recently been prepared. Such of the Returns as are written in English have been printed in full in Toulmin Smith's " English Gilds."

See also **MONASTIC FOUNDATIONS, &c.**

HANAPER ACCOUNTS.

ACCOUNTS OF THE CLERK OF THE HANAPER. (MISCEL-
LANEA, EXCHEQUER, Q. R.)   Edward I. to Elizabeth.

Accounts of the Receipts and Issues by the Clerk of
the Hanaper, with Writs, Receipts, and other documents
subsidiary thereto.   These include accounts of the Fees
received on Charters, Patents, and Commissions passing
the Great Seal, specifying the names of the persons to
whom such Charters, &c., were granted; and also Accounts
of the payments of salaries, allowances, and other disbursements by the Clerk of the Hanaper to various Officers of
the Court of Chancery.
Calendar.   1 Vol. MS.

ACCOUNTS OF THE CLERKS OF THE HANAPER.   1562 to
1827.
[*Audit Office,* " *Declared Accounts,*" *Bundles* 1354 *to*
1420.]

HOSPITALS.

ACCOUNTS OF THE RECEIVERS-GENERAL AND PAYMASTERS
OF CHELSEA HOSPITAL.   1680 to 1827.
[*Audit Office,* " *Declared Accounts,*" *Bundles* 1466 *to*
1488.]

HOSPITALS AND INFIRMARIES (VARIOUS), ACCOUNTS OF.
1653 to 1809.
[*Do., Bundles* 1503 *to* 1528.]

GREENWICH HOSPITAL ACCOUNTS (LAND REVENUE
OFFICE).   13 vols.   1702–1724.
Accounts of the Household expenses and of repairs and
other Works.

HUNDRED ROLLS.

HUNDRED ROLLS.   2 & 3 Edward I. and 7 & 8 Edward I.

The Hundred Rolls contain the Inquisitions taken by
virtue of two Special Commissions issued in the second and
seventh years of Edward I. respectively, by which the
Commissioners were directed to summon juries to inquire
into the King's rights, royalties, and prerogatives, and into
the frauds and abuses connected therewith.
By them the Crown was furnished with evidence of " all
the demesne lands of the Crown, whether ancient or newly
acquired by escheat or purchase; of the manors, &c.
formerly in the hands of the Crown, the persons holding
the same, by what authority, and how alienated; of
the tenants in capite and tenants in ancient demesne: of
the losses sustained by the Crown (in military services and

HUNDRED ROLLS—(continued).

HUNDRED ROLLS, &c.—(continued).

otherwise) by sub-infeudations made by such tenants; of alienations to the church under the pretext of gifts in frankalmoigne; of wardships, marriages, escheats, and suits and services withholden and subtracted; of the fee-farms of the Crown, hundreds, wapentakes, and tythings; of courts, wreck of the sea, free-chase, free-warren, and other jura regalia; of the oppressions of the nobility, clergy, and others claiming such rights; of exactions by excessive and illegal tolls in fairs, and for murage, pontage, &c.; of exactions by sheriffs, escheators, and other ministerial officers; and of the illegal exportation of wools, &c., &c." Similar inquiries appear to have been held by the Justices Itinerant, both at earlier and subsequent dates. The Returns to some of these are placed with the Hundred Rolls, but they are more generally enrolled on the Assize Rolls amongst the " Placita Coronæ " and " Placita de Quo Warranto."

A portion only of the Inquisitiones Hundredorum or Hundred Rolls, was returned into Chancery and deposited in the Tower of London; the remainder, so far as they exist, together with the Rolls called " Extract Hundred Rolls," from which the deficiences can in many cases be supplied, being deposited with the Records of the Treasury of the Receipt of the Exchequer in the Chapter House.

Transcripts in full of most of the Hundred Rolls of Edward I., together with several Inquisitions, dated 39 Henry III,, have been printed by the Record Commission in 2 Vols. folio, with *Indices Nominum* and *Locorum.*

N.B.—The Titles of the several Hundred Rolls, as given in the printed volumes, do not appear in the original Rolls, but appear to have been compiled by the editors from the several Commissions and Articles of Inquiry.

The Hundred Rolls, both of the Tower and Chapter House Series, have now, for convenience of reference, been placed together in 8 Boxes, the contents of which are set out in the following List :—

HUNDRED ROLLS.

(The Rolls marked with an asterisk have not been printed.)

Bedford.	(Tower Series.)	7 Edw. I.	2 rolls.
„	(Chapter House.)	„	1 roll.
Bucks.	(Tower Series.)	„	5 rolls.
„	(Chapter House.)	39 Hen. III. ⎫ and ⎬ 3 Edw. I. ⎭	18 rolls.
Cambridge.	(Tower Series.)	7 Edw. I.	15 rolls.
„	(Chapter House.)	3 „	4 rolls.*
Derby.	(Tower Series.)	3 „	4 rolls.

HUNDRED ROLLS—(continued).

HUNDRED ROLLS, &c.—(continued).

Devon.	(Chapter House.)	3 Edw. I.	47 ms.
Dorset.	,,	3 ,,	4 ms.
Essex.	,,	2 ,,	3 rolls.
Gloucester	,,	2 ,,	5 ms.
,,	,,	2 ,,	1 roll.*
Hereford	,,	3 ,,	3 rolls.
Hertford	,,	3 ,,	1 roll.
Hunts	(Tower Series.)	7 ,,	5 rolls.
,,	(Chapter House.)	3 ,,	2 rolls.*
Kent.	,,	3 ,,	1 roll.
Lincoln.	(Tower Series.)	3 ,,	30 rolls.
London	(Chapter House.)	3 ,,	16 ms.
,,	,,	3 ,,	1 roll.

(An "Extract Roll.")

,,	(Tower Series.)	7 Edw. I.	26 ms.*
Middlesex.	,,	7 ,,	2 ms.*
Norfolk.	(Chapter House.)	3 Edw. I.	12 rolls.
,,	,,	Hen. III. (?)	1 roll, en-

titled "De Escheatis, et viduis et valettis," &c.*

Northampton.	(Chapter House.)	3 Edw. I.	2 rolls.
Nottingham.	(Tower Series.)	,,	4 rolls.
Oxford.	,,	7 ,,	18 rolls.
,,	(Chapter House.)	39 Hen.III. and 2 Edw. I.	7 rolls.
Rutland.	,,	3 ,,	1 roll.
Salop.	,,	39 Hen.III. and 2 Edw. I.	23 rolls.
Somerset	,,	2 Edw. I.	25 ms.
Southampton	,,	2 & 3 Edw. I.	5 rolls.
Stafford	,,	39 Hen. III.	1 roll.
,,	,,	39 Hen. III. and 3 Edw. I.	2 rolls.*
Suffolk.	,,	3 Edw. I.	9 rolls.

(Roll 9 not printed.)

Sussex.	,,	3 Edw. I.	1 roll.

(An "Extract Roll.")

,,	,,	3 Edw. I.	1 m.*
Warwick.	——————.	7 Edw. I.	A book

of 126 leaves containing Transcripts of the Inquisitions for the County of Warwick. [*Misc. Books,
Exchequer Q. R., Vol. 15.*] Not printed.

Wilts.	(Chapter House.)	39 Hen. III.	1 Roll.
,,	,,	3 Edw. I.	35 ms.
,,	,,	,,	1 Roll.*

HUNDRED ROLLS—(continued).

EXTRACT HUNDRED ROLLS &c. (in Box 8).

No. 1. Dorset, Northumberland, Essex, Norfolk, Suffolk, and Hertford.

No. 2. Lincoln, Oxford, Berks, Bucks, Beds, Cambridge, Hunts, Devon, and Cornwall.

No. 3. York, Somerset, Worcester, Gloucester, Leicester, Warwick, Notts, Derby, Stafford, Northampton, and Rutland.

No. 4. Norfolk, Suffolk, Essex, Hertford, Dorset, and Northumberland. (This Roll contains Verdicts " de Ministris" only, and is not printed.)

INQUISITIONES HUNDREDORUM. (EXCHEQUER Q. R.) 12 & 13 Edw. I. A bundle, formerly amongst the Miscellanea of the Queen's Remembrancer, containing Inquisitions and Extents of certain Hundreds in the Counties of Somerset and Dorset, Bucks, Northampton, &c.

INQUISITIONS RESPECTING LIBERTIES AND FRANCHISES IN DIVERS COUNTIES. 10 Edw. II. A bundle containing 79 Inquisitions, many of which are almost illegible. These have not been printed.

INQUISITIONS, "POST MORTEM," AND "AD QUOD DAMNUM," &c.

INQUISITIONS POST MORTEM.

The documents known as " Inquisitiones post mortem " or " Escheats," consist principally of the inquests which were held on the death of any of the King's tenants in capite by the escheator or escheators of the several counties or districts, who, either by virtue of Writs " de diem clausit extremum " to them directed, or " virtute officii " merely, summoned a jury to inquire upon oath of what lands, &c. such tenant was seized at the time of his death, by what rents or services they were held, and the name and age of the next heir, in order that the King might be duly informed of his right of escheat or wardship or other advantages thereby accruing to him.

If the heir was an adult, on his appearance in Court and performance of homage to the King, and on payment of a reasonable *fine* or *relief*, the livery and seisin of his lands was granted to him.

If, however, he was a minor, he and his lands remained in wardship until he could sue out his writ " de ætate probandâ," under which process witnesses were examined and their depositions returned into Chancery, when, on being proved of full age, he was released from his wardship.

INQUISITIONS POST MORTEM, &c.—(continued).

Inquisitions Post Mortem—(continued).

These " *Proofs of Age* " will be found amongst the Inquisitions post mortem. Proceedings " de probatione ætatis " are also entered on the earlier Coram Rege Rolls. [See " Ancient Kalendars of the Exchequer, &c." Vol. I. p. li.]

The earlier Inquisitions post mortem also include the Inquisitions " *ad quod damnum,*" and a great variety of other documents partaking of the nature of Returns to Writs of Inquiry issued out of the Chancery. Such are Inquisitions respecting Knights' Fees ; Extents of Manors ; Inquisitions as to the lands, &c. of Attainted Persons, of Felons, and of Idiots and Lunatics ; inquiries respecting the Liberties and Franchises of Cities and Boroughs, Rights of Fishery, Free-Warren, &c., and respecting the building and repairing of Castles and Bridges ; and Inquests held on appeals of murder and homicide, and respecting trespasses of various kinds and other misdemeanours. The Inquisitions *ad quod damnum,* from 1 Edward II. to 39 Henry VI. (with the exception of those of the reign of Richard II.), have been separated from the Inquisitions post mortem, and form a distinct class. Subsequent to the latter date they are again filed with the Inquisitions post mortem.

The series of Inquisitions post mortem commences with the earlier portion of the reign of Henry the Third. There is, however, amongst the Miscellanea of the Exchequer, Queen's Remembrancer, a roll of a somewhat similar nature, entitled " Rotulus de Dominabus et Pueris et Puellis de " donatione Regis in xij. Comitatibus," which contains Abstracts of Inquisitions taken in the 31st year of Henry the Second, for the purpose of ascertaining the wardships, reliefs, and other profits due to the King from the widows and orphans of his tenants in capite, and minutely describing their ages and heirship, with the quantity and value of their lands, and the stock thereon, &c., &c. See
FEUDAL TENURES.

There is also amongst the Inquisitions post mortem a Portfolio entitled " *Inquisitiones de Rebellibus, anno* 49 *Henry III.,*" which contains Inquisitions respecting the possessions of such persons as were implicated in the rebellion of the Earl of Leicester, which terminated with the battle of Evesham.

The series of Inquisitions post mortem terminates with the abolition of the Court of Wards and Liveries, which took place soon after the Restoration, a few Inquisitions only existing of a later date than 20 Charles I.

INQUISITIONS POST MORTEM, &c.—(continued).

INQUISITIONS POST MORTEM—(continued).

Transcripts of the Inquisitions post mortem were sent into the Exchequer, where they form a series known as "ESCHEATORS' INQUISITIONS," which in many instances supplies the deficiencies of the Chancery series.

On the establishment of the Court of Wards and Liveries in the year 31 & 32 Henry VIII., when the heir was found to be a minor, a Transcript was also transmitted to that Court.

Commissions of Inquiry respecting Escheats and Forfeitures, &c. of a later date than the series of Inquisitions post mortem, with the returns thereto, will be found amongst the "SPECIAL COMMISSIONS" from the Petty Bag Office and also amongst those of the Queen's Remembrancer's Department. See **COMMISSIONS.**

INQUISITIONS AD QUOD DAMNUM.

The Inquisitions ad quod damnum were taken by virtue of Writs addressed to the Escheators of the several counties or districts, when any Grant of a Market, Fair, or other privilege, or a License of Alienation of land was solicited, directing them to inquire, by means of a jury, whether such grant would be prejudicial to the interests of the King or of other persons. They were originally filed with the Inquisitions post mortem, but from 1 Edward II. to 39 Henry VI. (with the exception of those of Richard II.), form a distinct series. Subsequent to the latter date they are again filed with the Inquisitions post mortem.

From the commencement of the reign of James I., the Inquisitions ad quod damnum are amongst the "BREVIA REGIA," of the Petty Bag Office. See **CHANCERY FILES.**

A list of the several classes of Inquisitions post mortem or ad quod damnum, with the means of reference thereto, is appended.

Chancery.

INQUISITIONS POST MORTEM, &c. Henry III. to Charles I., and Miscellaneous (Eliz. to Car. II.)

Calendar. Hen. III. to Ric. III. Printed with Indices Nominum and Locorum. 4 Vols. folio.

Calendar. Hen. VII. in the press (1895.)

Indexes. Hen. VII. to Car. II. 9 Vols. M.S.*

See also **PALMER'S INDEXES.**

* These volumes will be superseded by the new Inventory of Chancery Inquisitions from Henry VII. to Charles II. which is in progress.

INQUISITIONS POST MORTEM, &c.—(continued).

Chancery—(continued).

INQUISITIONS AD QUOD DAMNUM. 1 Edw. II. to 39 Hen. VI.

Calendar. Edw. II. to Hen. VI. Printed in one volume folio, with Indices Nominum and Locorum.

[Before 1 Edw. II. and after 39 Hen. VI., and also for the reign of Richard II., see "INQUISITIONS POST MORTEM, &c." From and after the reign of James I., see "BREVIA REGIA" (PETTY BAG OFFICE).]

Exchequer, Queen's Remembrancer.

INQUISITIONS POST MORTEM (ESCHEATORS'). Henry III. to James I.

See "ESCHEATORS' ACCOUNTS AND INQUISITIONS," under the title **ESCHEATS, ATTAINDERS, AND FORFEITURES.**

Court of Wards and Liveries.

INQUISITIONS POST MORTEM. Henry VIII. to Charles I.

These are duplicates of the Chancery Series of Inquisitions post mortem which were returned into the Court of Wards and Liveries in all cases where the next heir was a minor.

Index. 34 Hen. VIII. to Car. I. 2 Vols MS.

INQUISITIONS POST MORTEM, TRANSCRIPTS OF. 2 to 23. Henry VIII. 6 Vols. [*Misc. Books, Vols.* 304 to 309.]
        Do. ABSTRACTS OF. 1 Eliz. to 15 Car. I. 9 Vols. [*Misc. Books, Vols.* 316 to 324.]
        Do. EXTRACTS FROM. 8 to 18 Hen. VIII. and Philip and Mary (co. Chester only). 2 Vols.
        [*Misc. Books, Vols.* 325-326.]
Chronological Index. 34 Hen. VIII. to 41 Eliz. 1 Vol.
        [*Misc. Books, Vol.* 312.]
Alphabetical Calendar. 1 Eliz. to 7 Jas. I. 1 Vol.
        [*Misc. Books, Vol.* 311.]
Calendar. 7 Eliz. to 15 Car. I. 1 Vol.
        [*Misc. Books, Vol.* 310.]
See also "*Palmer's Indexes,*" Vol. 104.

Duchy of Lancaster.

INQUISITIONS POST MORTEM. Edw. I. to Chas. I.

Calendar. Printed in the volumes entitled "Ducatus Lancastriæ" (Vol. 1, Pars Prima), with *Indices Nominum* and *Locorum.*

INQUISITIONS POST MORTEM, &c.—(continued).

Palatinate of Lancaster.

INQUISITIONS POST MORTEM. Ric. II. to Eliz. 2 Bundles.

Calendar. Printed. Report XXXIX., App., pp. 533–549.

Palatinate of Durham.

INQUISITIONS POST MORTEM, &c. Pontificate of Robert Nevill (1438–1457) to Chas. I. (*Cursitor's Records, Nos. 164 to 190.*) For Inquisitions prior to the Pontificate of Bp. Nevill, see INQUISITIONS POST MORTEM, REGISTERS OF.

Calendar. Report XLIV., App., pp. 310–542.

INQUISITIONS POST MORTEM, REGISTERS OF.

Abstracts or Transcripts of Inquisitions post mortem during the Pontificates of Bishops Beaumont, Bury, Hatfield, Fordham, Skirlawe, Langley, and Nevill. 1318 to 1442. 1 Vol. containing 314 leaves. (*Cursitor's Records, No. 2.*)

Calendar. Report XLV., App. I., pp. 153–282.

INQUISITIONS POST MORTEM, PROOFS OF AGE, AND ASSIGNMENTS OF DOWER, ABSTRACTS OF. Temp. Bishop Ruthall. 1509 to 1523. (*Cursitor's Records, No. 3.*) A manuscript of 63 pages.

Index Nominum at the end of the volume.

INQUISITIONS POST MORTEM, &c., ABSTRACTS OF. Temp. Bishops Bothe and James. 1457 to 1483. A manuscript of 93 folios. (*Cursitor's Records, No. 4.*) *Index Nominum* at the end of the volume.

INQUISITIONS POST MORTEM, ABSTRACTS OF, from the Pontificate of Bishop Beaumont (1318) to the reign of James I. Arranged *alphabetically* according to places. Imperfect, ending with the letter S. A manuscript of 363 leaves. [*Cursitor's Records, No. 5.*]

EXTENTS, &c. James I.

A manuscript book of a miscellaneous character, consisting of 568 pages, and containing (*inter alia*) extents of lands in the hands of the Bishop taken by virtue of Writs of diem clausit extremum, of Mandamus, of Scire facias, Extendi facias, &c. for intrusions into or alienation of lands and tenements without license.

[*Cursitor's Records, No. 7.*]

INQUISITIONS POST MORTEM, &c.—(continued).

Palatinate of Durham—(continued).

EXTENTS FOR ALIENATIONS WITHOUT LICENSE, &C. A Roll of 5 membranes. [*Cursitor's Records, No.* 198.]

INQUISITIONS AD QUOD DAMNUM, Geo. II. and Geo. III. A bundle of 35 instruments.
[*Cursitor's Records, No.* 197.]

Palatinate of Chester and Flint.

INQUISITIONS POST MORTEM, &C. Edw. III. to Car. I.

This series contains Inquisitions post mortem, Inquisitions ad quod damnum, Inquisitions as to Lunatics, Idiots, and Right of Way; proofs of Age; Assignments of Dower; Extents; Writs of Livery, &c.
Index. Report XXV., App., pp. 32–60.
Calendar. Edw. III. to Hen. VII. 1 Vol. MS. (arranged chronologically with an Index Locorum).
Index. Edw. III. to Car. II. 2 Vols. MS. (incomplete). Vol. 1 contains also references to Claims of Liberties.

IRELAND.

The principal documents relating to Ireland, in addition to the Series of "Irish State Papers" consist of the following :—

Chancery.

The "ROTULI HIBERNIÆ," or IRISH ROLLS, from 1 to 50 Edward III. See **CHANCERY ENROLMENTS (VARIOUS).**

Exchequer, Queen's Remembrancer.

IRISH EXCHEQUER DOCUMENTS. Henry III. to Richard III.

These are the Accounts of the successive Treasurers of Ireland of their receipts and expenses, which were rendered annually to the Exchequer in England pursuant to an order made in the 21st year of Edward I., with other documents relating to the transactions in that country and to the Mint and Exchange there. Two ecclesiastical taxations of Ireland, dated respectively A.D. 1302 and A.D. 1306, are also deposited with these documents. They are contained in 6 Rolls, of which a syllabus is given in the Deputy-Keeper's Fifth Report, App. II. The Irish Exchequer Documents have been elaborately described in the "Calendar of Documents relating to Ireland" published under the direction of the Master of the Rolls.
Calendar. 1 Vol. MS.

IRELAND—(continued).

Exchequer, Queen's Remembrancer—(continued).

MINISTERS' AND RECEIVERS' ACCOUNTS.

The Accounts of the possessions in Ireland of Roger Bigod, Earl of Norfolk, Thomas, Earl of Ormond, Elizabeth de Burgo, Lady of Clare, and others will be found with the General Series of Ministers' Accounts. (*See* Lists and Indexes, No. V., 1894.)

Exchequer, Treasury of the Receipt.

Documents relating to Ireland of various early dates, including Transcripts from the Memoranda Rolls of the Irish Exchequer from 1 Hen. V., to 12 Hen. VI. (printed in the "Rotuli Selecti"), Indentures of Fealty, &c., &c., will be found amongst the Miscellanea of the Exchequer.

REGISTRUM MUNIMENTORUM "LIBER A."

In this volume (fol. 416–420) will be found transcripts of several documents relating to Ireland, including Grants of the Seignory of Ireland and of the cities of Dublin and Limerick, &c. made by Henry III. to his eldest son Edward; of letters and obligations by the Prelates of Ireland and others; and of King John's letter declaring the reasons of his proceedings against William de Breosa.

Exchequer of Receipt.

CIVIL LIST ESTABLISHMENT FOR IRELAND, 1709.

One volume, containing a list of the Irish and French Pensioners, lists of Officers on full and half-pay, &c., &c. There are also amongst the Miscellanea of the Exchequer of Receipt accounts of the Military Establishments in Ireland, and of the soldiers levied or impressed for service there, from 43 Elizabeth to 20 James I. See **ARMY, NAVY, &c.**

State Paper Office.

Extents, &c., of the possessions of the dissolved Monasteries in Ireland. 3 Vols.

[*State Papers, Ireland, Folios. Vols.* 1 *to* 3.]

Papers relating to the "Adventurers for lands in Ireland" during the Commonwealth, with an Index. 14 Vols.

[*State Papers, Ireland, Vols.* 288–302.]

Ancient Maps. &c. 3 Vols. These include a Description of Ireland with a General Map and Plans of the principal Forts; Maps of the Provinces of Ulster and Munster, and numerous County and Baronial Maps made during the reigns of Elizabeth and James I.

[*State Papers, Ireland, Maps, Vols.* 1 *to* 3.

See also **STATE PAPERS, CALENDARS OF.**

IRELAND—(continued).

Calendar of Documents relating to Ireland. 1171 to 1307. 4 Vols., consisting of Excerpts from the Public Records of "all instruments and entries relating to Ireland." Printed in the Series of "Calendars of State Papers," &c.

Memoranda of Rolls, &c. relating to Ireland. Included in Ayloffe's "Calendar of Ancient Charters, &c." 1 Vol. 4to.

See also the "Liber Munerum Publicorum Hiberniæ," amongst the Record Publications (Ireland).

JEWELS.

Chancery.

Matters relating to the Crown Jewels are entered on the Close and Patent Rolls. See **CHANCERY EN-ROLMENTS.**

Exchequer, Queen's Remembrancer, and Treasury of the Receipt.

ACCOUNTS AND INVENTORIES OF THE CROWN JEWELS, &c. These will be found amongst the Accounts, &c. relating to the WARDROBE AND HOUSEHOLD, a complete Inventory of which is being prepared.

Numerous Indentures relating to the pawning of the Crown Jewels, &c., for the payment of troops, especially during the reign of Henry V., exist amongst the Accounts, &c., relating to the ARMY AND NAVY.

The following Inventories of Jewels are amongst the Miscellaneous Books from the Chapter House :—

INVENTORIES OF PLATE, JEWELS, AND, REGALIA Hen. VI. Vol. 84. [Printed in Palgrave's "Ancient Kalendars and Inventories of the Exchequer," Vol. II., pp. 241–258.]

ACCOUNTS OF THE JEWEL HOUSE. 24 Hen. VIII. Vol. 85. [Printed, as above, Vol. II., pp. 259–298.]

INVENTORIES OF THE ROYAL JEWELS, &c. 2 James I. Vol. 86. [Printed, as above, Vol. II., pp. 299–355, and Vol. III., p. 424.]

Exchequer of Receipt.

ACCOUNTS OF THE JEWELS, PLATE, &c., SOLD FOR HER MAJESTY'S USE (MISCELLANEA, EXCHEQUER OF RECEIPT.) 42 Elizabeth. 6 Rolls.

Entries relating to the purchase, &c. of Jewels will also be found on the Issue Rolls.

See **RECEIPTS AND ISSUES OF THE EXCHEQUER.**

JEWELS—(continued).

Land Revenue Office.

The following Inventories of Jewels, Plate, &c. are preserved at the Land Revenue Record Office.

An Inventory of the Wardrobe, Pictures, Statues, Plate, Jewels, Cabinets, Household Goods and effects of King Charles I., taken by the Commissioners appointed in 1649 for the sale thereof.

Inventories and Accounts of the Jewels of Queen Anne of Denmark, Consort of James I.

An Inventory of the Wardrobe and Jewels of Queen Elizabeth in 1599.

[*See* Record Commissioners' Report, 1800, p. 170.]

Audit Office and Pipe Office.

DECLARED ACCOUNTS OF THE MASTER AND TREASURER OF THE CROWN JEWELS, &c. 1546 to 1639.

JEWS.

Before the expulsion of the Jews from England, which took place about the year 1290, a considerable revenue was drawn from them by the King by way of *Tallages* (which were imposed at pleasure on the whole community, who were made to answer for one another, and if they made default on the days fixed for payment, were heavily fined); of *Fines* relating to law proceedings and *Amerciaments* for misdemeanours; and by means of the Fines and Compositions which they were compelled to pay for the King's goodwill and protection, and for license to trade or other privileges. In fact, the King seemed to be absolute lord of their estates and effects, and even of the persons of them and of their families, and "as they fleeced the subjects of the realm, so he fleeced them." [*Madox, Hist. of the Exchequer.*]

The *Receipt* or place appointed for the management of this Revenue of the *Judaism* was called *Scaccarium Judæorum*, or *Scaccarium Judaismi*, and formed a part of the Great Exchequer; certain persons being assigned to be Curators of this Revenue who were usually called *Custodes* or *Justiciarii Judæorum*, and who exercised jurisdiction in all affairs relating to the community, namely, in the Accounts of the Revenue, in Pleas upon Contracts made with the Jews, and in causes or questions touching their lands or chattels, or their Tallages, Fines, and Forfeitures.

When any Charter or Contract was made by the Jews one part of it was laid up in a public chest, called the *Chest of the Chirographs*, or of the Chirographers, such part being designated the *Pes Chirographi.*

JEWS—(continued).

The Chirographers who had the custody of all such Deeds or Contracts, were persons established for that purpose in those towns in which a considerable number of Jews resided, as at Lincoln, York, Oxford, &c., and generally consisted of Jews and Christians acting together. On the occasion of the goods and chattels of any Jew being forfeited, the Chirographs or Contracts relating to any debts due to him were transferred to the Exchequer for the King's benefit.

King Henry III. " out of his royal grace to the Jews, " and for the support of such of them as embraced the " Christian religion, and were destitute of livelyhood," founded a House at London, called the " *Domus Conversorum*," or House of the Converts, and endowed it with a competent revenue; the custody of the said House being generally granted to some clergyman of distinction, who was assisted by a chaplain and clerks.

The custody of the Domus Conversorum was committed by Edward II. to William de Ayremynne, then clerk or keeper of the Rolls of the Chancery, to whose office it was thenceforward attached, the ancient Hospital of the Converts being eventually represented by the present Rolls House. The converts in residence at any one time appear from the Accounts of the Keeper of the Domus Conversorum to have seldom exceeded four or five in number.

Exchequer, Queen's Remembrancer.

ACCOUNTS, &c. RELATING TO THE JEWS. Henry II. to Edward I.

These consist of Accounts of Debts owing to Jews in various counties, Receipts and Memoranda of the Tallages levied on them, and Extents and Inquisitions as to their lands and possessions, with enrolments of their Obligations and Charters before the Treasurers and Barons of the Exchequer.

Calendar, 1 Vol. MS.

ACCOUNTS OF THE KEEPER OF THE DOMUS CONVERSORUM. Edward III. to Elizabeth.

These are the Accounts of " the Keeper of the Rolls of " the King's Chancery, and of the Domus Conversorum," or House set apart for the reception of converted Jews, as well of the stipend of the Chaplain and Clerk there, as of the wages of the converts for the time being, who, however, were generally very few in number.

Descriptive Slips.

Two Rolls of Accounts of the Keeper of the Domus Conversorum, bearing dates 8–15 Edward I., formerly deposited amongst the Miscellanea of the Exchequer, Treasury of the Receipt, have been added to this Series.

JEWS—(continued).

Exchequer of Receipt.

JEWS ROLLS. John to 23 Edward I.

This series consists of 38 Rolls, containing yearly accounts of the receipts from the Tallages, and from the Fines and Amercements imposed on the Jews.

JEWISH CONTRACTS OR "STARRA." Temp. Henry III. and Edward I.

These are original contracts written in Hebrew, generally in the nature of Acquittances or Releases made by the Jews, and are very few in number, and of no great historical interest. Six documents of this nature are referred to in the Pipe Roll of 3 John, as having been produced by Robert, Earl of Leicester, in part discharge of a debt owing by him to Aaron the Jew of Lincoln, with which he was charged on the lands and chattels of the said Jew being seized into the King's hands.

Thirteen only of these documents exist in the Public Record Office, but a much larger collection is preserved in the Archives of the Dean and Chapter of Westminster Abbey.

Exchequer of Pleas.

PLEAS BEFORE THE JUSTICES OF THE JEWS. 3 Henry III. to 14 Edward I. 47 Rolls.

The following Documents relating to the Jews are amongst the " Miscellaneous Rolls, Chancery."

No. $\frac{1}{5}$. A Roll entitled " Scrutinium factum archæ chirographariorum Colecestriæ," containing a schedule of debts owing to the Jews by various persons.

4 Edw. I.

No. $\frac{1}{6}$. A similar Roll relating to the Jews of York.

4 Edw. I.

No. $\frac{1}{7}$. A Roll of Grants of the houses which belonged to the Jews in England. 19 Edw. I.

No. $\frac{1}{8}$. A Roll of the Sales of the houses of condemned Jews, made by order of the King. Temp. Edw. I.

JUDICIAL PROCEEDINGS. Court of Chancery (Equity Side).

The earlier proceedings of the Court of Chancery commence in the reign of Richard II., and show that the chief business of the Court at that period did not consist in actions relating to the uses of land, but in receiving and adjudicating on petitions addressed to the Chancellor in cases of assault and trespass and a variety of outrages cognizable at Common Law, but for which the petitioner was unable to obtain redress owing to the position or powerful connexions of his adversary.

JUDICIAL PROCEEDINGS. **Court of Chancery (Equity Side)**—(continued).

They are exceedingly valuable and interesting as illustrating the origin and variations in the mode of procedure in the Court of Chancery as a Court of equitable jurisdiction, besides teeming with curious information as to the manners and customs of the times.

From the reign of Richard II. to that of Philip and Mary, they are arranged chronologically according to the periods of the several Chancellorships, and a Calendar is in course of formation.

The arrangement of the Chancery proceedings subsequent to the appointment of the Six Clerks of the Court of Chancery is extremely complicated, and will be best explained by a brief description of the method pursued in filing the several documents in the Six Clerks' Office at the period when those officers were virtually the solicitors acting for the plaintiffs or defendants in each suit, the records being thus treated to a considerable extent as documents under the immediate control of each of the said officers, and falling into six divisions accordingly.

When a Bill was brought into the Office to be filed it was delivered to one of the subordinates (who were called Sworn Clerks or Clerks in Court) of any one of the Six Clerks, who thereupon entered the names of the plaintiff and defendant, together with that of his principal and his own names, in the *Bill Book*, which was always kept open in the office for that purpose. The Six Clerk, whose name was thus entered in the Bill Book, became thenceforward the " Plaintiff's Six Clerk " and his said subordinate the " Plaintiff's Clerk in Court." The Bill was then taken into the study of the Six Clerk to whom it belonged and placed upon the File, where it remained until an appearance was entered for one of the defendants.

The Sworn Clerk or Clerk in Court for the Defendant making appearance then took the Bill off the File and made a copy for his client, keeping the Bill in his possession until the Defendant's Answer was drawn up, when the Bill with the Answer annexed was redelivered to the Six Clerk of the Plaintiff. These Bills and Answers were kept in the Six Clerk's study during six clear Terms for purposes of reference, after which period they were taken down to the Record Rooms and sorted alphabetically into bundles according to the plaintiffs' names. If more than one Answer was made to a Bill, such subsequent Answers were not generally annexed to the Bill like the first Answer, but were filed with the Records of the Term in which they were made. It, however, frequently happened that when Answers were taken away by the Plaintiff's Clerk in Court to be copied they were not returned to the

JUDICIAL PROCEEDINGS. Court of Chancery (Equity Side)—(continued).

Six Clerk *for many years*, and consequently never put into their proper bundles. In case of the death of any such Clerk in Court the Records in his custody were delivered to the Six Clerk whom he represented; but not being in the proper order or method observed by the Six Clerks in keeping their records, were arranged alphabetically under the general head of " Pleadings," by which title they were distinguished from the " Study Matters " or proceedings taken annually from the Six Clerk's Study ; consequently in a suit of long standing a search for the various Answers has to be continued from bundle to bundle for a considerable period. Moreover, when a Bill was amended it was removed from its old bundles and placed on the File as if it were a fresh Bill; but the preceding Answers were not removed from their bundles, and consequently, after finding an Answer, it may become necessary to search forwards to find the Bill to which it belongs. The " Single Bills," or Bills to which no appearance was entered, were put in bundles by themselves and kept distinct from the " Study Matters," or " Pleadings." It frequently happened that when a Bill was taken off the File for the purpose of being copied, the Clerk in Court who so removed it did not return it directly to the Six Clerk from whose File it was taken, but instead passed it on to one of the other Clerks in Court or Sworn Clerks who appeared for some other Defendant, and if no Answer happened to be filed by such last-mentioned Clerk in Court the Bill was never returned to the Plaintiff's Six Clerk at all, but remained in the custody of the Clerk in Court to whom it had been delivered, and was in due course put away with the Records of the Six Clerk whom he represented. It thus often becomes necessary, if a Bill is not found in the Division of the Six Clerk with whom it was filed, to continue the search from Division to Division of the remaining Clerks.

N.B.—The difficulties of searching are also increased by the title of the suit being often varied according to the name of the particular defendant making answer.

The *Depositions in Country Causes*, or Depositions taken by Commission, remained for two years in the custody of the Clerk in Court or Sworn Clerk for the Plaintiff or Defendant, as the case might be, and were then placed with the Records of the Six Clerk whom he represented, being indexed in the same books as the Bills and Answers, but under a separate heading.

Commissions of Partition, with the returns thereto, will also be found amongst these Depositions.

JUDICIAL PROCEEDINGS. Court of Chancery (Equity Side)—(continued).

The *Depositions in Town Causes*, or Town Depositions, were kept in the Examiners' Office where they were taken, those prior to 1724 being sent to the Record Office in the Tower for safe custody. The Town Depositions were on *paper*; those taken in the Country on *parchment*, the Commission by which they were taken being generally annexed, together with an abstract of the Bill called the " Dedimus Bill."

The annexed list shows the several classes of documents belonging to the Equity side of the Court of Chancery, with the means of reference to each.*

ACCOUNTANT-GENERAL'S CERTIFICATES. 1726 to 1825. These are the Certificates made by the Accountant-General of the Court of Chancery of the payment of sums of money into Court. They consist of about 527 Bundles arranged alphabetically, according to the titles of the suits. Those of a later date than 1825 are kept at the Chancery Pay Office ; they are now called Paymaster-General's Certificates.

ADMINISTRATION SUMMONSES. See "CHANCERY PROCEEDINGS."

AFFIDAVITS. 1611 to 1869. From 1611 to 1819 these are arranged chronologically, Term by Term. After 1819 the Affidavits in each Term are arranged alphabetically according to the titles of the Causes or Matters. From Trinity 1828, inclusive, the Affidavits in *Matters* are generally kept distinct from those in *Causes*, and placed at the end of the alphabetical arrangement.

Registers of Affidavits. 1615 to 1746. 53 Vols., containing entries of the Affidavits in full.

Indexes { 1607 to 1755. 49 Vols.
{ 1781 to 1869. 99 Vols.

AWARDS AND AGREEMENTS. See "REPORTS AND CERTIFICATES."

Awards of Arbitrators respecting enclosures, &c. and in law suits of various kinds are enrolled on the early Close Rolls.

BILLS, ANSWERS, DEPOSITIONS, &c. See " CHANCERY PROCEEDINGS."

CHANCERY PROCEEDINGS. Richard II. to 1869. Under this title are included the Bills, Answers, Depositions, and

---

* The Chancery Masters' Documents, placed under the charge and superintendence of the Master of the Rolls pursuant to Statute 40 & 41 Vict. c. 55, are under special restrictions. *Vide* Report XL., App. No. 10.

JUDICIAL PROCEEDINGS. Court of Chancery
(Equity Side)—(continued).

CHANCERY PROCEEDINGS, &C.—(continued).

other Proceedings in Chancery suits which were formerly deposited in the Tower of London, and in the offices of the Record and Writ Clerks (formerly the "Six Clerks"), and of the Examiners of the Court of Chancery. They may be classified as follows :—

(1.) Chancery Proceedings (Early). Ric. II. to Philip and Mary, arranged under the names of the Lords Chancellors. [Calendar in progress.]

(2.) Chancery Proceedings. Elizabeth to Charles I. *Series I.* [Indexed.]

(3.) Do. (Supplementary). *Series II.* [List in progress.]

(4.) Do. (Miscellaneous). 102 Bundles. These will be eventually incorporated in *Series II.*

(5.) Chancery Proceedings. 1649 to 1842. Arranged in *Six Divisions,* bearing the names of the Six Clerks of the Court of Chancery respectively.

(6.) Chancery Proceedings. 1842 to 1869. Arranged alphabetically, year by year, under the general heading of " Pleadings."

(7.) Depositions (from the Examiners' Office) called "Paper" or "Town Depositions." 26 Hen. VIII. to 1853. These are arranged alphabetically in bundles, Term by Term.

(8.) Depositions, "Sealed " or Unpublished. 389 Bundles.

The means of reference are as follows :—

Bill Books. From about 1673 to 1852. 156 Vols. M.S. These contain entries of all the Bills filed in Chancery arranged alphabetically year by year, the names of the Six Clerks and Clerks in Court who appeared for the plaintiffs being given in the margin, thus enabling the searcher to refer to the Division in which the Records should be indexed and also to the " Cause Books " and " Clerk in Court's Books." From 1673 to 1713 the series is very imperfect. After 1842 the Bill Books contain, instead of the names of the Six Clerks, the numerical references to the Files of Pleadings and the names of the Vice-Chancellors.

Cause Books. From about 1620 to 1842. Each of the Six Clerks kept in his study a book called the " Cause Book," in which he entered in full the names of the Plaintiffs and Defendants in all suits in which the Bills were filed in his office, adding thereto the dates of the several Answers or Replications in the order in which they were filed. In the margin he entered the names of the Six Clerks and Sworn Clerks for the several

JUDICIAL PROCEEDINGS. Court of Chancery (Equity Side)—(continued).

CHANCERY PROCEEDINGS, &c.—(continued).

Defendants. When an answer was made by any of the Defendants in whose name he appeared, an entry thereof was also made by the Six Clerk in his Cause Book, with the date of filing such Answer. The Cause Books thus contain a complete record of the proceedings in every cause so far as relates to the time of filing Bills, Answers, and Replications. The entries are made alphabetically, under the Plaintiffs' names.

Clerk in Court's Books. From about 1713 to 1842. These were books kept by the several Clerks in Court or Sworn Clerks, in which they entered the dates of the Appearances and other proceedings in the suits with which they were concerned, together with the names of the *Solicitors* for the parties whom they represented, and the name of the *Six Clerk* for the other side.

Calendars and Indexes, as follows :—

Bills and Answers. Elizabeth. A *Calendar* printed by the Record Commission, in 3 Vols. folio, with Indexes of names and places. [Examples are prefixed of some of the earlier Chancery Proceedings from Ric. II. to Hen. VIII.]

Do. Elizabeth. 1 Vol. M.S. An *Index Nominum* only. [Some of the documents noticed in this Index are not included in the printed Calendar.]

Do. James I. 1 Vol. M.S. An *Index Nominum* only.

Do. James I. An *Index Locorum* in 3 Vols. M.S.

Do. Charles I. 4 Vols M.S. An *Index Nominum* only. (Printed by the Index Society.)

[Bills and Answers of the reigns of Elizabeth, James, and Charles will also be found in the Six Clerk's Books " Mitford I.," Vol. 17, and " Mitford V.," Vol. 22.]

Depositions (Country). Eliz., James, and Charles. 1 Vol. MS. An *Index Nominum* referring to the Depositions taken by Commission, or " Country " Depositions only. [There are also Depositions of Eliz., James, and Charles in the following " Six Clerks' Books," viz., " Bridges' Depositions," Vol. 6, " Collins' Depositions," Vol. 10, and " Whittington's Depositions," Vol. 32.]

Depositions (Town). Hen. VIII. to Mary. An *Index Nominum* in 1 Vol. MS.

Depositions (Unpublished). *Index*, 1 Vol. M.S.

Bills, Answers, and Depositions. 1649 to 1842. 59 Vols. MS., called " Six Clerks' Books." These are in Six Divisions, one for each of the Six Clerks, and contain the Bills, Answers, Replications, and *Country* Depositions, the

JUDICIAL PROCEEDINGS. Court of Chancery (Equity Side)--(continued).

latter being indexed separately. The name of the division in which search should be made may be obtained from the Bill Books, but it is sometimes necessary to search all Six Divisions. [See above.] Since the year 1714, the Six Clerks' Books are in three sets, extending respectively from 1714 to 1758, 1758 to 1800, and 1800 to 1842, with a supplementary volume, entitled " Records sorted since 1842," referring to such documents as were found in the several studies on the abolition of the Six Clerks. [Some of these documents are of comparatively early date.]

Do. 1842 to 1869. 94 Vols. MS. An *Alphabetical Index* to the Bills, Answers, Depositions, &c., arranged alphabetically under Plaintiffs' names and entitled " Index to Pleadings."

DECREES AND ORDERS, ENTRY BOOKS OF. 36 Hen. VIII. to 1869. These are the Entry Books kept by the Registrars of the Court of Chancery, and were formerly deposited in the Report Office.

They are divided into two series, distinguished as *" Reg. Lib. A."* and *" Reg Lib B."* respectively. The first series or *Reg. Lib. A.* commences in 36 Henry VIII. and, up to and including Trinity Term 1629 contains the entries of Decrees and Orders from A. to Z., inclusive. After Trinity Term 1629, this series contains letters A. to K. only.

The second series, or *Reg. Lib. B.*, commences in 1 Edw. VI., and contains entries of Decrees and Orders from A. to Z. inclusive, till Trinity Term 1629, after which date it contains those from L. to Z. only.

Indexes. 38 Hen. VIII. to 1869. 628 Vols. MS.

DECREE ROLLS. 26 Hen. VIII. to 1878. The Decree Rolls contain such Decrees, Orders, and Dismissions of the Court of Chancery, &c., as were *enrolled*, generally for the purposes of an appeal to the House of Lords. Any Decree or Order of the Court of Chancery (and also Orders by the Ecclesiastical Court in England "directing payment of any sum of money," and orders of the Court of Chancery in Ireland, and of the Incumbered Estates Court, Ireland, of a similar nature), might be enrolled within six months from the date thereof, but not later without special leave of the Court, and no enrolment of any Decree, &c. was allowed after the expiration of five years from the date thereof. In order to obtain the enrolment of any Decree or Order a *Docquet of Enrolment* setting forth the preliminary proceedings, and reciting the Decree or Order to be enrolled, was drawn up, which Docquet, after having been inspected by one of the Clerks

JUDICIAL PROCEEDINGS. Court of Chancery (Equity Side)—(continued).

DECREE ROLLS, &c.—(continued).

of Records and Writs, was signed by the Lord Chancellor, Lord Keeper, or Lords Commissioners of the Great Seal for the time being, and without such signature no Decree or Order could be enrolled. The original Docquets are preserved in Bundles from 26 Hen. VIII. Since the passing of the Judicature Act in 1875 the enrolment of Decrees and Orders of the Court of Chancery became unnecessary, with the exception of Orders confirming *Railway Schemes*, pursuant to Stat. 30 and 31 Vict. c. 127. The only other Orders enrolled subsequent to the passing of the above-mentioned Act are those of other Courts which it is intended to enforce by process issuing out of the Chancery Division, such as Orders of Irish Courts, under Stat. 41 Geo. III. c. 90. s. 5, and Orders of the Arches Court under 2 and 3 Wm. IV. c. 93. s. 2.

Calendars and Indexes. 14 Vols. MS., one of which is an *Index Locorum.*

PAYMASTER-GENERAL'S CERTIFICATES. Before 1825 see "ACCOUNTANT GENERAL'S CERTIFICATES." Since 1825 they are at the Chancery Pay Office.

PETITIONS. 1834 to 1869. These are arranged alphabetically in bundles, according to the date of *filing*, which is generally *subsequent* to that of the Order made on the Petition. It was not the practice to file the Petitions in Chancery suits prior to 1834. There is, however, a collection of "Appeal Petitions" extending from 1774 to 1869, and of "Corporation" or "Charity Petitions" from 1834 to 1845, to which there are separate Indexes.

Indexes. 16 Vols. MS.

PETITION BOOKS (LORD CHANCELLORS) 1756 to 1858. 43 Vols.

RAILWAY SCHEMES. These are filed with the "Pleadings," the Orders confirming them being enrolled on the DECREE ROLLS.

REPORTS AND CERTIFICATES. 1554 to 1869. These are the Original Reports made to the Court by the Masters in Chancery on the matters referred to them for their investigation and opinion, extending in date from 1544 to the abolition of the Masters in Chancery in 1848. Subsequent to the latter date they consist of the Certificates of the Chief Clerks and Taxing Masters, with the accounts, &c. thereto annexed. The Paymaster-General's Certificates are not included in this class

JUDICIAL PROCEEDINGS. Court of Chancery (Equity Side)—(continued).

REPORTS AND CERTIFICATES—(continued).

The Reports and Certificates together comprise 2,953 volumes, in which the documents are alphabetically arranged Term by Term. The last 24 volumes form a supplementary set of reports extending from 1703 to 1799, with some few of earlier date, and consisting principally of such documents as were too bulky to be bound up in their regular order. These documents are marked in the Indexes as "Not Bundled." The last volume consists of "Corporation Reports" (relating to Charities in various Boroughs) from 1836 to 1846.

Alphabetical Indexes. 1606 to 1869. 261 Vols.

The following documents were transferred from the Report Office, with the Reports, &c. above described :—

Awards and Agreements 1694 to 1844. 15 Bundles. These are the Awards given by Arbitrators, and the Agreements arrived at by consent between the parties in various suits. As a rule they appear to have been embodied in the Reports subsequently made by the respective Masters.

Exceptions to Reports, &c. 1756 to 1859. 44 Bundles. The nature of these documents is sufficiently explained by their Title.

REGISTRARS' COURT OR MINUTE BOOKS. 1639 to 1869. These contain the Notes taken in Court by the several Registrars on the hearing of the Causes, with Minutes of the decision of the Court, &c. They are arranged in Terms, there being generally one volume per Term for each Registrar, for which reason they are sometimes designated "Term Books." There are also "Cause Books" from 1735 to 1848, and "Cause Paper Books" from 1806 to 1843, which contain merely the titles of the Causes set down for hearing, day by day.

JUDICIAL PROCEEDINGS. Court of Chancery (Common Law Side).

The jurisdiction of the Court of Chancery was originally of two kinds : ordinary, or legal ; and extraordinary, or absolute. The *ordinary* jurisdiction was that "in which " the Lord Chancellor in his proceedings and judgments " was bound to observe the Order and Method of the Com- " mon Law "; in which cases the proceedings were usually in *Latin*, and were in later years filed at the Petty Bag Office. The *extraordinary* jurisdiction was that exercised by the Court in cases of *Equity*, the proceedings in which were commenced by *English Bill and Answer*.

JUDICIAL PROCEEDINGS. Court of Chancery (Common Law Side)—(continued).

The pleadings on the ordinary or Common Law Side of the Court consist of pleadings on Writs of Right, on Petitions and Monstrans de Droit, and respecting Recognizances acknowledged in the Court of Chancery, proceedings on Writs of Scire Facias for the repeal of Letters Patent, on Writs of Partition of Land in Co-parcenary and for Dower, on Traverses of Inquisitions or Offices (to prove that an Inquisition of lands or goods was defective or untruly made), and in all personal actions by or against any Officer of the Court.

PLEADINGS ON THE COMMON LAW SIDE OF CHANCERY. (TOWER SERIES.) Edward III. to Richard III.

DO. (ROLLS CHAPEL OFFICE SERIES.) Henry VII. to James I.

Inventory. Report IV., App. II., pp. 108–110.
Calendar. Henry VII. "Palmer's Indexes," Vol. 107.

DO. (PETTY BAG OFFICE SERIES.) James I. to Victoria.

93 Bundles endorsed "Proceedings and Judgments on Writs of Scire Facias, &c."
Indexes. 10 Vols. MS.

COUNTY PLACITA. John to Edward IV.

The documents known as "County Placita," so called from their being arranged according to Counties, consist of Transcripts of Proceedings in the King's Bench and other Courts, and of Feet of Fines and other Records brought into Chancery by Writ of Certiorari.

Index Locorum. Bedford to Wilts. 1 Vol. MS.
Calendar. Bedford to Norfolk. 1 Vol. MS.

PRECEDENT BOOKS (CURSITORS'). 3 Vols.

DO. (PETTY BAG). 6 Vols.

REMEMBRANCE ROLLS OF ORDERS. (PETTY BAG OFFICE.) 14 Car. I. to 2 Geo. II. 10 Rolls.

These contain entries of the Orders made with reference to proceedings on the Common Law Side of Chancery.

WRITS. See CHANCERY FILES.

WRITS, PRECEDENTS FOR. See PRECEDENT BOOKS.

JUDICIAL PROCEEDINGS. Court of Queen's Bench (Crown Side).

AFFIDAVITS (GENERAL). 1716 to 1858.

Indexes. 1738 to 1851. 15 Vols., called "Memoranda Books of Affidavits."

JUDICIAL PROCEEDINGS. Court of Queen's Bench (Crown Side)—(continued).

APPEARANCE BOOKS. 1725 to 1843. 13 Vols.

ASSIZE ROLLS, EYRE ROLLS, &c. John to Edward IV. 1,550 Rolls.

(See Lists and Indexes, No. IV., 1894.)

Under the general Title of "Assize Rolls, &c." are included:—

(*a*.) Rolls of the *Justices in Eyre*, who were originally sent at irregular intervals, as of five, six, or seven years throughout the Counties of England with Commission to hear more especially such causes as were termed Pleas of the Crown. The scope of their Commissions was gradually widened, and early in the reign of Henry the Third they were competent to hear pleas of every kind, their Rolls being generally arranged under the several heads of—

"Placita de Juratis et Assisis,"
"Placita Coronæ,"
"Placita Forinseca." (Pleas originated in the County in which the Justices then were, but relating to other Counties),
and
"Placita de Quo Warranto."
To these were sometimes added—
"Placita de Querelis,
Placita de Ragemannis,
and
"Deliberationes Gaolarum."

The Eyre Rolls were made up in Counties, there being generally several copies of each Roll, one for the King marked "Rex," and others bearing the names of the several Justices. No Justices in Eyre were appointed after 10 Edward III.

(*b*.) Rolls of the *Justices of Assize* (Justiciarii ad capiendas assisas), who appear to have been appointed for the purpose of avoiding the delay and inconvenience caused by the long intervals between the Eyres of the Justices Itinerant. By the Statute of Westminster, 13 Edward I., it was enacted that two Justices should be assigned before whom, and none other, Assises of novel disseisin, mort d'ancestor, and attaints should be taken, and who were to associate to themselves one or two of the knights of each shire and to take the assises and attaints therein three times in the year at the most.

JUDICIAL PROCEEDINGS. Court of Queen's Bench (Crown Side)—(continued).

ASSIZE ROLLS, EYRE ROLLS, &c.—(continued).

By the same Statute it was enacted that Inquisitions of trespass might be determined before the said Justices in pursuance of a Writ called the Writ of *Nisi Prius*, which directed the parties to appear on a certain day at one of the Benches at Westminster, " nisi prius Justiciarii venerint ad illas " partes ad capiendas assisas," unless the Justices should *first* come to that place to take the Assises, which they were certain to do, thus saving the parties much trouble and expense.

It being afterwards found that the Justices as assigned were often hindered by other duties from attending at the days and places appointed, it was further enacted by Statute 21 Edward I., that the Kingdom should be divided into four *Circuits*, and that eight Justices should be assigned, two for each Circuit, to take the Assises, &c., therein as aforesaid.

The number of Circuits was afterwards increased to six, at which it now stands, with the addition of a Circuit for North and South Wales.

By a Statute of 27 Edward I., the Justices of Assize were also empowered, after they had taken the assises, to deliver the gaols in their respective circuits. See GAOL DELIVERY ROLLS.

(c.) Rolls of the *Justices of Oyer and Terminer* (Justiciarii ad audiendum et terminandum), who were sent as occasion required to hear and determine one or more special causes, or under any extraordinary circumstances, as the occurrence of a great riot or insurrection, or the commission of heinous misdemeanours or trespasses in any particular county or district. The Justices of Oyer and Terminer were also frequently Justices of Gaol Delivery.

This class also includes a few original Commissions to take Special Assizes of Novel Disseisin, &c., with the proceedings thereon, and also Inquisitions and. Presentments of Jurors and other documents subsidiary to the Rolls of the Justices in Eyre and Justices of Assize.

Amongst the Assize Rolls are also to be found Pleas before the " Justices of Trailbaston," who were originally appointed by Edward I. to administer justice during his absence in the Scotch and French wars.

These Justices were of the nature of Justices of Assize, their name being derived from the " baston "

JUDICIAL PROCEEDINGS. Court of Queen's Bench (Crown Side)—(continued).

ASSIZE ROLLS, EYRE ROLLS, &c.—(continued).

or staff delivered to them as the badge of their office, which was to make Inquisition throughout the Kingdom touching the extortions of officers, intrusions into other men's lands, breaches of the peace and other offences.

The Placita de Quo Warranto enrolled on the Rolls of the Justices in Eyre consist of the pleadings and judgments on Writs of "Quo Warranto," which were in the nature of Writs of Right on behalf of the King against those who claimed or usurped any Office, Franchise, or Liberty, calling on them to show by what authority their claims were supported. These pleadings were first instituted as a consequence of the Inquisitiones Hundredorum or Hundred Rolls, taken by Commission in the 2nd and 7th years of Edward I., Articles of Inquiry thereon being delivered to the Justices in Eyre, for the purpose of holding pleas upon the claims therein stated.

These Articles were repeated from time to time in subsequent Commissions.

On the discontinuance of the Eyres in 10 Edward III., the Pleadings and Judgments on Writs of "Quo Warranto" or of "Quo titulo clamat" took place in the King's Bench or the Exchequer, and are enrolled on the "Coram Rege Rolls" or the "Memoranda Rolls" accordingly.

The "Placita de Ragemannis" which are occasionally found on the Eyre Rolls are the pleas taken under the Statute 4 Edward I. called the Statute of Rageman, which directed that Justices should go throughout the land to hear and determine all complaints and suits for trespasses committed within the 25 years then last past as well by the King's Bailiffs and Officers as by others. A Roll entitled "Veredicta de Ministris," containing such pleas in the 4th year of Edward the First, is placed with the Hundred Rolls.

By Statute 9 Edward III. it was established that the Justices of Assize, Gaol Delivery, and Oyer and Terminer should send in their Records to the Treasury of the Exchequer in Michaelmas Term every year, but this practice appears to have been discontinued in the reign of Edward IV.

The modern Justices of Assize and Nisi Prius go upon their Circuits by virtue of five several authorities :—

1. The Commission of the Peace.

JUDICIAL PROCEEDINGS. Court of Queen's Bench (Crown Side)—(continued).

ASSIZE ROLLS, EYRE ROLLS, &c.—(continued).

2. The Commission of Oyer and Terminer.
3. The Commission of General Gaol Delivery.
4. The Commission of Assize.
5. The Commission of Nisi Prius.

Their Records, which consist of Assize Rolls or Files, including original Indictments with the Verdicts thereon, Coroners' Inquisitions, Minute Books, Gaol Books or Calendars, and other proceedings, are preserved by the Clerks of Assize of the respective Circuits, and in some cases extend back as far as the reign of James I., whilst those of the Home Circuit begin in the reign of Philip and Mary.

[*Vide* Record Commissioners' Report, 1800, pp. 237–245].

The Records at Nisi Prius, with the Posteas thereon, appear, however, to have been generally handed to the parties concerned therein on their making application for them, Minute Books only of the Proceedings and Orders being kept by the Clerks of Assize.

The following collections of documents subsidiary to the Assize and Quo Warranto Rolls are amongst the " Miscellaneous Books " of the Exchequer Treasury of the Receipt :—

Vol. 87. Abstracts of Placita coram Rege, &c. Temp. John.
         [Printed in the " Placitorum Abbreviatio."]
Vol. 88. A book containing original Bills preferred to the *Justices of Trailbaston* in Com. Glouc., 14 Edw. II. ; to the *Justices in Eyre* in the *Channel Islands*, temp. Edw. I. ; and in the *Palatinate of Lancaster*, temp. Edw. III.
                 Edw. I.–Edw. III.
Vol. 89. Proceedings "de Quo Warranto " in Com. Bedford.
                 4 Edw. II.
Vol. 90. A Book containing Bills preferred to "H.de Berewick et sociis suis " at Preston, in the County of Lancaster, in the second year of the Dukedom ; and to the Justices Itinerant in the County of Bedford in the 18th year of Edw. III.
                 Edw. III.
Vol. 91. Proclamations of Outlawry in the County of Lincoln.
                 22 Edw. IV.–14 Hen. VII.

" BAGA DE SECRETIS." 17 Edward IV. to 53 George III.

The Records known under this Title consist of Indictments and Attainders for High Treason, and other State offences, with other proceedings on the Crown side of the Court, which, on account of their important or secret nature were kept apart. They were formerly kept under three keys, one of which was held by the Lord Chief Justice, another by the Attorney-General, and the third

JUDICIAL PROCEEDINGS. Court of Queen's Bench (Crown Side)—(continued).

" BAGA DE SECRETIS "—(continued).

by the Master of the Crown Office, the " BAGA " being deposited in a closet, which has long since disappeared.

The proceedings are placed in small bags or pouches, a *Descriptive Inventory* and *Calendar* of which is printed in the 3rd, 4th, and 5th Reports of the Deputy Keeper of the Public Records. Amongst these important records will be found the Trials and Convictions of Anne Boleyn, of Sir Walter Raleigh and others, of Guy Fawkes, of Sir Hardress Waller and the other regicides, of the adherents of the House of Stuart in 1715 and 1745, and other documents of the greatest historical interest.

The proceedings with regard to Perkin Warbeck's conspiracy in the reign of Henry VII., recently discovered and added to this series, are described in the Deputy Keeper's 54th Report, App. II.

BAILS, CALENDAR OF. 6 Jas. I. to 13 Will. III., 3 Rolls.

CONTROLMENT ROLLS. 1 Edward III. to 1843.

The Controlment Rolls may be sub-divided into three portions, the first of which is known as the *Bag Roll*, and contains Minutes of all Writs of Venire Facias and other Writs issued in each term; the second portion or *Controlment Roll* proper, contains Minutes of the Appearances and Pleas in each Term; and the third, or *Special Writ Roll*, contains enrolments in full of the Writs of Mandamus (which, when no return was made thereto, do not appear on the Crown Roll), and of other Special Writs. The Controlment Rolls form a distinct class of records, and do not refer in any way to the Coram Rege or Crown Rolls, except in so far as they exhibit a record or minute of the proceedings on the Crown side of the Court, term by term. There is one Controlment Roll for each year.

CONTUMACE CAPIENDO, ENROLMENT OF WRITS OF. 1844 to 1857. 1 Parcel. Before 1844 see CONTROLMENT ROLLS

CONVICTS, RETURNS OF. 1785 to 1827. 10 Bags.

CORAM REGE ROLLS. 5 Richard I. to 22 Victoria (1858). These Rolls are now sub-divided as follows :—

CURIA REGIS ROLLS. 5 Richard I. to 56 Henry III.

CORAM REGE ROLLS. 1 Edward I. to 13 William III.

CROWN ROLLS. 1 Anne (1702) to 22 Victoria (1858). (See Lists and Indexes, No. IV., 1894.)

Till the end of the reign of Henry III. when the Curia Regis became finally merged in the Court of King's Bench, the Rolls hitherto styled " Coram Rege Rolls " are more correctly termed " Rotuli Curiæ Regis," by which

JUDICIAL PROCEEDINGS. Court of Queen's Bench (Crown Side)—(continued).

CORAM REGE ROLLS—(continued).

name they are in fact described in the ancient calendars, and include the Placita "de Banco," as well as the Placita "Coram Rege." Since 1 Edward I. the Placita de Banco form a distinct class of enrolments. From 1 Edward I. to the first year of Queen Anne, the Placita Coram Rege, or Coram Rege Rolls, contain entries of all the proceedings in the Court of Queen's Bench, both on the Civil and Crown sides, the proceedings on the Crown side forming the latter part of each Roll, and being distinguished as the "Rex Roll." In 1702 the Pleadings in Civil Causes were separated and formed the "Pleas, or "Judgment Rolls" of the Court, the Placita Coram Rege being thenceforward known as the "Crown Rolls."

The Curia Regis Rolls from 6 Ric. I. to 1 John, have been printed in full, in two Vols. 8vo.

Abstracts of the Curia Regis and Coram Rege Rolls from Ric. I. to Edw. II. are printed in the "Placitorum Abbreviatio" with *Indices Locorum, Nominum, and Rerum.*

See also **AGARDE'S INDEXES.**

From 6 Charles I. to 1843 reference to the *Crown* causes enrolled on the Coram Rege or Crown Rolls is to be made by means of the "*Great Doggett Books,*" 17 Vols. MS.* These books contain entries of all pleas and other proceedings in the Court, term by term, specifying the date and number of the indictment, the date of the controlment or minute of the entry, and frequently the number of the Crown Roll, on which the proceedings are entered in full.

N.B.—The numbers in the left-hand margin of the books, when any such are given, refer to the Crown Roll of the same term. Those in the right-hand margin refer to the Crown Roll *of the same date as the Controlment specified,* thus: "By Controlment of Michaelmas last, Roll 7," means that the proceedings will be found on Roll 7 of the Crown Roll of that Term.

CORONERS' ROLLS. Henry III. to Henry VI. 256 Rolls.

These contain the enrolments of the Inquisitions taken before the King's Coroner on the occurrence of any sudden death, by misfortune or otherwise, which were directed to be returned by the Coroner to the Justices Itinerant at the next Gaol Delivery, or to be certified into the Court of King's Bench. They also include a few Rolls of Outlaws or of persons to be put in Exigent. (See Lists and Indexes, No. IV., 1894.)

---

* The Pleadings in *Civil* Causes from the year 1390, together with the Deeds enrolled, are indexed in the Doggett Rolls and Doggett Books of the Plea Side of the Court.

JUDICIAL PROCEEDINGS. Court of Queen's Bench (Crown Side)—(continued).

CURIA REGIS, ROLLS OF THE. See CORAM REGE ROLLS.

DEPOSITIONS. 1849 to 1857. 2 Bundles.

ERROR, RECORDS IN (FROM IRELAND). Geo. II. and Geo. III. 10 Rolls.

GAOL DELIVERY ROLLS. Edward I. to Edward IV. 221 Rolls. (See Lists and Indexes, No. IV., 1894.)

These include a number of Special Gaol Deliveries and Gaol Files, consisting of Writs, Panels of Jurors, Indictments, &c.

Gaol Deliveries are also enrolled on the Rolls of the Justices in Eyre. See ASSIZE ROLLS, EYRE ROLLS, &c.

INDICTMENTS (ANCIENT). Henry III. to Henry VII. 34 Bundles. Series imperfect.

INDICTMENTS (LONDON AND MIDDLESEX). 1675 to 1845.

These consist of the original Indictments found by the Grand Jury in the Court of King's Bench, of informations exhibited on the Crown Side of the Court, and also of such indictments, presentments, and convictions in London and Middlesex as were removed into the Court of King's Bench by Certiorari or Writ of Error.

Pye Books. 1673 to 1843. 11 Vols.

INDICTMENTS (OUT COUNTIES). 1625 to 1845.

These consist of such indictments, presentments, and convictions as were removed into the Court of King's Bench from other counties than London and Middlesex and of informations exhibited in the Court for offences committed in those counties. The earlier bundles contain also a few Coroner's Inquisitions.

Pye Books. 1661 to 1843. 5 Vols.

INDICTMENTS (LONDON AND MIDDLESEX AND OUT COUNTIES, AMALGAMATED). 1846 to 1858.

Indictment Book. 1844 to 1852. 1 Vol.

N.B. — The Indictments and other proceedings at Assizes are kept by the Clerks of Assize of the several Circuits.

INTERROGATORIES. 1701 to 1838. 6 Bundles.

JUDGMENTS, FILES OF. 1734 to 1824. 4 Bundles.

MANDAMUS, WRITS OF. See "CONTROLMENT ROLLS."

OUTLAWRY PROCEEDINGS. 1739 to 1844. 1 Bag.

POSTEAS, FILES OF. 1728 to 1839. 43 Bundles.

PROCESS BOOKS. 1737 to 1821. 8 Vols.

QUO WARRANTO ROLLS. See ASSIZE ROLLS, EYRE ROLLS, &c.

JUDICIAL PROCEEDINGS. Court of Queen's Bench (Crown Side)—(continued).

RULES, ENTRY BOOKS OF. 1589 to 1857. 70 Vols.

WRITS RETURNED, CALLED "RECORDS OF ORDERS." 1693 to 1858. These are contained in bags and consist of all Writs returned into the Crown side of the Court, except Writs of Certiorari to remove Indictments, &c. which are placed with the Indictments. They contain special cases reserved at Quarter Sessions, and certain classes of Writs, such as Writs of Attachment and Habeas Corpus, which do not appear upon the Bag or Controlment Rolls.

JUDICIAL PROCEEDINGS. Court of Queen's Bench (Plea Side).

ACCOUNTS OF MONEY PAID IN AND OUT OF COURT, CALLED "COURT MONEY BOOKS." 1675 to 1837. 30 Vols.

ACCOUNTS OF MONEY IN THE RECEIPT OF THE SIGNER OF THE WRITS. 1713 to 1780. 1 Vol.

AFFIDAVITS (GENERAL). 1733 to 1848. *Indexes.* 1733 to 1848. 38 Vols.

AFFIDAVITS OF DUE EXECUTION OF ARTICLES OF CLERK-SHIP. See **ATTORNEYS.**

BAILS, ENROLMENTS OF ENTRIES OF. 1664 to 1714.

COGNOVITS. 1825 to 1848. 90 Bundles. See also "WARRANTS OF ATTORNEY AND COGNOVITS."

COMMISSIONS AND DEPOSITIONS. 1832 to 1837. 1 Bag.

DOGGETT PAPERS OF ENTERING JUDGMENT. 1772 to 1839. 41 Bags. These are slips of paper containing the particulars and amount of the Judgment and Damages, the date of signing and the names before whom signed, with the number of the Roll and the names of the solicitors. They are tied up in terms and arranged alphabetically under the solicitors' names.

EJECTMENT, PROCEEDINGS IN.
An action of Ejectment was originally an action brought by one who had a lease for a term of years to recover the injury done to him by dispossession. It afterwards became converted into a method of trying titles to the freehold,— the Claimant making a formal entry on the premises, and being thus in temporary possession thereof, sealing and delivering a lease to some third person or lessee, who was then left upon the premises till the prior tenant entered thereon afresh and ousted him, or till some other person

JUDICIAL PROCEEDINGS. Court of Queen's Bench (Plea Side)---(continued).

EJECTMENT, PROCEEDINGS IN—(continued).

then called the *casual ejector*, either by accident or agreement came upon the land and ejected him. The lessee was thereupon entitled to his action of ejectment against the tenant or the casual ejector, as the case might be, for the recovery of his term with damages.

In the time of the Commonwealth, however, a new and more simple method of trying titles by Writ of Ejectment was introduced by Chief Justice Rolle, which continued in use till about the middle of the present century. This new method was based upon a series of legal fictions ; no actual lease was made, no actual entry by the Plaintiff, no actual ouster by the defendant ; but all were assumed for the sole purpose of trying the title. The usual course was to draw up a *Declaration*, in which a lease of the premises for a term of years was stated to have been made by him who claimed the title to a fictitious personage, *John Doe*, who is the nominal plaintiff in the action. It was also stated that Doe, the lessee, entered, and that the Defendant, *Richard Roe*, who is called the *casual ejector*, ousted him, for which ouster he brought this action. A written notice was then sent by the Defendant, Roe, to the tenant in possession of the lands, informing him of the action brought by John Doe, and transmitting him a copy of the declaration, at the same time assuring him that he, Roe, the Defendant, had no title at all to the premises, and should make no defence ; and therefore advising him to appear in court and defend his own title, otherwise he, the casual ejector, would suffer judgment to be had against him by default. On receipt of this friendly notice, the tenant must either appear by his Attorney at the beginning of the following term and *consent to a Rule* making him the Defendant instead of the *casual ejector*, or, if he does not so appear within the time appointed, on an affidavit being made of due service of the Declaration and Notice aforesaid, judgment is given by default against the casual ejector, and the tenant in possession is on such judgment turned out by a writ of *Habere facias Possessionem*.

When judgment in an action of Ejectment is allowed to go by default, it is entered in the Docket Book under the name of the casual ejector, Roe ; when, however, the tenant takes upon himself the defence of the action, it is entered under his, the real Defendant's name.

APPEARANCE BOOKS IN EJECTMENT. 1738 to 1836.

DECLARATIONS IN EJECTMENT 1728 to 1848.

JUDICIAL PROCEEDINGS. Court of Queen's Bench (Plea Side) —(continued).

RULES (CONSENT) IN EJECTMENT. *Series I.* 1720 to 1842

Do. *Series II.* 1721 to 1836.

Indexes. 1734 to 1848. 40 Vols. MS., as follows :—

From 1734 to 1790, 2 Vols., called " Alphabetical Index to Country Ejectments." From 1790 to 1848, 38 Vols., called " Rules for Judgment in Ejectment," which refer by number to the Declarations, the latter being generally found in the bundle of the Term preceding the date of the Rule.

ERROR, PROCEEDINGS IN. These are enrolled on the Plea or Judgment Rolls, and indexed separately in the Doggett Rolls or Doggett Books under the head of " Special Remembrances."

ERROR, WRITS AND TRANSCRIPTS OF RECORDS IN (FROM INFERIOR COURTS). 16 Bags.

ESSOIN ROLLS. Edw. III. to Hen. V. 74 Rolls.
Do. 3 Hen. VII. to 40 Geo. III. 1 Roll.

These contain entries of " Essoins " or " excuses " for non-appearance in answer to the Writs of Summons issued by the Court, and also of the Writs directing no essoin to be received in certain cases.

EXTRACT ROLLS, CALLED " EXTRACTA DE BANCO." EDW.III. to Hen. IV. 140 Rolls.

JUDGMENTS on POSTEAS AND INQUIRIES, ENTRY BOOKS OF. 1760 to 1838. 16 Vols.

MARSHALS' DOCQUETS OF COMMITMENTS. 1730 to 1822. 1 Bag.

MARSHALS' SURRENDER AND COMMITTITUR BOOKS. 1719 to 1838. 22 Vols.

OUTLAWRIES, EXTENTS, AND INQUISITIONS IN. Geo. III. to Vict. 1 Portfolio.

OUTLAWRIES, DOGGETT BOOKS OF. 1684 to 1840. 3 Vols.

PLEA OR JUDGMENT ROLLS. 1702 to 1848. Before 1702 see " CORAM REGE ROLLS " (QUEEN'S BENCH, CROWN SIDE). The Judgment Rolls are very imperfect, owing to the frequent neglect of Solicitors to carry in the Roll to be filed after Judgment had been duly signed. Where the particular Roll is wanting the only evidence of the Judgment is contained in the " Entry Books of Judgments, Issues, and other entries," the Doggett Papers of signing Judgments, and in the Entry Books of Rules in which the Rule to sign Judgment should appear.

JUDICIAL PROCEEDINGS. Court of Queen's Bench (Plea Side)—(continued)

PLEA OR JUDGMENT ROLLS—(continued).

Doggett Rolls. 1390 to 1655. Before 1702 the Doggett Rolls and other Indexes refer to the " Coram Rege " or " Crown Rolls " with which the Plea Rolls were then incorporated.

Doggett Books. 1656 to 1839. 331 Vols., arranged alphabetically under Defendants' names.* (In these books the *Enrolments of Deeds, &c.* and the *Proceedings in Error* are entered at the beginning of each Term under the head of " Special Remembrances.")

" *Special Remembrance Rolls.*" 1595 to 1648. References to the Deeds enrolled and Proceedings in error only.

Entry Books of Judgments, &c. 1736 to 1848. Entries of all Judgments, &c., arranged chronologically. 92 Vols.

Day Books of Judgments, &c. 1736 to 1848. Alphabetical Indexes to the Entry Books. 87 Vols.

PRISONERS' PAPERS. 1 Parcel.

PRISONERS' RULES OF DISCHARGE. 1729 to 1838. 21 Vols.

RULES, ENTRY BOOKS OF. 1603 to 1848.

WARRANTS OF ATTORNEY TO CONFESS JUDGMENT. 1802 to 1825. 335 Bundles, arranged alphabetically.

DO. (FROM VARIOUS COURTS). 1822 to 1825. 20 Bundles.

WARRANTS OF ATTORNEY AND COGNOVITS. 1822 to 1848. 1,437 Bundles. Arranged chronologically.

WARRANTS OF ATTORNEY, ENTRY BOOKS OF. 1822 to 1848. 54 Vols.

These are Registers of the Warrants of Attorney in various Courts filed in the Queen's Bench, pursuant to Stat. 3 Geo. IV. cap. 39.

Index. 1841 to 1848. 10 Vols.

WRITS AND POSTEAS. Eliz. to Will. IV. 1 Package.

WRITS (JUDICIAL). *Series I.* 1629 to 1848. 92 Bundles.

WRITS (SPECIAL, ORIGINAL). *Series II.* 1629 to 1844. 142 Bundles.

---

* These were discontinued by virtue of the Statute 2 Vict., cap. 11, by which the Registration of Judgments in the Court of Common Pleas was instituted.

JUDICIAL PROCEEDINGS. Court of Queen's Bench (Plea Side)—(continued).

WRITS (HABEAS CORPUS, &c.). 1649 to 1684. 12 Bags.
(Amongst these will be found many Presentments before Commissioners of Sewers and other documents of importance as returned to Writs of Recordari facias.)

WRITS OF REPLEVIN. 1764 to 1835. 4 Portfolios.

WRITS OF SCIRE FACIAS, ENROLMENTS OF. 1617 to 1826. 8 Bundles.

WRITS, INDEXES TO, CALLED "ALPHABET BOOKS." 1751 to 1832. 67 Vols.

JUDICIAL PROCEEDINGS. Court of Common Pleas.

AFFIDAVITS (GENERAL). 1704 to 1849.
Index. 1838 to 1847. 2 Vols.

COMMON ROLLS. See PLEA ROLLS or "COMMON ROLLS."

CROWN DEBTS, REGISTERS OF. 1839 to 1848. 10 Vols., entitled "The Index to Debtors and Accountants to the Crown."
Lexicographical Index. 1839 to 1850. 11 Vols.

DE BANCO ROLLS. 1 Edw. I. to 24 Hen. VII. 987 Rolls. (See Lists and Indexes, No. IV., 1894.)
The "Placita de Banco," and the Plea Rolls or Common Rolls of the Common Bench prior to the 25th year of Elizabeth, contain, in addition to the Personal Plea Rolls of that Court, the Pleas of Land or Common Recoveries, including the Proceedings on Writs of Right and in all real actions, and the Inrolments of Deeds and other writings. In Easter 25 Elizabeth the Pleas of Land and Deeds enrolled were formed into distinct Rolls, known as "Recovery Rolls."
Before 1 Edward I., when the Court of Common Pleas was finally separated from the Curia Regis, many Placita de Banco or Common Pleas will be found with the Rolls of that Court. See CORAM REGE ROLLS (QUEEN'S BENCH, CROWN SIDE).
See **LE NEVES INDEXES** to the Feet of Fines and Placita de Banco.

EJECTMENT, DECLARATIONS IN (with Affidavits of service annexed). 1704 to 1837. After 1837, see "AFFIDAVITS, GENERAL."
Do., CONSENTS IN. 1727 to 1774. After 1774 these are filed with the Declarations.
Indexes. 1728 to 1809. 2 Vols., called "Ejectment Books."
Do. 1815 to 1837. 1 Vol.
(For a description of Proceedings in Ejectment, see Judicial Proceedings of the Queen's Bench, Plea Side.)

JUDICIAL PROCEEDINGS. Court of Common Pleas—(continued).

ESSOIN ROLLS. 10 Hen. III. to 38 Geo. III.

These Rolls contain entries of excuses for non-appearance to the summons of the Court.

EXTRACT ROLLS. 1–17 Edw. III.

These contain entries of Memoranda of Interlocutory Pleadings in suits pending in the Court of Common Pleas, which appear to have been subsequently entered on the Placita de Banco.

JUDGMENTS, &c., REGISTERS OF. 1838 to 1849. 24 Vols.

These contain entries of Judgments in various Courts registered in the Common Pleas pursuant to the Statute 1 & 2 Vict. See also " CROWN DEBTS, REGISTERS OF."

NISI PRIUS RECORDS, ENTRIES OF. 1644 to 1837. 22 Vols.

OUTLAWRY BOOKS. 1821 to 1848. 4 Vols.

OUTLAWRY, REVERSALS OF. 10 Geo. II. to 1859. 4 Vols.

PLEA ROLLS OR "COMMON ROLLS." 1 Henry VIII. to 1859. 3,084 Rolls. Before Henry VIII., see " DE BANCO ROLLS."

Prior to Easter 25 Elizabeth the Plea or Common Rolls include Pleas of Land or Common Recoveries, Proceedings on Writs of Right and in all real actions, and Deeds Enrolled. From and after that date these proceedings form a distinct class of Rolls, called " Recovery Rolls "

Doggett Rolls. 1509 to 1859.
Prior to 1779, when the Prothonotaries' Offices were united, there are separate Rolls for each of the three Prothonotaries.

Doggett Books. 29 Car. II. to 1839.
These are Entry Books of Judgments under Defendants' names.*

Judgments, Day Books of. 1838 to 1859. 21 Vols. MS.
Do. (Account). 1800 to 1858. 48 Vols. MS.
Judgment Books (Common). 1651 to 1802. 32 Vols.
Do. (Special). 1679 to 1802. 11 Vols.

POSTEAS, FILES OF. 1689 to 1852, and Miscellaneous.

These are the Records of the Final Judgments in the several causes which should be annexed to or entered on

---

* These were discontinued by virtue of the Statute 2 Vict., cap. 11, by which the Registration of Judgments in the Court of Common Pleas was instituted.

JUDICIAL PROCEEDINGS. Court of Common Pleas—(continued).

POSTEAS, FILES OF—(continued).

the Issue Roll, thus converting it into a Judgment Roll. This, however, was frequently neglected, and the "Posteas," so called from the word with which they commenced, have been tied up in distinct bundles, sometimes called "Riders" or Final Judgments. There is also a box containing Riders and Final Judgments from Eliz. to Geo. II.

Index. 1718 to 1858. 10 Vols. MS.

RECOVERY ROLLS. 25 Elizabeth, Easter, to 1837. 1,004 Rolls.

Before Easter 25 Elizabeth, see PLEA ROLLS or "COMMON ROLLS."

REMEMBRANCE ROLLS (PROTHONOTARIES'). 6 Hen. VIII. to 1799.

Prior to the year 1770 these contain entries of all Rules for Judgment, &c., and also of Præcipes, &c. in Pleas of Land or Common Recoveries. After 1770 the Præcipes for Recoveries are entered on a separate series called "REMEMBRANCE ROLLS FOR RECOVERIES."

REMEMBRANCE BOOKS (SECONDARIES'). 1800 to 1837. 38 Vols. Entries of Rules only.

REMEMBRANCE BOOKS (MASTERS'). 1838 to 1859. 22 Vols. Entries of Rules only.

RIDERS AND FINAL JUDGMENTS. See "POSTEAS."

RULES, ENTRIES OF. See "REMEMBRANCE ROLLS" and "REMEMBRANCE BOOKS."

WARRANTS OF ATTORNEY TO CONFESS JUDGMENT. 1820 to 1849.

WARRANTS OF ATTORNEY TO SUE AND DEFEND. 1769 to 1837.

(For Admissions to sue and defend by guardians, from 1834 to 1850, see "Remembrance Roll for Recoveries," No. 88.)

WRITS OF COVENANT. Edw. III. to Will. IV. 64 Bags.

WRITS OF CAPIAS, WRITS FILED, &c., &c. 1800 to 1859. 114 Bags.

WRITS FILED, INDEX TO. 1838 to 1859. 3 Vols.

WRITS OF ENTRY AND SEISIN. 1801 to 1833. 94 Bags.

WRITS OF INQUIRY. 1650 to 1854. 222 Packages.

WRITS OF RIGHT. Proceedings in real actions, as on Writs of Right, Inquisitions in Partition, Pleas of Ancient Demesne, &c., subsequent to Easter 25 Elizabeth are enrolled on the "Recovery Rolls" and indexed in the "Recovery Indexes." Prior to that date they will be found on the De Banco Rolls or Common Rolls.

JUDICIAL PROCEEDINGS. Court of Exchequer (Queen's Remembrancer's or Equity Side).

AFFIDAVITS (ORIGINAL). 1572 to 1841.

APPEARANCES, ENTRIES OF. 1588 to 1841. 19 Vols.

BILLS, ANSWERS, REPLICATIONS, AND REJOINDERS. Eliz. to 1841 and Miscellaneous.

> *Bill Books.* Eliz. to 1841. 34 Vols. MS. Arranged chronologically, in Counties.
> *Calendar.* Elizabeth. 1 Vol. MS. (Bedford to Kent only.)
> *Index.* Jas. I. to Victoria. 1 Vol. MS. An Alphabetical Index to the "Miscellaneous Bills and Answers."
> *Do.* Uncertain Dates. 2 Vols. MS.

CERTIFICATES OF SALE AND TRANSFER OF BANK STOCK. 1820 to 1841. 4 Vols.

DECREES AND ORDERS:

> Decrees and Orders (Original). 22 Eliz. to 14 Car. II.
> Decrees (Original). 17 Car. II. to 1841.
> Orders (Original). 16 Car. II. to 1842.
> Decrees and Orders (Supplementary). 16 Eliz. to 12 Geo. I. and unarranged. 22 Portfolios.

DECREES AND ORDERS, ENTRIES OF.

> *Series I.* (Decrees and Orders). 1 Eliz. to 3 Jas. I. 29 Vols.
> *Series II.* (Decrees and Orders). 1 Jas. I. to 1 Car. I. 37 Vols.
> *Series III.* (Decrees and Orders). 1 Car. I. to 13 Car. II. 39 Vols.
> *Series IV.* (Decrees only). 2 Jas. I. to 4 & 5 Vict. 57 Vols.
> *Series V.* (Orders only). 13 Car. II. to 1850. 94 Vols.

[Since 1841 these Books contain Revenue Orders only.]
See also **MEMORANDA ROLLS OF THE EXCHEQUER.**

> *Calendar of Decrees and Orders.* 1 Eliz. to 3 Jas. I. 3 Vols. MS.
> *Do. of Decrees only.* 1 to 31 Eliz. and Jas. I. to Car. II., known as "Vanderzee's Index." 1 Vol. MS.
> *Chronological Index to Decrees and Orders.* James I. and Charles I. In progress.
> *Index to Decrees.* 7 Charles I. to 1841. 13 Vols MS.
> *Index to Orders.* (Imperfect.) 1686 to 1841. 25 Vols. MS.
> *Index Locorum.* Eliz. to Geo. III. 1 Vol. Printed, known as "Martin's Index to the Exchequer Records."

JUDICIAL PROCEEDINGS. Court of Exchequer (Queen's Remembrancer's or Equity Side)—(continued).

DEPOSITIONS TAKEN BEFORE THE BARONS OF THE EXCHEQUER, CALLED "BARONS' DEPOSITIONS." Eliz. to 1841.
    Calendar. Elizabeth. [After the reign of Elizabeth, the Barons' Depositions are arranged alphabetically.]

DEPOSITIONS TAKEN BY COMMISSION. Eliz. to 1841, and Miscellaneous.

Calendar.	1 Eliz. to 22 Jas. I. Report XXXVIII., App., No. 2.
Do.	1 Car. I. to 24 Car. I. Report XXXIX., App., No. 2.
Do.	24 Car. I. to 4 Jas. II. Report XL., App., No. 1.
Do.	1 Wm. and Mary to 13 Geo. I. Report XLI., App., No. 1.
Do.	George II. Report XLII., App., No. 1.
Do.	George III. 3 Vols. MS.
Do.	George IV. to Victoria. 1 Vol. MS.
Index Nominum.	1 to 33 Eliz., 1 Vol. MS.
Do.	1 to 22 Jas. I., 3 Vols. MS.
Calendar.	Eliz. to Vict. (Miscellaneous), 1 Vol. MS.
Index.	Do. 2 Vols. MS.

INFORMATIONS, PLEAS, AND WRITS. Eliz. to Vict. 10 Portfolios.

INFORMATIONS OF INTRUSION, TRANSCRIPTS OF. Temp. Car. I.
    [*Misc. Books, Augmentation Office, Vol.* 164.]

INFORMATIONS OF INTRUSION. 33 Geo. II. to 6 Vict. 1 Portfolio.
    Do. (ATTY. GEN. v. LORD CHURCHILL.) 1836 to 1843. Relating to the Forest of Whichwood, Co. Oxon. 1 Portfolio.
    See also **MEMORANDA ROLLS OF THE EXCHEQUER.**

MINUTE BOOKS (COMMON). 1616 to 1821. 140 Vols.

MINUTE BOOKS (EXCHEQUER CHAMBER). 1695 to 1841. 46 Vols.

OUTLAWRIES. Chas. I. to Vict. 1 Package.

OUTLAWRY BOOKS. 1639 to 1841. 4 Vols.

PETITIONS (ORIGINAL). Geo. III. to 1841. 15 Portfolios.
    Chronological Inventory.

JUDICIAL PROCEEDINGS. Court of Exchequer (Queen's Remembrancer's or Equity Side)— (continued).

REPORTS AND CERTIFICATES. 1648 to 1841.

Original Reports by the Masters or Deputy Remembrancers with Certificates of the purchase, sale, or transfer of Bank Stock. See also "CERTIFICATES OF SALE."

Index. 1648 to 1841. 5 Vols.

REVENUE PROCEEDINGS:—

Extents and Inquisitions for Debt. 1685 to 1837.

Informations relating to the Excise. Geo. III. to Victoria.

Index. 1798 to 1830. 2 Vols.

Indentures of Appraisement. (Valuations of goods seized for breaches of the Excise laws.) 1649 to 1827.

Do. 1837 to 1850.

License Books. 1637 to 1797. 4 Vols.

These contain Licenses granted to persons to compound where vessels or goods have been seized in consequence of informations raised against them.

Seizure Books and Entries of Writs of Appraisement. 1607 to 1843. 9 Vols.

Miscellaneous Papers in Revenue Causes. 72 Packages.

Index. 1 Vol. MS., called "Index to Papers."

Proceedings in Revenue Causes are also enrolled on the **MEMORANDA ROLLS OF THE EXCHEQUER.**

The Orders relating to Revenue proceedings are to be found in the " ENTRY BOOKS OF DECREES AND ORDERS."

WEY NAVIGATION CLAIMS.

A bundle of claims of persons interested in the navigation of the River Wey, made pursuant to Statute 23 Car. II.

WRITS AND POSTEAS. Will. and Mary to 1850. 28 Packages.

WRITS, JUDICIAL. 1666 to 1714. 13 Bags.

WRITS, ORIGINAL JUDICIAL. 1646 to 1830. 156 Bags.

JUDICIAL PROCEEDINGS. Court of Exchequer of Pleas or Common Law Side.

ACCOUNTS OF MONEY PAID IN AND OUT OF COURT. 1690 to 1775. 3 Vols.

AFFIDAVITS (GENERAL). 1830 to 1855.

APPEARANCE BOOKS. 28 Eliz. to 12 Anne. 35 Vols.

JUDICIAL PROCEEDINGS. Court of Exchequer of Pleas or Common Law Side—(continued).

COGNOVITS. See "WARRANTS OF ATTORNEY AND COGNOVITS."

EJECTMENT, PROCEEDINGS IN.
Affidavits on motion in Court in Ejectment. 1778 to 1837.
Declarations in Ejectment with Affidavits annexed. 1838 to 1849.
Index to Ejectments. 1830 to 1852. 2 Vols.
For a description of Proceedings in Ejectment, see JUDICIAL PROCEEDINGS OF THE COURT OF QUEEN'S BENCH (PLEA SIDE).

ERROR, TRANSCRIPTS OF PROCEEDINGS IN. 13 Bundles.

JEWS' PLEA ROLLS. 3 Hen. III. to 14 Edw. I. 47 Rolls.
These contain the Pleas before the Justices of the Jews. See **JEWS.**

PLEA ROLLS. 53 Hen. III. to 1855. (See Lists and Indexes, No. IV., 1894.)
Repertories. Edward IV. to Hen. VII. 1 Package.
Alphabetical Calendar. 1293 to 1820. 21 Vols. ⎱
Chronological Calendar. 1293 to 1820. 18 Vols. ⎰
These consist of selections of the more important pleadings and enrolments.
Calendar of Tythe-Suits enrolled in the Exchequer of Pleas. Edw. IV. to George III. Report II., App. II., pp. 249–272.
Doggett Books. Eliz. to 1837. 51 Vols.
Entry Books of Judgments. 1830 to 1855. 100 Vols.
Alphabetical Index to Ditto. 1830 to 1855. 46 Vols.

MINUTE BOOKS. 1657 to 1830. 74 Vols.

PLACITORUM FORMULARE. 1 Vol.

ORDER BOOKS. 3 Edw. VI. to 1830. 81 Vols.

OUTLAWRY BOOKS. 1832 to 1869. 2 Vols.

RULE BOOKS. 1811 to 1854. 43 Vols.

WARRANTS OF ATTORNEY AND COGNOVITS. 1803 to 1855.

WRITS, CALLED "BILLS AND WRITS." Edw. III. to 1855.

WRITS RETURNED (LONDON AND MIDDLESEX). 1843 to 1855.

Do. (OUT COUNTIES). 1843 to 1855.

WRITS, INQUISTIONS, POSTEAS, &c. 2 Portfolios.

WRITS AND TRANSCRIPTS OF JUDGMENTS FROM THE COURT OF GREAT SESSIONS IN WALES. 1 Portfolio.

JUDICIAL PROCEEDINGS. Court of Exchequer (Lord Treasurer's Remembrancer's Side).

Pleadings and Judgments on Writs of " *Quo titulo clamat*" and " *Quare maneria, &c. in manibus regis seisiri non debent,*" on *Claims of Liberties and Privileges* by Cities, Boroughs, and Towns, and Proceedings relating to the Accounts of Sheriffs, &c., and to the Fines, Issues, and Amerciaments due to the Exchequer from the Courts at Westminster and other jurisdictions are enrolled on the Memoranda Rolls of the Lord Treasurer's Remembrancer. See **MEMORANDA ROLLS OF THE EXCHEQUER.**

There are also the following distinct classes of documents :—

MINUTE BOOKS. 3 Jas. II. to 35 Geo. III. 4 Vols.

These books contain Minutes of Orders on the Lord Treasurer's Remembrancer's side of the Exchequer entered Term by Term, and also of the Admissions of Officers of that court.

ORDERS, ENTRY BOOKS OF. 35 Car. II. to 3 & 4 Will. IV. 18 Vols.

Do. (Drafts.) 1819 to 1832. 24 Vols.

ORDERS ENTRY BOOK OF. ˙21 Car. II. to 6 Geo. III. 1 Vol. entitled " Orders of Court," containing Comptroller's copies of Orders.

Do. 1685 to 1738. 1 Vol., entitled " Loane Orders," containing Orders for the repayment of Loans to the King, &c.

WRITS RETURNABLE, ENTRIES OF (CALLED " LEVY BOOKS "). 1805 to 1834. 7 Vols.

These contain entries of the sums to be levied by the Sheriffs of the several counties from various persons whose names are specified, with the reasons for such levy. The entries are described as " Writs Returnable " on such a date, where no Writs were issued " No Levy " being put against the name of the Sheriff.

WRITS AND INQUISITIONS FOR DEBT, &c. Eliz. to Geo. IV. 15 Portfolios.

JUDICIAL PROCEEDINGS. Exchequer (Courts of Augmentations and of the General Surveyors).

Court of Augmentations.

BILLS, ANSWERS, &c. Henry VIII. 2 Vols.

[*Misc. Books, Vols.* 20 *and* 23.]

See also SURVEY, COURT OF.

JUDICIAL PROCEEDINGS. Exchequer (Courts of Augmentations and of the General Surveyors) —(continued).

Court of Augmentations—(continued).

DEPOSITIONS. Henry VIII. to Edward VI. 26 Vols.
[*Misc. Books, Vols* 108 *to* 133.]
Index. Hen. VIII. to Edw. VI. 1 Vol. MS. (copied from No. 21,291 of the Additional MSS. in the British Museum), referring to some of the Miscellaneous Books above mentioned.

DECREES AND ORDERS. Henry VIII. to Edward VI. 15 Vols.
[*Misc. Books, Vols.* 91 to 105.]
Calendar. Henry VIII. to Edw. VI. 2 Vols. MS.
Index Locorum. Do. 2 Vols. MS.

INFORMATIONS and other proceedings in the COURT OF AUGMENTATIONS. Hen. VIII. 1 Vol.
[*Misc. Books, Vol.* 165.]

MINUTE BOOK. 38 Henry VIII.
A volume entitled "Liber Comparentium," containing Minutes of Orders in various Causes depending in the Court of Augmentations, entered day by day.
[*Misc. Books, Vol.* 3.]
Do. 1634. 1 Vol.
[*Misc. Books, Vol.* 329.]

ORDERS OF THE COURT OF AUGMENTATIONS concerning Arrears. 38 Hen. VIII. to 1 Edw. VI. 1 Vol.
[*Misc. Books, Vol.* 328.]

SURVEY, COURT OF; ANSWERS, &c. (EXCHEQUER, TREASURY OF THE RECEIPT.) Hen. VIII. to Edw. VI. Six volumes, containing the *Answers* to Proceedings in the *Court of Augmentations,* with a few Bills presented in the same Court.

MISCELLANEOUS PROCEEDINGS. Henry VIII. to Philip and Mary. 15 Packages.

WRITS, PRECEDENT BOOK OF. A volume called "Liber Brevium," containing Transcripts of Writs of various kinds issuing out of the Exchequer.
[*Misc. Books, Vol.* 169.]
There is also amongst the Miscellanea of the Treasury of the Receipt of a Roll containing examples of a great number of Writs compiled apparently in the reign of Edward IV.

Court of General Surveyors.

BILLS, ANSWERS, &c. Hen. VIII. 3 Vols.
[*Misc. Books, Augmentation Office, Vols.* 19, 21, and 22.]

JUDICIAL PROCEEDINGS. Exchequer (Courts of Augmentations and of the General Surveyors)—(continued).

Court of General Surveyors—(continued).

DECREES AND ORDERS. 34 to 38 Hen. VIII.

[*Misc. Books, Augmentation Office, Vol.* 106.]
This volume was kept pursuant to the Statute 33 Hen. VIII. cap. 39, establishing the Court of General Surveyors, by which it was enacted that the Clerk of the Court should enter in a book the appearances of all persons summoned to appear in the said Court, and all Acts, Decrees, and Orders therein made. From 38 Hen. VIII. the business of this Court was annexed to the new Court of Augmentations then established.

Calendar. Report XXX., App., pp. 166–196.

MINUTE BOOKS. 6 to 18 Hen. VIII. and 34 to 38 Hen. VIII. 2 Vols.
[*Misc. Books, Augmentation Office, Vol.* 313*a.* and 313*b.*]

JUDICIAL PROCEEDINGS. Exchequer (Court of First Fruits and Tenths).

PLEA ROLLS. Mary to George II. 19 Rolls.
Index. 1 Vol. MS.

PRECEDENT BOOK. 1 Vol.

PROCESS BOOKS. 29 Hen. VIII. to 1817. 13 Vols.

WRITS AND MISCELLANEOUS DOCUMENTS. Henry VIII. to William IV. 21 Packages.

JUDICIAL PROCEEDINGS. Courts of Wales and Chester (Equity Side).

BILLS, ANSWERS, &c. (CHANCERY.)
Chester Circuit. (Flint, Denbigh, and Montgomery.) 1750 to 1830.
Index. Geo. II. to Geo. IV. 1 Vol. MS.
North Wales Circuit. (Anglesey, Carnarvon, and Merioneth.) 1712 to 1830.
Bill Books. 5 Anne to 1 Will. IV. 3 Vols. MS.
Brecon Circuit. (Brecon, Radnor, and Glamorgan.) 2 & 3 Will. and Mary to 1 Will. IV.
Bill Books. 3 Anne to 1 Will. IV. 3 Vols. MS.
Carmarthen Circuit. (Carmarthen, Pembroke, and Cardigan.) 1 & 2 Wm. and Mary to 1 Will. IV.
Index. 4 Geo. II. to 1 Will. IV. 2 Vols. MS.

DECREES AND ORDERS. (CHANCERY).
Chester Circuit. (Flint, Denbigh, and Montgomery.)
Minute Books of Decrees and Orders. 6 Geo. II. to 1 Will. IV.

JUDICIAL PROCEEDINGS. Courts of Wales and Chester (Equity Side)—(continued).

DECREES AND ORDERS. (CHANCERY)—continued.[1]

North Wales Circuit. (Anglesea, Carnarvon, and Merioneth.)

Entry Books of Decrees and Orders. 7 Geo. I. to 4 Geo. IV.

Rule and Order Books. 4 Geo. I. to Will. IV.

Brecon Circuit. (Brecon, Radnor, and Glamorgan.)

Decree Book. 9 Anne to 16 Geo. III.

Order Books. 3 Anne to 34 Geo. III.

Minute Books. 3 Geo. I. to 4 Geo. IV.

Do. (Registrar's.) 4 to 11 Geo. IV.

Carmarthen Circuit. (Carmarthen, Pembroke, and Cardigan.)

Order Book. 19 Geo. II. to 3 Geo. III.

BILLS, ANSWERS, &c. (CHESTER EXCHEQUER.)

Chester and Flint. Hen. VIII. to Geo. IV. This series comprises the Bills, Answers, Depositions, and other Proceedings in the Exchequer of Chester.

Calendar and Index. Hen. VIII. to Phil. & Mary. Report XXV., App., pp. 23–31.

Index. 1 to 60 George III. 1 Vol. MS.

DECREES AND ORDERS (CHESTER EXCHEQUER.)

Chester and Flint. Entry Books of Decrees and Orders. 7 Eliz. to 19 Geo. II.

Do. (on Confessions). 5 Eliz. to 2 Will. and Mary.

Minute Books of Decrees and Orders. 32 Eliz. to 49 Geo. III.

See also RULE BOOKS.

PLEAS IN THE EXCHEQUER OF CHESTER. 38 Hen. VI. to 20 Car. II. 37 Rolls.

These consist of a few Traverses of Inquisitions post mortem and of Pleas at the Great Sessions, &c. returned into the Exchequer upon Writs of Certiorari.

Inventory. Report XXI., App., pp. 44–46.

PLEAS, INQUISITIONS, &c. (NORTH WALES), TRANSCRIPTS OF. Edw. III. to Henry VI.

[*Misc. Books, Exchequer, Augmentation Office, Vols.* 166 *and* 167.]

PORTMOTE, PENTICE, AND CROWNMOTE COURTS (CHESTER), PROCEEDINGS IN THE. 5 Edw. VI. to 2 Geo. III. 40 Rolls.

These consist of such proceedings in the said Courts as were returned into the Exchequer on Writs of Certiorari.

RULE BOOKS. (CHESTER EXCHEQUER.)

Chester and Flint. 13 Eliz. to 10 Geo. IV.

JUDICIAL PROCEEDINGS. Courts of Wales and Chester (Equity Side)—(continued).

" SEAL BOOKS " (CONTAINING ISSUES OF THE EXCHEQUER SEAL).

Chester and Flint. *Five Series.*
Series I. 3 Jas. I. to 1 Will. IV.
" II. 40 Eliz. to 56 Geo. III.
" III. 14 Car. II. to 54 Geo. III.
" IV. 24 Geo. III. to 1 Will. IV.
" V. 7 & 8 Geo. III. to 32 Geo. III.

These are merely entries of the Fees paid for Writs, Copies, &c.

JUDICIAL PROCEEDINGS. Courts of Wales and Chester (Common Law Side).

ASSIZE ROLLS, EYRE ROLLS, &c. '(Chester, Flint, and Macclesfield.) 35 Edw. I. to 15 Hen. VII. 15 Rolls.
(*See* Lists and Indexes, No. IV., 1894.)

CALENDAR ROLLS.
Chester. 39 Edw. III. to 38 Hen. VIII.
Flint. 21 Edw. III. to 13 Hen. VIII.
Radnor. 1 Mary to Commonwealth.
Glamorgan. 1 Mary to 48 Eliz.
Cardigan. 33 Hen. VIII. to 44 Eliz.
Pembroke. 33 Hen. VIII. to 20 Jas. I. and 26 Car. II.

These Rolls contain enrolments of the Calendar of Indictments and Pleas of the Crown which was usually filed with the Indictments themselves on the Gaol Files, and give the names of all persons indicted at the Great Sessions with the offences charged against them, and also abstracts of all Coroners' Inquests.

CROWN BOOKS. (Chester and Flint.)
Chester. 2 Eliz. to 10 Anne.
Flint. 24 Hen. VIII. to 16 Car. I.
Chester and Flint. 31 Geo. III. to 1 Will. IV.

These books contain notes or Memoranda of the Indictments, Presentments, Orders, and Sentences in Crown Causes. There are in all 10 Volumes.

ESSOIN ROLLS. (Chester.) 17 Edw. III. to 22 Hen. VII. 11 Rolls.

GAOL FILES.
Anglesey. 1 Geo. IV. to 1 Will. IV.
Brecon. 1 Eliz. to 1 Will. IV.

JUDICIAL PROCEEDINGS. Courts of Wales and Chester (Common Law Side)—(continued).

GAOL FILES—(continued).

Cardigan. 34 Hen. VIII. to 11 Geo. IV.
Carmarthen. 4 Edw. VI. to 11 Geo. IV.
Carnarvon. 4 Geo. II. to 1 Will. IV.
Denbigh. 17 Hen. VIII. to 1 Will IV
Glamorgan. 33 Hen. VIII. to 1 Will. IV.
Merioneth. 4 Anne to 1 Will. IV.
Montgomery. 1 Mary to 60 Geo. III.
Pembroke. 1 Edw. VI. to 1 Will. IV.

These consist of the documents filed by the Prothonotary in his capacity as Clerk of the Crown, and correspond to the " Mainprize Files " of Chester and Flint.

INDICTMENT ROLLS. (Chester, Macclesfield, and Flint.) 22 Edw. I. to 12 Hen. VII. 31 Rolls.

These Rolls contain Indictments, Presentments, and Inquisitions before the Justices of Chester at Chester, and in their Eyres ; and before Justices appointed by Special Commission, Sheriffs in their Tours, and the Coroners.

(*See* Lists and Indexes, No. IV., 1894.)

MAINPRISE FILES.

Chester. 3 Eliz. to 1 Will. IV.
Flint. 30 Hen. VIII. to 1 Will. IV.

These contain in addition to the Records of Bails, from which they take their name, all processes and documents filed in criminal causes, and also the Inquisitions taken before the Coroners. They correspond to the " Gaol Files " of the remaining counties.

MAINPRISE ROLLS (containing entries of Bails only).

Chester. 27 Edw. I to 38 Hen. VIII.
Flint. 18 Ric. II. to 20 Hen. VIII.
Macclesfield. 49 Edw. III to 20 Ric. II.
Montgomery. 37 Hen. VIII.
Radnor. 1 Mary to 8 Eliz.
Glamorgan. 33 Hen. VIII. to 6 Eliz.
Carmarthen. 37 Hen. VIII. to 4 Edw. VI.
Carnarvon. 34 Hen. VIII.

MINUTE BOOKS (PROTHONOTARIES').

Chester and Flint. 2 to 14 Geo. II.
Chester. 15 Geo. II. to 1 Will. IV.
Flint. 15 Geo. II. to 56 Geo. III.
Glamorgan. 1 to 13 Anne.
See also " RULES, ENTRY BOOKS OF."

OUTLAWRY ROLLS. (Chester.) 2 Edw. IV. to 1 Edw. V. 2 Rolls.

JUDICIAL PROCEEDINGS. Courts of Wales and Chester (Common Law Side)—(continued).

PLEA ROLLS.

Chester. 44 Hen. III. to 1 Will. IV.
Calendar of Deeds, Inquisitions, and Writs of Dower enrolled on the Chester Plea Rolls. Hen. III. to Hen. VIII. Printed in Reports XXVI. to XXX.
Docket Rolls. 32–38 Hen. VIII.
Docket Books. I Hen. VIII. to 1 Will. IV. These relate to Fines and Recoveries only.
Anglesey. 18 Eliz. to 1 Will. IV.
Docket Rolls. 8 Jas. I. to 2 Geo. IV.
Docket Books. 1 Geo. IV. to 1 Will. IV.
Brecon. 34 Hen. VIII. to 1 Will. IV.
Docket Rolls. 1 Eliz. to 20 Car. I.
Docket Books. 23 Car. I. to 41 Geo. III. (Brecon only.)
    Do. 5 Geo. II. to 1 Will. IV. (Brecon and Radnor.)
Cardigan. 33 Hen. VIII. to 1 Will. IV.
Docket Rolls. 1 Jas. I. to 6 Geo. II.
Carmarthen. 33 Hen. VIII. to 1 Will. IV.
Docket Rolls. 1 Eliz. to 6 Geo. II.
Carnarvon. 10 Ric. II. to 1 Will. IV.
Docket Rolls. 18 Eliz. to 59 Geo. III.
Docket Book. 1 Geo. IV. to 1 Will. IV.
Denbigh. 33 Hen. VIII. to 1 Will. IV.
Docket Rolls. 11 Eliz. to 31 Geo. III.
Flint. 12 Edw. I. to 1 Will. IV.
Docket Rolls. 15 Jas. I. to 9 Will. III.
Glamorgan. 33 Hen. VIII. to 1 Will. IV.
Docket Rolls. 37 Hen. VIII. to 16 Car. I.
Docket Books. 23 Car. I. to 42 Geo. III.
    Do. 20 Geo. II. to 1 Will. IV.
Merioneth. 1 Edw. VI. to 1 Will. IV.
Docket Rolls. 18 Eliz. to 59 Geo. III.
Docket Book. 1 Geo. IV. to 1 Will. IV.
Montgomery. 33 Hen. VIII. to 1 Will. IV.
Docket Rolls. 38 Hen. VIII. to 1 Will. IV.
Pembroke. 34 Hen. VIII. to 1 Will. IV.
Docket Rolls. 36 Hen. VIII. to 1653.
Radnor. 33 Hen. VIII. to 1 Will. IV.
Docket Rolls. 1 Mary to 20 Car. I.
Docket Books. 23 Car. I. to 49 Geo. III.
    Do. 5 Geo. II. to 1 Will. IV. (Brecon and Radnor.)

A List of all the Plea Rolls of Wales and Chester is contained in the List of Plea Rolls. (Lists and Indexes, No. IV., 1894.)

JUDICIAL PROCEEDINGS. Courts of Wales and Chester (Common Law Side)—(continued).

QUO WARRANTO ROLLS.

Chester. 27 to 31 Edw. III. and 15 Hen. VII. 3 Rolls.

Do. 15 Hen. VII. 2 Rolls.

The latter are paper Rolls containing recitals of the Liberties and Privileges of the Monasteries of Vale Royal and St. Werburgh, in the form of pleadings on Writs of Quo Warranto. (They are apparently drafts.)

QUO WARRANTO, ORIGINAL WRITS OF. 14 Hen. VII. 1 Roll.

RULES, ENTRY BOOKS OF, OR "RULE AND MINUTE BOOKS." (PROTHONOTARIES'.)

Chester and Flint. 1 to 35 Eliz.

Chester. 35 Eliz. to 1 Will. IV.

Flint. 17 Hen. VIII. to 1 Will. IV.

Denbigh and } 7 Geo. II. to 1 Will. IV.
Montgomery }

North Wales Circuit (Anglesey, Carnarvon, and Merioneth). 24 Geo. III. to 1 Will. IV.

Brecon Circuit (Brecon, Radnor, and Glamorgan). 12 Geo. I. to 10 Geo. IV.

Carmarthen Circuit (Carmarthen, Pembroke, and Cardigan). 13 Car. II. to Geo. III.

SHERIFFS' TOURN ROLLS, &c.

Chester. 31 Edw. III. to 18 Edw. IV. 7 Rolls.

Do. Flint. 16 Edw. III. to 1 Hen. IV. 1 Roll.

These Rolls contain Indictments, presentments, &c., similar to those found on the Indictment Rolls.

WARRANTS OF ATTORNEY, ROLLS OF.

Chester. 34 Edw. III. to 30 Hen. VIII.

The Warrants of Attorney are generally enrolled on the Plea Rolls. These few Rolls, however, form a distinct series of enrolments.

JUDICIAL PROCEEDINGS. Duchy of Lancaster.

AFFIDAVITS, REPORTS, CERTIFICATES, ORDERS, PETITIONS, &c. Elizabeth to 1800. 26 Bundles.

BILLS AND ANSWERS, DEPOSITIONS, &c. Hen. VII. to 1835.

The "Pleadings" or proceedings by Bill and Answer in the Chancery of the Duchy of Lancaster, more properly called the Court of Duchy Chamber at Westminster, commence in the reign of Henry VII. From that reign to the end of Elizabeth they are bound in volumes, the reference to these being by the printed Calendar (in three volumes) called "Ducatus Lancastriae."

JUDICIAL PROCEEDINGS. Duchy of Lancaster —(continued).

BILLS AND ANSWERS, DEPOSITIONS, &c.—(continued).

From Hen. VII. to Philip and Mary the Pleadings form two distinct Series, the first of which is described as "Pleadings, Surveys, &c.," and calendared in "Ducatus Lancastriæ," Vol. I. (*Pars Secunda*).

The second Series consists of a number of Pleadings found in the Duchy Office after the first had been printed, and bears the title of "Depositions, Examinations, &c." This is calendared in "Ducatus Lancastriæ," Vol. II. (*Pars Tertia*).

From 1 James I. the Bills, Answers, and Replications are arranged chronologically in bundles, each bundle containing the four Terms of the year, and are referred to by means of Alphabetical Indexes under the names of Plaintiffs and Defendants respectively according to the nature of the document filed, the Bills being indexed in the Plaintiff's name, and the Answers, if any, in the names of the several Defendants.

The Depositions, Examinations, and Surveys subsequent to the reign of Philip and Mary form a distinct set of bundles, to which there is a Manuscript Calendar. See DEPOSITIONS AND SURVEYS.

Calendar of Pleadings, &c. Hen. VII. to Elizabeth. 3 Vols. folio, entitled "Ducatus Lancastriæ."

Alphabetical Indexes. 1 Jas. II. to 1832. 6 Vols. MS.

DEPOSITIONS, SURVEYS, &c. Elizabeth to George II.

Prior to the reign of Elizabeth the Depositions and Examinations in suits pending in the Duchy Chamber are bound up with the Pleadings and calendared in the printed volumes known as "Ducatus Lancastriæ." From 1 Elizabeth they are preserved in yearly bundles, the Surveys of inclosures, encroachments, waste lands, &c. taken by Commission under the Duchy Seal forming separate bundles.

Calendar. 1 Eliz. to Geo. III. 1 Vol. MS., entitled "Surveys and Depositions."

DECREES AND ORDERS, ENTRY BOOKS OF. Edw. IV. to 1825. 47 Vols.

Indexes. Hen. VII. to 1835. 14 Vols. MS. (Vol. 14 is an Index Locorum from 1699 to 1796, arranged under Counties.) See also "Ayloffe's Calendars."

As it sometimes happens that Decrees made by the Court have never been enrolled, in the event of a Decree not being found in the Books of Decrees the bundles of *Draft Decrees* should also be searched.

DRAFT DECREES. Hen. VIII. to Geo. I. 142 Bundles.

DRAFT INJUNCTIONS. 12 Jas. I. to 1748. 23 Bundles.

JUDICIAL PROCEEDINGS. Palatinate of Durham (Crown Side).

ASSIZE CALENDARS. (Returns of Prisoners Committed.) 1805 to 1861. 6 Bundles.

COSTS OF PROSECUTIONS, &c. 1828 to 1876. 56 Bundles.

DEPOSITIONS. 1843 to 1877. 60 Bundles.

GAOL DELIVERY, COMMISSIONS OF. 1781 to 1876. 39 Bundles.

INDICTMENTS. 1713 to 1877. 166 Bundles.

INDICTMENT BOOKS. 1753 to 1876. 7 Vols.

MINUTE BOOKS. 1770 to 1784 and 1810 to 1876. 10 Vols.

PARDONS. 1816 to 1863. 2 Bundles.

RECOGNIZANCES. 1843 to 1877. 61 Bundles.

JUDICIAL PROCEEDINGS. Palatinate of Durham (Equity Side).

REGISTRARS' RECORDS.

AFFIDAVITS. 1657 to 1812. 26 Bundles.

BILLS, ANSWERS, REPLICATIONS, AND REJOINDERS. 1576 to 1840. 159 Bundles.

BILLS OF COSTS. 1702 to 1775. 4 Bundles.

COMMISSIONS, INTERROGATORIES, AND DEPOSITIONS. 1560 to 1803. 86 Bundles.

ORDERS, DECREES, AND REPORTS. 1613 to 1778. 137 Bundles.
      Do.   (MINUTES AND DRAFTS OF.) 1755 to 1829. 8 Bundles.

ORDERS AND DECREES, REGISTRARS' ENTRY BOOKS OF. 1633 to 1850. 7 Vols.

CURSITOR'S RECORDS.

INTERROGATORIES AND DEPOSITIONS. 1672 to 1768. 33 Bundles.

SIGNIFICAVITS FOR WRITS DE EXCOMMUNICATO CAPIENDO. 1700 to 1765. 3 Bundles.

JUDICIAL PROCEEDINGS. Palatinate of Durham (Common Law Side).

PROTHONOTARY'S RECORDS.

COGNOVITS AND WARRANTS OF ATTORNEY. 1828 to 1853. 17 Bundles.

DECLARATIONS AND OTHER PLEADINGS. 13 & 14 Car. II. to 15 and 16 Victoria. 178 Bundles.
      Indexes. 13 Car II. to 1774.

JUDICIAL PROCEEDINGS. Palatinate of Durham (Common Law Side).

EJECTMENTS, APPEARANCES TO. 4 Anne to 4 Geo. I. 1 Bundle.

JUDGMENT ROLLS. 20 Hen. VII. to 1844. 220 Rolls.
Index to Judgments. 24 Car. II. to 1728. 2 Vols.
[Prothonotary's Indexes No. 2.]

JUDGMENTS, FILES OF. 19 Car I. to 1853.

POSTEAS. 1751 to 1865. 6 Bundles.

JUDICIAL PROCEEDINGS. Palatinate of Lancaster (Crown Side).

ASSIZE ROLLS. See Lists and Indexes, No. IV., 1894.).
1–10 Henry D. of Lancaster. 8 Rolls.
The foregoing Rolls are deposited with the Records of the Duchy of Lancaster.
The earlier Assize Rolls relating to the County of Lancaster will be found in the general Series of Eyre and Assize Rolls. (See Lists and Indexes, No. IV., 1894.)
The following are with the Records of the Palatinate :—
    1–14 Hen. VI. 1 Roll.
    20–30   ,,   1 Roll.
    20 Hen. VI. (Fines and Amercements.) 1 Roll.
    22 Hen. VI. (Do.   .) 1 Roll.
    5–17 Edw IV. (Gaol Delivery.) 1 Roll.
And from 16 Hen. VIII. to 6 Victoria.

BAIL ROLLS. 22 to 38 Hen. VIII. 16 Rolls.

CORONERS' INQUISITIONS. 14 Car. II. to 3 Geo. IV. 51 Bundles.

DEPOSITIONS, INFORMATIONS, AND EXAMINATIONS.
In bundles, from 1808 to 1867, including the Lancashire Special Gaol Delivery (Fenian Trials) of 1867.

INDICTMENTS, WRITS OF ASSIZE, &c. 3 Hen. VI. to 38 Hen. VIII. 22 Bundles.

INDICTMENTS, &c. 17 Hen. VIII. to 4 Will. IV. 27 Bundles.

INDICTMENTS, CALENDARS TO.
    17 Edw. IV.   ⎫
    16–21 Hen. VIII. ⎬3 Rolls.
    26–35 Hen. VIII.⎭

INDICTMENTS, RECOGNIZANCES, VERDICTS, AND OTHER PROCEEDINGS, 1810 to 1867. In Bundles, entitled, "Nomina Ministrorum." These include the Lancashire Special Gaol Delivery (Fenian Trial) of 1867.

MINUTE BOOKS (CROWN OFFICE). 2 Jas. II. to 1828. 8 Vols.

JUDICIAL PROCEEDINGS. Palatinate of Lancaster (Crown Side)—(continued).

ORDER BOOKS (CROWN OFFICE). 10 Geo. II. to 1831. 4 Vols.

OUTLAWRY ROLLS. John of Gaunt to 1 Edward VI. 4 Rolls.

RECOGNIZANCES. 35 Car. II. to 52 Geo. III. 15 Bundles.

RECOGNIZANCE BOOKS. 41 Geo. III. to 8 Geo. IV. 2 Vols.

RULE BOOKS (CROWN OFFICE). 30 Geo. III. to 2 Victoria. 2 Vols.

JUDICIAL PROCEEDINGS. Palatinate of Lancaster (Equity Side).

CHANCERY RECORDS.

AFFIDAVITS. 1793 to 1836. 9 Bundles.
    Do.   ENTRIES OF. 1610 to 1678. 4 Vols.

APPEARANCE BOOKS. 1641 to 1703. 3 Vols.

BILLS. Henry VII. to 1853.
From Henry VII. to 1800 the Chancery Bills are bound in volumes, 91 in number; subsequent to the latter date they are in yearly bundles. 136 Vols. and Bundles.

ANSWERS. Edw. IV. to 1858.
Prior to 1710 the Answers are bound in volumes; from and after that date in yearly bundles. 251 Vols. and Bundles.
Bill Books. Edw. IV. to 1734. 10 Vols.
    Do.   1639 to 1648. 2 Vols. (Bills and Answers.)

CONSENTS. 1793 to 1836. 1 Bundle.

INTERROGATORIES, DEPOSITIONS, AND EXAMINATIONS. 24 Eliz. to 1853. 273 Bundles.

REPLICATIONS, DEMURRERS, EXCEPTIONS, &c. 1601 to 1846. 21 Bundles.

DECREES AND ORDERS, &c., ENTRY BOOKS OF. 15 Hen. VIII. to 1784. 27 Vols.

MINUTE BOOK (REGISTRAR'S). 1704 to 1713. 1 Vol.

JUDICIAL PROCEEDINGS. Palatinate of Lancaster (Common Law Side).

PROTHONOTARY'S RECORDS.

AFFIDAVITS. The Affidavits are filed with the " SESSIONAL PAPERS."
    Indexes. 1813 to 1838. 4 Vols., called " Pye Books."

JUDICIAL PROCEEDINGS. Palatinate of Lancaster (Common Law Side)—(continued).

JUDGMENTS, FINAL, &C.

Final Judgments (Draft). 20 Geo. III. to 52 Geo. III. 6 Vols.

Posteas (Draft). 51 Geo. III. to 11 Vict. 4 Vols.

Verdicts, Minutes of, 1839 to 1847. 1 Bundle.

See also "PANELS OF JURORS."

PANELS OF JURORS. 1811 to 1848. 75 Bundles.

These documents are useful as containing the Verdicts in the Suits entered on the Plea Rolls.

PLEA ROLLS. 2 Henry IV. to 11 Victoria. 767 Rolls.

Docquet Rolls. 1 to 15 John of Gaunt (1362 to 1377), and 6 Henry VI. to 34 Geo. II.

Docquet Rolls of Issues. 2 Car. I. to 8 Geo. I.

Docquet Books of Issues. 41 Geo. III. to 11 Vict. 6 Vols.

PRECEDENT BOOKS. 5 Vols.

REMEMBRANCERS' BOOKS. 8 Will. III. to 20 Geo. II. 3 Vols.

RULE BOOKS. 7 Geo. II. to 8 Vict. 15 Vols.

RULES, MINUTES OF. 7 Geo. II. to 36 Geo. III. 3 Vols.

RULES (CONSENT). 2 Geo. IV. to 16 Vict. 1 Bundle.

RULES IN EJECTMENT. 1811–1821. 1 Bundle.

RULES OF REFERENCE. 41 Geo. III. to 11 Vict. 4 Vols.

SESSIONAL PAPERS. Henry VIII. to 1847. 219 Bundles.

These contain the Original Issues, Affidavits, and other Pleadings in Suits in the Court of Common Pleas at Lancaster.

Indexes called "Pye Books." 2 Car. II. to 14 Geo. II. 6 Vols.

WRITS. 9 Hen. VI. to 1846. 703 Bundles.

Writ Books. 1712 to 1845. 22 Vols.

JUDICIAL PROCEEDINGS (VARIOUS).

High Court of Admiralty.

The principal Records of the High Court of Admiralty, which are not open to inspection except by permission of the Registrar of the Admiralty Court, are as follows :—

INSTANCE COURT.

ACT BOOKS. 1524 to 1744. 76 Vols.

Calendars. 1631 to 1673. 17 Vols.

ASSIGNATION BOOKS. 1673 to 1767. 126 Vols.

LIBELS, ALLEGATIONS, DECREES, AND OTHER PROCEEDINGS. 1533 to 1772.

WARRANT BOOKS. 1540 to 1772. 78 Vols.

JUDICIAL PROCEEDINGS (VARIOUS)—(continued).

High Court of Admiralty—(continued).

PRIZE COURT.

ACT BOOKS AND ASSIGNATION BOOKS. 1643 to 1770. 74 Vols.
    Calendars. 1653 to 1744. 21 Vols.

EXAMINATIONS, &c. 1664 to 1783.

LETTERS OF MARQUE, CALENDARS AND ENTRIES OF 1624 to 1762. 42 Vols.
    Do.   (during the American War). 40 Vols.

SENTENCE BOOKS. 1643 to 1766. 42 Vols.
    Do.   (during the American War). 15 Vols.

APPEAL COURT.

ASSIGNATION BOOKS. 1689 to the end of the American War. 45 Vols.

PRIZE PAPERS. 1744 to 1810.

The MUNIMENT BOOKS of the High Court of Admiralty from 1660 to 1815 are deposited in the Admiralty Registry at Somerset House.

In these books are entered the Appointments of Vice-Admirals, &c. &c.

Court of Chivalry, Court Military, or Earl Marshal's Court.

PLACITA EXERCITUS REGIS IN SCOTIA. 24 Edw. I. 1 Roll. [*Scottish Documents (Exchequer, Treasury of the Receipt), Box 93, No. 15.*]

PROCEEDINGS IN THE COURT OF CHIVALRY (MISCELLANEOUS ROLLS, &c., CHANCERY). Bundle 10.

    No. 1. Proceedings in a cause of Arms between Lovell and Morley.   9–10 Ric. II.

    No. 2.   Do.   between Richard le Scrope and Robert Grosvenor (on the behalf of Scrope).   12 Ric. II.

    No. 3.   Do.   do.   (on the behalf of Grosvenor).   13 Ric. II.

    No. 4. Proceedings "in causa depredationis" between Roches and Hanley.   12–10 Ric. II.

    No. 5. Proceedings between Wm. Gerard of London and John Chamberlayn of Calais, concerning the spoliation and detention of a prisoner.   22 Ric. II.

The following Proceedings in the Court of Chivalry are amongst the Domestic State Papers:—

Report of the proceedings of a Court of Chivalry held in the Painted Chamber, Westminster, by Earl Marshal Arundel, with a full description of the Court.   24 Nov. 1623.

        [*S. P., Dom., James I., Vol.* 154, *No.* 74.]

JUDICIAL PROCEEDINGS (VARIOUS)—(continued).
Court of Chivalry, &c.—(continued).

PROCEEDINGS IN THE COURT OF CHIVALRY, &c.—(continued).

Petition of Sir Thos. Harris, Bart., to the King, stating that one Simon Leake, who was employed to obtain for him a certificate of descent, preparatory to his creation as a Baronet, had entered a suit against him in the *Court of Chivalry* for having unduly obtained that certificate, and detailing the proceedings thereon. 21 March 1625.

[*S. P., Dom., James I., Vol.* 185, *No.* 92.]

Proceedings in the Court of Chivalry on an appeal of High Treason by Donald, Lord Reay, against David Ramsey. (Printed in State Trials, Vol. III., p. 483.)

[*S. P., Dom., Car. I., Vol.* 217.]

Proceedings in Courts of Chivalry will also be found at the Herald's College, where the Courts were formerly held.

Ecclesiastical Courts.

ARCHES, PROCEEDINGS IN THE COURT OF, &c.

There are a few Certificates of Legitimacy and other proceedings of early dates in the Court of Arches, and in the Consistory Courts, amongst the Miscellanea of the Exchequer. The later Records are in the custody of the Registrar of the Court.

DELEGATES' PROCESSES. 1609 to 1823.

These consist of 872 volumes containing the Processes or Copies of the Papers in Causes heard before the Court of Delegates. Transferred from the Registrars' Office of the High Court of Admiralty.

They are not open to inspection, except by permission of the Registrar of the Admiralty Court.

MINUTE BOOKS OF THE COURT OF HIGH COMMISSION FOR THE EXERCISE OF ECCLESIASTICAL JURISDICTION. 1634 to 1636 and 1639 to 1640. 4 Vols.

These are amongst the Domestic State Papers, and are calendared in the published " Calendars of State Papers, &c.

Marshalsea and Palace Courts.

MARSHALSEA COURT, PROCEEDINGS OF THE. (EXCHEQUER, TREASURY OF THE RECEIPT.) Edward I. to Henry VI. 29 Rolls, called " Placita Aulæ."

The " Placita Aulæ Hospitii Domini Regis," or Pleas before the Marshal of the King's Household, consist of

JUDICIAL PROCEEDINGS (VARIOUS)—(continued).
Marshalsea and Palace Courts—(continued).

MARSHALSEA COURT, PROCEEDINGS OF THE, &c.— (continued).

actions of trespass by or against the King's domestic servants or relating to trespasses committed within the verge of the Court, that is to say, within 12 miles of the Royal residence.

MARSHALSEA COURT, ACCOUNTS OF FINES AND AMERCIAMENTS IN THE. (EXCHEQUER, QUEEN'S REMEMBRANCER.
Edward I. to Elizabeth.
Calendar. 1 Vol. MS.

PALACE COURT, RECORDS OF THE. Charles I. to 1849.

The principal Records of the Palace Court, removed to the Public Record Office in 1850, consist of Bundles of Affidavits, Declarations, Records or Judgments, and other proceedings extending from about 1644 to 1849.

A detailed *Inventory* of these Records is given in the Deputy Keeper's Report XII., pp. 15–16.

Peveril Court.

The principal Records of the Court of the Honor of Peveril, abolished by Stat. 12 & 13 Vict. c. 101, consist of the following :—

Books of Pleadings. 1682–1697.
      ,,   Actions. 1686–1786.
      ,,   Issues and Judgments. 1755–1761.
Minute Books. 1729–1806.
Præcipe Books. 1808–1850.
Bundles of " Papers." 1846–1849.

A detailed *Inventory* of these Records is given in the Deputy Keeper's Report XVI., App., pp. 43 and 44.

Court of Requests.

BILLS, ANSWERS, DEPOSITIONS, &c. Henry VIII. to Charles I. In Bundles.
Indexes. Henry VIII. to Car. I. 4 Vols. MS.
Calendar. Elizabeth. 1 Vol. MS.
These refer to a very small portion of the proceedings. A new Calendar is in progress.

MISCELLANEOUS BOOKS. 208 Vols., vix. :—
    Affidavit Books. Eliz. to Charles I. 31 Vols.
                                         [Nos. 119–149.]
      Index. 13–16 Car. I. 1 Vol.   [No. 150.]
    Appearance Books. Hen. VIII. to Car. I. 14 Vols.
                                         [Nos. 104–117.]

198

JUDICIAL PROCEEDINGS (VARIOUS)—continued).
Court of Requests—(continued).
MISCELLANEOUS BOOKS—(continued).

Commissions Returned. 1–16 James I. 1 Vol.
[No. 208.]

Note Books. Eliz. to Car. I. 20 Vols.
[Nos. 151–170.]

Order Books. Eliz. to Car. I. 65 Vols.
[Nos. 39–103.]

Order and Decree Books. Hen. VII. to Car. I. 38 Vols. [Nos. 1–38.]

Process Books. Eliz. to Car. I. 28 Vols.
[Nos. 171–197.]

Replications, Book of. 1632–1636. 1 Vol. [No. 207.]

Witness Books. Eliz. to Car. I. 9 Vols.
[Nos. 198–206.]

Court of Star Chamber.

STAR CHAMBER PROCEEDINGS. Henry VII. to Charles I.

These consist of the Bills, Answers, Depositions, and other pleadings in the Court of Star Chamber from the reign of Hen. VII. to its final abolition.

They are exceedingly numerous and of great importance as illustrating both public and private history.

None of the Orders or Decrees of this Court are known to exist. In the Report of a Committee of the House of Lords made in 1719, it is stated that "the last notice of "them that could be got was that they were in a house "in St. Bartholomew's Close, London," and it is to be feared that they have been destroyed.

Index. Henry VIII. 1 Vol. MS. (Incomplete.)

Do. Elizabeth. 4 Vols. MS.

The foregoing Indexes refer to a very small portion of the proceedings.

ACCOUNTS OF FINES AND AMERCEMENTS IMPOSED IN THE STAR CHAMBER. (EXCHEQUER, Q. R.) Henry VIII. to James I.

Descriptive Slips.

Court of Wards and Liveries.

BILLS, ANSWERS, DEPOSITIONS, &c. Henry VIII. to Car. I. In Bundles (under arrangement).

Calendar. Henry VIII. to Car. I. 4 Vols. These refer to a portion of the Proceedings only. The greater part are unindexed.

[*Misc. Books, Vols.* 281 *to* 284.]

JUDICIAL PROCEEDINGS (VARIOUS) —(continued).

Court of Wards and Livories—(continued).

MISCELLANEOUS BOOKS, as follows :—

Affidavit Books.   14 Jas. I. to 21 Car. I.   16 Vols.
[Nos. 562–477.]

Decree Books.   15 Eliz. to 21 Car. I.   20 Vols.
[Nos. 84–102a.]

Minute Books.   2 Jas. I. to 14 Car. I.   4 Vols.
[Nos. 241–244.]

Process Books.   19 Hen. VIII. to 14 Car. I.   18 Vols.
[Nos. 233–240.]

Process, Certificates of.   1 to 20 James I.   3 Vols.
[Nos. 39–41.]

Order Books.   1 Edw. VI. to 24 Car. 1.   48 Vols.
[Nos. 514–561.]

KNIGHTHOOD, ORDERS OF.

THE STATUTES AND ORDINANCES OF THE MOST NOBLE
ORDER OF THE GARTER, "REFORMED, EXPLAINED, AND
DECLARED ANEW," BY KING HENRY THE EIGHTH.   1 Vol.
[*Misc. Books, Exchequer, Tr. of the Receipt,* Vol. 92.]
Documents relating to the Order of the Garter are also
contained in Vol. 113 of the said series of Miscellaneous
Books.

STATUTES OF THE ORDER OF THE GARTER AS ORDAINED
BY KING EDWARD VI.
A manuscript on vellum, probably drawn up by Sir Wm
Cecil, the Chancellor of the Order, Anno 6 Edw. VI.
[*S. P. Dom., Edw. VI., Vol.* 17.]

STATUTES OF THE ORDER OF ST. MICHAEL, founded by
Louis XI. of France.
A beautifully illuminated volume amongst the records
of the Exchequer, Treasury of the Receipt.

WINDSOR, ESTABLISHMENT OF THE POOR KNIGHTS OF.
1 Elizabeth.
A volume, richly illuminated, containing the Indentures
of Foundation and Ordinances for the government of the
"Thirteen Poor Knights of Windsor."

LEASES (CROWN).

The Manors and lands belonging to the Crown were in
ancient times "let to farm" by the King's High or Chief
Justiciar or by the Justices Itinerant, the duty afterwards
devolving on the Treasurer of the Exchequer.

When, however, particular lands were withdrawn from
the control of the Exchequer and placed under the direct
supervision of persons thereto appointed, the power of

LEASES (CROWN)—(continued).

granting leases was vested in the hands of such officers; thus by Statute 6 Henry VIII. the King's "General Surveyors" were empowered to let the Crown Lands under their control for 21 years, their "Bills of Lease" being sufficient warrant to the Lord Chancellor for the preparation of the Letters Patent; and on the erection of the Courts of the *General Surveyors* and of the *Augmentations of the Revenues of the Crown* the power of granting leases under its own Seal was vested in each of the said Courts.

The two Courts above mentioned were dissolved by Letters Patent of the 38th year of Henry VIII. and embodied into a new "*Court of Augmentations*" endowed with similar powers, which in its turn was dissolved by Letters Patent of 1 Mary, all Warrants for Leases being thenceforward directed to be passed by the *Lord Treasurer*, and the Leases, if the yearly rents of the land exceeded 40s. a year, to pass under the *Great Seal of England*, and, if the rents did not exceed that value, under the *Seal of the Court of Exchequer*.

By the same Letters Patent the Leases of the Court of Augmentations were directed to be placed in the custody of the *Clerk of the Pipe*.

The power of granting leases of the lands, &c. under its control was also vested in the *Court of Wards and Liveries* and continued therein till the abolition of that Court.

Leases of lands, &c. under the jurisdiction of the Duchy of Lancaster, and of the several Counties Palatine of Chester, Durham, and Lancaster were made under their respective Seals and form distinct series. See **LEASES (DUCHY OF LANCASTER)** and **CHANCERY ENROLMENTS (CHESTER, DURHAM, AND LANCASTER).**

The more modern method of obtaining a Crown Lease was as follows :—

A petition or memorial for a lease was preferred to the Treasury, which was referred to the Surveyor-General of Crown Lands to be reported on. A *Warrant* was thereupon issued to the Surveyor-General to make a *Constat*, or to obtain from the Auditor a *Particular* of the Premises as described in former Leases. The *Constat* or *Particular* was then rated by the Surveyor-General, which *rate* contained a specification of the term of years, and of the reserved rent and fine, with the covenants and provisoes ; the *Constat*, *Particular*, and *Rate* being sent to the Treasury.

A warrant was then issued from the Treasury to the *Clerk of the Pipe* to prepare the lease to be passed under the Seal of the Court of Exchequer, a copy of the Draft of

LEASES (CROWN)—(continued).

the Lease which was called the *Transcript* being transmitted to the Chancellor of the Exchequer, and, after receiving his signature and that of the Lords of the Treasury, returned to the Pipe Office.

The Lease was then ingrossed, signed by the Clerk of the Pipe, and transmitted to the Chancellor to receive the Exchequer Seal, after which it was enrolled in the Office of the *Auditor*.

By authority of the Statute 1 and 2 George IV. cap. 52., Leases are granted by the *Commissioners of Woods, Forests, and Land Revenues*, by sufficient Warrant from the Treasury, both the Great Seal and the Exchequer Seal being dispensed with.

For Leases by private persons, see **DEEDS EN-ROLLED.**

The following are the principal classes of documents relating to **CROWN LEASES :—**

Chancery.

Leases of Crown Lands are enrolled on the Patent Rolls, and may be referred to by means of the general Indexes to those Rolls.

References to Crown Leases from Charles I. to Will. III. enrolled on the Patent Rolls are also contained in " Palmer's Indexes," Vol. 69, and in Vol. 38 a List is given of the " Long Leases " of Crown Lands made during the reigns of Charles I. and Charles II.

Exchequer, Queen's Remembrancer.

COUNTERPARTS OF CROWN LEASES.

1677 to 1831. 26 Packages.

Index. 1 Vol. MS.

Exchequer, Augmentation Office.

LEASES BY VARIOUS QUEENS.

Henry VII.—Henry VIII. Three volumes containing original Indentures of Leases by Elizabeth, Queen of Hen. VII., and by Katharine of Arragon, Anne Boleyn, Jane Seymour, and Katharine Parr, wives of Henry VIII.

[*Misc. Books, Vols.* 176–178.]

LETTERS PATENT AND INDENTURES. Henry VIII. 6 Vols.

[*Misc. Books, Vols.* 238–243.]

Index. Report XLIX., App., pp. 209–360.

LEASES, COPIES OF.

Philip and Mary. Six volumes containing copies of Leases (on paper).

[*Misc. Books, Vol.* 179 *to* 184.]

Index. Report XLIX., App., pp. 209–360.

LEASES (CROWN)—(continued).

Exchequer, Augmentation Office—(continued).

LEASES, COUNTERPARTS OR TRANSCRIPTS OF. Henry VIII.
to James I. 51 Packages.
Index. Eliz. to James I. 1 Vol. MS. (References to
these Transcripts are also given in the Index to " PAR-
TICULARS OF LEASES," referred to below.)

LEASES AND PENSIONS, ENROLMENTS OF. 28 to 38
Henry VIII.
Five volumes, containing enrolments of Letters Patent
granting Leases and Pensions.
[*Misc. Books, Vols.* 232 *to* 236.]
Index. Report, XLIX., App., pp. 209–360.

LEASES, ENROLMENTS OF. 28 & 29 Henry VIII. to
3 James I.
Twenty-one volumes, arranged chronologically. The
series is complete from 28 & 29 Henry VIII. to 5 Philip
and Mary. Since the latter date the 34th to the 38th years
of Elizabeth and the 3rd year of James I. are alone
represented.
[*Misc. Books, Vols.* 209 *to* 229.]
Index. Report, XLIX., App., pp. 209–360.

LEASES, ENROLMENTS OF. 3 to 43 Elizabeth 8 Boxes.
Index. 1 Vol. MS.

LEASES BY THE SURVEYORS-GENERAL, ENROLMENTS OF,
34 to 38 Henry VIII. 1 Volume.
[*Misc. Books, Vol.* 230.]
Calendar. Report XXV., App., pp. 1–22.

LEASES, PARTICULARS FOR.
[Henry VIII.] Seventeen volumes, containing original
Particulars for Leases collected from different parts of the
Augmentation Office in 1837, and arranged alphabetically
under Counties. The date of the majority of them may
be attributed to the reign of Henry VIII.
[*Misc. Books, Vols.* 185 *to* 201.]

Henry VIII. and Edward VI. Six volumes, containing
Particulars for Leases, in many cases extracted from the
Rentals of the possessions of dissolved Monasteries, &c. in
various counties. The last volume contains Particulars
for Leases in the county of York only, temp. Edw. VI.
[*Misc. Books, Vols.* 204 *to* 208b.]

Elizabeth. Two volumes, containing Transcripts of
Particulars for Leases in various counties, temp. Elizabeth.
[*Misc. Books, Vols.* 202, 203.]

Henry VIII. to James I. 42 Portfolios, three of which
contain the " Particulars for Leases in Reversion."
Index. Elizabeth to James I. 4 Vols. MS.

LEASES (CROWN)—(continued).

Exchequer, Augmentation Office—(continued).

LEASES IN REVERSION, PARTICULARS FOR. Elizabeth (1564 to 1592). 3 Portfolios.

Index. 1 Vol. MS.

LEASES, REPERTORY OF. 9 & 10 Elizabeth, and 25 to 40 Elizabeth.

A Repertory or Calendar of Leases under the Exchequer Seal in various counties, arranged chronologically.
[*Misc. Books, Vol.* 231.]

LEASES SURRENDERED TO THE CROWN AND VARIOUS. Henry VIII. and Edward VI. 9 Packages.

Exchequer, Lord Treasurer's Remembrancer.

LEASES, COUNTERPARTS OF, AND PARTICULARS FOR. 1566 to 1822.

A collection of Counterparts of Crown Leases with, in many cases, the Particulars attached (sometimes the Particulars only existing without the Counterpart), with a few Particulars of Fee-Farm Rents, arranged in 28 Portfolios.

These documents are numbered consecutively from 1 to 6,702.

Index Nominum. 1 Vol. MS.

LEASES, ENROLMENTS OF. Eliz. to Geo. III. 4 Rolls.

The first Roll contains Enrolments of *Leases and Patents* of the 32nd and 33rd years of Elizabeth ; the second, *Enrolments of Leases* of the lands of *Recusants* during the Commonwealth ; and the third and fourth, *Enrolments of Leases* from the reign of Charles II. to that of George III., inclusive.

LEASES, ENTRY BOOKS OF. 1750 to 1812.

Eleven volumes, containing Entries of Crown Leases, in full, each volume having an *Index Nominum.*

LEASES, DRAFTS OF. Eliz. to Geo. IV. Eight packages, called " Drafts of Demises."

LEASES, ABSTRACTS OF. 1 Eliz. to 52 Geo. III. 12 Vols.
Do.   Elizabeth and James I. 1 Vol.
Do.   1 to 26 Elizabeth.
[*Vide S. P. Dom. Eliz., Vol.* 166.]

Exchequer of Receipt.

Crown Leases from 1599 to 1696 are entered in the AUDITORS' PATENT BOOKS.

See **RECEIPTS AND ISSUES OF THE EXCHEQUER.**

Court of Wards and Liveries.

LEASES, ENTRIES OF. 20 Hen. VIII. to 45 Eliz. 5 Vols.
[*Misc. Books, Vols.* 187 *to* 191.]

LEASES, PARTICULARS FOR. 35 Eliz. to 21 Car. I. 4 **Vols.**
[*Misc. Books, Vols.* 192 *to* 195.]

LEASES (CONVENTUAL).

The classes known as " Conventual Leases " consist of such Transcripts or Counterparts of Leases made by the several Monastic Establishments as fell into the hands of the Crown on the dissolution of those houses. Many Conventual Leases will be found in the several Series of Ancient Deeds. See **DEEDS (ANCIENT).**

CONVENTUAL LEASES. (AUGMENTATION OFFICE.) Richard II. to Henry VIII. 29 Portfolios. Arranged in Counties.
Calendar and Index Locorum. 1 Vol. MS.
Do. (EXCHEQUER, Q. R.) Henry VIII. 1 Package. Formerly No. 895 of the Bundles of Ancient Miscellanea of the Exchequer, Queen's Remembrancer.
Descriptive Slips. 1 Vol. MS.

LEASES (DUCHY OF LANCASTER).

LEASES, BOOKS OF INROLMENT OF. Henry VII. to 13 CHARLES I. 11 Vols.
Index, in the volume entitled " Index to Leases Henry VIII. to George II."

—— ENTRY BOOKS OF (NORTH AUDITOR'S). Henry VII. to George III. 35 Vols.
Inventory. Report XXX., App. 1, *p.* 5.

——. Do. (SOUTH AUDITOR'S). Henry VIII. to George III. 22 Vols.
Inventory. Report XXX., App. 1, *p.* 5.

LEASES (DRAFT). Hen. VIII. to 1760. 104 Bundles.
[*Div. XIV.*]
The particulars are in most cases prefixed to the Draft.
Calendar. Hen. VIII. to Geo. II. 1 Vol. called " Index to Leases."

LEASES, COUNTERPARTS OF, &c. Edw. VI. to 1758.
[*Div. XV. Bundles* 1 *to* 61.]

LEASES IN REVERSION. 8 to 44 Eliz. and Jas. I. 7 Bundles.
[*Div. XIV. Bundles* 50 *to* 55 *and* 71.]

LEASES, SURRENDERS OF. 1660 to 1705.
[*Div. XV. Bundles* 47 *and* 48.]

See also **CHARTERS AND GRANTS.**

LE NEVE'S INDEXES.

A collection of 37 volumes, referring chiefly to the Feet
of Fines and De Banco Rolls, as follows :—

Vol. 1 -	Bedford -	Ric. 1. to Ric. 3.	A Calendar to the Feet of Fines, with an Index Locorum.
Vol. 2 -	Berks - -	Ric. 1. to Ric. 3.	Do. do.
Vol. 3 -	Bucks - -	Ric. 1. to Ric. 3.	Do. do.
Vol. 4 -	Cambridge -	Ric. 1. to Edw. 4.	Do. do.
Vol. 5 -	Cornwall -	Ric. 1. to Ric. 3.	Do. do.
Vol. 6 -	Cumberland and Devon.	Ric. 1. to Edw. 4.	Do. do.
Vol. 7 -	Derby - -	Ric. 1. to Ric. 3.	Do. do.
Vol. 8 -	Dorset - -	Ric. 1. to Ric. 3.	Do. do.
Vol. 9 -	Essex - -	Ric. 1. to Ric. 3.	Do. [no Index Locorum].
Vol. 10 -	Gloucester and Herts.	John to Ric. 3., Ric. 1. to Ric. 3.	Do. [with Indices Locorum].
Vol. 11 -	Various Counties	3 Jas. 1. (East. and Trin.)	An Index to the Feet of Fines, referring apparently to some Entry Book.
Vol. 12 -	Divers Counties	Ric. 1. to Edw. 2.	A Calendar to the Feet of Fines of Divers Counties or Unknown Counties, with an Index Locorum. [See also vol. 26.]
Vol. 12a	Divers Counties	Hen. 2. to Edw. 2.	A revised Calendar of " Feet of " Fines of Unknown, " Various, and Divers " Counties." [1870.]
Vol. 13 -	Divers Counties	Edw. 3. to Hen. 6.	A Calendar to the Feet of Fines of Divers Counties, with an Index Locorum.
Vol. 14 -	Do. -	Edw. 6. to Phil. & Mar.	Do. do.
Vol. 15 -	Do. -	3 to 5 Eliz. -	A Calendar to the Feet of Fines.
Vol. 16 -	Bucks -	Ric. 1. to Hen. 3.	Abstracts of Feet of Fines, with an Index Locorum.
Vol. 17 -	Do. -	Ric. 1. to Hen. 6.	A Calendar to the Feet of Fines, with Indices Nominum and Locorum.
Vol. 18 -	Yorks - -	Hen. 6. - -	A Calendar to the Feet of Fines, with an Index Locorum.
	Do. -	Ric. 1. and John	Do. do.
	City of York -	Edw. 4. and Ric. 3.	Abstracts of Feet of Fines.

LE NEVE'S INDEXES—(continued).

Vol. 19 -	Yorks -	Hen. 3. to Edw. 1.	Abstracts of Feet of Fines [with an Index Locorum].
Vol. 20 -	Do. -	Edw. 2. and Edw. 3.	Do. do.
Vol. 21 -	Do. -	Ric. 2. to Hen. 5.	Do. [with Indices Locorum].
Vol. 22 -	England, &c. -	Ric. 3. and Hen. 7.	A Calendar to the Feet of Fines, with Indices Locorum and Nominum for Ric. 3. [The Index Locorum for Hen. 7. is in Vol. 26.]
Vol. 23 -	Do. -	Temp. Hen. 8. -	Abstracts of Feet of Fines of various years.
Vol. 24 -	Do. -	Temp. Hen. 8. -	Do. do.
Vol. 25 -	Southampton -	Ric. 1. to Edw. 1.	A Calendar to the Feet of Fines.
Vol. 26 -	Hunts - -	John to Ric. 2. -	An Index Locorum to the Feet of Fines.
	Westmoreland - Do. -	John to Edw. 4. 40 Hen. 3. and 7 & 20 Edw. 1.	Abstracts of Feet of Fines. Abstracts of Assize Rolls, &c.
	Divers Counties	John to Edw. 2.	An Index Locorum to Feet of Fines (referring to Vol. 12).
	Do. -	Edw. 3. to Edw. 6.	An Index Nominum to Feet of Fines (referring to Vol. 13).
	Do. -	Edw. 4. -	Abstracts of Fines, with Indices Nominum and Locorum.
	England, &c. -	Hen. 7. - -	An Index Locorum to the Feet of Fines, for the whole reign of Hen. 7., referring to the Calendar in Vol. 22.
Vol. 27 -	Wilts - -	John to Edw. 4.	An Index Locorum to the Feet of Fines.
Vol. 28 -	Beds to Middlesex.	1 to 24 Hen. 7. -	An Index Locorum to the Placita de Banco, arranged in Counties.
Vol. 29 -	Norfolk to Wilts	Do. -	Do. do. [This vol. contains also an Index Locorum to the Placita de Banco, temp. Ric. 3. and Edw. 5., and to the Deeds enrolled on the Placita de Banco in the reign of Hen. 7.]
Vol. 30 -	Bedford to Dorset.	Edw. 2. -	Indices Locorum to the Placita de Banco and to the Feet of Fines.
Vol. 31 -	Ebor to Lincoln	Edw. 2. -	Do. do.
Vol. 32 -	Middlesex to Sussex.	Edw. 2. -	Do. do.

LE NEVE'S INDEXES—(continued).

Vol. 33 -	Warwick to Wigorn, &c.	Edw. 2.	-	Indices Locorum to the Placita de Banco and to the Feet of Fines.
				[This Index contains also an Index Locorum to the Deeds enrolled in the reign of Edw. 2.]
Vol. 34 -	List of De Banco Rolls.	Edw. 1. to Hen. 7.		
Vol. 35 -	Bedford to Wilts, &c.	Hen. 8. -	-	An Index Locorum to the Feet of Fines. [Those relating to Manors or Churches only are indexed.]
	Bedford to Wilts, &c.	Edw. 4.	-	An Index Locorum to the Placita de Banco and to the Deeds enrolled temp. Edw. 4.
	Bedford to Wilts, &c.	Phil. & Mar.	-	An Index Locorum to the Feet of Fines.
Vol. 36 -	Entries of Searches.	-	-	A volume containing Notes of Searches made at various times in the Talley Office at Westminster, with *references* to the *Records*, and a *General Index.*
Vol. 37 -	Extracts from Domesday Book, &c.	-	-	A volume containing Extracts from Domesday Book and the Black Book of the Exchequer, a List of Monasteries, and other notes. *See also* "Agarde's Indexes," vols. 24, 29, 38, 39, 53, and 54.

LIVERY OF LANDS.

Writs to Escheators, &c. for the Livery of Lands are entered on the Fine Rolls. See **CHANCERY ENROLMENTS.**

Warrants from the Court of Wards for Special and General Liveries will be found in the Privy Seal and Signed Bill Bundles. See **PRIVY SEALS AND SIGNED BILLS, &c.**

LIVERIES, BOOKS OF. (COURT OF WARDS AND LIVERIES.) Hen. VIII. to Charles I. 30 Vols.

["*Miscellaneous Books*" (*Court of Wards, &c.*). Vols 54 to 83. *See also Vols.* 173 *to* 179.]

LIVERY, WRITS OF, &c. (PALATINATE OF CHESTER.) Eliz. to Car. I.

Alphabetical Calendar. Report XXVI., App., pp. 32–35.

GENERAL AND SPECIAL LIVERIES. (DUCHY OF LANCASTER.) Temp. Eliz. 2 Files.

[*Div. XII. Bundle* 46.]

Calendar. Report XXXIX., App., pp. 549–562.

LOANS AND BENEVOLENCES.

Accounts and Assessments relating to Loans and Benevolences will be found amongst the Subsidy Rolls. See
TAXATION.

LOANS, DOCUMENTS RELATING TO. (EXCHEQUER, TREASURY OF THE RECEIPT.) Edw. III. to Car. I.

These consist of Letters Patent, &c. for the repayment of Loans to the King, with Commissions to raise money on loans and the returns thereto, &c., &c. They are amongst the Miscellanea.

LOANS, LETTERS PATENT AND PRIVY SEALS FOR. (EXCHEQUER. TREASURY OF THE RECEIPT.) Hen. VII. to Car. I.

REGISTER OF THE NAMES OF CONTRIBUTORS TO A LOAN. 1590. 1 Vol. [*S.P. Dom., Eliz., Vol.* 236.]

LUNACY AND IDIOTCY.

The custody of the lands and persons of Idiots and Lunatics was of old times vested in the King as a royal prerogative, which was confirmed and established by Stat. 17 Edward II. cap 10.

Prior to the establishment of the Court of Wards and Liveries by Henry VIII., and also subsequent to its abolition, the jurisdiction over Idiots and Lunatics was entrusted to the Lord Chancellor, by whom all grants were made of the custody of their persons and estates. These Grants were made out by the *Clerk of the Custodies* and originally enrolled on the PATENT ROLLS. From the period of the Commonwealth, however, they were entered on separate rolls, and subsequently in books which were kept in the office of the *Clerk of the Custodies,* and afterwards transferred to that of the *Secretary of Lunatics.*

The Grants of Custodies, together with the bonds given by the *Committees,* or persons to whom such custody was entrusted, were also entered in DOCKET BOOKS, which exist at the Lunacy Office, from the reign of Charles II. to the present time; as also the Accounts, Affidavits, Reports, and Orders relating to the estates of lunatics, &c.

The appointment of *Committees* of the persons and estates of lunatics, and the examination of their accounts, were, under certain circumstances, vested in the Masters of the Court of Chancery.

LUNACY, COMMISSIONS AND INQUISITIONS OF. (CHANCERY, PETTY BAG OFFICE.) Charles I. to 1852. These consist of commissions *de lunatico inquirendo* with the returns thereto, arranged alphabetically. 24 Bundles.
Index. 1 Vol. MS.

LUNACY AND IDIOTCY—(continued).

LUNACY COMMISSIONS, &c.—(continued).
Do. 1853 to 1869. 8 Bundles, arranged chronologically.
Indexes at the Crown Office, Queen's Bench.

Inquisitions on Writs "*de lunatico inquirendo*" of earlier dates are placed with the "INQUISITIONS POST MORTEM."

LUNACY COMMISSIONS, &c. (PALATINATE OF LANCASTER.)
Car. II. to Will. IV. 1 Bundle.

MANORS, EXTENTS OF, &c.

A *Manor* appears to have constituted originally a certain circuit of ground granted by the King to some Baron or man of worth, as an inheritance for him and his heirs, with the exercise of such jurisdiction within the said compass as the King saw fit to grant, and subject to the performance of such services and yearly rents as were by the grant required.

The greater Barons, who thus held a large extent of territory under the Crown, frequently granted out to inferior persons smaller manors, to be held from themselves as superior lords, and rendering to them similar rents and services, the superior lord being then called the Lord Paramount over all such manors, and his seignory being frequently termed an *Honour*, especially if it had belonged to an ancient feudal Baron, or had been at any time in the hands of the Crown. In imitation of this practice, the inferior lords began to carve out and grant to others on similar terms still more minute estates, till the superior lords observed, that by this process of sub-infeudation they lost all their feudal profits, as wardships, marriages, escheats, &c., which fell into the hands of the mesne or middle lords, who were the immediate superiors of the tenant or occupier of the land; and also, that the mesne lords were so impoverished by the diminution of their estates, that they were disabled from performing the services due from them. This occasioned, firstly, a provision in the Great Charter of 9 Henry III. "that no man " should either give or sell his land without reserving " sufficient to answer the demands of his lord," and afterwards the Statute of "*Quia Emptores*," 18 Edward I., which directs that, in all sales or feoffments of lands, the feoffee shall hold the same, *not of the immediate feoffor but of the chief lord of the Fee,* and subsequent to which no new manors were created.

In 4 Edward I. a Statute was framed known as the " Extenta Manerii," [*Statutes of the Realm, Vol.* 1, *p.* 242] containing directions for extending and surveying manors which, although there is no evidence of any general survey

MANORS, EXTENTS OF, &c.—(continued).

throughout the kingdom being then taken, appears to have resulted in numerous *Extents* or *Surveys* being taken from time to time, many of which will be found amongst the Inquisitions Post Mortem, and also amongst the "Miscellanea" of the Exchequer, Queen's Remembrancer, of which a separate collection has been formed.

Numerous Surveys of Manors exist also amongst the " SPECIAL COMMISSIONS" of the Exchequer, Queen's Remembrancer.   See **COMMISSIONS.**

Depositions relating to the Customs and Boundaries of Manors and Decrees thereon are frequently referred to in the Calendar of " DEPOSITIONS TAKEN BY COMMISSION" (EXCHEQUER, Q. R.), printed in Reports XXXVIII., XXXIX., and XL., and in Martin's " INDEX TO THE EXCHEQUER RECORDS."

Decrees relating to the Customs and Boundaries of Manors are frequently enrolled on the CHANCERY DECREE ROLLS, to which there is an *Index Locorum.*

See also **RENTALS AND SURVEYS.**

MANUMISSIONS.

Deeds of manumission of villeins will be found amongst the several series of Ancient Deeds and Charters.   See **DEEDS (ANCIENT).**

There is amongst the Duchy of Lancaster Records a volume containing entries of Manumissions in the reign of Elizabeth.

[*Duchy of Lanc., Div. XI., No.* 101.]

The original Instruments of Manumission, with Certificates of the Lands and Goods of Bond Men and Bond Women in several Counties, are amongst the Miscellaneous Records of the Duchy.

[*Div. XXV., B.B., Nos.* 1 *to* 3.]

MAPS, PLANS, AND CHARTS.
State Paper Office.

A collection of Maps, Plans, and Charts (English, Colonial, and Foreign) partly MS. and partly engraved, contained in 34 Vols. and 10 Cases.

Alphabetical Index.   1 Vol. MS.

Maps of Ireland. See **IRELAND.**

Maps and Plans of Manors belonging to the Duchy of Lancaster. See **SURVEYS.**

Maps and Plans annexed to Inclosure Awards.   See **DEEDS ENROLLED** (p. 81).

MARKETS AND FAIRS.

Grants of Markets and Fairs are enrolled on the Charter and Patent Rolls.   See **CHANCERY ENROLMENTS.**

MARKETS AND FAIRS—(continued).

There is also amongst the Miscellaneous Rolls, &c. of the Court of Chancery a File of Grants and Claims of Markets, Fairs, Free Warren, &c. (Bundle 6), which is calendared in "Palmer's Indexes," Vol. 106.

A List of all Markets and Fairs granted under the Seal of the Duchy of Lancaster is contained in the volume known as "Great Ayloffe," fol. 46–47.

For Inquisitions "ad quod damnum" taken prior to granting a Market or Fair, see **INQUISITIONS**.

Chronological List of Grants of Markets and Fairs. John to Edw. IV. ["*Palmer's Indexes," Vol.* 93.]*

MEMORANDA ROLLS OF THE EXCHEQUER.

Memoranda Rolls. (Exchequer, Queen's Remembrancer.) 1 Henry III. to 1848.

The Memoranda Rolls of the Queen's Remembrancer of the Exchequer contain enrolments of Writs of Scire Facias for the recovery of debts due to the Crown with the proceedings thereon—of Informations on Seizures made in the several Ports of goods forfeited for nonpayment of customs or for unlawful importation—of Transcripts of Outlawries and other proceedings whereby lands or goods were forfeited to the Crown—of Special Commissions of Inquiry with the Returns thereto—of Informations of Intrusion on the Royal Forests and Wastes, &c.— and of Recognizances and Bonds of various kinds, such as those entered into by Printers and Publishers, &c., &c.

They also contain enrolments of Grants and Letters Patent for several purposes, of Warrants and Constitutions under the Sign Manual, of many Decrees and Orders in causes on the Equity side of the Exchequer, and of such Deeds and Instruments between private individuals as were acknowledged before the Barons of the Exchequer.

The Coming of the Sheriffs and other Accountants to the Exchequer to make their half-yearly Profers, and the States and Views of the Public Accounts of the Kingdom with others matters concerning the collection of the Revenue are also entered on these rolls in the same manner as on the rolls of the Lord Treasurer's Remembrancer.

Repertories.† 1 Edw. I. to 32 Charles II.

Indexes called "Agenda Books." 35 Hen. VIII. to 12 Victoria. 35 Vols.

Martin's "Index to the Exchequer Records." 1 Vol. 8vo.

Do. (Lord Treasurer's Remembrancer.) 1 Hen. III. to 5 Wm. IV.

---

* This List has been recently printed by the Royal Commission on Market Rights, &c.
† Prior to the reign of Edward III. these Repertories are very meagre.

MEMORANDA ROLLS OF THE EXCHEQUER—
(continued).

MEMORANDA ROLLS, &c.—(continued).

The Memoranda Rolls of the Lord Treasurer's Remembrancer contain the enrolments of the Coming of Sheriffs, Bailffs, Escheators, &c. to the Exchequer to make their Profers and to render their Accounts—of Recognizances or acknowledgments of debt to the King and others—of Commissions and Letters Patent—of the " Communia" or Common Matters or business of the Court in each Term such as Pleadings and Judgments on Writs of *quo titulo clamat*, and *quare maneria, &c. in manibus Regis seisiri non debent*—of Claims of Liberties, Franchises, and Privileges by Cities, Boroughs and Towns, &c.—of Pleadings respecting the Fines, Issues and Amerciaments contained in the Rolls of Estreats returned into the Exchequer from the Courts at Westminster and other jurisdictions—of Proceedings relating to the Accounts of Sheriffs, Escheators, and Bailiffs, and of a variety of matters relating to the charge and discharge of the King's Debtors and Accountants—of States and Views of the Accounts of Sheriffs and other Accountants—of the Presentations and Admissions of Officers of the Court—of Bails or " Manucaptions "—of Fines for Homage or Reliefs—of the " Precepta " or Orders of the Court made with respect to the Accounts of Sheriffs and others—and of the Writs and Process of various kinds issuing from the Lord Treasurer's Department.

They also contain the Enrolments of such Deeds and Instruments as were acknowledged before one of the Barons of the Exchequer and enrolled for safe custody.

Repertories (General). 1 Edw. III. to 1653.

Repertories to " Fines and Reliefs." Edw. I. to Edw. III.

Repertories to " Manucapciones." 20 Hen. VII. to 12 Eliz.

Repertories to " Precepta." 1 Edw. III. to 1 Jas. I.

Repertories to " States and Views of Accounts." 1 Edw. III. to 14 Jas. I.

Indexes, called " Agenda Books." 2 Jas. I. to 3 Will. IV. 9 Vols.

Do. called " Madox's Index." Various Dates. 3 Vols. containing selections from the Memoranda Rolls. (Incorporated in Jones's *Index to the Records.*)

Abstracts from the Memoranda Rolls. 8 Hen. III. to 26 Edw. I. 4 Vols.

" *Tayleure's Index* " to the Memoranda and Originalia *Rolls.* 1 Vol. MS. arranged alphabetically under places. (The references are incorporated in *Jones's Index.*)

MEMORANDA ROLLS OF THE EXCHEQUER—
(continued).

MEMORANDA ROLLS, &c.—(continued).

Jones's Index to the Records. Selections from the Memoranda and Originalia Rolls arranged alphabetically under places and printed in 2 Vols. folio. Vol. I. relates to the Originalia Rolls only from Hen. VIII. to Anne. Vol. 2, to the Memoranda Rolls from Hen. III. to Geo. II.

EXCHEQUER PROCEEDINGS SUBSIDIARY TO THE MEMORANDA ROLLS. (EXCHEQUER, Q. R.) Henry III. to James I.

These consist of Bills and Petitions of Accountants, Informations and Pleadings thereon, Writs of Distringas, Writs and Returns of various kinds, and other Memoranda relating to the business of the Exchequer, being, in fact, the original documents in connexion with the proceedings enrolled on the Memoranda Rolls of the Queen's Remembrancer. In the earlier bundles are also contained many Transcripts from the Assize Rolls and from the Placita coram Rege, Placita coram Baronibus de Scaccario, and Placita de Banco.

Descriptive Slips.

Pleas before the Barons of the Exchequer, with Extents and Inquisitions of various kinds. Temp. Edward III. 1 Vol. [*Misc. Books (Augmentation Office), Vol.* 487.]

" BREVIA DE SCACCARIO." 1 to 8 Elizabeth.

Two vols. containing copies of Writs issued by the Queen's Remembrancer of the Exchequer against sundry Debtors and Accountants to the Crown.

[*Misc. Books (Augmentation Office), Vols.* 26 *and* 27.]

MINES.

MINES, ACCOUNTS OF. (EXCHEQUER Q. R.) Edward I. to Charles I.

Accounts of the receipts and expenses of the royal mines in Devon and Cornwall, including the wages of workmen, expenses of implements, &c., together with Rolls of the " Cunagium Stanni " or " Stannary Rolls " thereto belonging.

Similar accounts formerly existing amongst the Miscellanea of the Treasury of the Receipt and amongst the Records relating to the Duchy of Cornwall have been added to this class.

ACCOUNTS OF THE CUNAGIUM STANNI. 13 Elizabeth to 1611. 2 Vols.

[*Misc. Books (Augmentation Office), Vols.* 353 *and* 354.]

MINISTERS' AND RECEIVERS' ACCOUNTS.

Under this title may be included the yearly Accounts of
all *Bailiffs, Farmers, Reeves, Collectors, Receivers,* and
other Officers or Ministers of such Manors and Lands
belonging to the Ancient Demesne of the Crown as did
not form part of the *Firma Comitatus* or yearly Farm of
the Sheriff, and also of such lands as were acquired from
time to time by escheat, forfeiture, or otherwise.

Amongst them will be found also numerous Accounts
as rendered to the Lords of the several Manors, &c. by
their respective Bailiffs or Farmers anterior to the date
of their acquisition by the Crown.

The Ministers' Accounts of the lands in the hands of the
Crown were at first entered, together with the Sheriffs'
Accounts, on the PIPE ROLLS, and subsequently, when from
the ever-increasing business of the Exchequer these Rolls
increased in bulk to an unmanageable degree, on a separate
series of Rolls called the Rolls of "FOREIGN ACCOUNTS,"
that is to say, of such accounts as were foreign to the
Sheriff's jurisdiction. It appears, however, to have been
the practice of the Bailiffs, Reeves, and other "Ministers"
to bring with them to the Exchequer on the occasion of
their yearly audit a *Compotus* or Account of their Receipts
and Expenses, and also a Roll of the *Particulars* of such
Accounts which, after comparison with the Accounts or
Abstracts thereof entered on the Pipe Rolls or the Foreign
Rolls, were left by the Accountants in the Treasury of the
Exchequer, where they form a large and important class of
documents containing the minutest details of the management and revenue of the various lands, manors, and tenements in the hands of the Crown from a very early period.

Early in the reign of Henry VII., in order to ensure a
more speedy payment of his revenues than could have been
arrived at by following the ordinary course of the Exchequer, an informal practice was introduced by which
certain lands were withdrawn from the direct survey or
control of that Court, and the Accounts thereof taken by
word of mouth before " *Special Commissioners* " appointed
for that purpose, by whom the sums received were paid
into the Treasury of the King's Chamber.

This was followed by the appointment, in the third year
of Henry VIII., of " *General Surveyors and Approvers of
the King's Lands,*" who were legally authorised to call the
Accountants before them to the King's Chamber instead
of to the Exchequer itself, which hitherto was the only
lawful method, and by Statute 33 Hen. VIII. c. 39, in
order to render the said General Surveyors entirely independent of any other Court or Jurisdiction, a Court was
erected called the " *Court of the General Surveyors of the
King's Lands,*" and consisting of the King's Surveyors,

MINISTERS' AND RECEIVERS' ACCOUNTS, &c.
—(continued).

a Treasurer, Attorney, Master of the Woods, Auditors, Receivers, and other officers, under the survey of which were placed all lands accruing to the Crown by *Attainder, Escheat,* or *Forfeiture.*

By a previous Statute (27 Hen. VIII. cap 27) a Court had been erected for the management of the vast revenues arising from the possessions of the dissolved Monasteries under the title of the *Court of the Augmentations of the Revenues of the Crown,* within the survey of which were placed not only the revenues of the *dissolved Monasteries,* but also all lands, &c. acquired or to be acquired by *Purchase or Exchange.* This Court comprised a Chancellor who was empowered to make gifts, grants, &c. under the Seal of the Court, a Treasurer, Attorney, Solicitor, and Particular Auditors and Receivers.

Both the above-mentioned Courts were dissolved by Letters Patent of the 38th year of Henry VIII., and a *"New Court of the Augmentations"* erected, with full jurisdiction over all the revenues heretofore in the survey of the said abolished Courts, and over all honors, castles, seignories, manors, lands, &c. within England, Wales, Calais, and the Marches thereof, which might thereafter come to the King by any Act of Parliament or by any Gift, Grant, Surrender, Bargain and Sale, or by Forfeiture, Attainder, or Escheat. A proviso was, however, inserted that such honours, &c. as were already in the survey of the Court of Exchequer or of the Duchy of Lancaster should continue in the same.

The principal Officers of this Court consisted of—
A Chancellor.
Two General Surveyors.
A Treasurer.
Two Masters of the Woods (one for the North and one for the South side of Trent).
Two Surveyors of the Woods.
Ten Auditors of the Revenues.
Two Auditors of Imprests, &c.
Eleven Receivers.
Particular Surveyors for each County.
An Attorney, Solicitor, Clerk, &c., &c.

This Court was in turn abolished by authority of the Stat. 1 Mary, cap. 10, and the business thereof transferred to the Exchequer. The ancient mode of collecting the revenues through the Sheriffs was not, however, restored, the several Ministers and Receivers rendering their Accounts, as heretofore, to the *Auditors of the Exchequer,* now called the *Auditors of the Land Revenue,* and the sums due from them being paid directly to the Receipt of the Exchequer, instead of to a Treasurer.

MINISTERS' AND RECEIVERS' ACCOUNTS, &c.
—(continued).

In the 32nd year of Henry VIII. a "*Court of Wards*" was established for the especial management of the revenues arising from the possessions of Minors, Idiots, and Lunatics, and other profits incident to the Tenures in Capite, and in the following year the Liveries of Lands were subjected to the jurisdiction of the same Court, which was thenceforward known as the "*Court of Wards and Liveries.*" The principal Officers of this Court consisted of a Master, an Attorney, a Receiver-General, two Auditors, and Particular Auditors and Receivers, by whom a distinct series of Accounts relating to the possessions of Wards and Minors was rendered to the Exchequer, which Accounts exist from the establishment of the Court to the final abolition of Feudal Tenures at the Restoration.

Subsequent to the Restoration the *Gross Sums* only arising from each particular district, in which no variation was thenceforward made, were accounted for by the several Receivers, no record being kept of the rents by which they were made up, the persons by whom they were payable, or the lands out of which they issued, and the Accounts of the Bailiffs, Reeves, or other local Collectors being no longer returned to the Exchequer.

With that period, therefore, the Ministers' Accounts as a series may be said to terminate. The Rentals and other documents relating to the management of the Crown property of a subsequent date will be found at the office of the Land Revenue Records and Inrolments.

The following list represents the principal classes of Ministers' and Receivers' Accounts, arranged according to the Courts to which they belong.

A General Inventory of all the Ministers' Accounts prior to the reign of Henry VII. has been issued (Lists and Indexes, No. V., 1894).

Exchequer, Queen's Remembrancer.

MINISTERS' ACCOUNTS (GENERAL SERIES). Henry III. to Richard III.

These consist mainly of original Accounts and Particulars of Accounts of the Bailiffs, Reeves, and other Ministers of such Honours and Lands as formed part of the Ancient Demesne or from time to time came into the hands of the Crown by escheat, forfeiture, or otherwise (including the Temporalities of various Religious Houses), which were formerly preserved amongst the so-called Ancient Miscellanea of the Queen's Remembrancer's Department, the collection comprising 880 Bundles or Parcels, a brief list of which is given in the Appendix to the Deputy Keeper's 20th Report, pp. 95-111. With these however, have been incorporated analogous docu-

MINISTERS' AND RECEIVERS' ACCOUNTS, &c.
—(continued).

Exchequer, Queen's Remembrancer—(continued).

ments formerly preserved in the Chapter House at Westminster, in the Office of Land Revenue Records, and in the Tower of London.

The contents of these Rolls are set out at length in the General Inventory above referred to.

MINISTERS' ACCOUNTS (GENERAL SERIES). Henry VII. to Charles II.

In this class are included the Ministers' Accounts of the Courts of General Surveyors and of the Augmentations, and those which subsequent to the abolition of those Courts were preserved in the Augmentation Office of the Exchequer and the Office of Land Revenue Records, with which have been incorporated the Accounts of the Court of Wards and Liveries and also those of the Duchy of Cornwall between the above-mentioned dates.

These are at present arranged chronologically, but in order to facilitate the production of consecutive Rolls they will shortly be re-arranged county-wise, and a General Inventory of them will be issued.

Such an Inventory has already been completed for the reign of Henry VII. There is a Chronological List of the remainder of these Accounts in 3 Vols.

ALIEN PRIORIES, &c., ACCOUNTS OF. 22 Edw. I. to 22 Edw. IV.

These consist of the Accounts of Bailiffs and other Ministers, relating to the possessions of the Alien Religious Houses in England, and also of laymen who were foreign subjects.

The Alien Priories were cells or small convents established by and subordinate to such foreign monasteries as held possessions in this country. Some of these were conventual, that is to say, choosing their own priors and applying the revenues they received to their own use and benefit, paying an obvention or acknowledgment only to the foreign house; whilst others were entirely dependent thereon and transmitted thereto the whole of their revenues. For this reason their estates were generally confiscated on the breaking out of a war between England and France, being, however, restored to them on the return of peace. Such confiscations took place in the reigns of Edward I., Edward II., Edward III., and Richard II. The Alien Priories were finally dissolved by Act of Parliament 2 Henry V., and all their estates vested in the Crown, except some lands granted to the College of Fotheringay. A full description of these Priories is printed in Dugdale's Monasticon, Vol. VI., Pt. II., pp. 985–1119.

MINISTERS' AND RECEIVERS' ACCOUNTS, &c.
—(continued).

Exchequer, Queen's Remembrancer—(continued).

ALIEN PRIORIES, &c.—(continued).

These Accounts are included in the General Inventory of Ministers' Accounts, Henry III. to Richard III. (Lists and Indexes, No. V. 1894).

BISHOPS' TEMPORALITIES, ACCOUNTS OF. Henry III. to Richard III.

These consist chiefly of Bailiffs' and Ministers' Accounts of the possessions of the various Bishoprics whilst they were in the hands of the Crown during the vacancies of the respective sees. They are included in the General Inventory above referred to.

Subsequent to the reign of Richard III. these accounts are included in the General Series of Ministers' Accounts.

CONTRARIANTS' LANDS, ACCOUNTS OF, &c. Edward II.

The Ministers' Accounts relating to Contrariants' Lands are included in the General Inventory of Ministers' Accounts, Henry III. to Richard III.

There are also amongst the Records of the Exchequer, Lord Treasurer's Remembrancer, three large Rolls belonging apparently to the Series of "Foreign Accounts," containing very full Accounts of the issues of the lands and tenements of the "Contrariants" in various counties, from 14 to 20 Edward II.

KNIGHTS TEMPLARS, ACCOUNTS OF THE POSSESSIONS OF THE. Edward II. These are included in the General Inventory above mentioned.

There are also amongst the Records of the Exchequer, Lord Treasurer's Remembrancer, three large Rolls containing accounts of the possessions of the Knight's Templars, with a *Repertory* thereof (see below).

An Inquisition taken in 1185 by Geoffrey FitzStephen, Master of the Order of Knights Templars, as to their possession in England, will be found amongst the Miscellaneous Books of the Queen's Remembrancer's Office.

[Vol. 16.]

Exchequer, Augmentation Office.

MINISTERS' ACCOUNTS, BOOKS OF. Henry VII. to Edward VI.

41 volumes, consisting chiefly of Receivers' and Receiver-Generals' Accounts.

[*Misc. Books, Vols.* 268 *to* 308.]

MINISTERS' ACCOUNTS, ARREARS OF. Henry VII. to James I. 10 Vols.

[*Misc. Books, Vols.* 7 *to* 14, *Vol.* 25, *and Vol.* 28.]

MINISTERS' AND RECEIVERS' ACCOUNTS, &c.
—(continued).

Exchequer, Augmentation Office—(continued).

MINISTERS' ACCOUNTS, VIEWS OF. Henry VIII. to James I. 13 Vols.

[*Misc. Books, Vols.* 442 *to* 454.]

TREASURERS' ACCOUNTS. 28 Hen. VIII. to 1 Mary. 10 Rolls.

These contain an Account of all moneys received or paid by the Treasurer of the Court of Augmentations, specifying the amounts received from the Particular Receivers of the Revenues of the dissolved Monasteries, &c. in the various Counties throughout England and Wales, with the sums produced by the sale of their Jewels, Plate, and Ornaments; the Fines or Compositions received for the Toleration and Continuance of certain Religious Houses; and the various sums received by Sales of Lands, &c., with an exact description of the premises sold, the name of the purchaser, and date of purchase, &c.

The payments comprise the Fees and Wages to Officers of the Court, Annuities to Royal and other personages, Pensions to the Abbots, Priors, and others of the dissolved Monasteries, and payments of various kinds made by Warrant of the Chancellor of the Court of Augmentations or otherwise.

WOODS, ACCOUNTS OF SALES OF. Henry VIII. to James I. 2 Vols.

Do. Henry VIII. to Elizabeth. 6 Vols.

[*Misc. Books, Vols.* 457 *to* 462.]

Exchequer, Lord Treasurer's Remembrancer.

CONTRARIANTS' LANDS, ENROLLED ACCOUNTS OF. 14 to 20 Edward II. 3 Rolls.

QUEEN'S LANDS, ENROLLED ACCOUNTS OF. Edw. III., Ric. II., and Hen. IV.

These contain Enrolments of Accounts relating to the lands and possessions of Philippa, Anne, and Johanna, Queens of England. A brief summary of the Accounts only is given.

TEMPLARS' LANDS, ENROLLED ACCOUNTS OF. Edward II.

Three large Rolls containing enrolments of the Accounts of the possessions of the Knights Templars in various Counties, which were seized into the King's hands on the expulsion of that Order.

Repertory. 1 Roll.

FOREIGN ACCOUNTS, ROLLS OF. Edw. III. to Car. II 23 Rolls.

See REVENUE ROLLS.

MINISTERS' AND RECEIVERS' ACCOUNTS, &c.
—(continued).
Court of Wards and Liveries.

The Accounts of the Bailiffs and Receivers of the Possessions of Minors and of other Royal Wards under the Survey of the Court of Wards and Liveries have been incorporated with the General Series of Ministers' Accounts. The following Accounts made up in the form of Books remain with the MISCELLANEOUS BOOKS of the Court.

VIEWS OF ACCOUNTS. 37 Hen. VIII. to 9 Car. I. 38 Vols.
[*Nos.* 1 *to* 38.]

BOOKS OF ARREARS. Hen. VIII. to 21 Car. I. 12 Vols.
[*Nos.* 42 *to* 53.]

RECEIVER-GENERALS' ACCOUNTS. 26 Hen. VIII. to 17 Car. I. 71 Vols.
[*Nos.* 361 *to* 431.]

FEODARIES' ACCOUNTS. 33 Hen. VIII. to 15 Car. I. 82 Vols.
[*Nos.* 432 *to* 513.]

The following Accounts relating to the possessions of Wards are amongst the Miscellaneous Books of the Treasury of the Receipt :—

Vol. 212. Declarations of Accounts of the possessions of Wards. 21 Hen. VII.
Vol. 246. Docket Book of Sales of Wards. 18-20 Hen. VIII.
Vol. 247. Ministers' Accounts of the possessions of Wards. 20–21 Hen. VII.
Vol. 248. Do. 22–23 Hen. VII.
Vol. 249. Feodaries' Account, Kent. 43 Eliz. to 5 Jas. I.

Duchy of Lancaster.

MINISTERS' AND RECEIVERS' ACCOUNTS. Edward I. to George III.

A Calendar and Index to this Collection, which consists of Ministers' Accounts, Accounts of Particular Receivers, and Receivers' Declared Accounts, is printed in Report XLV., App. 1, pp. 1–152. Those of an earlier date than Henry VII. are included in the General Inventory of Ministers' Accounts. (Lists and Indexes, No. V. 1894).

RECEIVER-GENERAL'S ACCOUNTS, &c. Edw. III. to 1771.
[*Dir. XXVIII.*]

These consist of the Accounts of the Keeper of the Wardrobe and Treasurer of the Household and of the Receiver-General's Accounts, and States of the Revenue of the whole Duchy of Lancaster. They include Treasurer's and Comptroller's Accounts of the Town and Marches of Calais from 8 to 18 Henry VII.
Descriptive Catalogue. Report XXX., App., pp. 35–88.

MINISTERS' AND RECEIVERS' ACCOUNTS, &c.
—(continued).

Principality of Wales and Palatinate of Chester.

The Ministers' Accounts relating to Wales and Chester prior to the reign of Henry VII., including the Chamberlain's and Receiver-General's Accounts, are included in the General Inventory of Ministers' Accounts above referred to.

Those of a later date than Richard III. will be found in the General Series of Ministers' Accounts (Henry VII. to Charles II.)

Ireland.

MINISTERS' ACCOUNTS. Edw. I. to Edw. III.

These relate to the possessions of Roger Bigod, Earl of Norfolk, Thomas, Earl of Ormond, Elizabeth de Burgo, Lady of Clare, and others, and are included in the General Inventory above referred to.

MINT.

In 1848 a Royal Commission was appointed to inquire into the constitution, management, and expense of the Mint, and the Report of the Commissioners, which was presented to Parliament in the following year, contains a complete history of the several Mints.

The Accounts and other documents relating thereto include the following :—

MINT, ACCOUNTS, &c., RELATING TO THE. (EXCHEQUER, QUEEN'S REMEMBRANCER.) Henry III. to George II.

These consist of the accounts of the " Custos Cambii et Monetæ " (at London and Canterbury), from Henry III to Henry VIII.; of the *Controller of the Mint*, from Henry III. to Elizabeth ; of the *Master of the Mint*, from Edw. I. to Geo. II.; and of Miscellaneous Documents relating to Mint and Coinage, including those formerly preserved in the Treasury of the Receipt of the Exchequer.

Calendar. 1 Vol. MS.

Do. (AUDIT OFFICE AND PIPE OFFICE.)

Accounts of the Wardens of the Mint, 1536 to 1815.

Do. of the Masters and Workers. 1626 to 1827.

Do. of Purchases and Sales of Tin. 1603 to 1665, and 1703 to 1725.

Controlment Rolls. 10 James I. to 18 Charles II.

Miscellaneous Accounts. 1547 to 1706.

See List of " Declared Accounts " (Lists and Indexes, No. II. 1893).

MINT—(continued).

MINT, ACCOUNTS, &c.—(continued).

The following documents relating to the Mint are amongst the Miscellaneous Books of the Treasury of the Receipt:—

Vol. 99. Book of Charges of the Old Mint House at the Tower. 18 Henry VIII.

Vol. 100. Assay Rolls and other documents relating to the Mint. Henry VIII. to Geo. I.

Vol. 101. Memoranda relating to the Trial of the Pix.

ROTULUS EMPTIONUM ARGENTI FACTARUM IN CAMBIO LONDONIÆ, &c. 50–55 Henry III.

[*Misc. Rolls, &c. (Chancery) No.* $\frac{18}{3}$.]

TRIALS OF THE PIX, PROCEEDINGS ON. (EXCHEQUER, Q. R.) 1603 to 1824. 1 Package.

Documents relating to the Mint will also be found amongst the Treasury Records.

MISCELLANEOUS BOOKS.

The principal classes of Miscellaneous Books preserved in the Public Record Office are those of the Queen's Remembrancer's Department in the Exchequer, of the Treasury of the Receipt of the Exchequer or Chapter House, and of the Augmentation Office in the Exchequer. A brief list of each class is appended.

Many of these books are more fully described in the present volume under the heads to which they belong, and those which contain Court Rolls, Ministers' Accounts, or Rentals and Surveys, will be exhaustively dealt with in the Lists of those documents now in progress.

Exchequer, Queen's Remembrancer.

Vol.		
1	A "Breviate" of Domesday Book, with other Memoranda.	Temp. Edw. I.
2	The Red Book of the Exchequer.	—
3	Book of Aids - - - - -	20 Edw. III.
4	Book of Knight's Fees - - - -	6 Hen. VI.
5	Testa de Nevill. (Vol. I.)	—
6	Do. do. (Vol. 2).	—
7	Book of Fifteenths and Tenths - - -	3 Hen. V.
8	Transcript of the Great Cowcher of the Duchy of Lancaster. (Vol. 1.)	—
9	Transcripts of Statutes - - - -	John to Ric. II.
10	Do. - - - -	Edw. III. to Hen. VI.
11	Do. - - - -	Edw. IV. to Hen.VIII.
12	The Black Book of the Exchequer, or Liber Niger Parvus.	
13	Pope Nicholas' Taxation. Vol. 1 (York).	—
14	Do. Vol. 2 (Canterbury).	—
15	Tenures in Warwick (Transcripts of the Inquisitiones Hundredorum).	—
16	Templars' Lands, Inquisition concerning - -	31 Hen. II.

MISCELLANEOUS BOOKS—(continued).

Exchequer, Queen's Remembrancer—(continued).

Vol.		
17	Transcript of Kirkby's Quest - - -	Temp. Edw. I.
18	Rental, &c. of the Priory of Holy Trinity, London	—
19	Chartulary of Torre Abbey.	
20	Do. Godstowe Nunnery.	—
21	Do. Coventry Priory.	—
22	Do. Warwick College.	—
23	Do. Newstead Priory.	—
24	Do. Malmesbury Abbey.	—
25	Do. Chertsey Abbey.	—
26	Do. Oseney Abbey.	—
27	Do. St. Augustine's Monastery, Canterbury.	—
28	Do. Ramsey Abbey.	—
29	Do. Langdon Abbey.	—
30	Visitation of the Archdeaconry of Norwich - -	Temp. Edw. III.
31	Cardinal Pole's Pension Book - - -	2 & 3 Philip & Mary.
32	The Book of Common Prayer, deposited pursuant to the Act of Uniformity.	14 Car. II.
33	Enrolments of Deeds of Bargain and Sale - -	Temp. Hen. VIII.
34	Do. do. - -	,,
35	Accounts of the Voyages of Martin Frobisher (Vol. 1.)	Temp. Eliz.
36	Do. do. (Vol. 2.)	,,
37	Humberstone's Survey. (Vol. 1) - - -	,,
38	Do. (Vol. 2.) - - -	,,
39	Surveys of Religious Houses in Somerset, Wilts, Gloucester, and Worcester.	,,
40	Survey of the Possessions of the Archbishop of Canterbury.	1616–17.
41	Survey of the Possessions of Thomas Lord Paget and Charles Paget.	1585.
42	Survey of the Possessions of Leonard Dacre -	1589.
43	Survey of the Manor of Claxby, co. Lincoln -	Temp. Eliz.
44	Survey of the Manor of Eltham, co. Kent - -	3 Jas. I.
45	Survey of the Possessions of Thomas, Duke of Norfolk, and Philip, Earl of Arundel, in London and Middlesex.	32 Eliz.
46	Survey of the Possessions of the same in Norfolk, Suffolk, Cambridge, and Essex.	31 Eliz.
47	Survey of the Honor of Penrith and of Inglewood Forest.	17 Jas. I.
48	An Ancient Repertory of Escheators' Accounts.	—
49	A Book of Notes of Old Indentures - -	Temp. Edw. VI.
50	A Book of Payments in connection with the Post	Temp. Philip & Mary.
51	Book of Obligations for Survey of Woods -	Eliz. & Jas. I.
52	A Book relating to the Sale of Crown Lands -	8 Jas. I.
53	Copies of Leases by Queen Anne in 14 James I., also Copies of Orders made by the Trustees for the sale of Fee Farm Rents.	A.D. 1650 to 1653.
54	Copies of Leases granted by Robert Earl of Holland	A.D. 1655 to 1669.
55	Account Books of the Stewards of Lords Warwick and Holland.	—
56	Do. do.	—
57	Do. do.	—
58	Do. do.	—
59	Do. do.	—
60	A Journal relating to the removal of the Records of the Court of Exchequer.	A.D. 1822.

MISCELLANEOUS BOOKS—(continued).

Exchequer, Treasury of the Receipt.

Vol.			
1	Army and Navy Receipts and Payments - -		Hen.VII. & Hen.VIII.
2	Charges of the Army and Navy - -		3–5 Hen. VIII.
3	Army, Navy, and Ordnance Payments - -		Hen.VII. & Hen.VIII.
4	Payments of the Royal Ordnance, &c. - -		5 & 6 Hen. VIII.
5	Expenses of building the Henry Grace Dieu, &c. -		Temp. Hen. VIII.
6	Accounts of the Royal Dockyard at Portsmouth -		14 & 15 Hen. VIII.
7	Navy and Ordnance Accounts - -		Temp. Hen. VII.
8	Indentures of the King's Ordnance - -		,,
9	Expenses of the Army to and from France - -		Temp. Hen. VIII.
10	Naval and Ordnance Receipts and Payments -		Hen.VII. & Hen.VIII.
11	Expenses, &c. of the Navy - -		Temp. Hen. VIII.
12	Expenses of the Navy - -		4 & 6 Hen. VIII.
13	Inventory of the Stores of the Royal Navy - -		6 Hen. VIII.
14	Accounts for money for King's voyage to Scotland, &c.		Temp. Hen. VII.
15	Account of Military Stores - -		,,
16	Certificates of Musters, Hereford - -		Temp. Hen. VIII.
17	Do.	Dorset - - -	,,
18	Do.	Stafford -	,,
19	Do.	South'ton - -	,,
20	Do.	Denbigh - - -	,,
21	Do.	Lincoln - -	,,
22	Do.	Norfolk - -	,,
23	Do.	York, N. R. - -	,,
24	Do.	Surrey - - -	,,
25	Do.	Norfolk - - -	,,
26	Do.	Monmouth - -	,,
27	Do.	Worcester - -	,,
28	Do.	Oxford and Suffolk -	,,
29	Do.	Dorset - -	,,
30	Do.	York, E.R. - -	,,
31	Do	Hereford - - -	,,
32	Do.	York and Ainsty (City of).	,,
33	Do.	Anglesea and Merioneth -	,,
34	Do.	Yorkshire (Craven and Booland).	,,
35	Do.	Worcester - -	,,
36	Do.	Do. - -	,,
37	Do.	York, W.R. - -	,,
38	Do.	Do. - -	,,
39	Do.	York, E.R. - -	,,
40	Do.	Northumberland - -	,,
41	Do.	York, N.R. - -	,,
42	Do.	South Wales - -	,,
43	Do.	York, W.R. - -	,,
44	Do.	York, N.R. - - -	,,
45	Do.	Sussex - - -	,,
46	Do.	Wilts - - -	,,
47	Do.	Beds, North'ton, and Notts.	,,
48	Do.	Salop - - -	,,
49	Do.	North Wales - -	,,
50	Do.	Sussex - - -	,,
51	Do.	Dorset - - -	,,
52	Do.	Gloucester - -	,,
53	Do.	Cornwall - - -	,,
54	Do.	Rutland - - -	,,
55	Do.	Do. - - -	,,
56	Cornwall, Duchy of, Book of Arrears of the Receivers-General.		Hen.VII. & Hen.VIII.
57	Charters, &c., of Edmund, late Earl of Cornwall, Transcripts of.		Temp. Edw. I.

MISCELLANEOUS BOOKS—(continued).

Exchequer, Treasury of the Receipt—(continued).

Vol.		
58	An Ecclesiastical Taxation in the Diocese of Coventry and Lichfield.	Temp. Hen. VII.
59	A Certificate as to Monastic Pensions in the West Riding of Yorks.	6 Edw. VI.
60	An Ecclesiastical Taxation in the Diocese of Rochester.	Temp. Hen. VII.
61	An Ecclesiastical Taxation in the Archdeaconry of Richmond.	Temp. Hen. VIII.
62	An Ecclesiastical Taxation in the Diocese of Lincoln.	Temp. Hen. VI.
63	Original Renunciations of Papal Supremacy -	Temp. Hen. VIII.
64	Do. do.	,,
65	Book of Values of all Spiritual Promotions - -	,,
66	Inventories of the goods and chattels of the Duke of Ireland and others.	11–12 Ric. II.
67	Transcripts of Kirkby's Quest for the County of York	Temp. Edw. I.
68	Do. do. - - - - -	,,
69	Extents of Knights' Fees of the Honor of Richmond	9–10 Edw. I.
70	Lists of Knights' Fees in the County of Kent -	Temp. Edw. II.
71	Transcript of the Testa de Nevill for the County of Lincoln, and a Ledger Book of the Abbey of Barlinges.	—
72	A Book of Knights' Fees in several Counties entitled, "Feoda in Capite," compiled by the Master of the Court of Wards.	34 Hen. VIII.
73	An Account of the Knights' Fees in the County of Kent, compiled by the Feodary of that County.	35 Hen. VIII.
74	An Account of the Tenures of Manors in the County of Gloucester.	18 Eliz.
75	Transcripts of Arrentations in divers Forests -	9–35 Edw. I.
76	Perambulations, Pleas, &c., relating to Sherwood Forest.	Hen. III. to Edw. III.
77	The "Black Book" of the Forests - - -	30 Hen. VIII.
78	Accounts of Payments made by the Constable of Gascony.	4 Edw. II.
79	Accounts relating to Harfleur and Ponthieu -	Temp. Edw. III. & Hen. V.
80	Do. Ponthieu and Gascony -	Temp. Edw. III.
81	Accounts, &c., relating to Gascony - - -	,,
82	Accounts of the Bishopric of Tournay - -	23 Hen. VII.
83	Original Examinations in the Chancery of Brittany	Temp. Hen. VIII.
84	Inventories of Plate, Jewels, and Regalia - -	Temp. Hen. VI.
85	Accounts of the Jewel House - - - -	24 Hen. VIII.
86	Inventories of the Royal Jewels, &c. - - -	2 Jas. I.
87	Abstracts of Placita Coram Rege, &c. (printed in the "Placitorum Abbreviatio").	Temp. John.
88	Bills preferred to the Justices of Trailbaston -	Edw. I. to Edw. III.
89	Placita de Quo Warranto in Com. Bedford -	4 Edw. II.
90	Bills preferred to the Justices Itinerant in the Counties of Lancaster and Bedford.	Temp. Edw. III.
91	Proclamations of Outlawry in Com. Lincoln -	14 Hen. VII.
92	The Statutes and Ordinances of the Most Noble Order of the Garter.	—
93	A Book containing the names of Freemen of the London Companies.	Temp. Hen. VIII.
94	A Book containing the Petitions of Prisoners in Ludgate, &c.	,,
95	Accounts of the Lands, &c., of Sir John Hussey -	,,
96	Woods, Accounts of Sales of - - - -	Hen. VIII. to Jas. I.
97	Do. do. - - - -	Hen. VIII. to Eliz.
98	Accounts of the Manors of Skernyng and Wendlyng, co. Norfolk.	,,

MISCELLANEOUS BOOKS—(continued).
Exchequer, Treasury of the Receipt—(continued).

Vol.		
99	Book of Charges of the Old Mint House at the Tower.	18 Hen. VIII.
100	Assay Rolls and other documents relating to the Mint.	Hen. VIII. to Geo. I.
101	Memoranda relating to the Trial of the Pix.	—
102	Cardinal's Colleges, Accounts, &c., relating to -	Temp. Hen. VIII.
103	Do. do. -	,,
104	Do. do. -	,,
105	Do Transcripts of Grants to -	,,
106	Do. Statutes of - - - -	,,
107	Household Accounts of the Abbot of Ramsey -	21 Hen. VII. to 24 Hen. VIII.
108	Household Accounts of Holy Trinity Priory, London.	5-6 Hen. VIII.
109	Documents relating to Christ Church, Oxford -	Temp. Hen. VIII.
110	Ordinances relating to a Chantry in the Chapel of Allhallows, Barking.	Temp. Edw. IV.
111	Ordinances of St. George's Chapel, Windsor.	—
112	Instructions as to the Foundation of a Chantry at Campsey, co. Suffolk.	—
113	Documents relating to St. George's Chapel, Windsor	—
114	Commissions and Instructions to ascertain the value of Ecclesiastical Possessions.	26 Hen. VIII.
115	Dockets of the Submissions of Monasteries and Inventories of their Possessions.	30 Hen. VIII.
116	Instructions as to the Suppression of the Monasteries	—
117	Memoranda of the Monasteries surrendered to Cardinal Wolsey.	—
118	Depositions, &c., relating to Aske's Rebellion -	Temp. Hen. VIII.
119	Do. do. -	,,
120	Do. do. -	,,
121	Letters, &c., relating to disturbances in North of of England.	,,
122	Documents relating to Aske's Rebellion - -	,,
123	Liber Receptorum (Receipts of the Exchequer) -	Hen.VII. & Hen.VIII.
124	Receipts and Payments to the Treasury - -	Temp. Hen. VII.
125	Receipt Book of the Exchequer - - -	1-2 & 7-8 Hen. VII.
126	Receipt Book of the Exchequer - - -	13-20 Hen. VII.
127	Do. do. - - -	9-20 Hen. VIII.
128	Tellers' Book of the Exchequer - - -	1-27 Hen. VIII.
129	Extracts from the Pells Records.	—
130	Accounts of Receipts and Issues of the Exchequer	Temp. Hen. VII.
131	Do. do. -	9-13 Hen. VII.
132	Do. do. -	21 Hen. VIII.
133	Do. do. -	Temp. Hen. VIII.
134	Account of John Savile, Teller of the Exchequer -	12 Chas. I.
135	Orders, &c., for Payments from the Exchequer -	1655 to 1708.
136	Receipt Book for Salaries, Pensions, &c. - -	1710.
137	Calendar of Charters, &c., of the Archbishopric of Canterbury.	—
138	Inventory of the Deeds, &c., of Christ Church, Canterbury.	—
139	Catalogue of Deeds, &c., of Thomas Cromwell -	21-25 Hen. VIII.
140	A similar Catalogue - - -	Temp. Hen. VIII.
141	Do. - - -	24 Hen VIII.
142	Do. - - - -	,,
143	Do. - - - -	,,
144	Transcripts of the Letters of Privy Seal, &c., of Edward the Black Prince.	20-21 Edw. III.
145	States of Accounts of the Sheriffs throughout England.	21 Hen. VII.
146	Declarations " de minutis particulis " of the sheriffs throughout England.	19 Hen. VIII.

MISCELLANEOUS BOOKS—(continued).
Exchequer, Treasury of the Receipt--(continued).

MISCELLANEOUS BOOKS—(continued).

Exchequer, Treasury of the Receipt—(continued).

Vol.		
183	Butlerage and Prisage, Accounts of (London) -	Temp. Hen. VIII.
184	Do. Do. (Southampton	,,
185	Customs Accounts - - - - -	13–14 Hen. VII.
186	An Inventory of the Treaties remaining in the Treasury of the Exchequer.	—
187	A Calendar of Papal Bulls, &c. relating to Aquitaine.	Temp. Edw. II.
188	Transcripts of Ancient Treaties between France and England.	Temp. Hen. V.
189	Register of the Acts of Homage and Fealty by the Nobility, &c. of Aquitaine.	Temp. Edw. III.
190	Documents relating to Scottish affairs - -	Edw. III. to Eliz.
191	Documents relating to the Marches of Scotland and Wales.	Temp. Hen. VIII.
192	Instructions to Ambassadors at the Court of the King of Arragon.	,,
193	A Treatise on the Tropes and Figures of Scripture	—
194	Fragments of Legal Treatises, &c.	—
195	Treatises on Legal Subjects, &c.	—
196	Treatises on Theological Subjects.	—
197	Armestrong's Sermons &c.	—
198	An Ancient Legal Common Place Book.	—
199	A Book entitled " Carta Feodi."	—
200	Petitions, &c. relating to the Marches of Wales -	1 & 2 Ph. & Mary.
201	Expenses of the Royal Household - - -	14–16 Edw. I.
202	Wardrobe Accounts - - - - -	22–23 Edw. I.
203	Do. - - - -	12–14 Edw. III.
204	Do. - - - -	15–18 Edw. III.
205	Household Expenses of Queen Philippa -	23–24 Edw. III.
206	A Book of Orders of the Household (from S.P. Dom.).	Temp. Edw. IV.
207	Account of the Receivers of Elizabeth, Queen of Edward IV.	6–7 Edw. IV.
208	Accounts of the Clerk of the Marshalsea of the Household.	7–8 Hen. VII.
209	Accounts of the Keeper of the Great Wardrobe -	15 Hen. VII.
210	Household Expenses of Elizabeth, Queen of Henry VII.	17 Hen. VII.
211	Book of Receipts by the King - - -	21–23 Hen. VII.
212	Book of Declarations as to Revenues - - -	21 Hen. VII
213	Do. Do. - -	17–20 Hen. VII.
214	Books of King's Payments - - - -	21 Hen. VII. to 1 Hen. VIII.
215	Do. Do. - - - -	1–9 Hen. VIII.
216	Do. Do. - - - -	9–12 Hen. VIII.
217	Expenses of Revels, &c. - - - -	1–11 Hen VIII.
218	Household Expenses of the Earl of Devon -	10 Hen. VIII.
219	Do. of Princess Mary -	12–13 Hen. VIII.
220	Do. of the Duke of Buckingham -	12 Hen. VIII.
221	Account of the Treasurer of the Chamber -	14 Hen. VIII.
222	Household Accounts of Princess Mary	14–15 Hen. VIII.
223	Household Accounts of Katharine Countess of Devon.	16 Hen. VII.
224	Accounts of the Keeper of the Great Wardrobe -	16–17 Hen. VIII.
225	Household Expenses of Henry Earl of Devon	17 Hen. VIII.
226	Receipts and Payments of the Earl of Northumberland.	6–18 Hen. VIII.
227	Expenses at Greenwich - - - -	18 & 19 Hen. VIII.
228	Accounts of Revels, &c. - - - -	Temp Hen. VIII.
229	Do. - - - -	,,
230	Regulations of the Royal Household (the " Liber Niger of Edw. IV."). A Transcript, formerly in the State Paper Office.	,,

MISCELLANEOUS BOOKS—(continued).
Exchequer, Treasury of the Receipt—(continued).

Vol.		
231	Regulations of the Royal Household (the "Statutes of Eltham"). Formerly in the State Paper Office.	17 Hen. VIII.
232	An Account of the Wages of the Royal Household	Temp. Hen. VIII.
233	Expenses of the Diet of the King's Household	-
234	Ordinances of the Great Wardrobe - -	6 Chas. I.
235	Expenses of Repairs, &c., at Hampton Court -	Temp. Hen. VIII.
236	Do. do. -	"
237	Do. do. -	"
238	Do. do. -	"
239	Do. do. -	"
240	Do. do. -	"
241	Do. do. - -	22-23 Hen. VIII.
242	Do. do. - -	25 & 26 Hen. VIII.
243	Do. do. - -	26 & 28 Hen. VIII.
244	Do. do. -	28 & 29 Hen. VIII.
245	Do. do. - -	29 & 30 Hen. VIII.
246	Book of Sales of the King's Wardships -	18-20 Hen. VIII.
247	A Book of Wards - - - -	19-21 Hen. VII.
248	Do.	22-23 Hen. VII.
249	Feodaries' Account for the County of Kent -	41 Eliz. to 4 Jas. I.
250	Accounts of Works at Tykenhull -	17 Hen. VIII.
251	Accounts of Works, &c., at Westminster -	22-23 Hen. VIII.
252	Do. do. -	"
253	Warrants for the delivery of Records.	
254	Berwick-on-Tweed and the Marches, Accounts of the Receiver-General, &c.	Temp. Hen. VIII.
255	Gresham Domestic Accounts - -	Temp. Ph. and Mary.
256	Lord Cromwell's Accounts - - -	Temp. Hen. VIII.
257	Certificates as to the exportation of Wheat, &c.	"
258	Particulars for Grants of the Possessions of Colleges and Chantries.	Temp. Edw. VI.
259	Do. do.	"
260	Index to the foregoing - - -	"
261	Register of Grants of Crown Lands - -	1-4 Edw. VI.
262	Accounts of the Constable of Windsor Castle -	24 Hen. VII. to 10 Hen. VIII.
263	Do. do. - -	10 to 20 Hen. VIII.
264	Do. do. - -	20 to 31 Hen. VIII.

Exchequer, Augmentation Office.

Vol.		
1	Acquittances, Enrolments of - - -	34 Hen. VIII. to 1 Edw. VI.
2	Acts of Parliament relating to the Court of Augmentations, copies of.	3 to 28 Hen. VIII.
3	Appearance Book of the Court of Augmentations -	38 Hen. VIII.
4	Army Accounts - - - -	5 Hen. VIII.
5	Do. - - - -	1647 to 1652.
6	Do. - - - -	1648 to 1650.
7	Arrears, Account Book of. (Lands attainted) -	Temp. Hen. VIII.
8	Do. do. -	30 Hen. VIII.
9	Do. do. -	"
10	Do. do. -	32 Hen. VIII.
11	Do. do. -	"
12	Do. do. -	35 Hen. VIII.
13	Do. do. -	Temp. Hen. VIII.
14	Account Book of the Revenue of North Wales -	14 Jas. I.
15	Assessment and Arrentation of Lands in the Duchy of Cornwall.	9 Eliz.
16	Audley's Lands, Papers relating to - -	36 Hen. VIII. to 29 Eliz.

MISCELLANEOUS BOOKS—(continued).

Exchequer, Augmentation Office—(continued).

Vol.		
17	Augmentations, Papers relating to the establishment of the Court of.	Hen. VIII.
18	Battle Abbey, Rentals of, &c.	Temp. Hen. III.
19	Bills and Answers in the Court of General Surveyors.	35 Hen. VIII.
20	Bills and Answers in the Court of Augmentations -	Temp. Hen. VIII.
21	Do. do. General Surveyors	"
22	Bills, Answers, and Miscellaneous Proceedings in the Court of General Surveyors.	"
23	Bills, Answers, and Miscellaneous Proceedings in the Court of Augmentations.	"
24	Bishoprics, Henry the Eighth's Scheme of.	—
25	Arrears, Account Book of - - - - -	Temp. Hen. VIII.
26	"Brevia de Scaccario" (Transcripts of Writs and Returns).	1 to 9 Eliz.
27	Do. do. -	8 Eliz.
28	Arrears, Account Book of - - - -	Temp. Hen. VIII.
29	"Cartæ Antiquæ Diversorum Regum" (Original Letters Patent, &c.).	—
30	Do. do.	—
31	"Cartæ Miscellaneæ" (Ancient Deeds) - -	Vol. I.
32	Do. do. - -	Vol. II.
33	Do. do. - -	Vol. III.
34	Do. do. - -	Vol. IV.
35	Do. do. - -	Vol. V.
36	Do. do. - -	Vol. VI.
37	Do. do. - -	Vol. VII.
38	Do. do. - -	Vol. VIII.
39	Do. do. - -	Vol. IX.
40	Do. do. - -	Vol. X.
41	Do. do. - -	Vol. XI.
42	Do. do. - -	Vol. XII.
43	Do. do. - -	Vol. XIII.
44	Do. do. - -	Vol. XIV.
45	Do. do. - -	Vol. XV.
46	Do. do. - -	Vol. XVI.
47	Do. do. - -	Vol. XVII.
48	Do. do. - -	Vol. XVIII.
49	Do. do. - -	Vol. XIX.
50	Do. do. - -	Vol. XX.
51	Do. do. - -	Vol. XXI.
52	Do. do. - -	Vol. XXII.
53	Do. do. - -	Vol. XXIII.
54	Do. do. - -	Vol. XXIV.
55	Chartulary of Acornbury Priory.	—
56	Do. of Battle Abbey ("Registrum de Bello")	—
57	Do. do. (Rentals and Custumals).	—
58	Do. of the Beauchamps, of Hatch, co. Somerset.	—
59	Do. of Robert Hulle of Spaxton, co. Somerset.	—
60	Do. do. (a copy)	—
61	Do. of Pershore Abbey.	—
62	Do. of the Manors of Munden (Herts) and Wendon (Essex).	—
63	Do. of Worcester Cathedral.	—
64	Assessment of a Loan in the West Riding of York; Accounts relating to Warwick College, &c.	Temp. Hen. VIII.
65	Chester, Register of Royal Letters and Writs addressed to the Justices and Chamberlains of.	25 to 39 Edw. III.

MISCELLANEOUS BOOKS—(continued).
Exchequer, Augmentation Office—(continued).

Vol.				
66	Chester, Views of Accounts of the Chamberlain of			34 to 36 Hen. VIII.
67	Colleges and Chantries, Particulars for the Sale of			Hen. VIII. & Edw.VI.
68	Do.	do.		—
69	Cornwall, Duchy of, Acquittances	-	-	1 to 6 Jas. I.
70	Do.	do.	-	8 to 14 Jas. I.
71	Do.	do.	-	17 Jas. I. to 1 Chas. I.
72	Do.	do.	-	19 Jas. I.
73	Do.	do.	-	6 Chas. I.
74	Do.	do.	-	7-8 Chas. I.
75	Do.	do.	-	21 Chas I. to 1650.
76	Do.	Misc. Papers	-	1612 to 1621.
77	Cornwall, Valuations for a Muster in several Hundreds in the County of.			Henry VIII.
78	Do.	do.	-	,,
79	Court Rolls (Various)	-	-	Edw. III.to Hen.VIII.
80	Do.	-	-	Edw.IV. to Hen.VIII.
81	Do.	-	-	Hen. VIII. to Jas. I.
82	Do.	-	-	Hen. VIII.
83	Do.	-	-	35–36 Hen. VIII.
84	Do.	-	-	7-44 Eliz.
85	Do.	-	-	Phil. & Mary.
86	Do.	-	-	Edw. IV. to Mary.
87a	Defective Titles, Particulars for the Amendment of			1581 to 1627.
87b	Do.	do.	-	1600 to 1606.
88	Do.	do.	-	1613 to 1637.
89a	Do.	do.	-	1618 to 1638.
89b	Do.	do.	-	1630 to 1638.
90	Do.	do.	-	1619 to 1631.
91	Decrees and Orders of the Court of Augmentations, Vol. I.			28 Hen. VIII. Mich. to 29 Hen. VIII. Trin.
92	Do.	do.	Vol. II.	29 Hen. VIII. Mich. to 30 Hen. VIII. Trin.
93	Do.	do.	Vol. III.	33 Hen. VIII. Mich.
94	Do.	do.	Vol. IV.	34 Hen. VIII. Hil.
95	Do.	do.	Vol. V.	31 Hen. VIII. East. to 32 Hen. VIII. Trin.
96	Do.	do.	Vol. VI.	31 Hen. VIII. Mich
97	Do.	do.	Vol. VII.	32 Hen. VIII. Hil.
98	Do.	do.	Vol. VIII.	32 Hen. VIII. Mich.
99	Do.	do.	Vol. IX.	33 Hen. VIII. East to 33 Hen. VIII. Trin.
100	Do.	do.	Vol. X.	30 Hen. VIII. Mich. to 31 Hen. VIII. Trin.
101	Do.	do.	Vol. XI.	33 Hen. VIII. Hil.
102	Do.	do.	Vol. XII.	34 Hen. VIII. East. to 34 Hen. VIII. Trin.
103	Do.	do.	Vol. XIII.	34 Hen. VIII. Mich. to 35 Hen. VIII. East.
104	Do.	do.	Vol. XIV.	35 Hen. VIII. East. to 38 Hen. VIII. Trin.
105	Do	do.	Vol. XV.	1 to 7 Edw. VI.
106	Decrees of the Court of General Surveyors		-	34 to 38 Hen. VIII.
107	Account Book of the Receiver-General of the Queen Anne of Denmark.			13 Jas. I.

MISCELLANEOUS BOOKS—(continued).
Exchequer, Augmentation Office—(continued).

Vol.			
108	Depositions of the Court of Augmentations -		32–33 Hen. VIII.
109	Do. do.		33 Hen. VIII.
110	Do. do. -	-	34 Hen. VIII.
111	Do. do. -	-	37 Hen. VIII.
112	Do. do. •	-	38 Hen. VIII.
113	Do. do. -	-	Hen. VIII. & Edw. VI.
114	Do. do. -	-	3 Edw. VI.
115	Do. do. •	-	4 Edw. VI.
116	Do. do. -	-	,,
117	Do. do. -	-	Temp. Hen. VIII.
118	Do. do. -	-	,,
119	Do. do. -	-	,,
120	Do. do. -	-	,,
121	Do. do. -	-	,,
122	Do. do. -	-	Hen. VIII. & Edw. VI.
123	Do. do. -	-	,,
124	Do. do. •	-	Temp. Hen. VIII.
125	Do. do. -	-	,,
126	Do. do. -	-	36 Hen. VIII.
127	Do. do. -	-	,,
128	Do. do. -	-	6 Edw. VI.
129	Do. do. -	-	,,
130	Proceedings in the Courts of Augmentations and General Surveyors.		Temp. Hen. VIII.
131	Do. do. -		,,
132	Do. do. -		,,
133	Do. do. -		Temp. Edw. VI.
134	Depositions of the Court of Augmentations (pp. 1–25) and Court Rolls of Newton, co. Lanc. (pp. 26–117).		Temp. Hen. VIII. ,,
135	Fee-Farm Rents, Particulars and Certificates of Sale of.		1626 to 1653.
136	Do. do. -		1649.
137	Do. do. -		1650.
138	Views of Accounts of the Receiver-General of the Queen's Lands.		10–11 Jas. I.
139	Fee-Farm Rents, Minute Book of Trustees for the Sale of.		1650.
140	Fee-Farm Rents, Accounts of the Sale of -	-	,,
141	Do. Contracts, &c., for the Sale of	-	1650 to 1655.
142	Do. do.	-	1650 to 1658.
143	Do. do.	•	,,
144	Do. do.	-	1651, &c.
145	Fotheringay College, Accounts of -	-	29 Hen. VIII. to 2 Edw. VI.
146	Do. do. -	-	37 Hen. VIII.
147	Do. Statutes of.		—
148	Foundation of the Chapel of West Braynford	-	21 Hen. VII.
149	Chartulary of the Chantry of Chalgrave.		—
150	Foundation of the Chantry of Chiddingstone		9 Hen. VII.
151	Grants, Transcripts of - - -	-	Edw. VI. to Jas. I.
152	Do. - - -	-	Jas. I. & Chas. I.
153	Do. - - -		,,
154	Do. - - -	•	,,
155	Do. - - -		Various dates.
156	Grant to Sir Thos. Wyatt of the Manor of Boxley, co. Kent, Particulars for the.		Hen. VIII.
157	Grants of Offices, Particulars for - -	-	,,
158	Do. do. - -	-	,,
159	Defective Titles, Particulars for the Amendment of.		1623–1634
160	Household Book of Sir A. Denny, keeper of the Palace at Westminster.		34 Hen. VIII. to 2 Edw. VI.

MISCELLANEOUS BOOKS—(continued).
Exchequer, Augmentation Office—(continued).

Vol.			
161	Household Accounts of Queen Katharine Parr	-	35 Hen. VIII.
162	Indentures, Inrolments of	- - -	2 to 28 Hen. VIII.
163	Do.	- - -	21 to 25 Hen. VIII.
164	Informations, &c., in the Exchequer relating to Leicester and Barkby, Transcripts of.		Temp. Chas. I.
165	Informations and other proceedings in the Court of Augmentations.		Temp. Hen. VIII.
166	Pleas and Inquisitions as to the Rights and Privileges of the Principality in North Wales, Transcripts of.		Edw. III. to Ric. II.
167	Brief Valors of Lands in the hands of the Crown in several Counties.		Phil. & Mary.
168	Presentments as to Concealed Lands in the County of Northampton.		Temp. Eliz.
169	Precedents for Writs (" Liber Brevium ") -		Temp. Edw. III.
170	Presentments as to Concealed Lands in the County of Lancashire.		Temp. Eliz.
171	Inventories of possessions of attainted persons in Yorkshire.		Temp. Hen. VIII.
172	Inventories of the Goods, &c., of Monasteries in Warwickshire and Staffordshire.		,,
173	Contracts for the purchase of Crown Lands	-	1649 to 1651.
174	Do. do.	-	1650 to 1653.
175	Leases of Rectories, &c., Repertory to	- -	Temp. Hen. VIII.
176	Leases by Elizabeth, Queen of Henry VII. and by Katharine of Arragon.		Hen. VII. & Hen. VIII.
177	Leases by Anne Boleyn and Jane Seymour	-	Temp Hen. VIII.
178	Leases by Katharine Parr	- - -	,,
179	Leases. Copies of*	- - - -	Phil. & Mary.
180	Do.	- - - -	,,
181	Do.	- - - -	,,
182	Do.	- - - -	,,
183	Do.	- - - -	,,
184	Do.	- - - -	,,
185	Leases, Particulars for, Beds. to Cambridge	-	Hen. VIII.
186	Do. Cheshire to Devon	-	,,
187	Do. Dorset to Essex	-	,,
188	Do. Glouc. to Hunts.	- -	,,
189	Do. Kent	- -	,,
190	Do. Lanc. to Linc.	- -	,,
191	Do. Lond. and Middx.	-	,,
192	Do. Monmouth to Northton	-	,,
193	Do. Northumbd. to Rutland	-	,,
194	Do. Salop to Southton	-	,,
195	Do. Stafford and Suffolk	-	,,
196	Do. Surrey to Warwick	-	,,
197	Do Westmoreld. to Worcester	-	,,
198	Do. Yorkshire (Part 1)	-	,,
199	Do. Yorkshire (Part 2)	-	,,
200	Do. Wales (Counties)	-	,,
201	Do. Wales (Dioceses)	-	,,
202	Do. Various Counties	-	Eliz.
203	Do. do.	-	,,
204	Do. Ebor, Devon, Dorset, &c.	-	Hen. VIII.
205	Do. Somerset and Devon		,,
206	Leases, Particulars for, and Rentals, Yorks	-	,,
207	Do. do.	-	,,
208a	Do. do. Divers Counties		,,
208b	Leases, Particulars for, Yorks.	- -	Edw. VI.
209	Leases, Inrolments of*	- - -	28–29 Hen. VIII.
210	Do.	- - -	29 & 30 Hen. VIII.

* Indexed in the Deputy Keeper's 49th Report.

MISCELLANEOUS BOOKS—(continued).

Exchequer, Augmentation Office—(continued).

Vol.			
211	Leases, Inrolments of *	- - - - -	30 & 31 Hen. VIII.
212	Do.	- - - - -	31 & 32 Hen. VIII.
213	Do.	- - - -	32 & 33 Hen. VIII.
214	Do.	- - - - -	33 & 34 Hen. VIII.
215	Do.	- - -	34 Hen. VIII.
216	Do.	- - - -	35 & 36 Hen. VIII.
217	Do.	- - - -	37 & 38 Hen. VIII.
218	Do.	- - -	38 Hen. VIII. and 1 Edw. VII.
219	Do.	- - - - -	2 Edw. VI.
220	Do.	- - - -	3 Edw. VI.
221	Do.	- - - - -	4 Edw. VI.
222	Do.	- - - -	5 Edw. VI.
223	Do.	- - - -	,,
224	Do.	- - - - -	6 Edw. VI.
225	Do.	- - - -	7 Edw. VI.
226	Do.	- - - -	1 to 5 Phil. & Mary.
227	Do.	- - - - -	34 to 36 Eliz.
228	Do.	- - -	37 & 38 Eliz.
229	Do.	- - - -	3 Jas. I.
230	Leases of the Surveyors-General †	- -	34 to 38 Hen. VIII.
231	Leases, Repertory of	- - - -	9 & 10 and 25 to 40 Eliz.
232	Leases and Pensions, Inrolments of *	- -	28 to 30 Hen. VIII.
233	Do.	do.	- - -	30 & 31 Hen. VIII.
234	Do.	do.	- -	30 to 32 Hen. VIII.
235	Do.	do.	- -	31 to 34 Hen. VIII.
236	Do.	do.	- -	35 to 38 Hen. VIII.
237	Inquisitions, &c., as to the possessions of the "Pilgrims of Grace."		29 Hen. VIII.
238	Letters Patent and Indentures, Inrolments of *	-	Hen. VIII
239	Do.	do.	-	,,
240	Do.	do.	-	,,
241	Do.	do.	-	,,
242	Do.	do.	-	,,
243	Do.	do.	-	Jas. I.
244	Monastic Pensions, Original Warrants for *	-	28 Hen. VIII.
245	Do.	List of	- -	Hen. VIII.
246	Do.	do.	- - -	,,
247	Do.	(to Incumbents of Colleges and Chantries), Warrants for.	Edw. VI.
248	Do.	Accounts of the payment of	-	31 to 33 Hen. VIII.
249	Do.	do.	-	32 Hen. VIII.
250	Do.	do.	-	33 Hen. VIII.
251	Do.	do.	-	34–35 Hen. VIII.
252	Do.	do.	-	35 Hen. VIII.
253	Do.	do.	-	36 Hen. VIII.
254	Do.	do.	-	37 Hen. VIII.
255	Do.	do.	-	38 Hen. VIII.
256	Do.	do	-	1 Edw. VI.
257	Do.	do.	-	2 Edw. VI.
258	Do.	do	-	3 Edw. VI.
259	Do.	do.	-	4 Edw. VI.
260	Do.	do.	-	5 Edw. VI.
261	Do.	do.	-	6 Edw. VI.
262	Do.	do.	-	1 Mary.
263	Memoranda, obligations, &c.	-	Temp. Hen. VII.
264	Memoranda concerning Bailiffs' and Collectors' Accounts.		4 Edw. VI.
265	Do.	do.		,,
266	Do.	do.		,,
267	Do.	do.		Edw. VI. & Phil. & Mary.

* Indexed in the Deputy Keeper's 49th Report.
† Indexed in the Deputy Keeper's 25th Report.

MISCELLANEOUS BOOKS—(continued).
Exchequer, Augmentation Office—(continued).

Vol.	Ministers' and Receivers' Accounts, as follows :—	
268	Receiver-General's Accounts of Cottingham, co. York.	1 to 7 Hen. VIII.
	Views of Accounts of the Priory of Christ-church Twynham, co. Southampton.	35 to 38 Hen. VIII.
269	Collectors' Accounts of the Priory of St. Thomas of Acon, London.	11 to 18 Hen. VIII.
270	Do. do.	19 to 29 Hen. VIII.
271	Bailiffs' Accounts of Lands Exchanged (Hanworth, &c.).	18 to 26 Hen. VIII.
272	Bailiffs' Accounts of the Monastery of St. Alban's.	17-18 Hen. VIII.
273	Bailiffs' Accounts of Lands exchanged - -	18-19 Hen. VIII.
	Views of Accounts of Lands Forfeited - -	23 to 33 Hen. VIII.
274	Bailiffs' Accounts of the Monastery of St. Alban's.	21-22 Hen. VIII.
275	Receiver-General's Account of Sir Wm. Brereton's Lands in Cheshire.	22-23 Hen. VIII., 24-25 Hen. VIII.
276	Views of Accounts of Sir John Savage's Lands in Cheshire and other Counties.	22-23 Hen. VIII., 25-26 Hen. VIII.
277	Do. do.	24-25 Hen. VIII.
278	Receivers' Accounts of Possessions of dissolved Monasteries in several Counties.	27-28 Hen. VIII.
279	Views of Receivers' Accounts in several Counties	27 to 36 Hen. VIII.
280	Ministers' Accounts of the possessions of dissolved Monasteries in Nottinghamshire.	27-28 Hen. VIII.
281	Ministers' Accounts in Northumberland and Cumberland.	27 to 29 Hen. VIII.
282	Ministers' Accounts and Receiver-General's Accounts of Attainted Lands in York and Lincoln.	28 to 35 Hen. VIII.
283	Accounts and Rental of Merivale Abbey, co. Warwick.	13-14 Hen. VII.
	Accounts of the Church of Eccles, co. Lanc. -	28-29 Hen. VIII.
284	Receivers' Accounts of the Possessions of Dissolved Monasteries in the County of Stafford.	29 to 32 Hen. VIII.
285	Ministers' Accounts of Attainted Lands in the Counties of York, Lincoln, &c.	,,
286	Do. do. - -	,,
287	Receivers' Accounts of the Possessions of Dissolved Monasteries in the County of Leicester.	29 to 36 Hen. VIII.
— 288	Accounts and Views of Accounts of attainted lands in the counties of York, Lancaster, &c.	29 to 35 Hen. VIII.
289	Receivers' Accounts of the possessions of dissolved Monasteries in the Counties of Hereford, Lancaster, York, and Northampton.	29 to 36 Hen. VIII.
290	Receivers' Accounts of the possessions of dissolved Monasteries in the County of Warwick.	29 to 38 Hen. VIII.
291	Receivers' Accounts of the possessions of dissolved Monasteries in the County of Salop.	,,
292	Receivers' Accounts of the possessions of dissolved Monasteries in the County of Worcester.	,,
293	Receivers' Accounts of the possessions of dissolved Monasteries in the Counties of Hereford, Stafford, Salop, and Worcester.	30 to 32 Hen. VIII.
294	Receivers' Accounts of the possessions of dissolved Monasteries in the Counties of Northampton, Warwick, and Leicester.	31-32 Hen. VIII.
295	Ministers' Accounts of the Monastery of Bury St. Edmunds, co. Suffolk.	32 33 Hen. VIII.
296	Receivers' Accounts of Buckingham's Lands -	14-15 Hen. VIII. and 20-21 Hen. VIII.
	Receivers' Accounts of the Monastery of Evesham, co. Worcester.	33-34 Hen. VIII.

MISCELLANEOUS BOOKS—(continued).
Exchequer, Augmentation Office—(continued).

Vol.	Ministers' & Receivers' Accounts, as follows (cont.):—	
297	Receivers' Accounts of the possessions of dissolved Monasteries in the Counties of Northampton, Warwick, Leicester, and Rutland.	34–35 Hen. VIII
298	Receiver-General's Account of attainted Lands in the Counties of York and Lancaster.	34–36 Hen. VIII.
299	Receiver-General's Account of attainted Lands in the Counties of Rutland, Suffolk, Lancaster, Chester, and York.	,,
300	Ministers' Accounts and Views of Accounts of the Monastery of Whalley, co. Lancaster, and of Jarvaulx, co. York.	29 to 31 Hen. VIII.
301	Account Book of the Receipts and Expenses of Fotheringay College.	35 to 38 Hen. VIII.
302	Receivers' Accounts of Queen Katharine's Lands in Somerset and Dorset.	36 to 38 Hen. VIII.
303	Receivers' Accounts of the possessions of dissolved Monasteries in the Counties of Northampton, Warwick, Leicester, and Rutland.	37–38 Hen. VIII.
304	Receiver-General's Accounts of attainted Lands in the Counties of York and Lancaster.	28–29 Hen. VIII.
	Accounts of the Surveyors of the Queen's Lands of Fines, &c. received in various Counties.	37 Hen. VIII.
305	Views of Accounts and Memoranda relating to the Counties of Hereford and Worcester.	28–38 Hen. VIII.
306	Receiver-General's Accounts of Sheriff Hutton, co. York.	1–7 Hen. VIII.
307	Receivers' Accounts of Buckingham's Lands in divers Counties.	15–21 Hen. VIII.
	Receivers' Accounts of attainted Lands in the Counties of York and Lincoln.	29–32 Hen. VIII.
308	Views of Accounts of Monastic and other Lands in the hands of the Crown.	1–3 Edw. VI.
309	Entry Book of Grants of the Offices of Bailiffs, &c.	2 to 45 Eliz.
310	Do. do. -	1 to 22 Jas. I.
311	Do. do. -	1 Chas.I.to 28 Chas.II.
312	Ministers' Accounts of the Bishopric of Winchester.	2 Chas. I.
	Receiver-General's Account of the same -	3 Chas. I.
	Valor of the Bishopric - - -	4 Edw. VI.
313A	Rough Minute Book of the General Surveyors of the King's Lands.	6 to 31 Hen. VIII.
313B	Minute Book of the Court of General Surveyors -	34 to 38 Hen. VIII
314	Minute Book of the Commissioners for the sale of Crown Lands.	1649 to 1659.
315	Navy Accounts - - - - -	5 Hen. VIII.
316	Do. - - - - -	Temp. Hen. VIII.
317	Do. - - - - -	,,
318	Patents for Offices, Entries of - - -	34 to 38 Eliz
319	Do. do. - - -	39 to 43 Eliz.
320	Do. do. - - -	44 Eliz. to 1 Jas.
321	Do. do. - - -	1 to 4 Jas. I.
322	Do. Abstracts of - - -	1 to 5 Jas. I.
323	Do. Entries of - - -	5 to 21 Jas. I.
324	Do. Abstracts of - - -	5 to 22 Jas. I.
325	Do. Entries of - -	22 Jas. I. to 19 Car. I.
326	Do. do. - -	9 to 11 Will. 3.
327	Obligations - - - - -	1 Edw. VI. to 1 & 2 Ph. & Mary.
328	Orders of the Court of Augmentations concerning Arrears.	38 Hen. VIII.
329	Orders, Rough Entries of - - -	9–10 Car. I.
330	Precedent Book for Charters.	—

MISCELLANEOUS BOOKS—(continued).
Exchequer, Augmentation Office—(continued).

Vol.		
331	Privy Seals of the Court of Augmentations	33 Hen. VIII.
332	Purchase and Exchange, Inrolments of Deeds of	Temp. Hen. VIII.
333	Do. do.	,,
334	Do. do.	Temp. Edw. VI.
335	Receipts and Payments at Calais (Treasurers' Account).	Temp. Hen. IV.
336	Receipts and Payments by the Court of Augmentations.	33–34 Hen. VIII.
337	Do. do.	35–36 Hen. VIII.
338	Do. do.	36–37 Hen. VIII.
339	Do. do.	37–38 Hen. VIII.
340	Do. do.	1 Edw. VI.
341	Do. do.	2 Edw. VI.
342	Do. do.	3 Edw. VI.
343	Do. do.	4 Edw. VI.
344	Do. do.	,,
345	Do. do.	4–5 Edw. VI.
346	Do. do.	5 Edw. VI.
347	Do. do.	6 Edw. VI.
348	Do. do.	6–7 Edw. VI.
349	Do. do.	1 Mary.
350	Receipts in the Counties of Chester, Flint, Montgomery and Denbigh.	7 Chas. I.
351	Receipts in the County of Northampton (church offerings, &c.)	1–2 Ph. & Mary.
352	Recognizances in the Court of Augmentations	34–35 Hen. VIII.
353	Stannary Courts (Cornwall and Devon) Accounts of.	15 to 29 Eliz.
354	Do. do.	30 Eliz. to 9 Jas. I.
355	Views of Accounts of the Collectors of Customs, &c., at Exeter and Dartmouth.	5 to 8 Eliz.
356	Views of Accounts of Subsidies in Various Counties.	43–44 Eliz.
	Surveys, Rentals, &c., as follows :—	
357	Surveys of the Honor of Ampthill, co. Beds.	33 Hen. VIII.
358	Do. Manors of Ampthill, co. Beds., and Viellston and Kingdon, co. Devon.	6 Jas. I.
359	Surveys of the Manors of Arreton and W ellow, in the I. of Wight.	,,
360	Surveys of the Manors of Aylsham and Wymondham, co. Norfolk.	19 Jas. I.
361	Surveys of the Commandery of Balsall, co. Warwick, and Book of Sale relating to Suppressed Monasteries in Herts.	32 Hen. VIII.
362	Valors of the Dioceses of Bangor and St. Asaph	27 Hen. VIII.
363	Rental of Gorley, co. Hants, and Ministers' Accounts of Beaulieu.	32 Hen. VIII.
364	Survey of Beaumanor, co. Leicester, and arrears of Ministers' Accounts.	33 Hen. VIII.
365	Survey of the Manor and Honor of Berkhampstead, co. Berks.	5 Jas. I.
366	Survey of the Honor of Berkhampstead, co. Berks.	14 Jas. I.
367	Rentals of Berkhampstead Manor, co. Berks	32 Hen. VIII. & 1 & 2 Ph. & Mary.
368	Survey of Bowcombe, in the I. of Wight, and Valor of the possessions of Lady Elizabeth Warner in the County of Kent.	6 Jas. I. & 4 Eliz.
369	Surveys of the Manors of Brampton, co. Hants, Barnsley, co. York, and of the Borough of Wallingford, co. Berks.	29 Hen. VIII., & 4 & 6 Jas. I.
370	Rentals of Crown Lands in the Counties of Cornwall, Somerset, Gloucester, and Wilts.	34 Hen. VIII. to 20 Chas. I.

MISCELLANEOUS BOOKS—(continued).

Exchequer, Augmentation Office—(continued).

Vol.

Surveys, Rentals, &c., as follows (*cont.*) :—

371	Survey of Calais and the Marches - -	2 & 3 Ph. & Mary.
372	Do. do.	"
373	Surveys and Rentals of divers Priories in Carnarvon, Radnor, Beds, and Middx., with some Ministers' Accounts.	1 Edw. VI.
374	Rentals of divers Chantries in Worcestershire -	"
375	Valors of Colleges, Chantries, &c., in Sussex -	"
376	Valors of possessions of the Priories of Carlisle and Wetheral in Cumberland, Westmoreland, and Northumberland.	31 Hen. VIII.
377	Rental of Queen Catherine's possessions in England.	28 Chas. II.
378	Rental and Survey of the Priory of Chalcombe, co. Northampton.	Temp. Edw. III
379	Survey of the Manor of Cheltenham, co. Gloucester.	2 Jas. I.
380	Surveys of the Manors of Drakelow, Rudheath, Shuttington, Alvecote, Spalding, and Crowland, in the cos. of Chester, Warwick, and Lincoln.	6 Chas. I.
381	Rentals of South Clifton, Coddington, Winthorpe, Newark, Besthorpe, Gretton, and Balderton, in co. Notts.	Temp. Eliz.
382	Rentals, Valors, &c., relating to Holme Cultram and other Religious Houses in Cumberland, Northumberland, and York.	Temp. Hen. VIII.
383	Valor of the possessions of Thomas Earl of Derby, with declaration of Receiver's Accounts.	15 Hen. VIII.
384	Surveys of the Marquess of Exeter's Lands, co. Devon, and of the Manor of Stanwell, co. Middlesex, with divers Ministers' Accounts.	Temp. Hen. VII. & Hen. VIII.
385	Rentals of the possessions of Cecilia, Marchioness of Dorset, in Cornwall, Devon, Somerset, Dorset, and Wilts.	15 to 17 Hen. VIII.
386	Rental of the Manor of Dungemarsh belonging to Battle Abbey.	Temp. Hen. V.
387	Survey of the Manor of Emneth, co. Norfolk -	5 Jas. I.
388	Surveys of the Manors of Ewelme, co. Oxford, Freshwater, co. Southampton, and Carnanton, co. Cornwall.	6 Jas. I.
389	Rentals, &c., of Gillingham and other places in Kent;	18 Hen. VIII.
	Surveys of Barrow and other places in Lincolnshire.	9 Chas. I.
390	Valors of the Bishopric of Exeter (2 Hen. VII.), and of the possessions assigned to the Bishopric of Bristol, &c.	Temp. Hen. VIII.
391	Survey of the County of Hertford - -	3 & 4 Ph. & Mary.
392	Valor of the Deanery of Higham, co. Norfolk -	26 Hen. VIII.
393	Survey of Lord Hussey's Lands in Lincoln, Rutland, and Hunts.	29 Hen. VIII.
394	Surveys of the Manors of Kingswood and Bisley, in the cos. of Gloucester and Wilts.	2 & 6 Jas. I.
395	Surveys of Moulton Harrington, co. Lincoln, and of the Town of Southampton.	5 Jas. I.
	Survey of the possessions held by William, Lord Howard, in right of his wife.	32 Hen. VIII.
396	Survey of Woodsales in Lichfield Forest, co. Rutland, and	5 Edw. VI.
	Survey of the Manors of Shefford and Campton (Camelton), co. Beds.	3 Jas. I.

MISCELLANEOUS BOOKS—(continued),
Exchequer, Augmentation Office—(continued).

Vol.	Surveys, Rentals, &c., as follows (cont.):—	
397	Surveys of Monasteries called "Paper Surveys," Bucks to London.	Temp. Hen. VIII.
398	Do. do. Monmouth to Wilts.	„
399	Do. do. Bucks to Notts.	„
400	Do. do. Salop to Wilts.	„
401	Do. do. York.	„
402	Do. do. Beds to Wales.	„
403	Do. do. Northants and Leic.	„
404	Do. do. Warwick.	„
405	Rentals of Dore, co. Hereford, Missendon, co. Bucks, Fotheringhay, co. Northampton, and Sawtry, co. Hunts, with Memoranda relating to Monasteries in Cumberland, Westmorland, Northumberland, and York.	„
406	Surveys of Monasteries called "Paper Surveys," Berks to Warwick.	„
407	Rental and Terrier of the Lordships of Oye and Marke, near Calais.	22 Edw. IV.
408	Rentals and Surveys of monasteries, Chester to Warwick.	Hen. VII. & Hen. VIII.
409	Rentals and Surveys (various) -	„
410	Do. do.	„
411	Title to Sapperton and other Lands belonging to Sir Henry Pool.	18 Jas. I.
412	List of Incumbents of Rectories, &c., belonging to the Collegiate Church of St. Mary, Southwell, co. Notts, with amount of stipends.	18 Hen. VIII.
413	Surveys and Rentals (various) -	Edw. VI. & Jas. I.
414	Survey of the manor of Stockton, co. Norfolk -	5 Jas. I.
415	Valor of Lands assigned by the King to Churches and Colleges in Oxford and Cambridge, and other Miscellaneous Papers.	Hen. VIII. to Edw. VI.
416	Rentals of Calstock and other manors in Cornwall.	3 & 4 Ph. & Mary.
417	Survey of Crown Lands in Glamorgan -	1 & 2 Ph. & Mary.
418	Valor of Sir John Russell's Lands -	Temp. Hen. VIII.
419	Surveys and Rentals (various) -	Hen. VIII. to Jas. I.
420	Surveys of the possessions of Glastonbury Abbey, co. Somerset, and of divers Monasteries in co. Wilts.	31 to 32 Hen. VIII.
421	Surveys of the Manors of Thorley, Ugaton, and Niton, in the Isle of Wight.	6 Jas. I.
422	Rental of Thornbury, co. Gloucester -	17 Hen. VII.
	Surveys of Ashton Keynes, co. Wilts, and Rosedale, co. York.	Temp. Jas. I.
423	Valors of Monasteries, &c. in Wales -	Temp. Hen. VIII.
424	Survey of Walsingham Parva, co. Norfolk -	„ „
425	Survey of the Manor of Westham, Essex -	3 Jas. I.
426	Valor of the possessions of the Cathedral Church of Westminster in divers Counties.	Temp. Hen. VIII.
427	Accounts and Miscellaneous Papers relating to Whalley and other Monasteries.	„ „
428	Views of Accounts (various) -	Temp. Edw. VI.
429	Surveys of Woods in divers Counties -	Hen. VIII.–Eliz.
430	Do. do. -	„ „
431	Surveys of Woods in Devon and Cornwall -	3 Edw. VI.

MISCELLANEOUS BOOKS—(continued).
Exchequer, Augmentation Office—(continued).

Vol.	Surveys, Rentals, &c., as follows (*cont.*):—	
432	Rentals of Wrington, co. Somerset, and Accounts	33–36 Hen. VIII.
433	Survey and Rental of Wye, co. Kent - -	Temp. Hen. VI.
434	Do. do.	,,
435	Notes of divers Rents belonging to Syon Abbey	Temp. Edw. IV.
436	Proceedings in the Court of Augmentations between the Abbess of Syon and the Mayor of Rye, relating to Gateborough Marsh, co. Sussex.	Temp. Hen. VIII.
437	Accounts of the King's Treasurer in France -	Temp. Edw. III.
438	Do. do.	,,
439	Account Book of Sir Edward Cavendish, Treasurer of the King's Chamber.	2 Edw. VI.
— 440	Survey of the University of Cambridge - -	37 Hen. VIII.
— 441	Survey of the University of Oxford - - -	,,
442	Views of Ministers' Accounts in the Counties of Southampton, Wilts, and Gloucester.	31 Hen. VIII.
443	Views of Ministers' Accounts in the County of York.	32 Hen. VIII.
444	Views of Ministers' Accounts in the County of Gloucester.	32–34 Hen. VIII.
445	Views of Accounts of the Monastery of Tewkesbury and others, co. Gloucester.	35 to 37 Hen. VIII.
446	Views of Accounts of the Monastery of Romsey and others, in Gloucester and Wilts.	Hen. VIII.
447	Views of Accounts of the Monastery of Cirencester, co. Gloucester.	,,
448	Views of Accounts of Gower Land and other Lands in Wales.	,,
449	Views of Accounts of the Monastery of Jarvaux and Bridlington, &c., co. York.	,,
450	Views of Accounts of the Priory of Kington, &c., co. Wilts.	,,
451	Views of Accounts of Colleges and Chantries in the County of Notts.	5 Edw. VI.
452	Views of Accounts of the possessions of Monasteries in the County of Gloucester.	Edw. VI.
453	Views of Accounts of the possessions of Monasteries in the Counties of Wilts and Chester.	—
454	Views of Accounts of the possessions of Monasteries in the Counties of Lincoln, Notts, Derby and Chester.	10 Jas. I.
455	Wardrobe Accounts - - - -	28 Hen. VIII.
456	Do. - - - - -	31 Hen. VIII.
457	Woods, Accounts of Sales of, &c. - -	35 Hen. VIII.
458	Do. do. - -	Hen. VIII. to Eliz.
459	Do. do. - -	Hen. VIII. to Ph. & Mary.
460	Do. do. - -	,,
461	Do. do. - - -	Edw. VI.
462	Woods, Certificates of - - -	Ph. & Mary.
463	Miscellaneous Accounts, &c. - - -	28 to 36 Hen. VIII.
464	Certificates of Musters, co. Berks - -	Hen. VIII.
465	Prest Money, Account of, co. Berks.	—
466	Certificates of Musters, co. Norfolk - -	,,
467	Customs Accounts, London - - -	3 Jas. I.
468	Channel Islands, Accounts relating to the. (A Transcript).	—
469	Will of King Henry VIII., Transcript of the.	—
470	Declaration of the Revenue of the Queen (Anne of Denmark).	13 Jas. I.
471	Accounts relating to various Guilds and Chantries in Lichfield, co. Stafford, and to the repairs of houses, &c., belonging to the same.	Temp. Ph. & Mary.

MISCELLANEOUS BOOKS—(continued).
Exchequer, Augmentation Office—(continued).

Vol.				
472	Miscellaneous Letters and Papers - - -	Hen. VIII.
473	Do. do. - - -	,,
474	Do. do. - - -	,,
475	Do. do. - - -	,,
476	Do. do. - - -	,,
477	Do. do. - - -	,,
478	Do. do. - - -	,,
479	Do. do. - - -	,,
480	Do. do. - - -	,,
481	Various Accounts and Orders of Committees during the Commonwealth.	—
482	Transcripts from the Close Rolls - - -	1 Hen. VII.
483	Transcripts of Letters of Administration from the Registers of the Court of Probate.	Temp. Commonwealth.
484	Account of Fees paid in the Courts of King's Bench and Common Pleas.	—
485	Customs Accounts, Newcastle-on-Tyne - -	40 Eliz.
486	Papers relating to Earl Rivers - - -	Temp. Edw. IV.
487	A Collection of Original Writs and Returns in the Exchequer.	Temp. Edw. III.
488	Rentals of the Manor of Wye, &c., co. Kent - -	9 Edw. III.
489	Valuation of the Bishopric of Hereford with Transcripts of Deeds, &c.	Temp. Edw. III.
490	Regulæ Monachorum (a collection of Monastic Rules and Regulations).	—
491	Ministers' Accounts, Rentals, &c., of Sotwell, and other places in Oxfordshire.	Temp. Hen. VIII.
492	Statutes, &c. of Warwick College.	—
493	Final Concords, &c. in the Court of the Abbot of Battle at Wye, co. Kent.	Temp. Edw. III.
494	Valuations and Inventories of dissolved Monasteries in Southampton, Wilts, Cambridge, and Gloucester.	Temp. Hen. VIII.
495	Church Goods, Inventories of, Cambridge -	Edw. VI.
496	Do. do. Oxon and Derby -	,,
497	Do. do. Herts - - -	,,
498	Do. do. Middlesex - -	,,
499	Do. do. Norfolk - - -	,,
500	Do. do. do. - - -	,,
501	Do. do. do. - - -	,,
502	Do. do. do. - - -	,,
503	Do. do. do. - - -	,,
504	Do. do. do. - - -	,,
505	Do. do. do. - - -	,,
506	Do. do. Norwich - -	,,
507	Do. do. Lincoln and Notts -	,,
508	Do. do. Stafford - - -	,,
509	Do. do. Suffolk - - -	,,
510	Do. do. Suffolk - - -	,,
511	Do. do. Surrey - - -	,,
512	Do. do. Surrey - - -	,,
513	Do. do. Warwick - -	,,
514	Do. do. Wilts - - -	,,
515	Do. do. York, E.R. - -	,,

MISCELLANEOUS ROLLS, &c. (CHANCERY).

This is a collection of Rolls and Bundles formerly preserved in the Tower of London, and frequently referred to as the "Tower Miscellaneous Rolls," a brief Inventory of which is printed in the Deputy Keepers 2nd and 3rd

Q

MISCELLANEOUS ROLLS, &c.—(continued.)

Reports. Several Bundles containing original Letters Patent, Petitions, and Writs of Privy Seal have been removed from this series and added to their proper classes. The remainder have been classified as far as possible under the subjects to which they relate, as shown below, and are described in detail in the present volume under the Titles indicated. A List of the unclassified Rolls and additional documents, comprising Bundles 16 to 21, is appended.

Bundle.		
1	ARMY AND NAVY ACCOUNTS - See ARMY AND NAVY.	Edward I. to Edward IV.
2	CHANNEL ISLANDS DOCUMENTS - See CHANNEL ISLANDS.	Edward I. to Elizabeth.
3	DEEDS (ANCIENT) TRANSCRIPTS OF, and DEEDS OF PARTITION. See DEEDS (ANCIENT).	Henry III. to Edward VI.
4	ECCLESIASTICAL DOCUMENTS - See ECCLESIASTICAL MATTERS.	Edward I. to Commonwealth.
5	FRANCE, DOCUMENTS RELATING TO - See FRANCE.	Edward I. to Henry VIII.
6	GRANTS OF MARKETS AND FAIRS - See MARKETS AND FAIRS.	John to Henry VI.
7	HOMAGE ROLLS - - - See SCOTLAND.	19 to 24 Edward I.
8	KNIGHTS' FEES, INQUISITIONS AND ROLLS OF. See FEUDAL TENURES.	Henry III. to Henry IV.
9	MARSHALSEY OF THE ARMY, ROLLS OF THE See ARMY AND NAVY.	Edward I. and Edward II.
10	PROCEEDINGS IN THE COURT OF CHIVALRY See JUDICIAL PROCEEDINGS.	9 to 22 Richard II.
11	SCUTAGE ROLLS - - - See ARMY AND NAVY.	John to Edward III.
12	SEWERS, PROCEEDINGS BEFORE COMMISSIONERS OF. See SEWERS.	Edward II. to Henry VI.
13	SPECIAL COMMISSIONS, EXTENTS, AND INQUISITIONS. See RENTALS AND SURVEYS.	Richard II. to Henry VIII.
14	TREATIES AND DIPLOMATIC DOCUMENTS - See TREATIES.	Henry III. to Henry VII.
15	WARDROBE AND HOUSEHOLD ACCOUNTS - See WARDROBE AND HOUSEHOLD.	John to Elizabeth.

MISCELLANEOUS ROLLS (UNCLASSIFIED), as follows:—

Bundle 16.		
No. 1 -	A composition made between the Archbishop of Canterbury and Gilbert de Clare respecting the services to be rendered by the latter for certain Lands, &c., held by him from the said Archbishop.	42 Hen. III.
No. 2 -	A Roll of Grants of the Lands, &c., of the rebels.	50 Hen. III.
No. 3 -	Accounts of the purchase of Silver for the mint.	50-55 Hen. III.
No. 4 -	An Account of repairs, &c., at Woodstock -	3 Edw. I.
No. 5 -	A Schedule of the Debts owing to the Jews at Colchester.	4 Edw. I.
No. 6 -	A Schedule of the Debts owing to the Jews at York.	,,
No. 7 -	Accounts of Works, &c., at certain of the Royal Palaces.	,,

MISCELLANEOUS ROLLS, &c.—(continued).

MISCELLANEOUS ROLLS (UNCLASSIFIED), &c.—(continued).

Bundle 16.

No. 8	-	Enrolments of Warrants to divers Merchants for the exportation of wool.	5-6 Edw. I.
No. 9	-	Writs "de custodia commissa" of the Royal Castles and Manors.	9, 10 Edw. I.
No. 10	-	A Roll of Grants of the Houses which belonged to the Jews in England.	19, 20 Edw. I.
No. 11	-	Exemplification of a Plea in the King's Bench between the Prior of Tynmouth and the Burgesses of Newcastle on-Tyne.	20 Edw. I.
No. 12	-	An Account of Works, &c., at the Palace of the Archbishop of York in London.	25 Edw. I.
No. 13	-	A Roll of Letters Patent relating to Loans by Foreign Merchants.	26 Edw. I.
No. 14	-	A Roll of Letters Obligatory made by certain Abbots to divers Merchants.	„
No. 15	-	An Account of Debts due from the King to divers Merchants for goods purchased.	31-33 Edw. I.
No. 16	-	Enrolment of Special Pleadings at Bury St. Edmunds concerning matters in dispute between the Abbot and the Burgesses.	33 Edw. I.
No. 17	-	Extracts from Domesday Book of the Lands of Gilbert de Gand in various Counties.	Temp. Edw. I.
No. 18	-	Particulars of the Sales made by Order of the King of the Houses forfeited by the condemned Jews.	„
No. 19	-	An Extract from Domesday Book of the Terra Regis in Derbyshire.	„
No. 20	-	Enrolment of Writs for Trials at the Great Assize.	1-20 Edw. II.
No. 21	-	Exemplification of a Plea relating to the Inheritance of John de Walrond with Transcripts of the Inquisitions taken on her death.	3 Edw. II.
No. 22	-	Writs of Resumption of the Grants made by the King.	3, 5 Edw. II.
No. 23	-	A List of the sums owing to the Ecclesiastics of the County of York for Grain and Cattle supplied to the King.	4 Edw. II.
No. 24	-	Memoranda relating to the delivery of the Great Seal to Adam de Osgodby.	5 Edw. II.
No. 25	-	A Roll of presentments before the "Custodes Pacis" of the County of Somerset.	7 Edw. II.

Bundle 17.

No. 1	-	Writs of "exigi facias" directed to the Justices of Trailbaston in Com. Essex.	9 Edw. II.
No. 2	-	The record, &c. of the Judgment pronounced on the Mortimers by the Justices thereto assigned.	16 Edw. II.
No. 3	-	A File of Writs relating to the dissolution of the Knights Templars.	17 Edw. II.
No. 4	-	The record, &c. of the sentence on the Adherents of Thomas Earl of Lancaster.	18 Edw. II.
No. 5	-	A List of the Royal Castles in England and Wales, with the names of the Constables of those in England.	Temp. Edw. II.
No. 6	-	A List of the Collectors and Controllers of Customs in various ports, &c., compiled from the Rolls of the Exchequer.	„
No. 7	-	A Writ and Inquisition relating to the Goods and Debts of the Society of the Scala of Florence.	1 Edw. III.
No. 8	-	An Inquisition relating to the repair of Hethbeche Bridge, co. Notts.	„

Q 2

MISCELLANEOUS ROLLS, &c.—(continued).

MISCELLANEOUS ROLLS (UNCLASSIFIED), &c.—(continued).

Bundle 17.

No. 9	A Compendium or Epitome of the Statutes of Edward III.	1–36 Edw. III.
No. 10	Transcript of " Placita de Quo Warranto " relating to the Wapentake of Newark, co. Notts.	3 Edw. III.
No. 11	Memoranda of Rolls delivered out of and received into the Chancery.	4–10 Edw. III.
No. 12	A Roll of Grants, &c., made by Queen Philippa.	,,
No. 13	A " Passage Roll " - - - -	14–15 Edw. III.
No. 14	A Roll of Writs " de warantia dierum " -	15–30 Edw. III.
No. 15	The Tenor of Proceedings between the King and John, son of Edmund late Earl of Kent, concerning the Farm of the Town of Ailesbury.	22 Edw. III.
No. 16	The Tenor of the Indictments, &c. against John Fermour, knight, at Chelmsford.	25 Edw. III.
No. 17	The Tenor of the Indictments, &c. against John FitzWalter at Chelmsford.	,,
No. 18	Extracts from the Pipe Rolls of the Allowances, &c. made to the Knights Templars and the Brethren of St. John of Jerusalem, returned into Chancery by Writ of Certiorari.	26 Edw. III.
No. 19	A Transcript of Proceedings in the Exchequer relating to the Town of Berwick on Tweed.	28 Edw. III.
No. 20	An Extract from Domesday Book relating to the Lands of the Church of Hertford.	29 Edw. III.
No. 21	A Transcript of the Will of Johanna, widow of William de Hanampstede of London.	43 Edw. III.
No. 22	An Account of the whole revenue of the Prince of Wales.	47–49 Edw. III.
No. 23	A Transcript of Proceedings before the King's Justices in Ireland relating to the Advowson of the Church of Ardeath.	49 Edw. III.
No. 24	An Account of the wages of carpenters, &c. employed in re-building a mill.	Temp. Edw. III.
No. 25	An Account of the wrongs inflicted on William de Malkeney by ships of the Bishop of Winchester.	,,

Bundle 18.

No. 1	Proceedings between John le Bret and Nicholas de Baukwell relating to the Manor of Williamthorp, &c.	Temp. Edw. III.
No. 2	Proceedings before the Council on the claim of the Earl of Warwick to franchises in Gowerland with a Roll of evidences relating thereto.	,,
No. 3	A Roll containing a recital of the proceedings against the Despensers, with an Account of the Ceremony to be observed at the Coronation of the New King.	1 Edw. III.
No. 4	A long Roll of Depositions of Witnesses relating to the Jurisdiction of the Castle and Lordship of Curte.	Temp. Edw. III.
No. 5	A " Passage Roll " - - - -	1 & 2 Rich. II.
No. 6	An Indenture between William de Burstall Keeper of the Rolls of the Chancery, and his successor, witnessing the delivery of the Records.	5 Rich. II.
No. 7	An Assessment on the Burgesses of Bury St. Edmund of a Fine of 2,000 marks imposed on them for certain Transgressions.	11 Rich. II.

MISCELLANEOUS ROLLS, &c.—(continued).

MISCELLANEOUS ROLLS (UNCLASSIFIED), &c.—(continued).

Bundle 18.

No. 8	-	A Roll of the names of the Clergy and Laity in the County of Essex who took the Oath against annulling any of the Statutes passed in the then present Parliament.	11 Rich. II.
No. 9	-	Transcript of a Plea of Debt before one of the sheriffs of London (Forde v. Lomelyn and others).	19 Rich. II.
No. 10	-	Transcript of Proceedings in the Court of Admiralty between John Sampson, of Plymouth, and John Curteys, of Lostwithiel.	15 Rich. II.
No. 11	-	Transcript of Proceedings in the Court of Admiralty between John Gernesey and John Henton, of Bridgwater.	5 Hen. IV.
No. 12	-	Transcripts of Documents relating to Ireland	Temp. Hen. IV.
No. 13	-	Appointments of Mayors and Constables of the Staple.	1–10 Hen. VI.
No 14	-	A List of the Creditors of John late Duke of Norfolk, with the sums owing to them.	10 Hen. VI.
No. 15	-	The Tenor of Proceedings in the Exchequer relating to the possessions of Gilbert de Gaunt in the County of Lincoln.	13 Hen. VI.
No. 16	-	A roll of proceedings on a Traverse of Office for John le Scrop of Masham.	16 Hen. VI.
No. 17	-	Transcript of proceedings in the Exchequer relating to Wool taken by the King's enemies from certain merchants of Boston.	20 Hen. VI.
No. 18	-	A Copy of Certain Articles which the Earl of Somerset prays to have exemplified under the Great Seal, with the King's Answers thereto.	21 Hen. VI.
No. 19	-	A Roll consisting of a Petition and Sign Manual Warrant for a Grant of Certain Liberties to St. Mary's College, Cambridge.	22 Hen. VI.
No. 20	-	A Roll of Evidences relating to an enfeoffment to Thomas Tropenall and his heirs by Robert Hurdall of lands in Chikkelade and Hyndon, co. Wilts.	33 Hen. VI.
No. 21	-	Agreement between the Chancellor and Scholars of the University of Oxford and the Mayor and Burgesses of the same town, with Proceedings before the Council on matters in dispute between them.	18 Edw. I.
No. 22	-	The tenor of Proceedings before the Council between the Prior of Coventry and Queen Isabella.	10 Edw. III.
No. 23	-	Petition to Parliament of the Provost and Scholars of the College of St. Mary and St. Nicholas, Cambridge, with draft of Letters Patent annexed. [*Printed in " Rot. Parl." Vol. V., pp. 87–103.*]	23 Hen. VI.
No. 24	-	Petition to Parliament of the Town of Shrewsbury, with Schedule annexed. [*Printed in " Rot. Parl." Vol. V., pp. 121–127.*]	,,
No. 25	-	Petition to Parliament for a confirmation of Privileges to Eton College, with draft of Letters Patent annexed. [*Printed in " Rot. Parl." Vol. V., pp. 75–87.*]	,,

MISCELLANEOUS ROLLS, &c.—(continued).

MISCELLANEOUS ROLLS (UNCLASSIFIED), &c.—(continued).

Bundle 19.

No. 1	An Account of the "Wrongs and Losses sustained by Richard Southall at the hands of Sir John Huddlestone."	34 Hen. VI.
No. 2	Memoranda of Escheats and Outlaws	35-37 Hen. VI.
No. 3	The Petition of Ralph, Lord Cromwell, Treasurer of England.	Temp. Hen. VI.
No. 4	The Pedigree of Lord Fitzhugh	"
No. 5	The Pardon of Humphrey, Duke of Gloucester, and Eleanor, his wife.	"
No. 6	Lists of the Clergy and Laity in the Counties of Notts and Berks who had taken the oath directed by the King's Writ.	"
No. 7	A Roll containing Regulations for the Lords of the Council.	8 Hen. VI.
No. 8	A Writ and Return relating to the Advowson of Bedington, co. Surrey.	15 Edw. IV.
No. 9	A Paper Roll containing Instructions by the Parliament of Ireland to the Commissioners sent by them to entreat succour and relief.	Edw. IV.
No. 10	An Account of the Revenues of the Crown in Ireland.	Temp. Hen. VII.
No. 11	A List of the Manors appointed to the King for the term of his life.	"
No. 12	A Roll of proceedings in the Court of the Bishop of Norwich.	13 Eliz.
No. 13	An Inventory of the Goods, &c., in the Houses of John Sutton in the City of London.	20 Eliz.
No. 14	Proceedings in the Consistory Court of the Bishop of Bath and Wells.	37 Eliz.
No. 15	A Roll of Ordinances for the King's Council	1-3 Hen. VI.
No. 16	A Transcript of Proceedings in the Exchequer relating to certain ships belonging to Merchants of Newcastle-on-Tyne taken by the King's enemies.	29 Hen. VI.
No. 17	A Roll of Writs to Collectors of Subsidies for the delivery of a fifteenth to the Merchants of Lucca.	4 Edw. I.
No. 18	Appointments of Collectors of a thirtieth granted in aid of the Welsh War.	11 Edw. I.
No. 19	A Transcript of the Taxation of the Abbot of Woburn towards the Clerical Subsidy.	11 Edw. III.
No. 20	A List of Persons appointed throughout the Kingdom to Collect a Subsidy in Wool, &c.	14 Edw. III.
No. 21	Appointments of the Collectors of a Subsidy	3 Hen. IV.
No. 22	Memorandum as to the delivery of certain Records to the Keeper of the Rolls of Chancery.	2 Hen. IV.
No. 23	Names of Sheriffs and Escheators who have found security before the Barons of the Exchequer.	Temp. Hen. VI.
No. 24	List of Persons in the County of Dorset taking the oath to support the establishment of the King's succession.	26 Hen. VIII.
No. 25	Account of Michael Locke of the expenses of the voyage of Martin Frobisher to the "Meta Incognita," certified into Chancery by Writ.	26 Eliz.

Bundle 20.

No. 1	Portion of a roll of payments out of the Great Wardrobe.	43 Hen. III.
No. 2	Roll of wages of Sergeants at Arms	12 Edw. I.

MISCELLANEOUS ROLLS, &c.—(continued).

MISCELLANEOUS ROLLS (UNCLASSIFIED), &c.—(continued).

Bundle 20.

No. 3	-	Claims for allowances on their account by the Peruchi.	Temp. Edw. III.
No. 4	-	Debts claimed by the Merchants of the Scala of Florence.	Temp. Edw. III.
No. 5	-	Claims for allowances on their Account by the Bardi.	Temp. Edw. III.
No. 6	-	Expenses on behalf of a messenger of the King of Arragon.	Temp. Edw. I.
No. 7	-	Fragment of Account of Expenses of the Abbot of Welbeck and other Envoys to Norway.	Temp. Edw. I.
No. 8	-	Expenses of Francesco d'Accorso in going to the Parliament of Paris.	3 Edw. I.
No. 9	-	Fragment of an Account of Wages of masons, carpenters, and other workmen.	Temp. Hen. III.
No. 10	-	Charter Party of the ship "Saint Yves," of St. Malo.	30 Hen. VI.
No. 11	-	Note of Account between the officers of the Staple at Calais and John Felde.	Temp. Hen. VI.
No. 12	-	Fragment of an Account of the expenses of Messengers and other Payments out of the Wardrobe.	Temp. Edw. IV.
No. 13	-	Document relating to the Debts of Peter Passapayre, dated at Bordeaux.	44 Edw. III.
No. 14	-	Fragment of an Account of various Receipts and Payments for Matters in Gascony.	18 Edw. III.
No. 15	-	Draft of an Indenture appointing John Donati of Florence and others Master and Officers of the Mint.	30 Edw. III.
No. 16	-	Accounts of Mariners' Wages paid at Sandwich.	21 Edw. III.
No. 17	-	Return of ships arrested for the King's service.	32 Edw. III.
No. 18	-	Proceedings as to Piracy before Robert de Herle, Admiral of the Fleet.	35 Edw. III.
No. 19	-	Memorandum as to the shipment of certain Provisions at Boston to be taken to Sluys.	25 Edw. I.
No. 20	-	Bond for good behaviour by the Captains of certain ships of Bayonne.	11 Edw. III.
No. 21	-	A Collection of Warrants for various payments addressed to the Treasurer at War.	10 Hen. V.
No. 22	-	Portions of Returns to Commissions of Array in several Counties.	Edw. I. to Edw. III.
No. 23	-	Commission of Array and Return thereto for the Duchy of Lancaster.	33 Edw. III.
No. 24	-	Valuation of Victuals for the purposes of the expedition to Scotland.	3 Edw. II.
No. 25	-	Memorandum as to Victuals for the Navy -	Temp. Edw. III.

Bundle 21.

No. 1	-	A file of Writs of Scutage - - -	14 Hen. III.
No. 2	-	A file of Miscellaneous Memoranda formerly incorporated with the Parliamentary Petitions and Royal Letters.	—
No. 3	-	A file of documents relating to the will of Drew Barentyn, Citizen and Alderman of London.	—
No. 4	-	An Account of fines for respite of Knight-service.	6 Edw. I.
No. 5	-	A file of Writs of Summons to attend the marriage of Eleanor, the King's daughter.	21 Edw. I.
No. 6	-	A file of documents relating to ships and mariners.	Edw. I. to Edw. III.

MISCELLANEOUS ROLLS, &c.—(continued).

MISCELLANEOUS ROLLS (UNCLASSIFIED), &c.—(continued).

Bundle 21.

No. 7	-	A file of documents relating to Commissions of Array and Musters.	Edw. I. to Edw. III.
No. 8	-	A file of documents relating to landowners who ought to take up Knighthood.	Edw. I. to Ric. II.
No. 9	-	A file of Writs summoning men at arms to Portsmouth, &c.	20 Edw. III.

MONASTIC FOUNDATIONS, &c.

Under the general name of Monastic Foundations may be included those Cathedral and Collegiate Churches, Abbeys, Priories, Colleges, Hospitals, Friaries, and other ecclesiastical bodies which were suppressed at different times by authority of Parliament.

The *Monastic Cathedral Churches* were those in which the Bishop held the place of Abbot, the greater part of which were reconstituted subsequent to the dissolution of the Religious Houses by Henry VIII.

The *Collegiate Churches* and *Colleges* consisted of a number of Secular Clergy, living under the government of a Dean, Warden, Provost, or Master, and having for the more solemn performance of divine service, Chaplains, Singing men, and Choristers belonging to them.

The *Abbeys* were societies of Religious Persons, presided over by an Abbot or Abbess, some of which were so considerable that their Abbots were summoned to Parliament as Peers of the Realm, and wore Mitres, having many of the attributes of a Bishop within the limits of their respective Houses.

The *Priories* were similar societies to the Abbeys, ruled, instead of by an Abbot, by a Prior or Prioress, who in the Abbeys were only subordinate officers. They were of two kinds: *Firstly*, those in which the Prior held full sway as entirely as if he were an Abbot and was chosen by the convent, as the Cathedral Priors and most of those of the Austin Order. *Secondly*, such as were Cells, subordinate to some great Abbey by whose Abbot the Prior was placed and displaced at will. Some of these were altogether subject to their respective Abbeys, who sent them what officers and monks they pleased, taking their revenues into the common stock of the Abbey; others consisting of a stated number of monks who had a Prior sent them from the Abbey, and paid a yearly pension as an acknowledgment of their subjection, but acted in other matters as an independent body, and had the rest of their revenues for their own use.

Alien Priories were such as were Cells to foreign Monasteries, by whom they were established to collect and administer the revenues of such manors &c. as they held

MONASTIC FOUNDATIONS, &c.—(continued).

in this country. These also were of two kinds, some being conventual, that is to say, having Priors of their own choosing, and paying only the ancient "apport" to the foreign house, whilst others were entirely dependent on the foreign houses, to whom they returned all their revenues. For this reason their estates were generally seized during the wars between England and France, being restored to them on the conclusion of peace.

Hospitals were houses established by royal patents for the relief of poor and impotent people, and were capable of receiving gifts and grants in perpetuity. There were generally two or three Ecclesiastics attached to each Hospital, one as Master or Prior, and the others as Chaplains or Confessors.

Friaries were houses erected for the occupation of Friars, who, being by profession Mendicants, were supposed to have no property, and their houses were seldom endowed. The accounts of their possessions, therefore, show little more than the sites of their respective Houses, with the adjacent gardens, &c.

Chantries were endowments of lands or other revenues for the maintenance of one or more priests to say daily mass for the souls of the founder and his relations and benefactors, sometimes at a particular altar, and often in little chapels added to cathedral and other churches for that purpose.

Free Chapels were places of religious worship, exempt from all jurisdiction of the Ordinary, some of which having been originally built upon the manors and ancient demesnes of the Crown for the use of the King and his retinue, had been granted away together with such estates, retaining their original freedom from jurisdiction; others again having again been built and endowed by private persons with the special license of the Crown.

Preceptories were small communities of Knights Templars established in various parts of the country under the government of the so-called "Præceptores Templi," for the management and administration of their estates, being in fact Cells to the principal house in London.

Commanderies were similar institutions belonging to the Knights Hospitallers, or Knights of St. John of Jerusalem.

The first of these religious foundations to undergo the process of confiscation, to which by their ever-increasing revenues they were all eventually doomed, was that of the Knights Templars, who, on the suppression of that Order by Clement V., were distributed into several convents, their possessions being transferred to the rival Order of St. John of Jerusalem.

MONASTIC FOUNDATIONS, &c.—(continued).

The Alien Priories, the revenues of which, as has already been mentioned, were generally seized into the King's hands on the breaking out of a war, were the next to fall, an Act of Parliament being passed in the second year of Henry V., by which they were entirely suppressed, and their possessions confiscated to the King's use. With the revenues of these Priories several Colleges were subsequently almost entirely endowed, as that of All Souls, in Oxford, founded by Archbishop Chicheley in 1437, and Eton College, and King's College, Cambridge, founded by Henry VI. about 1441.

In 1497 the Bishop of Ely, with the King's consent, suppressed St. Rhadegund's nunnery in Cambridge, and with the revenues thereof founded Jesus College.

In 1505 Margaret, Countess of Richmond and Derby, founded Christ's College, Cambridge, and obtained the Pope's license to suppress the Abbey of Creyke, in Norfolk, and to settle its revenues on that College, and similar suppressions of the smaller monasteries for the purpose of endowing seats of learning were of not unfrequent occurrence prior to the reign of Henry VIII.

In April 1524, Cardinal Wolsey, being desirous of founding two Colleges, viz., one at Ipswich (his birthplace), and one at Oxford, and " finding, that there were " several mean monasteries in England in which both " the revenues and the number of the religious were " two small to keep up regular discipline, church ser-" vice, and hospitality," obtained a bull from Pope Clement VII. for suppressing the Priory of St. Frideswide, in Oxford; and another in September of the same year, for the suppression of as many small monasteries as were needed to raise a revenue not exceeding 3,000 ducats per annum.

In June 1525, the royal consent was obtained thereto, and Commissioners appointed to carry the suppression into effect. In 1528 and 1529 several other bulls were granted for similar purposes, and thus the way may be considered to have been paved towards a general dissolution.

On the casting off of the Papal Supremacy by Henry the Eighth, although the Religious Houses generally subscribed to an acknowledgment of the sovereign as the supreme head of the church, but little faith was placed in the sincerity of their allegiance, and the King being evidently resolved on their destruction, had little difficulty in finding suitable pretexts. In the 27th year of his reign, an Act was passed for the dissolution of all the Religious Houses whose incomes were less than 200l. a year, the loose and vicious lives of the monks and nuns in the smaller houses, and the misapplication of their revenues

MONASTIC FOUNDATIONS, &c.—(continued).

(as appeared by the visitations thereof made), being alleged as reasons for breaking them up and transferring their occupants to the greater monasteries, "in which, " thanks be to God, religion is right well observed and " kept up," their revenues, however, being applied to the King's use.

By this Act, about 380 houses were dissolved and a revenue of about 30,000l. per annum accrued to the royal Exchequer, besides 100,000l. in plate and jewels.

By another Act passed in the same reign, a new Court was established, called the "Court of the Augmentations of the Revenues of the Crown," under the survey of which the revenues of all the dissolved Monasteries were placed, together with all lands, &c. acquired by the Crown by purchase or exchange.

The suppression of these houses occasioned great discontent, and in 1536 a rebellion broke out in Lincolnshire headed by Doctor Makerel, the Prior of Barlings, who, styling himself "Captain Cobler," drew after him a great body of men, who were, however, soon dispersed and compelled to lay down their arms. Another and much more formidable insurrection broke out in Yorkshire, called the "Pilgrimage of Grace," on the termination of which the King resolved on the suppression of the rest of the Monasteries, and a new visitation thereof was appointed in 1537. This caused the greater Abbeys to be surrendered apace, many of them, having been implicated in the late rebellion, hoping by the voluntary surrender of their houses to save their lives.

Eventually, although there was no law compelling the Abbeys and Convents to surrender, they were almost all wrought upon to do so, and by an Act passed in the 31st year of the King's reign, all the Religious Houses, which since the passing of the former Act had been suppressed, forfeited, or given up, or should be so hereafter, were confirmed to the King and his successors, with all their rents, profits, and revenues, which were placed under the survey of the Court of Augmentations, with the exception of those attainted of treason, the revenues of which were accounted for at the Court of Exchequer.

In consequence of this Act, all the Abbots were prevailed upon to surrender, except those of Colchester, Glastonbury, and Reading, who could not be induced to do so, and were therefore accused of high treason, and executed, and their Abbeys forfeited by attainder.

The next year a bill was brought in for suppressing the Knights of St. John of Jerusalem, and thus the revenues of all the greater houses passed into the hands of the

MONASTIC FOUNDATIONS, &c.—(continued).

King, amounting to above 100,000l. per annum, including a large sum in plate and jewels.

The religious persons occupying these houses had, however, almost all of them something given them for their present subsistence, and pensions were assigned to them either for life or till they could be preferred to some other cure or dignity. The amount of these pensions was very considerable. Out of the revenues that came to his hands, however, the King managed to found six new Bishoprics, the Colleges of Christ Church, Oxford, and Holy Trinity, Cambridge, with Professorships of Divinity, Law, Physics, &c., in both Universities, besides laying out great sums of money in building and fortifying many Ports in the channel.

In 1545 further supplies were necessary for the maintenance of the wars with France and Scotland, and an Act was passed which, after reciting that the possessions of the Colleges, Chantries, Free Chapels, Guilds, &c., had been misapplied in various ways, and that in many cases not only the founders and donors thereof but other persons pretending to be such, and in some cases the priests or wardens themselves, had entered upon their lands, &c., and converted the profits thereof to their own use, declared that where such fraudulent practices had taken place the Chantries were thereby dissolved and their possessions forfeited to the King; and by direction of the same Act Commissioners were appointed to inquire into and make Certificates of the names of the various Chantries and their founders, the value of their lands, &c., and to take Inventories of their jewels, plate, and ornaments.

Few of the Chantries were disturbed, however, till the first year of Edward VI., when another Act was passed, by which all Chantries, &c. existing at any time within the five years preceding the date of the Act, and not already in the hands of the late or present King, were declared to belong to the Crown with all their lands and revenues, Commissioners being again appointed to make Certificate into the Court of Augmentations of all manors, lands, &c. belonging to the same, which were to be placed under the control of that Court and their revenues to be converted to the King's use. This was done accordingly, and these institutions were destroyed to the number of 90 colleges, 110 hospitals, and 2,374 chantries and free chapels.

A very elaborate account of the Monastic Foundations throughout England and Wales, with Transcripts of the Deeds of Foundation and of other Charters and Grants relating thereto, is contained in Dugdale's "Monasticon Anglicanum" which also contains Accounts of their possessions extracted from the Ministers' Accounts and from

MONASTIC FOUNDATIONS, &c.—(continued).

the Valor Ecclesiasticus; and copious references to Records from which similar information may be obtained, and also to the grants of the Sites of the several Religious Houses made at the time of the dissolution will be found in Tanner's "Notitia Monastica."

The following classes of documents illustrate this subject :—

ACKNOWLEDGMENTS OF SUPREMACY. (EXCHEQUER, TREASURY OF THE RECEIPT.)

These are the original Acknowledgments made by the several Religious Houses, &c., having in most cases the Conventual Seals attached, and bearing the signatures of the Abbots, Priors, and others.

Descriptive Inventory. Report VII., App. II., pp. 279–306.

ALIEN PRIORIES, &c., EXTENTS OF. (EXCHEQUER, Q. R.) 22 Edw. I. to 22 Edw. IV.

These consist of Extents and Inquisitions relating to the possessions of the Alien Religious Houses in England, and also of laymen who were foreign subjects. The Ministers' Accounts of such possessions have been added to the General Series of Ministers' Accounts, Henry III. to Richard III., and are set out at length in the Inventory of Ministers' Accounts. (Lists and Indexes, No. V., 1894.)

AUGMENTATION OFFICE ACCOUNTS (EXCHEQUER, Q.R.) Edward VI.

These consist of Rolls of the Pensions granted to the Incumbents and other ministers of the late dissolved colleges, chantries, &c., and of Commissions and Returns of Monastic Pensions made in the 6th year of Edward VI. See also "TREASURER'S ACCOUNTS."

CARDINAL WOLSEY'S INQUISITIONS. (CHANCERY.) Henry VIII.

Two volumes amongst the Inquisitions Post Mortem (formerly amongst the Miscellaneous Bundles of the Rolls Chapel Office), containing—

(1.) Inquisitions respecting the possessions of the several Monasteries, &c. surrendered to Cardinal Wolsey.
(2.) Inquisitions taken after Wolsey's death by the Commissioners specially appointed for that purpose.

Calendar. 1 Vol. MS.

MONASTIC FOUNDATIONS &c.—(continued).

CARDINAL WOLSEY'S INQUISITIONS, &c.—(continued).

The following is a List of the Religious Houses respecting which Inquisitions were taken:—

The Monasteries or Priories of—

Begham, co. Kent.
Blackmore, co. Essex.
Bradwell, co. Bucks.
Bromehill, co. Norfolk.
Canwell, co. Stafford.
Calceto, co. Sussex.
Daventree, co. Northampton
Dodness, co. Suffolk
St. Frideswide, co. Oxon.
Lesnes, co. Kent
Pray, co. Hertf.
St. Peter's, Ipswich, co. Suff.
Poghley, co. Berks.
Rumburgh, co. Suff.
Ravenston, co. Bucks.
Sandewall, co. Stafford.
Snape, co. Suff.
Tiptree, co. Essex.
Tonbridge, co. Kent.
Thoby, co. Essex.
Tykford, co. Bucks.
Wallingford, co. Berks.
Walton, co. Suff.
Wykes, co. Essex.

CARDINAL'S COLLEGES, DOCUMENTS RELATING TO.

Accounts, &c. relating to Cardinal's Colleges.
[*Misc. Books Exch. Tr. of Receipt, Vols.* 102, 103, and 104.]

Transcripts of Grants to Cardinal's Colleges, &c.
[*Do., Vol.* 105.]

Statutes of Cardinal's College.   [*Do., Vol.* 106.]

Terrier of Manors belonging to Cardinal's Colleges.
[*Do., Vol.* 163.]

Rental of the possessions of Cardinal's College, Oxford.
[*Do., Vol.* 164.]

Surrenders and Annexations to Cardinal's College. (Exchequer, Tr. of Receipt.) 4 Cases.

Wolsey's Patents. (Exchequer, Tr. of Receipt.) The original Grants by Cardinal Wolsey to the Colleges at Oxford and Ipswich of the possessions of the several Monasteries surrendered to him for their endowment and other documents connected therewith. 23 Boxes.

Abstracts of these are contained in the "Calendar of Letters and Papers, Henry VIII."

MONASTIC FOUNDATIONS, &c.—(continued).

CHARTULARIES.

The Monastic Chartularies were Registers kept by the several Religious Houses, in which were entered the Deeds and Charters from their various benefactors; Rentals and Surveys of their estates; Papal Letters and Bulls; and occasionally contemporary Chronicles of Events.

A great number of Chartularies remain in the hands of private individuals, or are scattered amongst the several Public Libraries, and of these a very complete List is printed in the "Collectanea Topographica." The following are deposited in the Public Record Office:—

Acornbury, Priory of.
> [*Misc. Books, Augmentation Office*, Vol. 55.]

Barlings, Abbey of.
> [*Misc. Books, Exch. Tr. of Receipt, Vol.* 71.]

Battle Abbey.
> [*Misc. Books, Augmentation Office, Vol.* 56.]

Burscough, Priory of St. Nicholas.
> [*Duchy of Lanc. Records, Div. XI., No.,* 6.]

Bury St. Edmund's, Abbey of.
> [Do.,   *No.* 5.]

Canterbury, Mon. of St. Augustine's.
> [*Misc. Books (Exch. Q.R.), Vol.* 27.]

Chertsey, Abbey of.
> [*Do.,*   *Vol.* 25.]

Coventry, Priory of.
> [*Do.,*   *Vol.* 21.]

Furness, Monastery of.
> [*Duchy of Lanc. Records, Div. XI., No.* 3.]

Gloucester, Abbey of St. Peter's.*
> [*Amongst the Records of the Court of Chancery.*]

Do.   Original Charters relating to the.   1 Box.
> [*Ibid.*]

Godstow, Nunnery of.
> [*Misc. Books (Exch. Q.R.), Vol.* 20.]

Kirkstall, Abbey of.
> [*Duchy of Lanc. Records, Div. XI., No.* 7.]

Langdon, Abbey of.
> [*Misc. Books, (Exch. Q. R.), Vol.* 29.]

Malmesbury, Abbey of.*
> [*Do.,*   *Vol.* 24.]

Newstead, Priory of.
> [*Do.,*   *Vol* 23.]

Oseney, Abbey of.
> [*Do.,*   *Vol.* 26.]

---

* Printed in the series of "Chronicles and Memorials, &c."

MONASTIC FOUNDATIONS, &c.—(continued).

CHARTULARIES—(continued).

Pershore, Abbey of.
[*Misc. Books, Augmentation Office, Vol* 61.]
Ramsey, Abbey of.*
[*Misc. Books (Exch., Q. R.), Vol.* 28.]
Selby, Abbey of.
[*Duchy of Lanc. Records, Div. XI., No.* 8.]
Torre, Abbey of.
[*Misc. Books (Exch., Q. R.), Vol.* 19.]
Warwick, College of St. Mary and Priory of.
[*Do., Vol.* 22.]
Warwick, College of St. Mary, Accounts, &c. of.
[*Misc. Books, Augmentation Office, Vol.* 64.]
Worcester, Cathedral Church of.
[*Do., Vol.* 63.]

COLLEGES AND CHANTRIES.

Certificates of Colleges and Chantries. (Augmentation Office.) Hen. VIII. and Edw. VI.

These consist chiefly of the Returns of the Commissioners appointed under the Act of 1 Edward VI. to inquire into the possessions of all Colleges, Hospitals, Chantries, Free Chapels, &c., the objects for which they were founded, the date of their foundation, names of the founders, and yearly value thereof. There are a few Returns only under the Act of 37 Hen. VIII. Others will be found amongst the Misc. Rolls, &c., Chancery, (Bundle 13) having been returned to that Court by virtue of Special Commissions.
Calendar. 1 Vol. MS.

Particulars for the Sale of Colleges and Chantries. (Augmentation Office.) Hen. VIII. and Edw. VI.

These are entered in two volumes amongst the Miscellaneous Books of the Augmentation Office. (Nos. 67 and 68.)
Calendar and Index Locorum. 1 Vol. MS.

Particulars for Grants relating to Colleges and Chantries. Edward VI. 2 Vols., with an *Index.*
[*Misc. Books, Exchequer, Tr. of the Receipt, Vol.* 258, 259, *and* 2 60.

Certificates of Colleges and Chantries in the County of Lancaster. Edward VI.
[*Duchy of Lanc. Records, Div. XVIII., No.* 26.
Do. in the County of Lincoln.
[*Do., No.* 25.]

MONASTIC FOUNDATIONS, &c.—(continued).

COLLEGES AND CHANTRIES—(continued).

Auditors' Particulars of lands belonging to Chantries in Lancashire, Yorkshire, and other Counties. Henry VIII. and Edw. VI.

[*Duchy of Lancaster Records, Div. XXV., Bundle U.*]

Certificates of Colleges, Chantries, and Guilds in the City of London. (Land Revenue Office.) Henry VIII. These are still in the Land Revenue Record Office, and consist of Certificates as to the Foundations and Endowments of Colleges, Chantries, Hospitals, &c., and also of the endowments of the different Crafts or Companies of the City of London.

Indentures of Foundation of Henry VII.'s Chapel at Westminster. (Exchequer, Treasury of the Receipt.) Two volumes magnificently bound in red velvet.

Transcripts of Charters, &c. relating to the Chantry of the Blessed Mary in St. Dunstan's in the West. 49 Edw. III.

[*Misc. Rolls, &c. (Chancery), No. $\frac{3}{15}$.*]

Transcripts of Charters, &c. relating to the Hospital of St. Bartholomew, near Oxford. John to Edw. I.

[*Do., No. $\frac{3}{25}$.*]

Inquisition, &c. concerning the state of the King's Free Chapel in the Castle of Hastings. 12 Edw. II.

[*Do., No. $\frac{4}{25}$.*]

Petition, &c. concerning Liberties granted to the College of St. Mary and St. Nicholas, Cambridge. 22 Henry VI.

[*Do., Nos. $\frac{18}{19}$ and $\frac{18}{23}$.*]

Petition &c., concerning a Confirmation of Liberties to Eton College. 23 Hen. VI.

[*Do., No. $\frac{18}{23}$.*]

A Roll relating to the Jurisdiction of the Bishop of Chichester in the King's Free Chapel at Hastings. Temp. Henry VI.

[*Do., No. $\frac{4}{24}$.*]

Foundation and Statutes of the College of Pleshey, co. Essex.

[*Duchy of Lancaster Records, Div. XXV., B. 10.*]

The following documents relating to Colleges and Chantries are amongst the Miscellaneous Books of the Exchequer, Treasury of the Receipt :—

Vol. 109. Documents relating to Christ Church College, Oxford. Hen. VIII.

Vol. 110. Ordinances relating to a Chantry in the Chapel of Allhallows, Barking. Edw. IV.

Vol. 111. Ordinances of St. George's Chapel, Windsor.

Vol. 112. Instructions as to the foundation of a Chantry at Campesey, in Suffolk.

Vol. 113. Documents relating to St George's Chapel, Windsor.

MONASTIC FOUNDATIONS, &c.—(continued).

COLLEGES AND CHANTRIES—(continued).

The following are amongst the Miscellaneous Books of the Augmentation Office:

Sacristan's Account of the College of Fotheringay, co. Northampton, &c. [*Vol.* 145.]

Accounts of the Master of Fotheringay College. [*Vol.* 146.]

Statutes of Fotheringay College. [*Vol.* 147.]

Indentures of Foundation of a Chapel, &c. at West Braynford. co. Midd. 21 Hen. VIII. [*Vol.* 148.]

Foundation and Statutes of a Chantry at Chalgrave, co. Oxon. 10 Hen. IV. [*Vol.* 149.]

Foundation of a Chantry at Chiddingstone, co. Kent. 9 Hen. VIII. [*Vol.* 150.]

Inquisitions and Presentments as to Chantry Lands in the County of Northampton. Temp. Elizabeth. [*Vol.* 168.]

A similar volume for the County of Lancaster. (Hundreds of Amounderness and Leylond.) [*Vol.* 170.]

Statutes of Warwick College. [*Vol.* 492.]

Many deeds relating to the foundation and endowment of Colleges and Chantries will be found amongst the " Cartæ Miscellaneæ " of the Augmentation Office and in other series of " ANCIENT DEEDS," &c.

See **DEEDS (ANCIENT)**.

CONVENTUAL LEASES. See **LEASES**.

HOUSEHOLD ACCOUNTS OF MONASTERIES, &c.

A great number of these, such as the Cellarers' Accounts, Sacristans' Accounts, Treasurers' Accounts, and so forth, will be found in the series of Ministers' Accounts of which they form a distinct branch. Such accounts are, however, frequently attached to the general Account of the Revenues of the Monastery. (*See* Lists and Indexes, No. V., 1894.)

The following are amongst the Miscellaneous Books of the Treasury of the Receipt:—

Vol. 107. Household Accounts of the Abbot of Ramsey. 21 Hen. VII. to 24 Hen. VIII.

Vol. 108. Do. of Holy Trinity Priory, London. 5-6 Hen. VIII.

KNIGHTS TEMPLARS, POSSESSIONS OF THE.

Inquisition concerning the possessions of the Knights Templars, taken by Geoffrey Fitz-Stephen, the Master of that Order, in 1185. [*Misc. Books, Exch., Q. R., Vol.* 16.]

Rolls of Accounts of the Templars' Lands. Temp. Edw. II. (Exchequer, L. T. R.) Three large Rolls.

Repertory. 1 Roll.

Writs relating to the dissolution of the Knights Templars and the seizure of their possessions. 17 Edw. II.

[*Misc. Rolls, &c., Chancery, No.* $\frac{4}{3}$.]

Extracts from the Pipe Rolls relating to allowances made to the Brethren of the Temple and of St. John of Jerusalem. 26 Edw. III.

[*Do* No. $\frac{17}{18}$.]

MONASTIC FOUNDATIONS, &c.—(continued).

LEASES AND PENSIONS.

Enrolments of Leases and Pensions. (Augmentation Office.) Henry VIII. to James I. 49 Vols.
Index. Report XLIX., App., pp. 209–360.
Books of Payment of Pensions. 37 Hen. VIII. to 1 Mary. 14 Vols. These contain accounts of the payment of pensions to "dyvers, being late religious persons," specifying their names, the Houses to which they respectively belonged, and the amounts paid to each.
[*Misc. Books (Augmentation Office), Vols.* 248 *to* 262.]
Warrants for Pensions. 28 Hen. VIII.

A volume containing original Warrants or Letters Patent for the payment of pensions to the Abbots, Priors, &c. of the dissolved Monasteries.
[*Misc. Books (Augmentation Office), Vol.* 244.]*
Do. Edward VI.

A similar volume containing Warrants for pensions to the Incumbents of the late Colleges and Chantries, &c.
[*Do., Vol.* 247.]*
Cardinal Pole's Certificate of Pensions. 2 & 3 Philip and Mary. A Certificate or Return, taken by virtue of an Indenture dated 24th Feb. 2 & 3 Philip and Mary, between the King and Queen of the one part and Cardinal Pole as Papal Legate of the other part, of all Fees, Annuities, Corrodies, or Pensions payable to Religious Persons throughout England and Wales.
[*Misc. Books (Exch. Q. R.), Vol.* 31.]
See also "AUGMENTATION OFFICE ACCOUNTS," "SUPPRESSION PAPERS," and "TREASURERS ACCOUNTS."

PENSIONS. See LEASES AND PENSIONS.

POSSESSIONS OF MONASTERIES, &c., ACCOUNTS OF THE (both prior and subsequent to the dissolution). See **MINISTERS' ACCOUNTS, &c.**

POSSESSIONS OF THE DISSOLVED MONASTERIES, &c., PARTICULARS FOR GRANTS OF THE. See **CHARTERS AND GRANTS.**

SUPPRESSION OF THE MONASTERIES, &c.

"Suppression Papers." (Exchequer Q. R.) Henry VIII
These consist of Views of Accounts of the possessions of Religious Houses in various Counties, with Accounts of the Pensions assigned to the Monks, Nuns, and Servants of the said Houses, &c., &c.
Descriptive Slips. 1 Vol. MS.

---

* Indexed in the Deputy Keeper's 49th Report.

MONASTIC FOUNDATIONS, &c.—(continued).

SUPPRESSION OF THE MONASTERIES, &c.—(continued).

Commission and Instructions to ascertain the value of Ecclesiastical Possessions. 26 Hen. VIII.

[*Misc. Books (Exch., Tr. of the Receipt), Vol.* 114.]

Dockets of the Submissions of the Monasteries and Abstracts of the Inventories of their possessions. 30 Hen. VIII.

[*Do.,*   *Vol.* 115.]

Instructions, &c. as to the Suppression of Monasteries.

[*Do.,*   *Vol.* 116.]

Inventories of the Goods of Friaries in various Counties. Temp. Hen. VIII.

[*Do.,*   *Vol.* 154.]

Do.   of Monasteries in various Counties.   Temp. Hen. VIII.

[*Do.,*   *Vol.* 155.]

Do.   &c. of Monasteries in the Counties of Southampton, Wilts, and Gloucester.   31 Hen. VIII.

[*Misc. Books (Augmentation Office) Vol.* 494.]

Do.   in the Counties of Warwick, Stafford, &c.

[*Do.,*   *Vol.* 172.]

Memoranda of Monasteries surrendered to Cardinal Wolsey.

[*Misc. Books (Exch., Tr. of the Receipt), Vol.* 117.]

A great number of documents relating to the Suppression of the Religious Houses will also be found amongst the "Letters and Papers," Henry VIII., calendared in the Series of "Calendars of State Papers."

SURRENDERS OF MONASTERIES. (AUGMENTATION OFFICE.) Henry VIII. 1 Case.

These are the original Deeds of Surrender, attested by the autograph signatures of the Abbots, Priors, and others, with, in most instances, the conventual seal attached.

Descriptive Catalogue. Report VIII., App. II., pp. 1-51.

See also CARDINAL'S COLLEGES.

The Deeds of Surrender are also enrolled on the Close Rolls.

SURVEYS AND RENTALS of the possessions of the dissolved Monasteries, &c.

See **RENTALS AND SURVEYS.**

TREASURER'S ACCOUNTS OF THE COURT OF AUGMENTATIONS. 28 Hen. VIII. to 1 Mary. 10 Rolls.

These contain an Account of all moneys received or paid by the Treasurer of the Court of Augmentations, specifying the Amounts received from the Particular Receivers of the revenues of the dissolved Monasteries, &c. through-

MONASTIC FOUNDATIONS, &c.—(continued).

TREASURER'S ACCOUNTS OF THE COURT OF AUGMENTA-
TIONS—(continued).

out England and Wales, with the sums produced by the
sale of their Jewels, Plate, and Ornaments; the Fines or
Compositions received for the Toleration or Continuance
of certain Houses; and the various sums received by Sales
of Lands, &c., with an exact description of the premises
sold, the name of the purchaser, and date of purchase, &c.

The payments comprise the Fees and Wages of
Officers of the Court, Annuities to Royal and other personages, Pensions to the Abbots, Priors, and others of the
dissolved Monasteries, and payments of various kinds made
by Warrant of the Chancellor of the Court of Augmentations or otherwise.

Inventory. Report XXI., p. 12.

VALUATIONS OF THE RELIGIOUS HOUSES &c.

The "Valor Ecclesiasticus" of 27 Henry VIII. gives a
Survey or Valuation of the possessions and revenues of all
the Religious Houses and Foundations throughout England and Wales.

See **ECCLESIASTICAL MATTERS.**

VISITATIONS OF HOSPITALS AND OTHER FOUNDATIONS.

Visitation of the Hospital of St. Leonard, Derby.
1 Edw. III. [*Misc. Rolls, &c. (Chancery), No.* $\frac{4}{18}$.]
Visitation of the King's Chapel in the Castle of Hastings.
19 Edw. III. [*Do.,* *No.* $\frac{4}{17}$.]
Visitation of the Hospital of St. Leonard, York. 39
Edw. III. [*Do.,* *No.* $\frac{4}{20}$.]
Visitation of the Hospital of St. Mary Bethlem, London.
4 Hen. IV. [*Do.,* *No.* $\frac{4}{21}$.]

NOMINA VILLARUM.

The documents known as "Nomina Villarum" consist
of the Returns to Writs issued in the ninth year of Edward II. to all the Sheriffs throughout England, directing
them to certify to the Exchequer the number of Hundreds
and Wapentakes within their respective Bailiwicks, what
Cities, Boroughs, and Townships there were within each
of such Hundreds or Wapentakes, and who were the
Lords thereof. These were required in relation to the
Military Levies granted in the Parliament at Lincoln in
9 Edward II., when it was directed that one man-at-arms
should be raised from every Township. The original
Returns were made on Rolls, a few of which are still
extant amongst the Records of the Lord Treasurer's
Remembrancer, as specified below.

NOMINA VILLARUM—(continued).

In the first year of Henry VII. it was noticed that these Rolls or Returns, being almost in daily use, had become so blind and frayed that they could scarcely be read or understood, and it was therefore ordered that they should be forthwith transcribed in a book to remain for ever in the Exchequer. This was done accordingly, as appears by the Memoranda Roll of Hilary, 1 Henry VII., but the volume thus framed has long since disappeared. A later Transcript of this volume, in the handwriting of Sir Henry Ellis, is, however, preserved amongst the Series of Transcripts made for the Record Commission, and other copies, more or less imperfect, exist amongst the Harleian MSS. and elsewhere.

These Transcripts, together with some of the original Returns, have been used in the compilation of the Returns printed in Palgrave's Parliamentary Writs, &c. Vol. II., Div. 3, pp. 297–416.

The original Rolls of Nomina Villarum hitherto found are eight in number representing the Counties of Beds and Bucks, Devon, Lincoln, Middlesex, Notts. and Derby, Salop and Stafford, Southampton, and Warwick respectively, the latter having been recently discovered.

[*Misc. Rolls, Exchequer, L. T. R. Bundle 2.*]

There are also amongst the records of the Queen's Remembrancer's Department five volumes called "Nomina Villarum," containing Certificates made to the Barons of the Exchequer by the Bailiffs of Liberties in various Counties of the names of the Towns, Hamlets, &c. within their respective Liberties with relation to the claims by the Lords thereof to Estreats, Felons' Goods, &c.

These volumes bear date in the reign of Charles II.

OATHS OF ALLEGIANCE, &c.

The Oaths of Allegiance and Supremacy, and also the Sacrament of the Lord's Supper, were by several Statutes and Ordinances enacted against Papists and Non-conformists directed to be taken by all persons holding offices, civil or military. The chief of these statutes were :—

(1.) The *Corporation Act* of 13 Car. II., by which no person could be legally elected to any office relating to the government of any City or Corporation unless within one year before accepting such office he had received the Sacrament of the Lord's Supper according to the rites of the Church of England, being at the same time enjoined to take the Oaths of Allegiance and Supremacy.

OATHS OF ALLEGIANCE, &c.—(continued).

(2.) The *Test Act*, 25 Car. II., Cap. II., by which all officers, civil and military, and persons having places of trust under his Majesty were directed to take the oath and make the declaration against transubstantiation in the Court of King's Bench or Chancery, and within six months after their admission to receive the Sacrament of the Lord's Supper in some public church, and to deliver into Court a Certificate thereof signed by the Minister and Churchwardens.

(3.) The " *Solemn Association* " entered into in 7 & 8 Will. III. by which the Parliament bound itself to defend his Majesty's person and Government against all plots and conspiracies, all persons bearing offices, civil or military, being enjoined to subscribe the Association to stand by King William under certain forfeitures and penalties.

The Oaths subscribed by Attorneys and Solicitors and by the Officers of the several Courts of Law are referred to under the heads of " Attorneys and Solicitors " and " Offices and Appointments " respectively.

OATH ROLLS. (CHANCERY.)

There are three sets of Oath Rolls which were transferred from the Petty Bag Office, viz.:—

1. Oaths of Allegiance and Test Oaths. Charles II. to Victoria. 36 Rolls, being the Original Oaths to which the signatures of the jurors were affixed.

2. Enrolments of Oaths. Charles II. to Anne. 7 Rolls. These include a Roll containing the names of all the officers and men in his Majesty's Fleet who had taken the Oaths of Allegiance and Supremacy. 12 Car. II.

3. Association Oath Rolls. 8 William III. These were subscribed by all persons bearing offices, pursuant to the " Solemn Association " entered into by the Parliament of William III. to defend his Majesty's person and Government against all plots and conspiracies. They are exceedingly voluminous, comprising upwards of 473 Rolls, and including all the Members of the House of Commons, the Freemen of all the City Companies, the Military and Civil Officers of the Crown, and the Clergy and Gentry throughout England and Wales.

OATHS OF ALLEGIANCE. (EXCHEQUER, QUEEN'S REMEMBRANCER.) Geo. I. to Geo. IV. 1 Portfolio.

OATHS OF ALLEGIANCE, &c.—(continued).

OATH ROLLS OR "SWEARING ROLLS." (QUEEN'S BENCH, CROWN SIDE.)   1673 to 1858.

Four Bags, containing Oath Rolls of various kinds, as Oaths of Allegiance, Sacrament and Test Oaths, Association Oath Rolls, temp. William III., and Oath Rolls of Naturalization from 1 to 12 Anne.

OATHS OF ALLEGIANCE, &c. (STATE PAPER OFFICE.)

A Collection of Original Instruments of Association for the defence of Queen Elizabeth, dated 19 Oct. 1584, and signed by various members of the Privy Council, by the dignified clergy of the Provinces of York and Canterbury, and by the gentry and principal persons of various counties and towns.

[S. P. Dom., Eliz., Vol. 174.]

SACRAMENT CERTIFICATES. (CHANCERY.)   1673 to 1789.

These are the Certificates, signed by the Minister and Churchwarden of each Parish, of such persons as had received the Sacrament of the Lord's Supper pursuant to the Test Act of 25 Charles II.

Do.   (QUEEN'S BENCH, CROWN SIDE.) 1676 to 1828.   10 Bags.

OFFICES AND APPOINTMENTS.

Chancery.

Grants of Offices of various kinds are enrolled on the PATENT ROLLS and may be referred to by means of the ordinary Calendars. A collection of references to Grants of Offices from Ric. III. to Car. II., arranged under Counties, is contained in "Palmer's Indexes," Vols. 108 and 109, and similar collections from Henry VIII. to Car. II. are contained in Vols. 136 and 137, in the first of these the entries being classified according to the nature of the offices. [See also Vols. 36, 57, 63, and 110.]

Surrenders of Offices are enrolled on the CLOSE ROLLS, on the SURRENDER ROLLS, and on the SPECIFICATION AND SURRENDER ROLLS.

There is a Bundle of Certificates of Surrenders of Offices amongst the Certificates (Various) from the Petty Bag Office.   See CERTIFICATES.

Special Commissions to inquire into Forfeitures of Offices. 5 Charles I. to 4 William IV. See COMMISSIONS.

ESCHEATORS AND CUSTOMERS.

The appointment of Escheators and also of the Searchers and other officers of the Customs are enrolled on the "FINE ROLLS" till the reign of Charles I., when that series became extinct; afterwards on the Patent Rolls, and subsequent

OFFICES AND APPOINTMENTS—(continued).
Chancery—(continued).
ESCHEATORS AND CUSTOMERS—(continued).

to the year 1725 on the "BISHOPS' PATENT ROLLS," which, in addition to the Appointments of Bishops, contained those of the Escheators and also of "Customers."

There are also amongst the Records transferred from the Petty Bag Office Bundles entitled "CUSTOMERS' PATENTS," containing the original Patents or Privy Seal Bills for such appointments from George I. to George III.

JUSTICES OF THE PEACE. Commissions of the Peace are enrolled on the back of the Patent Rolls.

The Commissions of the Peace of later dates are preserved at the Chancery Crown Office.

Writs of Dedimus Potestatem to swear Justices of the Peace, and also the Masters Extraordinary in Chancery, are amongst the "BREVIA REGIA" from the Petty Bag Office.

Lists of Justices of the Peace of various dates are also to be found amongst the Domestic State Papers, under the title "Liber Pacis."

LORDS LIEUTENANT OF COUNTIES.

The Commissions appointing Lords Lieutenant of Counties are enrolled on the back of the Patent Rolls and entered in the Index to those Rolls under the head of "Commissions." See also the volumes entitled "Liber Pacis" amongst the Domestic State Papers.

MASTERS EXTRAORDINARY IN CHANCERY.

Writs of Dedimus Potestatem to swear Masters Extraordinary are amongst the "BREVIA REGIA" from the Petty Bag Office.

OFFICERS OF THE COURT OF CHANCERY, ADMISSION ROLLS OF. 40 Eliz. to the present time (from the Petty Bag Office).

Index, 1 Vol. MS.

Orders for the payment of Salaries to the Masters and other Officers are entered in the Registrar's Entry Books of Decrees and Orders, and indexed under the title "Suitors' Fee Fund."

SHERIFFS.

The appointments of Sheriffs are entered on the Fine Rolls.

Sheriffs' Rolls (from the Petty Bag Office). 36 Henry VIII. to 16 Charles I. These consist of the enrolments of the Lists of persons proposed as Sheriffs, showing which names were duly pricked. Similar Rolls amongst the Miscellaneous Rolls of the Court of Chancery have been added to this Series.

OFFICES AND APPOINTMENTS—(continued).
Chancery(continued).
SHERIFFS—(continued).
Sheriffs' Rolls (from the Six Clerks' Office). 1700 to 1848.
100 Rolls.

There are amongst the Records of the Lord Treasurer's
Remembrancer four volumes called "Sheriffs' Books"
containing the names of the Sheriffs throughout England
from 1735 to 1832.

A complete List of all the Sheriffs of England from the
earliest period to the reign of William IV., extracted from
the Pipe Rolls and other sources has been completed and
will shortly be issued in the series of Lists and Indexes.

Exchequer, Queen's Remembrancer.
The appointments of Officers in the Queen's Remem-
brancer's Department are enrolled on the Memoranda
Rolls.

The Oaths of several Officers of the Exchequer are
entered in the Red Book and also in the Black Book of
the Exchequer.

There are also amongst the Records of the Queen's
Remembrancer two Rolls containing the Names of the
Barons of the Exchequer from 8 Edw. II. to 27 Eliz., and
of the *Treasurers of the Exchequer* from 6 Edw. II. to
14 Eliz.

Exchequer, Lord Treasurer's Remembrancer.
Presentations and Admissions of Officers are entered on
the Memoranda Rolls.
SHERIFFS' BOOKS. 1735 to 1832.
Four volumes, containing the names of the Sheriffs
throughout England.
ROLLS OF THE NAMES OF SHERIFFS, BAILIFFS, AND OTHER ACCOUNTANTS AT THE EXCHEQUER. 11 Henry VIII. and 31 Henry VIII.
[*Misc. Rolls, Nos. $\frac{2}{13}$ and $\frac{2}{14}$.*]

Exchequer, Augmentation Office.
GRANTS OF OFFICES. 33 Elizabeth to 19 Charles I. and 9 to 11 Wm. III.
Nine Volumes, entitled "Stewardships," containing enrolments of Grants of the Offices of Seneschals, Bailiffs
and Collectors of Rents, &c.
[*Misc. Books, Vols. 318 to 326.*]
PARTICULARS FOR GRANTS OF OFFICES. Henry VIII.
Two Volumes containing Particulars relating to the
granting of the Office of Bailiff or Collector of the Rents
of Lordships and Manors in various counties.
[*Misc. Books, Vols. 157 and 158.*]

OFFICES AND APPOINTMENTS—(continued).

Exchequer, Augmentation Office—(continued).

PARTICULARS FOR GRANTS OF OFFICES, &c.—(continued).

Elizabeth to Charles I. 3 Vols.

[*Misc. Books, Vols.* 309 *to* 311.]

Henry VIII. to Charles II. 22 Packages.

Exchequer of Receipt.

The Appointments of Officers are enrolled in the PATENT BOOKS and PRIVY SEAL BOOKS of the Pell Office.

Accounts of payments to Judges, Officers of the Court, Commissioners of the Treasury, the Chancellor of the Exchequer, the Auditor, Clerk of the Pells, the Tellers, and other Officers will be found in the "POSTING BOOKS." See **RECEIPTS AND ISSUES OF THE EXCHEQUER.**

Index to Appointments and Offices. Eliz. to 1827. 2 Vols.

These contain references to the Registrations of Grants of Offices and Appointments in the Patent Books and Rolls of the Auditor's Office. Vol. 1 is arranged alphabetically under the names of the *Persons;* Vol. 2 under the names of the several *Offices or Appointments.*

Domestic State Papers.

A BOOK OF ALL THE OFFICES UNDER THE CROWN, with the amount of salaries, fees, and allowances attached to each; comprising Officers of the Courts of Revenue; Officers and Ministers of Justice; Officers in the various Departments of the Household; Keepers of the Royal Castles, Parks, and Forests; and Keepers of Forts and Garrisons in various Counties, &c., &c., the whole amounting to 84,428*l.* 2*s.* 5*d.* About 1588.

[*S. P. Dom., Eliz., Vol.* 221.]

"LIBER PACIS." 1577.

A Book containing the names of the Council in the North and of the Commissioners of Oyer and Terminer there; of the Council in the Principality of Wales; of the Judges on the Circuits; and of the Justices of the Peace in all the Counties in England and Wales.

[*S. P. Dom., Eliz., Vol.* 121.]

"LIBER PACIS." 1580.

A similar volume. [*S. P. Dom., Eliz., Vol.* 145.]

"LIBER PACIS." 1608.

A volume containing Lists of the Justices of Assize and of the Lords Lieutenant and Justices of the Peace throughout England and Wales.

[*S. P. Dom., Jas. I., Vol.* 33.]

OFFICES AND APPOINTMENTS—(continued).

Domestic State Papers—(continued).

"LIBER PACIS." 1632.

A Volume containing the names of all the Justices of the Peace throughout the Kingdom, with a List of the Lords Lieutenant.

[*S. P. Dom., Car. I., Vol.* 212.]

"LIBER PACIS." 1638.

A Book containing a List of all the Justices of the Peace for England and Wales; together with a List of all the able men fit for the wars in the County of Derby as returned in Dec. 1638, the total number being 17,308.

[*S. P. Dom., Car. I., Vol.* 405.]

Note. There is a "Liber Pacis" dated 2 Car. I. amongst "Miscellanea" of the Exchequer, Q. R.

Admiralty, High Court of.

APPOINTMENTS OF VICE-ADMIRALS, &c. are entered in the "Muniment Books" of the High Court of Admiralty, which are preserved at the Admiralty Registry from 1660 to the present time.

Duchy of Lancaster.

The Grants of Offices of early dates are enrolled in the "REGISTERS OF GRANTS, &c." [See **CHARTERS AND GRANTS.**] Those from Henry VII. to 1767 are in the class known as PRIVY SEALS AND BILLS FOR PATENTS OF OFFICES, &c. (Division XII.).

There is an *Index* to Grants of Offices, Annuities, Presentations, Warrants, &c. from Hen. VIII. to 1835 in 1 Vol. MS., entitled "*Index to Patents.*"

Palatinate of Chester.

An Alphabetical List of Officers of the Palatinate of Chester in the counties of Chester and Flint and North Wales from the earliest period to the extinction of the Welsh Judicature, with the dates of Appointment and references to the Records, is printed in the Appendix to the 31st Report, pp. 169–261.

PALMER'S INDEXES.

A collection of private Indexes purchased from the executors of Thos. Palmer, Esq., formerly Chief Clerk of the Record Office at the Rolls Chapel, consisting of Calendars and Indexes to the Patent Rolls, Close Rolls, Inquisitions Post Mortem, and other Records of the Court of Chancery, arranged principally with reference to the names of *Manors* and *Places.*

Vol. 1, A.	Patent Rolls -	Edw. 5. -	A calendar.
	Close Rolls -	19 & 20 Hen. 7.	"Indentures de Suffragiis."
	Charter Rolls -	Ric. 3. to Hen. 8.	A calendar, with Index Locorum.

PALMER'S INDEXES—(continued).

Vol. 1, A.	Patent Rolls -	Ric. 3. - -	A calendar arranged under Counties.
	Do. -	Hen. 7. - -	A calendar of Entails created and Reversions granted by Patent, temp. Hen. 7.
	Do. -	26 to 30 Hen. 8.	A calendar.
Vol. 2, B.	Do. -	Ric. 3. - -	A calendar, with Indexes of Counties, Persons, and Places.
	Close Rolls -	Ric. 3. - -	Do. do.
	Do. -	Hen. 7. - -	Do. do.
	Patent Rolls -	Hen. 7. - -	An *Index Locorum* to the Cal. of Pat. Rolls, temp. Hen. 7. contained in the three following vols.
Vol. 3, C.	Do. -	Hen. 7. and Hen. 8.	A calendar arranged in Counties. [*Bedford* to *Kent*.]
Vol. 4, D.	Do. -	Do. -	Do. [*Lincoln* to *Rutland*.]
Vol. 5, E.	Do. -	Do. -	Do. [*Surrey* to *Westmoreland*.]
Vol. 6, F.	Do. -	Hen. 7. to 14 Eliz., and 23 to 26 Eliz.	A calendar for the county of *York* only.
Vol. 7, G.	Do. -	Hen. 7. to 14 Eliz., and 23 to 26 Eliz.	A calendar for the county of *Essex* only.
Vol. 8, H.	Do. -	Edw. 6. -	A calendar arranged in Counties. [*Anglesea* to *Notts*.]
Vol. 9, I.	Do. -	Do. -	Do. [*Northampton* to *Westmoreland*.]
Vol. 10, K.	Do. -	Phil. & Mar. -	A calendar arranged in Counties. [England, Wales, and Ireland.]
Vol. 11, L.	Do. -	1 to 14 Eliz., and 23 to 26 Eliz.	Do. [All English Counties, except *York* and *Essex*, for which *see* Vols. 6 and 7.]
Vol. 12, M.	Do. -	15 to 22 Eliz. -	A calendar, arranged chronologically, for England and Wales. [Index Locorum in Vol. 153.]
Vol. 13, N.	Do. -	26 to 32 Eliz -	Do. do. [Index Locorum as above.]
Vol. 14, O.	Do. -	33 to 37 Eliz., and 12 & 13 Chas. 2.	Do. do. [Index Locorum as above.]
Vol. 15, P.	Do. -	38 to 45 Eliz. -	Do. do. [Index Locorum in Vols. 30 to 33.]

PALMER'S INDEXES—(continued).

Vol. 16, Q.	Patent Rolls -	1 to 14 Jas. 1. -	A calendar, arranged in Counties. [*Berks* to *Norfolk*.]	
Vol. 17, R.	Do. -	3 to 5 Jas. 1., temp. Chas. 1., and 1655.	A calendar, arranged chronologically [with Memoranda, arranged alphabetically, of Special Grants, Enrolments, Acts of Parliament, &c., &c.].	
Vol. 18, S.	Do. -	6 to 8 Jas. 1. -	A calendar, arranged chronologically. [Index in Vol. 35.]	
Vol. 19, T.	Do. -	9 to 12 Jas. 1. -	Do. do.	
Vol. 20, V.	Do. -	12 to 15 Jas. 1.	A calendar, arranged chronologically. [Index in Vol. 35.]	
Vol. 21, W.	Do. -	16 to 22 Jas. 1.	Do. do.	
Vol. 22, X.	Do. -	1 to 16 Chas. 1.	A calendar, arranged in Counties. [*Berks* to *Kent*.]	
Vol. 23, Y.	Do. -	Do. -	Do. [*Lanc.* to *Wilts*], and also Welsh Counties, America, and West Indies, Channel Islands, &c. The English Counties only are indexed.	
Vol. 24, Z.	Do. -	1 to 14 Chas. 1.	A calendar, arranged chronologically. [This vol. contains a complete calendar of the Ditchfield Grant of 4 Chas. 1.]	
Vol. 25, H.R.	Do. -	Chas.2.to Geo.2.	Abstracts of *Grants, Licences*, &c., with an index to the Counties; also a list of *Charters of Incorporation*, &c., from Chas. 2. to Geo. 2.	
Vol. 26 -	Do. -	1 Mar. to 2 & 3 Phil. & Mar.	Abstracts of Grants, with an *Index Locorum*. [*See also* Vol. 34.]	
Vol. 27 -	Do. -	3 & 4 to 5 & 6 Phil. & Mar.	Abstracts of Grants, &c., arranged chronologically. [Index in Vol. 34.]	
Vol. 28 -	Do. -	1 to 5 Jas. 1. -	Do. [Index in Vol. 34.]	
Vol. 29 -	Do. -	14 to 31 Chas. 2.	Do. [Index in Vols. 30 to 33.]	
Vol. 30 -	Do. -	Hen. 8. to Geo. 2.	*Indices Locorum* [Bedford to Durham] referring to calendars contained in Vols. 3 to 24 inclusive, in " Liber H.R." (Vol.25),and to the Abstracts of Grants in Vol. 29.	

PALMER'S INDEXES—(continued).

Vol. 31 -	Patent Rolls -	Hen. 8. to Geo. 2.	*Indices Locorum* [Essex to Rutland], referring as above.
Vol. 32 -	Do. -	Do. -	*Indices Locorum* [Northampton to Somerset], referring as above.
Vol. 33 -	Do. -	Do. -	*Indices Locorum* [Salop to Westmoreland], referring as above.
Vol. 34 -	Do. -	Hen. 7. to Geo. 2.	*Indices Locorum* [York, &c.]. This Vol. consists of 10 divisions, referring as noted on the fly-leaf of the volume.
Vol. 35 -	Do. -	6 to 22 Jas. 1. -	*Indices Locorum*, arranged in Counties, referring to Vols. 18 to 21.
Vol. 36 -	Do. -	Mary, Phil. & Mary, Eliz.	References to *Grants of Offices, Commissions, Licences, Creations*, and *Incorporations*.
Vol. 37 -	Do. -	22 to 31 Eliz. -	A chronological calendar.
Vol. 38 -	Do. -	Hen. 7. to Will. 3.	A "General Alphabetical Index" to *Charters of Incorporation of Boroughs and Companies, Grants of Privileges, Licences* of various kinds, and other matters of importance selected from the Patent Rolls.
Vol. 39 -	Do. -	Eliz. - -	A calendar arranged alphabetically under Counties, A. to L.
Vol. 40 -	Do. -	Eliz. - -	A calendar arranged alphabetically under Counties, L. to Z.
Vol. 41 -	Do. -	Chas. 2. to Will. 3.	A chronological calendar.
Vol. 42 -	Patent, Close, and Charter Rolls, &c.	Hen. 3. to Edw. 4.	References arranged alphabetically under names of Places, to the Patent, Close, and Charter Rolls, Inq. post mortem, &c., formerly in the Tower of London, Letters A. and B.
Vol. 43 -	Do. -	Do. -	Do. C. to G.
Vol. 44 -	Do. -	Do. -	Do. H. to L.
Vol. 45 -	Do. -	Do. -	Do. M. to R.
Vol. 46 -	Do. -	Do. -	Do. S. to Z.
Vol. 47 -	Do. -	Do. -	An *Index Locorum* to the five preceding volumes.

PALMER'S INDEXES—(continued).

Vol. 48 -	Patent Rolls -	12 & 13 Chas. 2.	References to *Grants of Lands, Offices,* and *Presentations* in England, Wales, &c., arranged in Counties.
Vol. 49 -	Do. -	Edw. 6. -	A calendar, arranged in Counties, from *Anglesea* to *Ebor.*
Vol. 50 -	Do. -	Do. -	Do. *Ebor* to *Notts.*
Vol. 51 -	Do. -	Do. -	Do. *Northampton* to *Southampton.*
Vol. 52 -	Do. -	Do. -	Do. *Anglesea* to *Middlesex.*
Vol. 53 -	Do. -	Do. -	Do. *Norfolk* to *Wilts,* &c. [The earlier portion of this appears to be a copy of the foregoing calendar in vols. 49 to 51.]
Vol. 54 -	Do. -	Phil. & Mar. -	A calendar with an *Index Locorum,* an Index to the *Advowsons* granted, and an Index entitled "*Possessiones,*" giving the names of the owners of the lands, &c., before they came into the hands of the Crown.
Vol. 55 -	Do. -	1 to 25 Eliz. -	A calendar to the Grants of *Lands* only. [*Index Locorum* in vol. 151.]
Vol. 56 -	Do. -	27 & 28 Eliz. -	A calendar.
Vol. 57 -	Do. -	Ric. 3., Jas. 1., and Chas. 1.	A collection of references to *Grants* and *Commissions* of various kinds, with copies of certain Warrants, Licences, &c. [Apparently a book of rough memoranda only.]
Vol. 58 -	Do. -	1 to 3 Jas. 1. -	A calendar, with an Index Locorum.
Vol. 59 -	Do. -	4 to 6 Jas. 1. -	A calendar with an Index to the counties.
Vol. 60 -	Do. -	7 to 8 Jas. 1. -	Do. do.
Vol. 61 -	Do. -	9 to 12 Jas. 1. -	A calendar without Index [*see* vol. 64].
Vol. 62 -	Do. -	12 to 15 Jas. 1.	A calendar with an Index to the counties.
Vol. 63 -	Do. -	1 to 9 Jas. 1. -	A calendar to the *Grants of Offices.*
Vol. 64 -	Do. -	9 to 12 Jas. 1. -	A fair copy of Vol. 61, with an *Index Locorum.*

PALMER'S INDEXES—(continued).

Vol. 65 -	Patent Rolls -		16 to 22 Jas. 1.	A calendar with an *Index Locorum*.
Vol. 66 -	Do. -		1 to 4 Chas. 1. -	A calendar with an Index to the counties.
Vol. 67 -	Do. -		5 to 21 Chas. 1.	Do. do.
Vol. 68 -	Do. -		Chas. 2. (divers years).	A calendar with an *Index Nominum*.
	Do. -		Jas. 2. to Will. 3.	A complete calendar.
Vol. 69 -	Do. -		Chas. 1. to Will. 3.	References to *Leases from the Crown* for a term of years, enrolled in the Patent Rolls.
	Do. -		Chas. 2. to Will. 3.	References, in chronological order, to *Patents and Charters*, Grants of *Offices and Commissions*, and *Grants in Perpetuity*.
Vol. 70 -	Do. -		Hen. 8., Edw. 6., and Eliz.	References, arranged alphabetically under names of Places, to Grants, Inq. post mortem, &c., in the Counties of Bucks, Cambridge, Chester, Cumberland, Norfolk, and Warwick. [The grants will be found in the calendars marked A. to Z.]
Vol. 71 -	Close Rolls -		Hen. 8. - -	A calendar with an *Index Locorum*. [A list is appended of the Summons to Parliament, Surrenders of Monasteries, and other Special matters enrolled during the above period.]
Vol. 72 -	Do. -		22 to 25 Chas. 2.	An abstract of the Deeds Enrolled, particularly of the *Bargains and Sales* made by the Trustees for the sale of *Fee-farm Rents*, &c., with an *Index Locorum*.
Vol. 73 -	Fee-farm Rents	Chas. 2. -		A vol. containing copies of (1.) The Act of Parliament for advancing the sale of Fee-farm Rents; (2.) The Act vesting the power of sale in Lord Hawley and others; and (3.) The grant by Charles II. of Fee-farm Rents in divers counties to Lord Hawley and the other trustees.
Vol. 74 -	Delinquents' Lands.	Commonwealth -		Abstracts of Claims to the Estates of Delinquents, arranged alphabetically under the names of the Delinquents, and giving the names of the claimants and particulars of the estates.

PALMER'S INDEXES—(continued).

Vol. 75 -	Fine Rolls	-	Edw. 5. to Phil. & Mar.	A calendar, arranged alphabetically, under *Names of Persons*, with an *Index Locorum*.
Vol. 76 -	Do.	-	Eliz. to Chas. 1.	A chronological calendar. [*Index Locorum and Nominum*, in vol. 77.]
Vol. 77 -	Do.	-	Do. -	Indices Locorum and Nominum.
Vol. 78 -	Close Rolls	-	Commonwealth -	A calendar of the *Bargains and Sales* of *Crown Lands* and of *Delinquents' Estates* made during the Commonwealth.
Vol. 79 -	Do.	-	Do. -	An *Index Locorum* to the foregoing calendar.
Vol. 80 -	Do.	-	Do. •	A calendar of the Bargains and Sales of *Church Lands*, made during the Commonwealth.
Vol. 81 -	Do.	-	Do. -	An *Index Locorum* to the foregoing calendar.
Vol. 82 -	Charter, Patent, and Close Rolls.		John to Edw. 6.	References · relating to the *County of York*, arranged chronologically.
	Inquisitions post mortem.		Hen. 3. to Ric. 3.	Do. do.
Vol. 83 -	- - -		- - -	An *Index Locorum* to the foregoing calendar.
Vol. 84 -	Patent Rolls	-	Hen. 7. to Chas. 1.	Two vols. in one, containing references to grants of lands, &c., in *Wales* (including Monmouth), arranged in Counties.
Vol. 85 -	Do.	-	Phil. & Mar. -	Abstracts of Grants, arranged under Counties.
Vol. 86 -	Do.	-	12 to 18 Chas. 2.	Do. do.
Vol. 87 -	Do.	-	Ric. 3. to 20 Hen. 8., and temp. Hen. 8.	Abstracts of Grants of lands, with an *Index Locorum*.
Vol. 88 -	Do.	-	21 to 34 Hen. 8.	Do. do.
Vol. 89 -	Do.	-	35 to 38 Hen. 8.	Do. [*Index Locorum* in Vol. 152.]
Vol. 90 -	Do.	-	Edw. 5. to Hen. 7.	Entries of *Patents*, arranged chronologically, with a list of *Charters and Commissions*.
Vol. 91 -	Inquisitions post mortem		Hen. 7. to 5 Chas. 1.	Full abstracts of the *Inq. post mortem* for the county of Cambridge.

PALMER'S INDEXES—(continued).

Vol. 92 -	Inquisitions post mortem.	Hen. 8. to Phil. & Mar.	The same for the county of *York*.
Vol. 93 -	Fairs and Markets.	John to Edw. 4.	A *Chronological List* of the Grants of *Fairs and Markets* enrolled on the Patent, Charter, and Close Rolls.
Vol. 94 -	Inq. post mortem, &c.	Hen. 3. to Ric. 3.	A calendar to the Inq. post mortem for the counties of *Berks*, *Bucks*, and *Cambridge*, with references to the Patent, Close, and other Rolls for the same period. [*Indices Nominum* for Berks and Bucks].
Vol. 95 -	Do. -	Do. -	*Indices Locorum* only for the counties of Chester, Derby, and Devon. [The calendar to which they refer is not in this collection.]
Vol. 96 -	Do. -	Do. -	A calendar to the Inq. p. m. for the county of *Essex*, with an *Index Locorum*. This vol. contains also references to Inq. p. m. and other records, under the headings "Citra" and Ultra Trentam," and "Co. Durham."
Vol. 97 -	Do. -	Do. -	A calendar of the Inq. p. m., &c., for the counties of *Kent*, *Leicester*, and *Middlesex*. [No Index.]
Vol. 98 -	Do. -	Do. -	A similar calendar for the counties of *Northumberland*, *Oxford*, and *Suffolk*.
Vol. 99 -	Do. -	Do. -	A similar calendar for the counties of *Sussex*, *Warwick*, and *Wilts*, with *Indices Locorum* for Sussex and Wilts.
Vol. 100	Do. -	Hen. 7. to Jas. 1.	Abstracts of Inq. post mortem in *Suffolk*, giving the date of the death and the Name, &c., of the next Heir.
Vol. 101	Do. -	Hen. 7. to Chas.1.	A similar volume for the county of *Northampton*, with an *Index Locorum*.
Vol. 102	"Primus Liber Cedularum."	Hen. 7. to Mar.	A collection of materials touching the *Descent* of various families, the Lands they possessed, their Tenure, &c., extracted apparently from books at the Heralds' College, with an *Index Locorum*.

PALMER'S INDEXES—(continued).

Vol. 103	"Secundus Liber Cedularum."	1 to 28 Eliz. -	A similar volume to the foregoing, with *Indices Nominum and Locorum.*
Vol. 104	Inq. post mortem, *Court of Wards.*	Hen. 8. to Chas. 1.	An *Index Nominum*, referring to abstracts of Inq. post mortem amongst the Miscellaneous Books of the Court of Wards.
Vol. 105	Extents of Manors.	21 to 22 Eliz. -	Extents of manors, &c., in Various Counties, a book belonging apparently to the Court of Wards and Liveries.
Vol. 106	Miscellaneous Rolls, Chancery, &c.	John to Edw. 4.	A volume containing references to the Miscellaneous Rolls formerly in the Tower of London.
Vol. 107	Common Law Proceedings, Chancery.	Hen. 7. - -	A vol. entitled "Placita et Tra "versa super Inquisitiones," &c.
Vol. 108	Patent Rolls -	Ric. 3. to Jas. 2.	References to grants of *Offices, Liberties,* &c., in England, Scotland, Wales, and Ireland, arranged under Counties, A to L.
Vol. 109	Do. -	Do. -	Do. L to W.
Vol. 110	Do. -	Jas. 1. - -	References to *Grants of Offices* in England and Wales.
Vol. 111	Placita Coronæ -	Hen. 3. and Edw. 1.	Selections from the Placita Coronæ, &c., of Inquisitions as to services in various Counties from Gloucester to York.
Vol. 112	Patent Rolls -	1 to 3 Jas. 1. -	A chronological calendar of Grants.
Vol. 113	Inq. post mortem.	Hen. 7. to Chas. 1.	Abstracts of Inq. p. m. in the county of *Leicester.*
Vol. 114	Patent Charter, and Close Rolls, &c., &c.	Hen. 3. to Edw. 4.	Miscellaneous references arranged alphabetically (for the letters A and B only).
Vol. 115	Patent Rolls -	3 Edw. 6. -	A chronological calendar.
Vol. 116	Do. -	17 to 30 Hen. 8.	Do. do.
Vol. 117	Patent and Close Rolls, &c.	John to Hen. 6.	Miscellaneous references, arranged under the heads of Admiralty, Constableship of England, Cinque Ports, Ireland, Isle of Man, Oxford University, Parliaments, Scotland, Tower of London, Visitations, Wales, &c., &c.

PALMER'S INDEXES—(continued).

Vol. 118	Patent Rolls -	16 to 27 Chas. 2.	References to Grants, arranged alphabetically under names of Places.
Vol. 119	Do. -	Edw. 5. to Hen.7.	A chronological calendar.
Vol. 120	Inq. post mortem.	Hen. 7. and Hen. 8.	An Index Nominum, from A to L.
Vol. 121	Precedents of the office of Escheator.	- - -	A collection of Forms and other matters relating to the Escheator's Office, entitled "Liber Præsidentium Specialium."
Vol. 122	Miscellaneous References.	- - -	A list of references to various Records in the Rolls Chapel, since Ric. 3., proposed to be printed as a supplement to "Rymer's Fœdera."
Vol. 123	Grants of Fee-farm Rents.	Hen. 8. to Chas. 1.	A list of grants of *Fee-farm Rents* in England and Wales, arranged under Counties.
Vol. 124	Patent and Close Rolls, &c.	Hen. 8. to Geo. 2.	*Miscellaneous references* of various dates from Hen. 8. to Geo. 2., arranged alphabetically, and *Abstracts* of *Grants, &c.*, Chas. 2. to Will. & Mar.
Vol. 125	Inq. post mortem.	Hen. 7. to Eliz. -	Abstracts of Inq. p. m. relating to *London.*
Vol. 126	Do. -	Do. -	Do. relating to *Middlesex.*
Vol. 127	Patent Rolls -	Hen. 8. to Jas. 2.	Abstracts of Grants, &c., in the county of *Leicester.*
Vol. 128 and 129.	- - -	- - -	Two vols., entitled "Guide "Books in searching this "Series."
Vol. 130	Notes concerning the Manor of Secroft.	- - -	A volume containing a copy of the Grant of the *Manor of Secroft,* temp. Jas. 1., with copious Notes and references concerning the same manor.
Vol. 131	Borough of Hertford.	1622 - -	A copy of an Inquisition relating to the Borough and Town of Hertford.
Vol. 132	Patent Rolls, &c.	Hen. 7. to Edw. 6.	Miscellaneous references to Grants, &c., arranged in Counties.
Vol. 133	Do. -	Anne to Geo. 2.	An *Alphabetical List* of Grants, &c., on the Patent Rolls.

PALMER'S INDEXES—(continued).

Vol. 134	" Book of Entries."	1696 to 1701 -	Memoranda of Commissions and other matters passing the Great Seal, entered alphabetically according to the Subjects.
Vol. 135	" Grants, &c., Court of Chancery and Court of Augmentations."	- - -	Copies of grants to the Clerk of the Enrolments, &c., with Notes concerning the Court of Augmentations, the Fees at the several Law Courts, &c.
Vol. 136	Patent Rolls -	Ric. 3. to Chas. 2.	References to *Grants of Offices, &c.*
Vol. 137	Do. -	Hen. 8. to Chas. 2.	References to Patent Rolls, principally to *Grants of Offices,* &c.
Vol. 138	Do. -	Jas. 1. to Chas. 1.	References to *Special Licences, Pardons, Gaol Deliveries, Forfeitures,* &c., arranged under subjects.
Vol. 139	Do. -	Various reigns -	Miscellaneous references, arranged alphabetically under *Names of Places,* being apparently memoranda of Searches made from 1809 to 1818.
Vol. 140	Do. -	Temp. Eliz. -	References to Grants, &c., in various counties, from *Bedford* to *Huntingdon.*
Vol. 141	Patent Rolls and Liveries.	Ric. 3. to Eliz. -	References to the Patent Rolls, arranged under Counties; also an alphabetical *Index Nominum of Liveries* from 1 to 6 Eliz.
Vol. 142	Inq. post mortem	Hen. 3. to Ric. 3.	Abstracts of Inq. p. m. in the county of *Essex.*
Vol. 143	Patent, Charter, and Close Rolls, &c.	John to Edw. 4.	*Indices Locorum* only, arranged under Counties, referring to some volume not in this collection.
Vol. 144	Do. -	Hen. 3. to Ric. 3.	References to *Charters, Inquisitions, post mortem,* &c., &c., for the counties of *Chester, Cornwall, Dorset,* and *Westmoreland.*
Vol. 145	Patent Rolls -	Edw. 6. -	Abstracts of Grants, &c., arranged in Counties from *Salop* to *Wilts.*
Vol. 146	Abstracts of Sign Manuals.	8 Jas. 1. to 7 Chas. 1.	

PALMER'S INDEXES—(continued).

Vol. 147	Catalogue of Surveys.	Hen. 7. to Commonwealth.	Entitled " Catalogue of Surveys " in the Office of James West, " Esq., 1793," and referring to the Surveys now preserved in the Land Revenue Record Office.
Vol. 148	Parliament Rolls	4 Edw. 3. to 9 Hen. 5.	An " Abstract of all the Parliament Rolls in the Tower " of London."
Vol. 149	- - -	26 to 45 Eliz. -	An Index Locorum, referring to some Calendar not yet identified.
Vol. 150	- - -	26 to 45 Eliz. -	Do. do.
Vol. 151	Patent Rolls -	1 to 25 Eliz. -	An Index Locorum, referring to Vol. 55.
Vol. 152	Do. -	35–38 Hen. 8. -	Do. referring to Vol. 89.
Vol. 153	Do. -	15 to 37 Eliz. -	A rough Index Locorum referring to Vols. 12, 13, and 14.

PAPAL BULLS.

PAPAL BULLS.   John to Henry VIII.

A collection of original Papal Bulls and Letters brought together from various sources and including those formerly preserved in the Tower of London, an Inventory of which is printed in the Deputy Keeper's 5th Report. A Catalogue of these documents, many of which have been printed in Rymer's " Fœdera " and elsewhere, is in preparation.

A number of Papal Bulls and Letters will also be found amongst the State Papers of Henry VIII. (See Calendar of " Letters and Papers, &c.")

The " Golden Bull " of Clement VII., confirming the title of Defender of the Faith on Henry VIII., so-called from the seal of solid gold which on that occasion took the place of the ordinary leaden " Bulla," is amongst the records of the Exchequer, Treasury of the Receipt.

Copies of Papal Bulls will also be found in the Red Book of the Exchequer, in the " Registrum Munimentorum," and in several of the Monastic Chartularies deposited in the Public Record Office.

PAPISTS, RECUSANTS, AND NON-CONFORMISTS.

The penalties imposed on Papists for the exercise of their religion, and the restrictions on the education of

PAPISTS, RECUSANTS, AND NON-CONFORM-
ISTS—(continued).

their children as enforced by various statutes from Elizabeth to George I., were both numerous and severe.

If any *English* priest of the Church of Rome came to England from beyond the seas, or tarried in England three days without conforming to the church, he was guilty of high treason.

If the children of Papists were educated at home, and the schoolmaster did not repair to church, or was not allowed by the Bishop of the Diocese, the parents were liable to forfeit 10*l.* a month, and the schoolmaster 40*s.* a day. If they sent their children abroad for education they were liable to forfeit 100*l.*, and the children so sent were disabled from inheriting, purchasing, or enjoying any lands, tenements, or other profits.

Saying Mass was punishable by a forfeiture of 200 marks; hearing it, by a forfeiture of 100 marks.

All persons refusing to conform to the rites and ceremonies of the Church of England as by law established were, under several Statutes passed in the earlier part of Elizabeth's reign, subject to various penalties for such " Recusancy " as it was termed, no distinction being made between the Papists and other Non-conformists, and absence from church alone, unaccompanied by any other act, being sufficient to constitute such recusancy. In the 35th year of the same reign a Statute was, however, passed against *Popish* Recusants as distinguished from *Protestant* Recusants, by which the former were punishable by a fine of 20*l.* for every month during which they absented themselves from church, and by disabilities of various kinds, being also condemned within three months of their conviction as Popish Recusants either to submit and renounce their religious opinions, or, if required by four justices, to abjure the realm.

By Statute 11 & 12 Will. III. it was enacted that a person educated in or professing the Popish Religion who did not, within six months after attaining the age of 16, take the Oaths of Allegiance and Supremacy, and subscribe the Declaration against Popery prescribed by Stat. 30, Car. II., should, so far as regarded himself, be disabled from inheriting or taking lands by descent, devise, or limitation, and that during his life his next of kin, being a Protestant, should enjoy the said lands without accounting for the profits ; and that such a person should be incapable of purchasing lands, and all estates, interests, or profits made or suffered to his use or in trust for him should be void. Papists were also subjected to the burden of a double Land Tax.

By Statute 1 Geo. I. they were required under certain penalties therein mentioned to register their names and

PAPISTS, RECUSANTS, AND NON-CONFORMISTS — (continued).

estates; and by Statute 3 Geo. I. the obligation was imposed on them of enrolling their Deeds and Wills. The following documents bear on this subject :—

[See also **OATHS OF ALLEGIANCE, &c.**]

PAPISTS, RETURNS OF. (EXCHEQUER, Q. R.) George I.

Returns by the Clerks of the Peace of the several counties of the Names and Estates of Papists registered pursuant to the Statutes of the 1st and 9th years of Geo. I., with a few certificates by the Land Tax Commissioners of the payment by certain Papists of the double assessment on their estates, &c. 1 Portfolio.

Index. 1 vol. MS.

PAPISTS IN LANCASTER, RETURNS OF. (QUEEN'S BENCH, CROWN SIDE.) George I.

These contain names of those Papists in the County of Lancaster who had been summoned to take the Oath of Allegiance pursuant to Statute 9 Geo. I., but who did not appear. 1 Parcel.

The Deeds and Wills of Papists enrolled pursuant to the several Statutes on that behalf are to be found on the Close Rolls of the Court of Chancery and also on the Recovery Rolls of the Court of Common Pleas. See **DEEDS ENROLLED.**

Lists of all those Papists who had registered their Estates pursuant to the Statute 1 Geo. I., will be found amongst the "FORFEITED ESTATES PAPERS." See **ESCHEATS, ATTAINDERS, AND FORFEITURES.**

RECUSANT ROLLS. (EXCHEQUER, L. T. R.) 34 Elizabeth to 1 & 2 William and Mary. *Pipe Office Series.* 82 Rolls.

Do. (do.) 34 Elizabeth to 1 & 2 William and Mary. *Chancellor's Series.* 63 Rolls.

These contain the Accounts of the pecuniary Penalties inflicted on *Recusants*, that is to say, on such persons "as did not repair to any Church or Chapel or usual place " of Common Prayer to hear Divine Service;" and also of the lands seized into the King's hands on account of the sums due to the Exchequer in consequence of such recusancy.

Lists of Welsh Recusants will be found in the "CROWN BOOKS" for the Counties of Chester and Flint. See **JUDICIAL PROCEEDINGS.**

Certificates of Recusants' Estates sequestered during the Commonwealth, and of "Popish Recusants and Persons Concealed," from Anne to George I., will be found amongst the CERTIFICATES (VARIOUS) from the Petty Bag Office. See **CERTIFICATES.**

PAPISTS, RECUSANTS, AND NON-CONFORM-ISTS—(continued).

RECUSANT ROLLS, &c.—(continued.)

Papers relating to the discovery of a Jesuits' College at Clerkenwell, including a "list of all the Jesuits in this Province." 1628. [*S. P. Dom., Car. I., Vol.* 99.]

Accounts of the Receivers and Collectors of the Revenues arising from the Estates of Popish Recusants and of attainted persons. 1557, 1602 to 1605, and 1627 to 1734. [*Audit Office, " Declared Accounts," Bundles* 359 to 363.]

Accounts of moneys received from the principal Recusant clergy for providing Horses and Lances for Her Majesty's service in the Low Countries. 1585 to 1589. ·
[*Audit Office, " Declared Accounts," Bundle* 1592.]

NON-CONFORMISTS, LICENSES TO.

Licenses for Non-conformist Preachers and Teachers, and for places to be used as Meeting-houses, with other Memoranda relating thereto. 1672.
[*S. P. Dom., Car. II., Vol.* 321.]

An Entry Book of similar Licenses. 1672.
[*S. P. Dom., Entry Book, Car. II., Vol.* 38*a*.]

A similar Book in which the entries are classified as "Congregational" and "Presbyterian."
[*S. P. Dom., Entry Book, Car. II., Vol.* 38*b*.]

PARLIAMENTARY PROCEEDINGS.

The Records of Parliament preserved in the Public Record Office consist of the ORIGINAL PETITIONS and PLEADINGS IN PARLIAMENT from Edw. I. to Edw. IV.; of the PARLIAMENT ROLLS, on which were entered the daily transactions of the Assembly and the Bills and Petitions thereto presented, together with the Answers to the same, and on which, from the first year of Richard III., the several Acts of Parliament were formerly enrolled; of the STATUTE ROLLS or enrolments of the Acts of Parliament from Edw. I. to Edw. IV., with volumes of Transcripts of Statutes from John to Henry VIII.; of such PRIVATE ACTS of Parliament as have been certified into Chancery from the reign of Henry VIII. to that of George III. inclusive (the enrolment of Private Acts having been finally discontinued in the 35th year of Elizabeth); and of the WRITS OF SUMMONS of Peers, and WRITS AND RETURNS OF MEMBERS of the House of Commons from the earliest period to the present reign.

An alphabetical list of these documents is appended :—

PARLIAMENT ROLLS. (CHANCERY.) 5 Edward II. to 48 & 49 Victoria.

The "Rotuli Parliamentorum," or Rolls of Parliament prior to the reign of Richard III., contain entries of the

PARLIAMENTARY PROCEEDINGS—(continued).

PARLIAMENT ROLLS, &c.—(continued.)

several transactions in Parliament, including the adjournments and all other common and daily occurrences and proceedings from the opening to the close of each Parliament, with the several Petitions or Bills and the answers given thereto, not only on public matters on which the Statutes were afterwards framed, but also on private concerns. In some few instances the Statutes drawn up in form are entered, but in general the petitions and answers only, in which case the entry of itself furnishes no evidence that the petition and answer were at any time put into the form of a Statute. The Acts of Parliament from 6 Edw. I. to 8 Edw. IV., when drawn up in the form of Statutes, are enrolled on the Statute Rolls.

The Acts of Parliament commenced to be regularly enrolled on the Parliament Rolls in the first year of Richard the Third, and from that date to 3 Charles I. inclusive, the Parliament Rolls continue to contain, in addition to the Acts enrolled, Petitions and other miscellaneous proceedings of Parliament ; the latter, however, disappeared by degrees, the Parliament Rolls then consisting of the Acts enrolled only.

From Richard III. to 25 Henry VIII. they contain all the Acts, both public and private, passed in every session, with the introductory forms of presentation and the concluding forms of assent.

From 25 Hen. VIII. to 35 Elizabeth several of the Private Acts and afterwards all the Private Acts are omitted, their titles only being noticed.

From 16 Car. I. to 31 George II. the Rolls contain nothing but the Public Acts and the titles of the Private Acts, without any other parliamentary matter, and from 32 Geo. II. the titles of the Private Acts are also omitted.

In Feb. 1849 the engrossments and enrolments ceased, and Acts printed on vellum were substituted.

Such Private Acts as were removed into Chancery by Writ of Certiorari for the purpose of exemplification or otherwise, will be found in the "Certiorari Bundles" referred to below, under the heading of "PRIVATE ACTS OF PARLIAMENT, &c."

The Original Acts, both public and private, are kept at the Parliament Office.

In addition to the Chancery Series, there are Parliament Rolls of various dates from the 18th to the 35th of Edward I. amongst the Records of the Exchequer Treasury of the Receipt, and many Transcripts of Acts and Pleadings in Parliament will be found amongst the PARLIAMENTARY PROCEEDINGS of the Exchequer, Queen's Remembrancer, referred to below.

PARLIAMENTARY PROCEEDINGS—(continued).

An ancient Transcript of the Rolls of Parliament from the 18th to the 35th years of Edward I., and for the 12th year of Edward II., known as the "Vetus Codex," is preserved amongst the Records formerly in the Tower of London.

See VETUS CODEX, OR PLACITA PARLIAMENTARIA.

The Parliament Rolls (collected from various sources), together with many of the original Petitions to Parliament, from 6 Edward I. to 19 Henry VII. have been printed in 6 Vols. folio, entitled "Rotuli Parliamentorum," with an elaborate *Index*, in 1 Vol.

The "Statutes" from 6 Edward I. to Queen Anne are printed in 9 Vols., entitled "Statutes of the Realm," with *Indexes* in 2 Vols.

The "Acts and Ordinances" of the Parliament from 1640 to 1656 were printed by Henry Scobell, the Clerk of the Parliament in 1658 by special order of the Parliament. The original Records of these Acts being destroyed at the Restoration, this Volume forms the only evidence of the proceedings of the Long Parliament.

Indexes to Parliament Rolls, from 1 Richard III., to 48 & 49 Victoria, 10 Vols. (part MS. and part printed).

PARLIAMENT ROLLS. (EXCHEQUER, TREASURY OF THE RECEIPT.) 18 to 35 Edward I. 10 Rolls.

These are printed in the "Rotuli Parliamentorum" referred to above.

PARLIAMENT PAWNS. *See* "SUMMONS TO PARLIAMENT, WRITS OF."

PARLIAMENTARY AND OTHER PETITIONS. (CHANCERY, AND EXCHEQUER.) Edward I. to Henry VII.

These consist of original Petitions of ancient date now brought together from various sources, and including Petitions to the King, to the King and Council, and to Parliament, with others addressed to the Chancellor in his executive capacity, and to various Officers of State. A great number of Petitions to the King from the inhabitants of Gascony and other French provinces will also be found in this collection.

Many of the Petitions to Parliament have been printed in the "Rotuli Parliamentorum."

An Alphabetical List of all these "Ancient Petitions" has been issued. (Lists and Indexes, No. I., 1892.)

PARLIAMENTARY PROCEEDINGS—(continued).

PARLIAMENTARY AND OTHER PROCEEDINGS. (CHAN-
CERY.)

A collection of Transcripts of Statutes, Pleadings, and
other proceedings in Parliament and before the Council,
formerly amongst the Miscellaneous Records in the Tower
of London.

PARLIAMENTARY PROCEEDINGS. (EXCHEQUER, Q. R.)
13 Edward I. to James I.

These consist of Pleadings, Transcripts of Statutes and
other proceedings in Parliament of the highest interest
and importance, many of which have been printed in the
"Rotuli Parliamentorum," the "Statutes of the Realm,"
and in Cole's "Documents illustrative of English History,"
published by the Record Commissioners.

The greater portion of these were formerly preserved
with the so-called Miscellanea of the Exchequer, Queen's
Remembrancer, but numerous documents of a similar
nature from the Records of the Treasury of the Receipt of
the Exchequer have been added to the collection, a complete catalogue of which has been made, including the
Parliamentary and other Proceedings of the Court of Chancery above mentioned. The Petitions to Parliament
formerly in this class have been added to the collection of
"Parliamentary and other Petitions," described above.

PARLIAMENTARY WRITS, AND WRITS OF MILITARY
SUMMONS, &c. Collected from various sources.

Transcripts, Chronological Abstract and Calendar.
Edw. I. and Edw. II. Printed in 4 Vols. or Parts, edited
by Sir F. Palgrave.

Transcripts. Edw. III. to Edw. IV. 55 Vols. MS.

Chronological Abstract. 1 to 51 Edw. III. 8 Vols. MS.

The foregoing volumes contain Transcripts from various
classes of Records consisting of Writs of Summons of
Peers to Parliament, Writs and Returns for the election
of Members of the House of Commons, Writs for levying
the Expenses of Knights, Citizens, and Burgesses, Writs
of Military Summons addressed to such as were generally
considered Barons of the Realm, Writs for the performance
of Military Service addressed to the Sheriffs of Counties,
Commissions of Array, and other documents relating to
Military Service, or affording evidence of the names of
individuals attending or deliberating in Parliaments or
Councils, &c. *Vide* Preface to the first volume of "Parliamentary Writs," &c.

PARLIAMENTARY PROCEEDINGS—(continued).

PRIVATE ACTS OF PARLIAMENT CERTIFIED INTO CHAN-
CERY. (ROLLS CHAPEL OFFICE SERIES.) Henry VIII.
to George III.

These consist of a series of Bundles called " CERTIORARI
BUNDLES," containing transcripts of such Private Acts
of Parliament as were brought into Chancery by Writ of
Certiorari for the purpose of being exemplified under the
Great Seal.

Do. (PETTY BAG OFFICE SERIES.) James I. to
George III.

A collection similar to the foregoing, removed from the
Petty Bag Office.

Index (to both Series). 1 Vol. MS.

A bundle of " Acts of Parliament passed in Ireland,"
and enrolled in the 10th year of Charles I., exists amongst
the Miscellaneous Bundles of the Rolls Chapel Office.

STATUTE ROLLS. 6 Edw. I. to 8 Edw. IV.

These contain the enrolments of the Statutes when
formally drawn up. The series is very imperfect, consisting
of six Rolls only, which, however, are supplemented by
Transcripts of Statutes apparently sent into the Chancery
for the purpose of being exemplified under the Great Seal,
and now placed with the Parliamentary Proceedings
described above.

See **CHANCERY ENROLMENTS (VARI-
OUS).**

STATUTES, TRANSCRIPTS OF. John to Richard II.

A Volume containing Transcripts of Statutes, commencing with those of Marlborough and Runnymede,
together with entries of a great number of Writs, an
Article entitled " Prerogativa Regis," &c., &c.

[*Misc. Books (Exchequer, Q. R.), Vol. 9.*]

Do. Edw. III. to Henry VI. A similar volume,
beautifully illuminated, with an Index to the Subjects.

[*Do., Vol. 10.*]

Do. Edw. IV. to Henry VIII. A similar volume,
extending from 1 Edw. IV. to 7 Hen. VIII.

[*Do., Vol. II.*]

Do. A compendium or epitome of the Statutes of
Edward the Third. 1–36 Edw. III.

[*Misc. Rolls, &c., Chancery, No. $\frac{17}{9}$.*]

See also PARLIAMENTARY PROCEEDINGS.

PARLIAMENTARY PROCEEDINGS—(continued).

Summons of Peers to Parliament, Writs of.

These are enrolled on the back of the Close Rolls till 21 Hen. VIII., after which date they were filed at the Petty Bag Office, and are described as "Parliament Pawns."

Transcripts in full. 49 Hen. III. to 1685. Printed in 1 Vol., entitled "Dugdale's Summons to Parliament."

See also Parliamentary Writs, &c.

Summons to Parliament, Writs of, called "Parliament Pawns." (Chancery, Petty Bag Office.) 21 Hen. VIII. to 1818.

These consist of the enrolments of Writs of Summons of Peers to Parliament. They are put up in three Parts or Bundles, to which there is an Index.

Before 21 Hen. VIII. the Writs of Summons are enrolled on the back of the Close Rolls.

Vetus Codex, or Placita Parliamentaria. (Chancery.)

A Volume amongst the Tower Records (sometimes called the Black Book of the Tower), containing an ancient transcript of the Rolls of Parliament from 18 to 35 Edw. I. and of the 12th year of Edw. II.

It is not known by whom or on what occasion this transcript was made, but it is referred to in the Parliament Roll 6 Ric. II., Part 2, m. 26, as being then in the Tower of London.

The "Vetus Codex" is printed in Ryley's Placita Parliamentaria, with an Appendix of illustrative Records. See Parliament Rolls.

Writs and Returns of Members to Parliament. (Chancery.) 3 Edw. I. to 1 Victoria.

These are the original Writs for the election of Knights and Burgesses to serve in Parliament, with the Returns thereto. They are contained in 288 Portfolios or Bundles, the *Single Returns* being kept distinct from the *General Returns.* Abstracts of these returns, giving the name of every member returned to serve in Parliament from the earliest period to 1880 with the name of the constituency represented, so far as they can be ascertained therefrom, have been printed in Return to two orders of the House of Commons, dated respectively 4 May 1876 and 9 March 1877; the information given being checked and supplemented by reference to the Books of Parliamentary Returns preserved at the Crown Office. An Index has been made to these Abstracts, and published in two Volumes.

PARLIAMENTARY PROCEEDINGS—(continued).

NOTES OF DEBATES IN THE HOUSE OF COMMONS from March 21 to June 9, 1628.

These are partly in shorthand, and contain brief particulars by Sir E. Nicholas of a great number of speeches of which there is no other known report. (*Vide* Calendar of Domestic State Papers.)

[*S. P. Dom., Car. I., Vol.* 97.]

PARTITION OF LANDS.

Chancery.

COMMISSIONS OF PARTITION.

Partition suits in Chancery were commenced by Bill in the ordinary manner, a Commission being thereupon issued, which, with the return thereto, was returned into the Six Clerks' Office. These Commissions will be found amongst the "Depositions taken by Commission."

See **JUDICIAL PROCEEDINGS.**

DEEDS OF PARTITION.

These are generally enrolled on the Close Rolls.

The following Deeds of Partition, with a few Assignments of Dower, each forming a distinct roll, are amongst the Miscellaneous Rolls, &c., Chancery (Bundle 3):—

No. 3. Partition of the Manors of Northerek, Hillington, Combes, and Helmingham, in the County of Suffolk, amongst the heirs of Roger, the son of Peter Fitz Osbert. 34 Edw. I.

No. 7. Partition of the lands, &c. of Gilbert de Clare, formerly Earl of Gloucester. (The pourparty of Hugh Daudeley and his wife.) 11 Edw. II.

No. 8. Do. (The pourparty of Hugh le Despenser and his wife.) 11 Edw. II.

No. 9. An extent of the possessions of the Earldom of Clare. 11 Edw. II.

No. 10. Partition of the lands, &c. of Gilbert de Clare. (The pourparty of Roger Damory and his wife.) 11 Edw. II.

No. 13. Partition of the Manor of Thaxted amongst the heirs of Giles Badlesmere. 21 Edw. III.

No. 14. Partition of the lands, &c. of Giles Badlesmere in Ireland. 25 Edw. III.

No. 17. Partition of the possessions of Humphrey de Bohun, Earl of Hereford, in Herefordshire and the Marches of Wales. 4 Ric. II.

No. 18. Partition of the lands, &c. of Thomas Beauchamp, Earl of Warwick. 4 Hen. IV.

No. 19. Assignment of Dower to Anne, widow of Edmund, late Earl of Stafford. 5 Hen. IV.

No. 20. Partition of lands, &c. in Glamorgan, between Joan, widow of Richard Vernon and others. 13 Hen. IV.

No. 21. Assignment of Dower to Margaret, widow of John Darcy. 14 Hen. IV.

No. 22. Partition of the lands, &c. of Humphry de Bohun, Earl of Hereford. (The pourparty of Anne, Countess of Stafford.) Hen. V.

PARTITION OF LANDS—(continued).

Chancery—(continued).

DEEDS OF PARTITION—(continued).

No. 23. Partition of the lands, &c. of Edmund, Earl of March.
3 Hen. VI.
No. 24.   Do.   do.   · 3 Hen. VI.
No. 25. Partition of the lands, &c. of Joan, late Countess of
Kent.   21 Hen. VI.
No. 26. Partition of the lands, &c. of the late Earl Marshal.
(2 Rolls.)   Temp. Hen. III.
No. 27. Partition of the Knights' Fees, &c. of Thomas de
Clifford, Knight.   Temp. Hen. VI.

PETITIONS.

Petitions to the King and Council and to Parliament.
See **PARLIAMENTARY PROCEEDINGS.**
Petitions of various kinds, addressed to the Sovereign
and to the principal Officers of State, will be found in the
Series of Domestic State Papers and amongst the other
Records of the Home Office.
See **STATE PAPERS, CALENDARS OF,** and
DEPARTMENTAL RECORDS.
Petitions in connexion with proceedings in the several
Courts of Law are described under the head of **JUDICIAL
PROCEEDINGS.**

PIRACY.

Matters relating to Piracy are entered on the early Close
Rolls, and frequent references thereto appear in the
Domestic State Papers.

PIRATES, ABSTRACTS OF PROCEEDINGS AGAINST.

A volume containing Abstracts of proceedings against
the receivers and aiders of Pirates in all the maritime shires
of England and Wales, with lists of ports, creeks, and
havens, names of Commissioners for trial of piracies, &c.
1577 to 1579.   [*S. P. Dom., Eliz., Vol.* 135.]

PIRATES' GOODS.

A few Inventories of the goods of Pirates, several of
which relate to one " Clinton Atkinson," described as a
" Sea Rover," will be found amongst the Miscellanea of
the Exchequer.

POST OFFICE.

ACCOUNTS OF THE MASTERS AND COMPTROLLERS OF THE
POSTS. 1566 to 1639.
Do.   OF THE RECEIVERS-GENERAL. 1695 to 1827.
Do.   OF THE ACCOUNTANTS-GENERAL. 1746 to 1827.
The above are amongst the " Declared Accounts " of
the Audit Office.
See **DEPARTMENTAL RECORDS.**

PRISONS (QUEEN'S BENCH AND FLEET).

Queen's Bench Prison.

COMMITMENT BOOKS. 1719 to 1862. 54 Vols.

COMMITMENTS, ABSTRACT BOOKS OF. 1780 to 1815. 21 Vols.

Do., ENTRY BOOKS OF. 1785 to 1862. 25 Vols.

Do., TO STRONG ROOM. 1847 to 1862. 3 Vols.

DECLARATION BOOKS. 1747 to 1856. 18 Vols.

DISCHARGES. 1780 to 1862. 79 Packages.

EXECUTION BOOKS. 1758 to 1851. 10 Vols.

INQUISITIONS POST MORTEM ON PRISONERS. 1747 to 1839.

Amongst the Records of the Queen's Bench, Crown Side.

PRISONERS, ALPHABETICAL LISTS OF. 1778 to 1862. 32 Vols.

PRISONERS' PAPERS. (VARIOUS.)

These consist of Petitions, Rules, and other documents relating to prisoners in the Queen's Bench, and are placed with the Records of the Queen's Bench, Plea Side.

MISCELLANEOUS BOOKS. 39 Vols.

Fleet Prison.

COMMITMENT BOOKS. 1699 to 1842. 50 Vols.

COMMITMENTS (ARRANGED NUMERICALLY). 160 Bundles.

DISCHARGES. 43 Bundles.

N.B.—The Registers of Marriages, &c. of both the Queen's Bench and the Fleet Prison are at the General Register Office, Somerset House.

PRIVY COUNCIL.

The Acts and Proceedings of the Privy Council, from the Registers preserved in the Privy Council Office and elsewhere, have been published by the Record Commissioners in 7 Vols. royal 8vo., extending in date from 10 Richard II. to 33 Henry VIII.

A New Series, of which ten volumes extending from 1542 to 1578, have been issued, has been commenced under the direction of the Master of the Rolls.

The Council Books and other Proceedings during the time of the Commonwealth, are amongst the Records of the State Paper Office.

Proceedings before the Council of early date will be found in the collection of "Parliamentary and other Proceedings (Chancery)." The following are amongst the "Miscellaneous Rolls, &c." Chancery :—

PRIVY COUNCIL—(continued).

No. 11. A roll containing "Regulations for the Lords of the Council." (Printed in Rot. Parl. Vol. IV., pp. 343–344.) 8 Hen. VI.

No. 12. A roll entitled, "Ordinances for the King's Council." 1–3 Hen. VI.

PRIVY SEALS, SIGNED BILLS, &c.

The usual methods by which the Lord Chancellor was authorized to affix the Great Seal to Charters and Letters Patent or Close prior to the reign of Henry VIII. were by a Writ or Bill under the Privy Seal, by a Royal Sign Manual or Signed Bill, by a Letter under the Privy Signet, or by a Fiat or Warrant of the King or of one of the higher Officers of State.

The WRIT OF PRIVY SEAL commenced with the name and titles of the sovereign, and addressing the Lord Chancellor by name directed the issuing of documents under the Great Seal in due form, concluding with the datal clause, "under our Privy Seal," and giving the regnal year of the sovereign.

The BILL OF PRIVY SEAL omitted the royal style and the name of the Chancellor, and was used principally for directing the issue of Letters of protection and safe conduct.

The SIGN MANUAL or SIGNED BILL consisted of the Bill or Petition addressed to the King beseeching the granting of his Letters Patent to which the Sign Manual had been affixed, and which was then delivered to the Lord Chancellor as his authority for carrying out the prayer of the petition. To this Bill a schedule was sometimes annexed containing the form of the Letters Patent to be issued, which, when separate, also bore the Royal Sign Manual. The Bill and Schedule were, however, more frequently written on the same piece of parchment. In some cases the form of the Letters Patent only is preserved with the royal signature at the top. With the Sign Manuals are frequently found documents in the form of Petitions or Drafts of Letters Patent which are without the Sign Manual, but which bear evidence of having been delivered to the Chancellor for execution.

The SIGNET LETTER differed from the Writ of Privy Seal by omitting from the face of the document both the name and titles of the King and of the person to whom it was addressed, commencing merely with the words, "By the King," and being couched more in the form of a modern letter. It was more frequently written in English or French than in Latin, and bore the name of the person to whom it was addressed on the outside. The regnal year was sometimes omitted in the datal clause

PRIVY SEALS, SIGNED BILLS, &c.—(continued).

which was "under our Privy Signet" instead of "under our Privy Seal." A great number of the Signet Letters or Letters Missive, subsequent to the reign of Henry V., have also the Sign Manual at the commencement.

The FIAT or Warrant was issued either by the King himself or by one of the higher Officers of State, as the Lord Treasurer, the Lord High Admiral, the Steward of the Household, &c. The Royal Fiats were generally for Letters of Protection and Safe-Conduct, and occasionally for Commissions and Appointments, those of the Officers of State relating generally to the appointment of Deputy Officials and to matters of minor import.

Subsequent to the passing of the Act "concerning the "Clerks of the Signet and Privy Seal" in the 27th year of Henry the Eighth the process to be followed in order to obtain the passing of Letters Patent was somewhat complicated, several stages having in ordinary cases to be passed through in succession, in the course of which the following documents were, according to the circumstances, brought into requisition :—

1. A WARRANT under the Royal Sign Manual, addressed to the Attorney-General or Solicitor-General, or both of them, directing the preparation of a Bill for the signature of the sovereign, which was technically called the "King's Bill" or "Queen's Bill."

2. The KING'S OR QUEEN'S BILL which was made out by the Clerk of the Patents at the "Patent Bill Office" according to the precedents preserved in his Office, or in new and special cases from drafts transmitted with the Warrants, or drawn up by him and submitted to the Attorney or Solicitor-General to be perused and settled. The King's Bill contained the whole form of the Charter, Grant, or Patent to be issued in the words in which it was to pass the Great Seal, with the exception only of the Royal style at the beginning and the testing clause at the end, but with the addition at the foot of the Bill of a Docket signed by the Attorney or Solicitor-General, or both of them, explaining the contents of the Bill, and specifying the authority by which it was drawn up. It was engrossed on parchment and transmitted to the office of the Secretary of State for the Home Department to receive the Royal signature, transcripts being sent to the Privy Signet Office and the Privy Seal Office to be made use of in the further stages of the Patent.

3. The BILL OF PRIVY SIGNET or SIGNET BILL. This was prepared by one of the Clerks of the Privy Signet from the transcript of the King's Bill sent to the Signet Office from the Patent Bill Office, by collating it with the original King's Bill bearing the Royal Sign Manual

PRIVY SEALS, SIGNED BILLS, &c.—(continued).

(which was lodged in the Signet Office for that purpose), completing it, and affixing the Privy Signet thereto together with his own signature.

The Privy Signet Bill was then addressed by him to the Lord Privy Seal, and forwarded to his office as the authority for making out the Writ of Privy Seal.

4. THE WRIT OF PRIVY SEAL. On the receipt of the Privy Signet Bill, the Keeper of the Records in the Privy Seal Office prepared the Bill or Writ of Privy Seal by adding the formal parts to the Transcript of the King's Bill received by him from the Patent Bill Office, and presented it to the Lord Privy Seal in order that the Seal might be affixed thereto. The Privy Signet Bill which was the authority to the Lord Privy Seal for so doing was generally kept by him in his private possession, which accounts for the existence of Privy Signets in so many libraries and private collections. This practice was, however, discontinued in 1831, since which date they are preserved in the Privy Seal Office.

The Writ of Privy Seal was then presented to the Lord Chancellor, who signed a memorandum called the *Recepi* at the foot of the same, and this signature was the authority to the proper Officers for the preparation of the Letters Patent, and for affixing the Great Seal.

The Writs of Privy Seal were transmitted annually to the Six Clerks' Office, and on the abolition of that office to the Clerks of Records and Writs, for enrolment on the Patent Rolls, of which records they form to a great extent the original instruments. The enrolment was however in many cases neglected, and the Bundles of Privy Seals, should a grant not be found on the Patent Rolls, will often supply the deficiency. From the Six Clerks' Office the Bundles of Privy Seals, &c., together with the enrolments, were transmitted to the Petty Bag Office, and thence to the Chapel of the Rolls. They are now enrolled at the Enrolment Office in Chancery, and thence transferred along with the Patent Rolls to the Public Record Office.

5. SIGNED BILLS. The Signed Bill was a Bill under the Royal Sign Manual obtained by the direct intervention of the Lord Chancellor or Lord Keeper, who directed a Bill to be prepared by the Clerk of the Crown, to which he procured the Royal signature. According to the usage of the Chancery the Great Seal was then affixed to the Letters Patent by the authority of the Bill so signed, without any previous Warrant under the Sign Manual, and without the subsequent authorities of the Privy Signet and Privy Seal, by which three out of the four mandatory documents above described were dispensed with. The Signed Bills were chiefly used for Letters

PRIVY SEALS, SIGNED BILLS, &c.—(continued).

Patent appointing the Judges, Attorneys and Solicitors General, and other legal appointments (with the exception of the Masters of the Rolls, Vice Chancellors, and Masters in Chancery, whose appointments passed under the Privy Seal).

6. IMMEDIATE WARRANTS. When it was necessary that the Letters Patent should pass the Great Seal with more than usual expedition, a Warrant was prepared by the Secretary of State for the Home Department in a form styled Immediate, the effect of which was to dispense with the Bill of Privy Signet and the Writ of Privy Seal. This Warrant having received the Royal Sign Manual empowered the Attorney-General to direct the preparation of the King's or Queen's Bill accordingly. This was *entered* at the Privy Signet and Privy Seal Offices, but no Bill or Writ was issued thereon. The Statute of 27 Henry VIII., which recognizes this practice, directs, however, that the usual fees shall be paid at the said offices.

The Signed Bills, the Immediate Warrants and the King's or Queen's Bills thereon are all included in the bundles of Writs of Privy Seal.

In addition to the documents above described the Privy Seal and Signed Bill Bundles contain COMMISSIONS of various kinds, PROCLAMATIONS, LEASES, WARRANTS OF THE COURT OF WARDS FOR THE LIVERY OF LANDS, LICENSES OF ENTRY, WINE LICENCES, &c., &c. The King's or Queen's Bills from 1660 to the present time are amongst the Home Office Records (to which Department the business of the Privy Signet Office was transferred on its abolition), and are known under the title of "SIGNET OFFICE BILLS."

PROCLAMATIONS.

An Order having been made by the Privy Council for a Proclamation, whether for holding of Parliaments or any other purpose, the same was transmitted to the Crown Office, where the Proclamation was drawn up by the Clerk of the Crown, and, after having been submitted to the Law Officers for their approval, was engrossed and received the Royal Sign Manual. The Proclamations so signed were then transmitted to the Lord Chancellor's Office for the Great Seal to be affixed, and being returned to the Crown Office they were then transmitted annually to the Six Clerks' Office for enrolment with the Signed Bills and Privy Seals, and are entered on the back of the Patent Rolls.

The original Proclamations will be found in the Privy Seal and Signed Bill Bundles.

PRIVY SEALS, SIGNED BILLS, &c.—(continued).

There are also amongst the Domestic State Papers collections of printed PROCLAMATIONS extending from James I. to George III. (See Lists and Indexes, No. III., 1894.)

The following are the principal Series of Privy Seals, Signed Bills, &c. as at present arranged :—

PRIVY SEALS, SIGNED BILLS, &c. (CHANCERY) called "WARRANTS FOR THE GREAT SEAL." Henry III. to Victoria.

These include the Series formerly preserved in the Tower of London and the Rolls Chapel respectively. They have now been amalgamated and arranged in strict chronological order up to the end of the reign of Richard III. From the reign of Henry VII. to the present time they are arranged in monthly Bundles.

Those of the reign of Henry VIII. are included in the *Calendar of Letters and Papers* relating to that reign, and a *Calendar* to those of the first seven years of Charles I. has been made, which is printed in the Appendix to the 43rd Report.

SIGN MANUAL WARRANTS. (STATE PAPER OFFICE.) James I. and Charles I. Thirty Volumes, containing original King's Bills or Warrants for the Great Seal, and forming Vols. 4 to 33 of the Series of "Warrant Books." References to these are included in the printed "Calendars of State Papers."

SIGNET OFFICE BILLS. (HOME OFFICE.) 1661 to 1851. 387 Bundles.

These are arranged in monthly Parcels or Files, and form a continuation of the "Sign Manual Warrants" or "King's Bills" from the State Paper Office.

Docquet Books (from the Signet Office). 1584 to 1835. 35 Vols.

Indices Nominum. 1584 to 1829. 11 Vols.

Docquet Books (from the Patent Office). 1617 to 1850. 19 Vols.

PRIVY SEALS, DOCKETS OF AND WARRANTS FOR. (Amongst the Harleian MSS.) 1634 to 1711.

These documents formerly belonged to the Duke of Newcastle as Lord Privy Seal, in the reign of Queen Anne, and are now deposited with the Harleian MSS. in the British Museum.

Calendar. Car. I. to Anne. Printed. Report XXX., App., pp. 360–503.

Do. Do. 1 Vol. MS., with Indices Nominum and Locorum. [*Transcripts, Series II., No.* 20.]

PRIVY SEALS, SIGNED BILLS, &c.—(continued).

PRIVY SIGNET BILLS OR "WARRANTS FOR THE PRIVY
SEAL." (EXCHEQUER, TREASURY OF THE RECEIPT.)
Series I. (under arrangement).
Series II. Henry VIII. to Charles I., 120 Bundles.
Index. 3 Vols. MS.

PRIVY SEAL BOOKS AND ROLLS. (EXCHEQUER OF RECEIPT,
PELLS' AND AUDITORS' DEPARTMENTS.) Elizabeth to
Victoria.
See **RECEIPTS AND ISSUES OF THE
EXCHEQUER.**

PRIVY SEALS AND WARRANTS FOR ISSUES. (EXCHEQUER
OF RECEIPT.) Henry III. to William IV.

These consist of Writs of Privy Seal for payments out
of the Exchequer, including Writs of Liberate and Solvatis.
They are useful as supplying defects in the series of Issue
Rolls. Prior to 1 Henry IV. this collection is very
imperfect.

WARRANTS FOR THE DELIVERY OF RECORDS. (EXCHE-
QUER, AUGMENTATION OFFICE.) 24 Henry VII. to 1635.
1 Box.

PRIVY SEALS AND SIGNED BILLS. (DUCHY OF LANCAS-
TER.) 1 Hen. VII. to 1767. 43 Bundles.
Index, entitled "Index to Grants in Fee." 1 Vol. MS.

PRIVY SEALS, SIGNED BILLS, LETTERS MISSIVE, &c.
(PALATINATE OF LANCASTER.) Ric. II. to Hen. VII.
3 Bundles.

PRIVY SEALS, SIGNED BILLS, AND WARRANTS. (CHESTER
AND FLINT.) Hen. VII. and Hen. VIII.
Alphabetical Calendar. Report XXVI., App., pp.
16–31.

REBELLIONS.

Records of the *Trials and Convictions of Rebels* and of
all persons attainted of High Treason are contained in the
class of documents known as the "BAGA DE SECRETIS,"
deposited with the Records of the Queen's Bench, Crown
Side.

A *Calendar* and *Index* to the contents of the Baga de
Secretis, which extend from the reign of Edw. IV. to that
of George III. inclusive, are contained in the Deputy
Keeper's Third, Fourth, and Fifth Reports.

There are also COMMISSIONS OF INQUIRY RESPECTING
TREASON, with the Returns thereto, from 5 Charles I. to
Anne, amongst the Special Commissions from the Petty
Bag Office.

REBELLIONS—(continued).

Attention may also be directed to the following Miscellaneous References to Rebellions and Rebels :—

EARL OF LEICESTER'S REBELLION. Temp. Henry III.

Proceedings against the Earl of Leicester and other rebels in pursuance of the Dictum de Kenilworth, 51 Henry III., and other documents, consisting of:—

1. A roll entitled "Terræ rebellium datæ fidelibus," containing a brief notice of many forfeited lands, with the names of the persons who had formerly held them and of those to whom they had been given by the King. (Amongst the Miscellanea of the Exchequer.)

2. Four rolls entitled "Placita de Terris datis et occu-"patis occasione turbacionis in regno Angliæ," containing the record of the proceedings in consequence of the Dictum de Kenilworth in the counties of Essex, Northampton, Suffolk, and Cambridge respectively. [These rolls form part of the regular series of Assize Rolls.]

The foregoing are printed in full in the "Rotuli Selecti" by Joseph Hunter.

3. "Inquisitiones de Rebellibus." 49 Henry III. One portfolio containing Inquisitions respecting the possessions of such persons as were implicated in the "Bellum de Evesham." (This is placed with the regular series of Inquisitions post mortem, &c.)

4. A roll entitled "De terris duellionum a Rege diversis personis concessis." 50 Henry III.
[*Misc. Rolls, Chancery, No. ⅙.*]

EARL OF LANCASTER'S REBELLION. Temp. Edward II.

Record and process of the sentence against certain adherents of Thomas, Earl of Lancaster. 18 Edw. II.
[*Misc. Rolls, Chancery, No. 4/7.*]

Full Accounts of the possessions of the so-called "Contrariants," or adherents of Thomas, Earl of Lancaster, will be found amongst the Ministers' and Receivers' Accounts and also amongst the Enrolled Accounts of the Lord Treasurer's Remembrancer.

See **MINISTERS' AND RECEIVERS' ACCOUNTS.**

EARL OF KENT'S REBELLION. 1 Henry IV.

"Placita Coronæ aulæ Hospitii domini Regis," concerning the rebellion of Thomas Holand, Earl of Kent. 1 Henry IV.
[*Placita Aulæ. Roll 28.*]

REBELLIONS—(continued).

PERKIN WARBECK'S REBELLION. Temp. Henry VII.

The Indictments and other proceedings against the adherents of Perkin Warbeck will be found in the "Baga de Secretis."

There is also amongst the Miscellanea of the Exchequer a roll of 33 membranes containing an account of the Fines imposed upon those who had favoured or adhered to the rebels against the Lord the King—"Michael Joseph, " James, late Lord Audeley, and a certain man of " infamous character, Peter Warbek, born in Flanders." 12 Henry VII.

ASKE'S REBELLION, OR THE "PILGRIMAGE OF GRACE." Temp. Henry VIII.

Depositions, &c. relating to Aske's Rebellion. Three Vols.

[*Misc. Books, Exch., Treasury of the Receipt, Vols.* 118, 119 *and* 120.]

Letters and Papers relating to the disturbances in the North of England. Temp. Henry VIII.

[*Do.*, *Vol.* 121.]

Documents relating to Aske's Rebellion.

[*Do.*, *Vol.* 122.]

Inquisitions, &c. concerning the possessions of those who took part in the rebellion called " The Pilgrimage of Grace." 29 Hen. VIII.

[*Misc. Books, Augmentation Office, Vol.* 237.]

Accounts of the possessions of the " Pilgrims of Grace." See **MINISTERS' AND RECEIVERS' ACCOUNTS.**

Calendar. 1 Vol. MS., called " Index to Attainders."

BABINGTON'S CONSPIRACY, DOCUMENTS RELATING TO. Elizabeth.

These are amongst the Miscellanea of the Exchequer and consist of Inventories of the goods and chattels of Anthony Babington, Chidiock Tichebourne, and others attainted of High Treason as participators in " Babington's Conspiracy."

DUKE OF NORFOLK'S CONSPIRACY. Elizabeth.

Surveys of the possessions of the Earls of Northumberland and Westmoreland, and of Sir John Neville, Leonard Dacre, and other rebels, taken by Commission dated 18 March 1569. Two large volumes, amongst the Miscellaneous Books of the Exchequer Queen's Remembrancer, known as " Homberstone's Survey."

THE GUNPOWDER PLOT.

The Depositions, Examinations, and other papers relating to the " Gunpowder Treason," including the anonymous letter written to Lord Monteagle, the Con-

REBELLIONS—(continued).

THE GUNPOWDER PLOT—(continued).

fessions signed by Guido Fawkes himself, letters of Father Garnett, and other papers of the greatest interest, are contained in two volumes belonging to the Domestic Series of State Papers.

THE DUKE OF MONMOUTH'S REBELLION.

An account of the proceedings against the rebels and other prisoners in the Counties of Southampton, Wilts, Dorset, Devon, and Somerset, who were tried before Lord Jeffreys in the so-called "Bloody Assize," is appended to a Warrant dated 12 Nov. 1685, directing the issuing of Commissions to inquire into their lands and possessions.

[*Treasury Letter Book*, 1684–1686, *Vol.* 3, *pp.* 187–197.]

THE REBELLIONS OF 1715 AND 1745.

The Trials and Convictions of the adherents of the House of Stuart who took part in the risings of 1715 and 1745 are contained in the BAGA DE SECRETIS.

Lists of all the persons attainted in connexion with the rebellion of 1715, with Rentals, Surveys, and other Papers relating to their estates, will be found amongst the PROCEEDINGS OF THE COMMISSIONERS OF FORFEITED ESTATES, an Inventory of which is printed in Report V., App. II., pp. 97–130.

RECEIPTS AND ISSUES OF THE EXCHEQUER.

The Exchequer was at first a general name signifying as well the place where the Revenue was supervised and managed as the place where it was paid in, that part of it in which the money was received and issued being called the *Thesaurus* or Treasury, the phrase "*in thesauro liberarit*" being generally used to signify that an accountant had delivered money into the Exchequer. In process of time this became known as the *Inferius Scaccarium*, the *Lower Exchequer*, or *Exchequer of Receipt*, the branch which exercised the management of the Revenue with its several Departments being called the *Upper Exchequer* or *Exchequer of Account*.

Although the Exchequer of Receipt was the principal place for the receipt and issuing of the Royal revenue, payments and issues were sometimes made at the *Camera Regis* or King's Chamber, and also at the *King's Wardrobe* in the Tower of London, and at a Treasury in the New Temple.

Several other inferior Receipts or Treasuries called Exchequers were also established for particular purposes, and in various parts of the realm.

When any money was to be paid into the Exchequer by a Sheriff or other Accountant the proper place was at the Office of the four *Tellers* or *Numeratores Scaccarii* in

RECEIPTS AND ISSUES OF THE EXCHEQUER—
(continued).

the Exchequer of Receipt. There the amount was entered in a book, and immediately transcribed on a slip of parchment called a *Bill* or *Tellers' Bill*, and thrown down a pipe into the Tally Court, where a *Tally* was struck or levied. A Tally was a stick (generally of hazel), prepared by an Officer called the Tally Cutter, on which notches were cut indicating the sum specified in the Teller's Bill, in addition to which the sum was written on two sides of it by the Tally Writer, and it was then cleft from end to end through the notches, one of the parts being retained by the Chamberlain of the Exchequer and the other given to the party paying in the money in order to be used in his discharge at the Exchequer of Account, where the Tallies on which allowance was claimed were carefully compared with the Counter-Tallies from the Chamberlain's Office.

The Teller's Bill was entered by the Clerk of the Pells on the Receipt Rolls, called the *Pellis Introitus, Pellis Receptœ*, or Pell of Receipt, and then filed by the Auditor, who also entered the same and afterwards made *Certificate* thereof to the Lord Treasurer.

By Stat. 23 Geo. III., cap. 82, Tallies were directed to be abolished, and indented Check Receipts to be substituted, but this did not come into operation till the removal of the Chamberlains in 1826.

When the Tallies were discontinued, a Memorandum of the Teller's Bills sent into the Tally Court called the *Bill of the Day*, was made by the Clerk of the Introitus, which was sent to the Principal Office to enable the Clerk of the Cash Book to charge the Tellers at the close of each day. An account of each head of the Revenue was also entered in the *Daily Receipt Book*, the moneys received by each Teller being kept distinct, and at the end of every week a total made of each branch of Revenue. A *General Receipt Book* was also kept, in which was inserted the total amount of Revenue received during the week, classed under heads, separating that of England and Scotland.

The *Issues* from the Exchequer were in earlier times made by virtue of a Writ or Mandate from the King under the Great or Privy Seal, directed sometimes to the Chief Justiciar and Barons, but most commonly to the Treasurer and Chamberlains of the Exchequer; the Writ most generally used being called a Writ of Liberate. These Writs were put into execution by *Orders* or *Warrants* from the Lord Treasurer, directed to the Auditor of the Receipt, which were his authority for drawing up an Order on one of the Tellers for the payment of the sum, which Order was then signed by the Lord

RECEIPTS AND ISSUES OF THE EXCHEQUER—
(continued).

Treasurer or Under Treasurer, and forwarded by the Auditor to the Teller named.

In and subsequent to the reign of Charles II. an additional authority was issued by the Treasurer, called a *Letter of Direction*, describing the particular funds out of which the money was to be paid, &c.

The Writs of Liberate or Privy Seal were of two kinds, one of which was final, directing the payment of a certain sum at a fixed time, the other, which directed several payments to be made from time to time, being called a Writ or Privy Seal *Current* or *Dormant*, several Orders being frequently grounded on a single Writ.

Sometimes issues were made from the Royal Treasuries by way of *Prest* or *Imprest*, that is to say, money *advanced* for certain purposes for which the persons receiving it became accountable at the Exchequer of Account.

An account of all moneys issued was entered by the Clerk of the Pells on the Issue Roll called the *Pellis Exitus* or Pell of Issue, stating by whom the sums were paid, and by what Warrant.

Yearly or half-yearly *Declarations or Views* of the Receipts and Issues of the Exchequer were made to the Lord Treasurer by the Auditor of the Receipt, or by the Clerk of the Pells, and during the reign of Henry VIII. *Half-yearly Declarations*, showing the *State of the Royal Treasury*, were made to the King by the Under-Treasurer.

The ancient constitution of the Receipt of the Exchequer was abolished by Stat. 4 Wm. IV., cap. 15, the Auditor, Tellers, Clerk of the Pells, and other subordinate officers being then replaced by a Comptroller-General of the Exchequer with an Assistant Comptroller and the necessary Clerks and Assistants.

On the abolition of the Office of the Comptroller-General of the Exchequer as a separate office, which took place in 1867 pursuant to Stat. 28 & 29 Vict. c. 93, the records of that office, in continuation of those of the Ancient Receipt of the Exchequer, were transferred to the Public Record Office.

The following are the principal Records relating to the business of the Exchequer of Receipt :—

ACCOUNT BOOKS (AUDITORS'). 1782 to 1834. 27 Vols.

Do.   (COMPTROLLER-GENERAL'S) :—

Great Britain. 1835 to 1867. 14 Vols.
Ireland. 1837 to 1867. 12 Vols.
Revenue Quarterly, Ireland. 1837 to 1846. 1 Vol.
Revenue Yearly, Ireland. 1838 to 1867. 2 Vols.

RECEIPTS AND ISSUES OF THE EXCHEQUER—
(continued).

ACQUITTANCE OR RECEIPT BOOKS. 1629-32 and 1693-1706. 2 Vols.

These contain the Acquittances or Receipts for sums paid to various private individuals, and furnish an interesting series of Autographs of distinguished persons, such as those of Gibbons, Wren, and others.

ANNUITIES. See FEES AND ANNUITIES.

ASSIGNMENT BOOKS (AUDITORS'). 1622 to 1834. 32 Vols.

These contain the Deeds of Assignment, whereby pensions, annuities, and other payments out of the Exchequer were alienated in whole or in part; and also Letters of Attorney, Letters of Administration, and Probates of Wills, with other like documents, as recorded in the Office of the Auditor of the Receipt.

From 1791 to 1834 these Volumes contain Letters of Attorney *only*, the Assignment Books forming a separate series, consisting of five Vols.

Inventory. 1622–1834. Report VII., App. II., p. 32.

Descriptive Catalogue. 1622–1738. Report V., App. II., pp. 292–295.

ASSIGNMENT BOOKS (PELLS'). 1677 to 1704. 18 Vols.

These are called "Bankers' Assignments," and contain entries of Deeds, Wills, and Administrations relative to the transfer of shares in the interest of the Loans made to King Charles II. by several Bankers, and payable at the Exchequer.

Descriptive Catalogue. 1677 to 1703-4. Report VI., App. II., pp. 228–230.

ASSIGNMENT BOOKS (GOLDSMITHS').

First Series. 1676 to 1713. 11 Vols.

Second Series. 1678 to 1688. 17 Vols.

In the year 1677 great loans were advanced to the Government by the "Goldsmiths" or Bankers of London on the credit of the hereditary revenue of the Excise, to pay the interest of which terminable Annuities were secured and charged upon that Revenue, by Letters Patent granted to the several contractors or principal creditors, who in their turn made Assignments of divers portions of those Annuities to the persons who had contributed to such Loans. The foregoing are Entry Books of these Assignments; in Series I. the Assignments being collected under the names of the individual bankers to whom the original Assignments were made by the Crown, and in Series II. the same Assignments being entered in chronological order.

Description and Inventory. Reports IV., App. II. p. 167; and V., App. II., p. 246.

ASSIGNMENTS OF ORDERS ON BANKERS' ANNUITIES. 1704 to 1717. 2 Vols.

RECEIPTS AND ISSUES OF THE EXCHEQUER—
(continued).

ATTORNEY, LETTERS, WARRANTS, AND POWERS OF.
"Letters of Attorney." 1706 to 1768. 8 Vols. These relate to "Annuities," &c.
"Powers of Attorney." 1745 to 1787 and 1801 to 1829. 8 Vols. These contain Powers from various Public Officers to enable a third party to receive their salaries at the Receipt of the Exchequer.
Indexes to the foregoing. 4 Vols.
See also ASSIGNMENT BOOKS.
"Entry Book of Letters of Attorney of Nevis and St. Christopher's Debentures." 1707. 1 Vol.

BILLS OF THE DAY. See RECEIPT BOOKS (DAILY).

"BLOOD MONEY" CERTIFICATES. 1649 to 1800. 3 Bundles, containing Certificates of the conviction of highwaymen and other felons, and of the names of the persons by means of whom such convictions were obtained, stating the amount of the rewards due to them in respect thereof. The receipts of the persons mentioned are endorsed on the Certificates.

BREVIATES OF ISSUES. See POSTING BOOKS, or PRIVY SEALS (DORMANT).

CASH BOOKS (AUDITORS'). 1800 to 1834. 35 Vols.

CERTIFICATE BOOKS (PELLS'). 1611 to 1670. 9 Vols.
These consist of entries of the Certificates, made weekly or otherwise, of the Receipts, Issues, and "Remains" of the four Tellers of the Exchequer, showing the precise state of the revenue and expenditure from week to week. Brief entries of "Tellers' Remains," or the sums remaining in the hands of the four Tellers, are also contained in the "POSTING BOOKS OF ISSUES ON PRIVY SEALS."
Description and Inventory. Report VI., App. II., pp. 241–246.

CERTIFICATE BOOKS, CALLED "TELLERS' WEEKLY CERTIFICATE BOOKS."
1610 to 1665. 14 Vols.
and
1813–1835. 5 Vols.

CERTIFICATE BOOKS (AUDITORS'). 1704 to 1834. 20 Vols.

CIVIL LIST ISSUES. 1812 to 1834. 7 Vols., containing a summary of the Revenue set apart to be applied for the Civil List.

CONSOLIDATED FUND BOOKS. 1757 to 1834. 45 Vols., containing Accounts of the income of the Consolidated Fund and of the charges thereon. There are also original Letters touching payments out of the Consolidated Fund, &c., from 1809 to 1834.

RECEIPTS AND ISSUES OF THE EXCHEQUER—
(continued).

DEBENTURE BOOKS (AUDITORS'). 1569 to 1608. 34 Vols.
called "Tellers' Views of Receipts and Issues," or Yearly
Views of the Payments of Fees, Salaries, Annuities, and
Pensions, by the four Tellers of the Exchequer, forming
the "Auditors' Accounts of Payments upon Debentures."
Descriptive Catalogue. Report II., App. II., pp. 243–
246.
Do. 1619 to 1691. 24 Vols.
called "Auditors' Debenture Books."
Descriptive Catalogue. Report V., App. II., pp. 295–
299.
Do. 1696 to 1834. 55 Vols.
called "Auditors' Debenture Books."
See also PAYMENTS BY ROYAL WARRANT or "SOLU-
TIONES PER WARRANTA."

DECLARATION BOOKS (AUDITORS'). 1625 to 1699.
Brief Declarations of the Receipts and Issues of the
Exchequer, and of the state thereof, as certified to the Lord
Treasurer by the Auditor of the Receipt, in half-yearly
volumes. 31 Vols. [There is also amongst the Miscel-
lanea a volume containing "Auditors' Declarations of
Issues," from 1544 to 1560.]
Descriptive Catalogue. 1625 to 1699. Report II.,
App. II., pp. 235–237.

DECLARATION BOOKS (PELLS'). 1555 to 1792.
Half-yearly Declarations of the Receipts and Issues of
the Exchequer, made by the Clerk of the Pells.
Descriptive Catalogue. Report VI., App. II., pp. 232–
243.

DECLARATIONS OF THE STATE OF THE TREASURY (UNDER-
TREASURER'S). 24 Hen. VII. to 38 Hen. VIII. 26 Vols.
Do. DRAFTS OF. Temp.
Hen. VIII. 3 Vols.
Descriptive Catalogue. Report II., App. II., pp. 195–
199.

ENTRY BOOKS (AUDITORS'). 1833 to 1835. 4 Vols.

ESTABLISHMENT OF THE PRINCESS CHARLOTTE OF WALES,
SALARIES, &c. OF THE. 1806 to 1814. 1 Vol.

EXCHEQUER BILLS, ISSUE BOOKS OF. 1744 to 1834, and
of various dates from 1696 to 1855. 26 Vols., consisting
of Entry Books of the Weekly Issues on Exchequer Bills.
Do. (Second Series), 1778 to
1833. 17 Vols., called "Issue Books."
Do., CERTIFICATES OF. 1666 to 1862;
56 Vols., called "Certificates of Exchequer Bills issued."
Do. Do. 1714 to 1726.

RECEIPTS AND ISSUES OF THE EXCHEQUER—
(continued).

EXCHEQUER BILLS, CERTIFICATES OF—(continued).

Entitled "Certificates of Exchequer Bills authorized to be issued by Parliament" (anno 1697, anno 1720, and anno 1723 respectively). 8 Vols.

Do., REGISTERS OF. 1793–1794. 9 Vols.

Do., WARRANTS AND CONTRACTS FOR. 1696 to 1834. 14 Vols.

Do., PAYMASTER'S CERTIFICATES. 1839 to 1834. 1 Vol.

Do., ACCOUNTS AND REPORTS RELATING TO. 1697 to 1731 and 1722–3. 1 Vol.

Do., ACCOUNTS OF THE RECEIVERS AND PAYMASTERS, &c. 1697 to 1828. (Amongst the "Declared Accounts" of the Audit Office.)

FEES AND ANNUITIES, BREVIATES OF. 43 Eliz. to 1698. 37 Vols. (in 4 Bundles), entitled "Breviates of Fees and Annuities payable at the Exchequer."

Do., ASSURANCES, WILLS, &C. RELATING TO ANNUITIES. 1691–1711. 7 Vols.

See also "ASSIGNMENT BOOKS" and "DEBENTURE BOOKS."

IMPREST BOOKS (PELLS'). 1682 to 1790 and 1826 to 1834. 15 Vols.

These Books contain entries by the Auditor of the Receipt of the Exchequer of the sums paid to various public officers by way of "Imprest" or Advance (of which they were to render an account), to be by them disbursed in their respective Departments, pursuant to the authorities therein specified. The last volume is in tabular form, and appears to bear a closer relation to the series called "General Imprest Rolls." There is an *Index Nominum* at the end of each volume.

Description and Inventory. Report VII., App. II., pp. 217–218.

IMPREST BOOKS (PELLS'). 1569 to 1678. 11 Vols. Called "Imprest Certificate Books."

IMPREST ROLLS, GENERAL (AUDITORS'). 1788 to 1834. 7 Vols.

These contain short entries of the issues week by week, mentioning to whom and for what purpose, but not giving the authority for the payment.

IMPREST ROLLS OF THE EXCHEQUER. 22 Elizabeth to 1760. (Amongst the Records of the Audit Office.)

These contain the Accounts of sums advanced to the Treasurers of the Army, Navy, and Ordnance, the Paymasters of the Works, &c., &c.

ISSUE BOOKS (AUDITORS'). See "ORDER BOOKS."

RECEIPTS AND ISSUES OF THE EXCHEQUER—
(continued).

ISSUE BOOKS (PELLS'). 1597 to 1834. 483 Vols.

These Books contain entries of all payments made at the Receipt of the Exchequer, and are in fact duplicates, or rather drafts, of the Issue Rolls since the final establishment of the Record of Expenditure called the "Pell of Issue."

All payments being made either upon *Debentures* (which are grounded on Letters Patent), or upon *Orders* (which are grounded on Letters of Privy Seal), the entries consist of the whole tenor of one, and of the substance of the other, respectively. They were set down in the same manner as the entries in the Receipt Books, day by day, as the several authorities for payment were presented ; for no money could be paid by any Teller until the Clerk of the Pells had testified the recording of the Issue, by writing his *Recordatur*, with the date of the entry in his Book or Roll, on the Debenture or Order by virtue of which the payment was to be made.

They are, like the Receipt Books, furnished with Indexes from the time of the Commonwealth, and are thereby rendered more consultable than the Issue Rolls. Since the time when the engrossing of the Issue Rolls ceased they have become the principal record or "Pell" itself; and therefore, from and after Easter Term 1797, are the only authentic Records of the expenditure of the Exchequer.

Description and Inventory. Report III., App. II., pp. 175–187.

Indexes, called "Alphabets to Issue Books," 1822 to 1832. 22 Vols.

ISSUE ROLLS (PELLS'). 6 Hen. III. to 19 Edw. IV. and from 9 Eliz. to 1797. 1215 Rolls.

Do. (AUDITORS'). 1 Edward I. to 19 Edw. IV. 357 Rolls.

The *Issue Rolls, Pelles Exitus,* or *Pells of Issue* contain the entries made by the Clerk of the Pells of all payments made out of the Revenues of the Crown by the Lord High Treasurer and the Chamberlains of the Exchequer, commencing in the reign of Henry III., and being continued in a regular series to the end of the reign of Edward IV., similar Rolls being also made up by the Auditor of the Receipt. From the reign of Edward IV. to that of Elizabeth the regular engrossing of the rolls appears to have ceased ; being, however, re-established in the latter reign, and thence continued until 1797, after which date the entries are in Books.* •

---

* Accounts of Issues during the period for which the Issue Rolls are wanting will be found on the "Tellers' Rolls."

RECEIPTS AND ISSUES OF THE EXCHEQUER—
(continued).

ISSUE ROLLS (AUDITORS')—(continued).

A translation of the Issue Roll of 34 Edward III. has been printed in full, together with extracts of the Issue Rolls from Henry III. to Henry VI., by F. Devon.

ISSUES. See RECEIPTS AND ISSUES.

ISSUES, BREVIATES OF. See "POSTING BOOKS."

JEWS ROLLS. John to 23 Edward I.

These contain yearly accounts of the receipts from Tallages and other imposts on the Jews.

JORNALIA ROLLS. 21 Edward I. to 1 Edward II.

These contain entries of the total amount of the Receipts and Issues of the Exchequer, day by day, and week by week. They consist of two bundles containing 18 rolls.

LIBERATE ROLLS. 10 Henry III. to 33 Edward I.

These rolls contain precepts directing the payment of sums of money to the Keeper of the Wardrobe, the officers of the Exchequer, and for disbursements of the Crown generally. They also contain orders to Sheriffs to deliver possession of lands or goods which had been extended. There is a series of similar rolls amongst the records of the Court of Chancery extending from the reign of John to that of Henry VI. See **CHANCERY ENROLMENTS.**

MISCELLANEOUS EXCHEQUER PAPERS, called "Thorpe's Exchequer Papers." 1469 to 1685.

A collection of original Letters, Warrants, &c. relating to the business of the Exchequer purchased from Mr. Markham John Thorpe (by whom they had been bought at an auction) in August 1844, and bound in seven volumes.

ORDER BOOKS (PELLS'). 1597 to 1698. 88 Vols.

These are Entry Books containing the substance of the Orders and Warrants made from time to time by the Lord Treasurer directing payments to be made by the Tellers of the Exchequer in pursuance of Writs of Privy Seal. The Privy Seal being a Warrant to the Treasurer but not to the Tellers, the Lord Treasurer on receipt of such a Writ, or of a Warrant from the Sovereign or the Privy Council grounded on or referring to one, found it necessary to charge some Teller to issue and pay the whole or part of the sum therein specified, as the case might require; thus many Orders were frequently made upon the Privy Seal or Warrant.

These Orders were signed by the Lord Treasurer and Under-Treasurer, or, in later times, by three or more of the Commissioners of the Treasury, but were not complete

RECEIPTS AND ISSUES OF THE EXCHEQUER—
(continued).

ORDER BOOKS (PELLS')—(continued).

even when thus signed until subscribed with a direction
to some Teller by name for the payment of the whole or
part of the sum specified out of some particular branch
of the Revenue; for which purpose a *Letter of Direction*
was sent to the Auditor from the Treasury specifying the
Revenue upon which the sum was to be charged. Thus
the original Order served to the Teller as a cheque to a
banker, and (together with the Receipt of the person to
whom the money was paid) was retained among his
Vouchers until his Account was examined by the Auditor,
with whom it was finally lodged. No Order was, however, permitted to be paid by any Teller until it had been
recorded in the "Order Books" of the Pell Office.

These Books are of great use in facilitating researches
for payments which are valuable for historical purposes,
inasmuch as, although the Privy Seal Books afford the
original authority for the miscellaneous expenditure of the
Crown, the evidence of the actual payments made thereon
must be sought either in the Issue Rolls or Books, or
which is much better, in the Order Books, from which all
payments of salaries and annuities are excluded, the
labour of searching being thereby much reduced.

Description and Inventory. Report VI., App II.,
pp. 221–226.

[Selections from the Order Books above described
during the reign of James I., which include many curious
and important entries, have been printed in 1 Vol. 8vo.,
entitled "Issues of the Exchequer, James I.," edited by
F. Devon.]

ORDER BOOKS (AUDITORS'). 1619 to 1678, and 1697.
29 Vols.

These books are similar in their contents to those of
the Pell Office, but slightly different in form.

Descriptive Catalogue. Report II., App. II., pp., 228–
231 ; and Report V., App. II., pp. 299, 300.

Do. (Series II.) called "ISSUE BOOKS."
1760 to 1834. 150 Vols. After 1834, see ORDERS AND
TREASURY WARRANTS.

ORDERS (AUDITORS'), entitled "MODERN TELLERS'
VOUCHERS." 1560 to 1669, and 1701 to 1834.

The original orders, contained in 81 Parcels or Bundles.

ORDERS (EARL CAMDEN'S). 1806 to 1812. 11 Vols.

ORDERS (FOR PENSIONS PAID BY LORD THURLOW).
1782 to 1808. 2 Vols.

ORDERS (FOR "PERMANENT CHARITIES"). 1789 to 1808.

A parcel of loose documents, filling up the chasms in
Lord Thurlow's volumes.

RECEIPTS AND ISSUES OF THE EXCHEQUER—
(continued).

ORDERS AND RECEIPTS RELATING TO THE COMMITTEE FOR
THE PUBLIC REVENUES. 1648 to1652. 1 Bundle.
ORDERS AND WARRANTS. See TREASURY ORDERS AND
WARRANTS, and WARRANTS, ORIGINAL.
ORDERS AND TREASURY WARRANTS (COMPTROLLER-
GENERAL'S). 1834-1865. 29 Vols.
    Do.   Ireland. 1837-1867. 30 Vols.
    Do.   REGISTERS OF, CALLED " CREDITS."
England. 1834-1867. 39 Vols.
Ireland. 1837-1867. 31 Vols.
PATENT AND PRIVY SEAL BOOKS AND ROLLS.

In this series are enrolled all Letters Patent granting
offices, annuities, pensions, or honours to which pecuniary
emolument are attached, and also Privy Seals and Warrants for the payment of money out of the Exchequer.
Amongst these will be found Inrolment Books of the
Letters of Privy Seal issued by Oliver and Richard
Cromwell during the Commonwealth, and of the " Letters
Patent for Fees and Annuities" granted by Charles I. at
Oxford from 1643 to 1646, and of Letters Patent under
the Great Seals of Oliver and Richard Cromwell, and in
the name of " The Keepers of the Liberties of England,"
from 1654 to 1660 inclusive. They are classified as
follows :—

(a.) PATENT BOOKS (PELLS'). 1597 to 1834. 46 Vols.

These are Books of Inrolment of Letters Patent, Royal
Sign Manual Warrants for Pensions, Treasury Constitutions and Appointments to Offices kept by the Clerk of
the Pells.
Descriptive Catalogue. Report IV., App. II., pp. 182-
186.
A Calendar of the contents of Vols. 11 and 12 of this
Series, extending from 1643 to 1646, and from 1654 to
1660 respectively, is printed in Report IV., App. II., pp.
187-200.

(b.) PATENT BOOKS (AUDITORS').

First Series. 1509 to 1834. 56 Vols.
These are Entry Books of Letters Patent granting
Offices, Pensions, and Honours with *pecuniary emoluments.*
Descriptive Catalogue. 1509 to 1663. Report II.,
App. II., pp. 205 209.
Second Series. 1599 to 1696. 12 Vols., called
" Auditors' Patents for Tallies," containing entries of
Letters Patent relating to Grants *of or from the Revenues
of the Crown* or charged thereupon, *Crown Leases, Annui-
ties,* and other Patents.
Descriptive Catalogue. Report II., App. II., pp. 209-
211.

RECEIPTS AND ISSUES OF THE EXCHEQUER—[1]
(continued).

(c.) PATENT ROLLS (AUDITORS'). 7 to 17 James I. 9 Rolls.
Inventory. Report VII., App. II., p. 29.

(d.) PATENT AND PRIVY SEAL ROLLS (PELLS'). 2 to 17 James I. 6 Rolls.
Descriptive Catalogue. Report IV., App. II., pp. 210, 211.

(e.) PATENTS AND PRIVY SEALS (FOR BARONETS), ENTRIES OF. James I. to James II. 9 Vols., so called, containing accounts of the sums paid by various persons for Patents of Baronetcy.

(f.) PRIVY SEAL BOOKS (PELLS'). 1597 to 1834. 59 Vols.
These volumes contain entries of all the Letters of Privy Seal addressed to the Treasurer and Chamberlains of the Exchequer, directing the payment of any money out of the Receipt of the Exchequer, and also of the Royal Warrants grounded thereon. Similar Entry Books or Books of Enrolment were also kept by the Auditors of the Exchequer.
Descriptive Catalogue. Report IV., App. II., pp. 203–208. [No. 13 of this Series contains the Privy Seals of *Oliver* and *Richard Cromwell*, a Calendar of which is printed in Report V., App. II., p. 246.]

(g.) PRIVY SEAL BOOKS (AUDITORS'). 1 Henry VII. to 14 Henry VIII. (1 Vol.) ; and 1570 to 1834 (32 Vols.).
These are similar Entry Books to those of the Clerk of the Pells.
Descriptive Catalogue. Report II., App. II., pp. 211–219 ; and Report V., App. II., p. 291.
Do., called "Enrolments of Privy Seals, Assignments, Warrants, and Letters of Attorney." 1620 to 1707. 7 Vols.
Descriptive Catalogue. Report II., App. II., pp. 219–221.

(h.) PRIVY SEAL ROLLS (AUDITORS') 9 to 17 James I. 6 Rolls.
Inventory. Report VII., App. II., p. 31.

PAYMENTS BY ROYAL WARRANT, BOOKS OF. 1 to 28 Elizabeth. 17 thin Vols., entitled "Solutiones factæ per Warranta Reginæ per Numeratores Scaccarii," containing abstracts of all payments out of the Exchequer by Writs of Privy Seal, Warrants, &c. reduced under distinct heads according to the several kinds of Warrants issued.
Descriptive Catalogue. Report II., App. II., pp. 246–247.

PAYMENTS OUT OF THE CONSOLIDATED FUND. See "CONSOLIDATED FUND BOOKS."

PAYMENTS, BOOKS OF (RELATING TO THE WARDROBE AND HOUSEHOLD). 1571 to 1593. 10 Vols.

RECEIPTS AND ISSUES OF THE EXCHEQUER—
(continued).

PAYMENTS, TELLERS' VIEWS OF. See "RECEIPTS AND ISSUES, TELLERS' VIEWS OF."

PENSIONS. See PATENT AND PRIVY SEAL BOOKS, &c.

PENSIONS PAID BY LORD THURLOW. See ORDERS.

"PERMANENT CHARITIES." See ORDERS.

POSTING BOOKS (PELLS'). *First Series,* 1597 to 1628, called "Breviates of Issues upon Letters of Privy Seal" or "Privy Seals, Dormant."

A large proportion of the payments made out of the Exchequer being made by virtue of Privy Seals which were not satisfied by a single payment, but operated as the authority for *successive payments* at intervals, the Clerk of the Pells *posted* into a book, under the names of the individuals, offices, departments, or services referred to, abstracts of all the Privy Seals then in force, with references to the places of their enrolment in his "Privy Seal Book," the payments made thereon from time to time being specified in the margin. He was thus enabled to ascertain how far every Privy Seal was satisfied, and whether there remained sufficient of the original sum specified therein to warrant any payment directed by an Order on that authority. Such Privy Seals as did not *expire* in a single Issue were technically described as *dormant;* they were not *dead,* but *sleeping.* Hence, these books have been called "Dormant Privy Seals"; though, as they contain Abstracts only of those documents, which are entered in full in the "Privy Seal Books," the name "Posting Books" by which the more modern books of a similar nature were known in the Pell Office has been thought to describe them more clearly. They furnish a convenient and comprehensive clue to the contents of the Issue Roll, and omitting the ordinary payments of salaries and pensions, exhibit all the great expenditure of the Crown for purposes naval and military, domestic and foreign.

Descriptive Catalogue. Report IV., App. II., pp. 169–171.

POSTING BOOKS (PELLS'). *Second Series.* 1718 to 1834.

These Books contain brief entries of all Payments on Debentures arranged under the names of the several Grantees, including those to Members of the Royal Family, the Salaries of the various Officers of the Treasury and Exchequer, of Judges and Law Officers, of Secretaries of State, Political and Foreign Ministers, &c., &c., and of Perpetuities and Pensions. There is an Index Nominum at the end of each volume.

Descriptive Catalogue. Report IV., App. II., pp. 177–179.

RECEIPTS AND ISSUES OF THE EXCHEQUER— (continued).

POWERS OF ATTORNEY. See ASSIGNMENT BOOKS, and ATTORNEY, WARRANTS, LETTERS, AND POWERS OF.

PRÆSTITA ROLLS. (EXCHEQUER, Q. R.) John to James I.

These consist of Accounts of the payments made to various Officers of the Royal Household and others at the Exchequer of Receipt on account of their Salaries, Wages, &c., or for the performance of special duties as messengers or otherwise, or the execution of works and repairs. The first of these Rolls, dated 7 John, is printed in the "Selections from the Miscellanea of the Queen's Remembrancer," published by the Record Commission.

There is also a Præstita Roll of the 12th year of King John amongst the Miscellaneous Enrolments of the Court of Chancery; and a similar Roll dated Michaelmas, 43 Henry III., will be found amongst the Miscellanea of the Exchequer of the Receipt.

PRIVY SEALS AND WARRANTS FOR ISSUES. Henry III. to William IV. 218 Parcels.

Prior to 1 Henry IV. the series is very imperfect.

PRIVY SEAL BOOKS, &c. See PATENT AND PRIVY SEAL BOOKS, &c.

PRIVY SEALS (DORMANT). See POSTING BOOKS.

RECEIPT BOOKS (AUDITORS'). 1570 to 1709. 128 Vols.

These contain an account of all Payments into the Exchequer for every half year, under the names of the several Tellers receiving the same, and subdivided under the several species of Revenue so received.

They form an almost perfect series from 1570 to 1642 inclusive, with three books of the time of the Commonwealth, five of the reign of Charles II., and one of that of Queen Anne.

Descriptive Catalogue. Report II., App. II., pp. 237–243.

Do., called " Bills of the Day," or " Daily Receipt Books." 1801 to 1834. 32 Vols.

Do. (PELLS'). 1559 to 1834. 516 Vols.

These books contain copies of all the Tellers' Bills, as thrown down by them upon the table of the Tally Court on the payment of revenues into the Exchequer; stating the County or Place from which the revenue arose, the name of the Accountant rendering the same, the amount, and the name of the Teller to whose hands the money was paid. From these Books the Receipt Rolls, of which they form the drafts or duplicates, were engrossed, and in default or absence of the Roll the Book serves authoritatively as

RECEIPTS AND ISSUES OF THE EXCHEQUER—
(continued).

RECEIPT BOOKS (PELLS')—(continued).

the Pell of Receipt. The enrolling of the Receipts being discontinued in the year 1782, from that date to the year 1834 the Receipt Books form the only Record of the Income of the Exchequer. From the year 1641 each Book (with few exceptions) is furnished with an Index.

Description and Inventory. Report III., App. II., pp. 156–169; and Report IV., App. II., p. 166. [A Calendar of certain Privy Seals from 1666 to 1670, enrolled in Vol. 515 of this series, is printed in Report IV., App. II., p. 208.] Before 1559 see RECEIPT ROLLS.

RECEIPT BOOKS (COMPTROLLER-GENERAL'S):—
Great Britain. 1834 to 1866. 20 Vols.
Ireland. 1837 to 1867. 18 Vols.

These form a continuation of the Auditors' Receipt Books.

RECEIPT BOOKS (for sums paid to private individuals).
See ACQUITTANCE AND RECEIPT BOOKS.

RECEIPT ROLLS (PELLS'). 14 John to 22 George III. 1110 Rolls.

Do. (AUDITORS'). 5 Henry III. to 10 Eliz. 555 Rolls.

The Receipt Rolls, Pelles Receptæ, or Pells of Receipt, were anciently engrossed from the "Tellers' Bills," or, before they were invented, from the Tallies, and subsequently from the Receipt Books, and contain copies of all the Tellers' Bills, &c. as thrown down by them upon the table of the Tally Court on the payment of revenues into the Exchequer. Prior to the reign of Edward I. the series of these Rolls is irregular, but from the first year of that reign to the 22nd of George III., when the engrossing of the Receipts on Rolls was discontinued, it is nearly perfect. Since Easter 1782 the RECEIPT BOOKS are the only Records of the income of the Exchequer.

RECEIPTS, ABBREVIATES OF (PELLS'). 1562 to 1643. 68 Vols.

These books contain abridged entries of all payments of Revenues into the Exchequer, very briefly extracted out of the Receipt Book.

Descriptive Catalogue. Report III., App. II., pp. 171–173.

RECEIPTS AND ISSUES, ACCOUNTS OF. Henry VII. to Henry VIII.

A few rough Entry Books of Receipts and Issues, belonging chiefly to the reigns of Henry VII. and Henry VIII., will be found amongst the Miscellaneous Books of the Exchequer Treasury of the Receipt. (See p. 226.)

RECEIPTS AND ISSUES OF THE EXCHEQUER—

(continued).

RECEIPTS AND ISSUES, BRIEF DECLARATIONS OF (AUDITORS'). 1 Car. I. to 1699. 31 Vols.

RECEIPTS AND ISSUES, TELLERS' VIEWS OF. 11–12 Elizabeth to 1608. 34 Vols.

RECEIPTS AND PAYMENTS, WEEKLY CERTIFICATES OF (PELLS'). 1611 to 1670. 9 Vols.

REVENUE, ACCOUNTS OF THE. 1786 to 1834. 23 Vols.
These are the Yearly, Quarterly, and Weekly Accounts of the Revenue made from the Exchequer to the Lords of the Treasury. There is also amongst the Miscellanea a Synopsis of the Revenue Accounts for the reign of George IV.

REVENUE, RECEIPTS AND ORDERS RELATING TO THE 1648 to 1652.
A bundle of Receipts and Orders relating to the Committee for the Public Revenues during the Commonwealth.

SUPPLY CASH BOOKS. 1817 to 1833. 18 Vols., containing apparently entries of the Supplies for the various Public Departments.

TELLERS' BILLS. Henry VI. to George III. 39 Bundles containing the original "Tellers' Bills," or accounts of money paid into the Receipt of the Exchequer, on narrow slips of parchment.

TELLERS' BOOKS OR ROLLS. Henry IV. to Charles I. 155 Rolls.
These are the Rolls of Accounts of Receipts and Issues kept by the four Tellers of the Exchequer. They are valuable as supplying information for periods when the Issue Rolls are wanting.

TELLERS' CERTIFICATE BOOKS. See CERTIFICATE BOOKS.

TELLERS' REMAINS. See POSTING BOOKS.

TELLERS' VIEWS OF ACCOUNTS. 1 Eliz. to 9 James I. 37 Vols.
These consist of Views (otherwise called "Brief Declarations") of the Receipts and Issues of the four Tellers as certified to the Lord Treasurer by the Auditor of the Receipt of the Exchequer.
Descriptive Catalogue. Report II., App. II., pp. 233–234. See also RECEIPTS AND ISSUES, TELLERS' VIEWS OF.

TELLERS' VOUCHERS. See ORDERS (AUDITORS').

TREASURY LETTERS. 1793 to 1834. 30 Vols., containing Letters of direction from the Treasury to the Auditors of the Exchequer. See ORDER BOOKS.

RECEIPTS AND ISSUES OF THE EXCHEQUER—
(continued).

TREASURY LETTERS (COMPTROLLER-GENERAL'S) :—
Great Britain. 1834–1867. 56 Vols.
Ireland. 1837–1867. 31 Vols.
Reference Books or Indexes. England. 1834–1865.
12 Vols.
Ireland. 1837–1865. 4 Vols.

TREASURY ORDERS AND WARRANTS. 1547 to 1788.
Original Orders and Warrants to the Tellers of the
Exchequer for payments bearing the signatures of the
Lord High Treasurer and others. 20 Portfolios.
See also ORDERS, and WARRANTS, ORIGINAL.

UNDER-TREASURERS' DECLARATIONS. See DECLARATIONS.

VOUCHERS. See ORDERS.

WARDROBE DEBENTURES, &c. Various dates. 58 Parcels.
These consist of original Debentures or Notes of sums
owing in the Great Wardrobe, which were paid at the
Exchequer of Receipt, the Debenture being thereupon
cancelled and retained as a voucher. They were formerly
amongst the Records of the Treasury of the Receipt of
the Exchequer. The payments are recorded on the Issue
Rolls.

WARRANT BOOKS (PELLS'). 1617 to 1790.
These contain Entries of the Warrants of the successive
Lords Treasurers and Under-Treasurers (1) for striking
Tallies ; (2) for drawing Orders and Debentures for Issues,
being the Ordinary Money Warrants ; (3) for Issues cut
of the Royal Aid and other special Revenues ; (4) for the
payment of Interest on Bankers' Loans ; (5) for the payment of Arrears to the Servants, &c. of Charles II. ; (6)
relative to the Funds of the South Sea Company ; and
(7) relative to payments out of the Sales of Forfeited
Estates.
Descriptive Catalogue. Report V., App. II., pp. 282–
289.

WARRANT BOOKS (AUDITORS'). 1626 to 1790. 70 Vols.
These are the Auditors' Entry Books of Warrants of
various kinds in several series.
Descriptive Catalogue. Report II., App. II., pp. 221–
228. (See also Report V., App. II. p. 292.)

WARRANTS FOR ISSUES. See PRIVY SEALS AND WARRANTS
FOR ISSUES.

WARRANTS, ORIGINAL. 1794 to 1834. 88 Vols., containing
Original Royal and Treasury Warrants for the Issue of
Money at the Receipt of the Exchequer.
Descriptive Catalogue. Report VIII., App. II., pp. 193–
198. See also TREASURY ORDERS AND WARRANTS.

REGISTERS, AND BOOKS OF REMEMBRANCE.

Under this Title are included the several Entry Books of
Official Memoranda, and of documents of special importance, which were compiled at a very early period by the
Officers of the Exchequer and others for the use of their
respective Departments. Such are the Black Books of
the Treasury of the Receipt and of the King's Remembrancer's Department, the Red Book of the Exchequer,
the Registrum Munimentorum, and others, the contents
of which are fully described below. To these have been
added certain ancient Kalendars and Inventories of the
Exchequer, giving Lists of Charters, Treaties, &c., and
of the Royal Jewels and other Articles of Value deposited
in the Treasury.

The Book of Aids, the Liber Feodorum, and other
volumes consisting exclusively of Returns of Knights'
Fees, are described under the head of **FEUDAL
TENURES.**

The Black Book of the Admiralty, which includes the
" Laws of Oleron," stated to have been made by Richard I.
when he was at the Isle of Oleron, and said to be "the
" most excellent collection of sea-laws in the world," is
in the custody of the Registrar of the Admiralty Court.

BLACK BOOK OF THE EXCHEQUER OR "LIBER NIGER."
(EXCHEQUER, TREASURY OF THE RECEIPT.)

The contents of this volume are as follows :—

1. A Table or perpetual Calendar for finding the Dominical
Letters, &c.
2. A Calendar or Almanac containing Memoranda of remark-
able occurrences and of appointments of various Officers
of the Exchequer.
3. Drawings of the emblems of the four Evangelists, accompanied by verses from the several Gospels (probably
used for the purpose of administering oaths).
4. Drawings of the Crucifixion, the Virgin and Child, St.
Michael, &c., with Latin and English verses and
miscellaneous entries.
5. The " Dialogus de Scaccario," a Treatise on the ancient
constitution and practice of the Exchequer. (There is
another copy of this treatise in the Red Book.)
6. The Oath of the Teller of the Exchequer.
7. The Oath of the Messenger of the Exchequer.
8. A Survey of the Manor of Isleworth. Edw. III.
9. A Deed of sale of timber at Bodyham. 50 Edw. III.
10. Admissions of Chamberlains, Tellers, and Clerks of the
Pells. Hen. VI. and Edw. IV.
11. A collection of rhymes and idle verses.
12. Tables for the calculation of salaries, apparently of the
reign of Edw. II.
13. Miscellaneous entries relating to the Receipt of the Exchequer, Admissions of Officers, Orders of Court, Writs
and other Memoranda of a similar description from
19 Edw. II. to 1715, a few original instruments being
annexed or inserted.

REGISTERS, AND BOOKS OF REMEMBRANCE
---(continued).

BLACK BOOK OF THE EXCHEQUER OR "LIBER NIGER PARVUS." (EXCHEQUER, QUEEN'S REMEMBRANCER.)

This was compiled about the same time as the Red Book (Temp. Henry III), and contains many similar entries. The contents are as follows:—

1. The Will of Henry II.
2. Treaty between Henry I. and Robert Earl of Flanders, dated at Dover. 6 Id. Martii. [Printed in Rymer's Fœdera.]
3. Treaty between the same, dated 16 Kal. Junii. [Printed in Rymer's Fœdera.]
4. Treaties between Henry II., Earl Theodoric, and Philip, Earl of Flanders. [Printed in Rymer's Fœdera.]
5. Acknowledgment of the Homage due from the subjects of the Earl of Flanders to Henry II. [Printed as above.]
6. Agreement between Henry II. and William King of Scotland. [Printed as above.]
7. Four Bulls of Pope Alexander. Temp. Hen. II. [Printed as above.]
8. Certificates or "Chartæ" by the several Tenants in Capite of the number of Knights' Fees held by them returned into the Exchequer in the 14th year of Henry II.
9. An account of the Royal Household (Temp. Henry II.), entitled "Constitutio domus Regis de procurationibus."
10. Carta Stannarii Domini Regis.
11. Carta Hamelini Comitis Warren'.
12. Carta Walteri Croc.
13. Carta Henrici de Clinton.
14. Carta Aliciæ de Bella Aqua.
15. Carta Domini Coventrensis.
16. Confirmatio Decani et Capituli Lichfeldensis.
17. Charter to W. de Braosa.
18. Carta Scabinorum et proborum hominum de Sancto Andomaro.
19. The pledges for the sons of W. de Braosa.
20. Henor Boloniæ. (A List of the Knights' Fees, &c. belonging to the Honour.)

RED BOOK OF THE EXCHEQUER OR "LIBER RUBEUS." (EXCHEQUER, QUEEN'S REMEMBRANCER.)

The Red Book of the Exchequer consists of two distinct portions or subdivisions, the first of which comprises the original entries made at the time the volume was compiled (none of which are of a later date than 15 Henry III.), and is distinguished from the rest of the volume by the regularity and beauty of the handwriting, by the illumination, and by the entries being in double columns. By this portion, however, one half only of the volume is occupied, the rest being filled by entries in the hands of later scribes, many of which are of great curiosity and value, but have been made with little regard to the uniformity or beauty of the volume.

The greater part of these entries belong to the period of Edward I., with a few of the reigns of Edward II., Edward III., and Richard II.

Since the latter reign nothing appears to have been added (with the exception of one grant in the reign of

REGISTERS, AND BOOKS OF REMEMBRANCE
—(continued).

RED BOOK OF THE EXCHEQUER &c.—(continued).

Henry V.) till the reign of Elizabeth, when the blank leaves of the volume appear to have been used by the Officers of the Exchequer for official Memoranda of various kinds entered quite at random.

The contents of the First Portion are as follows :—

1. The Laws of Henry I. " De libertate Ecclesiæ et tocius Angliæ observandâ."
2. "Constitutio Domûs Regis" (Temp. Hen. II.). This is also in the Black Book.
3. The " Dialogus de Scaccario." (Also in the Black Book.)
4. A collection made from the Pipe Rolls by Adam de Swereford (temp. Hen. III.) of all the Scutages levied between 2 Hen. II. and 13 John, showing the number of Knights' Fees accounted for by each Tenant in Capite.
5. Transcripts of the Certificates or " Chartæ " by the several Tenants in Capite of the number of Knights' Fees held by them returned into the Exchequer in 14 Hen. II. [These are also in the Black Book.]
6. A Return of the Serjeanties in the different Counties.
7. Inquisitions respecting Knights' Fees and other Tenures in Capite. 12 & 13 John.
8. Similar Inquisitions respecting the Knights' Fees of escheated Honours. 13 John.
9. An account of the Knights' Fees held by the Tenants of the Duke of Normandy, with the service due from them.

The additional entries may be classified as follows :—

(I.) Lists of Knights' Fees, &c. and Official Memoranda, as follows :—

1. Excerpts from the Pipe Rolls of Henry II. and Richard I.
2. A large collection of the Feudal Tenures in various Counties, with the sums paid thereon in the reigns of Henry II. and Richard I.
   A list of Knights' Fees in the County of Chester. 37 Hen. III.
4. Accounts of Castle Guard Rents belonging to Dover, Windsor, Newcastle-on-Tyne, &c. Temp. Hen. III.
5. A collection of Ordinances by the King and Council respecting the practice of the Exchequer in the reigns of Edw. II. and Edw. III.
6. The Oaths of the several Officers of the Exchequer (in the handwriting of the reign of Elizabeth), together with those of the Lord Mayor of London and of the Mayors and Bailiffs of other Cities and Towns, and of the Escheators, Sheriffs, Justiciars, and Members of the King's Council, with other Memoranda relating to the business of the Court and various documents relating to the Mint and Coinage.

(II.) Public Charters, Statutes, and Diplomatic Documents, as follows :—

1. Transcripts of Charters of William the Conqueror, Henry I., Henry II., and Henry III., including an Inspeximus of Magna Charta and the Charter of Liberties of 9 Hen. III.
   [The copies of these Charters printed in the Statutes of the Realm," and in Rymer's " Fœdera " have

REGISTERS, AND BOOKS OF REMEMBRANCE
—(continued).

RED BOOK OF THE EXCHEQUER—(continued).

been either taken from or collated with those in the Red Book.]

2. Transcripts of Statutes of Henry III., Edward I., and Edward II. [Printed in the Statutes of the Realm.]

3. Letters and Treaties relating to the affairs of the Emperor Frederic II. (brother-in-law of Henry III.), and to negotiations with France, Flanders, and Scotland.

(III.) Papal Bulls and Letters.

These consist of Transcripts of Bulls and Letters concerning the Papal authority, of various dates, including a Declaration by Wm. Marshall Earl of Pembroke and others in the name of the magnates of Ireland, protesting against the absolution by Pope Innocent of the subjects of the King of England from their allegiance, the famous Letter from Robert Grosteste, Bishop of Lincoln to Pope Innocent IV. in 1253; and a Catalogue of Papal Bulls delivered into the Exchequer.

(IV.) Title Deeds, &c. of the Royal Possessions.

These consist of Transcripts of Grants and Conveyances to the King from various persons, including Quit-claims from Piers de Gaveston of several Manors received by him from Edward II.; documents relating to the possessions of Isabella de Fortibus Countess of Albemarle (Temp. Edward I.), who had made the King her heir; and Charters and Grants to the King from John de Warrenna Earl of Surrey, Ralph Pipard Knight, Gilbert Peche Knight, Hugh de Plessetis, the Bishop of Winchester, and many others.

A very full Report by Mr. Hunter on the composition and contents of the Red Book of the Exchequer, from which the foregoing particulars are taken, is contained in the Report of the Record Commissioners for the year 1837, pp. 165–177.

This volume is now being edited for the "Rolls Series" of publications.

REGISTRUM MUNIMENTORUM. (EXCHEQUER, TREASURY OF THE RECEIPT.)

Two volumes generally referred to as "Liber A" and "Liber B," being Registers or "Books of Remembrance," formed in the reign of Edward I. They contain Transcripts of Papal Bulls and of Treaties and other diplomatic documents during the reigns of Henry III. and Edward I., a List of which is appended.

Contents of "LIBER A."

1. Table of Contents, with references to the Chests, &c. in which the originals of the documents transcribed in the volume were deposited.

2. Papal Bulls relating to the grant of the tenths of ecclesiastical benefices for the recovery of the Holy Land.

3. Papal Bulls relating to Guy and Aymeric de Montfort, monitions addressed to the Kings of Scotland and Princess of Wales, excommunications of the King's enemies, &c., &c.

REGISTERS, AND BOOKS OF REMEMBRANCE
—(continued).

REGISTRUM MUNIMENTORUM—(continued).

4. Documents relating to the disputes between Hugh, Count of March and Angouleme, and Henry III.
5. Documents relating to the marriage of Margaret daughter of Edward I. with John son of the Duke of Brabant.
6. Documents relating to the Treaty of Marriage of the Maid of Norway.
7. Documents relating to the marriages between Joanna daughter of Henry King of Navarre and a son of Edward I., and between Elizabeth daughter of Edw. I. and John the son of Florence Count of Holland.
8. Papal Bulls, &c. relating to the marriage between Alphonso son of Peter King of Aragon and Eleanor daughter of Edward I.
9. Further documents relating to the marriage of the Maid of Norway.
10. Grants, conveyances, &c. made to the Crown, obligations and securities for payment of moneys to the King, grants of aids and subsidies, and other miscellaneous documents.
11. Documents relating to the election of the Prior of St. Swithin's, Winchester, &c.
12. Constitutions made by John Peckham, Archbishop of Canterbury, in the Council held at Reading. (Printed by Wilkins.)
13. Award by Richard King of the Romans as to the manner in which the Earl of Gloucester is to proceed to the Holy Land, &c.
14. Transcripts of the Statute of Westminster pro Mercatoribus, 13 Edw. I.; and of the Statute of Gloucester, 6 Edw. I.
15. Miscellaneous documents, including the Will of Edw. I.; Papal Bulls, &c. relating to the liberation of Aymeric de Montfort; Inquisitions concerning the Parks of Fremantle and Howden; Leagues with Castile; Letters from English prelates concerning the war against the Welsh, &c.
16. Letters, submissions, homages, and other documents relating to the affairs of Wales during the reigns of Henry III. and Edward I.
17. Grants of the Seigniory of Ireland and of the Cities of Dublin and Limerick, &c. made by Henry III. to his eldest son Edward; Letters and obligations from the Prelates of Ireland, and other documents relating to that country.
18. Treaties of Peace with Norway, &c.

Contents of "LIBER B."

1. Tables of Contents.
2. Treaties and Diplomatic Documents between France and England.
3. Letters from the Count of Savoy, the Magistrates of various towns in Ponthieu, &c.
4. Letters of Homage and other documents relating to France.
5. Deed of Covenant for money lent to Prince Edward by St. Louis in aid of his pilgrimage to the Holy Land, with other documents relating thereto.
6. Treaties and Correspondence with Florence Count of Holland, and with Castile, &c.

REGISTERS, AND BOOKS OF REMEMBRANCE
—(continued).

REGISTRUM MUNIMENTORUM—(continued).

7. Documents relating to the Truces between Philip King of France and Alphonso King of Arragon.
8. Treaties between Edward I. and Guy, Count of Flanders.
9. Documents relating to the Treaty at Tarrascon between Alphonso King of Arragon and Charles King of Sicily.
10. Letters, &c. relating to the liberation of the Prince of Salerno, made captive by the King of Arragon.
11. Letters, Treaties, and other documents relating to the affairs of Arragon and Sicily.
12. Homages, Pleas, Grants, and other documents relating to Gascony. Temp. John and Henry III.
13. The Charters of Oleron, surrendered by the community on account of their trespasses.
14. Privileges granted to the Bastida of Valence in the Agennois.
15. Grants of lands, demesnes, &c. made by Henry III. to his son Edward, both in England and Wales and beyond the Seas.
16. Various documents relating to Gascony.
17. Documents relating to Gascony, Ponthieu, the Agennois, &c.

KALENDARE DE BULLIS PAPALIBUS, &c. (EXCHEQUER, TREASURY OF THE RECEIPT.) Edward II.

This Calendar, also known as " Bishop Stapleton's Calendar," was compiled about the year 1323, under the direction of Walter Stapleton, Bishop of Exeter, who at that time held the office of Treasurer. It contains a description of all the documents then in the Treasury, methodically arranged under the heads of Papal Bulls, Charters, &c., the various chests, &c. in which they were deposited being noted in the margin, with drawings of the *signs* by which they were distinguished. [Printed in Palgrave's "Ancient Kalendars and Inventories of the Exchequer," Vol. 1, pp. 1–155.]

LIBER MEMORANDORUM CAMERARII. (EXCHEQUER, TREASURY OF THE RECEIPT.) 39 Edw. III. to 35 Hen. VIII.

This volume contains the Memoranda made from time to time by the Chamberlains or their deputies as well of the Muniments as of the Jewels and other articles deposited in the Treasury or delivered out of the same. Many valuable instruments are inserted at full length, and others are annexed to the leaves and bound up therewith.

[Printed in Palgrave's " Ancient Kalendars and Inventories of the Exchequer."]

KELLAWE'S REGISTER. (PALATINATE OF DURHAM.) 1311 to 1316.

This volume is a record of all the Acts and Proceedings of the Palatinate, whether relating to ecclesiastical or

x

REGISTERS, AND BOOKS OF REMEMBRANCE
—(continued).

KELLAWE'S REGISTER. (PALATINATE OF DURHAM)—(continued).

temporal matters during the Pontificate of Richard de Kellawe, Bishop of Durham, from A.D. 1311 to A.D. 1316. A brief description of this Register, with an Index of Persons and Places, is printed in Report XXX., App., pp. 99–120, and the Register has been published in the Series of "Chronicles and Memorials," in 4 Vols. 4to, edited by Sir Thos. Duffus Hardy.

RENTALS AND SURVEYS.

Under the general title of Rentals and Surveys a collection has been made of the numerous Rentals or Rent Rolls, Terriers, Extents, and Surveys or Valuations of Monastic and other possessions which formerly existed amongst the Miscellanea of the Queen's Remembrancer's Department, of the Treasury of the Receipt of the Exchequer, and of the Augmentation Office, with a few documents of the like nature amongst the Records transferred from the Tower of London and the Records of the Principality of Wales and Palatinate of Chester.

These have been arranged as far as possible in Counties, and an Inventory of them has been prepared.

Numerous Rentals and Surveys will also be found in the several series of "Miscellaneous Books," described on pp. 222–241.

The *Extents of Manors* in the nature of returns to Writs of Extendi Facias or to Special Commissions out of the Exchequer drawn from the sources above mentioned form a separate collection, an Inventory of which is in progress.

The Surveys belonging to various Courts and offices which exist as distinct classes or groups are described on pp. 341–345.

REVENUE ROLLS.

Under this title may be classed the several Rolls, with the documents subsidiary thereto, by means of which the Crown Revenue was accounted for at the Pipe Office of the Court of Exchequer. The business of this Office, which derived its name from the fancied resemblance of its functions to those of a pipe or conduit,—"for as water " is conveyed from many fountains and springs by a pipe " into the cistern of a house and from thence into the " several offices of the same, so this golden and silver " stream is drawn from several courts (as fountains of " justice and other springs of revenue), reduced and col- " lected into one pipe, and by that conveyed into the

REVENUE ROLLS—(continued).

" cistern of his Majesty's Receipt,"—consisted of recording on the Great Roll, there called the Pipe Roll, the King's determined debts and certain revenue, and of levying the same by process addressed to the Sheriffs of the several counties, who, with the Bailiffs and other accountable officers, were first summoned into the Exchequer to be duly apposed as to the various items in charge against them for which they subsequently accounted at the Pipe Office, receiving therefrom their formal discharge or " Quietus."

The Revenues of the Crown under the Feudal System were of two kinds, either *certain* or *casual*, both of which were accounted for almost entirely by the Sheriffs of the several counties, cities, and towns, to whom as the King's Farmers the custody of his lands, tenements, and other possessions was committed.

The *certain* Revenue consisted of the rents and services due to the King from the tenants of the various manors, lands and tenements held by grant or lease from the Crown, the charge of the whole of which was committed to the Sheriff under the title of " Corpus Comitatus " or the Farm of the whole shire, and was grounded on the *Estreats* or *Extracts* from the Rolls of Chancery of all Charters, Letters Patent, Writs, and other documents for which any rent or consideration was to be rendered, which were sent into the Exchequer under the title of " Originalia " or " Originals," in order that any rents or reservations due thereon might be collected by means of the process issuing out of the latter Court. [See ORIGINALIA ROLLS.]

The *casual* Revenue consisted of the Fines, Issues, Amerciaments, and Forfeited Recognizances in the various Courts of Law and before the Justices of the Peace, and of the profits of lands, tenements, goods, and chattels seized into the King's hands by virtue of writs of outlawry, or de diem clausit extremum, &c., and other profits arising from the royal prerogative.

The several processes by means of which these were accounted for to the Exchequer were as follows :—

(1.) Twice in the year, at the Terms of Hillary and Trinity respectively, a Writ was issued from the Pipe Office of the Exchequer which was called the *Summons of the Pipe*, and was addressed to the Sheriffs throughout England, directing them to appear before the Treasurer and Barons of the Exchequer, bringing with them *whatever they owed* to the King and all debts thereunder written.

To this Writ, which was returnable in the following term, was annexed a Transcript from the Great Roll of the Pipe of the whole charge against the Sheriff.

REVENUE ROLLS—(continued).

On the appointed day the Sheriff appeared by his Under-Sheriff or Attorney, and was *apposed*, at first in open court, and afterwards before the Cursitor Baron, on his account.

This *apposal* consisted of examining the several items of charge expressed in the Writ or Summons of the Pipe one by one, and placing them to the Sheriff's Account or otherwise, according to the answers made by him. It was so called because the Court then decided what items the Sheriff should *apponere* or place to account.

If the Sheriff had levied any of the debts specified in the schedule annexed to the Writ of Summons to each of such items he said *tot*, meaning thereby that he charged himself with the whole sum, or *so much* as was therein expressed. The letter T. was thereupon set against that particular sum in the margin of the Pipe Roll, which is called "totting" it. If he had not received the whole of the money the remainder of the item was nichilled thus, "Recd. [so much]" "*nil* the rest." If any sums due to the Crown had been paid at the Receipt of the Exchequer, as was sometimes done, the Sheriff did not tott that particular item, because he had not actually levied it. He was still, however, charged therewith, but conditionally only, the item being marked O, or O'ni., that is to say, *oneratur, nisi habeat sufficientem exonerationem*. In such cases the Sheriff had to produce the Record or Book of the Clerk of the Pells, showing that the sum had been actually paid, on doing which he received an order of discharge, and "Exon'." was entered against that item on the margin of the Pipe Roll. If the Sheriff had not received any particular item, he answered *nil*, and such item was thereupon said to be *nichilled*. These nichilled items were afterwards put into a schedule called the *Schedule of the Pipe*, which was sent down to the Lord Treasurer's Remembrancer in order that process might be issued against the defaulters. Upon this Schedule the Lord Treasurer issued what was called the *Long Writ* or Prerogative Writ, which combined in itself every species of compulsory process known to the law being at once a *non omittas, fieri facias, capias, and extent*, and also a writ of *diem clausit extremum, attachment, and distringas*.

Towards the end of the reign of Edward the Third, in consequence of the great increase of the *casual* revenue caused by the establishment of the Justices of the Peace, the recognizances taken by whom were so numerous and so frequently forfeited that the Clerk of the Pipe was totally unable to transcribe all the estreats on the Pipe Roll, two new officers were appointed to assist the

REVENUE ROLLS—(continued).

Clerk and the Comptroller of the Pipe in the discharge of their duties, called respectively the *Clerk of the Foreign Estreats* and the *Foreign Apposer.*

The duties of the Clerk of the Foreign Estreats were to receive from the Clerks of the Judges of the several Courts, the Clerks of Assize, Clerks of the Peace, Town Clerks, and others the *Estreats* or *Extracts* of the several Fines, Issues, Amerciaments, and forfeited recognizances in their several Courts, and to enter them on rolls called Estreat Rolls, from which he afterwards made out the Writs of Summons to the Sheriffs of the different counties, called the *Summons of the Green Wax,* calling them to account at the Exchequer for the issues of Casual revenue or of the Green Wax in the same way as the Summons of the Pipe called them to account for the *certam* or fixed Revenue.

The Summons of the Green Wax, so called because the Estreats annexed to the Writ were under a Seal in Green Wax, were issued twice a year at the same time as the Summons of the Pipe, and were answered in the same manner. The apposal of the Sheriff on the casual revenue or Green Wax, took place, however, before the *Foreign Apposer,* who was specially appointed for that purpose, instead of before the Cursitor Baron, the Clerk of the Estreats attending him with the Estreat Rolls and marking them according to the Sheriff's answers in the same way as the Pipe Rolls were marked on his apposal on the summons of the Pipe.

On this apposal the Clerk of the Estreats also marked on the Rolls the claims made by the *Bailiffs of Liberties.* If any Fines or other Issues were claimed by the Lord or Grantee of any Liberty in respect of such Liberty, a claim on his behalf was made by his Bailiff in open Court, and the decision pronounced on such claim by the Foreign Apposer, whether allowed or not, was thereupon entered on the Estreat Roll, and the item dealt with accordingly. After the Sheriffs had been apposed, the Foreign Apposer extracted from the Estreat Rolls whatever sums had been totted, and transmitted a copy thereof to the Pipe Office, which was called an *Escrow* or *Scroll.* They were then recorded by the Clerks of the Pipe Office on the Great Roll, and charged on each Sheriff under the head of "Nova Oblata," or accounts of the current year.

The following may be regarded as the principal Revenue Rolls:—

PIPE ROLLS. 31 Henry I. to 2 William IV. 676 Rolls.*

The Pipe Rolls or Great Rolls of the Exchequer contained the yearly charge against the Sheriffs of the several

---

* There is also a small collection of "Norman Pipe Rolls," or Great Rolls of the exchequer of Normandy, extending from 30 Henry II. to the reign of King John, the whole of which have been printed by the Society of Antiquaries.

REVENUE ROLLS—(continued).

Pipe Rolls—(continued).

counties as drawn up and engrossed by the Clerk of the Pipe and specifying the various rents, farms and debts due from them to the King in their capacity as Farmers or Collectors of his Revenues.

Sometimes the Sheriff accounted merely as the *Custos* or Bailiff of the shire, the rents paid to him in that capacity being particularised one by one, but more generally the greater part of the rents due to the King within any one county were *let to farm* to the Sheriff at a fixed sum, such rents being then called Viscontiel rents, and the sum rendered by the Sheriff in lieu thereof being termed the ' Farm of the whole county," or *Firma de corpore comitatus.* This amount was accounted for by the Sheriff in a *gross sum*, without specifying the several Viscontiel rents by which it was made up, and was frequently subdivided into two amounts, specified as *blanco* and *numero* respectively. The difference between the two methods of computation was considerable, the *blanco*, or " blank silver," being the amount represented by silver, the fineness of which had been tested by combustion or melting down ; this was either real or nominal ; *real*, when a sample was actually put into the furnace and melted ; *nominal*, when 1s. in every 20s. was paid and accepted in lieu of the actual test. Farms, the rent of which was thus paid, were said to be *dealbated* or *blanched.*

The payment described as *numero*, or by tale, was the amount represented by the ordinary coinage without reference to the fineness of the silver. Both of these forms of payment were frequently made use of in accounting for the firma de corpore comitatus, according to the manner in which the rents had been answered to the Sheriff by the sub-tenants.

In addition to the Corpus Comitatus there were in each county certain *Gross Farms*, that is to say, rents charged upon particular persons, or on cities and towns, and accounted for separately on the Pipe Roll, either because, although written out to the Sheriff, they were to be answered for by the persons upon whom they were charged, or because they were such as had been reserved after the Farm of the county had been fixed at a certain sum.

The manors and lands which made up the Corpus Comitatus were frequently charged by the King with settled payments of Alms and Liveries, &c. for which an allowance or deduction was made from the Sheriff's Farm, as was also done in the case of the *Terræ datæ*, or lands granted away by the King, for the lands of which the Sheriff could, as a matter of course, be no longer held responsible.

REVENUE ROLLS—(continued).

PIPE ROLLS—(continued).

After the Firma de Corpore Comitatus had been accounted for, the next item put in the charge on the roll was the "Crementum Comitatus" (if any), that is to say, the rents of farms which had heretofore been particular farms to the Sheriff and were now thrown into the "Corpus Comitatus."

Then followed the "*Proficuum Comitatus*," or Profits of the Sheriff's Tourns and of the County Court (these were sometimes let to farm to the Sheriff for a fixed sum, called Firma de Proficuo), the *Escheats and Purprestures*, or amounts arising from forfeited lands and encroachments of wastes, &c.: (subsequent to the appointment of Escheators in the reign of Henry III., the escheated lands were accounted for by those officers instead of by the Sheriffs); the *Fines, Oblatus, Issues, and Amerciaments* and other profits and perquisites of courts; and the sums to be accounted for by way of *Aids, Tallages, Scutages,* and other feudal imposts.

At the end of Hilary and Trinity Terms in each year, two Writs, called respectively the *Summons of the Pipe* and the *Summons of the Green Wax* (or *Casual Revenue*) were issued from the Pipe Office to the Sheriffs of the several counties throughout England, and answered by them at the *Utas* or Octaves of Easter and Michaelmas Terms respectively, when they made their *Profers* or half-yearly prepayments on account of the Issues of their Bailiwicks and underwent their *apposal* or examination respecting the several items put in charge against them on the Pipe Roll, on which their answers were duly noted. The Summons issued in Hilary Term contained the "Corpus Comitatus" and the Farms that were in arrear the preceding year with the "Oblata" and "Placita Curiæ," &c., or casual revenue up to the end of that term; those sent out in Trinity Term containing the "Nova Oblata," and "Nova Placita," &c., or accounts of the current year, which was reckoned from Michaelmas to Michaelmas.*

CHANCELLOR'S ROLLS. 9 Henry II. to 3 William IV. 612 Rolls.

These were counter-rolls or duplicates of the Pipe Rolls made annually by the Comptroller of the Pipe who was anciently styled the "Clericus Cancellarii," or Clerk of the Chancellor, as the Clerk of the Pipe was in like manner

---

* The Pipe Rolls of 31 Hen. I. 2, 3, and 4 Hen. II., and Ric. I. have been printed, *in extenso*, by the Record Commission; and those from 5 to 13 Hen. II. by the "Pipe Roll Society."

REVENUE ROLLS—(continued).

styled the Clerk of the Treasurer. They served as a check upon the Pipe Roll, and from them the Comptroller of the Pipe twice in the year made out the process called the "Summons of the Pipe." The series is very imperfect. The Chancellor's Roll of 3 John has been printed by the Record Commission.

EXANNUAL ROLLS. Edw. I. to Geo. III. 15 Rolls.

By the Statute commonly called the Statute of Rutland, 12 Edw. I., it was ordained that the *Corpus Comitatus* instead of being written afresh every year in the Great Roll of the Pipe, should be written in a separate roll so as to avoid the repetition of the *Terræ datæ* in the Sheriff's Accounts which thereafter began with the words "Corpus hujus "comitatus annotatur in Rotulo, &c.," and then proceeded to the *Remanens firmæ post terras datas.* A roll entitled " De CorporibusComitatuum,"of the 12th year of Edward I., is placed with the regular series of Pipe Rolls of that date. At the same time it was directed that the matters which could not be collected, which were called *Dead Farms* and *Desperate Debts*, should not be repeated year by year on the Pipe Roll to the great burden of the officers of the Exchequer, but should be made up into a separate roll to be read yearly to the Sheriffs on passing their accounts, in order to see if any of them could be collected.

Some of these *Desperate Debts* are entered on the roll above referred to, called "de Corporibus Comitatuum," the remainder forming a distinct series called Exannual Rolls.

FOREIGN ACCOUNTS, ROLLS OF. 42 Edw. III. to Chas. II. 23 Rolls, including two rolls entitled " Rotuli de diversis Computis," extending from John to Edw. III.

In addition to the Accounts of the Sheriffs the early Pipe Rolls contain those of several other Accountants, as the Escheators or *Custodes Escætarum* ; the Farmers or Custodes of such Towns and Burghs as were not part of the Corpus Comitatus nor within the Sheriff's receipt ; the Custodes Cambii ; the Keepers of the Wardrobe ; the Treasurers of Ireland and others. These were at first placed at the end of the Great Roll in each year, but subsequently formed into distinct Rolls known as Foreign Rolls or Rolls of Foreign Accounts, that is to say, such as were Foreign to the Jurisdiction of the Sheriff.

Repertories. Edw. III. to Hen. VI.

An Inventory of all the Foreign Accounts from Henry III. to Richard III. inclusive whether enrolled on the Pipe Rolls, the Chancellor's Rolls, or the Rolls of Foreign Accounts has been nearly completed.

REVENUE ROLLS—(continued).

ORIGINALIA ROLLS. Henry III. to 1837. 1102 Rolls.

The "Originalia," or "Estreats of the Chancery," contain Transcripts in full from the Patent, Close, and Fine Rolls and other Chancery Enrolments of all Grants, Leases, Writs, or other documents wherein any rents were reserved to the Crown or for which any payment or service was to be rendered or done, which were transmitted to the Exchequer in order that such rents or payments might be duly put in charge to the Sheriffs on the Pipe Rolls.

The earlier Originalia Rolls also contained in addition to such "estreats," commissions for taking inquisitions, and various original writs issued from the Court of Chancery in respect of the Crown revenue which at a later period were issued under the authority of the Court of Exchequer, and are recorded on the Memoranda Rolls of that Court.

A brief Abstract of the rents, &c. reserved, and of the substance of the Originalia, was made by the Clerks of the Lord Treasurer's Remembrancer in the form of an Index or *Repertory*, and sent into the Pipe Office as particulars to be put in charge on the Great Roll, where they were termed "Parcels of the Pipe."

The making of these Repertories and the preparation of such particulars was termed, in official phrase, "Executing the Originals."

Abstracts. Hen. III. to Edw. III. Printed by the Record Commissioners from the Office Repertories, in 2 Vols., folio, entitled "Rotulorum Originalium Abbreviatio." With Indexes of Persons and Places.

Repertories. (General.) 11 Hen III. to 8 Geo. III., and 1821 to 1824.

Repertories, called "Originalia Abstracts." 12 Car. II. to 22 Geo. III.

Do. called "Originalia Extracts." 25 Hen. VI. to 16 Car. I.

Abstracts. Hen. VIII. 4 Vols. MS.

Calendar. Edw. I. to Eliz. 1 Vol. MS., entitled "References to Originals."

Do. Various dates. 1 Vol. MS., entitled "References to Charters and Grants to Corporations."

Do. Hen. VIII. to Anne. Printed in Vol. 1 of Jones's "Index to the Records."

REVERSIONS, ROLLS OF. Edw. III. to Hen. VIII.

Two rolls containing extracts from the Pipe Rolls and Originalia Rolls of the Issues and Profits which ought to be accounted for by reason of the reversion of lands and tenements on the expiration of leases or otherwise.

REVENUE ROLLS—(continued).

The following classes of documents may be regarded as subsidiary to the Revenue Rolls :—

AMERCIAMENTS. See FINES AND AMERCIAMENTS.

ESTREATS (CHANCERY). See ORIGINALIA ROLLS.

ESTREATS (FOREIGN). These are enrolled on the MEMORANDA ROLLS.

Repertories. 23 Hen. VII. to 31 Geo. III.

ESTREATS (FOREIGN), ROLLS OF. (EXCHEQUER, L. T. R.) 5 Edw. VI. to 5 Will. IV.

FINES AND AMERCIAMENTS, ACCOUNTS OF. (EXCHEQUER, Q. R.) Henry III. to James II.

These are accounts of the Issues of Fines and Amercements before the Justices of Assize, Justices of the Bench, and others in various counties, giving in many instances the names of the persons by whom such Fines were paid.

FINES AND AMERCIAMENTS, CLAIMS TO. (EXCHEQUER, L. T. R.) 1 Vol.

This volume contains an Abstract of all the claims to Fines and Amerciaments made by Lords of Liberties in the various Counties and Towns throughout England, with references to the Pipe Rolls on which such claims are recorded and wherein the Charters by virtue of which the claims were made are generally fully recited.

There are also five volumes entitled " Nomina Vilarum," Temp. Car. II. which contain the names of the Towns, Hamlets, &c. within the several Liberties throughout England as certified to the Barons of the Exchequer by the Bailiffs of such Liberties.

SUMMONS OF THE PIPE, WRITS OF. (EXCHEQUER, Q. R.) Edward II. to James I.

These are Writs addressed to the Sheriffs of the several Counties directing them to appear and account for their farms to the Treasurer and Barons of the Exchequer. They were issued twice in the year, and were accompanied by a roll containing a transcript from the Pipe Roll of the *charge* against the Sheriff showing the farms, debts, arrears, &c., for which he was to answer. They are valuable only as illustrating the process of business in the Exchequer.

See also **SHERIFFS' ACCOUNTS.**

ROYAL AND HISTORICAL LETTERS.

ROYAL AND HISTORICAL LETTERS. Richard I. to Henry VII.

Under the title of " Ancient Correspondence " a collection has been made of all the original Royal and Historical Letters formerly preserved in the Tower of London, in the Treasury of the Exchequer, and amongst the various classes of Miscellanea which have been recently examined.

ROYAL AND HISTORICAL LETTERS—(continued).

ROYAL AND HISTORICAL LETTERS—(continued).

These have been arranged as far as practicable in chronological order, and a Descriptive Catalogue of the whole series is in progress.

Selections from the Royal Letters of the reigns of Henry III. and Henry IV., in 3 Vols. 8vo., have been printed in the series of "Chronicles and Memorials."

ROYAL LETTERS, &c., TRANSCRIPTS OF.

There is amongst the Miscellanea of the Exchequer a roll containing transcripts of the Letters of Edward Prince of Wales, in the 33rd year of Edw. I.

A description of this roll is printed in the 9th Report, App. II., pp. 246–249.

A collection of original letters addressed to Edward the Black Prince (41 Edw. III.), and of Correspondence relating to the affairs of Gascony and Ponthieu in the reign of Edw. III., formerly bound in a volume and deposited with the Miscellaneous Books of the Treasury of the Receipt, has been added to the Series of "Ancient Correspondence."

There is also amongst the Miscellaneous Books of the Treasury of the Receipt (Vol. 144), an original Register of the Letters of Privy Seal of Edward the Black Prince extending from 20 to 21 Edw. III.

See also **REGISTERS, &c.**

ROYALISTS AND DELINQUENTS.

During the period of the Commonwealth the executive administration was carried on by a series of *Committees* under the supreme direction of the Council of State. Of these Committees there were two, the sole object of which was the seizure and confiscation of, or the levying of Fines and Compositions for, the estates of "Delinquents," that is to say of those who took the Royalist side in the Civil War or who came under the description of Papists or Recusants.

The first of these was the *Sequestration Committee,* by the rules of which, on an information of delinquency, if well grounded, the estate in question was seized and held until the accusation could be investigated. If the delinquency was proved to the satisfaction of the Committee the delinquent was deprived of his whole Estate, one-fifth being however allowed to him for the maintenance of his children, and one-fifth of the proceeds of the estate being allowed to the informer. In cases of Recusancy one-third of the estate was allowed to the Recusant.

In the course of a few years the Sequestration Committee, the working of which was very unfair and unsatis-

ROYALISTS AND DELINQUENTS—(continued).

factory, was entirely superseded by a *Committee for Compounding* for the Estates of Royalists and Delinquents, the object of which was to receive from the Delinquents themselves, both from those against whom no information had been made and from those who were already under sequestration,—

(1.) A confession of their delinquency.

(2.) A pledge of adherence to the present Government.

(3.) A full account on oath of their possessions, real and personal.

A legal Report was then made thereon and they were admitted to compound in proportion to the degree of their guilt.

One-half his estate was exacted from any delinquent member of Parliament, one-sixth from those who had taken part in the former or latter war, and one-third from those who had been active in both wars.

[*Calendar of State Papers.* 1649–50.]

The following are the principal records bearing on this subject:—

ROYALIST COMPOSITION PAPERS.

These are in two Series, the first of which comprises the Correspondence and Orders of the Commissioners for the sequestration and sale of the estates of the royalist nobility and gentry, and is contained in 113 folio volumes.

The second Series consists of 54 volumes, containing the original particulars, taken on oath, of the estates and personal property of those Royalists who were permitted to compound on payment of a fine, with the amount of the Compositions at which they were assessed.

A Calendar of the Proceedings of the Committee, for Compounding, including the volumes above described, has been published in the Series of "Calendars of State Papers, &c."

DELINQUENTS' ESTATES, PARTICULARS OF.

Two very large volumes, containing Entries of Particulars of Delinquents' Estates, Real and Personal, with an Index Nominum in a separate volume.

[*S. P. Dom. Commonwealth.* **G.** 55, 56, *and* 57.]

DELINQUENTS' ESTATES, REPORTS ON, &c.

Two Entry Books, containing Reports on Delinquents' Estates and Accounts of the Fines levied thereon.

[*S. P. Dom. Commonwealth.* **G.** 53 *and* G. 54.]

DELINQUENTS' ESTATES, SURVEYS OF.

1652 and 1653. Two Volumes.

[*S. P. Dom. Commonwealth.* **G.** 58 *and* G. 59.]

ROYALISTS AND DELINQUENTS—(continued).

DELINQUENTS' ESTATES, BARGAINS AND SALES OF.
Commonwealth. Enrolled on the Close Rolls.
[*See "Palmer's Indexes," Vols.* 78 *and* 79.]
Do., ABSTRACTS OF CLAIMS TO.
Commonwealth.
[*See "Palmer's Indexes," Vol.* 74.]
Do., CERTIFICATES OF. (CHANCERY
PETTY BAG OFFICE.) 1 Bundle.

SCOTLAND.

The principal classes of documents relating to Scotland, in addition to the Scottish Series of State Papers, and the collection of "Border Correspondence," consist of the "Rotuli Scotiæ," or SCOTCH ROLLS, described under the head of **CHANCERY ENROLMENTS (VARIOUS);** the "Great Roll of Scotland," on which are recorded the chief steps of the process amongst the competitors for the crown of Scotland in the reign of Edward I.; the "Ragman Roll" containing the enrolments of the "Homage Bills," or submissions of the Prelates, Nobility, and Commonalty of Scotland to Edward I.; the original "Homage Bills" therein referred to; Accounts, &c. relating to various Scottish Castles; and Indentures of Wardenship of Berwick and the Marches, &c., &c., the references to which are as follows:—

HOMAGE ROLLS. (CHANCERY.) 19–24 Edw. I.
These consist of five rolls, amongst the Miscellaneous Rolls, &c. formerly preserved in the Tower (Bundle 7), the first two of which, sometimes called the "Great Roll of Scotland," are duplicates, and relate to the competition for the crown of Scotland between Balliol, Bruce, and others. (Printed in Rymer's "Fœdera, &c.," Vol. II., pp. 542–600.)
Nos. 3, 4, and 5 are triplicates of the so called "Ragman Roll," which contains the enrolments of the submissions of the Scottish nobility to Edward I.

SCOTTISH DOCUMENTS. (CHANCERY).
Henry III. to Charles II. Two Portfolios, placed with the Miscellaneous Rolls, &c., containing a large variety of documents relating to Scottish affairs. Most of these are referred to in Mr. Bain's "Calendar of Documents relating to Scotland," or printed in Stevenson's "Documents illustrative of the History of Scotland."

Do. (EXCHEQUER, TREASURY OF THE RECEIPT.)
Edward I. to Elizabeth.
These consist of Diplomatic and other Documents relating to the affairs of Scotland from the reign of Edward I. to that of Elizabeth, with a few of earlier date, including the original Submissions or HOMAGE

SCOTLAND—(continued).

SCOTTISH DOCUMENTS, &C.—(continued).

BILLS of the Scottish nobility to Edward I. They are
contained in 5 Portfolios (numbered 1 to 5) and 96 Boxes
(numbered 6 to 101). Most of these documents have
been printed either in Rymer's "Fœdera," in Palgrave's
"Documents illustrative of the History of Scotland," or
in Stevenson's Collections on the same subject.

SCOTLAND, ACCOUNTS, &C. RELATING TO. (EXCHEQUER
Q. R.) Edw. I. to Edw. III.

These consist of a few Sheriffs' and Bailiffs' Accounts
relating to Edinburgh, Roxburgh, and Berwick-on-Tweed,
an Account of the Chamberlain of Scotland dated 1329,
with some Inquisitions and subsidiary documents.

The Accounts of the Keepers of several Scottish
Castles and the Indentures of Wardenship of Berwick
and the Marches will be found amongst the Accounts, &c.
relating to the ARMY AND NAVY.

A bundle of Inquisitions as to the possessions of Scots
in several counties of England dated 24 Edward I. will be
found with the SHERIFFS' ACCOUNTS. See p. 304.

LAWS OF THE MARCHES. Edward VI. 2 Vols.

[S. P. Dom. · Edw. VI. Addenda. Vols. 5 and 6.]

A *Calendar* of various Documents in the Public Record
Office relating to Scotland from 1108 to 1509, edited by
Mr. Joseph Bain, under the direction of the Deputy Clerk
Register of Scotland, has been published in four volumes.
See also **STATE PAPERS, CALENDARS OF.**

SEALS.

There are amongst the Records formerly in the Chapter
House, and also amongst those of the Augmentation
Office, several boxes of loose Seals.

Seals of the various Monasteries, &c. will be found
attached to the ACKNOWLEDGMENTS OF SUPREMACY.

There is also amongst the Chapter House Records a
small box containing "FORGED SEALS," temp. Hen. VI.

An *Inventory* of the Seals originally attached to the
"BARONS' LETTER" of 29 Edward I. is printed in
Report VIII., App. II., pp. 185–188.

A separate collection of ANCIENT DEEDS having Seals
attached is now being formed, a *Catalogue* of which will
be issued in due course.

An Account of the Graver of the Mint for making
Seals for the late Queen Elizabeth, and for James I. on
his accession, extending from 1600 to 1609, will be found
amongst the "DECLARED ACCOUNTS" of the Audit
Office. [*Bundle* 2120.]

SEWERS, COMMISSIONS AND LAWS OF.

The Commissioners of Sewers were in early reigns appointed at the pleasure of the Crown, " in all parts of the Realm wherever needful," by Commission under the Great Seal, granted *pro re nata*, such Commissions to endure for five, and sometimes for 10 or 15 years.

By Statute 23 Hen. VIII. it was enacted that the Commissions were to be at the discretion and nomination of the Lord Chancellor, Lord Treasurer, and Chief Justices, and to continue for 10 years unless repealed by a new Commission. The duties of the Commissioners of Sewers were to over-look the repairs of sea-banks and sea-walls, and the cleansing of rivers, public streams, and ditches &c. for the carrying off of water, and were limited to the county for which they were specially appointed. They were empowered to make Laws and Ordinances for the carrying out of such repairs and to assess and levy such rates as they deemed necessary for that purpose. They might decree the sale of lands in default of payment of such rate, but their Decrees were to be certified into Chancery and to have the royal assent ; and the Commissioners were subject to the jurisdiction of the Court of King's Bench.

The Commissions of Sewers are enrolled on the dorse of the Patent Rolls.

PROCEEDINGS BEFORE THE COMMISSIONERS OF SEWERS. (CHANCERY.) Edw. II. to Hen. VI.

A bundle amongst the " Miscellaneous Rolls, &c." (No. 12), containing Transcripts of Proceedings before various Commissioners of Sewers and of Proceedings in the Court of King's Bench relating to sea-banks, &c. returned into the Court of Chancery pursuant to Writs of Certiorari.

SEWERS, LAWS OF, &c. (CHANCERY, PETTY BAG OF-FICE), as follows .—

Laws and Ordinances of Sewers. 42 Elizabeth to 1831. Two Bundles. These contain also several Commissions of Sewers with the Inquisitions thereon.
  Do.   Enrolments of. 8 Charles I. to 1714. Four Rolls.

Decrees relating to Bedford Level. · 16 & 17 Charles II. to 36 Charles II. Eight Bundles or Parts.
  Index. 1 Vol. MS.

SEWERS, DRAFT COMMISSIONS OF. (DUCHY OF LANCASTER.) 1660 to 1722. Three Bundles.

SHERIFFS'—ACCOUNTS, &c.

Exchequer, Queen's Remembrancer.

SHERIFFS' ACCOUNTS, PARTICULARS OF. Henry III. to James I.

These are the Particulars of the Accounts rendered to the Exchequer by the Sheriffs of the several counties of the issues of the manors and lands, goods and chattels, in their custody, and of their expenses in repairs of castles, provision of victuals, custody of prisoners, &c. &c. Amongst the documents subsidiary to these Accounts are many receipts from persons who received Annuities by direction of the King out of the moneys coming to the hands of the Sheriff, for which he claimed allowance. Amongst these Accounts is a Parcel entitled "Inquisi-" "tiones de terris Scotorum in diversis Comitatibus." 24 Edward I.

Descriptive Slips.

Exchequer, Lord Treasurer's Remembrancer.

SHERIFFS' ACCOUNTS OF SEIZURES, &c. Ric. III. to Car. II. 179 Rolls.

These rolls contain the Particulars of the various Seizures made by the Sheriff from year to year, with the total amount of which he was charged on the Pipe Roll. They are arranged in Counties, and contain full particulars relating to each Seizure, stating in what roll the Sheriff accounted for the same. They also contain an account of the Felons' Goods, Waifs, Strays, &c. taken possession of by the Sheriff by virtue of his office from year to year.

Repertories. 7 Edw. VI. to 13 Car. I.

SHERIFFS' ACCOUNTS, ENTRIES OF. 12 Wm. III. to 33 Geo. III. 4 Vols.

SHERIFFS' ACCOUNTS, STATES AND VIEWS OF. 21 Car. I, to 2 Wm. IV. 16 Vols.

States and Views of the Accounts of Sheriffs are also enrolled on the MEMORANDA ROLLS.

Repertories to States and Views. 1 Edw. III. to 14 Jas. I.

The following are amongst the Miscellaneous Books of the Exchequer, Treasury of the Receipt:—

Vol. 145. States of Accounts of the Sheriff's throughout England. 21 Hen. VII.

Vol. 146. Declarations "de minutis particulis" of the Sheriffs throughout England. 19 Hen. VIII.

Palatinate of Durham.

SHERIFFS' ACCOUNTS, &c. 1335 to 1624.

These are amongst the Miscellaneous Documents selected from the Auditors' Records when the latter were

SHERIFFS' ACCOUNTS, &c.—(continued).

Palatinate of Durham—(continued).

SHERIFFS'S ACCOUNTS, &c.—(continued).
returned to the custody of the Ecclesiastical Commissioners.
Descriptive List.

Duchy of Lancaster.

SHERIFFS' BILLS. 1684 to 1758. 6 Bundles including 1 bundle of Sheriffs' Oaths from 1733 to 1737.

SPECIAL COMMISSIONS AND RETURNS. See COMMISSIONS.

The following are amongst the Miscellaneous Rolls, &c. (Chancery):—

SPECIAL COMMISSIONS, EXTENTS, INQUISITIONS, &c. (*Miscellaneous Rolls, &c., Chancery, Bundle 13).*

File 1. Proceedings before the Council against John Northampton, Mayor of London, Richard Norbury, and John More, with Extents of their lands, goods, and chattels. 8 Ric. II.

File 2. Inquisitions as to the possessions of Alexander Nevill, Archbishop of York and others attainted by Act of Parliament. 11 Ric. II.

File 3. Inquisitions as to the possessions of John le Scrop de Masham, in connexion with a Petition of Right. 2 Hen. VI.

File 4. Inquisitions concerning Depopulation pursuant to Stat. 9 Hen. VIII. 9-10 Hen. VIII.

File 5. Special Commissions and Returns thereto relating to the possessions of certain Colleges and Chantries. 38 Hen. VIII.

SPECIFICATIONS OF PATENT INVENTIONS.

SPECIFICATIONS OF INVENTIONS, ENROLMENTS OF. (CHANCERY.)

Prior to the year 1849 the Specifications of Inventions were enrolled either at the Enrolment Office in Chancery, the Petty Bag Office, or the Rolls Chapel Office. Those enrolled at the Enrolment Office were entered on the Close Rolls together with the ordinary Indentures, &c., there being distinct sets of Rolls at the Petty Bag Office and Rolls Chapel Office respectively known as "Specifica-"tion and Surrender Rolls," on which the Surrenders of Offices, &c. were also enrolled.

From 1849 to 1853 inclusive the Specifications were enrolled at the Enrolment Office only, and during that period form a distinct branch of the Close Rolls, to which there is a seperate Index.

Disclaimers of Specifications are also enrolled as a distinct branch of the Close Rolls, consisting of six Parts or Rolls, the dates of which extend from 1854 to 1867 inclusive.

SPECIFICATIONS OF PATENT INVENTIONS—
(continued).

SPECIFICATIONS OF INVENTIONS, &c.—(continued).

The Specifications of a later date than 1853 are registered at the Great Seal Patent Office.

Calendar (to Specifications enrolled on the Close Rolls). Anne to 1 Geo. IV.

Printed. Reports VI., App. II., pp. 155–203; VII., App. II., pp. 189–210, and VIII., App. II., pp. 82–134.

Do. 1712 to 1840. MS. In the volume entitled " Rotuli Regis Caroli, &c." pp. 101–260.

Index. 1841 to 1848. See Index to " Indentures."

Do. 1849 to 1853. 1 Vol. MS.

N.B.—*Alphabetical, Chronological, and Reference Indexes to all Patents of Inventions have been published by the Patent Office.*

SPECIFICATION AND SURRENDER ROLLS. (PETTY BAG OFFICE SERIES.) 1712 to 1848.

287 Rolls or Parts, containing the Enrolments of Specifications of Inventions and of Surrenders of Offices, &c.

Index. 2 Vols. MS.

Do. (ROLLS CHAPEL OFFICE SERIES.) 1712 to 1848.

These consist of 140 Parts or Rolls, containing the Enrolments of such Specifications of Inventions as were enrolled at the Rolls Chapel Office, and also of Surrenders of Offices, &c. [See also the SURRENDER ROLLS described under the head of **CHANCERY ENROLMENTS (VARIOUS).**]

Calendar. 1712 to 1837. Printed. Reports VI., App. II., pp. 116–154; and VII., App. II., pp. 108–187.

Do. 1712 to 1848. MS. In the volume entitled " Rotuli Regis Caroli, &c."

SPECIFICATIONS OF PATENT INVENTIONS. (PATENT OFFICE SERIES.) 1852 to 1879.

These documents subsequent to the year 1851 are arranged in numerical order, each patent having its distinctive number, as shown in the various Indexes issued by the Patent Office.

STATE PAPERS, CALENDARS OF.

The State Papers spring from three great and original sources, namely, the Offices of the Secretaries of State for the Foreign, the Colonial, and the Home Departments, and in the State Paper Office were classified under those several denominations, the papers emanating from the Home Department being technically described as the *Domestic Papers* in contradistinction to those relating to the *Foreign* and *Colonial* interests of the nation, and the correspondence relating to Ireland and Scotland being also treated as distinct Series.

STATE PAPERS, CALENDARS OF—(continued).

The magnificent collection of Letters and Papers from the reign of Henry VIII. to that of Charles II., inclusive, has been rendered so familiar and easy of access to the student by the voluminous Calendars published from time to time under the direction of the Master of the Rolls that it will suffice for the purpose of the present volume to indicate the number of volumes already published and the dates between which they extend. For State Papers of an earlier date than Henry VIII. reference must be had to the Ancient Correspondence formerly preserved in the Tower described under the head of "Royal and Historical Letters, &c.," to the "Treaties and Diplomatic Documents" formerly in the Chapter House, and to the several classes of "Chancery Enrolments" on which documents of this nature were formerly entered.

The later records of the Home, Foreign, and Colonial Offices, together with those of the Admiralty, War Office, and other Departments of State are described under the head of "Departmental Records."

A brief account of the formation and History of the State Paper Office, showing the manner in which large masses of State Papers have become dispersed amongst Public Libraries and Private Collections, is given in the Introduction to the present volume.

The Calendars of State Papers in the Public Record Office already published are as follows:—

STATE PAPERS. Henry VIII. Selections of the most important Letters printed in full. 11 Vols. 4to. (Published under the authority of the Commissioners for publishing State Papers. 1830-1852.)

LETTERS AND PAPERS (FOREIGN AND DOMESTIC), of the reign of Henry VIII. 1509 to 1539. 14 Vols.

In addition to the State Papers and Correspondence relating to the reign of Henry VIII. preserved not only in the Public Record Office but in the British Museum, the Libraries of Oxford and Cambridge and elsewhere, these volumes contain Abstracts of all Grants from the Crown, Privy Seals, Accounts of the Army, Navy, and Ordnance, and other documents illustrating in any way the political, social, or religious history of the country during the reign of Henry VIII.

STATE PAPERS. (DOMESTIC SERIES.)
Edward VI. to James I. 1547 to 1625. 12 Vols.
Charles I. 1625 to 1649. 22 Vols.
Commonwealth. 1649 to 1660. 13 Vols.
Do.   1643 to 1660. A Calendar of the Proceedings of the Committee for Compounding, &c. 5 Vols.

STATE PAPERS, CALENDARS OF—(continued)

STATE PAPERS. (DOMESTIC SERIES.)—(continued).

Commonwealth. 1642 to 1656. A Calendar of the Proceedings of the Committee for the Advance of Money. 3 Vols.

Charles II. 1660 to 1671. 11 Vols.

STATE PAPERS. (FOREIGN SERIES.)

1547–1558. 2 Vols.

1558–1577. 11 Vols.

STATE PAPERS. (COLONIAL SERIES.)

America and West Indies. 1574 to 1676. 4 Vols.

East Indies, China, and Japan. 1513 to 1634. 5 Vols.

STATE PAPERS RELATING TO IRELAND.

Henry VIII. to Elizabeth. 1509–1597. 6 Vols.

Do. James I. 1603–1625. 5 Vols.

STATE PAPERS RELATING TO SCOTLAND. 1509 to 1603. 2 Vols.

These volumes include the Scottish Series of State Papers for the reigns of Henry VIII., Edw. VI, Mary, and Elizabeth, with an Appendix from 1543 to 1592; and a separate Series of Papers relating entirely to Mary Queen of Scots, during her detention in England from 1568 to 1587. The "Border Correspondence," from 1547 to 1577 inclusive, has been incorporated in the Foreign Series of State Papers.

HOME OFFICE PAPERS. 1760 to 1772. 3 Vols.

TREASURY PAPERS. 1557 to 1728. 6 Vols.

A *List of Printed Books*, containing State Papers, is given in the Deputy Keeper's 28th Report, pp. 140–141.

STATE PRISONERS.

ACCOUNTS OF THE CUSTODY OF PRISONERS OF WAR, &c. (EXCHEQUER, Q. R.) Edw. III. to Hen. VII.

These consist principally of Accounts of the Constables of various Castles and Fortresses, including the Tower of London, relating to the custody of Prisoners of War and to their Ransoms, &c. and will be found amongst the Accounts, &c. relating to the ARMY AND NAVY. (*See* p. 17).

EXPENSES OF THE DIET, &c. OF MARY QUEEN OF SCOTS, AND ALSO OF HER FUNERAL. 1584 to 1587.

[*Audit Office, "Declared Accounts."* *Bundle* 2119.]

EXPENSES OF STATE PRISONERS IN THE TOWER OF LONDON AND PAY OF THE GARRISON. 1551 to 1553.

[*Do.* *Bundle* 2298.]

See also **TOWER OF LONDON.**

341

STATUTE STAPLE.

STATUTE STAPLE, CERTIFICATES AND RECOGNIZANCES OF (CHANCERY.) Hen. VIII. to Anne.

By the Statute of the Staple of 27 Edward III. the Mayor and Constables of the Staple, in each town in which a Staple of Wools or other merchandise was established, were empowered to take and seal Recognizances or Obligations of Debts ; upon which, on default of payment, the Mayor might imprison the Debtor and attach his goods, to be afterwards sold for the satisfaction of the Creditor. If, however, the Debtor should not be found within the limits of the Staple in question the obligation was to be certified into the Chancery, from which Court process should thereupon issue. These Certificates and Recognizances consist of 43 Bundles, formerly deposited in the Rolls Chapel Office.

Inventory. Report IV., App. II., p. 110.

The Certificates and Recognizances of an earlier date than Hen. VIII., with extents and other proceedings on the Statute Staple, will be found amongst the "Brevia Regia" or CHANCERY FILES.

STATUTE STAPLE, PROCEEDINGS ON THE. (CHANCERY, PETTY BAG OFFICE.) Jas. I. to Geo. III.

Extents, re-extents, and other proceedings on the Statute Staple, formerly deposited in the Petty Bag Office, and known as "Writs of Execution." Those of an earlier date will be found amongst the "CHANCERY FILES." No proceedings have been taken upon Statutes Staple since 15 George III.

APPOINTMENTS OF MAYORS AND CONSTABLES OF THE STAPLE. 1-10 Hen. VI.
[*Misc. Rolls, &c. (Chancery), No.* $\frac{18}{13}$.]

ACCOUNTS OF THE STAPLE AT CALAIS. Hen. VII., and Hen. VIII.

These will be found amongst the Original Accounts &c. of the Exchequer relating to France.

PROCEEDINGS ON THE STATUTE STAPLE. Hen. VIII.
[*Misc. Books, Exchequer, Treasury of the Receipt, Vol.* 147.]

SURVEYS, &c.

The DOMESDAY SURVEY is described under the head of DOMESDAY BOOK.

For SURVEYS OF BISHOPRICS and other ECCLESIASTICAL BENEFICES, see **ECCLESIASTICAL MATTERS.**
See also **MONASTIC FOUNDATIONS, &c.**

SURVEYS, &c.—(continued).

The principal Collections of Surveys are the following:—

Chancery.

SURVEYS OF CHURCH LIVINGS. Temp. Commonwealth. 3 Vols.

These contain Returns of the number and value of the Ecclesiastical Benefices in various Counties made pursuant to an Ordinance of Parliament dated 20 Dec. 1649.

Vol. 1 contains the Returns for the Counties of Berks, Bucks, Essex, Gloucester, Hertford, Lancaster, and Lincoln.

Vol. 2 contains these for the County of Dorset only.

Vol. 3 those for the Counties of Middlesex, Norfolk, Northumberland, Oxford, Sussex, Westmoreland, Wilts, and Yorkshire.

The foregoing are the only original Returns known to exist, but there are in the Lambeth Library 24 large volumes containing official copies of these Returns, which in many cases supply their places when wanting.

SURVEY OF THE MANOR OF EAST GREENWICH. 1696.

This is amongst the SPECIAL COMMISSIONS from the Petty Bag Office. See **COMMISSIONS.**

Exchequer, Queen's Remembrancer.

For Surveys taken by Special Commissions issuing out of the Exchequer, see **COMMISSIONS.**

"Homberstone's Survey." 1569. Two large volumes containing a survey of the possessions of the Earls of Northumberland and Westmoreland, and of Sir John Nevill, Leonard Dacre, and other rebels, made by Edmund Hall and William Homberstone by virtue of a Commission dated 18 March 1569.

[*Misc. Books, Exchequer Q. R., Vols.* 37 *and* 38.]

Several other Books of Surveys will be found amongst the Miscellaneous Books of the Queen's Remembrancer's Department. (See p. 223.)

Exchequer, Augmentation Office.

SURVEYS (PARLIAMENTARY).

Commonwealth. 56 Portfolios. The "Parliamentary Surveys," so called as having been taken under the authority of the Parliament (A.D. 1649 to 1653), extend to all the Counties of England and Wales, and are of two kinds, one class being made "by virtue of a Commission "granted upon an Act of the Commons assembled in "Parliament for the Sale of the Honours, Manors, and "Lands" belonging to King Charles I., his Queen, and Prince, passed 16th July 1649; the other class was taken under a Commission grounded upon an Act of the

SURVEYS, &c.—(continued).

Exchequer, Augmentation Office—(continued).

SURVEYS (PARLIAMENTARY)—(continued).

Commons for the Sale of the Fee-Farm Rents belonging to the Commonwealth of England, which were formerly payable to the Crown of England, the Duchy of Lancaster, and the Duchy of Cornwall, passed 11 March 1649.

Some of the documents in this series are only copies of Evidences submitted to the Surveyors in the course of their labours, others being short Certificates by the Surveyors themselves. The great majority of the documents however are complete Surveys subscribed by the Surveyors. Similar Surveys relating to the Duchy of Lancaster exist amongst the Duchy Records now in the Public Record Office, those relating to the County of Cornwall being deposited in the Duchy of Cornwall Office

Calendar. Report VII., App. II., pp. 224–238 (Bedford to Lancaster); and Report VIII., App. II., pp. 52–81. (Leicester to York, &c.)

SURVEYS AND RENTALS (VARIOUS).

Surveys and Rentals. Henry VIII. to James I.

These consist of 79 volumes containing Surveys, Rentals, and Valuations of Lands, chiefly Monastic, in various counties and of various dates. Some of these are known as the "Paper Surveys."

See "Miscellaneous Books, Exchequer Augmentation Office," Vols. 357 to 435 (pp. 237–240).

Exchequer, Treasury of the Receipt.

SURVEYS, RENTALS, &c. (VARIOUS). 35 vols.

See "Miscellaneous Books, Exchequer, Treasury of the Receipt," Vols. 148 to 182 (p. 227).

Court of Wards and Liveries.

SURVEYS, BOOKS OF. 5 Hen. VIII. to 21 Elizabeth and 12 James I. 17 Vols.

[*Misc. Books, Vols.* 129 *to* 146.]

FEODARIES' SURVEYS. Hen. VIII. to Charles I. 287 Bundles.

These are original paper surveys and are arranged in Counties.

Duchy of Lancaster.

SURVEYS, BOOKS OF. Edw. VI. to Jas. II. 33 Vols.

Inventory. Report XXX., App., pp. 10–12.

"OLIVER CROMWELL'S SURVEYS."

These correspond to the "Parliamentary Surveys" of the Augmentation Office.

Inventory. Report XXX., App., pp. 40, 41.

SURVEYS, &c.—(continued).

Duchy of Lancaster—(continued).

SURVEYS OF WOODS, BOOKS OF. Eliz. to Jas. I. 13 Vols.
Some of these include Maps.
Inventory. Report XXX., App., p. 12.

SURVEYS OF RELIGIOUS HOUSES IN LANCASHIRE. Henry VIII.
[*Misc. Records, Div. XXV. Bundle G.*]

SURVEYS, &c. TAKEN BY COMMISSION. Eliz. to Geo. III.
72 Bundles. *Index.* 1 Vol. MS.

WARRANTS AND COMMISSIONS TO SURVEY, &c., DRAFTS OF.
13 Eliz. to 1785. 80 Bundles.
Inventory. Report XXX., App., pp. 9, 10.

ANCIENT MAPS AND PLANS.
These are chiefly descriptive of boundaries of manors
and of extents and valuations of premises viewed under
Special Commissions of Survey issued in suits pending in
the Duchy Court or otherwise. The Surveys to which
they belong are generally to be found in the bundles of
Surveys, &c. taken by Commission.
Inventory. Report XXX., App., pp. 39, 40.

EXTENTS FOR DEBTS. Eliz. to Car. II. 7 Bundles.
Inventory. Report XXX., App., p. 12.

SURVEYS, &c. (VARIOUS):—
Rentals of the Honor of Tutbury, co. Stafford. 2 Henry
V. A collection of Rentals of various Manors in the
Counties of Derby, Stafford, Notts, Leicester, and Warwick
belonging to the Honor of Tutbury, parcel of the Duchy
of Lancaster, taken by virtue of Letters Patent, dated
4 Feb., 2 Hen. V., 1 Vol., generally known as the Coucher
of the Honor of Tutbury.
[*Registers of Grants, &c. Div. XI. No. 4.*]
Extent of the Honor of Tickhill and Survey of Incles-
more, with Map.
[*Register of Grants, &c. Div. XI. No. 12.*]
Many other Surveys and Rentals will be found amongst
the Miscellaneous Records in Bundles. A List of these
has been made.

Palatinate of Chester.

EXTENTS AND RENTALS. Chester and Flint. Edw. III.
to Eliz.
These are incorporated with the General Series of
Rentals and Surveys. (See p. 322.)

CLAIMS OF LIBERTIES AND PRIVILEGES WITHIN THE
PALATINATE OF CHESTER. Temp. Hen. VI. (?)
These are indexed in the first volume of the MS. Index
to the Inquisitions post mortem.

SURVEYS, &c.—(continued).

Domestic State Papers.

A Survey of the Manors of Minster and Shurland in the Isle of Sheppey, taken by virtue of a Commission from the Exchequer. 27 Nov. 1573.

[*S. P. Dom., Eliz., Vol.* 87.]

Many other Surveys are incorporated in the Series of Domestic State Papers. [*Vide* printed Calendars.]

TAXATION.

The most ancient forms of *direct* Taxation were the *Hidage* and *Carucage* assessed on such lands as were not held by Military Service, the *Tallages* paid by the King's Ancient Demesnes and by the Cities and Towns, and the *Scutages* or compositions for non-performance of military service, which, at first merely arbitrary payments, came eventually to be levied by a regular assessment at so much for every Knight's Fee. A new kind of Tax in the form of a *Tenth, Fifteenth,* or other Part of all moveables belonging to the subject is said to have been introduced by Henry II. in order to defray the expenses of an expedition to Palestine, from which circumstance the first of such Taxes has been described as the *Saladin Tithe.*

Grants to the King of Tenths and Fifteenths or other proportions were made from time to time by the Commons in Parliament, new assessments being generally made at each fresh grant, the amount raised by such taxes being thus very uncertain.

In the 8th year of Edward III. it was, however, reduced to a certainty, a new valuation at the rate of a fifteenth being then made of every township, borough, and city in the kingdom, which, notwithstanding any alteration in the value of money or increase of personal property, remained for some time the fixed standard for future assessments; so that whenever the Commons granted the King a fifteenth every parish in England knew the proportion required from it.

Poll Taxes at the rate of so much a head on all persons above a certain age were also frequently granted by Parliament, as in the 51st year of Edward III. and the 2nd and 4th years of Richard II. respectively.

The term *Subsidy* has been applied generally to all the foregoing imposts, as also to the duties on Wools, Cloths, &c., which from time to time were granted to the King in aid of his expenses; the subsidy properly so called was, however, a Tax which came into use about the reign of Richard II., and was not imposed directly on property, but on persons according to the *reputed value* of their estates, at the rate of 4s. in the pound for lands and

TAXATION—(continued).

2*s*. 8*d*. for goods, those of *Aliens* being valued at a double rate. The valuation was, however, so very moderate that an entire subsidy of this kind did not amount to more than 70,000*l*.

In addition to the Subsidies from the Laity which were granted by the Commons in Parliament, similar grants, to be assessed on ecclesiastical preferments, were made by the Clergy in Convocation, which grants had, however, to be afterwards confirmed by Parliament. A Subsidy from the Clergy was at the rate of 4*s*. in the pound, according to the valuations of their livings made from time to time.

The Lay Subsidy was usually raised by Commissioners appointed by the Crown or the great officers of State; but during the Civil War between Charles I. and his Parliament the latter, having no other sufficient revenue, introduced the practice of making weekly and monthly assessments of a specific sum on the several Counties of the kingdom, which were levied by a pound rate on lands and personal estates, and these were continued during the whole of the Commonwealth. After the Restoration the ancient method of granting Subsidies seems to have been once, and once only, renewed, namely, in 1663, when four Subsidies were granted by the Temporalty and four by the Clergy. This was, in fact, the last time of raising supplies in that manner, from that time forward periodical assessments being made in the manner of the modern Land and Assessed Taxes.

The Land Tax as at present levied, although most of the above-mentioned imposts partook more or less of that nature, was finally established by the Statute 4 Wm. and Mary, c. 1, according to an assessment or valuation of all the estates throughout the kingdom made in the previous year. From the year 1693 to 1798 it continued to be an annual charge on the subject at rates varying from 4*s*. to 1*s*. in the pound, being made perpetual in the latter year at the rate of 4*s*. in the pound.

By the Act of 38 George III., by which it was made perpetual, the Land Tax was also made subject to *Redemption* or Purchase, the sums paid for such Redemption or Purchase being made applicable to the reduction of the National Debt.

Copies of the Assessments of the Land Tax for the year 1798 on each Parish and Division throughout England, the *quota* then fixed as payable by each Parish or Township remaining unchanged from that date to the present time, are preserved at the Land Tax Redemption Office. The *Parchment Duplicates* of such Assessments which, according to the Statute of 4 Wm. and Mary,

TAXATION—(continued).

were to be annually certified into the Exchequer, are amongst the Records of the Queen's Remembrancer's Department.

The *Hearth Tax*, a payment to the King of 2s. on every hearth "in all houses paying to church and poor," was first established by Statute 13 & 14 Car. II., although a similar payment under the name of "fumage" or "smoke-farthings" was a custom of great antiquity, mention thereof being made in Domesday Book. This tax, which was especially obnoxious on account of its inquisitorial nature, was finally abolished by Statute 1 Wm. and Mary. Six years later, however, a tax of 2s. was levied on all houses except cottages, and also a tax on all windows in such houses exceeding nine in number. The HEARTH TAX ROLLS are placed with the SUBSIDY ROLLS.

Amongst the various forms of *Indirect Taxation*, the accounts of which are to be found amongst the Records of the Exchequer, may be indicated Accounts of Collectors of Customs, of Butlerage and Prisage, of the duties on Cloth or Ulnage, and of the Subsidies on Wools, &c., &c.

SCUTAGE, ACCOUNTS OF COLLECTORS OF (EXCHEQUER, Q. R.)

The Accounts of Collectors of Scutages, Tallages, and other contributions of a like nature will be found amongst the Subsidy Rolls described below. The SCUTAGE ROLLS, which contain the Mandates for the relief from payment of Scutage of such persons as had personally or by deputy rendered the service due from them or had compounded therefor by a fine, are described under the head of **ARMY, NAVY, &c.**

SUBSIDY ROLLS. (EXCHEQUER, Q. R.) Henry III. to William and Mary.

These are sub-divided into two Series, "Clerical" and "Lay," and consist of the Rolls of Accounts, Assessments, Inquisitions, Certificates, and other documents relating to the assessing and collection of the "Tallages, Carucages, "Scutages, Aids, Subsidies, Loans, Benevolences, Contri- "butions, Reliefs, &c. granted to the King by the Clergy "in Convocation, or by the Laity in Parliament, or enjoyed "by him in virtue of the Royal Prerogative or ancient "prescriptive right."

As many of these Rolls contain the names of the persons assessed towards the payment of each subsidy, they are extremely valuable in the compilation of pedigrees, showing at once the precise hundred and township in which the family lived at the time of the assessment, and also to a certain extent their rank and position, which may be deduced from the amounts paid. The most valuable assessments for materials of this nature are the grants

TAXATION—(continued).

of 23 Edward I. and of the 1st and 6th years of Edward III., and the Poll Taxes of 51 Edward III. and the 2nd and 4th years of Richard II.

From the latter date to 14 Henry VIII. the rolls, with few exceptions, supply no names, but from 14 Henry VIII. to the reign of Charles the Second the lists of names are numerous and complete, especially in the HEARTH TAX ROLLS of the latter reign. The Subsidy Rolls cease about the year 1698, their place being supplied by the Accounts of LAND AND ASSESSED TAXES, which, however, do not contain the names of the person assessed, but only the Total Amount paid by each Parish.

The "CLERICAL SUBSIDIES" in the same manner show the names of the Churches, and sometimes of the clergy who paid the sums assessed on them.

There are also Rolls of "ALIEN SUBSIDIES," which contain accounts of the Subsidies assessed on Foreigners resident in England.

With the Subsidy Rolls are also placed the NONÆ ROLLS or "Inquisitiones Nonarum" of 14 & 15 Edward III. These specify the value of every benefice, distinguishing how far it exceeded or fell short of the valuation of Pope Nicholas in 1291, and stating the causes of such variation in glebe, tithe, endowment, appropriation, &c., and other circumstances connected therewith. They also include Lists of the Burgesses of the several Cities and Towns, with the sums at which they were assessed, and the names of those persons taxed at a fifteenth.

These Inquisitions were taken upon oath of the parishioners in every Parish, for the purpose of assessing a Subsidy of a 9th and a 15th granted in the 14th year of Edward III. The subsidy granted was a *ninth* of the corn, wool, and lambs in each Parish, and from the Cities and Towns a *ninth* of all moveables, whilst from Foreign Merchants, those who dwelt in forests and wastes, and "others that lived not of their gain or store" a fifteenth only was exacted. Many of these rolls, but not all of them, have been printed by the Record Commissioners in the volume entitled "Nonarum Inquisitiones."

With the Lay Subsidies were also formerly placed the "CERTIFICATES OF RESIDENCE," *i.e.*, documents under the hands and seals of the Commissioners for levying and assessing the Subsidies in the several Counties, certifying that the persons therein named were, at the time of a particular assessment, resident at the place specified in the Certificate, and had there been taxed to the amount due from them in respect of the said Subsidy, and were therefore exonerated from any further payment in that behalf.

TAXATION—(continued).

SUBSIDY ROLLS, &c.—(continued).

These afford valuable evidence of changes of residence, as they were given in order to prevent persons removing from one County to another being twice assessed towards the same Subsidy.

They belong chiefly to the reigns of Elizabeth and James I., and are now being arranged in alphabetical order.

Descriptive Inventory. (Clerical and Lay.) Reports II., App. II., pp. 132–189; III., App. II., pp. 3–104; IV., App. II., pp. 2–29; and V., App. II., pp. 2–32.

Descriptive Slips. (Clerical.) 26 Vols. MS. (Vol. 26 contains the Taxations of Popes Nicholas and Boniface.)

Descriptive Slips. (Lay.) 71 Vols. MS. (Numbered 27 to 97. Vol. 95 contains "Alien Subsidies" from Edw. III. to Ric. III., and Vols. 96 and 97 Subsidies in " Divers Counties.")

The following volumes relate to the collection of Subsidies, &c. :—

Fifteenths and Tenths, A Book of. 3 Henry V. A volume containing Particulars of the Collection of a Fifteenth and Tenth granted by the laity in the 3rd year of Henry the Fifth in all Counties and Cities throughout England. The Total Amounts only are given. [*Misc. Books (Exchequer, Q. R.), Vol.* 7.]

Accounts of the Collectors, of Subsidies in various Counties. 43 & 44 Elizabeth. 1 Vol.
[*Misc. Books (Augmentation Office), Vol.* 356.]

Names of the Contributors, &c. to a Loan granted to Queen Elizabeth in the year 1590, in the City of London and various Counties in England, with the sums demanded from each, none being of lower amount than 20*l*. [*S. P. Dom., Eliz., Vol.* 236.]

Ship-Money. An account of the money raised in Essex for fitting out a ship of 800 tons to be ready at Portsmouth on 1st March 1636-7. This account states the name of every inhabitant in each parish assessed to this tax, with the amount with which he was charged. [*S. P. Dom., Car. I., Vol.* 358.]

Papers relating to the case of Ship-money between the King and John Hampden. 1637, 1638.
[*S. P. Dom., Car. I., Vol.* 394.]

LAND AND ASSESSED TAXES.

Land and Assessed Taxes, Accounts of. (Exchequer, Q. R.) 1688 to 1830.

These include the *Parchment Duplicates* certified into the Exchequer pursuant to the Statute 4 Wm. and Mary, c. 1., giving the Total Amounts assessed in each Parish, &c., year by year, with the names of the Collectors.

TAXATION—(continued).

Those of the year 1798 are especially valuable, as in that year the *Quota* payable by each Parish became a *fixed amount*, and remains so to the present day, the Parchment Duplicates being the absolute evidence of the amount due in each case.

Land and Assessed Taxes, Entries of. (Exchequer, Q. R.) 1689 to 1834. 200 Vols.

   Do.   1693 and 1697. 2 Vols.

   Do.   called " Tax Books" (Exchequer, L. T. R.), in two series, as follows :

  Land Tax. 1689 to 1821. 10 Vols.

  Assessed Taxes. 1708 to 1822. 11 Vols.

Land and Assessed Taxes, Receiver-General's Accounts of. (Land Revenue Office.) 1688 to 1830. 58 Bundles.

BUTLERAGE AND PRISAGE.

Pincerna Regis, Accounts of the. (Exchequer, Q. R.) 8 Edw. I. to 17 Jas. I. These relate to the dues which the King's Butler was entitled to take on all importations of wine. They show the ports at which ships landed wine, the quantity landed, the amount taken for the King's use, &c., &c. Similar Accounts will be found amongst the Miscellanea of the Treasury of the Receipt.

Calendar. 1 Vol. MS.

Butlerage and Prisage, Accounts of. Henry VIII. Two Vols., one relating to *London* and the other to *Southampton.*

[*Misc. Books, Exch., Tr. of the Receipt, Vols.* 183 *and* 184.]

CUSTOMS.

The following Accounts, &c. relating to the collection of Customs are amongst the Records of the Exchequer, Queen's Remembrancer :—

Customs, Accounts of Collectors of. Edward II. to James I.

These are the Accounts of the Collectors of Customs in various Ports, with Files of Receipts and Acquittances and other documents subsidiary thereto. They are arranged under the names of the several Ports.

Descriptive Slips.

Customs (Dover Haven), Accounts of. Elizabeth.

Accounts relating to the dues levied in various ports on all vessels of a certain tonnage for the repair of Dover Haven, pursuant to Statute 23 Eliz. c. 6., entitled " An Act for the Repair of Dover Haven."

Descriptive Slips.

Customs. (Havener's Accounts.) Henry IV. and Henry VI.

Descriptive Slips.

TAXATION—(continued).

CUSTOMS—(continued)

Customs. (Searchers' Accounts.) Edw. II. to Elizabeth.
These are the Accounts of the Searchers of Customs in various ports of the money, goods, &c. forfeited by illegal exportation.

Descriptive Slips.

Forfeitures of Goods exported "contra proclamationem," Accounts of. Edward III. to Richard II.
These are the Accounts of Bailiffs, Searchers, and other Officers in various Ports of seizures of Money, Provisions, Cloth, Arms, Horses, &c. intended for exportation contrary to the King's proclamation.

Descriptive Slips.

The following are amongst the Miscellaneous Books of the Augmentation Office :—

Accounts of the Collector of Customs in the Ports of Exeter and Dartmouth. 8 Elizabeth. 1 Vol.

[*Misc. Books, Vol.* 355]

An Account of the Tonnage and Poundage collected in the Port of London for one whole year. 2–3 James I.

[*Do., Vol.* 467.]

A similar volume for the Port of Newcastle-on-Tyne. 40–41 Elizabeth. [*Misc. Books, Vol.* 485.]

ULNAGE.

Ulnagers' Accounts. (Exchequer, Q. R.) Edw. III. to James I.
These are Accounts of the Collectors of the Ulnage or Subsidy granted to the King on all cloths sold in each county. They contain very little information.

WOOLS, SUBSIDIES ON.

Wools, Accounts, &c., relating to. (Exchequer, Q. R.) Edward III.
These are Accounts of the Collectors of the Subsidies on Wools, &c., giving the amount of wool received from each person, with its value, and other documents subsidiary thereto.

The following Accounts, relating to various forms of Taxation, are amongst the " Declared Accounts " of the Audit Office and similar Accounts will be found in the Pipe Office Series. (*See* Lists and Indexes, No. II., 1893.) :—

Accounts of the Receivers-General of the Duties on Marriages, Births, and Burials (and also on Bachelors and Widowers), in certain counties and precincts. 1695 to 1706.

Butlerage and Prisage. Accounts of the Chief Butler of England. 1554 to 1673.

TAXATION—(continued).

DECLARED ACCOUNTS—(continued).

Customs :

Accounts of the Farmers, Commissioners, Collectors, and Comptrollers-General of the Customs. 1602 to 1827.

Do. of Receivers-General and Cashiers. 1672 to 1827.

Do. of the Comptrollers and Cashiers in the West Indies and America. 1684 to 1786.

Excise :

Accounts of the Commissioners and Governors of Excise. 1647 to 1849.

Hackney Coaches, Receiver-General's Accounts of the duty on. 1694 to 1828.

Hawkers' Licences, Receivers' and Commissioners' Accounts of. 1697 to 1828.

Hearth Tax. Accounts of the Receivers, &c. 1673 to 1684.

Salt, Duties on. Cash and General Accounts. 1694 to 1798.

Stamp Duties. Cash and General Accounts. 1694 to 1827.

TOWER OF LONDON.

ACCOUNTS OF THE CONSTABLE OF THE TOWER. (EXCHE-QUER, Q. R.) Edw. I. to Hen. VI.

These are accounts of the yearly expenses of the Constable of the Tower, including the costs of repairs, &c., and of the custody of various Scotch and Welsh prisoners, and will be found amongst the Accounts, &c., relating to the ARMY AND NAVY. (See p. 17.)

BILLS OF THE LIEUTENANTS OF THE TOWER. (EXCHE-QUER OF RECEIPT.) 1572 to 1765.

Two parcels containing Bills from the Tower of London for the Fees, &c. of the Officers there, and for the maintenance of State Prisoners from 1572 to 1605, and from 1634 to 1765 respectively.

ACCOUNTS OF THE MASTERS AND KEEPERS OF THE ARMOURY. 1556 to 1686.

[*Audit Office, " Declared Accounts." Bundles 2299 to 2301.*]

ACCOUNTS OF STATE PRISONERS AND PAY OF THE GAR-RISON. 1551 to 1553.

[*Do.* *Bundle* 2298.]

An *Index* to the " RECORDS IN THE CUSTODY OF THE " CONSTABLE OF THE TOWER OF LONDON, RELATING " TO THE STATE PRISONERS, GARRISON, &c.," which are contained in five volumes extending from 1660 to 1837 inclusive, is printed in the Appendix to the Deputy Keeper's Thirtieth Report, pp. 313–359. The volumes referred to are still at the Tower.

See also **WORKS AND BUILDINGS.**

TREATIES AND DIPLOMATIC DOCUMENTS.

As the Lord Chancellor was in ancient times not only the Keeper of the King's conscience but also his Secretary of State both for Home and Foreign Affairs, it is to the Rolls of the Chancery that we must look for the most complete record of the correspondence and negotiations with Scotland, Ireland, Wales, and Foreign Countries, and for the Appointments and Powers of Ambassadors, Letters of Safe Conduct, and other documents of a more or less diplomatic nature. These are enrolled on a series of rolls formerly known as the TREATY ROLLS, but which are now sub-divided into the several classes of ALMAIN ROLLS, FRENCH ROLLS, IRISH ROLLS, NORMAN ROLLS, ROMAN ROLLS, SCOTCH ROLLS, VASCON ROLLS, and WELSH ROLLS, described in the present volume under the title of **CHANCERY ENROLMENTS (VARIOUS).**

Documents of a similar nature will also be found on the Close and Patent Rolls, and numerous isolated documents relating to the same subject exist amongst the Miscellaneous Rolls of the Court of Chancery, including the "HOMAGE ROLLS," which relate to the competition for the Crown of Scotland between Balliol, Bruce, and others in the reign of Edward I.

A large and important collection of original Treaties and of documents subsidiary thereto from Henry I. to Henry VIII. known as "DIPLOMATIC DOCUMENTS" exists amongst the Records of the Treasury of the Receipt of the Exchequer formerly deposited in the Chapter House, and Transcripts of similar documents will be found in the several **REGISTERS AND BOOKS OF REMEMBRANCE** described under that title and also amongst the "Miscellaneous Books" of the Treasury of the Receipt, indicated in the following List.

There is also a large collection of TREATIES from Henry VIII. to 1837 and of "TREATY PAPERS" from about Henry VI. to George III. amongst the Records of the Foreign Office. See **DEPARTMENTAL RECORDS.**

See also **STATE PAPERS.**

DIPLOMATIC DOCUMENTS. (CHANCERY.) Henry III. to Henry VII.

A collection of diplomatic and other documents relating principally to the affairs of the French Provinces under the English rule. 4 portfolios.

The following are amongst the Miscellaneous Rolls, &c. (Bundle 14):—

No. 1. Enrolment of a Treaty between the Kings of England and France, dated 7 April 27 Hen. III., and of Writs of Dedimus Potestatem, &c. relating to Truces of the 14th and 26th years of Hen. III. 27 Hen. III.

TREATIES AND DIPLOMATIC DOCUMENTS—
(continued).

DIPLOMATIC DOCUMENTS. (CHANCERY)—(continued).

No. 2. Enrolment of a Treaty between the Kings of England and France, dated 20 May 1259, and of various Letters relating thereto.   43 Hen. III.
No. 3. Enrolments of Letters from the King of England to the Kings of France and Castile, the Pope, and others.
                                                8-10 Edw. I.
No. 4. Treaties and State Letters between the Kings of England, France, and Arragon.   14 Edw. I.
No. 5. Letters, &c. relating to a dispute between the King of England and the Comte de la Marche concerning the Castle of Montreuil.   18 Edw. I.
No. 6. Copies of Treaties and Letters between the King of England and Eric, King of Norway.   18 Edw. I.
No. 7. Letters of Credence for the Archbishop of Dublin and Anthony, Bishop of Durham, &c.   22 Edw. I.
No. 8. Writs for the restitution of ships and merchandise according to the Agreement between the subjects of the Kings of England and Portugal.   23 Edw. I.
No. 9. Letters and Drafts of Letters from the King to divers nobles of Gascony.   23 Edw. I.
No. 10. Drafts of Letters relating to the Treaty made between the Kings of England and France on the mediation of the two Cardinals sent by Pope Boniface.
                                                23 Edw. I.
No. 11. Treaties between the Kings of England and France, dated 23 Oct. 1298.   25 Edw. I.
No. 12. Letters from the King to the Papal See relating to the renewal of peace between England and France.
                                                25 Edw. I.
No. 13. A roll containing Transcripts of the submissions of the Proctors representing England, France, Burgundy, &c. in the Compromise made before Pope Boniface.
                                                26 Edw. I.
No. 14. A roll containing a Transcript of the procuration made by the representative of Burgundy. (Imperfect.)
                                                26 Edw. I.
No. 15. A roll, entitled "De superioritate maris Angliæ et "jure officii Admirallatus in eodem," containing Transcripts and Confirmations of Ordinances respecting the shipping and commerce between England, Bayonne, Flanders, &c.   26 Edw. I.
No. 16. Articles of the Peace between the Kings of England and France.   31 Edw. I.
No. 17. Articles relating to the homage of the Court of Flanders to the King of France.   Temp. Edw. I.
No. 18. Transcript of an Ordinance between the King of England, the Court of Flanders, and the people of Ghent.   Temp. Edw. I.
No. 19. Proposed Articles of a Treaty between England and France, with the answers thereto.   4 Edw. I.
No. 20. A roll containing copies of Letters from Louis X. and Philip VI. of France concerning peace between that country and England, and also of Petitions from English subjects to the French King, with the answers thereto.   8 Edw. II. and 7 & 8 Edw. III.
No. 21. Demands made at "Peitiers" to the King of France, with the responses thereto.   Edw. II.
No. 22. Articles relating to the homage due from the King of England to the King of France.   Edw. II.
No. 23. A Composition between the Kings of England and France relating to the Castle, &c. of Blaye.   Edw. II

TREATIES AND DIPLOMATIC DOCUMENTS—
(continued).

DIPLOMATIC DOCUMENTS. (CHANCERY)—(continued).

No. 24. Articles of inquiry as to the matters of dispute between England and other countries and the remedies, with the answers thereto. Edw. II.

No. 25. Proceedings relating to the surrender of the Isle of Oleron. 1 Edw. III.

No. 26. The form of declaration of homage to be made by the King of England for the Duchy of Aquitaine. 3 Edw. III.

No. 27. A roll relating to the matters of dispute between England and other countries, the remedies formerly provided and now to be corrected. 4 Edw. III.

No. 28. Enrolment of a Treaty between the Kings of England and France. (Imperfect.) 5 Edw. III.

No. 29. Proceedings of the Commissioners of the King of England and the Earl of Flanders at Bruges concerning the losses incurred by certain merchants. 8 Edw. III.

No. 30. A Transcript of the Certificates made to Edward I. concerning the dangers to be apprehended from the confederacies of the French, Scots, and others, with a List of the documents taken by the Bishop of Chester and the Earl of Lincoln to the Court of France. Edw. III.

No. 31. Letters of Credence, Instructions, &c. for William Fitz-Waryn and John de Langtoft concerning a Treaty between England and France. Edw. III.

No. 32. The Certificate of John Peres concerning the affairs and dangers which affect the King in the processes pending in the Court of France. Edw. III.

No. 33. A roll containing the reasons for assigning Commissioners, &c. to defend the King's rights in the negotiations with France. Edw. III.

No. 34. Negotiations, &c. between the Kings of England and Aragon touching the dispute between the latter and Philip de Valoys. Edw. III.

No. 35. Petitions, &c. relating to the losses inflicted on the People of Flanders and the subjects of the King of Castile and Leon. Hen. IV.

No. 36. A Treaty between the King of England and the Merchants of the Hanse Towns. 14 Edw. IV.

No. 37. Transcripts of Letters from the Archduke Maximilian to Henry VII., dated respectively the 14th, 19th, and 24th Sept. 1506. (Printed. Gairdner. I. 301–306.)

No. 38. Acknowledgments by Hen. III. of debts due from him to W. de Talma and W. Torco, Citizens of Agen. 38 Hen. III.

No. 39. List of witnesses before the King of France, concerning the Bastide of Agen, &c. Temp. Hen. III.

No. 40. Proceedings before Adam de Norfolk and John de Forgetter, the King's Commissioners, concerning the injuries alleged to be suffered by John de Greilli and Alexander de Bergerac through the construction of the Bastide of Sauveterre. 10 Edw. I.

No. 41. Petitions addressed to the Commissioners appointed by the Kings of England and France with regard to the losses sustained by English subjects. 25 Edw. I.

TREATIES AND DIPLOMATIC DOCUMENTS—
(continued).

DIPLOMATIC DOCUMENTS. (CHANCERY)—(continued).

No. 42. Matters in dispute between Edward, King of England, and Robert de Bruce. Temp. Edw. I.

No. 43. Memorandum concerning the question of referring to the Pope differences occurring between the Kings of England and Scotland. Temp. Edw. I.

No. 44. The certificate of William de Sardene, an officer of the Court of Canterbury, concerning the dangers to which the King is exposed owing to the claims of the Papacy, and showing how such dangers may be avoided. Temp. Edw. I.

No. 45. A roll containing a Notarial copy, dated 27 May 1311. of complaints by the French King of breaches of the late Truce, &c. 4 Edw. II.

No. 46. Draft of proceedings before the Proctors of the Kings of England and France. 5 Edw. II.

No. 47. Report of John de Benstede and Thomas de Cambridge, made to the Lord Chancellor, on the results of their mission from the King to various towns and districts of Gascony. 9 Edw. II.

No. 48. Tenor of proceedings and judgment in the Court of Antony Pessaigne, Seneschal of Aquitaine, in a dispute between Jordan de L'Isle and Alexander de Caumont. 11. Edw. II.

No. 49. Recapitulation of the pretexts for the war waged in Guienne between Edward II. of England and Charles IV. of France. 17 Edw. II.

No. 50. Roll of accusations against J. de Colom of Bordeaux, one of the King's Council in Gascony. Temp. Edw. II.

No. 51. Answers of the Seneschal of Gascony and the Agenois to the petitions of the nobles and others of the Agenois respecting their liberties and customs. Temp. Edw. II.

No. 52. Monition addressed to the Mayor and others of the town of Lynn by Elias de Jonestone, on behalf of the Bishop of St. David's and Sir Wm. Trussel, Commissioners appointed to carry into effect the treaties heretofore made between the Kings of England and France, against any infraction of the said Treaties by Ship-Masters. 11 Edw. III.

No. 53. Fragments of enrolments of instruments issued by Edward III. as Vicar-General of the Roman Empire. Temp. Edw. III.

No. 54. Petitions addressed by the Inhabitants of Cahors to Sir John Chandos, the King's Lieutenant, with the replies thereto. Temp. Edw. III.

No. 55. Matters concerning the foreign possessions of the English Crown, as to which the advice of certain persons is to be taken and certified to the King. Temp. Edw. III.

DIPLOMATIC DOCUMENTS. (EXCHEQUER, TREASURY OF THE RECEIPT.) Henry I. to James I.

A collection of Original Treaties and of documents subsidiary thereto contained in 35 boxes.

Calendar. Report XLV., App. I., pp. 285–380, and Report XLVIII., App., pp. 561–619.

TREATIES AND DIPLOMATIC DOCUMENTS—
(continued).

DIPLOMATIC DOCUMENTS. (EXCHEQUER, TREASURY OF THE RECEIPT.)—(continued).

The following are amongst the Miscellaneous Books of the Treasury of the Receipt:—

Vol. 186. An "Inventory of the Treaties remaining in the Treasury."

Vol. 187. A Calendar or Repertory of Papal Bulls, Treaties, &c. relating to the Duchy of Aquitaine. Edw. II.

Vol. 188. Transcripts of ancient Treaties between the Kings of England and France. Hen. V.

Vol. 189. Register of the Acts of Homage and Fealty by the nobility and others of the Duchy of Aquitaine.
Edw. III.

Vol. 190. Documents relating to Scottish Affairs. (Many of these are printed in Rymer's Fœdera.)
Edw. III. to Eliz.

Vol. 191. Documents relating to the Marches of Scotland and Wales. Hen. VIII.

Vol. 192. Instructions to Ambassadors at the Court of the King of Arragon. Hen. VIII.

TREATISES ON VARIOUS SUBJECTS.

ENGLAND, THE CONDITION OF.

"An account of the State of England in anno Domini 1600." By Thos. Willson. A manuscript of 87 pages, stating the claims of the several competitors for the Crown, with a description of the country and of Ireland the condition of the people; state of the revenue and expenses; the military and naval forces; &c., &c.
[*S. P. Dom., Eliz., Vol.* 280.]

AN ACCOUNT OF ENGLAND AND ITS INSTITUTIONS. A volume written apparently about the end of the reign of James I. [*S. P. Dom., Charles I., Vol.* 17A.]

TRADE AND VOYAGES OF DISCOVERY.

A volume containing copies and extracts of treaties, grants, &c. relating to trade and voyages of discovery from the time of Offa, King of Mercia, to the year 1586. Printed in "Hakluyt's Voyages."
[*S. P., Dom., Eliz., Vol.* 196.]

AURUM REGINÆ.

A Treatise on the Queen's claim to the Aurum Reginæ. 1607.
[*S. P., Dom., Jas. I., Vol.* 29.]

The following are amongst the Miscellaneous Books of the Exchequer, Treasury of the Receipt:—

Vol. 193. On the "Tropes and Figures of Scripture."

Vol. 194. Fragments of Legal Treatises, &c.

Vol. 195. Treatises on Legal Subjects, &c.

Vol. 196. Treatises on Theological Subjects.

Vol. 197. Armestrong's "Sermons, &c. on Popish Supremacy."

Vol. 198. Ancient Legal Common Place Book.

Vol. 199. A printed book entitled "Carta Feodi," found amongst the papers of the Court of Wards.

UNIVERSITIES.

ACCOUNTS, &c. RELATING TO THE UNIVERSITIES OF OX-
FORD AND CAMBRIDGE. (EXCHEQUER, Q. R.) Edw. III.
to Elizabeth.

These consist principally of Accounts of the Warden of
King's Hall, Cambridge, relating to the expenses of the
scholars, &c., with a few Warrants and Receipts for payment of Annuities, &c. by various Colleges in Oxford and
Cambridge.

Calendar. 1 Vol. MS.

SURVEYS OF THE UNIVERSITIES OF OXFORD AND CAM-
BRIDGE. (EXCHEQUER, AUGMENTATION OFFICE.) 37
Henry VIII.

A Survey or Valuation of all the possessions, as well
temporal as spiritual, of the various Colleges, Halls,
Hospitals, Chantries, and Chapels within the several
Towns and Universities of Oxford and Cambridge,
together with the expenses and reprises thereof, and full
particulars of the several Foundations, giving the names of
the Founders, date and conditions of foundation, stipends,
benefactions, &c.; taken by Commissioners appointed for
that purpose in the 37th year of Henry VIII. Two large
volumes.

[*Misc. Books, Vols.* 440 (*Cambridge*) *and* 441
(*Oxford*).]

The following volumes relating to the Unversities of
Oxford and Cambridge are amongst the Domestic State
Papers :—

A manuscript describing the FOUNDERS and BENE-
FACTORS of various COLLEGES IN CAMBRIDGE;
and the names of all those at present in the University.
1563?

[*S. P., Dom., Eliz., Vol.* 32.]

A COMMISSION AND DEPOSITIONS of Witnesses respecting a disputed election to the Mastership of ST.
JOHN'S COLLEGE, CAMBRIDGE. 1633.

[*S. P., Dom., Car. I., Vol.* 249.]

ENTRY BOOKS OF LETTERS, WARRANTS, &c. RELAT-
ING TO THE UNIVERSITIES. Charles II. 2 Vols.

[*Dom. Entry Books, Vols.* 27 *and* 53.]

See also the "ECCLESIASTICAL ENTRY BOOKS" in the
same series.

WALES.

The principal classes of documents relating to Wales, in
addition to the "Rotuli Walliæ" or WELSH ROLLS of the
reign of Edward I., and the PATENT OR REMEMBRANCE
ROLLS of the PALATINATE OF CHESTER, both of which

WALES—(continued).

are described under the head of **CHANCERY EN-ROLMENTS**, consist of the PLEA ROLLS and other Proceedings of the Courts of Great Sessions from 33 Henry VIII. (see **JUDICIAL PROCEED-INGS**), and of MINISTERS' AND RECEIVERS' ACCOUNTS, COURT ROLLS, INQUISITIONS POST MORTEM (Chester and Flint), FINES AND RECOVERIES, &c. described under the titles indicated.

The PLEA ROLLS of the Palatinate of Chester commence in the 44th year of Henry III., and a Calendar of the Deeds, Inquisitions, &c. enrolled thereon from Hen. III. to Hen. VIII. is printed in the Deputy Keeper's Reports, Nos. XXVI. to XXX. inclusive.

The STATUTA WALLIÆ of 12-13 Edward I. will be found amongst the PARLIAMENTARY PROCEEDINGS described on p. 285.

The RECORD OF CÆRNARVON, a collection of extents in the Counties of Caernarvon and Anglesey, taken principally in the 26th Edw. III., with an Extent of the Bishopric of Bangor and various other matters, is amongst the Harleian MSS. in the British Museum.

This volume was printed by the Record Commission in 1838.

Letters, Submissions, Homages, and other documents relating to the affairs of Wales during the reigns of Henry III. and Edward I. are contained in the REGISTRUM MUNIMENTORUM "LIBER A." See **REGISTERS AND BOOKS OF REMEMBRANCE**.

The GOLDEN GROVE BOOK, a Genealogical and Heraldic Collection relating to Wales, consisting of three volumes with an index volume, was in 1870 conditionally deposited in the Public Record Office, for the Public use, by its owner, the Earl of Cawdor.

WARDROBE AND HOUSEHOLD ACCOUNTS.

The King's Wardrobe, subsequently subdivided into a Great Wardrobe, a Wardrobe of the Household, and a Privy Wardrobe, was anciently one of the Royal Treasuries into which certain portions of the revenues of the Crown were paid, and from which disbursements were made, as well for military and naval as for civil and domestic expenses.

It represented, in fact, with regard to the expenditure of the State a group of government offices comprising an Admiralty, War Office, Foreign Office, and Lord Chamberlain's Department, and including the functions of a Keeper of the Privy Purse.

According to the author of Fleta, to the Treasurer of the Wardrobe were committed the expenses of the King

WARDROBE AND HOUSEHOLD ACCOUNTS—
(continued).

and his family, and in conjunction with a Clerk of the
Wardrobe, who was associated to him as comptroller, he
was to keep a record of whatever belonged to his office.

He was to keep the King's money, jewels, gifts, and
private receipts, and to make a separate roll thereof, to be
returned annually into the Exchequer.

In another roll were to be entered the daily and necessary expenses, which comprised the buying of horses and
carriages and many other articles; also gifts, alms and
oblations; the wages of knights and archers; the wages
of messengers, and foreign fees, presents or accommoda-
tions; and the expenses of the wardrobe, including the
buying of cloth, furs, wax, spices, linen and such like;
together with purchases of jewels, &c., goldsmiths' work,
and the wages of the royal falconers and huntsmen.

In the Day Book of the Comptroller of the Wardrobe
of the 28th year of Edward the First, preserved in the
library of the Society of Antiquaries, and printed by order
of the society in 1787, the issues of the Great Wardrobe
are classified under twelve heads, as follows:—

1. Alms and Oblations.
2. Necessaries for the Household; including the purchase of
horses for the King's use, the charges and expenses of
ambassadors and messengers, wages of servants and
expenses of household requisites.
3. Victuals and Stores for the use of the King's household,
and also for the use of the Army and of certain castles
and garrisons.
4. Gifts and rewards to messengers and servants coming
to the King, payments for the restoration of horses
killed or destroyed in the king's service, and expenses
of the support of prisoners.
5. Payments to knights and others of the Household of their
annual fees, and payments to foreign soldiers.
6. Wages of Archers, Men-at-Arms, and others.
7. Wages of foot soldiers and of artificers and workmen
employed in the wars, and also wages of seamen.
8. Expenses of messengers and others despatched on the
King's business.
9. Wages of the royal falconers and huntsmen and expenses
attending hawks and hounds.
10. Allowances for the robes of the knights and others of the
Household.
11. Accounts of the Jewels and goldsmiths' work bought
within the year or otherwise coming into the Wardrobe, and also Lists of the Jewels, &c. given away,
and of those remaining in the Wardrobe.
12. Accounts of the cloths, furs, wax, spices, and other
articles bought for the Wardrobe.

This will sufficiently indicate the nature of the Accounts
referred to below which, in addition to many similar
Comptroller's Account Books include Accounts of the
Clerks and Keepers of the Great Wardrobe, of the Ward-

WARDROBE AND HOUSEHOLD ACCOUNTS—
(continued).

robe of the Household, of the Privy Wardrobe, and of several minor royal Households.

The accounts of the Wardrobe of the Household relate more especially to diet and domestic expenses and are interesting and valuable as showing the movements of the King and his Court from day to day.

The Particulars of Accounts relating to the expenses of the ARMY AND NAVY, and of AMBASSADORS AND ENVOYS form distinct classes and are referred to in the present volume under the titles indicated.

The Accounts of the EQUITIUM REGIS or Royal Stables also form a distinct class as mentioned below.

From the reign of Elizabeth to the present time the Accounts of the Keepers of the Great Wardrobe and of the Royal Household, &c. will be found amongst the Records of the Lord Chamberlain's Department and also amongst the Declared Accounts of the Audit Office and Pipe Office. *See* **DEPARTMENTAL RECORDS.**

WARDROBE AND HOUSEHOLD ACCOUNTS (EXCHEQUER QUEEN'S REMEMBRANCER. 14 John to 56 George III.

These are original Accounts of all the Receipts and Issues of the Great and Privy Wardrobe and of the daily expenses of the Royal and minor royal Households as rendered to the Exchequer by the Clerks and Keepers of the Wardrobe, the Treasurer of the King's Chamber, and at a later period by the Cofferers and Comptrollers of the Household and others, with Receipts and other documents subsidiary to such accounts.

They include also numerous inventories of the Royal Jewels and Plate from a very early period.

The " Misæ Roll " or roll of daily expenses of 14 John belonging to this series is printed in full in Cole's " Selections from the Records of the Exchequer " published by the Record Commission.

With this series have been incorporated many similar Accounts formerly deposited with the Miscellanea of the Treasury of the Receipt of the Exchequer and a few rolls from the Miscellaneous Records of the Exchequer of Receipt.

An Inventory of all the Original Accounts of the Exchequer in which the foregoing are included has been completed and will shortly be issued in the series of " Lists and Indexes."

CLARE HOUSEHOLD ACCOUNTS. (EXCHEQUER QUEEN'S REMEMBRANCER). Edward I. to Edward III.

These are Accounts of the daily expenses of the Household of Elizabeth de Burgo Lady of Clare.

They will be included in the Inventory above mentioned.

WARDROBE AND HOUSEHOLD ACCOUNTS—
(continued).

EQUITIUM REGIS ACCOUNTS (EXCHEQUER QUEEN'S REMEMBRANCER). Edward I. to James I.

These relate to the expenses of the Royal Stud, the purchase of provender, wages of attendants, &c.

They will be included in the Inventory of Exchequer Accounts above mentioned.

Many Books of Accounts relating to the Wardrobe and Household will be found amongst the Miscellaneous Books of the Exchequer Treasury of the Receipt and a few amongst those of the Augmentation Office. *See* **MISCELLANEOUS BOOKS.**

The following rolls of Accounts are amongst the Miscellaneous Rolls, &c., Chancery. (Bundle 15) :—

No. 1. An account of expenses in provisions for the Royal Household.   Temp. John.

No. 2. An account of the Treasurer of the Wardrobe.   10 Hen. III.

No. 3. An account of cloth of gold, &c. sent to the Emperor and of the royal beds and robes.   19 Hen. III.

No. 4. An account of expenses of the Royal Household.   Temp. Hen. III.

No. 5. A List of presents given to and by the King. (Imperfect.)   Temp. Hen. III.

No. 6. A File of Accounts relating to the Receipts and Issues of the Wardrobe.   Temp. Hen. III.

No. 7. Accounts of the Wardrobe, "de minutis particulis."   3–8 Edw. I.

No. 8. An account of the expenses made for the Tournament at Windsor.   6 Edw. I.

No. 9. A roll of Ordinances of the Royal Household.   7 Edw. I.

No. 10. Expenses of the Royal Household.   8 Edw. I.

No. 11. Expenses of victuals in Gascony and Wales.   10 Edw. 1.

No. 12.   Do.   in Wales.   10–11 Edw. I.

No. 13. An account of Wines, &c. purchased for the King's use.   9–13 Edw. I.

No. 14. The Household expenses of Edward the King's son.   18 Edw. I.

No. 15.   Do.   at Langley.   18 Edw. I.

No. 16. An account of the King's Goldsmith.   24–25 Edw. I.

No. 17. The Household expenses of the Bishop of Coventry and Lichfield on an embassy.   25 Edw. I.

No. 18. The household expenses of Thomas of Lancaster and Henry his brother.   25 Edw. I.

No. 19. An account of the Clerk of the Wardrobe of the Cloth of Gold, &c. issued.   34 Edw. I.

No. 20. Expenses of Royal Household.   Temp. Edw. I.

No. 21.   Do.   Temp. Edw. I.

No. 22. A roll of Ordinances of the Household of Lord d'Eresby.   12 Edw. II.

No. 23.   Do.   of the Royal Wardrobe.   17 Edw. II.

No. 24. An account of the household expenses of William de Stowe.   Temp. Edw. III.

No. 25.   Do.   of the Lady Alicia de Brienne.   13 Hen. IV. to 1 Hen. V.

WARDROBE AND HOUSEHOLD ACCOUNTS—
(continued).

No. 26. The Ordinances of the King's Household.
23 Hen. VI.
No. 27. An Inventory of Furniture. &c.   Temp. Hen. VI.
No. 28. An Account of the New Years' Gifts made to and by
the Queen.   5 Eliz.
No. 29.   Do.   19 Eliz.
No. 30.   Do.   40 Eliz.
No. 31.   Do.   45 Eliz.

The following Books of "Accounts of the Clerk and
Comptroller of the Wardrobe" form a separate Bundle :—

No. 1. A Wardrobe Account Book.   6 Edw. I.
No. 2.   Do.   13 Edw. I.
No. 3.   Do.   14 Edw. I.
No. 4.   Do.   17 Edw. I.
No. 5.   Do.   18 Edw. I.
No. 6.   Do.   25 Edw. I.
No. 7.   Do.   25 Edw. I.
(a portion only).

WARDROBE AND HOUSEHOLD ACCOUNTS ENROLMENTS
OF. (EXCHEQUER, L.T.R.) 42 Henry III. to 1 Edward
IV. 10 Rolls, as follows:—

No 1. Accounts of the Clerk of the Wardrobe.
42 to 45 Henry III.
No. 2. Accounts of the Keepers of the King's Wardrobe.
9 Edw. II. to 22 Edw. III.
No. 3. Accounts of the Clerks and Purveyors of the Great
Wardrobe.   17 Edw. II. to 25 Edw. III.
No. 4. Accounts of the Keeper of the Wardrobe.
24 Edw. III. to 9 Ric. II.
No. 5. Accounts of the Keeper of the Great Wardrobe.
48 Edw. III. to 1 Hen. IV.
No. 6. Accounts of the Keeper of the Great Wardrobe.
6 Hen. IV. to 2 Edw. IV.
No. 7. Accounts of the Keeper of the Great Wardrobe.
Hen. IV. to Edw. IV. (much decayed)
No. 8. Accounts of the Keeper of the Great Wardrobe.
1 Hen. VII. to 1 Edw. VI.
No. 9. Duplicate Accounts.   Edw. II. & Edw. III.
No. 10. Duplicate Accounts.   Edw. III.

Accounts of the Wardrobe and Household are also
enrolled with other "Foreign Accounts," on the Pipe
Rolls and Chancellor's Rolls. A List of all these enrolments
is in preparation.

WARDROBE ACCOUNT BOOKS (EXCHEQUER OF RECEIPT).
Accounts of the Keeper of the Great Wardrobe.
18–19 Henry VIII. 1 Vol.
Expenses of the Great Wardrobe. 1561 to 1566. 5 Vols.
Accounts of the Privy Purse and Robes of Prince Henry.
6–7 James I. 1 Vol.
Accounts of the Cofferer and Keeper of the Great Wardrobe of the Household of Prince Charles.
1616–1625. 8 Vols.

WARDROBE AND HOUSEHOLD ACCOUNTS—

(continued).

Wardrobe Account Books, &c.—(continued).

Accounts of the Comptroller of the Household of Prince Charles. 1616–1625. 8 Vols.

Accounts of the Master of the Wardrobe and Robes to Prince Charles. 1617–1624. 12 Vols.

Accounts of the Receivers-General of the Revenues of Charles I. as Prince and as King. 1618–1640. 7 Vols.

Descriptive Catalogue. Report II., App. II., pp. 199–203; and Report V., App. II., pp. 289–290.

Wardrobe Account Books (Audit Office Records).

Accounts of the Expenses of Funerals and Coronations. 1619 to 1714. 6 Vols.

Books of Expenses of Revels. 1571 to 1588. 12 Vols.

See also Declared Accounts (pp. 88–89.)

An Account of the Household of Henry II., entitled " Constitutio Domus Regis de Procurationibus " is contained in the Black Book of the Exchequer (Liber Niger Parvus).

The following Books of Regulations of the Royal Household, formerly in the State Paper Office, have been added to the Miscellaneous Books of the Exchequer, Treasury of the Receipt.

Vol. 206. Orders and Regulations set down for the government of the Household of Edward IV. An attested copy by Sir J. Williamson of " a fair Manuscript " given to him by Dr. Barlow, Provost of Queen's College, " Oxford." 1 Vol.

Vol. 230. An elaborate Treatise on the early regulations of the Household of the Kings of England, known as the Liber Niger of the Household of Edward IV. 1 Vol.

Vol. 231. Articles devised at Eltham for the Establishment of the Royal Household, anno 17 Henry VIII., with Lists of Officers, their wages and diet, &c. 1 Vol.

The two last-mentioned volumes are printed in the collection of " Ordinances and Regulations for the Government of the Royal Household in various Reigns," published by the Society of Antiquaries in 1790.

WARDS AND MINORS.

Grants of the custody of the lands and persons of Wards and Minors, and Writs for the Livery of such Lands on the heir attaining his majority, are entered on the Patent and Fine Rolls respectively. See **CHANCERY ENROLMENTS.**

Inquisitions respecting the possessions of Wards and Minors and the Proofs of Age taken on suing out the Writ " de probatione ætatis " will be found amongst the **INQUISITIONS POST MORTEM.**

WARDS AND MINORS—(continued).

Accounts of the possessions of Wards and Minors are included in the general series of **MINISTERS' AND RECEIVERS' ACCOUNTS.**

A "Court of Wards," to which the office of Liveries was subsequently united, was instituted by Statute 32 Henry VIII. c. 46., for the purpose of superintending and regulating the inquiries made upon the death of the King's tenants as to the lands of which they died seised, and the name and age of the next heir &c., in order to ensure to the King his rights of marriage, wardship, relief, and primer seisin, and all such inquiries were subject to the jurisdiction of the Court until its final abolition by the Statute 12 Car. II. c. 24.

The Inquisitions returned into the Court of Wards and Liveries are referred to under the head of **INQUISITIONS POST MORTEM,** and its Judicial Proceedings under the head of **JUDICIAL PROCEEDINGS (VARIOUS).**

The remaining Records of the Court consist chiefly of "Miscellaneous Books" as follows :—

DOWER, INDENTURES, PATENTS, AND ASSIGNMENTS OF. Hen. VIII. and Edw. VI. 1 Vol.

[*Misc. Books. Vol.* 286.]

DOWERS, PARTICULARS FOR. 9 Eliz. to 11 Car. I. 2 Vols.

[*Do. Vols.* 287–288.]

EXTENTS, ATTACHMENTS, BONDS, AND RECOGNIZANCES, ENTRIES OF. Eliz. to Car. I. 118 Vols.

[*Do. Vols.* 583 *to* 700.]

EVIDENCES, BOOKS OF. 1556 to 1645. 4 Vols., and Calendar, 1 Vol. [*Do. Vols.* 180 *to* 184.]

See also "DEEDS, CHARTERS, EVIDENCES, &c. (ORIGINAL)" described under the head of **DEEDS (ANCIENT).**

INDENTURE BOOKS. Hen. VIII. to Car. I. 15 Vols.

[*Do. Vols.* 114 *to* 128.]

LIVERIES, BOOKS OF. Hen. VIII. to Car. I. 30 Vols.

[*Do. Vols.* 54 *to* 83.]

LIVERIES, PARTICULARS FOR. Hen. VIII. to Mary. 5 Vols. [*Misc. Books, Vols.* 578 *to* 582.]

PATENT AND DECREE BOOKS. Hen. VIII. to Jas. I. 11 Vols. [*Do. Vols.* 103 *to* 113.]

SURVEYS, BOOKS OF. 5 Hen. VIII. to 21 Eliz., & 12 Jas. I. 17 Vols. [*Do. Vols.* 129 *to* 146.]

There is also a collection of Surveys in Bundles known as "Feodaries Surveys," extending from Hen. VIII. to Car. I., and arranged in Counties.

WARDS AND MINORS—(continued).

WARDSHIPS, PETITIONS AND COMPOSITIONS FOR. 8 Jas. I.
to 20 Car. I. 7 Vols. [*Do.*   *Vols.* 214 *to* 220.]

WARDSHIPS, SALES OF, AND PREFERMENTS. Hen. VIII.
to Car. I. 18 Vols. [*Do.*   *Vols.* 147 *to* 164.]

MISCELLANEOUS BOOKS. Henry VIII. to Car. I. 196
Vols. [*Do.*   *Vols.* 165 *to* 360.]

The following volumes relating to the king's wardships
before the establishment of the Court of Wards are
amongst the Miscellaneous Books of the Exchequer,
Treasury of the Receipt :—

Vol. 246. Sales of King's Wardships.   18–20 Hen. VIII.
Vol. 247. A Book of Wards.   19–21 Hen. VIII.
Vol. 248. Do.   22–23 Hen. VIII.

WILLS (ROYAL AND PRIVATE).

ROYAL WILLS.

The Will of Henry II. is enrolled in the Black Book of
the Exchequer.

The Will of Edward I. is enrolled in the "Registrum
Munimentorum" (*Liber A. No.* 15).

The Wills of Richard II., Henry V., Henry VII., and
Henry VIII. are preserved amongst the Records of the
Treasury of the Receipt of the Exchequer, each forming a
separate volume.

A Copy of the Will of Henry VIII. forms Vol. 469 of
the Miscellaneous Books of the Augmentation Office.

WILLS OF PRIVATE PERSONS.

Many Wills of private persons are to be found in the
several Series of "Ancient Deeds" now in the course of
being catalogued. See **DEEDS (ANCIENT).**

Pursuant to Statute 1 Geo. I. the Wills of Roman
Catholics are enrolled on the CLOSE ROLLS.

Wills are also frequently enrolled on the DECREE ROLLS
of the Court of Chancery and on the RECOVERY ROLLS of
the Common Pleas. See **DEEDS ENROLLED.**

Letters of Administration and Probates of Wills relating
to Government Annuities, &c. are entered in the ASSIGN-
MENT BOOKS of the Exchequer of Receipt from 1622, and
previous to that date in the PATENT AND PRIVY SEAL
BOOKS of that Court. See **RECEIPTS AND
ISSUES OF THE EXCHEQUER.**

A Parliamentary Return in 1845 (*Sessional Paper,
H. C., 1845, No.* 249), exhibits the extraordinary number
of jurisdictions in which Wills are to be found, showing
that they are deposited in Parish Churches, private houses
of Registrars, with Lords of Manors, &c., &c.

WILLS (ROYAL AND PRIVATE)—(continued).

WILLS OF PRIVATE PERSONS—(continued).

Wills affecting lands or tenements in Middlesex or in Yorkshire are registered at the several District Registries established for those Counties. See **DEEDS, &c., REGISTRIES OF.**

By Statute 42 Geo. III. c. 99. Extracts of Wills from the Registries of the different Counties, Divisions, &c. are sent to the Legacy Duty Office, Somerset House.

The Original Wills filed in the Prerogative Court of Canterbury from 1383, and those of several other jurisdictions, are also preserved at Somerset House.

WORKS AND BUILDINGS.

ACCOUNTS OF THE CLERK OF THE WORKS. (EXCHEQUER, Q. R.) Edward III. to Elizabeth.

These are Accounts of the Works carried on in various Royal Palaces, Castles, Parks, &c., with Files of Receipts and other documents subsidiary thereto. Amongst them will be found a number of writs, receipts, and indentures in connexion with the account of Geoffrey Chaucer during the period in which he was Clerk of the King's Works.

ACCOUNTS OF WORKS AT WESTMINSTER AND THE TOWER. (EXCHEQUER, Q. R.) Henry III. to Philip and Mary.

These are Accounts by the Clerk of the Works of the Wages of Artificers, and expenses of materials in repairs and building executed in the Royal Palace at Westminster and in the Tower of London. They are voluminous, and contain much curious information. Similar Accounts will be found amongst the Miscellanea of the Treasury of the Receipt.

ACCOUNTS RELATING TO WINDSOR CASTLE AND CHAPEL. (EXCHEQUER, TREASURY OF THE RECEIPT.) Hen. VIII.

These are amongst the Miscellaneous Books (Vols 262 to 264) and consist of the Accounts of the Constable of Windsor Castle, and of Accounts of Repairs and Buildings in connexion therewith.

The earlier Accounts of the Constable of Windsor Castle will be found amongst the Accounts, &c. relating to the ARMY AND NAVY. (See p. 17.)

ACCOUNTS OF REPAIRS AT WESTMINSTER. (EXCHEQUER OF RECEIPT.) 44 Henry III. 2 Rolls.

These rolls give a most minute account of the expenses incurred for rebuilding, repairing, and enlarging part of the King's Palace at Westminster, and for decorating and

WORKS AND BUILDINGS—(continued).

ACCOUNT OF REPAIRS AT WESTMINSTER, &c.—(continued).

ornamenting the same, specifying the sums paid to each artist and workman, and whence the timber, stone, and other materials were obtained.

All the foregoing Accounts are included in the new Inventory of Original Accounts of the Exchequer.

ACCOUNTS OF WORKS AND BUILDINGS. (AUDIT OFFICE.) 1563 to 1827.

See **DEPARTMENTAL RECORDS.**

The following Accounts of Repairs at Royal Palaces, &c. are amongst the Miscellanea:—

Expenses of Repairs at Woodstock. 3 Edw. I.
[*Misc. Rolls, &c. (Chancery), No.* $\frac{16}{4}$.]

Expenses of the Royal Palaces. 4 Edw. I.
[*Do.* *No.* $\frac{1}{7}$.]

Expenses at the Palace of the Archbishop of York in London. 25 Edw. I.
[*Do.* *No.* $\frac{16}{12}$.]

Accounts of Works, &c. at the Palace of Westminster. 22–23 Hen. VIII.
[*Misc. Books, Exchequer, Treasury of the Receipt, Vols.* 251 *and* 252.

INDEX.

396

Wards and Minors, Possessions of, 365.
Warrant Books (Exchequer of Receipt), 315.
    „   „   (Home Office), 92.
    „   „   (Treasury), 93.
Warrants (Lord Chamberlain's Department), 93.
Warrants of Attorney (Queen's Bench, Plea Side), 174.
    „   „   (Common Pleas), 177.
    „   „   (Exchequer of Pleas), 181.
    „   „   (Palatinate of Durham), 191.
Warrants of Attorney, Rolls of (Chester), 189.
Warrants for Issues. See "Privy Seals and Warrants for Issues."
    „   „   Books of (Exchequer of Receipt), 315.
Warrants for the Great Seal, 295.
    „   „   delivery of Records, 296.
Watson's Roll, 48.
Welsh Rolls, 48.
West Indies. See "America and West Indies."
Westminster and the Tower, Accounts of Works at, 367.
Wey Navigation Claims, 180.
Wills (Royal), 366.
    , (of Private Persons), 366.
Windsor Castle and Chapel, Accounts relating to, 367.
    „ Poor Knights of, 199.
Winton Domesday, 97.
Wolsey's Inquisitions, 253.
    „ Patents, 254.
Woods, Sales of, 219.
    „ Special Commissions concerning, 62.
Wools, Subsidies on, 351.
Works and Buildings, Accounts relating to, 367.
Writs (Chancery). See "Chancery Files."
    „ (Queen's Bench, Crown Side), 171.
    „ (Queen's Bench, Plea Side), 174, 175.
    „ (Common Pleas), 177.
    „ (Exchequer, Q.R.), 180.
    „ (Exchequer of Pleas), 181.
    „ (Exchequer, L.T.R.), 182.
    „ (Palatinate of Lancaster), 194.
Writs and Miscellaneous Documents (Exchequer, Court of First Fruits, &c.), 184.
Writs "de excommunicato capiendo," Significavits for, 107.
Writs of Right (Chancery), 163.
    „ (Common Pleas), 177.
Writs and Returns of Members to Parliament, 287.

www.ingramcontent.com/pod-product-compliance
Lightning Source LLC
Chambersburg PA
CBHW031816270326
41932CB00008B/442